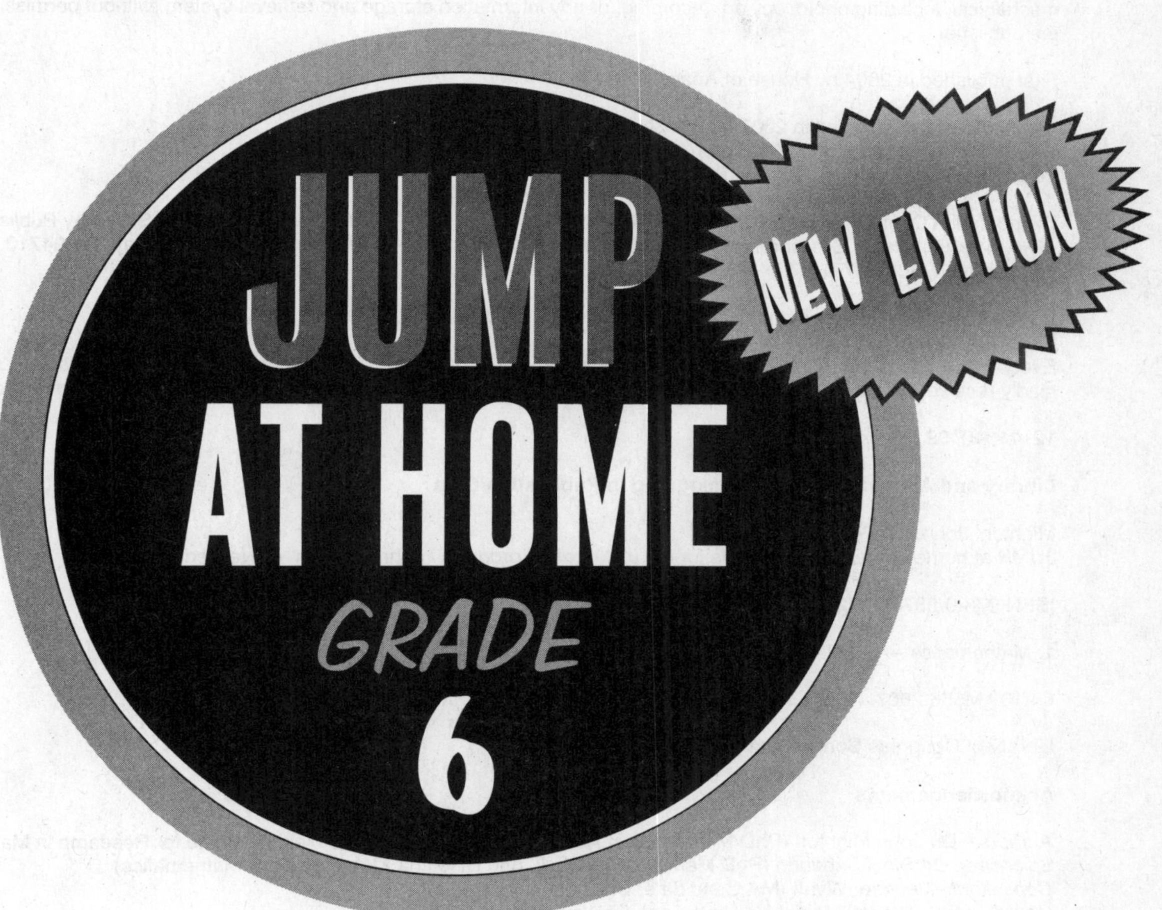

Worksheets for the JUMP Math Program

JOHN MIGHTON

First published in 2004 by House of Anansi Press Inc.

Revised edition published in 2007 by House of Anansi Press Inc.
110 Spadina Avenue, Suite 801, Toronto, ON, M5V 2K4
Tel. 416-363-4343 Fax 416-363-1017 www.anansi.ca

Distributed in Canada by HarperCollins Canada Ltd.
1995 Markham Road, Scarborough, ON, M1B 5M8
Toll free tel. 1-800-387-0117

Distributed in the United States by Publishers Group West
1700 Fourth Street, Berkeley, CA 94710
Toll free tel. 1-800-788-3123

Some of the material in this book has previously been published by JUMP Math.

12 11 10 09 08 2 3 4 5 6

Library and Archives Canada Cataloguing in Publication Data

Mighton, John, 1957–
JUMP at home grade 6 : worksheets for the JUMP math program / John Mighton. — New ed.

ISBN 978-0-88784-772-1

1. Mathematics — Problems, exercises, etc. I. Title.

QA139.M556 2007 j510'.76 C2007-906418-3

Library of Congress Control Number: 2007908577

Acknowledgements

Authors – Dr. John Mighton (PhD Mathematics, Ashoka Fellow, Fellow of the Fields Institute for Research in Mathematical Sciences), Dr. Sindi Sabourin (PhD Mathematics, BEd), and Dr. Anna Klebanov (PhD Mathematics)
Consultant – Jennifer Wyatt (MA Candidate, BEd)
Contributors – Betony Main, Lisa Hines, and Sheila Mooney
Layout – Katie Baldwin, Rita Camacho, Tony Chen, Lyubava Fartushenko, and Pam Lostracco

This book, like the JUMP program itself, is made possible by the efforts of the volunteers and staff of JUMP Math.

Cover design: The Bang

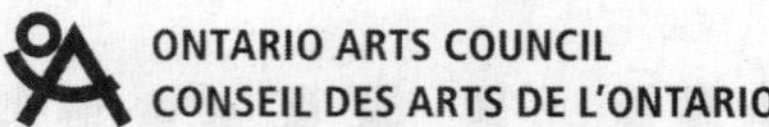

We acknowledge for their financial support of our publishing program the Canada Council for the Arts, the Ontario Arts Council, and the Government of Canada through the Book Publishing Industry Development Program (BPIDP).

Printed and bound in Canada

Contents

INTRODUCTION TO THE "JUMP AT HOME" WORKBOOKS

Based on my work with hundreds of elementary students, spanning fifteen years, I am convinced that all children can be led to think mathematically. Even if I am wrong, the results of JUMP suggest that it is worth suspending judgment in individual cases. A parent or teacher who expects a child to fail is almost certain to produce a failure. The method of teaching outlined in this book (or any method, for that matter) is more likely to succeed if it is applied with patience and an open mind.

If you are a parent and you believe that your child is not capable of leaning math, I recommend that you read *The Myth of Ability: Nurturing Mathematical Talent in Every Child* or *The End of Ignorance: Multiplying Our Human Potential*, and consult the JUMP website (at www.jumpmath.org) for testimonials from teachers who have tried the program and for a report on current research on the program.

You are more likely to help your child if you teach with the following principles in mind:

1) *If a child doesn't understand your explanation, assume there is something lacking in your explanation, not in your child.*

   When a teacher leaves a student behind, it is almost always because they have not taken responsibility for examining the way they teach. I often make mistakes in my lessons: sometimes I will go too fast for a student or skip steps inadvertently. I don't consider myself a natural teacher. I know many teachers who are more charismatic or faster on their feet than I am. But I have had enormous success with students who were thought to be unteachable because if I happen to leave a student behind I always ask myself: What did I do wrong in that lesson? (And I usually find that my mistake is neglecting one of the principles listed below.)

2) *In mathematics, it is always possible to make a step easier.*

   A hundred years ago, researchers in logic discovered that virtually all of the concepts used by working mathematicians could be reduced to one of two extremely basic operations, namely, the operation of counting or the operation of grouping objects into sets. Most people are able to perform both of these operations before they enter kindergarten. It is surprising, therefore, that schools have managed to make mathematics a mystery to so many students.

   A tutor once told me that one of her students, a girl in Grade 4, had refused to let her teach her how to divide. The girl said that the concept of division was much too hard for her and she would never consent to learn it. I suggested the tutor teach division as a kind of counting game. In the next lesson, without telling the girl she was about to learn how to divide, the tutor wrote in succession the numbers 15 and 5. Then she asked the child to count on her fingers by multiples of the second number, until she'd reached the first. After the child had repeated this operation with several other pairs of numbers, the tutor asked her to write down, in each case, the number of fingers she had raised when she stopped counting. For instance,

   15 5 3

   As soon as the student could find the answer to any such question quickly, the tutor wrote, in each example, a division sign between the first and second number, and an equal sign between the second and third.

   $15 \div 5 = 3$

   The student was surprised to find she had learned to divide in 10 minutes. (Of course, the tutor later explained to the student that 15 divided by five is three because you can add 5 three times to get 15: that's what you see when you count on your fingers.)

   In the exercises in the JUMP Workbook we have made an effort to break concepts and skills into steps that children will find easy to master. But the workbooks are far from perfect. Some pages are more cramped than we would have liked and some pages do not provide enough practice or preparation. The worksheets are intended as models for parents to improve upon: we hope you will take responsibility for providing your child with warm-up questions and bonus questions (see below for a discussion of how to create these questions), and for filling in any gaps our materials wherever you find them. We have made a serious effort to introduce skills and concepts in small steps and in a coherent order, so a committed parent should have no trouble seeing where they need to create extra questions for practice or where they need to fill in a missing step in the development of an idea.

3) *With a weaker student, the second piece of information almost always drives out the first.*

   When a teacher introduces several pieces of information at the same time, students will often, in trying to comprehend the final item, lose all memory and understanding of the material that came before (even though they may have appeared to understand this material completely as it was being explained). With weaker students, it is always more efficient to introduce one piece of information at a time.

I once observed an intern from teachers college who was trying to teach a boy in a Grade 7 remedial class how to draw mixed fractions. The boy was getting very frustrated as the intern kept asking him to carry out several steps at the same time.

I asked the boy to simply draw a picture showing the number of whole pies in the fraction 2 ½. He drew and shaded two whole pies. I then asked him to draw the number of whole pies in 3 ½, 4 ½ and 5 ½ pies. He was very excited when he completed the work I had assigned him, and I could see that he was making more of an effort to concentrate. I asked him to draw the whole number of pies in 2 ¼, 2 ¾, 3 ¼, 4 ¼, then in 2 1/3, 2 2/3, 3 1/3 pies and so on. (I started with quarters rather than thirds because they are easier to draw.) When the boy could draw the whole number of pies in any mixed fraction, I showed him how to draw the fractional part. Within a few minutes he was able to draw any mixed fraction. If I hadn't broken the skill into two steps (i.e. drawing the number of whole pies then drawing the fractional part) and allowed him to practice each step separately, he might never have learned the concept

As your student learns to concentrate and approach the work with real excitement (which generally happens after several months if the early JUMP units are taught properly), you can begin to skip steps when teaching new material, or even challenge your student to figure out the steps themselves. But if your student ever begins to struggle with this approach, it is best to go back to teaching in small steps.

4) *Before you assign work, verify that your student has the skills needed to complete the work.*

In our school system it is assumed that some students will always be left behind in mathematics. If a teacher is careful to break skills and concepts into steps that every student can understand, this needn't happen. (JUMP has demonstrated this in dozens of classrooms.)

Before you assign a question from one of the JUMP workbooks you should verify that your student is prepared to answer the question without your help (or with minimal help). On most worksheets, only one or two new concepts or skills are introduced, so you should find it easy to verify that your student can answer the question. The worksheets are intended as final tests that you can give when you are certain your student understands the material.

Always give a short diagnostic quiz before you allow your student to work on a worksheet. In general, a quiz should consist of four or five questions similar to the ones on the worksheet. The quizzes will help you identify whether your student needs an extra review before you move on.

5) *Raise the bar incrementally.*

Any successes I have had with weaker students are almost entirely due to a technique I use which is, as a teacher once said about the JUMP method, "not exactly rocket science." When a student has mastered a skill or concept, I simply raise the bar slightly by challenging them to answer a question that is only incrementally more difficult or complex than the questions I had previously assigned. I always make sure, when the student succeeds in meeting my challenge, that they know I am impressed. Sometimes I will even pretend I'm about to faint (students always laugh at this) or I will say "You got that question but you'll never get the next one." Students become very excited when they succeed in meeting a series of graduated challenges. And their excitement allows them to focus their attention enough to make the leaps I have described in *The Myth of Ability* and *The End of Ignorance.*

There is a growing body of evidence in cognition that suggests that the brain is plastic and that, through rigorous instruction, new abilities and forms of intelligence can emerge even in older students or in students who have struggled in a subject. The research has shown, however, that very little happens in the brain if a student's attention is not engaged. By raising the bar for your child — allowing them to succeed at a series of graduated challenges — you can help their brain work far more efficiently. (See *The End of Ignorance* for an account of new research in cognition.)

In designing the JUMP workbooks, I have made an effort to introduce only one or two skills per page, so you should find it easy to create bonus questions: just change the numbers in an existing question or add an extra element to a problem on a worksheet. For instance, if your child has just learned how to add a pair of three-digit numbers, you might ask your child to add a pair of four- or five-digit numbers. If you become excited when you assign more challenging questions, you will find that even a child who previously had trouble focusing will race to finish their work so they can answer a bonus question.

6) *Repetition and practice are essential.*

Even mathematicians need constant practice to consolidate and remember skills and concepts. Studies of chess players and other experts have shown that intuition, creativity and proficiency can develop out of rigorous practice and study. (See for instance the article "The Expert Mind" in *Scientific American*.) Practice doesn't have to be torture. By raising the bar, by allowing your child to make discoveries themselves, and by playing with subtle variations on patterns you can make practice fun.

7) *Praise is essential.*

We've found the JUMP program works best when teachers give their students a great deal of encouragement. Because the lessons are laid out in steps that any student can master, you'll find that you won't be giving false encouragement. (This is one of the reasons kids love the program so much: for many, it's a thrill to be doing well at math.)

We haven't observed a student yet – even among scores of remedial students – who couldn't learn math. When it is taught in steps, math is actually the subject in which children with attention deficits and learning disabilities can most easily succeed, and thereby develop the confidence and cognitive abilities they need to do well in other subjects. Rather than being the hardest subject, math can be the engine of learning for delayed students. This is one of JUMP's cornerstone beliefs. If you disagree with this tenet, please reconsider your decision to use JUMP. Our program will only be fully effective if you embrace the philosophy.

What Is JUMP Math?

JUMP Math is a philosophy and a set of materials and methods that aims to improve the teaching of mathematics and to help students enjoy and meet their potential in the subject.

The JUMP program is based on the belief that all children in the regular school system, even those diagnosed as having serious learning disabilities, or who are failing, can do well at math. Mathematics, rather than being the most difficult subject, is one in which children can most easily succeed, even at a young age, and can thereby develop the confidence and cognitive abilities they need to do well in other subjects.

JUMP is a registered not-for-profit organization and a charity.

About This Book

This book covers only part of the standard curriculum: it does not contain any material on Geometry, Probability, Statistics or Data Management and only partially covers the curriculum in Measurement. JUMP has published in-class versions of this book that cover the complete curriculum and that come with teacher manuals that have lesson plans for each worksheet. Significant discounts are available for teachers for class sets. For more information see the JUMP website (www.jumpmath.org).

The Fractions Unit

To prepare your child to use this book, you should set aside 40 to 50 minutes a day for three weeks to teach them the material in the JUMP Fractions Unit. You may print individual copies of the unit from the JUMP website at no charge The Fractions Unit has proven to be a remarkably effective tool for instilling a sense of confidence and enthusiasm about mathematics in students. The unit has helped many teachers discover a potential in their students that they might not otherwise have seen. In a recent survey, all of the teachers who used the Fractions Unit for the first time acknowledged afterwards that they had underestimated the abilities of some of their students. (For details of this study, see the JUMP website at www.jumpmath.org.)

Games

As much as possible make learning an adventure and a game for your child. Build lessons around the worksheets that allow your child to meet and overcome challenges, to solve puzzles and to make discoveries. For ways to turn your lessons into games see for instance the problem solving lesson in this introduction (pages viii-xii), the Modified Go Fish activity in Mental Math (page xxxv), and the activities with concrete materials (pages xiii-xxii). There are many standard games that help children develop a sense of numbers (like Cribbage or Monopoly) and an ability to reason and to make predictions and deductions (various card games and strategy games).

Sample Problem Solving Lesson

As much as possible, allow your child to extend and discover ideas on their own (without pushing them so far that they become discouraged). It is not hard to develop problem solving lessons (where your child can make discoveries in steps) using the material on the worksheets. Here is a sample problem solving lesson you can try with your child.

1. **Warm-up**
   Review the notion of perimeter from the worksheets. Draw the following diagram on grid paper and ask your child how they would determine the perimeter. (You may need to state that the drawings on the board are drawn to scale: 1 unit^2 = 1 cm^2.)

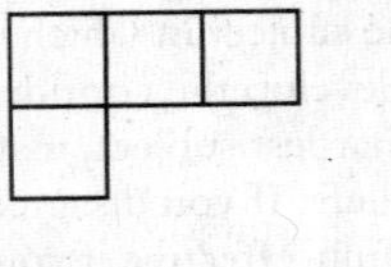

   Allow your child to demonstrate their method (e.g., counting the line segments, or adding the lengths of each side).

2. **Develop the Idea**
   Draw some additional shapes on grid paper and ask your child to determine the perimeter of each.

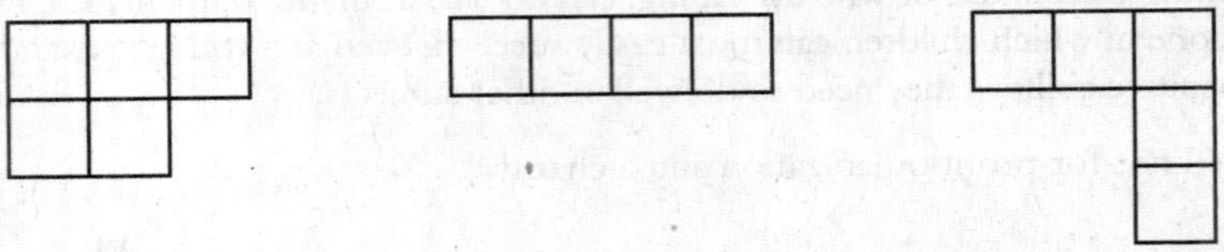

Check	Bonus	Try Again?
The perimeters of the shapes above are 10 cm, 10 cm and 12 cm respectively.	Have your child make a picture of a letter from their name on graph paper by colouring in squares. Then ask them to find the perimeter and record their answer in words.	Children may need to use some kind of system to keep them from missing sides. Suggest that your child write the length of the sides on the shape.

3. **Go Further**
   Draw a simple rectangle on the board and ask your child to again find the perimeter.

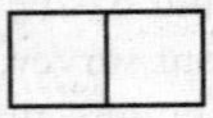

   Add a square to the shape and ask your child how the perimeter changes.

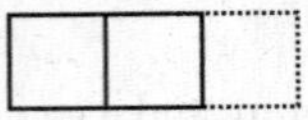

   Draw the following polygons on the board and ask your child to copy the four polygons on their grid paper.

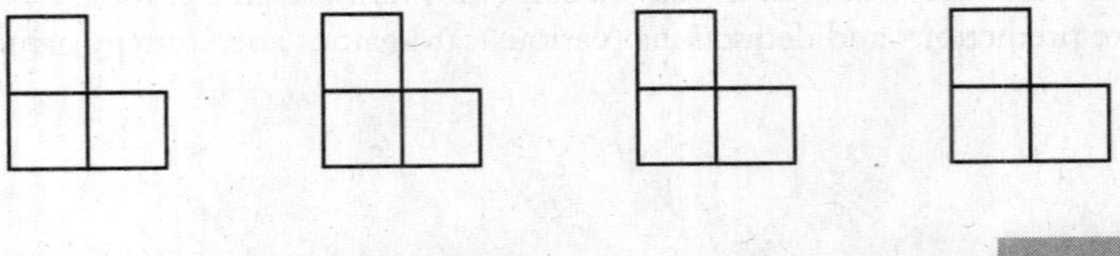

Sample Problem Solving Lesson *(continued)*

Ask your child how they would calculate the perimeter of the first polygon. Then instruct them to add an additional square to each polygon and calculate the perimeter again.

Check	Bonus	Try Again?
Have your child demonstrate where they added the shapes and how they found the perimeter. Ask your child to discuss why they think the perimeter remains constant when the square is added in the corner (as in the fourth polygon above).	▪ Ask your child to calculate the greatest amount the perimeter can increase by when you add a single square. ▪ Ask them to add 2 (or 3) squares to the shape below and examine how the perimeter changes. ▪ Ask them to create a T-table where the two columns are labelled "Number of Squares" in the polygon and "Perimeter" of the polygon (see the Patterns section for an introduction to T-tables). Have them add more squares and record how the perimeter continues to change.	Ask your child to draw a single square on their grid paper and find the perimeter (4 cm). Then have them add a square and find the perimeter of the resulting rectangle. Have them repeat this exercise a few times and then follow the same procedure with the original (or bonus) questions.

4. Another Step

Draw the following shape on the board and ask your child, "How can you add a square to the following shape so the perimeter *decreases*?"

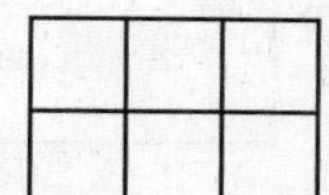

Check	Bonus	Try Again?
Discuss with your child why perimeter decreases when the square is added in the middle of the second row. You may want to ask them what kinds of shapes have larger perimeters and which have smaller perimeters.	Ask your child to add two squares to the polygons below and see if they can reduce the perimeter.	Have your child try the exercise again with six square-shaped pattern blocks. Have them create the polygon as drawn above and find where they need to place the sixth square by guessing and checking (placing the square and measuring the perimeter of the resulting polygon).

Sample Problem Solving Lesson *(continued)*

5. **Develop the Idea**
Hold up a photograph that you've selected and ask your child how you would go about selecting a frame for it. What kinds of measurements would you need to know about the photograph in order to get the right sized frame? You might also want to show your child a CD case and ask them how they would measure the paper to create an insert for a CD/CD-ROM.

Show your child on paper how the perimeter of a rectangle can be solved with an addition statement (e.g., Perimeter = 14 cm is the sum of 3 + 3 + 4 + 4). Explain that the rectangle is made up of two pairs of equal lines and that, because of this, we only need two numbers to find the perimeter of a given rectangle.

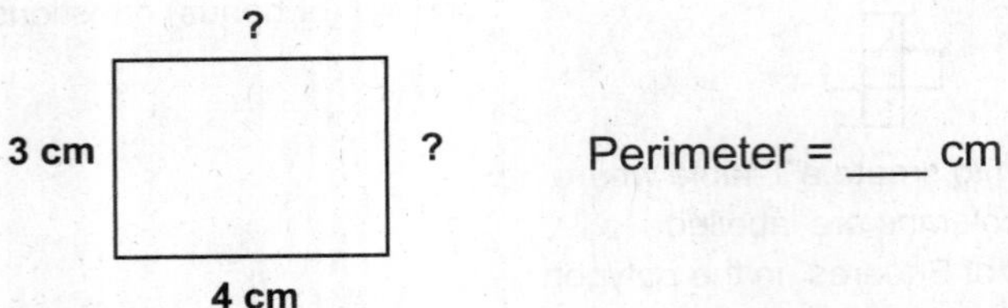

Perimeter = ___ cm

Show your child that there are two ways to find this:
a) Create an addition statement by writing each number twice: 3 cm + 3 cm + 4 cm + 4 cm = 14 cm
b) Add the numbers together and multiply the sum by 2: 3 cm + 4 cm = 7 cm; 7 cm × 2 = 14 cm

Ask your child to find the perimeters of the following rectangles (not drawn to scale).

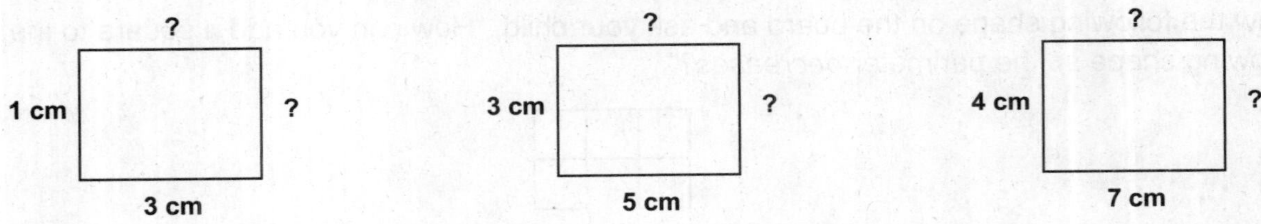

Check	Bonus	Try Again?
Take up the questions (the perimeters of the rectangles above, from left to right, are 8 cm, 16 cm and 22 cm).	Continue creating questions in this format for your child and gradually increase the size of the numbers.	Have your child draw a copy of the rectangle in a notebook and copy the measurements onto all four sides. Have them create an addition statement by copying one of the numbers and then crossing our the measurement: ~~4 cm~~ ~~1 cm~~ ~~1 cm~~ ~~4 cm~~ 4 cm 4 cm 1 cm + 1 cm

6. **Go Further**
Demonstrate on grid paper that two different rectangles can both have a perimeter of 10 cm.

Ask your child to draw all the rectangles they can with a perimeter of 12 cm.

Check	Bonus	Try Again?
After your child has finished, ask them whether they were able to find one rectangle, then two rectangles, then three rectangles.	Ask your child to find (and draw) all the rectangles with a perimeter of 18 cm. After they have completed this, they can repeat the same exercise for rectangles of 24 cm or 36 cm.	If your child finds only one (or zero) rectangles, they should be shown a systematic method of finding the answer and then given the chance to practise the original question. On grid paper, have your child draw a pair of lines with lengths of 1 and 2 cm each. 1 cm 2 cm Ask them to draw the other three sides of each rectangle so that the final perimeter will be 12 cm for each rectangle, guessing and checking the lengths of the other sides. Let them try this method on one of the bonus questions once they accomplish this.

7. Raise the Bar

Draw the following rectangle and measurements on paper:

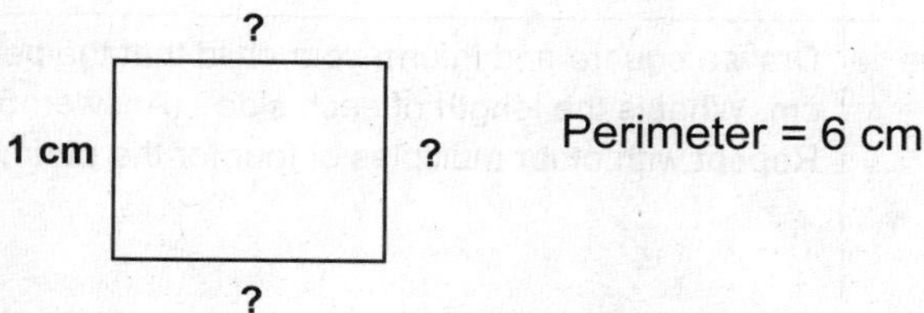

Ask your child how they would calculate the length of the missing sides. After they have given some input, explain to them how the side opposite the one measured will always have the same measurement. Demonstrate how the given length can be subtracted twice (or multiplied by two and then subtracted) from the perimeter. The remainder, divided by two, will be the length of each of the two remaining sides.

Draw a second rectangle and ask your child to find the lengths of the missing sides using the methods just discussed.

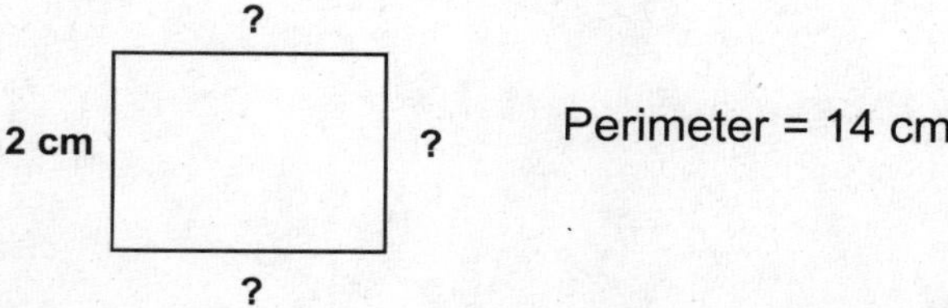

Sample Problem Solving Lesson *(continued)*

Check	Bonus	Try Again?
Check that your child can calculate the length of the sides (2 cm, 2 cm, 5 cm and 5 cm).	Give your child more problems like above. For example: ▪ Side = 5 cm; Perimeter = 20 cm ▪ Side = 10 cm; Perimeter = 50 cm ▪ Side = 20 cm; Perimeter = 100 cm ▪ Side = 65 cm; Perimeter = 250 cm Be sure to raise the numbers incrementally on bonus questions.	Give your child a simple problem to try (similar to the first demonstration question). ? / 1 cm ? Perimeter = 8 cm / ? Provide them with eight toothpicks (or a similar object) and have them create the rectangle and then measure the length of each side. Have them repeat this with more questions.

8. Assessment

Draw the following diagrams of rectangles and perimeter statements, and ask your child to complete the missing measurements on each rectangle.

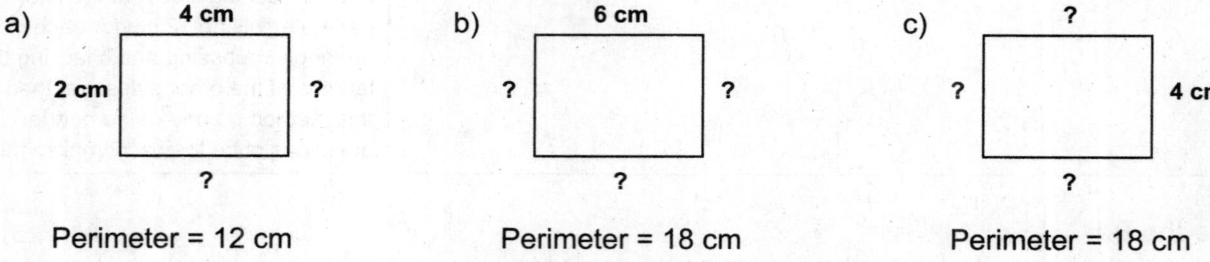

Check	Bonus
Answers for the above questions (going clockwise from the sides given): a) 2 cm, 4 cm b) 3 cm, 6 cm, 3 cm c) 5 cm, 4 cm, 5 cm	Draw a square and inform your child that the perimeter is 20 cm. What is the length of each side? (Answer: 5 cm.) Repeat with other multiples of four for the perimeter.

Activities with Concrete Materials

When you teach the material in this book you should try, whenever possible, to illustrate and explore the ideas on a worksheet with concrete materials and models. For most exercises in the workbook you can use simple materials, such as coins, paper money, counters (such as buttons or poker chips), rulers, and so on.

The most common materials that are used in schools to make models of whole numbers and decimals are base ten blocks, which are made of 1 cm by 1 cm cubes.

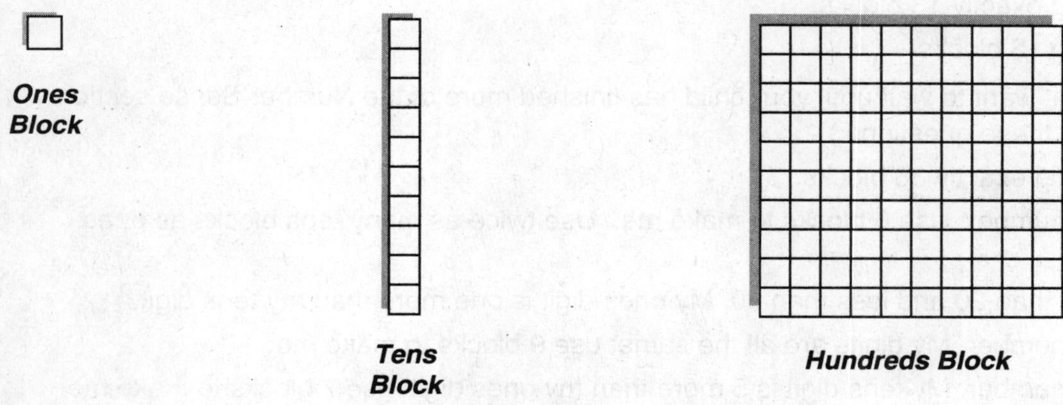

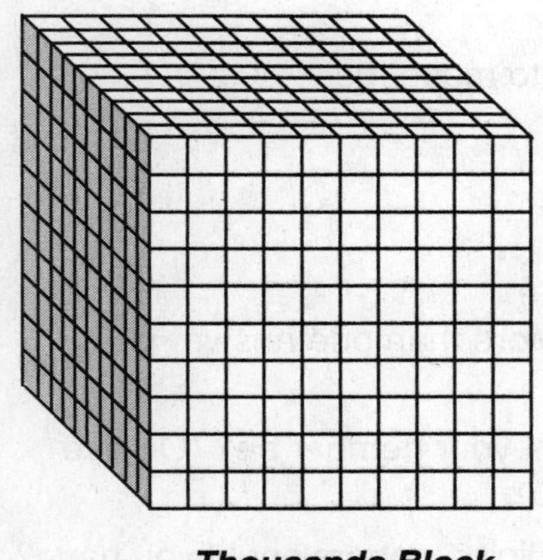

We have provided blackline masters of the ones, tens, and hundreds blocks (see page xl) that you can copy and cut out. To make a model of the thousands block, tape six hundreds blocks together to make a cube.

Activities with Concrete Materials

1. Give your child ones, tens, and hundreds blocks.

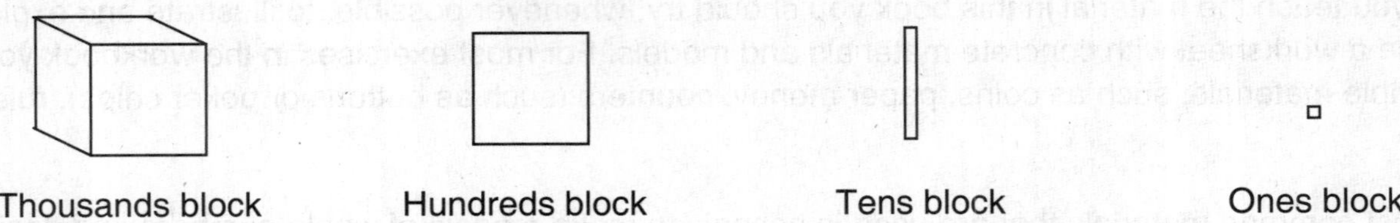

Instructions:

a) Show 17, 31, 252, etc. with base ten blocks.

b) Show 22 using exactly 13 blocks.

c) Show 31 using 13 blocks.

Harder: (You might want to wait until your child has finished more of the Number Sense section before you assign these questions.)

d) Show 315 using exactly 36 blocks.

e) I am a 2 digit number: Use 6 blocks to make me. Use twice as many tens blocks as ones blocks.

f) I am a greater than 20 and less than 30. My ones digit is one more than my tens digit.

g) I am a 3 digit number. My digits are all the same: use 9 blocks to make me.

h) I am a 2 digit number. My tens digit is 5 more than my ones digit: use 7 blocks to make me.

i) I am a 3 digit number. My tens digit is one more than my hundreds digit and my ones digit is one more than my tens digit: use 6 blocks to make me. What would I be if I was represented by 7 blocks?

j) Show 1123 using exactly 16 blocks. (There are 2 answers.)

k) I am a 4 digit number. My digits are all the same: use 12 blocks to make me.

2. *Wrap Up: Visualizing base ten materials*

Ask your child to imagine choosing some base ten blocks…

Instructions:

a) You have more tens than ones. What might your number be? (More than one answer is possible.)

b) You have the same number of ones and tens blocks. What might your number be? (Or give harder questions.)

c) You have twice as many tens blocks as ones blocks. What two digit numbers could you have?

d) You have six more ones than tens. What might your number be?

e) You have one set of blocks that make the number 13 and one set of blocks that make the number 22. Could you have the same number of blocks in both sets?

f) You have one set of blocks that make the number 23 and one set of blocks that make the number 16. Could you have the same number of blocks in both sets?

g) You have an equal number of ones, tens, and hundreds and twice as many thousands as hundreds. What might your number be?

NOTE: If some of the questions are too hard to solve by visualization, let your child sketch base ten models.

Activities with Concrete Materials

3. Give your child a set of cards with the numbers 1 to 8 on them.

   a) Ask them to arrange the cards in two rows as shown so that the difference between the number is as small as possible.

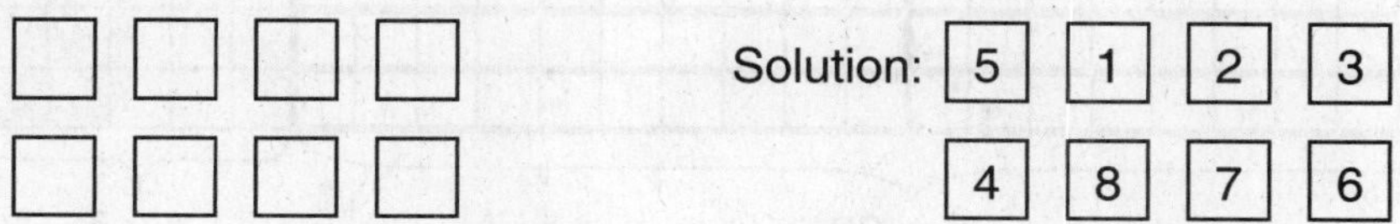

   b) Ask them to place the eight cards so that the three subtraction statements below are correct.

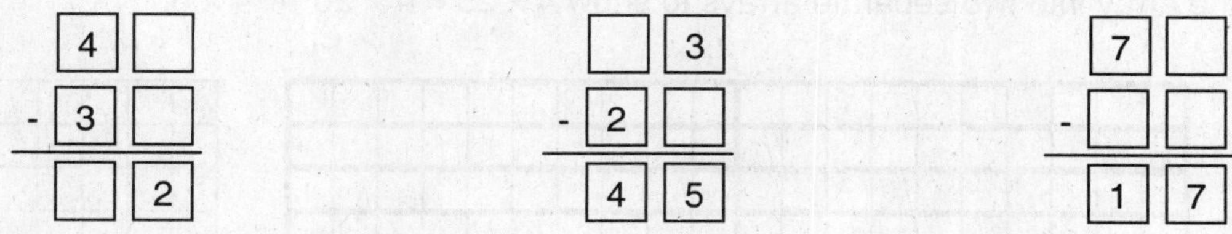

4. Your child can make base ten models to show how to break a product into smaller products. The picture at the top of worksheet NS6-20 on page 55 shows that $4 \times 22 = 4 \times 20 + 4 \times 2$. Ask your child to make a similar model to show that $4 \times 25 = 4 \times 20 + 4 \times 5$.

<u>Step 1:</u>
Make a model of 25 using 2 different colours of base ten blocks (one colour for the tens blocks and one colour for the ones blocks).

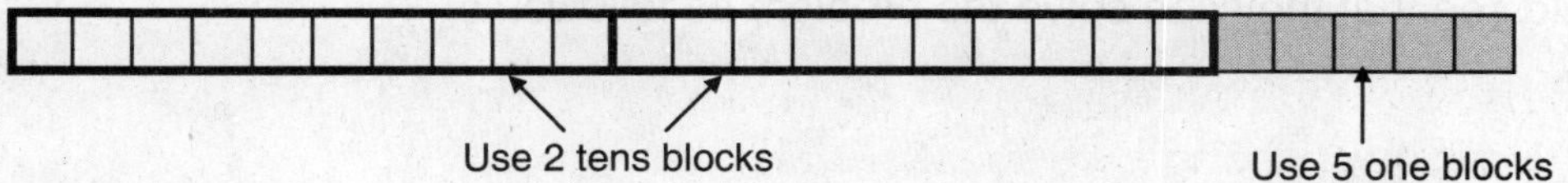

Activities with Concrete Materials

Step 2:

Extend the model to show 4 × 25.

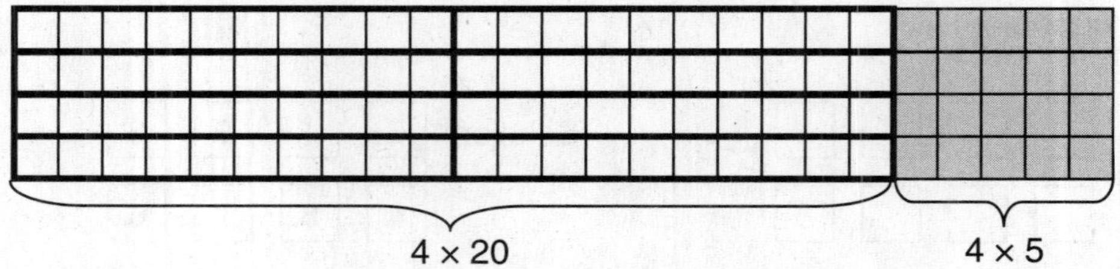

Step 3:

Break the array into two separate arrays to show 4 × 25 = 4 × 20 + 4 × 5.

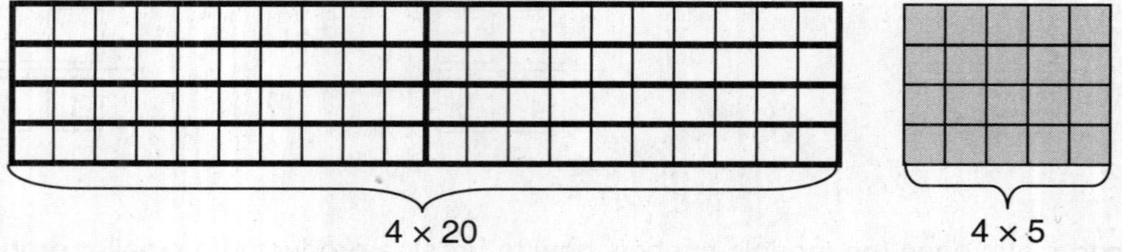

5. Give your child a set of base ten blocks and 3 containers large enough to hold the blocks. Ask them to make a model of 74 using the blocks. Point out that each of the tens blocks they used to make the model is made up of 10 smaller ones blocks. Then ask them to show how they would divide the 74 ones blocks in their model into the three containers as evenly as possible.

   Your child should see that they can solve the problem as follows:

   Step 1:

   Make a representation of 74.

   Step 2:

   Divide the tens blocks among the three containers as evenly as possible.

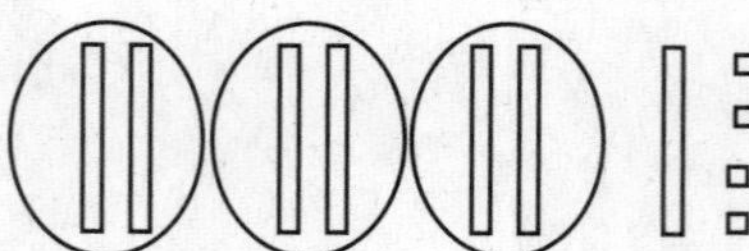

Your child should see that they can only place 2 tens blocks per container, with one left over (7 ÷ 3 = 2 R1). Point out to them that when they perform the standard long division algorithm, they are simply keeping track of the steps they followed in dividing up the tens blocks.

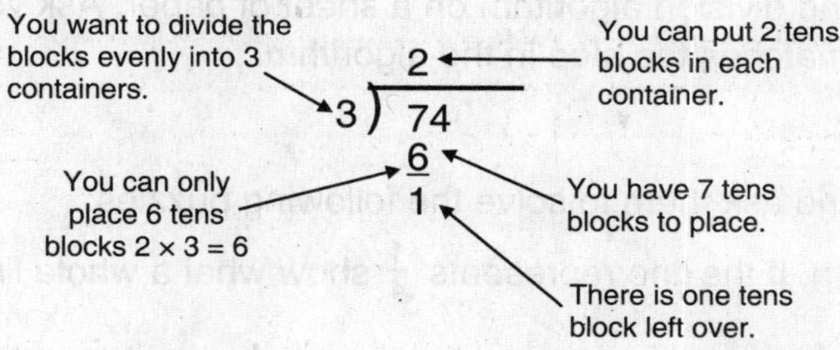
You want to divide the blocks evenly into 3 containers.
2
3) 74
6
1
You can put 2 tens blocks in each container.
You can only place 6 tens blocks 2 × 3 = 6
You have 7 tens blocks to place.
There is one tens block left over.

Step 3:
Your child should recognize that they can only divide up the remaining units if they regroup the tens block as ten ones.

In the long division algorithm, this step is equivalent to brining down the number in the ones column.

```
    2
3 ) 74
    6↓
    14  ← Regroup the tens block as 10 ones and
          put all your ones together – now you
          have 14 ones.
```

Step 4:
Divide the 14 ones among the 3 containers.

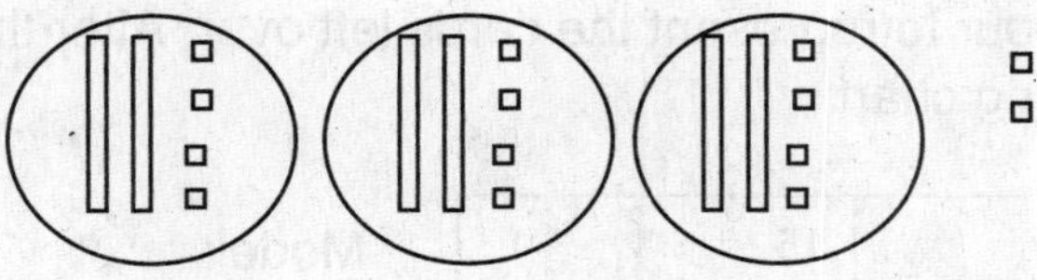

In the algorithm:

```
    24  ← You can put 4 ones
3 ) 74    blocks in each container
    6     (14 ÷ 3 = 4)
    14
    12  ← You can place 12 ones
     2    altogether (4 × 3 = 12)
        ← There are 2 left
          over.
```

Activities with Concrete Materials

After placing the 2 tens blocks and 4 ones blocks into each of the containers, you have placed 24 ones blocks altogether (and this is exactly the number you get on top of the division sign). Play the game with different numbers. Keep track of the steps your child takes with the blocks and write the equivalent step in the long division algorithm on a sheet of paper. Ask your child to explain on paper how the step they took matches the step in the algorithm.

6. Give your child a ruler and ask them to solve the following puzzles:

   a) Draw a line 1 cm long. If the line represents $\frac{1}{4}$ show what a whole line what look like.

   b) Line: 1 cm long. The line represents $\frac{1}{6}$ show the whole.

   c) Line: 2 cm long. The line represents $\frac{1}{3}$ show the whole.

   d) Line: 3 cm long. The line represents $\frac{1}{4}$ show the whole.

   e) Line: $1\frac{1}{2}$ cm long. The line represents $\frac{1}{2}$ show the whole.

   f) Line: $1\frac{1}{2}$ cm long. The line represents $\frac{1}{4}$ show the whole.

   g) Line: 3 cm long. The line represents $\frac{1}{4}$ show $\frac{1}{2}$.

   h) Line: 2 cm long. The line represents $\frac{1}{8}$ show $\frac{1}{4}$.

7. Give your child counters to make a model of the following problem:

Postcards come in packs of 4. How many packs would you need to buy to send 15 postcards? Write a mixed and improper fraction for the number of packs you would use.

Your child could use a counter of a particular colour to represent the post cards they have used and a counter of a different colour to represent the cards left over. After they have made their model, they could fill in the following chart:

Number of Postcards	15
Number of packs of 4 postcards (improper fraction)	$\frac{15}{4}$
Number of packs of 4 postcards (mixed fraction)	$3\frac{3}{4}$

Model:

4 postcards in each package

One left over

Here is another sample problem your child could try:

Juice cans come in boxes of 6. How many boxes would you bring if you needed 20 cans? What fraction of the boxes would you use?

Activities with Concrete Materials

8. Give your child blocks of 2 colours and have them make models of fractions of whole numbers using the method described at the top of the worksheet. Here are some fractions they might try:

   a) $\frac{3}{4}$ of 15 b) $\frac{3}{4}$ of 16 c) $\frac{3}{5}$ of 20 d) $\frac{2}{7}$ of 21

9. Ask your child to draw 4 boxes of equal length on grid paper and shade 1 box:

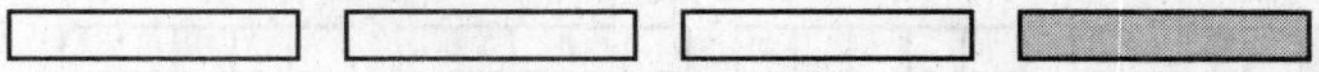

Point out to them that $\frac{1}{4}$ of the area of the boxes is shaded. Now ask them to draw the same set of boxes, but in each box to draw a line dividing the box into 2 parts:

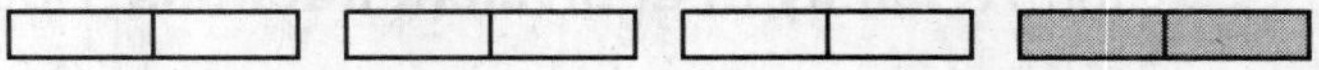

Now $\frac{2}{8}$ of the area is shaded. Repeat the exercise, dividing the boxes into 3 equal parts, (roughly: the sketch doesn't have to be perfectly accurate), then 4 parts, then five parts:

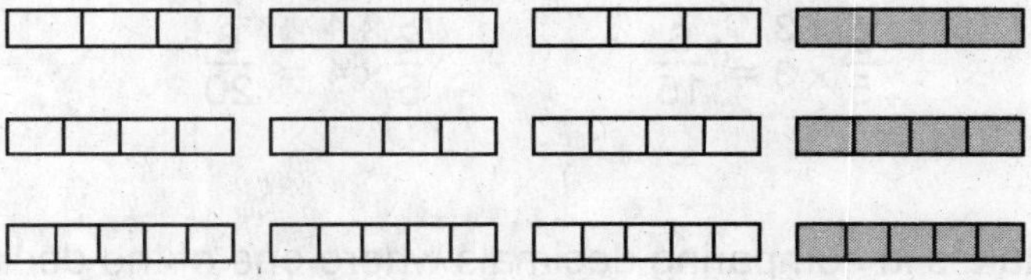

$\frac{3}{12}$ of the area is shaded

$\frac{4}{16}$ of the area is shaded

$\frac{5}{20}$ of the area is shaded

Point out to your child that while the appearance of the fraction changes, the same amount of area is represented:

$\frac{1}{4}, \frac{2}{8}, \frac{3}{12}, \frac{4}{16}, \frac{5}{20}$ all represent the same amount: they are equivalent fractions.

Ask your child how each of the denominators in the fractions above can be generated from the initial fraction of $\frac{1}{4}$:

Answer
Each denominator is a multiple of the denominator 4 in the original fraction:

$8 = 2 \times 4$ $12 = 3 \times 4$ $16 = 4 \times 4$ $20 = 5 \times 4$

Then ask them how each fraction could be generated from the original fraction.

Answer
Multiplying the numerator and denominator of the original fraction by the same number:

$\frac{1 \times 2}{4 \times 2} = \frac{2}{8}$ $\frac{1 \times 3}{4 \times 3} = \frac{3}{12}$ $\frac{1 \times 4}{4 \times 4} = \frac{4}{16}$ $\frac{1 \times 5}{4 \times 5} = \frac{5}{20}$

Activities with Concrete Materials

Point out that multiplying the top and bottom of the original fraction by any given number, say 5, corresponds to cutting each box into that number of pieces:

$$\frac{1 \times 5}{4 \times 5} \begin{array}{l} \leftarrow \text{there are 5 pieces in each box} \\ \leftarrow \text{there are } 4 \times 5 \text{ pieces altogether} \end{array}$$

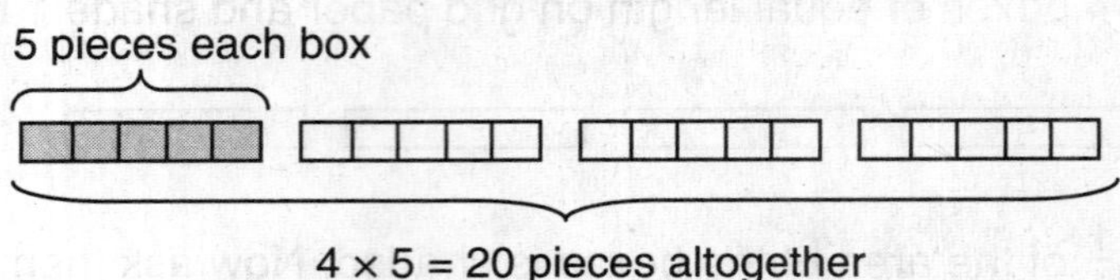

The fractions $\frac{1}{4}$, $\frac{2}{8}$, $\frac{3}{12}$, $\frac{4}{16}$ … form a **family of equivalent fractions**. Notice that no whole number greater than 1 will divide into both the numerator and denominator of $\frac{1}{4}$: $\frac{1}{4}$ is said to be reduced to lowest terms. By multiplying the top and bottom of a reduced fraction by various whole numbers, you can generate an entire fraction family. For instance, $\frac{2}{5}$ generates the family

$$\frac{2 \times 2}{5 \times 2} = \frac{4}{10} \qquad \frac{2 \times 3}{5 \times 3} = \frac{6}{15} \qquad \frac{2 \times 4}{5 \times 4} = \frac{8}{20}$$

10. Children often make mistakes in comparing decimals where one of the decimals is expressed in tenths and the other in hundredths. (For instance, they will say that .17 is greater than .2.) The following activity will help your child understand the relation between tenths and hundredths.

    Give your child a set of play-money dimes and pennies. Explain that a dime is a tenth of a dollar (which is why it is written as \$0.10) and a penny is a hundredth of a dollar (which is why it is written as \$0.01).

    Ask your child to make models of the amounts in the left-hand column of the chart below and to write as many names for the amounts as they can think of in the right-hand columns (sample answers are provided in italics):

Amount	Amount in Pennies	Decimal Names (in words)	Decimal names (in numbers)
2 dimes	*20 pennies*	*2 tenths (of a dollar)* *20 hundredths*	*.2* *.20*
3 pennies	*3 pennies*	*3 hundredths*	*.03*
4 dimes and 3 pennies	*43 pennies*	*4 tenths and 3 hundredths* *43 hundredths*	*.43* *.43*

You should also write various amounts of money on a sheet of paper and have your child make models of the amounts (e.g., make models of .3 dollars, .27 dollars, .07 dollars, etc). Also challenge them to make models of amounts that have 2 different decimal representations (e.g., 2 dimes can be written as .2 dollars or .20 dollars).

When you feel your child is able to translate between money and decimal notation, ask them to say whether they would rather have .2 dollars or .17 dollars. In their answer, they should say exactly how many pennies each amount represents (e.g., they must articulate that .2 represents 20 pennies and so it is actually the larger amount).

Amount (in dollars)	Amount (in pennies)
.2	
.15	

For extra practice, ask your child to fill in the right-hand column of the chart and then circle the greater amount. (Create several charts of this sort for them.)

11. Your child can learn to count forwards and backwards by decimal tenths using dimes.

Ask them to complete the following patterns using dimes to help them count. (Point out that a number such as 2.7, while not standard dollar notation, can be thought of as "2 dollars and 7 dimes."

Ask them to practise saying the money amounts in the sequences below out loud as they count up. For instance, for the sequence "2.7, 2.8, ____, ____," they would say: "2 dollars and 7 dimes, 2 dollars and 8 dimes, 2 dollars and 9 dimes," etc. This will help them see that the next term in the sequence is 3 dollars.

a) .2 , .3 , .4 , ____, ____, ____
b) .7 , .8 , .9 , ____, ____, ____
c) 2.7 , 2.8 , 2.9 , ____, ____, ____
d) 1.4 , 1.3 , 1.2 , ____, ____, ____

Activities with Concrete Materials

12. Give your child a set of base ten blocks and let them know that in the exercises below the hundreds block will represent the number 1 (the unit). This means that the tens block represents a tenth (0.1) and the ones block represents a hundredth (0.01).

    According to this convention, the number 3.25 would be represented as:

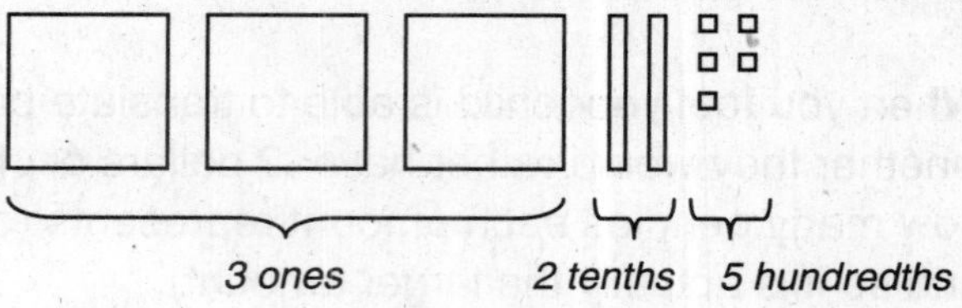

    3 ones 2 tenths 5 hundredths

    a) Start with these blocks:

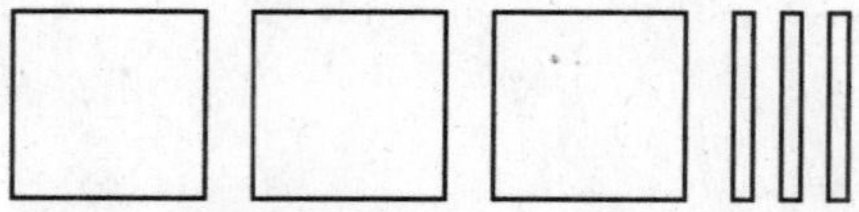

    - Add 2 blocks so that the sum (or total) is between 3.4 and 3.48.
    - Write a decimal for the amount you added.

    b) Take these blocks:

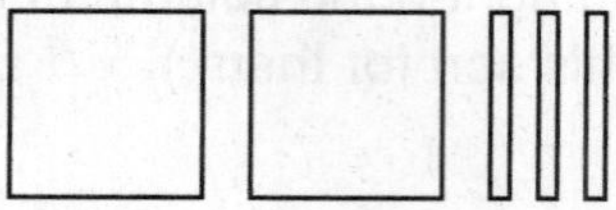

    - Add 2 blocks so that the sum (or total) is between 2.47 and 2.63.
    - Write a decimal for the amount you added.

    c) Take these blocks:

    - Add 2 blocks so that the sum (or total) is between 2.51 and 2.6.
    - Write a decimal for the amount you added.

13. Repeat the exercise of the preceding activity with the following instructions.
    PARENT: Make up more problems of this sort.

    a) Take these blocks:

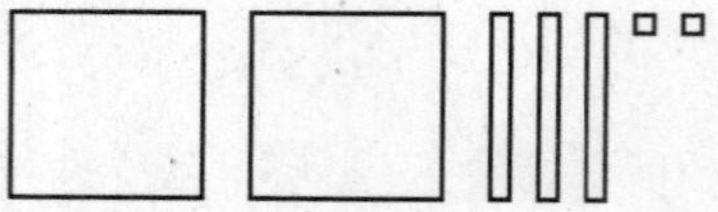

    - Take away 2 blocks so the result (the difference) is between 1.21 and 1.35.
    - Write a decimal for the amount you took away.

    b) Take these blocks:

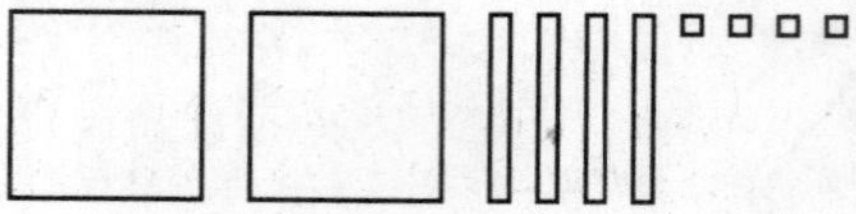

    - Take away 3 blocks so the result (the difference) is between 2.17 and 2.43.
    - Write a decimal for the amount you took away.

Mental Math Skills: Addition and Subtraction

PARENT:
If your child doesn't know their addition and subtraction facts, teach them to add and subtract using their fingers by the methods taught below. You should also reinforce basic facts using drills, games and flash cards. There are mental math strategies that make addition and subtraction easier: some effective strategies are taught in the next section. (Until your child knows all their facts, allow them to add and subtract on their fingers when necessary.)

To **add** 4 + 8, Grace says the greater number (8) with her fist closed. She counts up from 8, raising one finger at a time. She stops when she has raised the number of fingers equal to the lesser number (4):

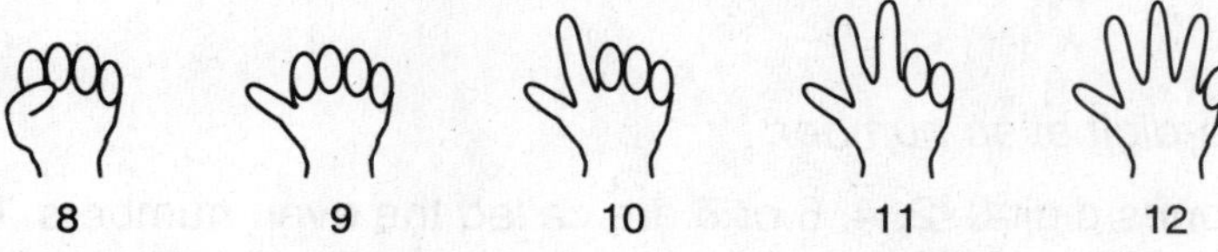

She said "12" when she raised her 4th finger, so: **4 + 8 = 12**

1. Add:

a) 5 + 2 = 7 b) 3 + 2 = 5 c) 6 + 2 = 8 d) 9 + 2 = 11

e) 2 + 4 = 6 f) 2 + 7 = 9 g) 5 + 3 = 8 h) 6 + 3 = 9

i) 11 + 4 = 15 j) 3 + 9 = 12 k) 7 + 3 = 10 l) 14 + 4 = 18

m) 21 + 5 = 26 n) 32 + 3 = 35 o) 4 + 56 = 60 p) 39 + 4 = 43

To **subtract** 9 – 5, Grace says the lesser number (5) with her fist closed. She counts up from 5 raising one finger at a time. She stops when she says the greater number (9):

She has raised 4 fingers when she stopped, so: **9 – 5 = 4**

2. Subtract:

a) 7 – 5 = 2 b) 8 – 6 = 2 c) 5 – 3 = 2 d) 5 – 2 = 3

e) 9 – 6 = 3 f) 10 – 5 = 5 g) 11 – 7 = 4 h) 17 – 14 = 3

i) 33 – 31 = 2 j) 27 – 24 = 3 k) 43 – 39 = 4 l) 62 – 58 = 16

PARENT:
To prepare for the next section (Mental Math), teach your child to add 1 to any number mentally (by counting forward by 1 in their head) and to subtract 1 from any number (by counting backward by 1)

Mental Math Skills: Addition and Subtraction *(continued)*

PARENT:
Children who don't know how to add, subtract or estimate readily are at a great disadvantage in mathematics. Children who have trouble memorizing addition and subtraction facts can still learn to mentally add and subtract numbers in a short time if they are given daily practice in a few basic skills.

<u>SKILL 1</u> – Adding 2 to an Even Number

This skill has been broken down into a number of sub-skills. After teaching each sub-skill, you should give your child a short diagnostic quiz to verify that they have learned the skill. I have included sample quizzes for Skills 1 to 4.

i) *Naming the next one-digit even number:*

Numbers that have ones digit 0, 2, 4, 6 or 8 are called the even numbers. Using drills or games, teach your child to say the sequence of one-digit even numbers without hesitation. Ask them to imagine the sequence going on in a circle so that the next number after 8 is 0 (0, 2, 4, 6, 8, 0, 2, 4, 6, 8, ...). Then play the following game: name a number in the sequence and ask your child to give the next number in the sequence. Don't move on until they have mastered the game.

ii) *Naming the next greatest two-digit even number:*

<u>Case 1 – Numbers that end in 0, 2, 4 or 6</u>
Write an even two-digit number that ends in 0, 2, 4 or 6 on a piece of paper. Ask your child to name the next greatest even number. They should recognize that if a number ends in 0, then the next even number ends in 2; if it ends in 2 then the next even number ends in 4, etc. For instance, the number 54 has ones digit 4, so the next greatest even number will have ones digit 6.

QUIZ

Name the next greatest even number:

a) 52 : 54 b) 64 : 68 c) 36 : 38 d) 22 : 24 e) 80 : 82

<u>Case 2 – Numbers that end in 8</u>
Write the number 58 on a piece of paper. Ask your child to name the next greatest even number. Remind them that even numbers must end in 0, 2, 4, 6 or 8. But 50, 52, 54 and 56 are all less than 58 so the next greatest even number is 60. Your child should see that an even number ending in 8 is always followed by an even number ending in 0 (with a tens digit that is one higher).

Name the next greatest even number:

a) 58 : 60 b) 68 : 70 c) 38 : 40 d) 48 : 50 e) 78 : 80

iii) *Adding 2 to an even number:*

Point out to your child that adding 2 to any even number is equivalent to finding the next even number: e.g., 46 + 2 = 48, 48 + 2 = 50, etc. Knowing this, your child can easily add 2 to any even number.

Mental Math Skills: Addition and Subtraction *(continued)*

QUIZ

Add:

a) 26 + 2 = 28 b) 82 + 2 = 84 c) 40 + 2 = 42 d) 58 + 2 = 60 e) 34 + 2 = 36

SKILL 2 – Subtracting 2 from an Even Number

i) *Finding the preceding one-digit even number:*

Name a one-digit even number and ask your child to give the preceding number in the sequence. For instance, the number that comes before 4 is 2 and the number that comes before 0 is 8. (Remember: the sequence is circular.)

ii) *Finding the preceding two-digit even number:*

Case 1 – Numbers that end in 2, 4, 6 or 8

Write a two-digit number that ends in 2, 4, 6 or 8 on a piece of paper. Ask your child to name the preceding even number. They should recognize that if a number ends in 2, then the preceding even number ends in 0; if it ends in 4 then the preceding even number ends in 2, etc. For instance, the number 78 has ones digit 8, so the preceding even number has ones digit 6.

QUIZ

Name the preceding even number:

a) 48 : 46 b) 26 : 24 c) 34 : 32 d) 62 : 60 e) 78 : 76

Case 2 – Numbers that end in 0

Write the number 80 on a piece of paper and ask your child to name the preceding even number. They should recognize that if an even number ends in 0 then the preceding even number ends in 8 (but the ones digit is one less). So the even number that comes before 80 is 78.

QUIZ

Name the preceding even number:

a) 40 : 38 b) 60 : 58 c) 80 : 78 d) 50 : 48 e) 30 : 28

ii) *Subtracting 2 from an even number:*

Point out to your child that subtracting 2 from any even number is equivalent to finding the preceding even number: e.g., 48 – 2 = 46, 46 – 2 = 44, etc.

QUIZ

Subtract:

a) 58 – 2 = 56 b) 24 – 2 = 22 c) 36 – 2 = 34 d) 42 – 2 = 30 e) 60 – 2 = 58

Mental Math Skills: Addition and Subtraction *(continued)*

SKILL 3 – Adding 2 to an Odd Number

i) *Naming the next one-digit odd number:*

Numbers that have ones digit 1, 3, 5, 7, and 9 are called the odd numbers. Using drills or games, teach your child to say the sequence of one-digit odd numbers without hesitation. Ask them to imagine the sequence going on in a circle so that the next number after 9 is 1 (1, 3, 5, 7, 9, 1, 3, 5, 7, 9, ...). Then play the following game: name a number in the sequence and ask your child to give the next number in the sequence. Don't move on until they have mastered the game.

ii) *Naming the next greatest two-digit odd number:*

Case 1 – Numbers that end in 1, 3, 5 or 7
Write an odd two-digit number that ends in 1, 3, 5, or 7 on a piece of paper. Ask your child to name the next greatest odd number. They should recognize that if a number ends in 1, then the next odd number ends in 3; if it ends in 3 then the next odd number ends in 5, etc. For instance, the number 35 has ones digit 5, so the next greatest odd number will have ones digit 7.

QUIZ

Name the next greatest odd number:

a) 51 : ______ b) 65 : ______ c) 37 : ______ d) 23 : ______ e) 87 : ______

Case 2 – Numbers that end in 9
Write the number 59 on a piece of paper. Ask your child to name the next greatest odd number. Remind them that odd numbers must end in 1, 3, 5, 7 or 9. But 51, 53, 55 and 57 are all less than 59. The next greatest odd number is 61. Your child should see that an odd number ending in 9 is always followed by an odd number ending in 1 (with a tens digit that is one higher).

QUIZ

Name the next greatest odd number:

a) 59 : ______ b) 69 : ______ c) 39 : ______ d) 49 : ______ e) 79 : ______

iii) *Adding 2 to an odd number:*

Point out to your child that adding 2 to any odd number is equivalent to finding the next odd number: e.g., 47 + 2 = 49, 49 + 2 = 51, etc. Knowing this, your child can easily add 2 to any odd number.

QUIZ

Add:

a) 27 + 2 = ____ b) 83 + 2 = ____ c) 41 + 2 = ____ d) 59 + 2 = ____ e) 35 + 2 = ____

Mental Math Skills: Addition and Subtraction *(continued)*

SKILL 4 – Subtracting 2 from an Odd Number

i) *Finding the preceding one-digit odd number:*

Name a one-digit odd number and ask your child to give the preceding number in the sequence. For instance, the number that comes before 3 is 1 and the number that comes before 1 is 9. (Remember: the sequence is circular.)

ii) *Finding the preceding two-digit odd number:*

Case 1 – Numbers that end in 3, 5, 7 or 9

Write a two-digit number that ends in 3, 5, 7 or 9 on a piece of paper. Ask your child to name the preceding odd number. They should recognize that if a number ends in 3, then the preceding odd number ends in 1; if it ends in 5 then the preceding odd number ends in 3, etc. For instance, the number 79 has ones digit 9, so the preceding odd number has ones digit 7.

QUIZ

Name the preceding odd number:

a) 49 : ______ b) 27 : ______ c) 35 : ______ d) 63 : ______ e) 79 : ______

Case 2 – Numbers that end in 1

Write the number 81 on a piece of paper and ask your child to name the preceding odd number. They should recognize that if an odd number ends in 1 then the preceding odd number ends in 9 (but the ones digit is one less). So the odd number that comes before 81 is 79.

QUIZ

Name the preceding odd number:

a) 41 : ______ b) 61 : ______ c) 81 : ______ d) 51 : ______ e) 31 : ______

iii) *Subtracting 2 from an odd number:*

Point out to your child that subtracting 2 from any odd number is equivalent to finding the preceding odd number: e.g., 49 – 2 = 47, 47 – 2 = 45, etc.

QUIZ

Subtract:

a) 59 – 2 = ___ b) 25 – 2 = ___ c) 37 – 2 = ___ d) 43 – 2 = ___ e) 61 – 2 = ___

SKILLS 5 and 6:

Once your child can add and subtract the numbers 1 and 2, then they can easily add and subtract the number 3: Add 3 to a number by first adding 2, then adding 1 (e.g., 35 + 3 = 35 + 2 + 1). Subtract 3 from a number by subtracting 2, then subtracting 1 (e.g., 35 – 3 = 35 – 2 – 1).

Mental Math Skills: Addition and Subtraction *(continued)*

PARENT: All of the addition and subtraction tricks you teach your child should be reinforced with drills, flashcards and tests. Eventually they should memorize their addition and subtraction facts and shouldn't have to rely on the mental math tricks. One of the greatest gifts you can give your child is to teach them their number facts.

SKILLS 7 and 8

Add 4 to a number by adding 2 twice (e.g., 51 + 4 = 51 + 2 + 2). Subtract 4 from a number by subtracting 2 twice (e.g., 51 – 4 = 51 – 2 – 2).

SKILLS 9 and 10

Add 5 to a number by adding 4 then 1. Subtract 5 by subtracting 4 then 1.

SKILL 11

Your child can add pairs of identical numbers by doubling (e.g., 6 + 6 = 2 x 6). They should either memorize the 2 times table or they should double numbers by counting on their fingers by 2s.

Add a pair of numbers that differ by 1 by rewriting the larger number as 1 plus the smaller number (then use doubling to find the sum): e.g., 6 + 7 = 6 + 6 + 1 = 12 + 1 = 13; 7 + 8 = 7 + 7 + 1 = 14 + 1 = 15.

SKILLS 12, 13 and 14

Add a one-digit number to 10 by simply replacing the zero in 10 by the one-digit number: e.g., 10 + 7 = 17.

Add 10 to any two-digit number by simply increasing the tens digit of the two-digit number by 1: e.g., 53 + 10 = 63.

Add a pair of two-digit numbers (with no carrying) by adding the ones digits of the numbers and then adding the tens digits: e.g., 23 + 64 = 87.

SKILLS 15 and 16

To add 9 to a one-digit number, subtract 1 from the number and then add 10: e.g., 9 + 6 = 10 + 5 = 15; 9 + 7 = 10 + 6 = 16. (Essentially, your child simply has to subtract 1 from the number and then stick a 1 in front of the result.)

To add 8 to a one-digit number, subtract 2 from the number and add 10: e.g., 8 + 6 = 10 + 4 = 14; 8 + 7 = 10 + 5 = 15.

SKILLS 17 and 18

To subtract a pair of multiples of ten, simply subtract the tens digits and add a zero for the ones digit: e.g., 70 – 50 = 20.

To subtract a pair of two-digit numbers (without carrying or regrouping), subtract the ones digit from the ones digit and the tens digit from the tens digit: e.g., 57 – 34 = 23.

Mental Math – Further Strategies

Further Mental Math Strategies

1. Your child should be able to explain how to use the strategies of "rounding the subtrahend (i.e., the number you are subtracting) up to the nearest multiple of ten."

Examples:

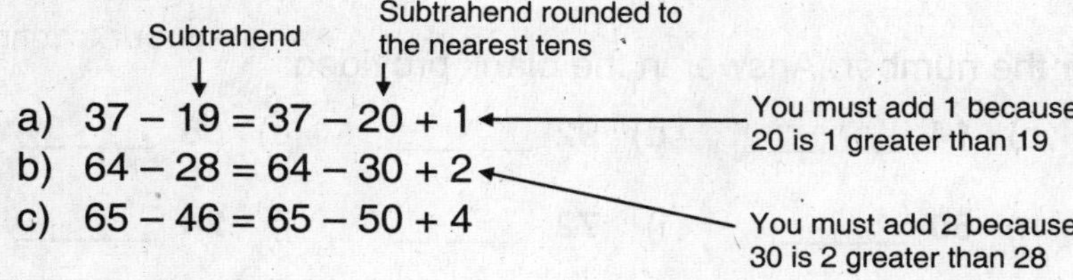
Subtrahend
Subtrahend rounded to the nearest tens
a) 37 – 19 = 37 – 20 + 1
b) 64 – 28 = 64 – 30 + 2
c) 65 – 46 = 65 – 50 + 4
You must add 1 because 20 is 1 greater than 19
You must add 2 because 30 is 2 greater than 28

Practice Questions:

a) 27 – 17 = 27 – ____ + ____
b) 52 – 36 = 52 – ____ + ____
c) 76 – 49 = 76 – ____ + ____
d) 84 – 57 = 84 – ____ + ____
e) 61 – 29 = 61 – ____ + ____
f) 42 – 18 = 42 – ____ + ____

PARENT: This strategy works well with numbers that end in 6, 7, 8 or 9.

2. Your child should be able to explain how to subtract by thinking of adding.

Examples:

Count by ones from 45 to the nearest tens (50)

Count from 50 until you reach the first number (62).

a) 62 – 45 = 5 + 12 = 17 ← The sum of counting up to the nearest ten and the original number is the difference.
b) 46 – 23 = 3 + 20 = 23
c) 73 – 17 = 6 + 50 = 56

} ← What method did we use here?

Practice Questions:

a) 88 – 36 = ____ + ____ = ____
b) 58 – 21 = ____ + ____ = ____
c) 43 – 17 = ____ + ____ = ____
d) 74 – 28 = ____ + ____ = ____
e) 93 – 64 = ____ + ____ = ____
f) 82 – 71 = ____ + ____ = ____

3. Your child should be able to explain how to "use doubles."

Examples:

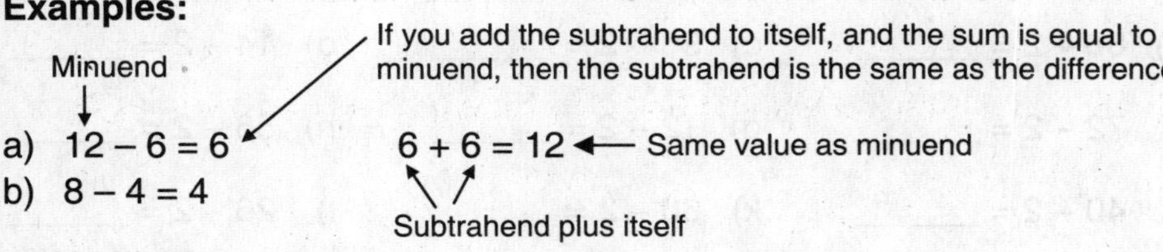
Minuend
If you add the subtrahend to itself, and the sum is equal to the minuend, then the subtrahend is the same as the difference.
a) 12 – 6 = 6
b) 8 – 4 = 4
6 + 6 = 12
Same value as minuend
Subtrahend plus itself

Practice Questions:

a) 6 – 3 = ____
b) 10 – 5 = ____
c) 14 – 7 = ____
d) 18 – 9 = ____
e) 16 – 8 = ____
f) 20 – 10 = ____

Mental Math Exercises

PARENT: Teaching the material on these Mental Math worksheets may take several lessons. Your child will need more practice than is provided on these pages. These pages are intended as a test to be given when you are certain your child has learned the materials fully.

PARENT: Teach skills 1, 2, 3 and 4 as outlined on pages xxiv-xxvii before you allow your child to answer Questions 1 through 12:

1. Name the <u>even</u> number that comes <u>after</u> the number. Answer in the blank provided:

a) **32** ______ b) **46** ______ c) **14** ______ d) **92** ______ e) **56** ______

f) **30** ______ g) **84** ______ h) **60** ______ i) **72** ______ j) **24** ______

2. Name the <u>even</u> number that comes <u>after</u> the number:

a) **28** ______ b) **18** ______ c) **78** ______ d) **38** ______ e) **68** ______

3. Add:

REMEMBER: Adding 2 to an even number is the same as finding the next even number.

a) 42 + 2 = ______ b) 76 + 2 = ______ c) 28 + 2 = ______ d) 16 + 2 = ______

e) 68+ 2 = ______ f) 12 + 2 = ______ g) 36 + 2 = ______ h) 90 + 2 = ______

i) 70 + 2 = ______ j) 24 + 2 = ______ k) 66 + 2 = ______ l) 52 + 2 = ______

4. Name the <u>even</u> number that comes <u>before</u> the number:

a) **38** ______ b) **42** ______ c) **56** ______ d) **72** ______ e) **98** ______

f) **48** ______ g) **16** ______ h) **22** ______ i) **66** ______ j) **14** ______

5. Name the <u>even</u> number that comes <u>before</u> the number:

a) **30** ______ b) **70** ______ c) **60** ______ d) **10** ______ e) **80** ______

6. Subtract:

REMEMBER: Subtracting 2 from an even number is the same as finding the preceding even number.

a) 46 − 2 = ______ b) 86 − 2 = ______ c) 90 − 2 = ______ d) 14 − 2 = ______

e) 54 − 2 = ______ f) 72 − 2 = ______ g) 12 − 2 = ______ h) 56 − 2 = ______

i) 32 − 2 = ______ j) 40 − 2 = ______ k) 60 − 2 = ______ l) 26 − 2 = ______

7. Name the <u>odd</u> number that comes <u>after</u> the number:

a) **37** ______ b) **51** ______ c) **63** ______ d) **75** ______ e) **17** ______

f) **61** ______ g) **43** ______ h) **81** ______ i) **23** ______ j) **95** ______

8. Name the <u>odd</u> number that comes <u>after</u> the number:

a) **69** ______ b) **29** ______ c) **9** ______ d) **79** ______ e) **59** ______

Mental Math Exercises *(continued)*

9. Add:

REMEMBER: Adding 2 to an odd number is the same as finding the next odd number.

a) 25 + 2 = 27 b) 31 + 2 = 33 c) 47 + 2 = 49 d) 33 + 2 = 35

e) 39 + 2 = 41 f) 91 + 2 = 93 g) 5 + 2 = 7 h) 89 + 2 = 91

i) 11 + 2 = 13 j) 65 + 2 = 67 k) 29 + 2 = 31 l) 17 + 2 = 19

10. Name the <u>odd</u> number that comes <u>before</u> the number:

a) **39** 37 b) **43** 41 c) **57** ______ d) **17** ______ e) **99** ______

f) **13** 11 g) **85** 83 h) **79** 7 i) **65** ______ j) **77** ______

11. Name the <u>odd</u> number that comes <u>before</u> the number:

a) **21** ______ b) **41** ______ c) **11** ______ d) **91** ______ e) **51** ______

12. Subtract:

REMEMBER: Subtracting 2 from an odd number is the same as finding the preceding odd number.

a) 47 − 2 = ______ b) 85 − 2 = ______ c) 91 − 2 = ______ d) 15 − 2 = ______

e) 51 − 2 = ______ f) 73 − 2 = ______ g) 11 − 2 = ______ h) 59 − 2 = ______

i) 31 − 2 = ______ j) 43 − 2 = ______ k) 7 − 2 = ______ l) 25 − 2 = ______

PARENT:
Teach skills 5 and 6 as outlined on page xxvii before you allow your child to answer Questions 13 and 14.

13. Add 3 to the number by adding 2, then adding 1 (e.g., 35 + 3 = 35 + 2 + 1):

a) 23 + 3 = ______ b) 36 + 3 = ______ c) 29+ 3 = ______ d) 16 + 3 = ______

e) 67 + 3 = ______ f) 12 + 3 = ______ g) 35 + 3 = ______ h) 90 + 3 = ______

i) 78 + 3 = ______ j) 24 + 3 = ______ k) 6 + 3 = ______ l) 59 + 3 = ______

14. Subtract 3 from the number by subtracting 2, then subtracting 1 (e.g., 35 − 3 = 35 − 2 − 1):

a) 46 − 3 = ______ b) 87 − 3 = ______ c) 99 − 3 = ______ d) 14 − 3 = ______

e) 8 − 3 = ______ f) 72 − 3 = ______ g) 12 − 3 = ______ h) 57 − 3 = ______

i) 32 − 3 = ______ j) 40 − 3 = ______ k) 60 − 3 = ______ l) 28 − 3 = ______

15. Fred has 49 stamps. He gives 2 stamps away. How many stamps does he have left?

47 stamps

16. There are 25 minnows in a tank. Alice adds 3 more to the tank. How many minnows are now in the tank?

28minnows

Mental Math Exercises *(continued)*

PARENT:
Teach skills 7 and 8 as outlined on page xxviii.

17. Add 4 to the number by adding 2 twice (e.g., 51 + 4 = 51 + 2 + 2):

a) 42 + 4 = ________ b) 76 + 4 = ________ c) 27 + 4 = ________ d) 17 + 4 = ________

e) 68 + 4 = ________ f) 11 + 4 = ________ g) 35 + 4 = ________ h) 8 + 4 = ________

i) 72 + 4 = ________ j) 23 + 4 = ________ k) 60 + 4 = ________ l) 59 + 4 = ________

18. Subtract 4 from the number by subtracting 2 twice (e.g., 26 – 4 = 26 – 2 – 2):

a) 46 – 4 = ________ b) 86 – 4 = ________ c) 91 – 4 = ________ d) 15 – 4 = ________

e) 53 – 4 = ________ f) 9 – 4 = ________ g) 13 – 4 = ________ h) 57 – 4 = ________

i) 40 – 4 = ________ j) 88 – 4 = ________ k) 69 – 4 = ________ l) 31 – 4 = ________

PARENT:
Teach skills 9 and 10 as outlined on page xxviii.

19. Add 5 to the number by adding 4, then adding 1 (or add 2 twice, then add 1):

a) 84 + 5 = ________ b) 27 + 5 = ________ c) 31 + 5 = ________ d) 44 + 5 = ________

e) 63 + 5 = ________ f) 92 + 5 = ________ g) 14 + 5 = ________ h) 16 + 5 = ________

i) 9 + 5 = ________ j) 81 + 5 = ________ k) 51 + 5 = ________ l) 28 + 5 = ________

20. Subtract 5 from the number by subtracting 4, then subtracting 1 (or subtract 2 twice, then subtract 1):

a) 48 – 5 = ______ b) 86 – 5 = ______ c) 55 – 5 = ______ d) 69 – 5 = ______

e) 30 – 5 = ______ f) 13 – 5 = ______ g) 92 – 5 = ______ h) 77 – 5 = ______

i) 45 – 5 = ______ j) 24 – 5 = ______ k) 91 – 5 = ______ l) 8 – 5 = ______

PARENT:
Teach skill 11 as outlined on page xxviii.

21. Add:

a) 6 + 6 = ______ b) 7 + 7 = ______ c) 8 + 8 = ______

d) 5 + 5 = ______ e) 4 + 4 = ______ f) 9 + 9 = ______

22. Add by thinking of the larger number as a sum of two smaller numbers. The first one is done for you:

a) 6 + 7 = 6 + 6 + 1 b) 7 + 8 = ____________ c) 6 + 8 = ____________

d) 4 + 5 = ____________ e) 5 + 7 = ____________ f) 8 + 9 = ____________

Mental Math Exercises *(continued)*

PARENT:
Teach skills 12, 13 and 14 as outlined on page xxviii.

23. a) 10 + 3 = ______ b) 10 + 7 = ______ c) 5 + 10 = ______ d) 10 + 1 = ______
e) 9 + 10 = ______ f) 10 + 4 = ______ g) 10 + 8 = ______ h) 10 + 2 = ______

24. a) 10 + 20 = ______ b) 40 + 10 = ______ c) 10 + 80 = ______ d) 10 + 50 = ______
e) 30 + 10 = ______ f) 10 + 60= ______ g) 10 + 10 = ______ h) 70 + 10 = ______

25. a) 10 + 25 = ______ b) 10 + 67 = ______ c) 10 + 31 = ______ d) 10 + 82 = ______
e) 10 + 43 = ______ f) 10 + 51 = ______ g) 10 + 68 = ______ h) 10 + 21 = ______
i) 10 + 11 = ______ j) 10 + 19 = ______ k) 10 + 44 = ______ l) 10 + 88 = ______

26. a) 20 + 30 = ______ b) 40 + 20 = ______ c) 30 + 30 = ______ d) 50 + 30 = ______
e) 20 + 50 = ______ f) 40 + 40 = ______ g) 50 + 40 = ______ h) 40 + 30 = ______
i) 60 + 30 = ______ j) 20 + 60 = ______ k) 20 + 70 = ______ l) 60 + 40 = ______

27. a) 20 + 23 = ______ b) 32 + 24 = ______ c) 51 + 12 = ______ d) 12 + 67 = ______
e) 83 + 14 = ______ f) 65 + 24 = ______ g) 41 + 43 = ______ h) 70 + 27 = ______
i) 31 + 61 = ______ j) 54 + 33 = ______ k) 28 + 31 = ______ l) 42 + 55 = ______

PARENT:
Teach skills 15 and 16 as outlined on page xxviii.

28. a) 9 + 3 = ______ b) 9 + 7 = ______ c) 6 + 9 = ______ d) 4 + 9 = ______
e) 9 + 9 = ______ f) 5 + 9 = ______ g) 9 + 2 = ______ h) 9 + 8 = ______

29. a) 8 + 2 = ______ b) 8 + 6 = ______ c) 8 + 7 = ______ d) 4 + 8 = ______
e) 5 + 8 = ______ f) 8 + 3 = ______ g) 9 + 8 = ______ h) 8 + 8 = ______

PARENT:
Teach skills 17 and 18 as outlined on page xxviii.

30. a) 40 − 10 = ______ b) 50 − 10 = ______ c) 70 − 10 = ______ d) 20 − 10 = ______
e) 40 − 20 = ______ f) 60 − 30 = ______ g) 40 − 30 = ______ h) 60 − 50 = ______

31. a) 57 − 34 = ______ b) 43 − 12 = ______ c) 62 − 21 = ______ d) 59 − 36 = ______
e) 87 − 63 = ______ f) 95 − 62 = ______ g) 35 − 10 = ______ h) 17 − 8 = ______

Mental Math (Advanced)

Multiples of Ten

NOTE:
In the exercises below, you will learn several ways to use multiples of ten in mental addition or subtraction.

I

542 + 214 = 542 + 200 + 10 + 4 = 742 + 10 + 4 = 752 + 4 = 756

827 − 314 = 827 − 300 − 10 − 4 = 527 − 10 − 4 = 517 − 4 = 713

Sometimes you will need to carry:

545 + 172 = 545 + 100 + 70 + 2 = 645 + 70 + 2 = 715 + 2 = 717

1. Warm up:

a) 536 + 100 = b) 816 + 10 = c) 124 + 5 = d) 540 + 200 =

e) 234 + 30 = f) 345 + 300 = g) 236 − 30 = h) 442 − 20 =

i) 970 − 70 = j) 542 − 400 = k) 160 + 50 = l) 756 + 40 =

2. Write the second number in expanded form and add or subtract one digit at a time. The first one is done for you:

a) 564 + 215 = 564 + 200 + 10 + 5 = 779

b) 445 + 343 = ______ = ______

c) 234 + 214 = ______ = ______

3. Add or subtract mentally (one digit at a time):

a) 547 + 312 = b) 578 − 314 = c) 845 − 454 =

II

If one of the numbers you are adding or subtracting is close to a number that is a multiple of ten, add the multiple of ten and then add or subtract an adjustment factor:

645 + 99 = 645 + 100 − 1 = 745 − 1 = 744

856 + 42 = 856 + 40 + 2 = 896 + 2 = 898

III

Sometimes in subtraction, it helps to think of a multiple of ten as a sum of 1 and a number consisting entirely of 9s (e.g., 100 = 1 + 99; 1000 = 1 + 999). You never have to borrow or exchange when you are subtracting from a number consisting entirely of 9s.

100 − 43 = 1 + 99 − 43 = 1 + 56 = 57 ← *Do the subtraction, using 99 instead of 100, and then add 1 to your answer.*

1000 − 543 = 1 + 999 − 543 = 1 + 456 = 457

4. Use the tricks you've just learned:

a) 845 + 91 = b) 456 + 298 = c) 100 − 84 = d) 1000 − 846 =

Mental Math Game: Modified Go Fish

PURPOSE:

If children know the pairs of one-digit numbers that add up to particular **target numbers**, they will be able to mentally break sums into easier sums.

EXAMPLE:

As it is easy to add any one-digit number to 10, you can add a sum more readily if you can decompose numbers in the sum into pairs that add to ten. For example:

$$7 + 5 = \underbrace{7 + 3}_{\text{These numbers add to 10.}} + 2 = 10 + 2 = 12$$

To help children remember pairs of numbers that add up to a given target number, I developed a variation of "Go Fish" that I have found very effective.

THE GAME:

Pick any target number and remove all the cards with value greater than or equal to the target number out of the deck. In what follows, I will assume that the target number is 10, so you would take all the tens and face cards out of the deck (aces count as one).

The dealer gives each player six cards. If a player has any pairs of cards that add to 10 they are allowed to place these pairs on the table before play begins.

Player 1 selects one of the cards in his or her hand and asks Player 2 for a card that adds to 10 with the chosen card. For instance, if Player 1's chosen card is a 3, they may ask Player 2 for a 7.

If Player 2 has the requested card, Player 1 takes it and lays it down along with the card from their hand. Player 1 may then ask for another card. If Player 2 does not have the requested card, they say, "Go fish," and Player 1 must pick up a card from the top of the deck. (If this card adds to 10 with a card in Player 1's hand, they may lay down the pair right away.) It is then Player 2's turn to ask for a card.

Play ends when one player lays down all of their cards. Players receive 4 points for laying down all of their cards first and 1 point for each pair they have laid down.

PARENT: If your child is having difficulty, I would recommend that you start with pairs of numbers that add to 5. Take all cards with value greater than 4 out of the deck. Each player should be dealt only four cards to start with.

I have worked with several children who have had a great deal of trouble sorting their cards and finding pairs that add to a target number. I have found that the following exercise helps:

Give your child only three cards, two of which add to the target number. Ask them to find the pair that adds to the target number. After your child has mastered this step with three cards, repeat the exercise with four cards, then five cards, and so on.

PARENT: You can also give your child a list of the pairs that add to the target number. As your child gets used to the game, gradually remove pairs from the list so that they learn the pairs by memory.

Hundreds Charts

1	2	3	4	5	6	7	8	9	10
11	12	13	14	15	16	17	18	19	20
21	22	23	24	25	26	27	28	29	30
31	32	33	34	35	36	37	38	39	40
41	42	43	44	45	46	47	48	49	50
51	52	53	54	55	56	57	58	59	60
61	62	63	64	65	66	67	68	69	70
71	72	73	74	75	76	77	78	79	80
81	82	83	84	85	86	87	88	89	90
91	92	93	94	95	96	97	98	99	100

1	2	3	4	5	6	7	8	9	10
11	12	13	14	15	16	17	18	19	20
21	22	23	24	25	26	27	28	29	30
31	32	33	34	35	36	37	38	39	40
41	42	43	44	45	46	47	48	49	50
51	52	53	54	55	56	57	58	59	60
61	62	63	64	65	66	67	68	69	70
71	72	73	74	75	76	77	78	79	80
81	82	83	84	85	86	87	88	89	90
91	92	93	94	95	96	97	98	99	100

1	2	3	4	5	6	7	8	9	10
11	12	13	14	15	16	17	18	19	20
21	22	23	24	25	26	27	28	29	30
31	32	33	34	35	36	37	38	39	40
41	42	43	44	45	46	47	48	49	50
51	52	53	54	55	56	57	58	59	60
61	62	63	64	65	66	67	68	69	70
71	72	73	74	75	76	77	78	79	80
81	82	83	84	85	86	87	88	89	90
91	92	93	94	95	96	97	98	99	100

1	2	3	4	5	6	7	8	9	10
11	12	13	14	15	16	17	18	19	20
21	22	23	24	25	26	27	28	29	30
31	32	33	34	35	36	37	38	39	40
41	42	43	44	45	46	47	48	49	50
51	52	53	54	55	56	57	58	59	60
61	62	63	64	65	66	67	68	69	70
71	72	73	74	75	76	77	78	79	80
81	82	83	84	85	86	87	88	89	90
91	92	93	94	95	96	97	98	99	100

How to Learn Your Times Tables in 5 Days

PARENT:
Trying to do math without knowing your times tables is like trying to play the piano without knowing the location of the notes on the keyboard. Your students will have difficulty seeing patterns in sequences and charts, solving proportions, finding equivalent fractions, decimals and percents, solving problems etc. if they don't know their tables.

Using the method below, you can teach your students their tables in a week or so. (If you set aside five or ten minutes a day to work with students who need extra help, the pay-off will be enormous.) There is really no reason for your students not to know their tables!

DAY 1: Counting by 2s, 3s, 4s, and 5s

If you have completed the JUMP Fractions unit you should already know how to count and multiply by 2s, 3s, 4s, and 5s. If you do not know how to count by these numbers you should memorize the hands:

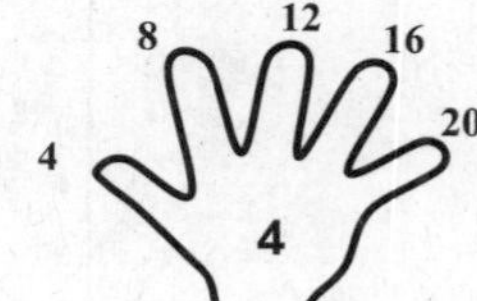

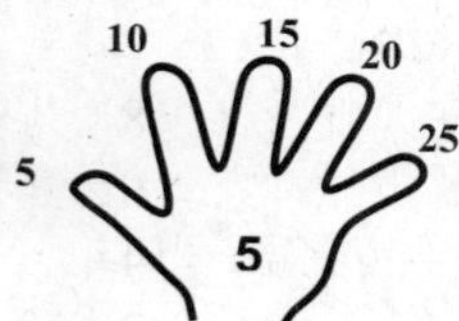

If you know how to count by 2s, 3s, 4s, and 5s, then you can multiply by any combination of these numbers. For instance, to find the product of 3 × 2, count by 2s until you have raised 3 fingers:

2

4

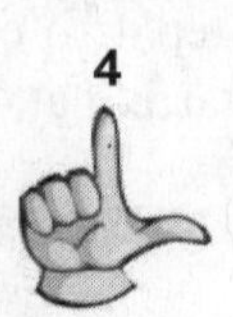

6

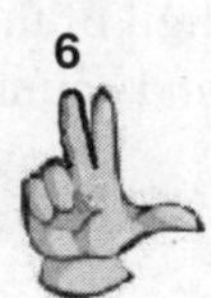

3 × 2 = 6

DAY 2: The 9 Times Table

The numbers you say when you count by 9s are called the **multiples** of 9 (0 is also a multiple of 9). The first ten multiples of 9 (after 0) are 9, 18, 27, 36, 45, 54, 63, 72, 81, and 90. What happens when you add the digits of any of these multiples of 9 (such as 1 + 8 or 6 + 3)? The sum is always 9!

Here is another useful fact about the 9 times table: Multiply 9 by any number between 1 and 10 and look at the tens digit of the product. The tens digit is always one less than the number you multiplied by:

9 × 4 = 36 — 3 is one less than 4

9 × 8 = 72 — 7 is one less than 8

9 × 2 = 18 — 1 is one less than 2

You can find the product of 9 and any number by using the two facts given above. For example, to find 9 × 7, follow these steps:

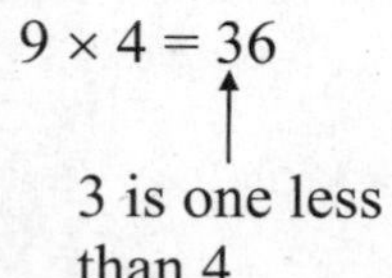

Subtract 1 from the number you are multiplying by 9: **7 – 1 = 6**

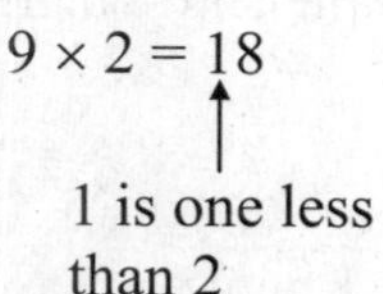

Now you know the tens digit of the product.

Step 2: $9 \times 7 = \underline{6}\ \underline{\ \ }$

These two digits add to 9.

$9 \times 7 = \underline{6}\ \underline{3}$

So the missing digit is 9 – 6 = **3**.
(You can do the subtraction on your fingers if necessary.)

Practise these two steps for all of the products of 9: 9×2, 9×3, 9×4, and so on.

DAY 3: The 8 Times Table

There are two patterns in the digits of the 8 times table. Knowing these patterns will help you remember how to count by 8s.

Step 1: You can find the ones digit of the first five multiples of 8, by starting at 8 and counting backwards by 2s.

8
6
4
2
0

Step 2: You can find the tens digit of the first five multiples of 8, by starting at 0 and counting up by 1s.

08
16
24
32
40

(Of course you do not need to write the 0 in front of the 8 for the product 1×8.)

Step 3: You can find the ones digit of the next five multiples of 8 by repeating step 1.

8
6
4
2
0

Step 4: You can find the remaining tens digits by starting at 4 and counting by 1s.

48
56
64
72
80

Practise writing the multiples of 8 (up to 80) until you have memorized the complete list. Knowing the patterns in the digits of the multiples of 8 will help you memorize the list very quickly. Then you will know how to multiply by 8.

$8 \times 6 = 48$

Count by 8 until you have 6 fingers up: 8, 16, 24, 32, 40, 48.

DAY 4: The 6 Times Table

If you have learned the 8 and 9 times tables, then you already know 6×9 and 6×8.

And if you know how to multiply by 5 up to 5×5, then you also know how to multiply by 6 up to 6×5! That is because you can always calculate 6 times a number by calculating 5 times the number and then adding the number itself to the result. The pictures below show how this works for 6×4:

6 × 4 { 5 × 4 } ← plus one more 4

5 fours — plus one more 4

$$6 \times 4 = 4 + 4 + 4 + 4 + 4 + 4$$

$$\mathbf{6} \times 4 = \mathbf{5} \times 4 + 4 = 20 + 4 = 24$$

Similarly: $\mathbf{6} \times 2 = \mathbf{5} \times 2 + 2$; $\mathbf{6} \times 3 = \mathbf{5} \times 3 + 3$; $\mathbf{6} \times 5 = \mathbf{5} \times 5 + 5$.

Knowing this, you only need to memorize 2 facts:

6 × 6 = 36 **6 × 7 = 42**

Or, if you know 6×5, you can find 6×6 by calculating $6 \times 5 + 5$.

DAY 5: The 7 Times Table

If you have learned the 6, 8, and 9 times tables, then you already know 6×7, 8×7, and 9×7.

And since you also already know $1 \times 7 = 7$, you only need to memorize 5 facts:

2 × 7 = 14 **3 × 7 = 21** **4 × 7 = 28** **5 × 7 = 35** **7 × 7 = 49**

If you are able to memorize your own phone number, then you can easily memorize these 5 facts!

NOTE: You can use doubling to help you learn the facts above: 4 is double 2, so 4×7 (28) is double 2×7 (14); 6 is double 3, so 6×7 (42) is double 3×7 (21).

Try this test every day until you have learned your times tables.

1. 3 × 5 = 15	2. 8 × 4 = ____	3. 9 × 3 = ____	4. 4 × 5 = ____
5. 2 × 3 = ____	6. 4 × 2 = ____	7. 8 × 1 = ____	8. 6 × 6 = ____
9. 9 × 7 = ____	10. 7 × 7 = ____	11. 5 × 8 = ____	12. 2 × 6 = ____
13. 6 × 4 = ____	14. 7 × 3 = ____	15. 4 × 9 = ____	16. 2 × 9 = ____
17. 9 × 9 = ____	18. 3 × 4 = ____	19. 6 × 8 = ____	20. 7 × 5 = ____
21. 9 × 5 = ____	22. 5 × 6 = ____	23. 6 × 3 = ____	24. 7 × 1 = ____
25. 8 × 3 = ____	26. 9 × 6 = ____	27. 4 × 7 = ____	28. 3 × 3 = ____
29. 8 × 7 = ____	30. 1 × 5 = ____	31. 7 × 6 = ____	32. 2 × 8 = ____

Base Ten Blocks

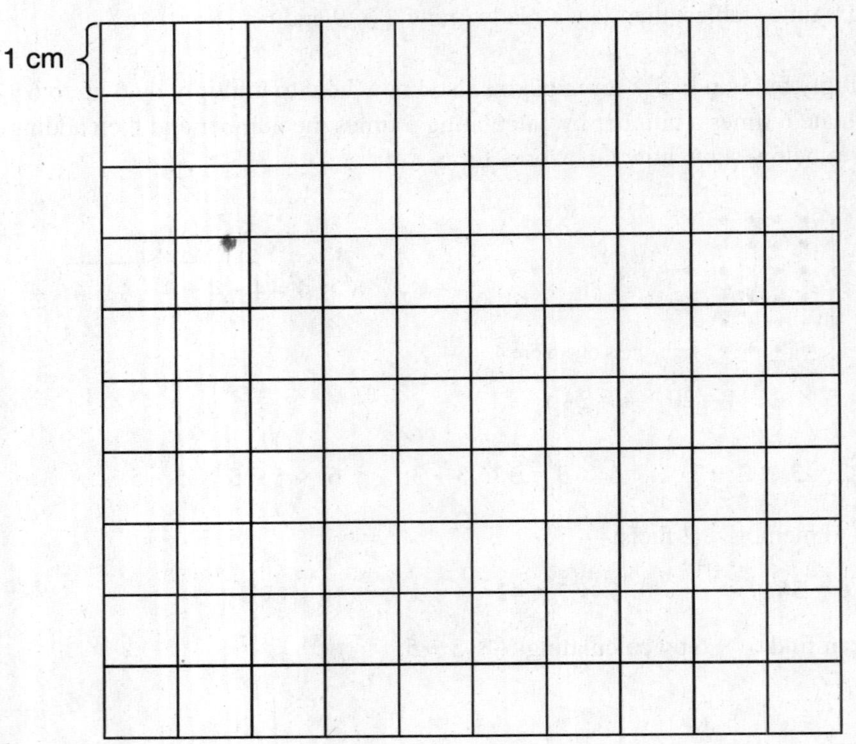

Hundreds Block

1 cm

1 cm

Ones Blocks

PA6-1: Increasing Sequences

In an **increasing sequence**, each number is greater than the one before it.

Deborah wants to continue the number pattern: 6 , 8 , 10 , 12 , ?

She finds the **difference** between the first two numbers:

6 7 8

(2)
6 , 8 , 10 , 12 , ?

She finds that the difference between the other numbers in the pattern is also 2. So the pattern was made by adding 2:

(2) (2) (2)
6 , 8 , 10 , 12 , ?

To continue the pattern, Deborah adds 2 to the last number in the sequence.

The final number in the pattern is 14:

(2) (2) (2) (2)
6 , 8 , 10 , 12 , 14

---

1. Extend the following patterns. Start by finding the gap between the numbers.

a) 2 , 5 , 8 , ___ , ___ , ___

b) 1 , 7 , 13 , ___ , ___ , ___

c) 2 , 7 , 12 , ___ , ___ , ___

d) 4 , 8 , 12 , ___ , ___ , ___

e) 1 , 6 , 11 , ___ , ___ , ___

f) 4 , 10 , 16 , ___ , ___ , ___

g) 2 , 12 , 22 , ___ , ___ , ___

h) 7 , 15 , 23 , ___ , ___ , ___

i) 31 , 34 , 37 , ___ , ___ , ___

j) 92 , 98 , 104 , ___ , ___ , ___

k) 12 , 23 , 34 , ___ , ___ , ___

l) 0 , 8 , 16 , ___ , ___ , ___

2. A plant that is 17 cm high grows 2 cm each day.

a) How high will the plant be after three days? 21 cm

b) In how many days will the plant be 27 cm high? 5 days

PA6-2: Decreasing Sequences

In a **decreasing sequence**, each number is less than the one before it.

Inder wants to continue the number pattern: 25 , 23 , 21 , ?

She finds the **difference** between the first two numbers: 25 24 23 (-2) 25 , 23 , 21 , ?

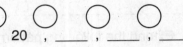

She finds that the difference between the other numbers in the pattern is also 2. So the pattern was made by subtracting 2. (-2) (-2) 25 , 23 , 21 , ?

The final number in the pattern is 19: (-2) (-2) (-2) 25 , 23 , 21 , 19

---

1. Extend the following patterns:

a) 18 , 15 , 12 , ___ , ___ , ___   b) 32 , 26 , 20 , ___ , ___ , ___

c) 52 , 47 , 42 , ___ , ___ , ___   d) 34 , 30 , 26 , ___ , ___ , ___

e) 51 , 46 , 41 , ___ , ___ , ___   f) 84 , 80 , 76 , ___ , ___ , ___

g) 62 , 51 , 40 , ___ , ___ , ___   h) 97 , 89 , 81 , ___ , ___ , ___

i) 71 , 64 , 57 , ___ , ___ , ___   j) 62 , 58 , 54 , ___ , ___ , ___

k) 82 , 73 , 64 , ___ , ___ , ___   l) 84 , 72 , 60 , ___ , ___ , ___

Use decreasing sequences to solve these problems:

2. Judi has saved $49. She spends $8 each day. How much money does she have left after 5 days?

3. Yen has a roll of 74 stamps. She uses 7 each day for 4 days. How many are left?

PA6-3: Extending a Pattern Using a Rule

1. Continue the following sequences by adding the number given:

a) (add 4) 41, 45, ______, ______, ______

b) (add 8) 60, 68, ______, ______, ______

c) (add 3) 74, 77, ______, ______, ______

d) (add 11) 20, 31, ______, ______, ______

e) (add 8) 61, 69, ______, ______, ______

f) (add 11) 31, 42, ______, ______, ______

2. Continue the following sequences by subtracting the number given:

a) (subtract 3) 25, 22, ______, ______, ______

b) (subtract 2) 34, 32, ______, ______, ______

c) (subtract 6) 85, 79, ______, ______, ______

d) (subtract 12) 89, 77, ______, ______, ______

e) (subtract 8) 57, 49, ______, ______, ______

f) (subtract 7) 57, 50, ______, ______, ______

BONUS

3. Create a pattern of your own. After writing the pattern in the blanks, say what you added or subtracted each time:

______, ______, ______, ______, ______ My rule: ______________________

4. Which one of the following sequences was made by adding 7? Circle it:
HINT: Check all the numbers in the sequence.

a) 4, 10, 18, 21 b) 4, 11, 16, 21 c) 3, 10, 17, 24

5. **72, 61, 50, 39, 28, ...**

Brenda says this sequence was made by subtracting 12 each time.
Sanjukta says it was made by subtracting 11.
Who is right?

____

____

PA6-4: Identifying Pattern Rules

1. What number was added to make the sequence?

a) 12, 17, 22, 27 add ____ b) 32, 35, 38, 41 add ____

c) 28, 34, 40, 46 add ____ d) 50, 57, 64, 71 add ____

e) 101, 106, 111, 116 add ____ f) 269, 272, 275, 278 add ____

2. What number was subtracted to make the sequence?

a) 58, 56, 54, 52 subtract ____ b) 75, 70, 65, 60 subtract ____

c) 320, 319, 318, 317 subtract ____ d) 191, 188, 185, 182 subtract ____

e) 467, 461, 455, 449 subtract ____ f) 939, 937, 935, 933 subtract ____

3. State the rules for the following patterns:

a) 419, 412, 405, 398, 391 subtract ____ b) 311, 319, 327, 335, 343, 351 add ____

c) 501, 505, 509, 513 ________ d) 210, 199, 188, 177, ________

e) 653, 642, 631, 620, 609 ________ f) 721, 730, 739, 748, 757, 766 ________

g) 807, 815, 823, 831 ________ h) 1731, 1725, 1719, 1713, ________

4. Use the first three numbers in the pattern to find the rule. Then fill in the blanks:

a) 52, 57, 62, 67, ____, ____ The rule is: Start at 52 and add 5

b) 78, 75, 72, ____, ____, ____ The rule is: ________________

c) 824, 836, 848, ____, ____, ____ The rule is: ________________

d) 1 328, 1 319, 1 310, ____, ____, ____ The rule is: ________________

5. **5, 11, 17, 23, 29, ...**

Tim says the pattern rule is: "Start at 5 and subtract 6 each time."
Jack says the rule is: "Add 5 each time."
Hannah says the rule is: "Start at 5 and add 6 each time."

a) Whose rule is correct? ________________

b) What mistakes did the others make? ________________

____

PA6-5: Introduction to T-tables

Claude creates an **increasing pattern** with squares. He records the number of squares in each figure in a chart or T-table. He also records the number of squares he adds each time he makes a new figure:

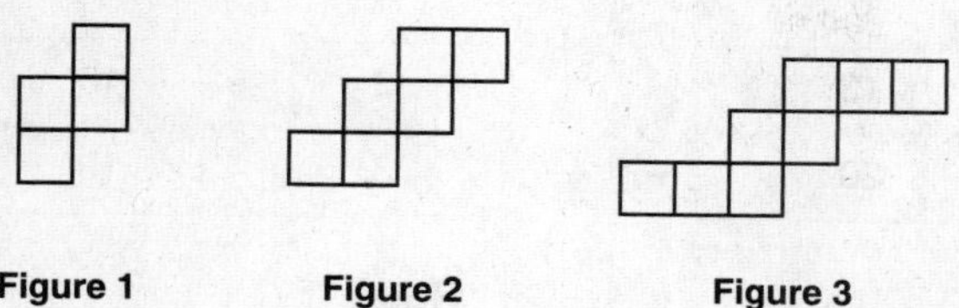

Figure	# of Squares
1	4
2	6
3	8

2, 2 — Number of squares added each time

The number of squares in the figures are 4, 6, 8, …

Claude writes a rule for this number pattern:

RULE: Start at 4 and add 2 each time.

---

1. Claude makes other increasing patterns with squares.
   How many squares does he add to make each new figure?
   Write your answer in the circles provided. Then write a rule for the pattern:

a)

Figure	Number of Squares
1	2
2	8
3	14

Rule:

b)

Figure	Number of Squares
1	3
2	9
3	15

Rule:

c)

Figure	Number of Squares
1	1
2	6
3	11

Rule:

d)

Figure	Number of Squares
1	1
2	8
3	15

Rule:

e)

Figure	Number of Squares
1	5
2	13
3	21

Rule:

f)

Figure	Number of Squares
1	11
2	22
3	33

Rule:

PA6-5: Introduction to T-tables *(continued)*

g)

Figure	Number of Squares
1	3
2	12
3	21

Rule:

h)

Figure	Number of Squares
1	6
2	13
3	20

Rule:

i)

Figure	Number of Squares
1	7
2	13
3	19

Rule:

2. Extend the number pattern. How many squares would be used in Figure 6?

a)

Figure	Number of Squares
1	2
2	10
3	18

b)

Figure	Number of Squares
1	4
2	9
3	14

c)

Figure	Number of Squares
1	7
2	11
3	15

3. After making Figure 3, Claude only has 35 squares left. Does he have enough squares to complete Figure 4?

a)

Figure	Number of Squares
1	4
2	13
3	22

YES NO

b)

Figure	Number of Squares
1	6
2	17
3	28

YES NO

c)

Figure	Number of Squares
1	9
2	17
3	25

YES NO

4. In your notebook, make a T-table to show how many shapes will be needed to make the fifth figure in each pattern:

a)  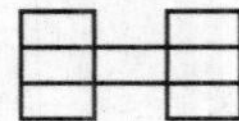 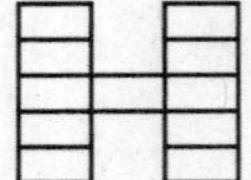

b) 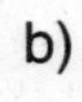 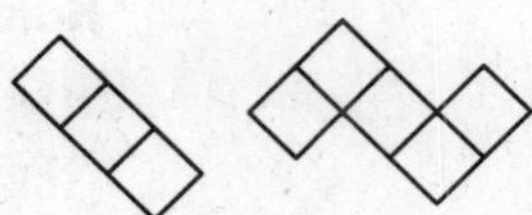 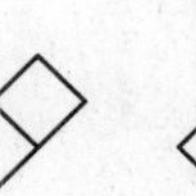 

PA6-6: T-tables

1. Count the number of line segments (lines that join pairs of dots) in each set of figures by marking each line segment as you count, as shown in the example:
HINT: Count around the outside of the figure first.

Example:

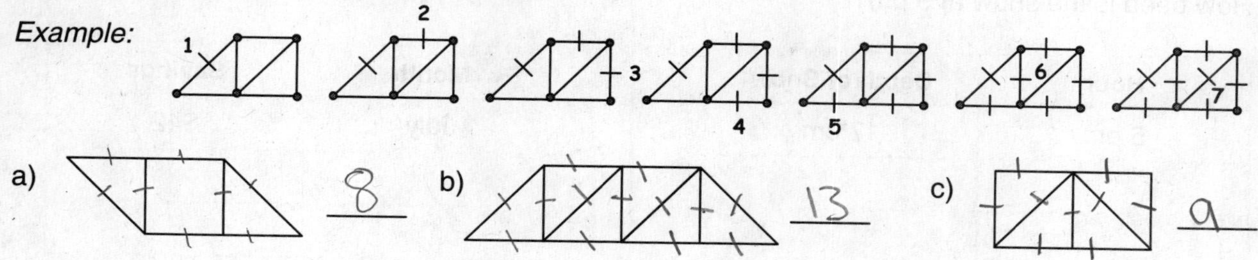

2. Continue the pattern below, then complete the chart:

Figure 1

Figure 2

Figure 3

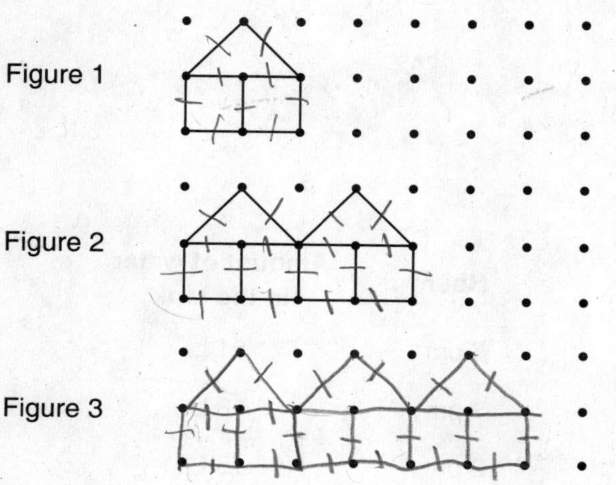

Figure	Number of Line Segments
1	9
2	17
3	27

a) How many line segments would Figure 4 have? ________

b) How many line segments would you need to make a figure with 5 triangles? ________

3. Continue the pattern below, then complete the chart:

Figure 1

Figure 2

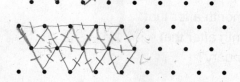

Figure 3

Figure 4

Figure	Number of Triangles	Number of Line Segments
1	3	6
2	6	13
3	9	19
4	12	25

a) How many line segments would Figure 5 have? 32

b) How many triangles would Figure 6 have? 14

PA6-6: T-tables *(continued)*

4. The snow is 17 cm deep at 5 pm.
   4 cm of snow falls each hour.
   How deep is the snow at 9 pm?

Hour	Depth of Snow
5 pm	17 cm

5. Philip has $42 in savings by the end of July. Each month he saves $9. How much will he have by the end of October?

Month	Savings
July	$42

6. Sarah's fish tank is leaking.
   At 6 pm, there are 21 L of water in the tank.
   At 7 pm, there are 18 L and at 8 pm, there are 15 L.

   a) How many litres of water leak out each hour?

   ____

   b) How many litres will be left in the tank at 10 pm?

   ____

   c) How many hours will it take for all the water to leak out?

   ____

Hour	Amount of water in the tank
6 pm	21 L
7 pm	18 L
8 pm	15 L
9 pm	
10 pm	

7. A store rents snowboards at $7 for the first hour and $5 for every hour after that. How much does it cost to rent a snowboard for 6 hours?

8. a) How many triangles would April need to make a figure with 10 squares?

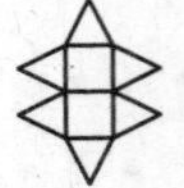
1
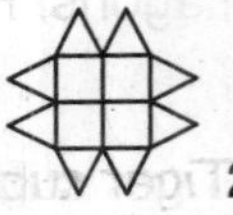
2
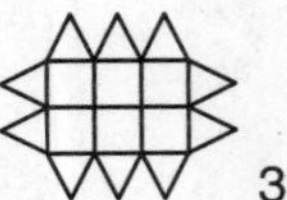
3

   b) April says that she needs 15 triangles to make the sixth figure. Is she correct?

9. Merle saves $55 in August. She saves $6 each month after that.
   Alex saves $42 in August. He saves $7 each month after that.
   Who has saved the most money by the end of January?

PA6-7: T-Tables (Advanced)

The **terms** of a sequence are the numbers or items in the sequence.

A **term number** gives the position of each item.

*This is **term number 4** since it is in the fourth position.*

4, 7, 10, 13, 16

1. Draw a T-table for each sequence to find the given term:

   a) Find the 5th term: 3, 8, 13, 18, … b) Find the 7th term: 42, 46, 50, 54,…

2. Ben says that the 6th term of the sequence 7, 13, 19,… is 53. Is he correct? Explain.

3. Find the missing terms in each sequence.

   a) 8, 12, _______, 20 b) 11, _______, _______, 26

   c) 15, _______, _______, 24, _______ d) 59, _______, _______, _______, 71

4.

Term Number	Term
1	13
2	15
3	18
4	19
5	21

Term Number	Term
1	25
2	29
3	34
4	37
5	41

Each T-Table was made by adding a number repeatedly.

Find and correct any mistakes in the tables.

5. Rita made an ornament using a hexagon (shaded figure), pentagons (dotted) and triangles.

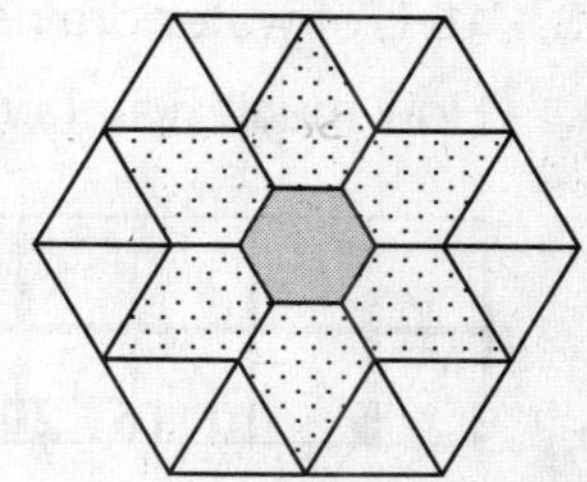

   a) How many pentagons does she need to make 7 ornaments?

   b) Rita used 6 hexagons to make ornaments.
   How many triangles and pentagons did she use?

   c) Rita used 36 pentagons. How many triangles did she use?

6. A newborn Siberian Tiger cub weighs 1 300 g. It gains 100 g a day.
A newborn baby weighs 3 300 g. It gains 200 g every week.

   a) A cub and a baby are born on the same day. Who weighs more after…

   i) 2 weeks? ii) 6 weeks?

   b) After how many weeks would the cub and the baby have the same weight?

PA6-8: Number Lines

Jacqui is on a bicycle tour 300 km from home. She can cycle 75 km each day.

If she starts riding towards home on Tuesday morning, how far away from home will she be by Thursday evening?

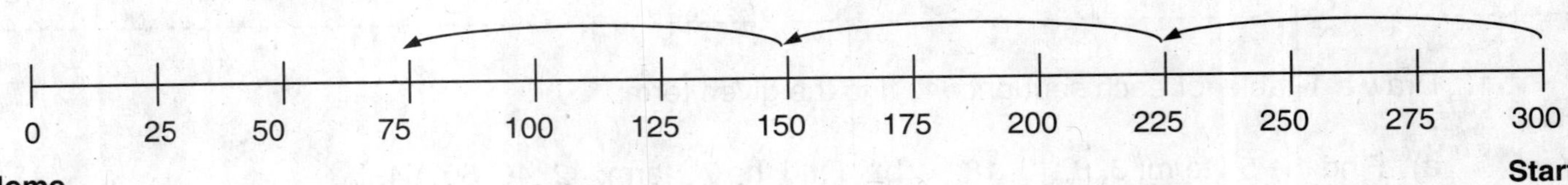

On Thursday evening, she will be 75 km from home.

1. On Wednesday morning Blair's campsite is 18 km from Tea Lake.
   He plans to hike 5 km towards the lake each day.
   How far from the lake will he be on Friday evening? 3km

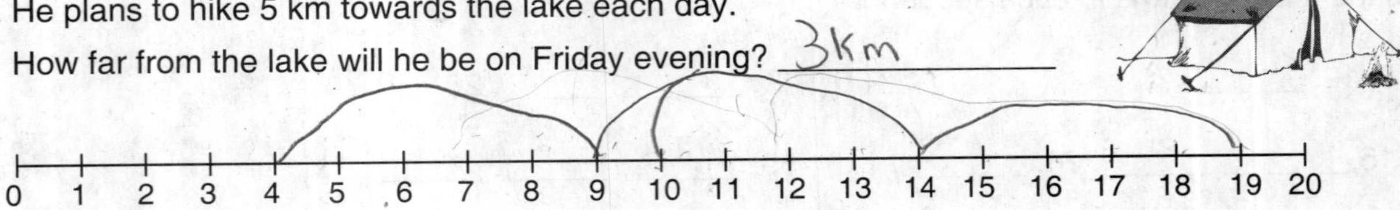

2. On Saturday morning, Samantha is 400 km from her home.
   She can cycle 75 km each day.
   How far from home will she be on Tuesday evening? __________

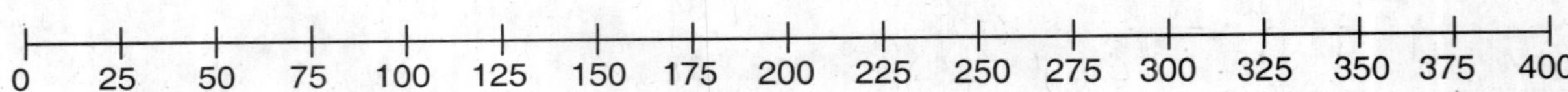

Draw and label a number line in the gird to solve the problem.

3. 15 L of water drains out of a 90 L tank each minute.
   How much water will be left after 5 minutes?

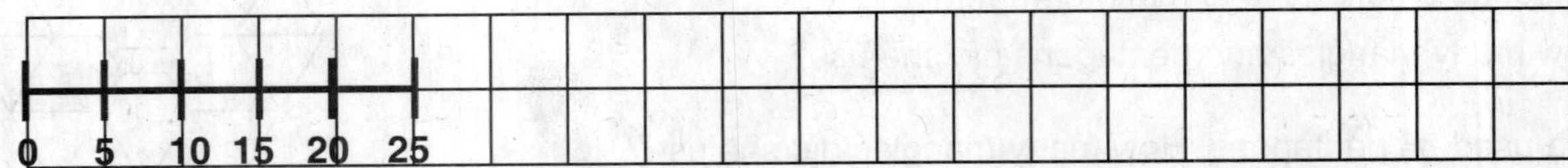

4. Brenda is 70 km from home.
   She can cycle 15 km an hour.
   How far from home will she be in 3 hours?

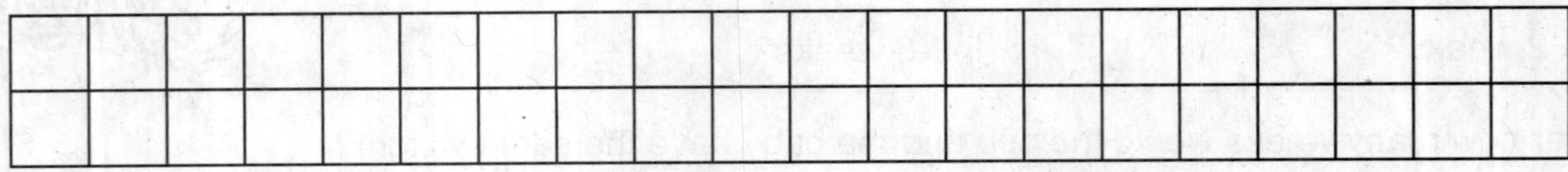

PA6-8: Number Lines

5. A grade six class is on a field trip 250 km from home.
   Their bus travels at a speed of 75 km each hour.
   How far from home will they be after 3 hours?

6. Paul plants 5 trees in a row.
   The nearest tree is 5 metres from his house. The farthest tree is 17 metres from his house.
   The trees are equally spaced.
   How far apart are the trees?
   HINT: Put Paul's house at zero on the number line.

7. Michael's house is 18 metres from the ocean.
   He is sleeping in a chair 3 metres away from his house (toward the ocean).
   The tide rises 5 metres every hour. How long will it take before his feet get wet?

8. Robert's bookcase has 5 shelves.
   The top shelf is 150 cm above the floor and the bottom shelf is 30 cm above the floor.
   How far apart are the shelves?

9. Aaron is training for football.
   He runs 5 metres forward and 2 metres back every 4 seconds.
   How far from where he started will he be after 16 seconds?

PA6-9: Lowest Common Multiples

The multiples of 2 and 3 are marked with Xs on the number lines below:

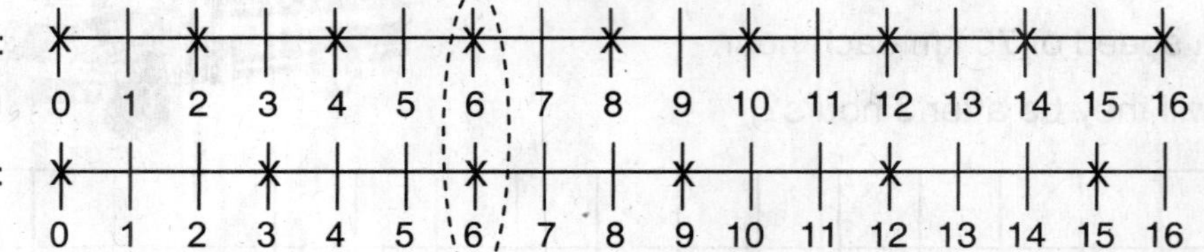

0 is a multiple of every number

The **lowest common multiple** (**LCM**) of 2 and 3 is 6: 6 is the least non-zero number that 2 and 3 both divide into evenly.

---

1. Mark the multiples of the given numbers on the number lines. What is the lowest common multiple of the pair?

a) **3:**

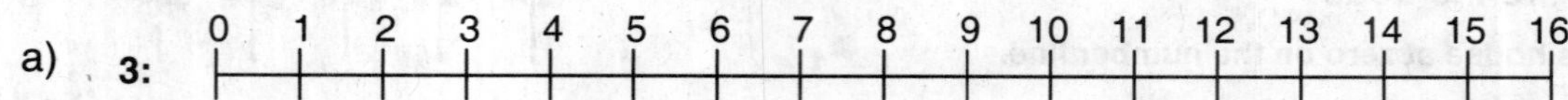

4:

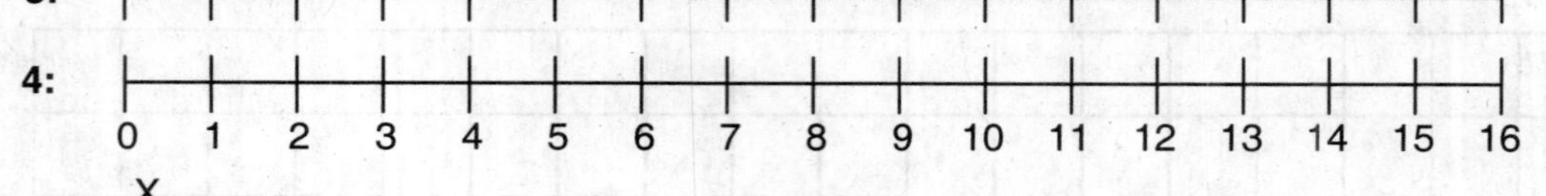

LCM = ______

b) **4:**

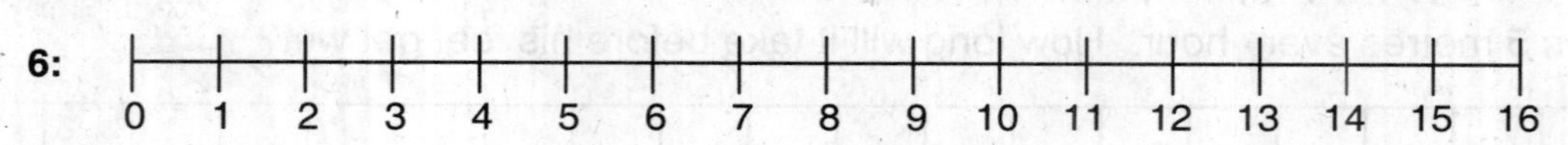

6:

0 1 2 3 4 5 6 7 8 9 10 11 12 13 14 15 16

LCM = ______

2. Find the lowest common multiple of each pair of numbers. The first one has been done for you:
HINT: Count up by the largest number until you find a number that both numbers divide into with no remainder.

a) 3 and 5

3: 3, 6, 9, 12, **15**, 18

5: 5, 10, **15**, 20

LCM = 15

b) 4 and 10

LCM = ______

c) 3 and 9

LCM = ______

d) 2 and 6

LCM = ______

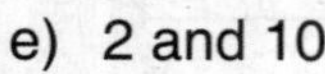

e) 2 and 10   f) 3 and 6   g) 3 and 12   h) 4 and 8   i) 8 and 10

j) 5 and 15   k) 6 and 10   l) 3 and 10   m) 6 and 8   n) 6 and 9

3. Paul visits the library every fourth day in January (beginning on January 4th).
Werda visits every sixth day (beginning on January 6th)
Nigel visits every 8th day (beginning on January 8th).

On what day of the month will they all visit the library together?

PA6-10: 2-Dimensional Patterns

TEACHER: Review ordinal numbers before beginning this page.

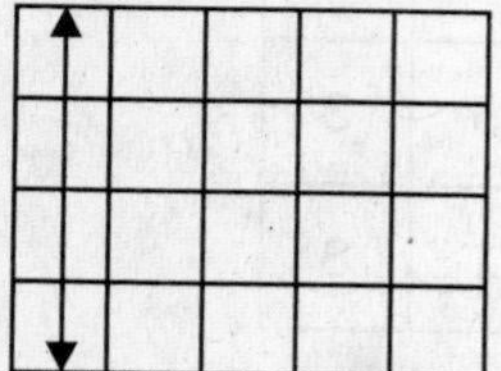

Columns run up and down.

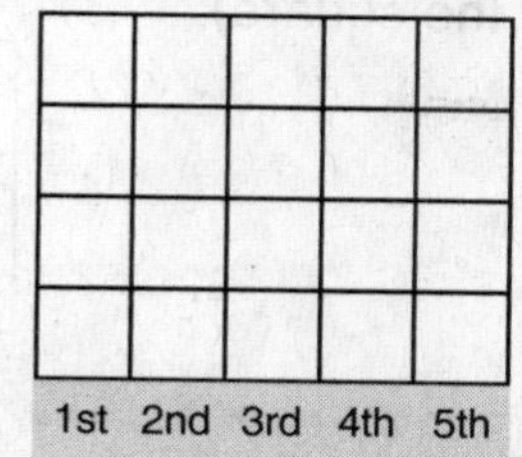

Columns are numbered left to right (in this exercise).

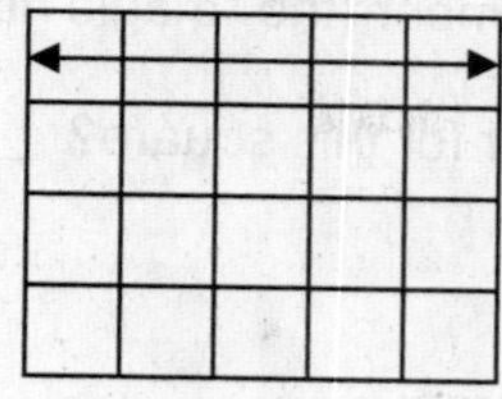

Rows run sideways.

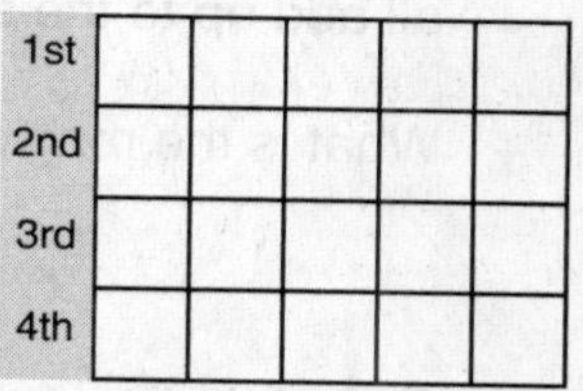

Rows are numbered from top to bottom (in this exercise).

---

1. Shade ...

a)

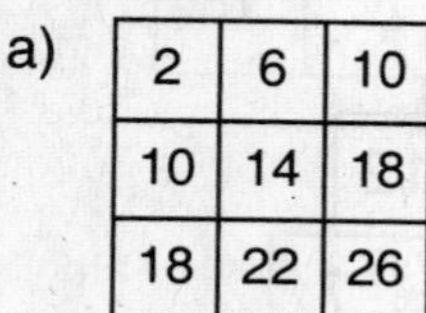

2	6	10
10	14	18
18	22	26

the 2nd row

b)

2	6	10
10	14	18
18	22	26

the 1st column

c)

2	6	10
10	14	18
18	22	26

the 3rd column

d)

2	6	10
10	14	18
18	22	26

the diagonals

(one is shaded here)

2. Describe the pattern in the numbers you see in each chart below:

NOTE: You should use the words "rows", "columns", and "diagonals" in your answer.

a)

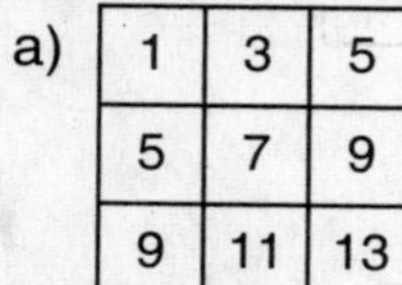

1	3	5
5	7	9
9	11	13

b)

6	12	18	24
12	18	24	30
18	24	30	36
24	30	36	42

c)

16	20	24	28
12	16	20	24
8	12	16	20
4	8	12	16

3. Make up your own pattern and describe it:

4. Place the letters X and Y so that each row and each column has two Xs and two Ys in it:

5. a) Which row of the chart has a decreasing pattern (looking left to right)?
   b) Which column has a repeating pattern?
   c) Write pattern rules for the first and second column.
   d) Describe the relationship between the numbers in the third and fourth columns.
   e) Describe one other pattern in the chart.
   f) Name a row or column that does not appear to have any pattern.

0	4	8	6	2
5	6	7	5	9
10	8	6	4	2
15	10	5	3	9
20	12	4	2	2

PA6-11: Extensions

1. In a magic square, the numbers in each row, column, and diagonal all add up to the same number (the "magic number" for the square):

   What is the magic number for this square? ______

2	9	4
7	5	3
6	1	8

2. Complete the magic squares:

a)

2		6
9	5	
4	3	

b)

	9	
10	5	12

c)

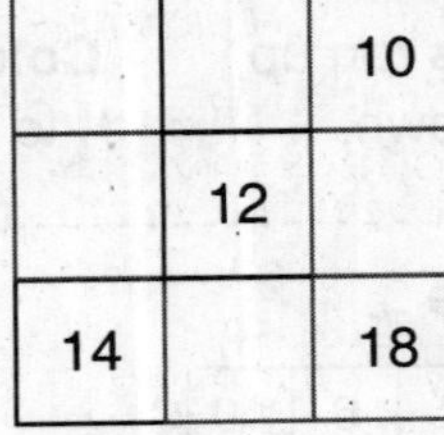

3. Here are some number pyramids:

5	
2	3

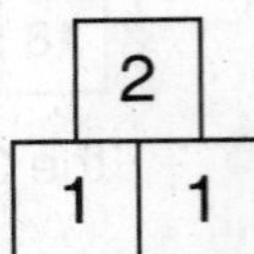

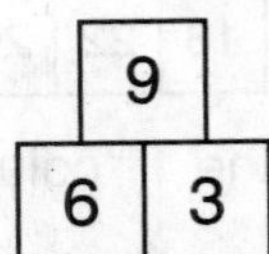

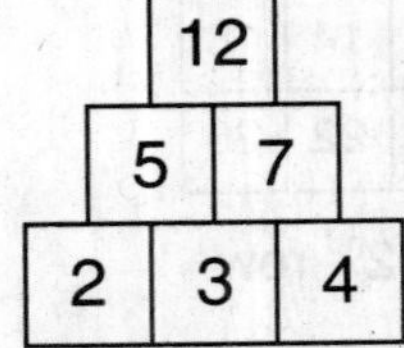

Can you find the rule by which the patterns in the pyramids were made? Describe it here:

4. Using the rule you described in Question 3, find the missing numbers:

a) 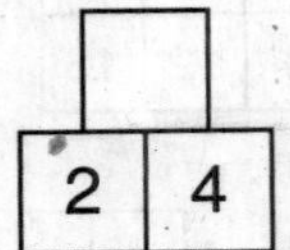

b) 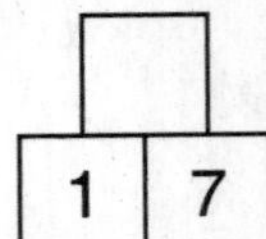

c) 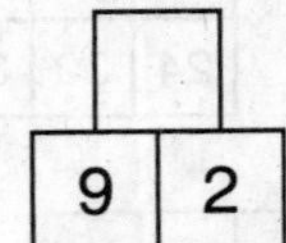

d) 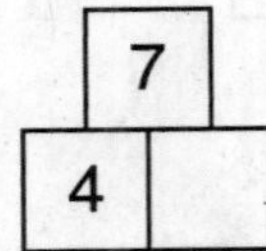

e) 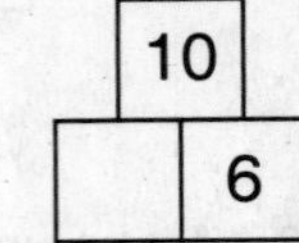

f) 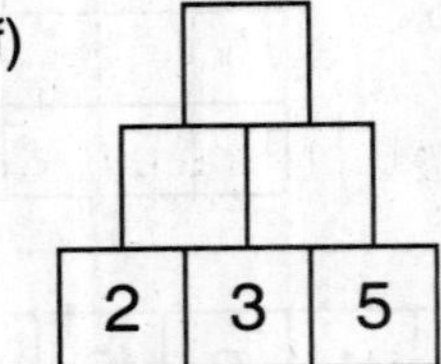

g) 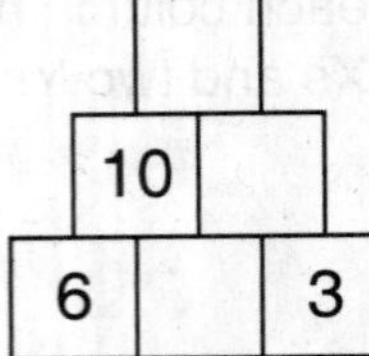

h) 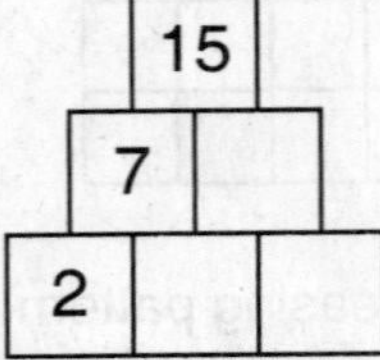

i) 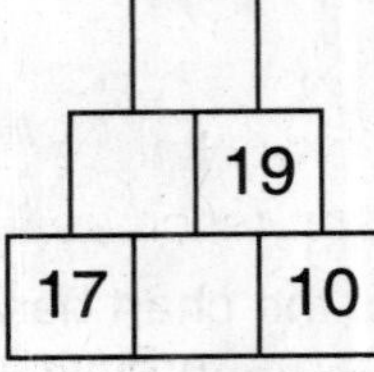

j) 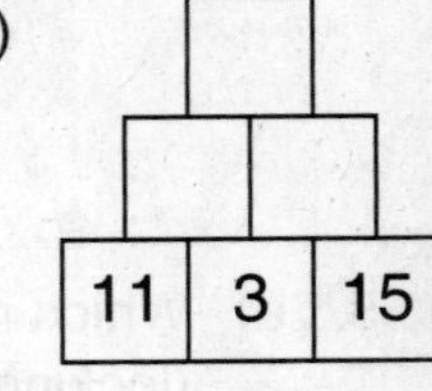

k) 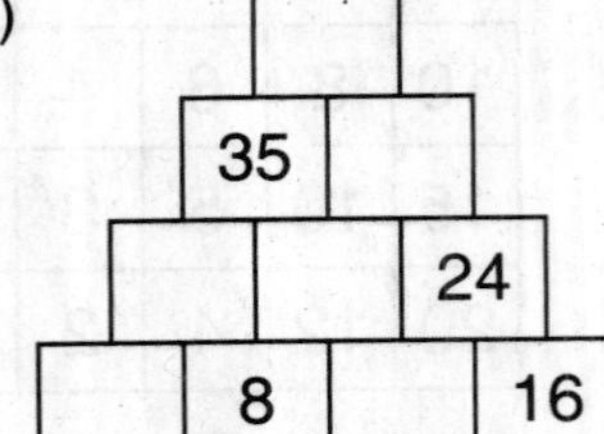

l) 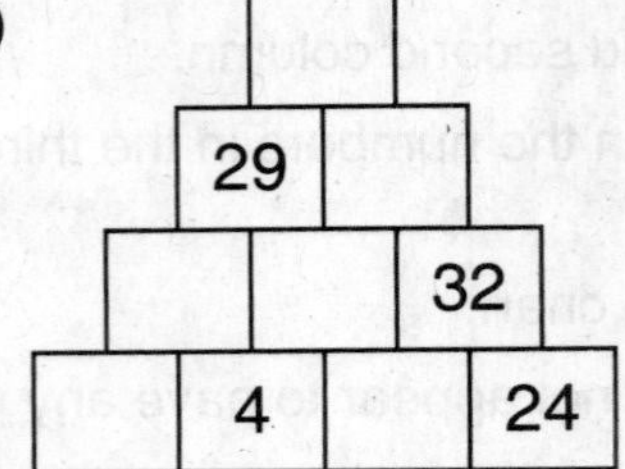

m) 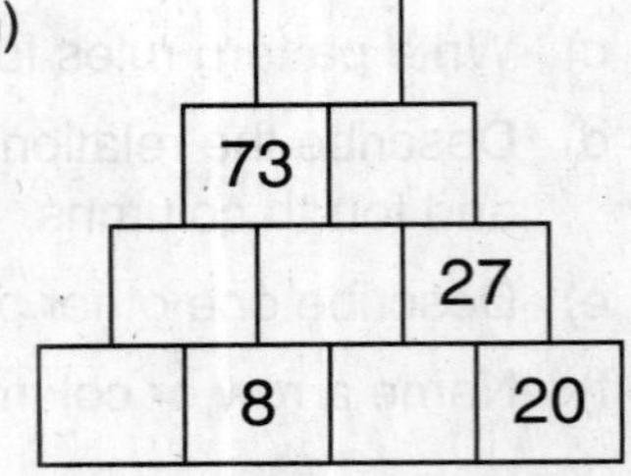

PA6-12: Finding Rules for T-tables – Part I

Andre makes a garden path using 6 triangular stones for every 1 square stone.

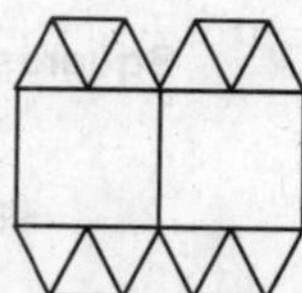
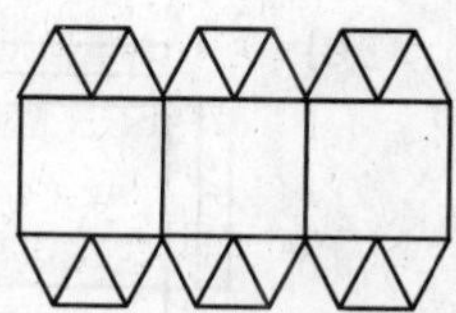

He writes an equation that shows how to calculate the number of triangles from the number of squares:

squares × 6 = triangles

or (for short): **6 × s = t**

Squares (s)	6 × s = t	Triangles (t)
1	6 × 1 = 6	6
2	6 × 2 = 12	12
3	6 × 3 = 18	18

---

1. Each chart represents a different design for a path. Complete the charts:

a)

Squares (s)	4 × s = t	Triangles (t)
1	4 × 1 = 4	4
2	4 × ☐ = 8	
3	4 × ☐ = 12	

b)

Squares (s)	3 × s = t	Triangles (t)
1	3 × ☐ = 3	
2	3 × ☐ = 6	
3	3 × ☐ = 9	

2. Write a rule that tells you how to calculate the number of triangles from the number of squares:

a)

Squares	Triangles
1	4
2	8
3	12

b)

Squares	Triangles
1	5
2	10
3	15

c)

Squares	Triangles
1	2
2	4
3	6

d)

Squares	Triangles
1	6
2	12
3	18

3. Wendy makes broaches using squares (s), rectangles (r), and triangles (t). Complete the chart. Write an equation (such as **4 × s = t**) for each design:

a) 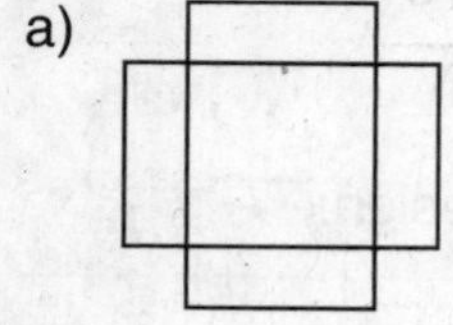

Squares (s)	Rectangles (r)
1	
2	
3	

b) 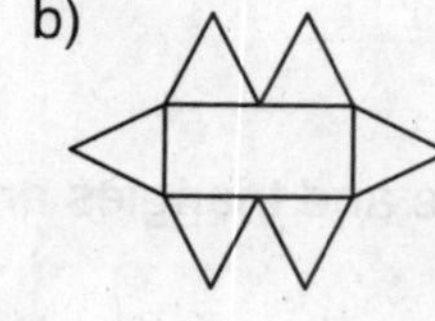

Rectangles (r)	Triangles (t)
1	
2	
3	

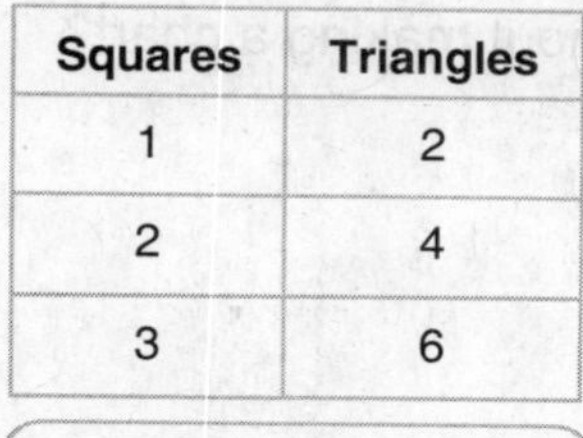

c)

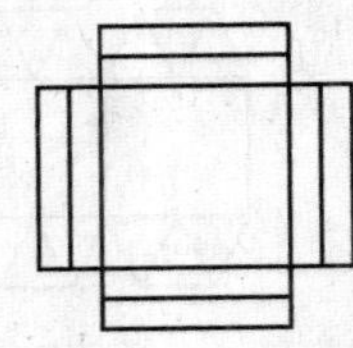

Squares (s)	Rectangles (t)

d)

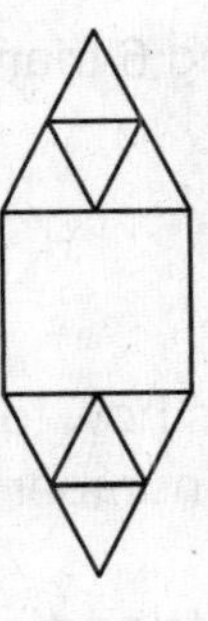

Squares (s)	Triangles (t)

e)

Squares (s)	Triangles (t)

f)

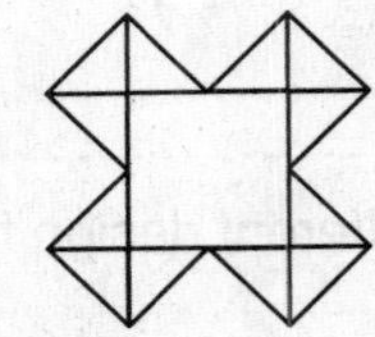

Squares (s)	Triangles (t)

4. Wendy has 39 triangles.

   Does she have enough triangles to make 7 broaches using the design here?

   How can you tell without making a chart?

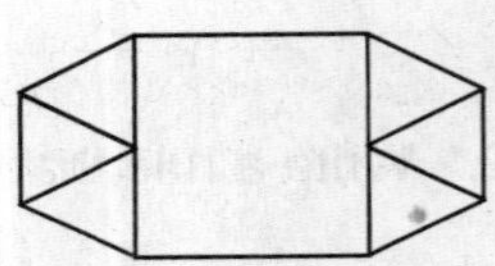

5. Create a design using squares (s) and triangles (t) to go with each equation:

   a) $6 \times s = t$

   b) $5 \times s = t$

6. Create a design with squares and triangles and then write an equation for your design:

In the auditorium, the number of chairs in each row is always 4 greater than the row number.
Kelly writes an equation that shows how to calculate the number of chairs from the row number:

row number + 4 = number of chairs (or **r + 4 = c** for short)

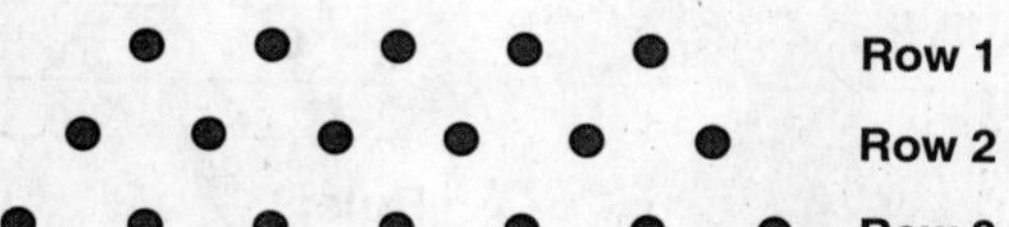

Row	r + 4 = c	Chairs
1	1 + 4 = 5	5
2	2 + 4 = 6	6
3	3 + 4 = 7	7

7. Each chart represents a different arrangement of chairs. Complete the charts:

a)

Row	r + 6 = c	Chairs
1	1 + 6 = 7	7
2	+ 6 =	
3	+ 6 =	

b)

Row	r + 9 = c	Chairs
1	+ 9 =	
2	+ 9 =	
3	+ 9 =	

8. Say what number you must add to the row number to get the number of chairs.
Write an equation using **r** for the row number and **c** for the number of chairs:

a)

Row	Chairs
1	5
2	6
3	7

Add 4

r + 4 = c

b)

Row	Chairs
1	8
2	9
3	10

c)

Row	Chairs
1	9
2	10
3	11

d)

Row	Chairs
7	12
8	13
9	14

9. Complete the charts. Then, in the box provided, write an equation for each arrangement of chairs:

a)

Row	Chairs

b)

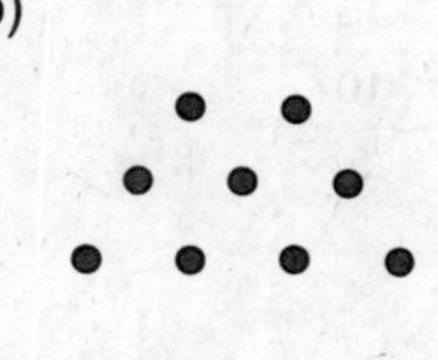

Row	Chairs

PA6-12: Finding Rules for T-tables – Part I *(continued)*

10. Apply the given rule to the numbers in the input column. Write your answer in the output column:

a)

INPUT	OUTPUT
1	
2	
3	

Rule:

Add 4 to the input.

b)

INPUT	OUTPUT
5	
6	
7	

Rule:

Subtract 4 from the input.

c)

INPUT	OUTPUT
3	
5	
6	

Rule:

Multiply the input by 6.

d)

INPUT	OUTPUT
32	
8	
40	

Rule:

Divide each input by 4.

e)

INPUT	OUTPUT
18	
19	
20	

Rule:

Add 10 to the input.

f)

INPUT	OUTPUT
4	
5	
6	

Rule:

Multiply the input by 8.

11. For each chart, give a rule that tells you how to make the output numbers from the input numbers.

a)

INPUT	OUTPUT
2	6
3	7
4	8

Rule:

b)

INPUT	OUTPUT
3	8
5	10
7	12

Rule:

c)

INPUT	OUTPUT
1	7
2	14
3	21

Rule:

d)

INPUT	OUTPUT
3	15
2	10
1	5

Rule:

e)

INPUT	OUTPUT
2	16
4	32
6	48

Rule:

f)

INPUT	OUTPUT
19	16
15	12
21	18

Rule:

PA6-13: Finding Rules for Patterns – Part I

Complete the T-table for each pattern.
Then write a rule that tells you how to calculate the second number from the first number.

1.

Number of Vertical Lines	Number of Horizontal Lines

Rule:

2.

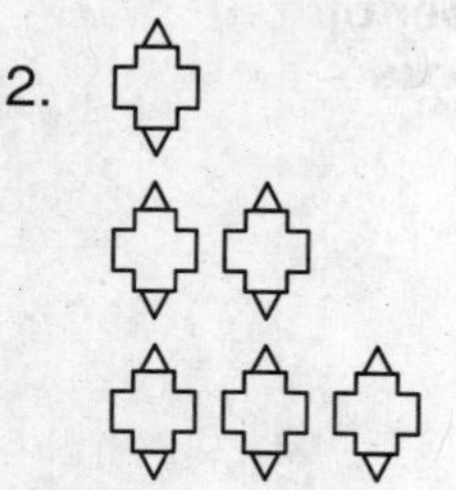

Number of Crosses	Number of Triangles

Rule:

3.

Number of Suns	Number of Moons

Rule:

4.

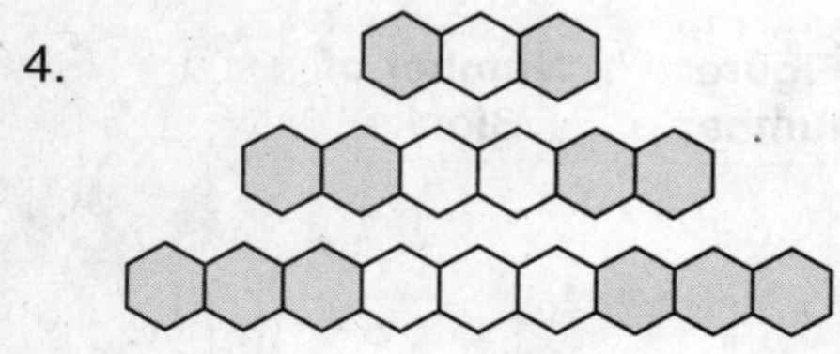

Number of Light Hexagons	Number of Dark Hexagons

Rule:

5.

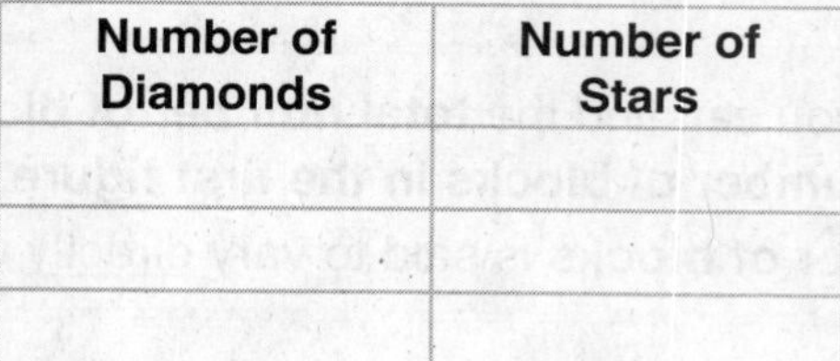

Number of Diamonds	Number of Stars

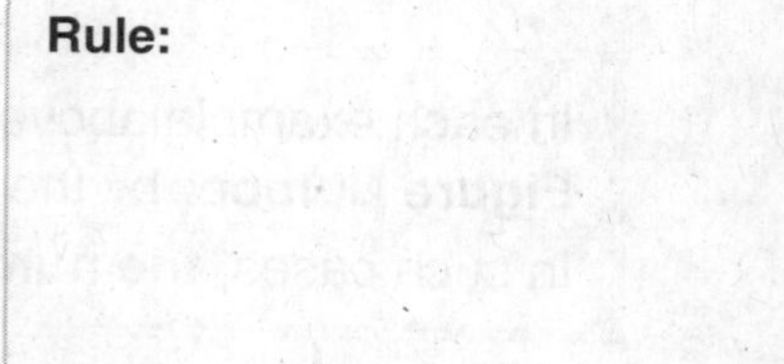

Rule:

6. Make a T-table and write a rule for the number of hexagons and triangles:

Figure 1 Figure 2 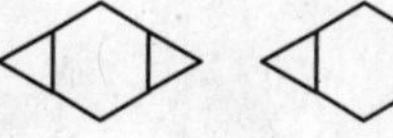 Figure 3 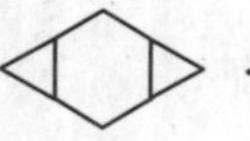 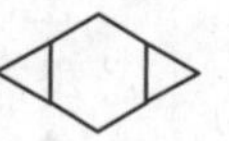 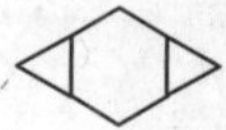

7. How many triangles are needed for 9 hexagons in the pattern in Question 6? How do you know?

PA6-14: Direct Variation

Fill in the chart and write a rule for the number of blocks in each figure, as shown in part a).

1. a)

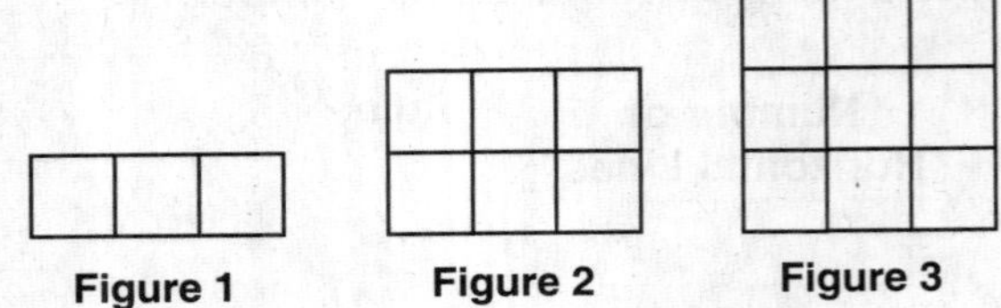

Figure 1 Figure 2 Figure 3

Rule: 3 × Figure Number

Figure Number	Number of Blocks
1	
2	
3	

b)

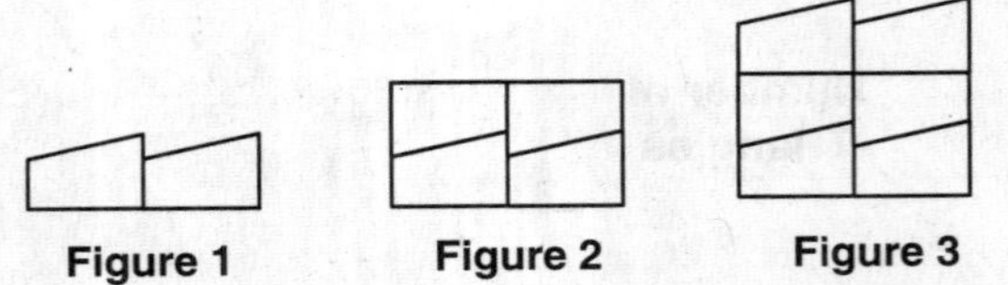

Figure 1 Figure 2 Figure 3

Rule: ______________________

Figure Number	Number of Blocks

c)

Figure 1 Figure 2 Figure 3

Rule: ______________________

Figure Number	Number of Blocks

d)

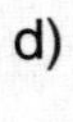

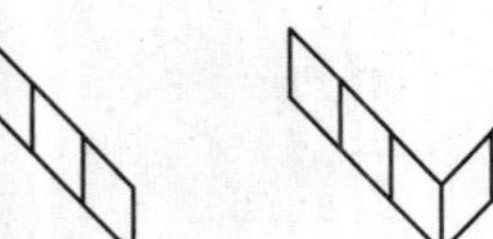

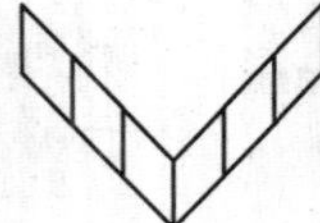

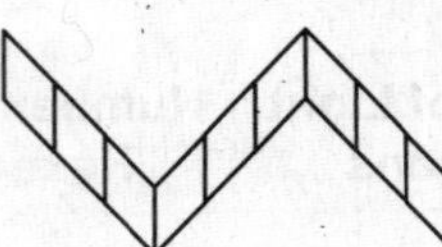

Figure 1 Figure 2 Figure 3

Rule: ______________________

Figure Number	Number of Blocks

In each example above, you can find the **total number of blocks** by *multiplying* the **Figure Number** by the **number of blocks in the first figure**.
In such cases, **the number of blocks** is said to vary directly with the Figure Number.

2. Circle the sequences where the number of blocks varies directly with the Figure Number:

a)

Figure Number	Number of Blocks
1	3
2	6
3	9

b)

Figure Number	Number of Blocks
1	4
2	7
3	10

c)

Figure Number	Number of Blocks
1	6
2	12
3	18

d)

Figure Number	Number of Blocks
1	5
2	10
3	16

PA6-15: Finding Rule for Patterns – Part II

1. In each pattern below, the number of *shaded* blocks increases directly with the Figure Number. The *total* number of blocks, however, does not increase directly.
   i) Write a rule for the number of *shaded* blocks in each sequence.
   ii) Write a rule for the *total number* of blocks in each sequence.

a)

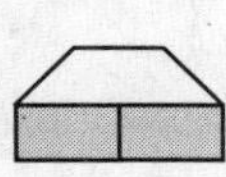
Figure 1

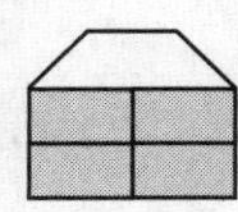
Figure 2

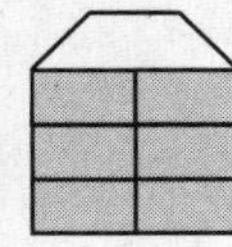
Figure 3

Rule for the number of shaded blocks:

2 × Figure Number

Rule for the total number of blocks:

2 × Figure Number + 1

b)

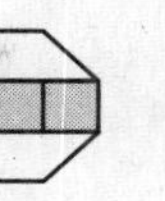
Figure 1

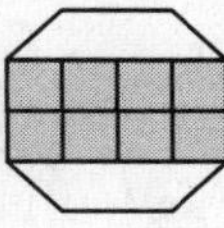
Figure 2

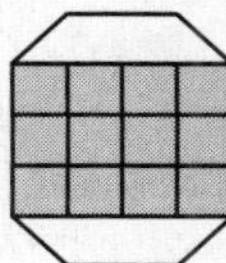
Figure 3

Rule for the number of shaded blocks:

____

Rule for the total number of blocks:

____

c)

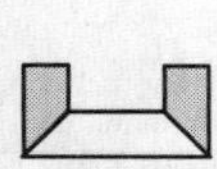
Figure 1

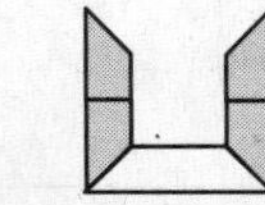
Figure 2

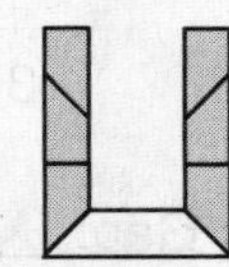
Figure 3

Rule for the number of shaded blocks:

____

Rule for the total number of blocks:

____

d)

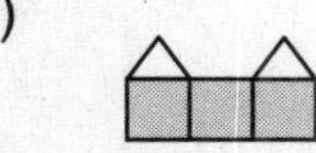
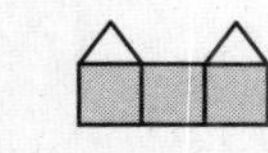
Figure 1

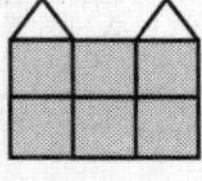
Figure 2

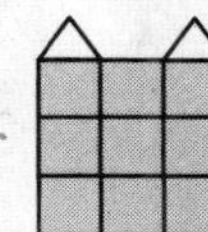
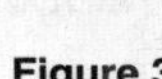
Figure 3

Rule for the number of shaded blocks:

____

Rule for the total number of blocks:

____

e) Rule for the number of shaded blocks:

____

Rule for the total number of blocks:

____

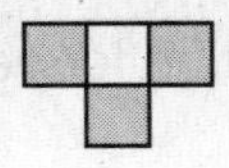
Figure 1

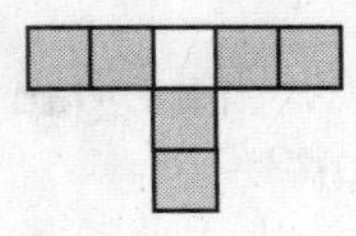
Figure 2

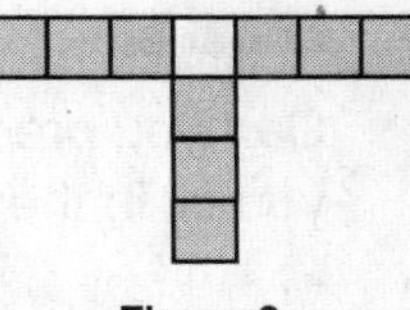
Figure 3

2. Draw or build a sequence of figures that might go with the following tables. Shade the part of each figure that varies directly with the Figure Number:

a)

Figure Number	Number of Blocks
1	5
2	7
3	9

b)

Figure Number	Number of Blocks
1	6
2	10
3	14

c)

Figure Number	Number of Blocks
1	7
2	10
3	13

PA6-16: Predicting the Gap Between Terms in a Pattern

1. Fill in the chart using the rule.

a) Rule: Multiply by 4 and add 3

INPUT	OUTPUT
1	
2	
3	

Gap: ____________

b) Rule: Multiply by 2 and add 3

INPUT	OUTPUT
1	
2	
3	

Gap: ____________

c) Rule: Multiply by 5 and add 4

INPUT	OUTPUT
1	
2	
3	

Gap: ____________

d) Rule: Multiply by 10 and add 1

INPUT	OUTPUT
1	
2	
3	

Gap: ____________

e) Compare the **gap** in each pattern above to the rule for the pattern. What do you notice?

____

____

2. For each pattern below, make a T-table as shown.

Fill in the total number of blocks (shaded and unshaded) and the gap.

Can you predict what the gap will be for each pattern before you fill in the chart?

Figure Number	Number of Blocks
1	
2	
3	

Figure 1
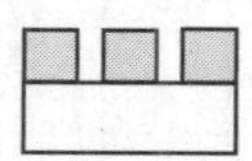

Figure 2
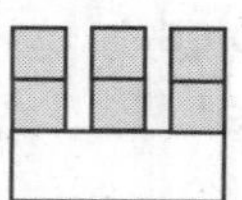

Figure 3
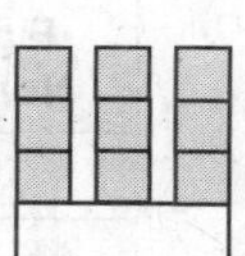

Figure 1
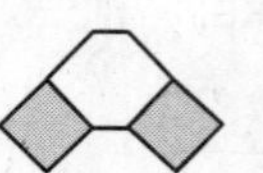

Figure 2
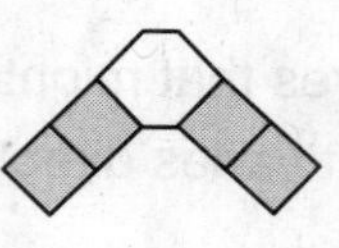

Figure 3
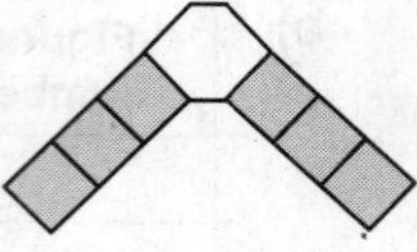

Figure 1
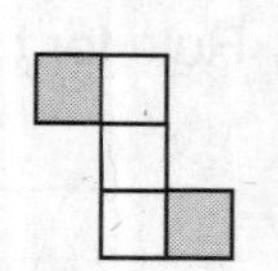

Figure 2
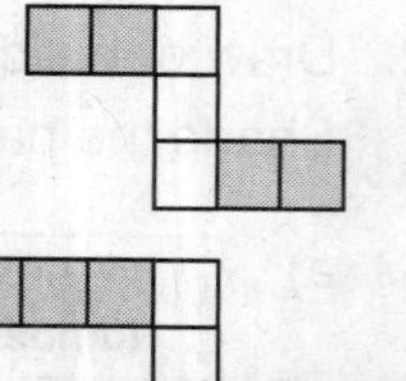

Figure 3
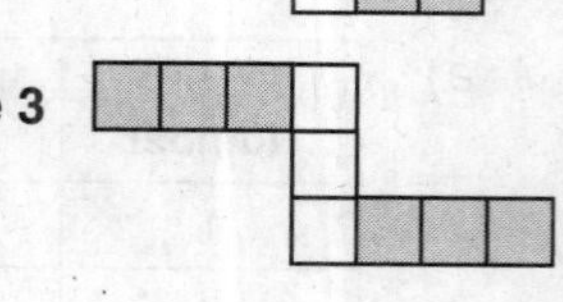

Can you write a rule for each pattern that tells how to find the number of blocks from the figure number?

PA6-17: Finding Rules for T-tables – Part II

In the T-table shown here, the output is calculated from the input by two operations:

INPUT	OUTPUT
1	5
2	8
3	11

To find the rule:

Step 1:
Find the step (or gap) between the numbers in the OUTPUT column.

INPUT	INPUT x GAP	OUTPUT	
1		5	
			3
2		8	
			3
3		11	

Step 2:
Multiply the INPUT numbers by the gap.

INPUT	INPUT x GAP	OUTPUT	
1	3	5	
			3
2	6	8	
			3
3	9	11	

Step 3:
What must you add to each number in the second column?

INPUT	INPUT x GAP	OUTPUT	
1	3	5	
			3
2	6	8	
			3
3	9	11	

Add 2

Step 4:
Write a rule for the T-table – **Rule:** Multiply the input by 3 and add 2

---

1. Use the steps above to find the rule that tells you how to calculate the OUTPUT from the INPUT:

a)

INPUT	INPUT x GAP	OUTPUT
1		9
2		13
3		17

Add ____

Rule: Multiply by ______ then add ______.

b)

INPUT	INPUT x GAP	OUTPUT
1		3
2		5
3		7

Add ____

Rule: Multiply by _______ then add ______.

c)

INPUT	INPUT x GAP	OUTPUT
1		7
2		10
3		13

Add ____

Rule: Multiply by _______ then add _______.

d)

INPUT	INPUT x GAP	OUTPUT
1		6
2		8
3		10

Add ____

Rule: Multiply by _______ then add ______.

PA6-17: Finding Rules for T-tables – Part II *(continued)*

2. Write a rule that tells you how to calculate the OUTPUT from the INPUT:

a)

INPUT	INPUT x GAP	OUTPUT
1		9
2		14
3		19

Multiply by _______ then add _______.

b)

INPUT	INPUT x GAP	OUTPUT
1		12
2		18
3		24

Multiply by _______ then add _______.

c)

INPUT	INPUT x GAP	OUTPUT
1		6
2		10
3		14

Multiply by _______ then add _______.

d)

INPUT	INPUT x GAP	OUTPUT
1		6
2		11
3		16

Multiply by _______ then add _______.

3. Write the rule that tells you how to calculate the OUTPUT from the INPUT:
NOTE: In this case you will have to subtract rather than add.

a)

INPUT	INPUT x GAP	OUTPUT
1		4
2		9
3		14

Multiply by _______ then subtract _______.

b)

INPUT	INPUT x GAP	OUTPUT
1		1
2		4
3		7

Multiply by _______ then subtract _______.

c)

INPUT	INPUT x GAP	OUTPUT
1		2
2		6
3		10

Multiply by _______ then subtract _______.

d)

INPUT	INPUT x GAP	OUTPUT
1		5
2		11
3		17

Multiply by _______ then subtract _______.

4. Write a rule that tells you how to make the Output from the Input: Each rule may involve either one or two operations.

a)

Input	Output
1	2
2	7
3	12
4	17

Rule:

b)

Input	Output
1	3
2	9
3	15
4	21

Rule:

c)

Input	Output
1	5
2	6
3	7
4	8

Rule:

d)

Input	Output
1	7
2	9
3	11
4	13

Rule:

e)

Input	Output
0	4
1	8
2	12
3	16

Rule:

f)

Input	Output
1	4
2	8
3	12
4	16

Rule:

BONUS

5. Find the rule by guessing and checking.

a)

Input	Output
5	27
6	32
7	37
8	42

Rule:

b)

Input	Output
4	7
5	9
6	11
7	13

Rule:

c)

Input	Output
57	63
58	64
59	65
60	66

Rule:

d)

Input	Output
2	7
4	13
6	19
8	25

Rule:

e)

Input	Output
10	31
9	28
3	10
1	4

Rule:

f)

Input	Output
8	13
4	5
3	3
7	11

Rule:

PA6-18: Applying Rules for Patterns – Part III

1. For each, draw Figure 4 and fill in the T-table.
   Then write a rule that tells you how to calculate the input from the output:

a) **1** **2** **3** **4**

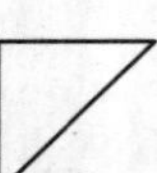

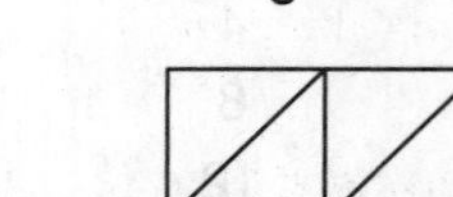

Figure	Number of Triangles
1	
2	
3	
4	

Rule for T-table: ____________________

Use your rule to predict how many triangles will be needed for Figure 9: __________

b) **1** **2** **3** **4**

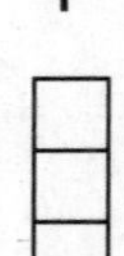

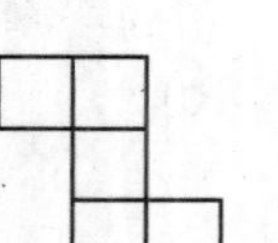

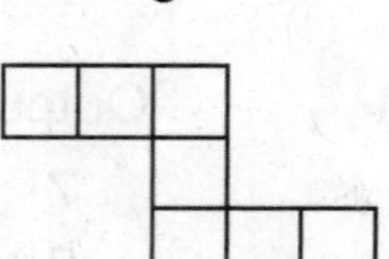

Figure	Perimeter
1	
2	
3	
4	

Rule for T-table: ____________________

Use your rule to predict the number of line segments in Figure 11: __________

c) **1** **2** **3** **4**

Figure	Number of Squares
1	
2	
3	
4	

Rule for T-table: ____________________

Use your rule to predict the number of squares needed for Figure 10: __________

d) **1** **2** **3** **4**

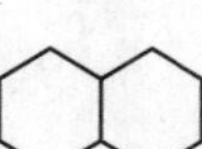

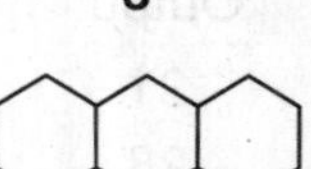

Figure	Perimeter
1	
2	
3	
4	

Rule for T-table: ____________________

Use your rule to predict the perimeter of Figure 23: __________

NS6-1: Introduction to Place Value

1. Write the place value of the underlined digit.

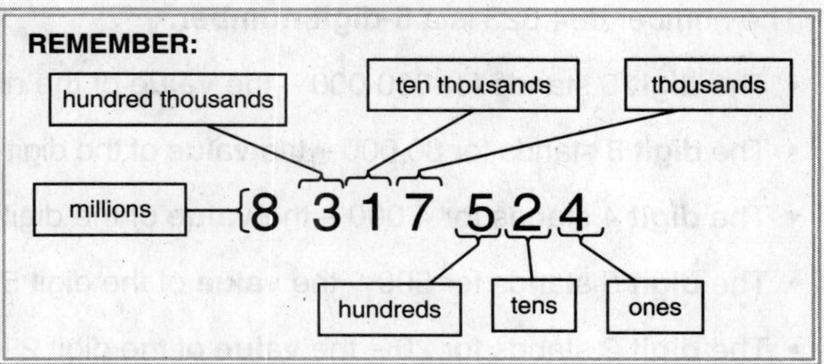

a) 56 2$\underline{3}$6 — tens

b) $\underline{1}$ 956 336

c) 8 $\underline{2}$56 601

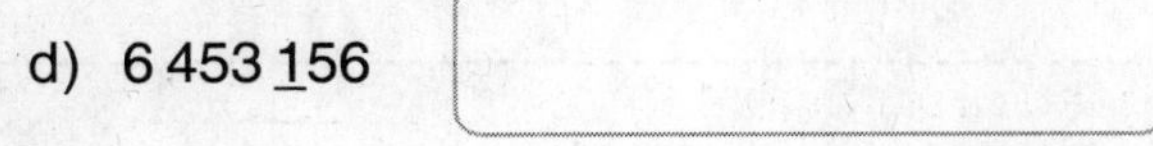

d) 6 453 $\underline{1}$56

e) 7 103 25$\underline{6}$

f) 2 5$\underline{8}$9 143

g) 92$\underline{3}$ 156

2. Give the place value of the number 5 in each of the numbers below.
HINT: First underline the 5 in each question.

a) 35 689

b) 5 308 603

c) 36 905

d) 215

e) 2 542

f) 3 451 628

g) 43 251

h) 152 776

i) 1 543 001

3. You can also write numbers using a place value chart.

Example:

4 672 953 would be:

millions	hundred thousands	ten thousands	thousands	hundreds	tens	ones
4	6	7	2	9	5	3

Write the following numbers into the place value chart.

	millions	hundred thousands	ten thousands	thousands	hundreds	tens	ones
a) 2 316 953	2	3	1	6	9	5	3
b) 62 507							
c) 5 604 891							
d) 1 399							
e) 17							
f) 998 260							

NS6-2: Place Value

The number 684 523 is a **6-digit number**.

- The **digit** 6 stands for 600 000 – the **value** of the digit 6 is 600 000
- The **digit** 8 stands for 80 000 – the **value** of the digit 8 is 80 000
- The **digit** 4 stands for 4 000 – the **value** of the digit 4 is 4 000
- The **digit** 5 stands for 500 – the **value** of the digit 5 is 500
- The **digit** 2 stands for 20 – the **value** of the digit 2 is 20
- The **digit** 3 stands for 3 – the **value** of the digit 3 is 3

1. Write the **value** of each digit.

a) 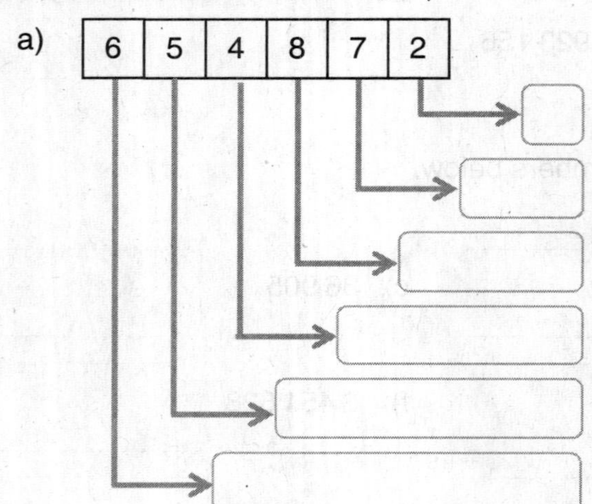

b) 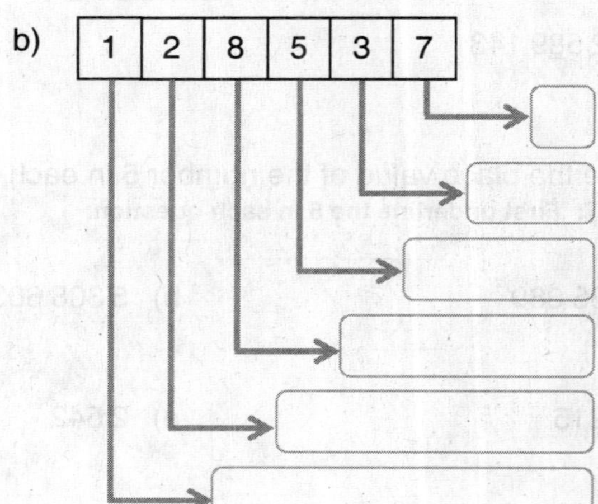

2. What does the digit 7 stand for in each number? The first one is done for you.

a) 8 476	b) 38 725	c) 93 726	d) 730 025
70			
e) 7 250	f) 64 297	g) 43 075	h) 382 457

3. Fill in the blanks.

a) In the number 4 523, the digit 5 stands for ______________ .

b) In the number 34 528, the digit 3 stands for ______________ .

c) In the number 420 583, the value of the digit 8 is ______________ .

d) In the number 75 320, the value of the digit 7 is ______________ .

e) In the number 723 594, the digit ______________ is in the ten thousands place.

PARENT: Model the two kinds of expanded form for your child (see page 32, Question 6 for details).

1. Write each number in expanded form. (numerals and words).

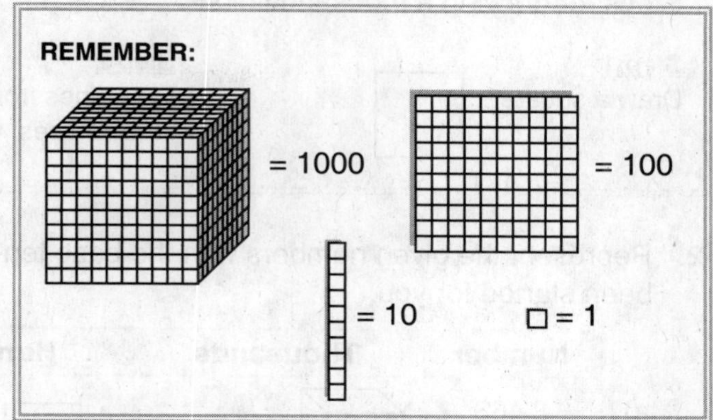

Example:

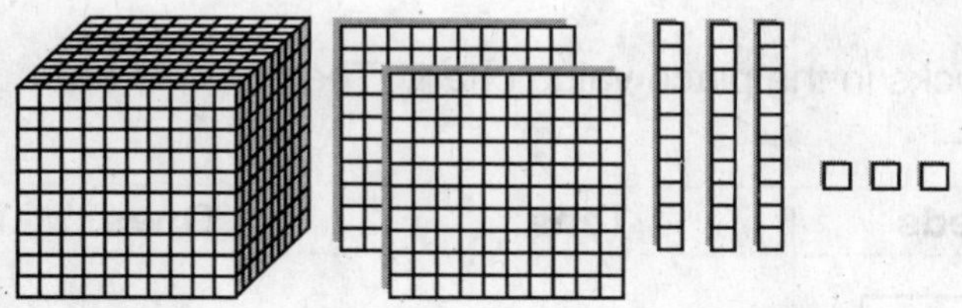

1 thousands + 2 hundreds + 3 tens + 3 ones = 1 233

a)

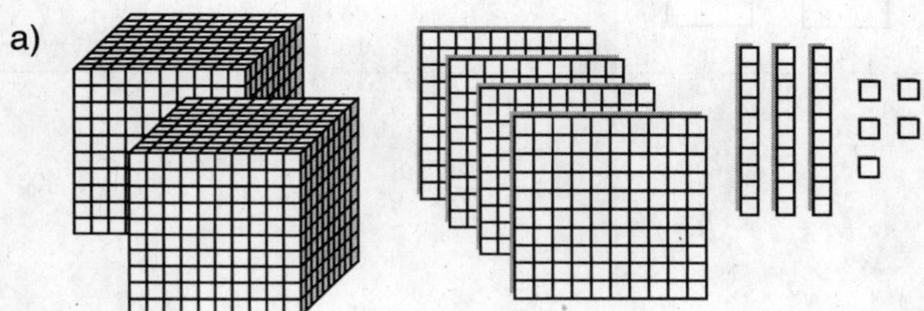

___ thousands + ___ hundreds + ___ tens + ___ ones = ______

b)

___ thousands + ___ hundreds + ___ tens + ___ ones = ______

c)

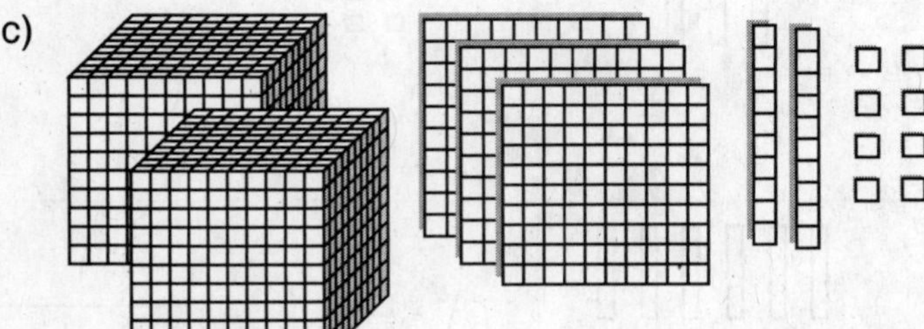

____ = ______

NS6-3: Representation with Base Ten Materials *(continued)*

Steps for drawing a thousands block:

Step 1: Draw a square:

Step 2: Draw lines from its 3 vertices:

Step 3: Join the lines:

2. Represent the given numbers with the base ten blocks in the place value chart. The first one has been started for you.

Number	Thousands	Hundreds	Tens	Ones
a) 3 468				
b) 1 542				
c) 2 609				

3. Write the numbers for the given base ten blocks.

	Thousands	Hundreds	Tens	Ones	Number
a)					______
b)					______

NS6-4: Representation in Expanded Form

1. Expand the following numbers using numerals and words. The first one is done for you.

   a) 2 536 784 = 2 millions + 5 hundred thousands + 3 ten thousands + 6 thousands + 7 hundreds + 8 tens + 4 ones

   b) 6 235 401 = ____________________

   c) 3 056 206 = ____________________

2. Write the number in expanded form (using numerals). The first one is done for you.

   a) 72 613 = 70 000 + 2 000 + 600 + 10 + 3

   b) 36 = ____________________

   c) 526 = ____________________

   d) 12 052 = ____________________

   e) 2 382 = ____________________

   f) 56 384 = ____________________

   g) 3 082 385 = ____________________

3. Write the number for each sum.

   a) 6 000 + 700 + 40 + 7 = ________

   b) 800 + 60 + 8 = ________

   c) 3 000 + 30 + 2 = ________

   d) 50 000 + 6 000 + 400 + 90 + 3 = ________

   e) 10 000 + 6 000 + 200 + 30 + 4 = ________

   f) 30 000 + 2 000 + 500 = ________

   g) 90 000 + 3 000 + 600 + 7 = ________

BONUS

   h) 300 000 + 2 000 000 + 5 + 70 000 + 200 = ________

4. Find the missing numbers.

   a) 2 000 + 600 + ________ + 5 = 2 645

   b) 4 000 + 200 + ________ + 5 = 4 285

   c) 40 000 + 3 000 + ________ + 10 + 5 = 43 715

   d) 80 000 + 5 000 + ________ + 60 + 3 = 85 263

   e) 20 000 + 6 000 + 300 + ________ = 26 302

   f) ________ + 400 = 9 400

   g) 6 000 + ________ = 6 080

   h) 80 000 + ________ + ________ = 87 005

   i) 300 000 + 90 000 + ________ + ________ = 390 702

NS6-4: Representation in Expanded Form *(continued)*

5. Write each number in expanded form. Then draw a base ten model.

Example: 3 152 = 3 000 + 100 + 50 + 2

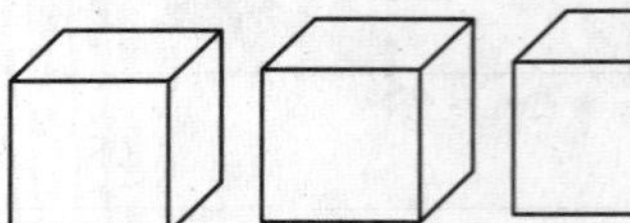
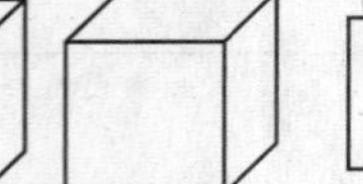

a) 4 354 =

b) 2 604 =

6. Represent the number 8 564 in four different ways – by sketching a base ten model, with number words, and in expanded form (2 ways).

Example: 234 – Two hundred thirty-four

234 = 2 hundreds + 3 tens + 4 ones *expanded form (using number words)*

234 = 200 + 30 + 4 *expanded form (using numerals)*

7. In the number 38 562, what is the sum of the tens digit and the thousands digit?

8. How many two-digit numbers have digits that add to twelve?

9. Using 5 blocks make (or draw) a model of a number such that…
   - The number is odd
   - There are twice as many thousands blocks as hundreds blocks

10. How many thousands blocks would you need to represent a million?

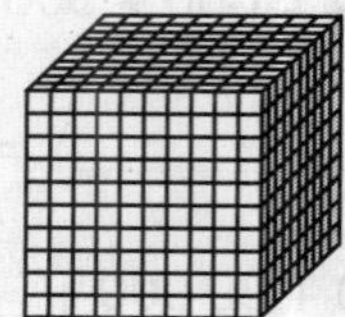

NS6-5: Comparing and Ordering Numbers

1. Write the **value** of each digit. Then complete the sentence.

a) 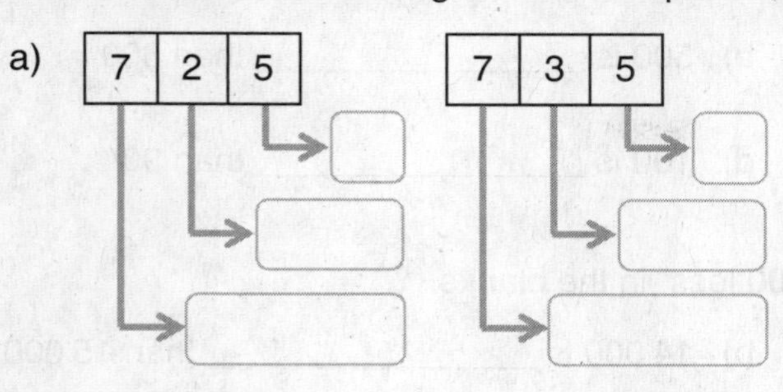

_______ is greater than _______

b) 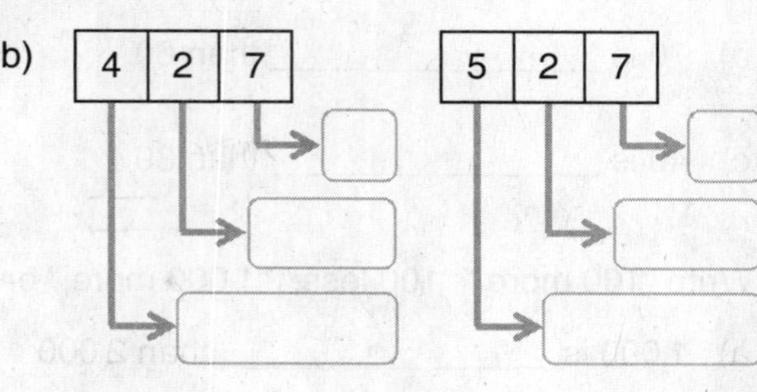

_______ is greater than _______

2. Circle the pair of digits that are different in each pair of numbers.
Then write the greater number in the box.

a) 83 752
83 762
83 762

b) 273 605
272 605

c) 614 852
614 858

d) 383 250
483 250

e) 812 349
813 349

f) 569 274
579 274

g) 323
324

h) 195 385
196 385

3. Read the numbers from left to right. Circle the first pair of digits you find that are different.
Then write the greater number in the box.

a) 641 583
641 597
641 597

b) 384 207
389 583

c) 576 986
603 470

d) 621 492
621 483

4. The inequality sign ">" in **7 > 5** is read "seven is greater than five."
The sign "<" in **8 < 10** is read "eight is less than ten."
Write the correct inequality sign in the box.

a) 8 653 [>] 8 486 b) 15 332 [ ] 16 012 c) 9 000 [ ] 7 999

d) 323 728 [ ] 323 729 e) 648 175 [ ] 648 123 f) 72 382 [ ] 8 389

g) 24 489 [ ] 38 950 h) 85 106 [ ] 83 289 i) 1 572 306 [ ] 1 573 306

NS6-6: Differences from 10 to 10 000

1. Write "10 more," "10 less," "100 more," or "100 less" in the blanks.

a) 70 is ________________ than 60
b) 500 is ________________ than 600
c) 40 is ________________ than 30
d) 100 is ________________ than 90

2. Write "100 more," "100 less," "1 000 more," or "1 000 less" in the blanks.

a) 1 000 is ________________ than 2 000
b) 14 000 is ________________ than 15 000
c) 5 900 is ________________ than 6 000
d) 70 000 is ________________ than 69 000

3. Write "1 000 more," "1 000 less," "10 000 more," or "10 000 less" in the blanks.

a) 7 000 is ________________ than 6 000
b) 13 000 is ________________ than 14 000
c) 40 000 is ________________ than 50 000
d) 60 000 is ________________ than 50 000
e) 8 000 is ________________ than 7 000
f) 40 000 is ________________ than 39 000

4. Write "10 000 more," "10 000 less," "100 000 more," or "100 000 less" in the blanks.

a) 200 000 is ________________ than 100 000
b) 70 000 is ________________ than 80 000
c) 160 000 is ________________ than 150 000
d) 400 000 is ________________ than 500 000
e) 19 000 is ________________ than 200 000
f) 800 000 is ________________ than 900 000

5. Circle the pair of digits that are different. Then fill in the blanks.

a) 385 237
395 237

385 237 is *10 000 less* than 395 237.

b) 291 375
291 475

291 375 is ________________ than 291 475.

c) 143 750
133 750

143 750 is ________________ than 133 750.

d) 522 508
532 508

522 508 is ________________ than 532 508.

e) 96 405
96 415

96 405 is ________________ than 96 415.

f) 3 752 582
3 751 582

3 752 582 is ________________ than 3 751 582.

NS6-6: Differences from 10 to 10 000 *(continued)*

6. Fill in the blanks.

a) ____________ is 10 more than 3 782
b) ____________ is 100 less than 39 927
c) ____________ is 100 more than 3 782
d) ____________ is 1 000 less than 15 023
e) ____________ is 10 000 more than 287 532
f) ____________ is 1 000 less than 23 685
g) ____________ is 10 000 more than 8 305
h) ____________ is 100 000 more than 4 253
i) ____________ is 100 000 less than 273 528
j) ____________ is 10 000 less than 178 253

7. Fill in the blanks.

a) 226 + 10 = ________
b) 28 573 + 10 = ________
c) 39 035 + 10 = ________
d) 42 127 + 100 = ________
e) 63 283 + 1 000 = ________
f) 58 372 + 10 000 = ________
g) 2 873 − 10 = ________
h) 485 − 10 = ________
i) 837 − 100 = ________
j) 32 487 − 1 000 = ________
k) 81 901 − 100 = ________
l) 25 836 − 10 000 = ________
m) 382 507 + 10 000 = ________
n) 1 437 652 − 100 000 = ________

8. Fill in the blanks.

a) 685 + ________ = 695
b) 302 + ________ = 402
c) 2 375 + ________ = 2 385
d) 2 617 + ________ = 2 717
e) 43 210 + ________ = 44 210
f) 26 287 + ________ = 26 387
g) 1 287 − ________ = 1 187
h) 6 325 − ________ = 6 315
i) 14 392 − ________ = 14 292
j) 386 053 − ________ = 376 053
k) 1 260 053 + 1000 = ________

BONUS

9. Continue the number patterns.

a) 6 407, 6 417, 6 427, ________ , ________
b) 46 640, 47 640, 48 640, ________ , ________
c) 624 823, 624 833, ________ , 624 853
d) ________ , 28 393, 28 403, 28 413

10. Circle the pair of digits that are different. Then fill in the blanks.

a) 827 325
827 335

827 325 is 10 less than 827 335

b) 382 305
482 305

________ is ________ greater than ________

c) 925 778
915 778

________ is ________ less than ________

NS6-7: Comparing Numbers (Advanced)

1. Write the number represented by the base ten materials in each box. Then circle the greater number in each pair.

HINT: If there is the same number of thousands, count the number of hundreds or tens.

a) (i)

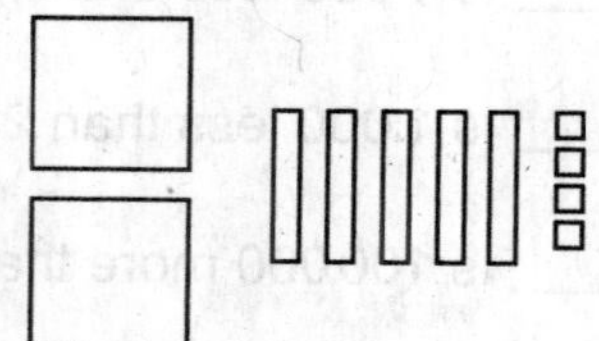

(ii)

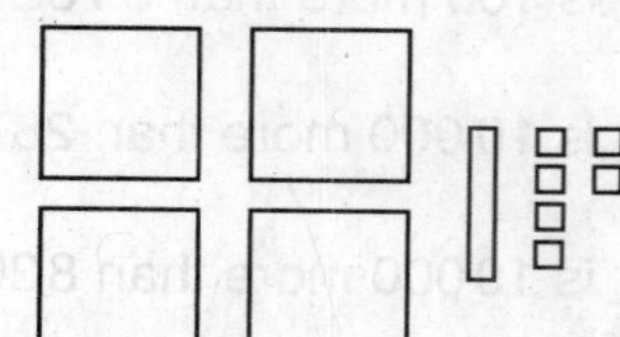

b) (i)

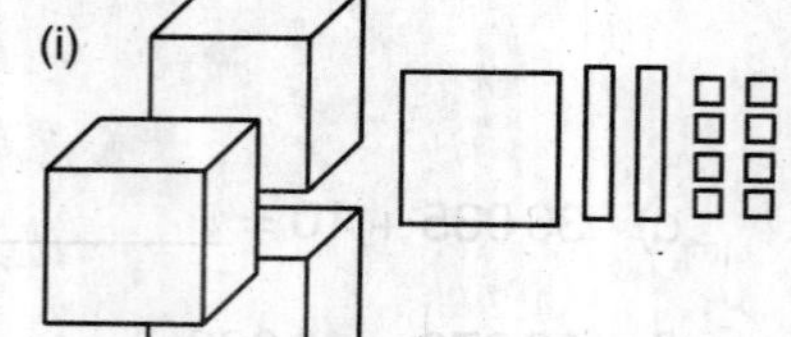

(ii)

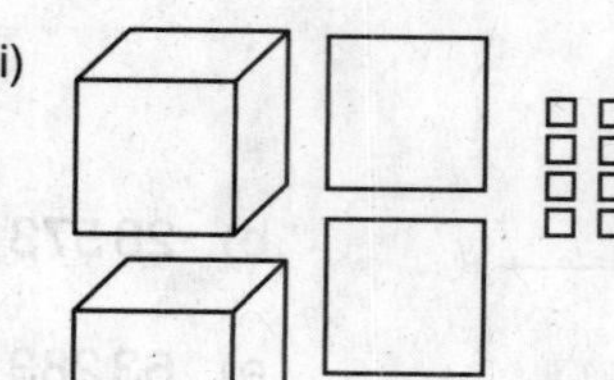

2. Circle the greater number in each pair.

a) 47 or forty-eight b) three thousand, five hundred seven or 3 508 c) ninety-four or 88

d) six hundred fifty-five or 662 e) 60 385 or sixty thousand four hundred twenty-five

3. List all the two-digit numbers you can make using the digits provided (using each digit only once). Then circle the greatest one.

a) 6, 7 and 8 b) 2, 9 and 4 c) 5, 2, and 0

4. Create the greatest possible <u>four-digit</u> number using the digits given. Only use each digit once.

a) 4, 3, 2, 6 ____________ b) 7, 8, 9, 4 ____________ c) 0, 4, 1, 2 ____________

5. Create the greatest possible number using these digits. Only use each digit once.

a) 3, 4, 1, 2, 8 ____________ b) 2, 8, 9, 1, 5 ____________ c) 3, 6, 1, 5, 4 ____________

6. Use the digits to create the greatest number, the least number and a number in between.

	Digits	Greatest Number	Number in Between	Least Number
a)	8 5 7 2 1			
b)	2 1 5 3 9			
c)	3 0 1 5 3			

NS6-7: Comparing Numbers (Advanced) *(continued)*

7. Arrange the numbers in order, starting with the <u>least</u> number.

   a) 683 759, 693 238, 693 231

   683759, 693231, 693238

   b) 473 259, 42 380, 47 832

   42380, 47832, 473259

   c) 385 290, 928 381, 532 135

   ______, ______, ______

   d) 2 575, 38 258, 195

   ______, ______, ______

8. What is the greatest number less than 10 000 whose digits are all the same? ______

9. Identify the greater number by writing > or <.

   a) 63 752 ☐ 63 750

   b) 927 385 ☐ 928 303

   c) 572 312 ☐ 59 238

   d) 1 230 075 ☐ 1 230 123

10.

City	Population
Ottawa	774 072
Hamilton	662 401
Kitchener	414 284

   a) Which city has a population greater than 670 000?

   ______

   b) Write the populations in order from least to greatest.

   ______

11. What is the greatest possible number you can create that has …

   a) 3 digits? ______ b) 4 digits? ______ c) 5 digits? ______

12. Using the digits 0, 1, 2, 3, 4, create an even number greater than 42 000 and less than 43 000.

13. Using the digits 4, 5, 6, 7, 8, create an odd number greater than 64 000 and less than 68 000.

14. What digit can be substituted for ☐ to make each statement true?

   a) 54 ☐ 21 is between 54 348 and 54 519.

   b) 76 ☐ 99 is between 76 201 and 76 316.

NS6-8: Regrouping

Nancy has 3 hundreds blocks, 14 tens blocks, and 8 ones blocks.
She exchanges 10 tens blocks for a hundreds block.

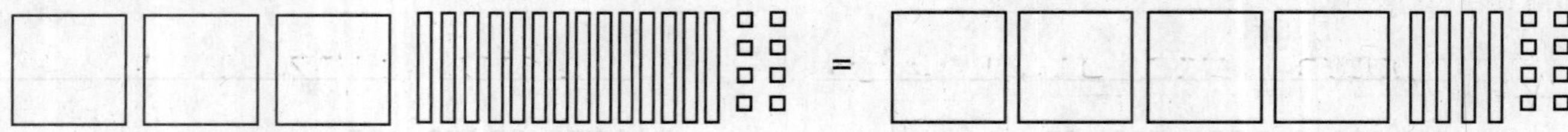

3 hundreds + 14 tens + 8 ones = 4 hundreds + 4 tens + 8 ones

---

1. Regroup 10 ones as 1 tens block.

a) 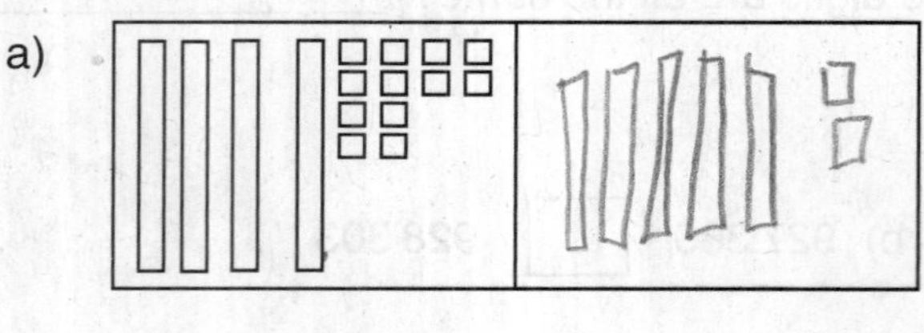

4 tens + 12 ones = 5 tens + 2 ones

b) 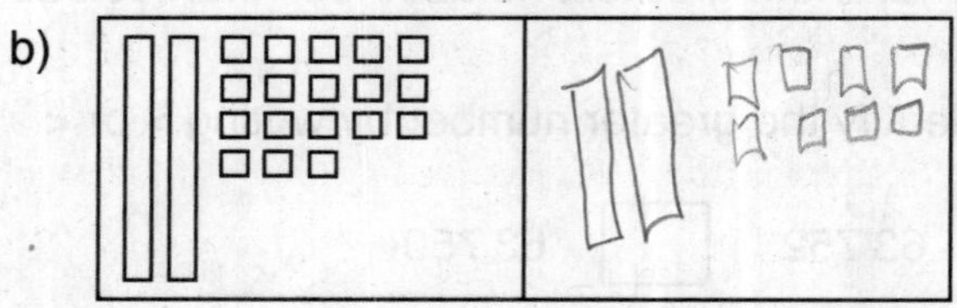

2 tens + 18 ones = 2 tens + 8 ones

2. Exchange ones for tens.

a) 53 ones = 5 tens + 3 ones b) 85 ones = 8 tens + 5 ones c) 14 ones = 1 tens + 4 ones

d) 27 ones = 2 tens + 7 ones e) 32 ones = 3 tens + 2 ones f) 16 ones = 1 tens + 6 ones

g) 11 ones = 1 tens + 1 ones h) 82 ones = 8 tens + 2 ones i) 93 ones = 9 tens + 3 ones

3. Complete the charts by regrouping 10 tens as 1 hundred.

a)

hundreds	tens
7	28
7 + 2 = 9	8

b)

hundreds	tens
6	24
6+2=8	4

c)

hundreds	tens
3	15
3+1=4	5

d)

hundreds	tens
6	36
6+3=9	6

e)

hundreds	tens
8	19
8+1=9	9

f)

hundreds	tens
2	20
2+2=4	0

4. Exchange tens for hundreds or ones for tens. The first one has been done for you.

a) 6 hundreds + 7 tens + 19 ones = 6 hundreds + 8 tens + 9 ones

b) 2 hundreds + 6 tens + 15 ones = 2 hund + 7tens + 5 ones

c) 8 hundreds + 28 tens + 9 ones = 10 hund + 8 tens + 8 ones

Rupa has 1 thousands block, 12 hundreds blocks, 1 tens block, and 2 ones blocks.

She regroups 10 hundreds blocks as a thousands block.

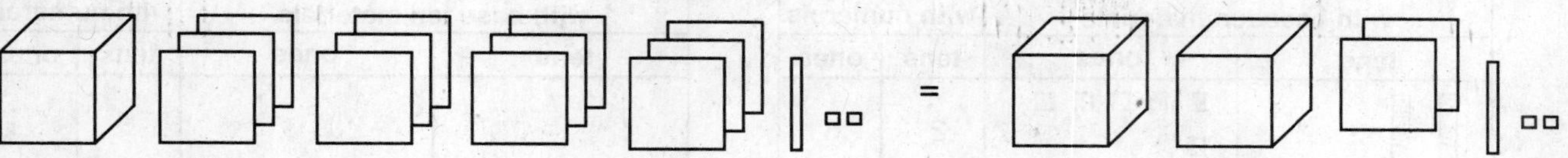

1 thousand + 12 hundreds + 1 ten + 2 ones = 2 thousands + 2 hundreds + 1 ten + 2 ones

5. Complete the charts by regrouping 10 hundreds as 1 thousand.

a)

thousands	hundreds
5	25
5 + 2 = 7	5

b)

thousands	hundreds
3	12
3+1=4	2

c)

thousands	hundreds
8	20
8+2=10	0

6. Exchange 10 hundreds for a thousand. The first one has been done for you.

a) 5 thousands + 23 hundreds + 2 tens + 5 ones = 7 thousands + 3 hundreds + 2 tens + 5 ones

b) 1 thousands + 54 hundreds + 2 tens + 6 ones = 6 thousands + 4 hundreds + 2 tens + 6 ones

c) 8 thousands + 15 hundreds + 3 tens + 0 ones = 9thousands + 5hundres + 3 tenst

7. Exchange thousands for ten thousands, hundreds for thousands, tens for hundreds, or ones for tens.

a) 2 thousands + 13 hundreds + 2 tens + 5 ones = 3 thousands + 3 hundreds + 2 tens + 5 ones

b) 5 thousands + 2 hundreds + 3 tens + 56 ones = 5 thosands+ 2hundres +8 tens + 6 Ones

c) 3 ten thousands + 27 thousands + 2 hundreds + 37 tens + 8 ones = 5tenthousands+ 7th-ousands+5 hundres+7 tens+8ones

8. Teresa wants to build a model of 6 thousand, 5 hundred and ninety.
She has 5 thousands blocks, 14 hundreds blocks and 30 tens blocks.

Can she build the model?

Use diagrams and numbers to explain your answer.

NS6-9: Adding With Regrouping

1. Add the numbers below by drawing a picture and by adding the digits. Use base ten materials to show how to combine the numbers and how to regroup. (The first one has been done for you.)

a) **26 + 36**

	with base ten materials		with numerals	
	tens	ones	tens	ones
26			2	6
36			3	6
sum		regroup 10 ones as ten	5	12
		after regrouping	6	2

b) **57 + 27**

with base ten materials		with numerals	
tens	ones	tens	ones

2. Add the ones digits. Show how you would regroup 10 ones as 1 ten. The first question has been done for you.

tens go here

a) 1 6 + 1 7 → tens box: 1, ones box: 3

ones go here

b) 2 4 + 3 6

c) 5 7 + 1 9

d) 7 3 + 1 9

e) 5 7 + 3 5

3. Add the numbers by regrouping. The first one has been done for you.

a) $\begin{array}{r} {}^{1}\ \ \\ 46 \\ +\ 25 \\ \hline 71 \end{array}$

b) $\begin{array}{r} 33 \\ +\ 48 \\ \hline \end{array}$

c) $\begin{array}{r} 72 \\ +\ 19 \\ \hline \end{array}$

d) $\begin{array}{r} 85 \\ +\ 17 \\ \hline \end{array}$

e) $\begin{array}{r} 47 \\ +\ 26 \\ \hline \end{array}$

f) $\begin{array}{r} 38 \\ +\ 43 \\ \hline \end{array}$

g) $\begin{array}{r} 69 \\ +\ \ 9 \\ \hline \end{array}$

h) $\begin{array}{r} 74 \\ +\ 19 \\ \hline \end{array}$

i) $\begin{array}{r} 43 \\ +\ 39 \\ \hline \end{array}$

j) $\begin{array}{r} 68 \\ +\ 29 \\ \hline \end{array}$

NS6-10: Adding 3-Digit Numbers

Simon adds **363 + 274** using base ten materials.

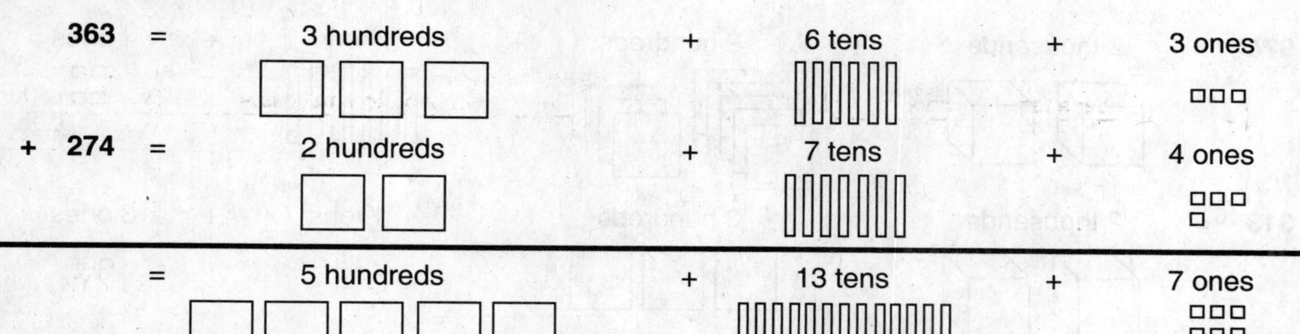

Then, to get the final answer, Simon regroups 10 tens as 1 hundred.

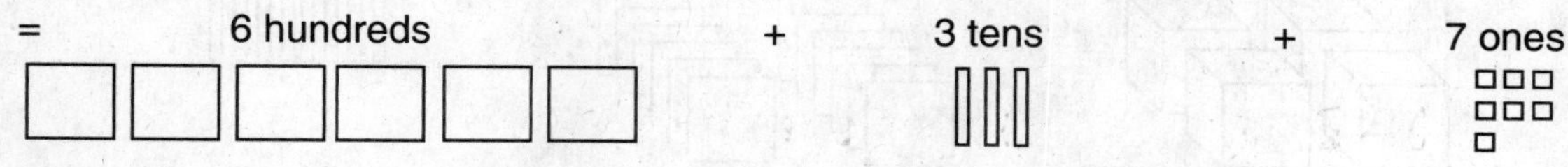

1. Add the numbers below, either by using base ten materials or by drawing a picture in your notebook. Record your work here.

483 = ____ hundreds + ____ tens + ____ ones
+ 245 = ____ hundreds + ____ tens + ____ ones
= ____ hundreds + ____ tens + ____ ones
after regrouping = ____ hundreds + ____ tens + ____ ones

2. Add. You will need to regroup. The first one is started for you.

a) [1] 364 + 253 = 17
b) [ ] 571 + 255
c) [ ] 652 + 94
d) 364 + 482
e) 447 + 172

3. Add, regrouping where necessary.

a) 168 + 323
b) 255 + 362
c) 295 + 123
d) 465 + 159
e) 457 + 303
f) 465 + 264

4. Add by lining the numbers up correctly in the grid. The first one has been started for you.

a) 449 + 346
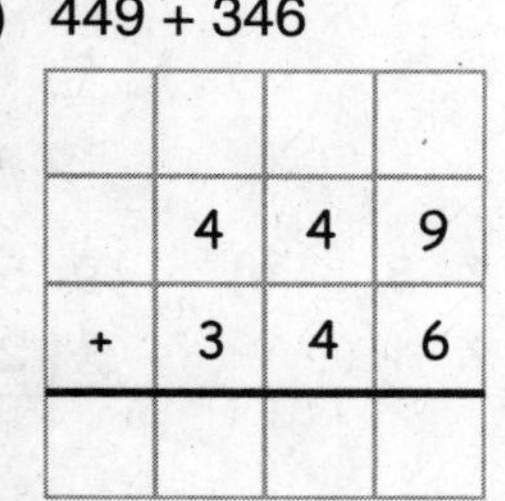

b) 273 + 456
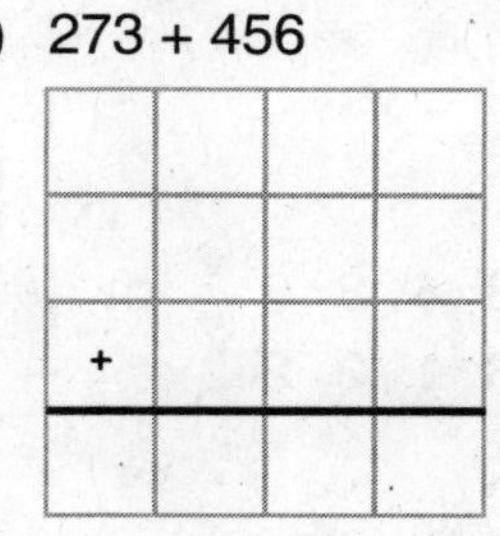

c) 832 + 109
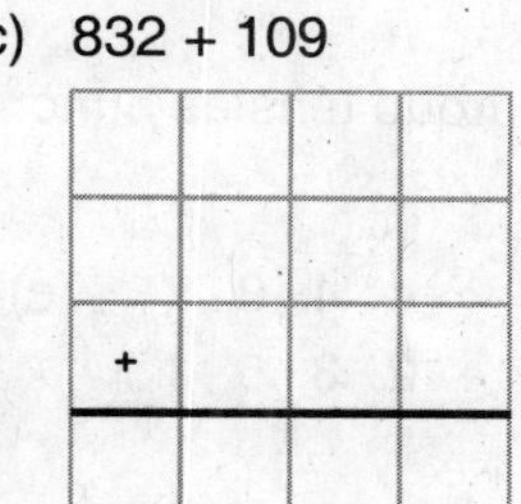

d) 347 + 72
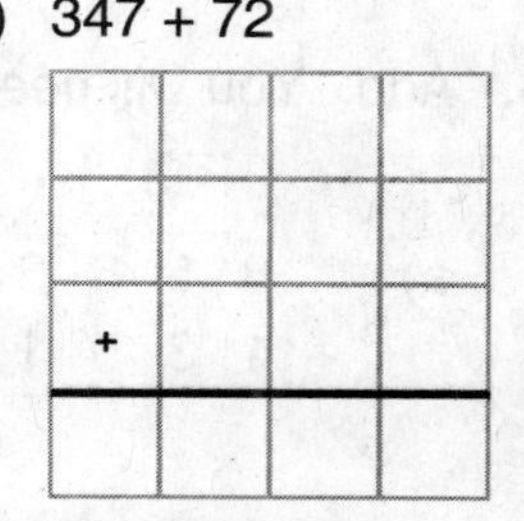

NS6-11: Adding Larger Numbers

Samuel adds **2 974 + 2 313** using base ten materials.

2 974 = 2 thousands + 9 hundreds + 7 tens + 4 ones

+ 2 313 = 2 thousands + 3 hundreds + 1 tens + 3 ones

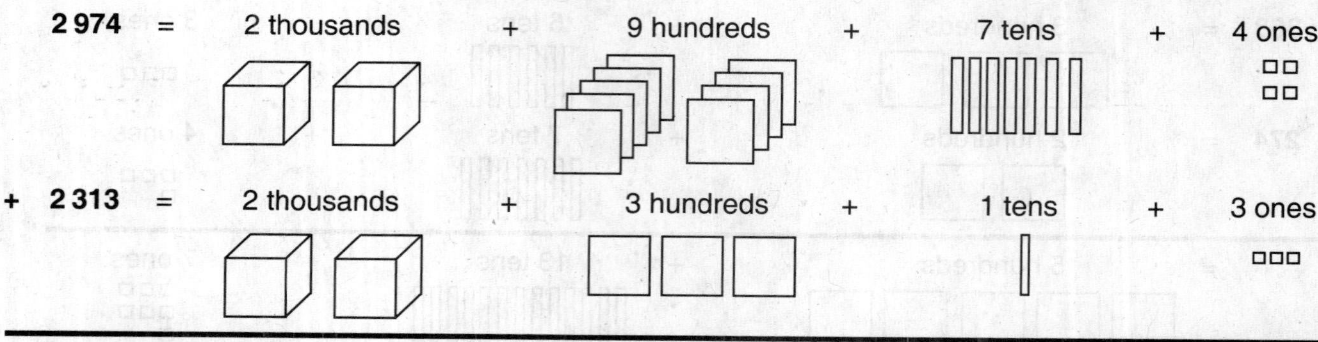

= 4 thousands + 12 hundreds + 8 tens + 7 ones

Then, to get the final answer, Samuel exchanges 10 hundreds for 1 thousand.

= 5 thousands + 2 hundreds + 8 tens + 7 ones

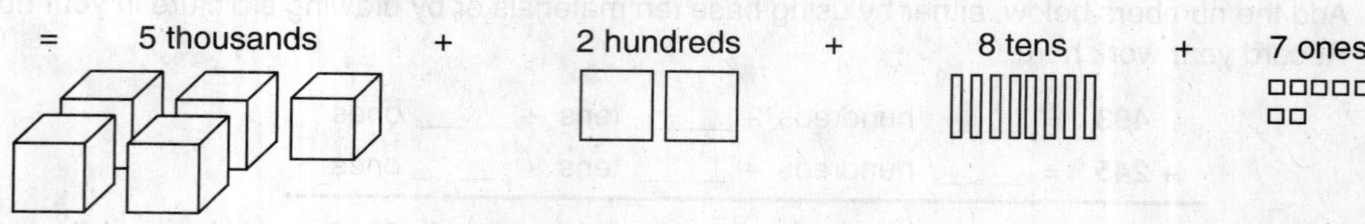

1. Add the numbers below, either by using base ten materials or by drawing a picture in your notebook. Record your work here.

5 486 = ____ thousands + ____ hundreds + ____ tens + ____ ones

+ 3 713 = ____ thousands + ____ hundreds + ____ tens + ____ ones

= ____ thousands + ____ hundreds + ____ tens + ____ ones

after regrouping = ____ thousands + ____ hundreds + ____ tens + ____ ones

2. Add. (You will need to regroup.) The first one is started for you.

a)
```
  4 6 8 3
+ 2 7 1 2
---------
    3 9 5
```
b)
```
  2 5 3 7
+ 4 6 2 1
```
c)
```
  8 6 5 4
+   7 2 4
```
d)
```
  3 1 7 4
+ 4 9 2 3
```
e)
```
  5 9 4 6
+ 2 4 3 2
```

3. Add. You will need to regroup tens as hundreds.

a)
```
  8 5 6 3
+ 1 3 5 1
```
b)
```
  4 4 8 7
+ 2 3 5 1
```
c)
```
  3 6 8 3
+ 3 1 3 2
```
d)
```
  2 4 7 8
+   2 7 1
```
e)
```
  9 5 9 3
+   2 5 2
```

NS6-11: Adding Larger Numbers *(continued)*

4. Add the following, regrouping or carrying where necessary.

a) 5 8 4 6 + 1 1 3 5

b) 3 5 6 4 + 2 8 1 3

c) 6 5 3 4 + 3 2 9 4

d) 8 8 5 4 + 1 0 6 3

e) 2 4 4 3 + 5 9 3 5

f) 6 7 5 2 + 2 3 3 4

g) 3 4 7 3 + 5 2 4 3

h) 5 6 7 5 + 9 2 3

i) 8 2 3 0 + 1 4 8 8

j) 2 5 4 8 + 3 4 8 1

5. Add by lining the digits up correctly in the grid. In some questions you may have to regroup twice.

a) 
2 468 + 7 431

b) 8 596 + 1 235

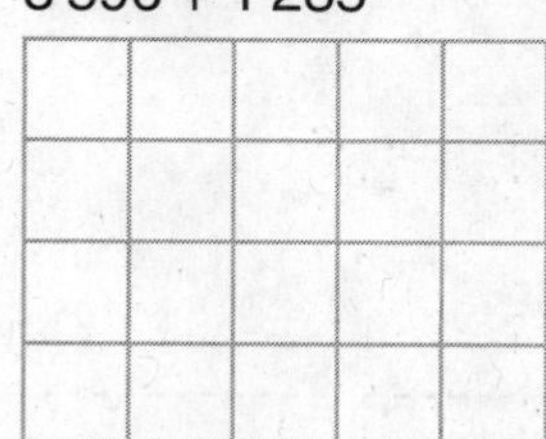

c) 6 650 + 2 198

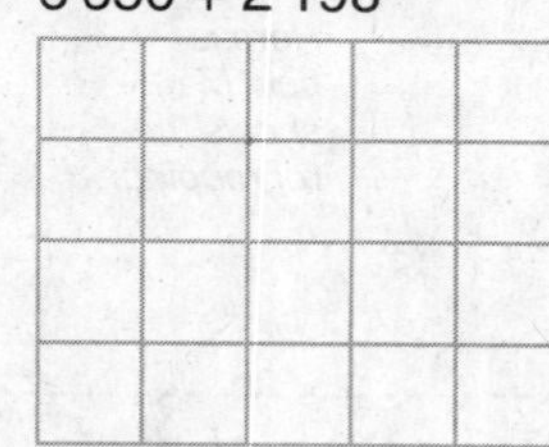

d) 8 359 + 48

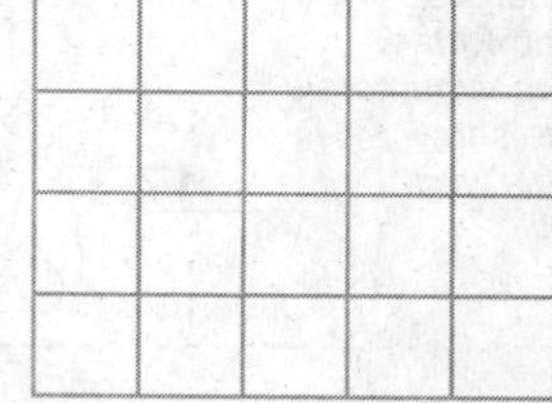

6. Add, regrouping where necessary.

a) 5 4 5 5 + 1 2 7 3

b) 7 3 2 4 6 + 1 8 3 8 2

c) 1 4 5 6 8 3 + 3 2 9 2 3 4

d) 2 3 5 2 7 5 + 5 1 2 9 1 3

e) 5 326 + 1 234 + 6 762

f) 3 658 + 6 343 + 4 534

g) 389 + 3247 + 712 + 52

7. A **palindrome** is a number (or word) that reads the same forward and backward.

For instance: 363, 51 815, and 2 375 732 are all palindromes.

For each number below, follow the steps shown here for the number 124.

Step 1: Reverse the digits. 124 → 421

Step 2: Add the two numbers. 124 + 421 = 545

Step 3: If the number you create is *not* a palindrome, repeat Steps 1 and 2 with the new number. Most numbers will eventually become palindromes if you keep repeating these steps.

Create palindromes from the following numbers.

a) 216 b) 154 c) 651 d) 23153 e) 371 f) 258 g) 1385

NS6-12: Subtraction

Mark subtracts **54 – 17** using base ten materials.

Step 1:
Mark represents 54 with base ten materials…

tens	ones
5	4

Here is how Mark uses numerals to show his work:

54
– 17

Step 2:
7 (the ones digit of 17) is greater than 4 (the ones digit of 54) so Mark regroups a tens block as 10 ones…

tens	ones
4	14

Here is how Mark shows the regrouping:

4 14
~~5~~ ~~4~~
– 1 7

Step 3:
Mark subtracts 17 (he takes away 1 tens block and 7 ones)…

tens	ones
3	7

And now Mark can subtract 14 – 7 ones and 4 – 1 tens:

4 14
~~5~~ ~~4~~
– 1 7
3 7

---

1. In these questions, Mark doesn't have enough ones to subtract. Help him by regrouping a tens block as 10 ones. Show how he would rewrite his subtraction statement.

a) **53 – 36**

tens	ones
5	3

	5	3
–	3	6

tens	ones
4	13

	4	13
	~~5~~	~~3~~
–	3	6

b) **65 – 29**

tens	ones
6	5

	6	5
–	2	9

tens	ones

	6	5
–	2	9

c) **45 – 27**

tens	ones
4	5

	4	5
–	2	7

tens	ones

	4	5
–	2	7

d) **53 – 48**

tens	ones
5	3

	5	3
–	4	8

tens	ones

	5	3
–	4	8

2. Subtract by regrouping. The first one is done for you.

a)

	7	12
	~~8~~	~~2~~
–	3	7
	4	5

b) 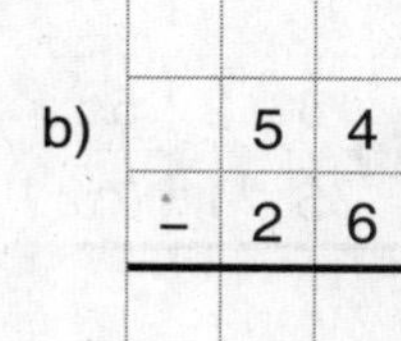

	5	4
–	2	6

c) 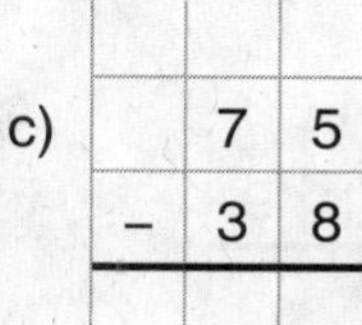

	7	5
–	3	8

d) 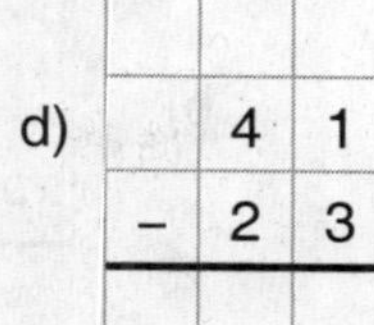

	4	1
–	2	3

e) 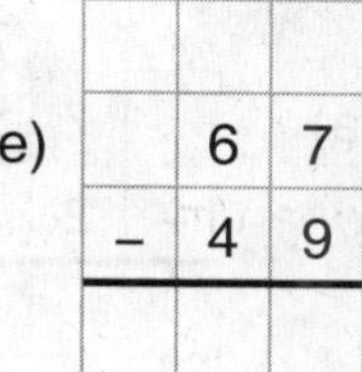

	6	7
–	4	9

3. For the questions where you need to regroup, write "Help!" in the space provided.
How do you know when you need to regroup? Write an answer in your notebook. If you are working with a partner, discuss.

a) 58 – 19   Help! ____ 8 is less than 9

b) 34 – 13 ______

c) 85 – 27 ______

d) 48 – 42 ______

e) 68 – 35 ______

f) 91 – 25 ______

g) 85 – 24 ______

h) 66 – 8 ______

i) 25 – 16 ______

j) 93 – 47 ______

k) 56 – 9 ______

l) 85 – 12 ______

4. To subtract 425 –182, Rita regroups a hundreds block for 10 tens blocks.

hundreds	tens	ones
4	2	5

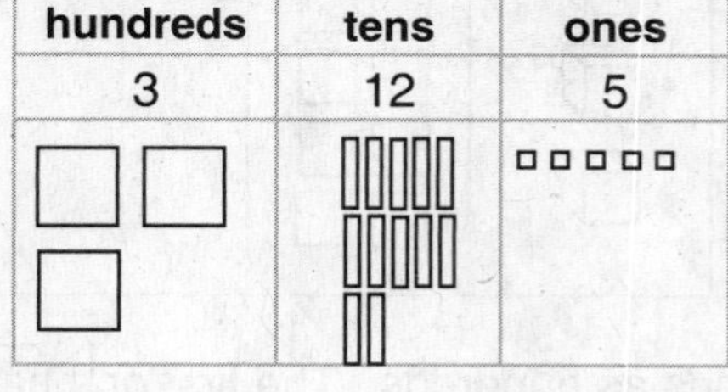

hundreds	tens	ones
3	12	5

hundreds	tens	ones
2	4	3

Subtract by regrouping <u>hundreds</u> as tens. The first one has been started for you.

a) 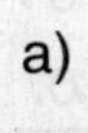 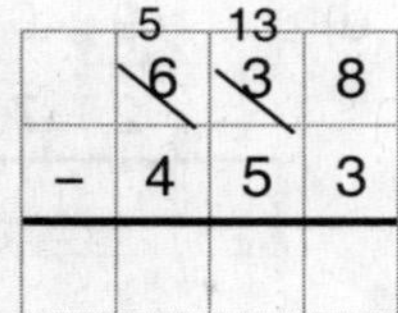

	5	13	
	~~6~~	~~3~~	8
–	4	5	3

b)

	8	5	4
–	3	7	2

c)

	7	5	5
–	3	8	2

d)

	4	2	3
–	1	8	2

5. Subtract by regrouping <u>tens</u> as ones. The first one has been started for you.

a)

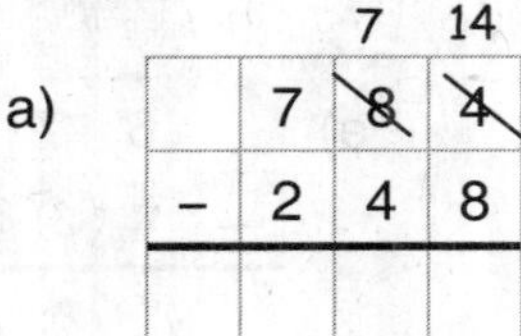

	7	~~8~~ 7	~~4~~ 14
–	2	4	8

b)

	3	4	3
–	2	1	9

c)

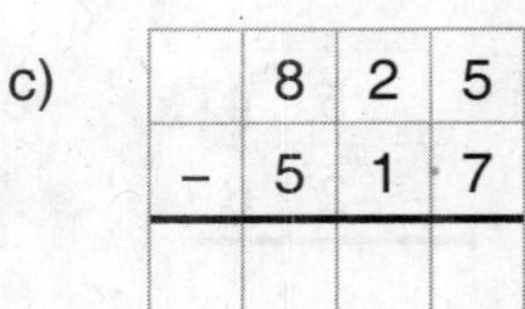

	8	2	5
–	5	1	7

d)

	6	7	1
–	3	1	6

6. For the questions below, you will have to regroup *twice*.

Example:

<u>Step 1</u>:
$$\begin{array}{r} {\scriptstyle 2\ 16} \\ 8\ \not{3}\ \not{6} \\ -\ 3\ 5\ 8 \\ \hline \end{array}$$

<u>Step 2</u>:
$$\begin{array}{r} {\scriptstyle 2\ 16} \\ 8\ \not{3}\ \not{6} \\ -\ 3\ 5\ 8 \\ \hline 8 \end{array}$$

<u>Step 3</u>:
$$\begin{array}{r} {\scriptstyle 12} \\ {\scriptstyle 7\ \not{2}\ 16} \\ \not{8}\ \not{3}\ \not{6} \\ -\ 3\ 5\ 8 \\ \hline 8 \end{array}$$

<u>Step 4</u>:
$$\begin{array}{r} {\scriptstyle 12} \\ {\scriptstyle 7\ \not{2}\ 16} \\ \not{8}\ \not{3}\ \not{6} \\ -\ 3\ 5\ 8 \\ \hline 7\ 8 \end{array}$$

<u>Step 5</u>:
$$\begin{array}{r} {\scriptstyle 12} \\ {\scriptstyle 7\ \not{2}\ 16} \\ \not{8}\ \not{3}\ \not{6} \\ -\ 3\ 5\ 8 \\ \hline 4\ 7\ 8 \end{array}$$

a)

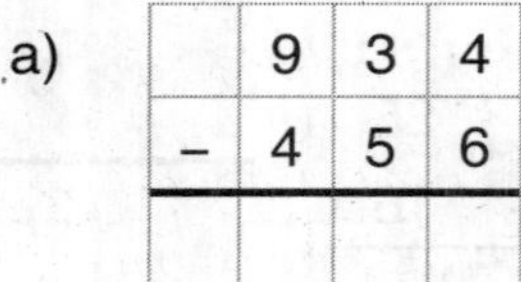

	9	3	4
–	4	5	6

b)

	7	4	7
–	2	6	9

c)

	5	3	2
–		5	9

d)

	8	9	2
–	4	9	5

7. To subtract 5 267 – 3 415, Laura regroups a thousands block as 10 hundreds blocks.

thousands	hundreds	tens	ones
5	2	6	7

thousands	hundreds	tens	ones
4	12	6	7

thousands	hundreds	tens	ones
1	8	5	2

Subtract by regrouping thousands as hundreds. The first one has been done for you.

a)

	~~4~~ 3	~~3~~ 13	5	8
–	1	5	2	6
	2	8	3	2

b)

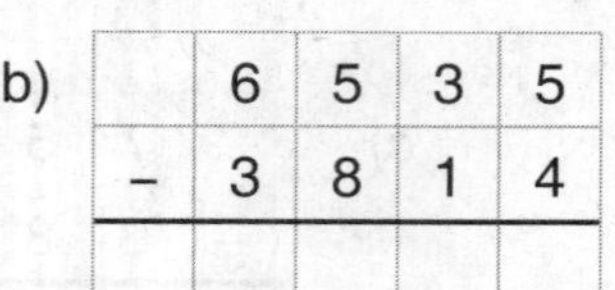

	6	5	3	5
–	3	8	1	4

c)

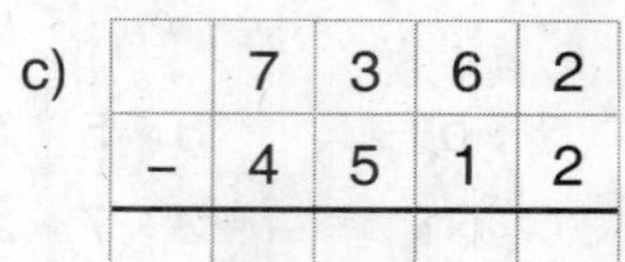

	7	3	6	2
–	4	5	1	2

d)

	9	0	6	3
–	2	7	0	2

NS6-12: Subtraction *(continued)*

8. In some of the questions below, you will need to regroup.

a)

	3	6	4	8
−	1	9	3	4

b)

	9	1	2	4
−	6	0	6	2

c)

	8	5	4	2
−	3	4	6	1

d)

3	2	8	3	9
−	4	6	2	8

9. In the questions below, you will have to regroup *three* times (i.e., regroup a ten as 10 ones, a hundred as 10 tens, and a thousand as 10 hundreds).

Example:

Step 1:

```
     1 13
  6 4 2̶ 3̶
− 3 7 4 6
        7
```

Step 2:

```
     1 13
  6 4 2̶ 3̶
− 3 7 4 6
        7
```

Step 3:

```
     11
   3 1̶ 13
  6 4̶ 2̶ 3̶
− 3 7 4 6
      7 7
```

Step 4:

```
     11
   3 1̶ 13
  6 4̶ 2̶ 3̶
− 3 7 4 6
    6 7 7
```

Step 5:

```
 13 11
   3 1̶ 13
  5 4̶ 2̶ 3̶
− 3 7 4 6
  2 6 7 7
```

a)

	9	5	4	2
−	1	7	6	3

b)

	6	4	3	7
−	2	6	7	8

c)

	4	5	6	3
−	1	7	9	5

d)

	7	8	4	3
−	4	8	6	5

10. In the questions below, you will have to regroup *two*, *three*, or *four* times.

Example:

Step 1:

```
 0 10
 1̶ 0̶ 0 0
−  7 5 6
```

Step 2:

```
    9
 0 10̶ 10
 1̶ 0̶ 0̶ 0
−  7 5 6
```

Step 3:

```
    9  9
 0 10̶ 10̶ 10
 1̶ 0̶ 0̶ 0̶
−  7 5 6
```

Step 4:

```
    9  9
 0 10̶ 10̶ 10
 1̶ 0̶ 0̶ 0̶
−  7 5 6
   2 4 4
```

a)

	1	0	0	0
−		4	6	8

b)

	1	0	0
−		3	2

c)

1	0	0	0	0
−	6	4	8	6

d)

	1	0	0	0	0
−		5	1	1	1

NS6-13: Adding and Subtracting

Answer the following questions in your notebook.

1. A school has 150 students.
   80 of the students are boys.

   How many are girls?

2. Raj has 150 stamps.
   Sharif has 12 fewer stamps than Raj.
   Cedric has 15 more stamps than Raj.

   How many stamps do the children have altogether?

3. Camile cycled 2 357 km one year and 5 753 km the next.

   How many km did she cycle altogether?

4. Two nearby towns have populations of 442 670 and 564 839 people.

   What is the total population of both towns?

5. A grocery store had 480 cans of soup.

   In one week they sold:

   - 212 cans of tomato soup
   - 57 cans of chicken soup
   - 43 cans of mushroom soup

   How many cans were left?

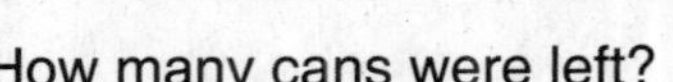

6. A box turtle can live 100 years.
   A rabbit can live 15 years.

   How much longer than a rabbit can a box turtle live?

7. In the number 432...

   - The 100s digit is one more than the tens digit
   - The 10s digit is one more than the ones digit

   Make up your own number with this property.

   _____ _____ _____

   Now write the number backwards.

   _____ _____ _____

   Next write these two numbers in a grid and subtract them (be sure to put the greater number on top).

   Try this again with several other numbers. You will always get 198!

   BONUS
   Can you explain why this works?

8. The shoreline of Lake Ontario is 1 146 km.

   The shoreline of Lake Erie is 1 402 km.

   How much longer is the shoreline of Lake Erie than the shoreline of Lake Ontario?

9. The Nile River is about 6 690 km long and the Amazon River is 6 440 km long.

   How much longer is the Nile River than the Amazon River?

NS6-14: Concepts in Number Sense

Answer the questions below in your notebook.

1. The chart below gives the area of some of the largest islands in Canada.

Island	**Area in km^2**
Baffin Island	507 450
Ellesmere Island	196 240
Newfoundland	108 860
Vancouver Island	31 290

a) Write the area of the islands in order from least to greatest.

b) How much greater than the area of the smallest island is the area of the largest island?

c) How much greater is the area of Ellesmere Island than Newfoundland?

d) The area of Greenland is 2 166 086 km^2.
Do Baffin Island and Vancouver Island *together* have an area greater than Greenland?

2. Use each of the digits 4, 5, 6, 7, 8 once to create…

a) the greatest odd number possible.

b) a number between 56 700 and 57 000.

c) an even number whose tens digit and hundreds digit add to 12.

d) a number as close to 70 000 as possible (explain how you know your answer is correct).

3. There are 390 000 species of plants and 1 234 400 species of animals.

How many more species of animals are there than plants?

4. Use the numbers 1, 2, 3, 4 once in each question.

a)

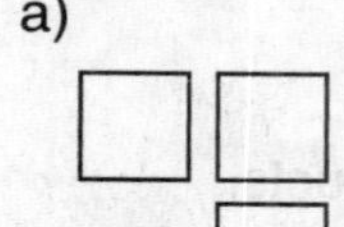

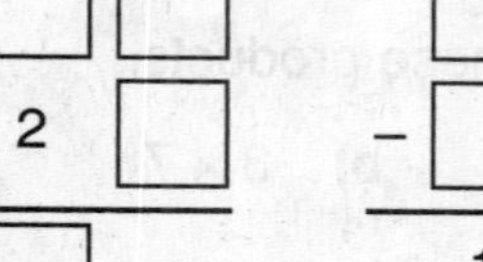

b)

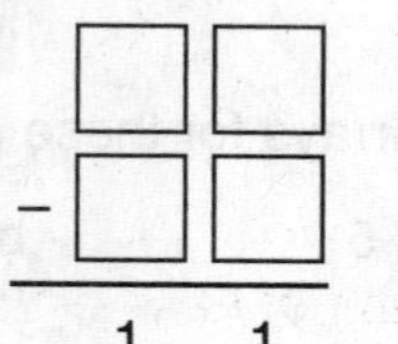

c)

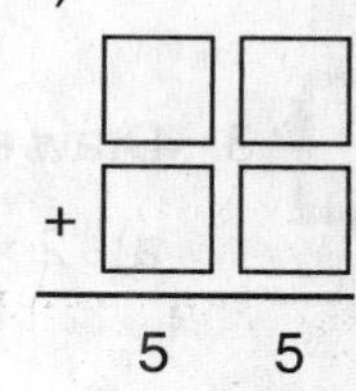

5. Here are some important dates in the history of science.

- In 1543, Copernicus published a book claiming the sun is the center of our solar system.
- In 1610, Galileo Galilei used his newly invented telescope to discover the moons of Jupiter.
- In 1667, Isaac Newton announced his law of gravity.

a) How long ago did Copernicus publish his book?

b) How many years passed between each pair of dates given?

NS6-15: Array and Factors

When you multiply a pair of numbers, the result is called the **product** of the numbers. You can represent a product using an **array**.

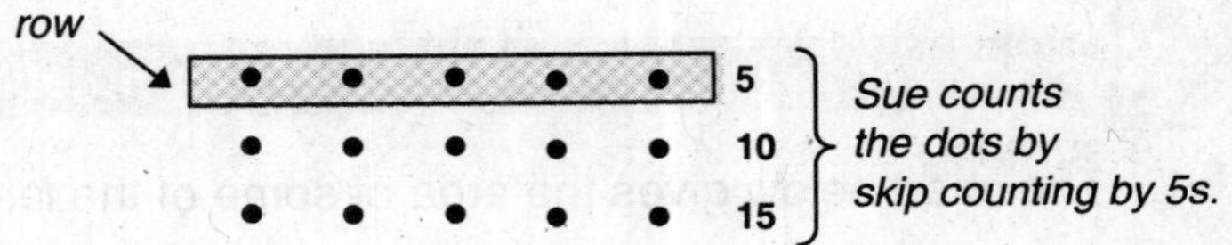

Sue writes a multiplication statement for the array: **3 × 5 = 15** (3 and 5 are called **factors** of 15)

---

1. Write a multiplication statement for each array.

a) 

b)

c) 

a) 3 rows
4 dots in each row
3 × 4 = 12

b) ____ rows
____ dots in each row
____

c) ________
____
____

2. Write a product for each array.

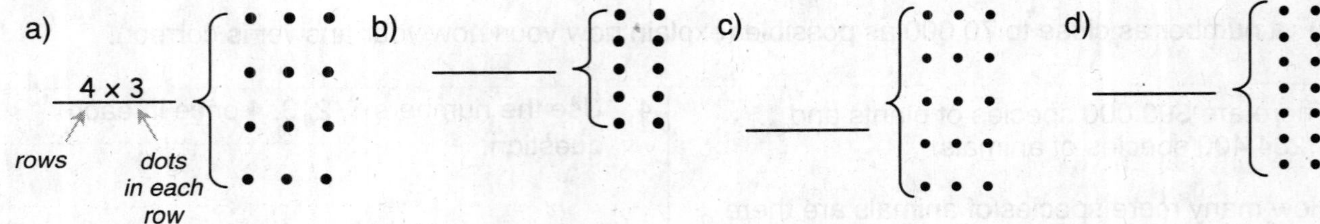

3. Draw arrays for these products.

a) 2 × 5 b) 3 × 7 c) 4 × 6 d) 1 × 8 e) 4 × 2

4. There are only *three* ways to arrange 4 dots in an array.
So there are only 3 ways to write 4 as a product of two factors.

1 × 4 = 4 **2 × 2 = 4** **4 × 1 = 4**

How many ways can you write each number as a product of two factors? (Draw arrays to help.)

a) 6 b) 8 c) 9 d) 10 e) 12

5. The numbers that appear beside the arrays in Question 4 are called the **factors** of 4.
The factors of 4 are the numbers 1, 2, and 4.

Write a list of factors for the numbers 6, 8, 9, 10, and 12.

NS6-16: Prime Numbers and Composite Numbers

A **prime** number has <u>two</u> distinct factors (no more, no less): itself and 1.

A **composite** number has <u>more than two</u> factors: at least one number **other than** itself and 1.

---

1. a) How many <u>distinct</u> factors does the number 1 have? _____ b) Is 1 a prime number? _____

2. List all the prime numbers less than 10: ____________________

3. List all the composite numbers between 10 and 20: ____________________

4. What is the greatest prime number less than 30? ____________________

5. Circle the prime numbers.

   1 25 14 13 17 20 27 15 12 18 29 33

6. Eratosthenes was a Libyan scholar who lived over 2000 years ago.
   He developed a method to systematically identify prime numbers.
   It is called **Eratosthenes' Sieve**.

   Follow the directions below to identify the prime numbers from 1 to 100.

   a) Cross out the number 1 (it is not prime).

   b) Circle 2, and cross out all the multiples of 2.

   c) Circle 3, and cross out all the multiples of 3 (that haven't already been crossed out).

   d) Circle 5, and cross out all the multiples of 5 (that haven't already been crossed out).

   e) Circle 7, and cross out all the multiples of 7 (that haven't already been crossed out).

   f) Circle all remaining numbers.

   You've just used **Eratosthenes' Sieve** to find all the prime numbers from 1 to100!

1	2	3	4	5	6	7	8	9	10
11	12	13	14	15	16	17	18	19	20
21	22	23	24	25	26	27	28	29	30
31	32	33	34	35	36	37	38	39	40
41	42	43	44	45	46	47	48	49	50
51	52	53	54	55	56	57	58	59	60
61	62	63	64	65	66	67	68	69	70
71	72	73	74	75	76	77	78	79	80
81	82	83	84	85	86	87	88	89	90
91	92	93	94	95	96	97	98	99	100

7. The prime numbers 3 and 5 differ by 2.
   Find three pairs of prime numbers less than 20 that differ by 2.

NS6-17: More Primes, Factors, and Composite Numbers

1. List all the factors of each number (the first one is done for you).

   a) 25: 1, 5, 25 ______ b) 8: ______

   c) 12: ______ d) 16: ______

   e) 9: ______ f) 18: ______

   g) 50: ______ h) 45: ______

   i) 60: ______ j) 42: ______

2. Put a check mark in front of the numbers that are composite numbers.

   ____ 30 ____ 31 ____ 32 ____ 33 ____ 34 ____ 35 ____ 36 ____ 37

3. Write a number between 0 and 20 that has …

   a) two factors: ______ b) four factors: ______ c) five factors ______

4. Cross out any number that is *not* a multiple of 4.

12	19	34	20	50	40

5. Write the three numbers less than 40 that have 2 and 5 as factors: ______ ______ ______

ADVANCED

6. Write three consecutive composite numbers. [ ] [ ] [ ]

7. Write five odd multiples of 3 between 10 and 40: ______ ______ ______ ______ ______

8. I am a prime number less than 10.
   If you add 10 or 20 to me, the result is a prime number.
   What number am I?

9. Which number is neither prime nor composite? Explain.

10. Find the **sum** of the first five composite numbers. Show your work.

11. How many prime numbers are there between 30 and 50? Explain how you know.

NS6-18: Prime Factorizations

Any composite number can be written as a product of prime numbers.
This product is called the **prime factorization** of the original number.

Example: Find a prime factorization of 20.

It can't be 10 × 2 (because the number 10 is a composite number).

5 × 2 × 2 is a prime factorization of 20.

---

1. You can find a prime factorization for a number by using a **factor tree**. Here is how you can make a factor tree for the number 20.

Step 1:
Find any pair of numbers (not including one) that multiply to give 20.

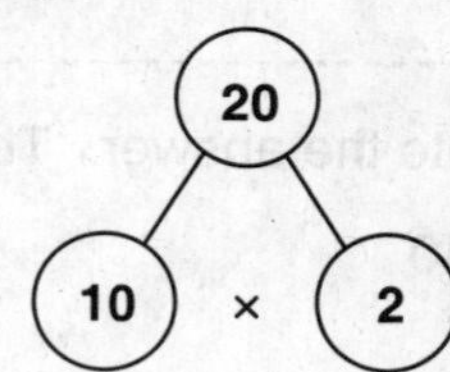

Step 2:
Repeat Step 1 for the numbers on the "branches" of the tree.

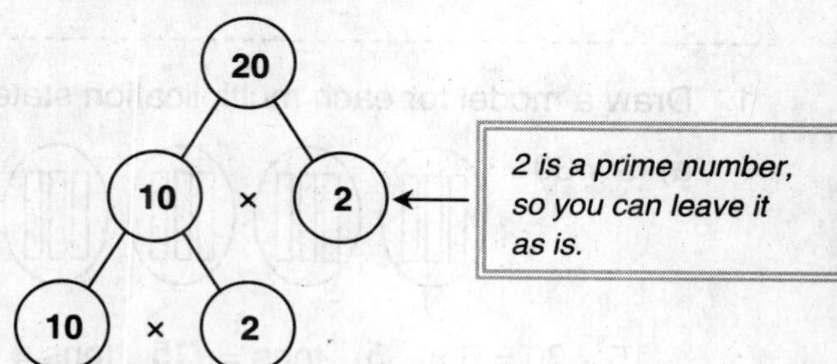

Complete the factor tree for the numbers below.

a)

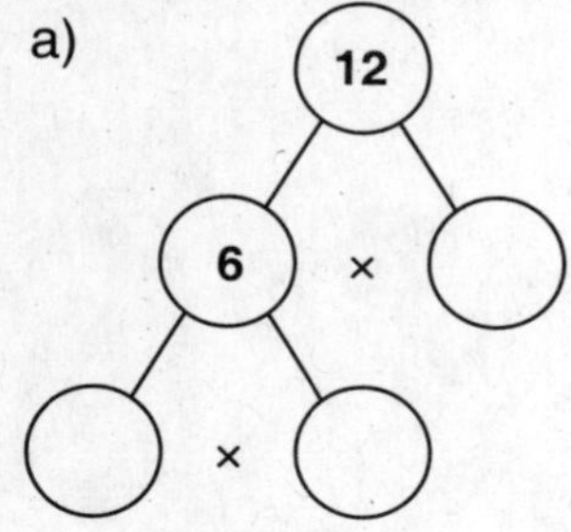

b)

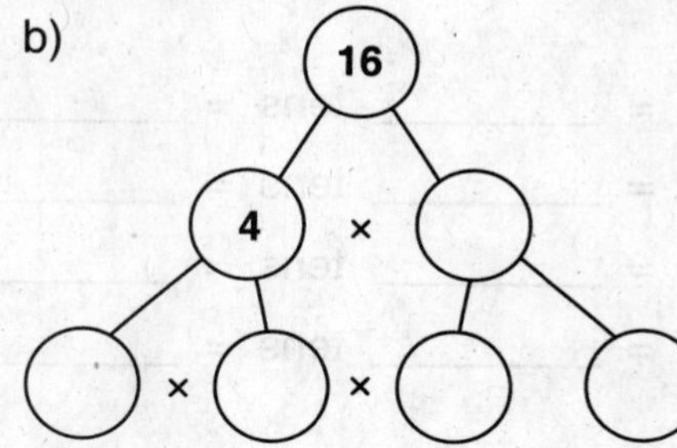

c)

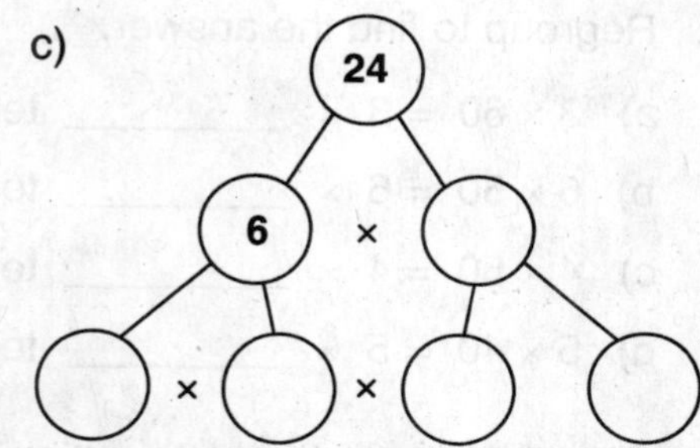

2. Write a prime factorization for each number below. The first one is started for you.
HINT: It helps to first find any factorization and then factor any composite numbers in the factorization.

a) 30 = 20 × 3 =

b) 18 =

c) 8 =

d) 14 =

3. Using a factor tree, find prime factorizations for:

a) 30 b) 36 c) 27 d) 28 e) 75

4. Here are some branching patterns for factor trees.
Can you find a factor tree for the number 24 that looks different from the tree in Question 1 c)?

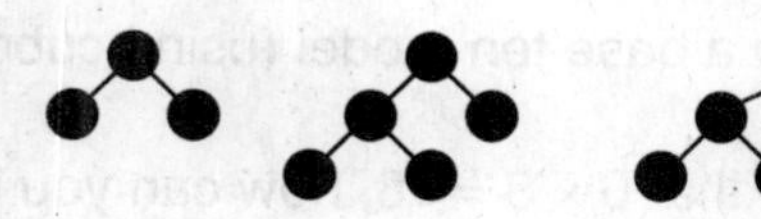

NS6-19: Multiples of 10

To multiply **4 × 20**, Allen makes 4 groups containing 2 tens blocks (20 = 2 tens).

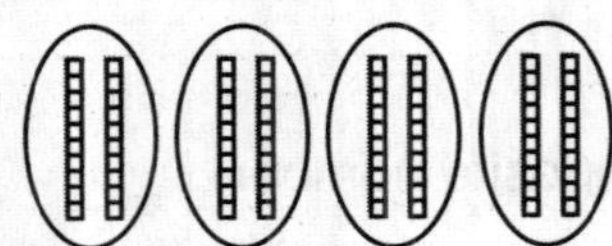

4 × 20 = 4 × 2 tens
= 8 tens
= 80

To multiply **4 × 200**, Allen makes 4 groups containing 2 hundreds blocks (200 = 2 hundreds).

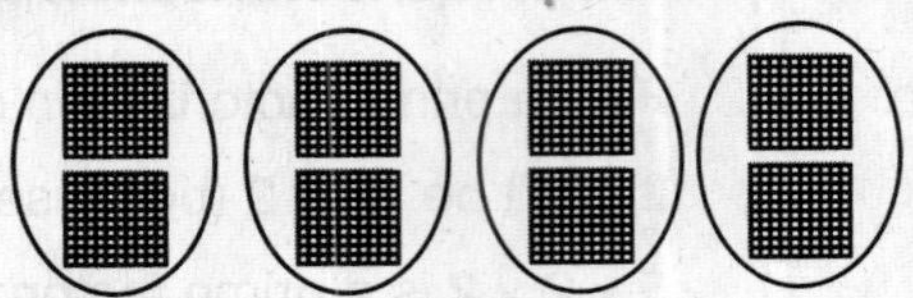

4 × 200 = 4 × 2 hundreds
= 8 hundreds
= 800

Allen notices a pattern:
4 × 2 = 8
4 × 20 = 80
4 × 200 = 800

1. Draw a model for each multiplication statement, then calculate the answer. The first one is done.

a) 5 × 30

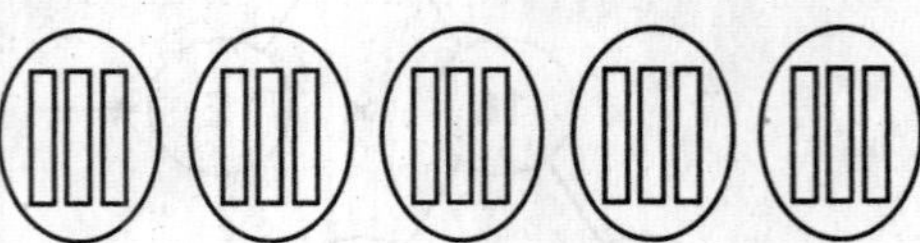

5 × 30 = 5 × 3 tens = 15 tens = 150

b) 3 × 40

3 × 40 = 3 × ____ tens = ____ tens = ____

2. Regroup to find the answer.

a) 3 × 60 = 3 × ________ tens = ________ tens = ________

b) 6 × 50 = 6 × ________ tens = ________ tens = ________

c) 4 × 50 = 4 × ________ tens = ________ tens = ________

d) 5 × 40 = 5 × ________ tens = ________ tens = ________

3. Complete the pattern by multiplying.

a) 5 × 3 = ______
5 × 30 = ______
5 × 300 = ______

b) 6 × 1 = ______
6 × 10 = ______
6 × 100 = ______

c) 3 × 4 = ______
3 × 40 = ______
3 × 400 = ______

d) 4 × 5 = ______
4 × 50 = ______
4 × 500 = ______

4. Multiply.

a) 7 × 30 = ______ b) 30 × 5 = ______ c) 3 × 40 = ______ d) 80 × 3 = ______

e) 4 × 400 = ______ f) 500 × 8 = ______ g) 5 × 80 = ______ h) 300 × 6 = ______

i) 3 × 900 = ______ j) 700 × 6 = ______ k) 8 × 20 = ______ l) 700 × 3 = ______

5. Draw a base ten model (using cubes to represent thousands) to show: 7 × 1 000 = 7 000.

6. Knowing that 6 × 3 = 18, how can you use this fact to multiply 6 × 3 000? Explain.

NS6-20: Mental Math

To multiply **4 × 22**,
Leela rewrites 22 as a sum: $22 = 20 + 2$

She first multiplies 4 by 20: $4 \times 20 = 80$

Next she multiplies 4 by 2: $4 \times 2 = 8$

Finally she adds the two results: $80 + 8 = 88$

So Leela can conclude that **4 × 22 = 88**.

This picture shows why Leela's method works:

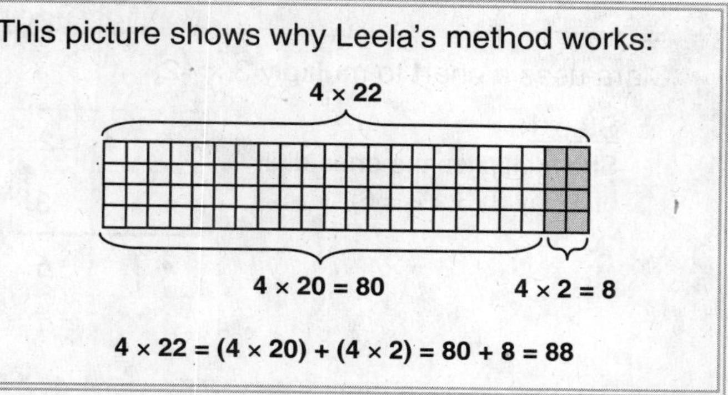

1. Use the picture to write the multiplication statement as a sum. The first one is started for you.

a)

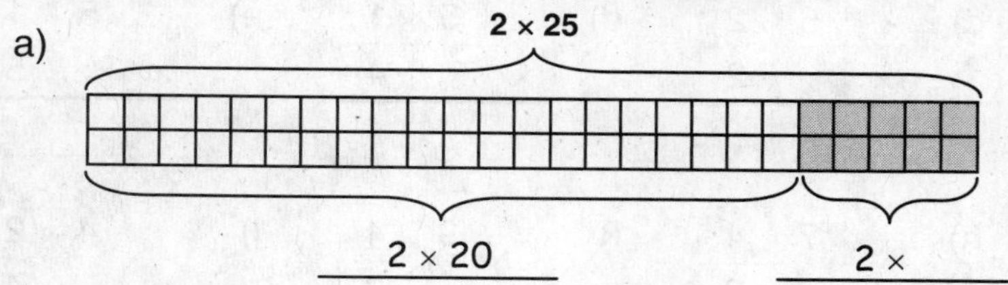

2 × 20 ______ 2 × ______

$2 \times 25 = (2 \times$ ____ $) + (2 \times$ ____ $)$

b)

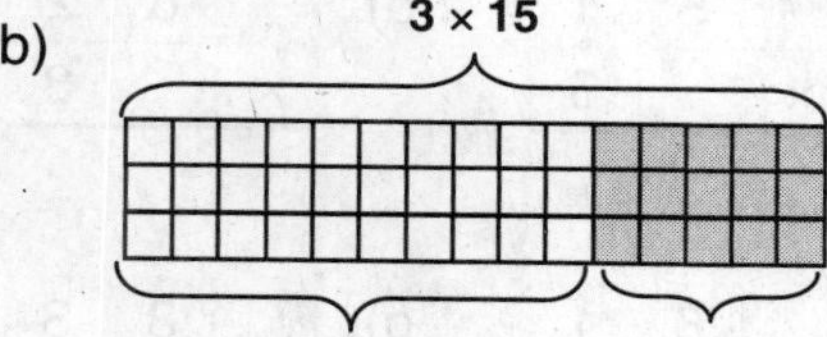

______ ______

$3 \times 15 = ($ ______ $) + ($ ______ $)$

2. Multiply using Leela's method. The first one has been done for you.

a) 5 × 13 = 5 × 10 + 5 × 3 = 50 + 15 = 65

b) 4 × 21 = ______ + ______ = ______ = ______

c) 3 × 43 = ______ + ______ = ______ = ______

d) 2 × 432 = 2 × 400 + 2 × 30 + 2 × 2 + 800 + 60 + 4 = 864

e) 3 × 312 = ______________________

f) 4 × 321 = ______________________

3. Multiply in your head by multiplying the digits separately.

a) 3 × 12 = ______ b) 3 × 52 = ______ c) 6 × 31 = ______ d) 7 × 21 = ______

e) 5 × 31 = ______ f) 3× 43 = ______ g) 6 × 51 = ______ h) 2 × 44 = ______

i) 4 × 521 = ______ j) 3 × 621 = ______ k) 5 × 411 = ______ l) 2 × 444 = ______

m) 3 × 632 = ______ n) 4 × 422 = ______ o) 4 × 212 = ______ p) 2 × 421 = ______

4. a) Stacy placed 821 books in each of 4 bookshelves. How many books did she place altogether?

b) Nickalo put 723 pencils in each of 3 boxes. How many pencils did he put in the boxes?

NS6-21: The Standard Method for Multiplication

Clara uses a chart to multiply 3 × 42:

Step 1:
She multiplies the ones digit of 42 by 3 (3 × 2 = 6).

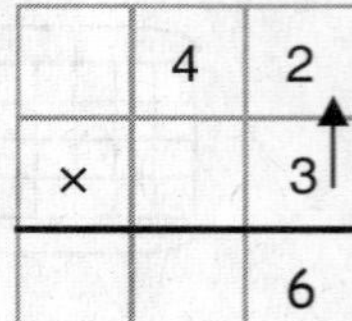

Step 2:
She multiplies the tens digit of 42 by 3 (3 × 4 tens = 12 tens).

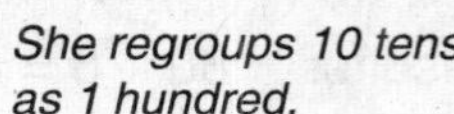

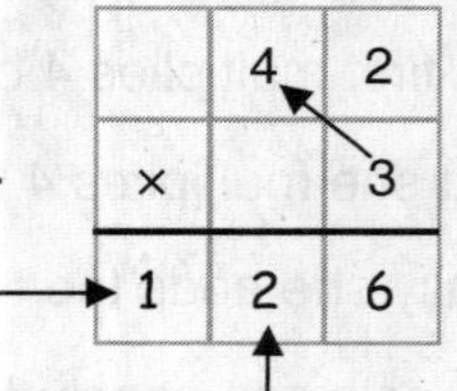

hundreds tens

1. Use Clara's method to find the products.

a)

	5	1
×		3

b)

	8	2
×		3

c)

	6	2
×		2

d)

	5	1
×		4

e)

	5	1
×		5

f)

	6	1
×		6

g)

	8	3
×		3

h)

	7	4
×		2

i)

	9	4
×		2

j)

	4	2
×		4

k)

	8	3
×		2

l)

	4	1
×		5

m)

	3	1
×		7

n)

	3	2
×		4

o)

	6	3
×		2

p)

	6	3
×		3

q)

	2	2
×		4

r)

	3	1
×		9

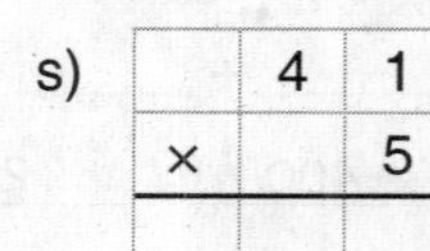

s)

	4	1
×		5

t)

	6	1
×		9

u)

	8	1
×		7

v)

	9	2
×		3

w)

	9	2
×		4

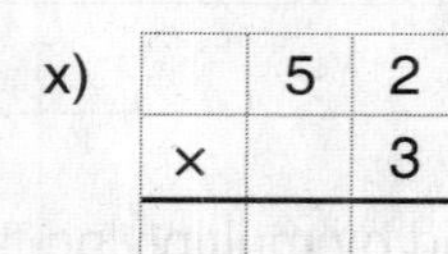

x)

	5	2
×		3

y)

	5	2
×		4

z)

	8	3
×		4

aa)

	9	3
×		2

bb)

	7	1
×		9

cc)

	5	3
×		3

dd)

	6	2
×		3

ee)

	4	4
×		2

ff)

	6	4
×		2

gg)

	5	1
×		5

hh)

	8	1
×		7

ii)

	9	3
×		3

2. Find the following products.

a) 3 × 63 b) 6 × 50 c) 5 × 61 d) 2 × 94 e) 4 × 42

NS6-22: Regrouping in Multiplication

Jane uses a chart to multiply 3 × 24:

Step 1:
She multiplies 4 ones by 3 (4 × 3 = 12).

She regroups 10 ones as 1 ten.

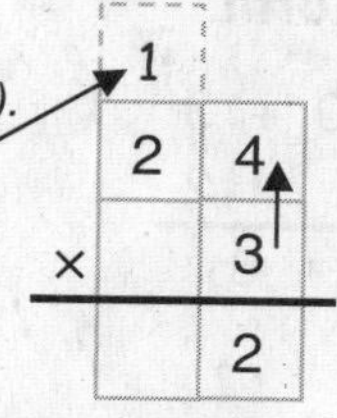

Step 2:
She multiplies 2 tens by 3 (3 × 2 tens = 6 tens).

She adds 1 ten to the result (6 + 1 = 7 tens).

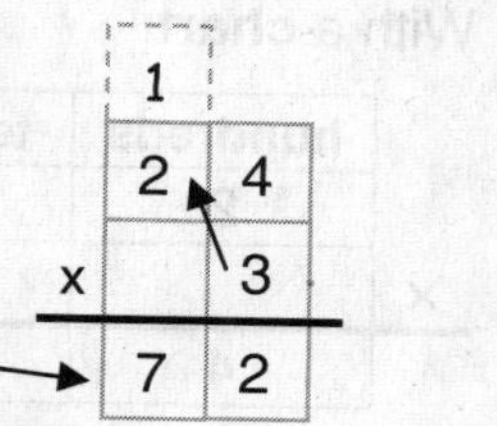

1. Using Alicia's method, complete the first step of the multiplication. The first one has been done.

a) carry: 1; 1 2 × 6 = 2
b) 2 5 × 3
c) 2 5 × 4
d) 1 6 × 6
e) 4 9 × 2

2. Using Alicia's method, complete the second step of multiplication.

a) carry: 1; 2 4 × 4 = 9 6
b) carry: 1; 3 5 × 3 = 5
c) carry: 2; 1 5 × 5 = 5
d) carry: 1; 1 3 × 6 = 8
e) carry: 2; 1 6 × 4 = 4

f) 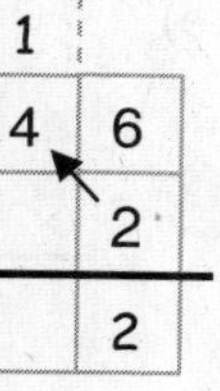

g) carry: 2; 4 8 × 3 = 4
h) carry: 1; 2 5 × 3 = 5
i) carry: 2; 2 9 × 3 = 7
j) carry: 3; 1 6 × 6 = 6

3. Using Alicia's method, complete the first and second steps of the multiplication.

a) 3 5 × 2
b) 1 5 × 6
c) 1 8 × 5
d) 2 5 × 3
e) 2 4 × 4

f) 2 7 × 5
g) 3 2 × 8
h) 3 5 × 6
i) 2 6 × 7
j) 4 6 × 8

NS6-23: Multiplying – 3-Digit by 1-Digit

Dillon multiplies **2 × 213** in three different ways.

1. With a **chart**:

	hundreds	tens	ones
	2	1	3
×			2
	4	2	6

2. In **expanded form**:

$$\begin{array}{r} 200 + 10 + 3 \\ \times\ 2 \\ \hline = 400 + 20 + 6 \\ = 426 \end{array}$$

3. With **base ten materials**:

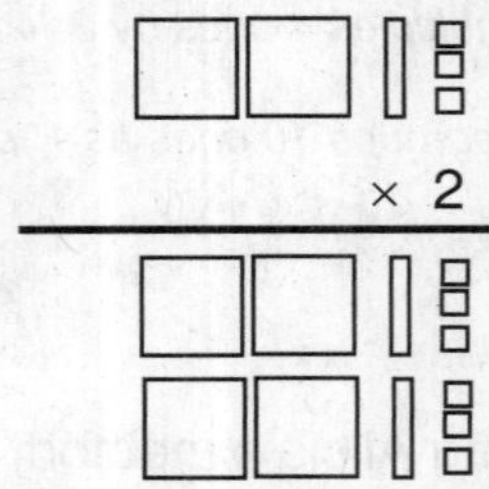

---

1. Rewrite the multiplication statement in expanded notation. Then perform the multiplication.

a) $\begin{array}{r} 234 \\ \times\ 2 \\ \hline \end{array}$ ______ + ______ + ______ × 2 = ______ + ______ + ______ = ______

b) $\begin{array}{r} 133 \\ \times\ 3 \\ \hline \end{array}$ ______ + ______ + ______ × 3 = ______ + ______ + ______ = ______

2. Multiply.

a) 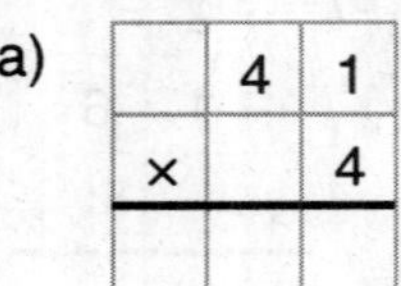

	4	1
×		4

b)

4	3	4
×		2

c)

3	1	2
×		3

d)

1	2	4
×		2

e)

3	2	3
×		3

3. Multiply by regrouping ones as tens.

a) 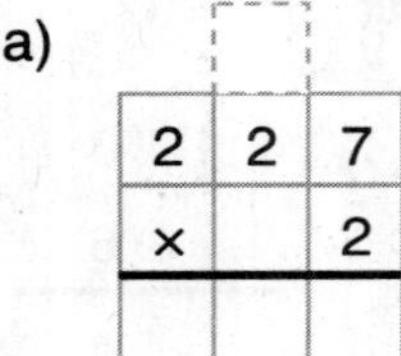

2	2	7
×		2

b) 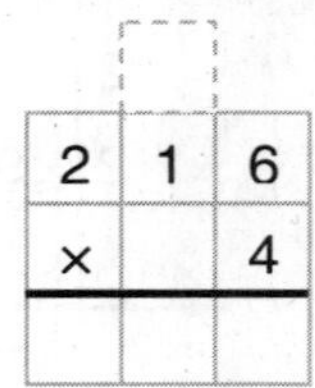

2	1	6
×		4

c) 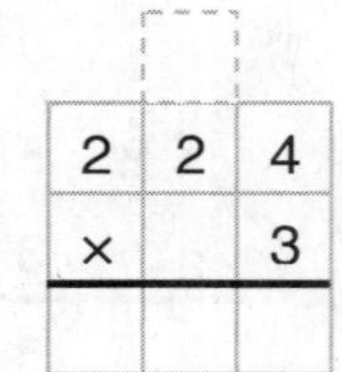

2	2	4
×		3

d) 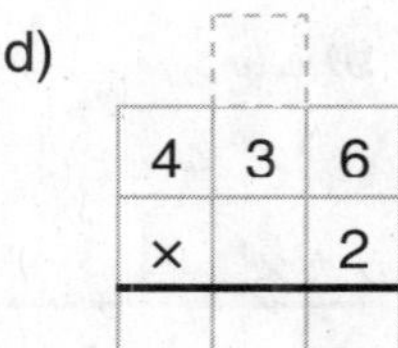

4	3	6
×		2

e)

1	1	6
×		6

4. Multiply by regrouping tens as hundreds. In the last question, you will also regroup ones as tens.

a) 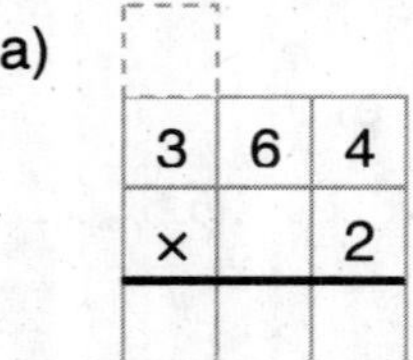

3	6	4
×		2

b) 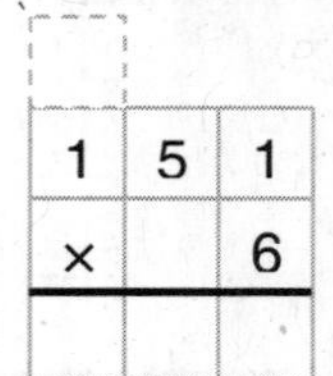

1	5	1
×		6

c)

2	4	2
×		4

d) 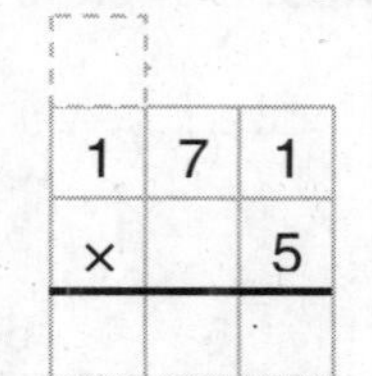

1	7	1
×		5

e) 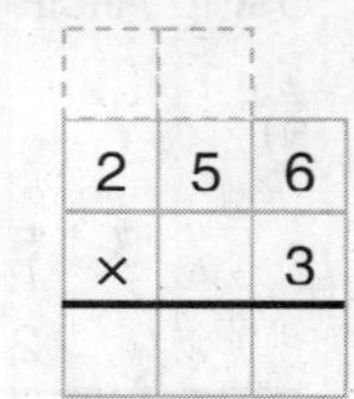

2	5	6
×		3

5. Multiply.

a) 5 × 134 b) 7 × 421 c) 6 × 132 d) 9 × 134 e) 8 × 124 f) 6 × 135

6. Draw a picture in your notebook to show the result of the multiplication.

a) 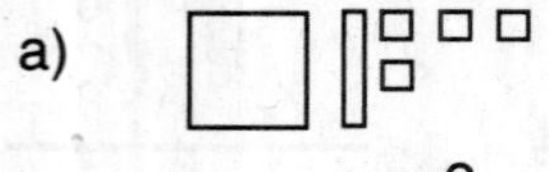 × 2

b) × 4

c) × 3

NS6-24: Multiplying by 10, 100 and 1000

1. a) Skip count by 10 fifteen times. What number did you reach? ______

   b) What is the product: 10 × 15 = ______

   c) Skip count by 100 fifteen times. What number did you reach? ______

   d) What is the product: 100 × 15 = ______

2. How many zeroes do you add to a number when you multiply the number by…

   a) 10? You add ___ zero. b) 100? You add ___ zeroes. c) 1000? You add ___ zeroes.

3. Continue the pattern.

a)	b)	c)
10 × 6 = ______	10 × 36 = ______	10 × 85 = ______
100 × 6 = ______	100 × 36 = ______	100 × 85 = ______
1000 × 6 = ______	1000 × 36 = ______	1000 × 85 = ______
10 000 × 6 = ______	10 000 × 36 = ______	10 000 × 85 = ______

4. Find the products.

a) 19 × 10 = ______	b) 10 × 56 = ______	c) 10 × 83 = ______
d) 42 × 100 = ______	e) 80 × 100 = ______	f) 13 × 100 = ______
g) 100 × 40 = ______	h) 10 × 23 = ______	i) 1 000 × 6 = ______
j) 572 × 10 = ______	k) 1 000 × 28 = ______	l) 93 × 1 000 = ______

5. Round each number to the **leading digit**.

   Then find the product of the rounded numbers.

> The first (non-zero) digit in a number – that is, the furthest to the left – is called the **leading digit**.

leading digit

a) 12 × 29

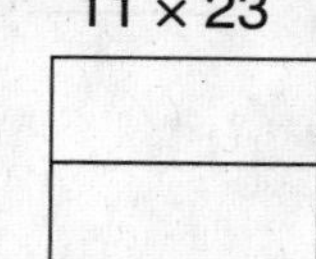

b) 11 × 23

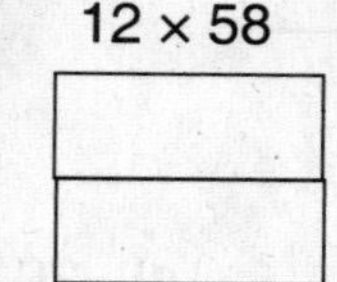

c) 12 × 58

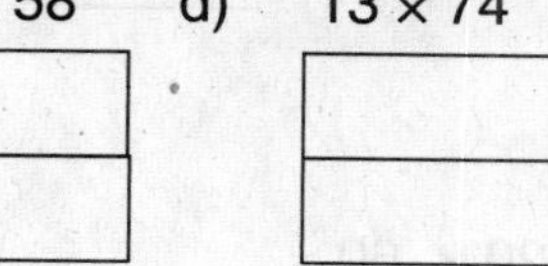

d) 13 × 74

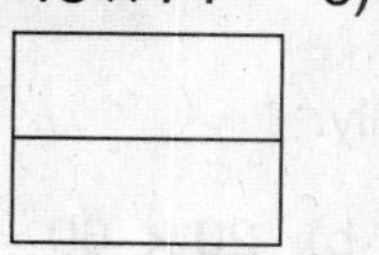

e) 68 × 110

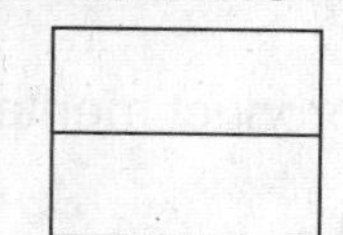

f) 61 × 120

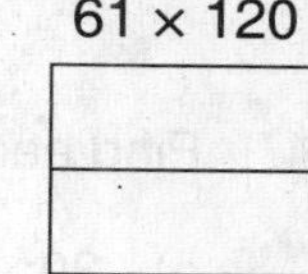

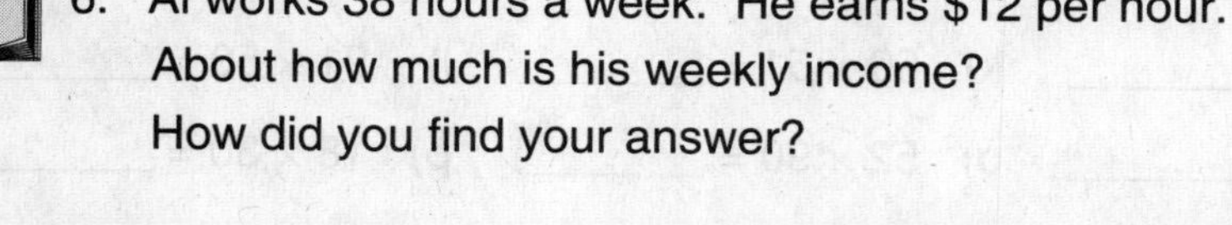

6. Al works 38 hours a week. He earns $12 per hour.
   About how much is his weekly income?
   How did you find your answer?

7. How many hundred dollar bills would you need to make …

   a) one hundred thousand dollars? b) one million dollars? Explain.

8. Which amount is worth more: 25 723 dimes or 231 524 pennies?

NS6-25: Mental Math – Multiples of Ten

Erin wants to multiply **20 × 32**.

She knows how to find 10 × 32, so she rewrites 20 × 32 as double 10 × 32.

20 × 32 = 2 × **10 × 32**
= 2 × 320
= 640

This picture shows why this works:

A 20 by 32 array contains the same number of squares as two 10 by 32 arrays.

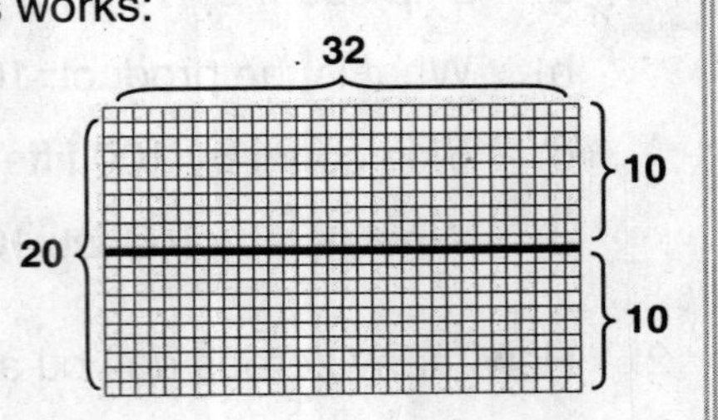

1. Write each number as a product of two factors (where one of the factors is 10).

a) 30 = 3 × 10 b) 40 = ______ c) 70 = ______ d) 50 = ______

2. Write an equivalent product for each array. The first one is done for you.

a)
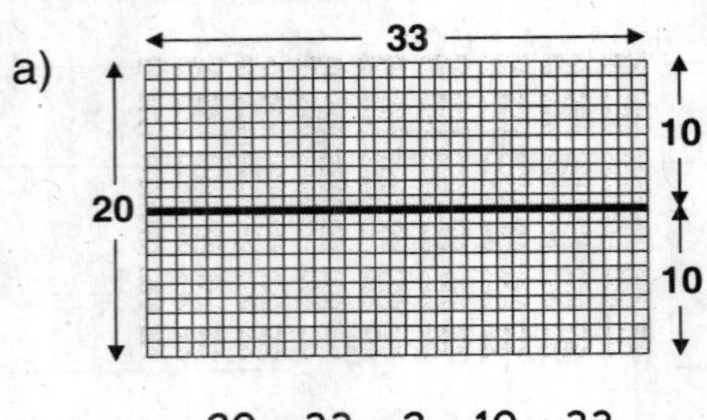

20 × 33 = 2 × 10 × 33

b)
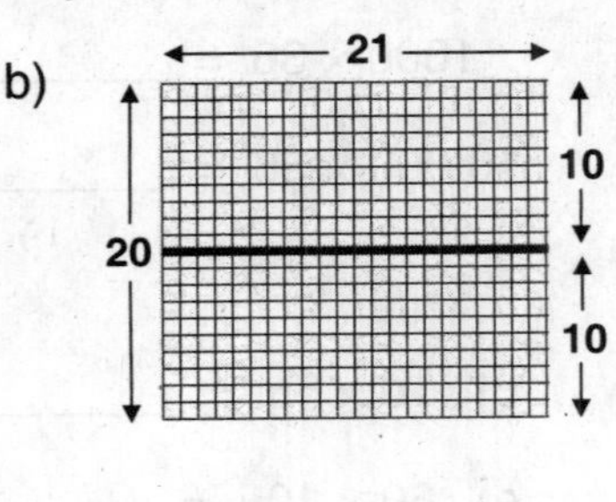

20 × 21 = ______

c)
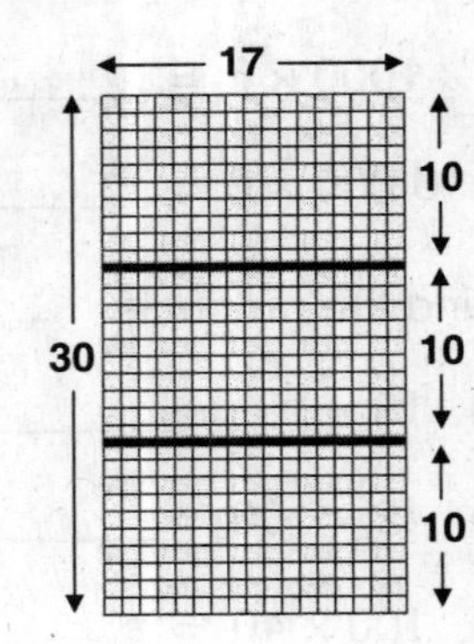

30 × 17 = ______

3. Find each product in two stages.

Step 1: Multiply the second number by 10
Step 2: Multiply the result by the tens digit of the first number

a) 20 × 24 = 2 × 240 = ______ b) 30 × 32 = ______ = ______ c) 40 × 12 = ______ = ______ d) 50 × 41 = ______ = ______

4. Find each product mentally.

a) 30 × 33 = ______ b) 20 × 60 = ______ c) 20 × 80 = ______ d) 40 × 34 = ______
e) 20 × 42 = ______ f) 30 × 83 = ______ g) 64 × 20 = ______ h) 30 × 74 = ______
i) 40 × 42 = ______ j) 30 × 53 = ______ k) 60 × 51 = ______ l) 91 × 50 = ______
m) 60 × 30 = ______ n) 80 × 40 = ______ o) 52 × 90 = ______ p) 18 × 30 = ______

5. Estimate each product. (Round each fator to the leading digit.)

a) 36 × 58 ≈ 40 × 60 = 2 400 b) 33 × 72 ≈ ______ c) 28 × 82 ≈ ______
d) 63 × 48 ≈ ______ e) 71 × 32 ≈ ______ f) 21 × 16 ≈ ______

NS6-26: Multiplying – 2-Digit by Multiples of Ten

Ed multiplies **20 × 37** by splitting the product into a sum of two smaller products.

20 × 37 = (20 × 7) + (20 × 30)
= 140 + 600
= 740

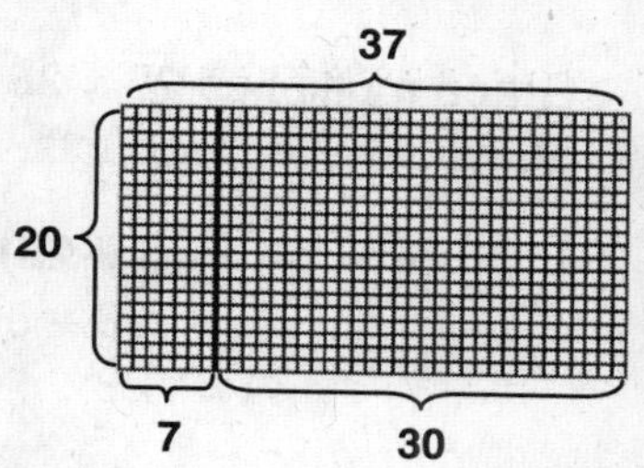

He keeps track of the steps of the multiplication in a chart.

	3	7
×	2	0
		0

Step 1:
Ed multiplies 2 × 7 = 14. He is really multiplying **20** × 7 so he first writes a zero in the ones place.

1		
	3	7
×	2	0
	4	0

Step 2:
Next, since 2 × 7 = 14, Ed writes the 4 in the tens place and the 1 at the top of the hundreds column.

1		
	3	7
×	2	0
7	4	0

Step 3:
Ed then multiplies **20** × **30** (= 600). As a short cut, he multiplies 2 × 3 = 6 and then he adds the 1 from the top of the hundreds column: 6 + 1 = 7 (= 700).

1. Practise the first two steps of the multiplication (given above). The first one is done for you.
NOTE: In one of the questions you will not need to regroup the hundreds.

a)

1		
	2	4
×	4	0
	6	0

b)

	1	6
×	7	0
		0

c)

	3	8
×	2	0

d)

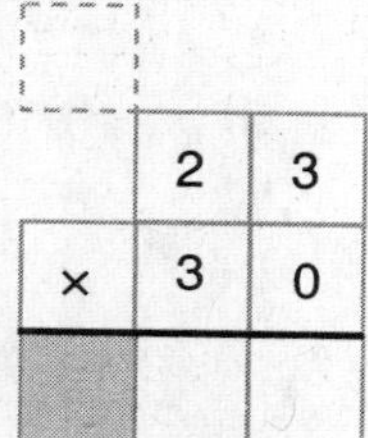

	2	3
×	3	0

e)

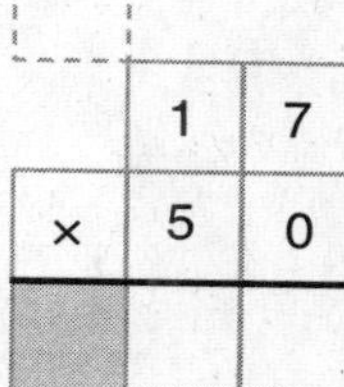

	1	7
×	5	0

2. Multiply.

a)

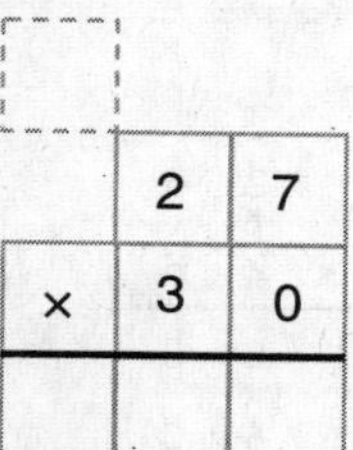

	2	7
×	3	0

b)

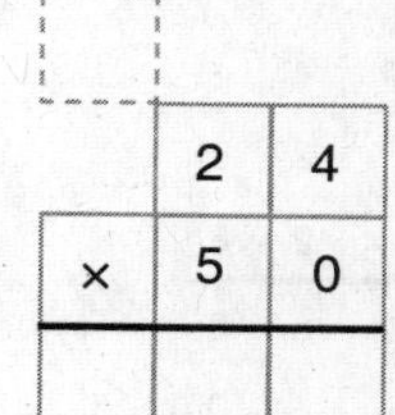

	2	4
×	5	0

c)

	2	3
×	6	0

d)

	2	3
×	8	0

e)

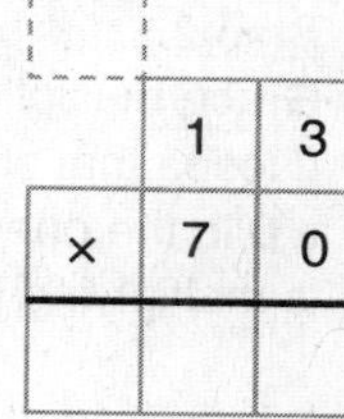

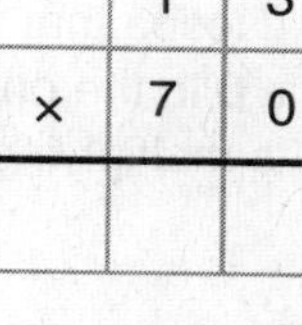

	1	3
×	7	0

f)

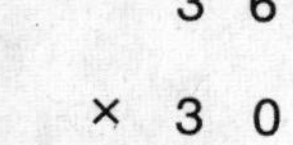

  3 6
× 3 0

g)
  4 2
× 2 0

h)
  2 6
× 4 0

i)
  1 2
× 6 0

j)
  3 2
× 7 0

3. Rewrite each product as a sum then find the answer.

a) 20 × 14 = (20 × 10) + (20 × 4) = 200 + 80 = 280

b) 30 × 23 = ____________________

c) 40 × 32 = ____________________

NS6-27: Multiplying – 2-Digit by 2-Digit

Grace multiplies **26 × 28** by splitting the product into a sum of two smaller products.

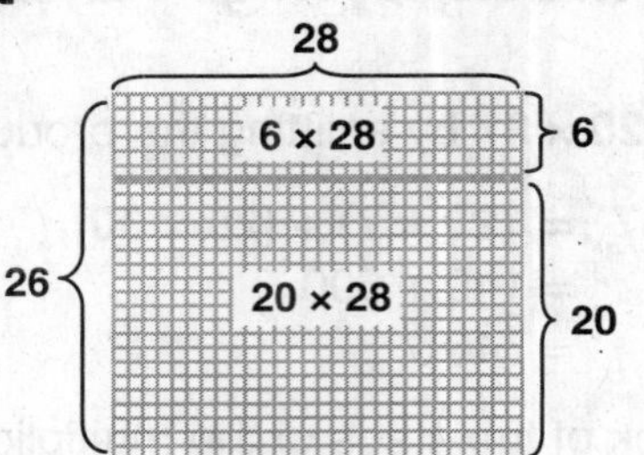

$$26 \times 28 = (6 \times 28) + (20 \times 28)$$
$$= 168 + 560$$
$$= 728$$

She keeps track of the steps of the multiplication using a chart.

Step 1:
She multiplies **6 × 28**:

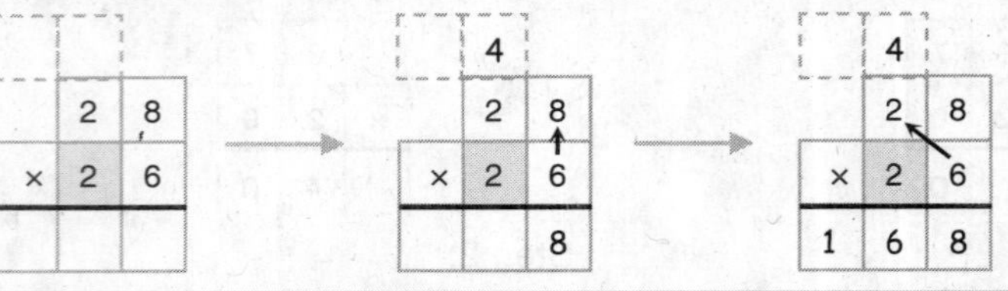

1. Practise the first step of the multiplication.

a)
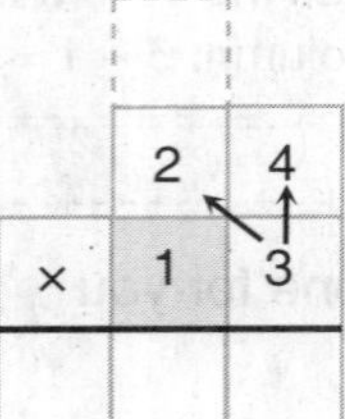

b)
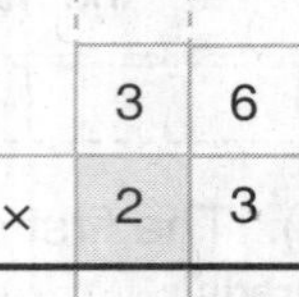

c)
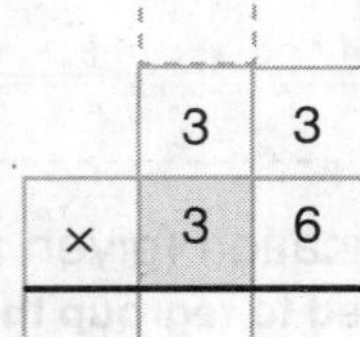

d)
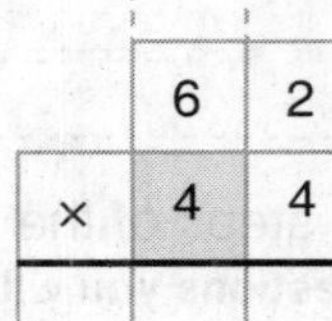

e)
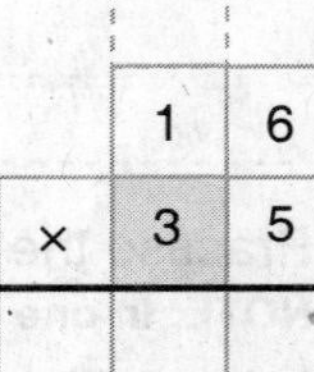

f)

	2	5
×	4	3

g)

	3	6
×	4	3

h)

	2	4
×	5	6

i)

	3	4
×	2	6

j)

	3	7
×	1	8

Step 2:
Grace multiplies **20 × 28**.
(Notice that she starts by writing a 0 in the ones place because she is multiplying by 20.)

	4	
	2	8
×	2	6
1	6	8
		0

1	4	
	2	8
×	2	6
1	6	8
	6	0

1	4	
	2	8
×	2	6
1	6	8
	6	0

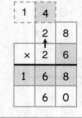

2. Practise the second step of the multiplication.

a)
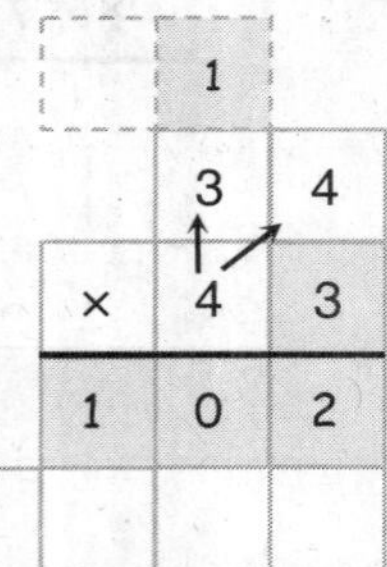

b)

	2	
	4	5
×	2	4
1	8	0

c)

	1	
	6	9
×	6	2
1	3	8

d)

	3	
	5	6
×	3	6
3	3	6

e)
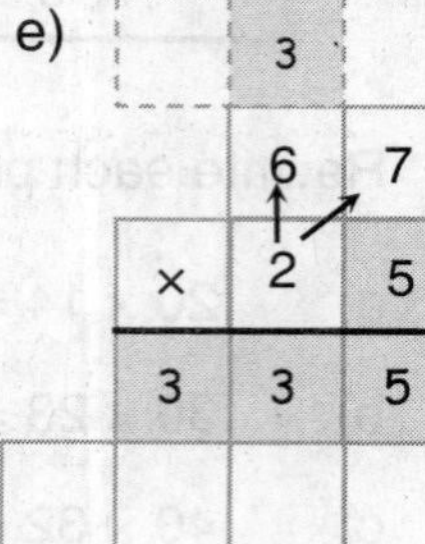

3. Practise the first two steps of the multiplication.

a) 35 × 26

b) 13 × 37

c) 32 × 54

d) 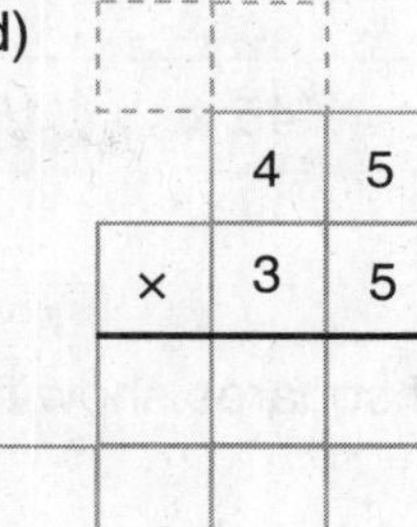
45 × 35

e) 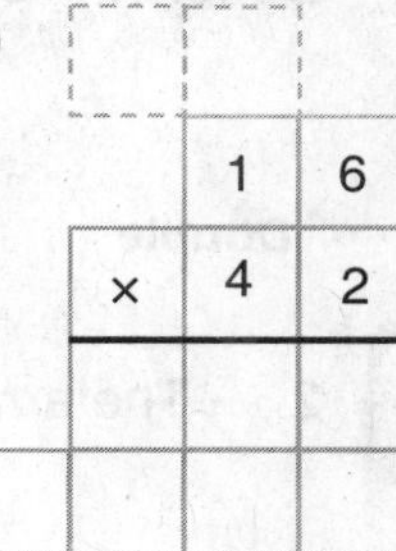
16 × 42

f) 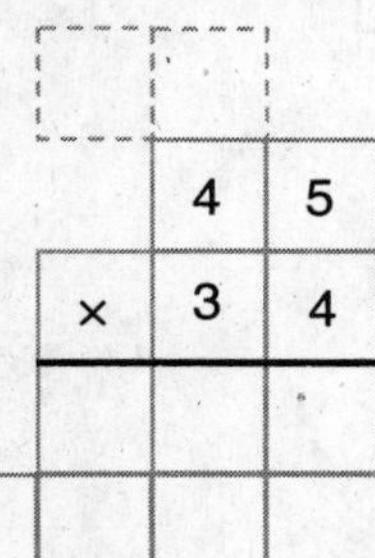
45 × 34

g) 23 × 45

h) 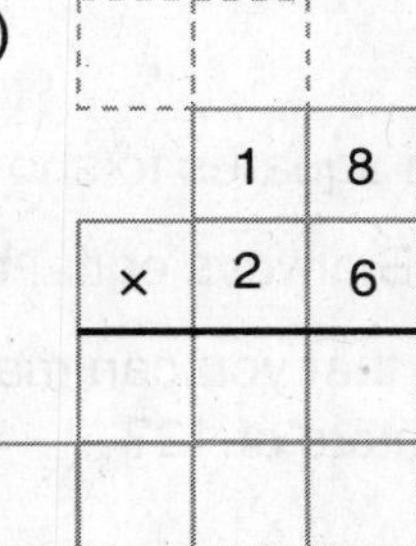
18 × 26

i) 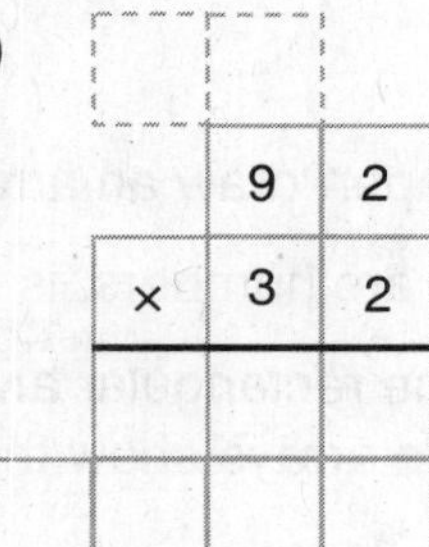
92 × 32

j) 75 × 63

Step 3:
Grace completes the multiplication by adding the products of **6 × 28** and **20 × 28**

4. Complete the multiplication by adding the numbers in the last two rows of the chart.

a) 28 × 26 (carries 1 4)
168
\+ 560
728

b) 54 × 68 (carries 2 3)
432
\+ 3240

c) 76 × 43 (carries 2 1)
228
\+ 3040

d) 27 × 63 (carries 4 2)
81
\+ 1620

e) 19 × 54 (carries 4 3)
76
\+ 950

5. Multiply.

a) 34 × 45
0

b) 19 × 64

c) 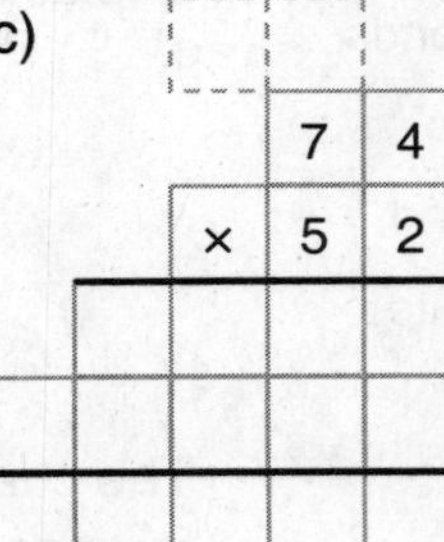
74 × 52

d) 54 × 34

e) 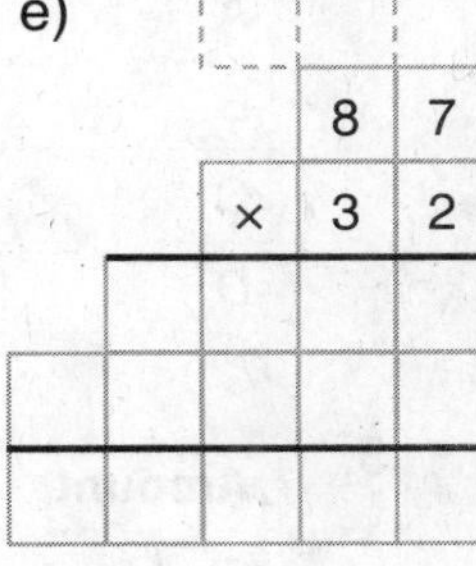
87 × 32

6. Find the products.

a) 35 × 23 b) 64 × 81 c) 25 × 43 d) 42 × 87 e) 13 × 94 f) 28 × 37

1. Double the ones and tens separately and add the result: $2 \times 36 = 2 \times 30 + 2 \times 6 = 60 + 12 = 72$.

	25	45	16	28	18	17	35	55	39
Double									

2. The arrays of squares show that $2 \times 3 = 3 \times 2$:

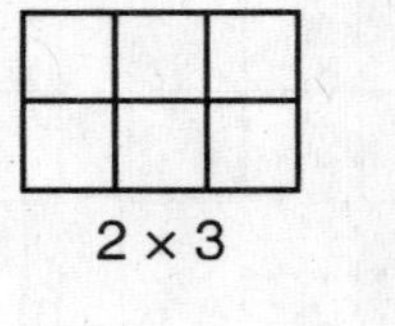

2×3

3×2

a) On grid paper, draw an array of squares to show that $7 \times 5 = 5 \times 7$

b) If A and B are numbers, is $A \times B$ always equal to $B \times A$? Explain.

c) Draw all the rectangular arrays that you can make using 12 squares. How do the arrays show the factors of 12?

3. Rearrange the products so you can find the answer mentally.

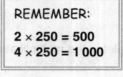

Example: $2 \times 8 \times 35$
$= 2 \times 35 \times 8$
$= 70 \times 8$
$= 560$

Example: $4 \times 18 \times 25$
$= 4 \times 25 \times 18$
$= 100 \times 18$
$= 1800$

REMEMBER:
$2 \times 250 = 500$
$4 \times 250 = 1\,000$

a) $2 \times 7 \times 25$ b) $4 \times 84 \times 25$ c) $2 \times 29 \times 500$

d) $4 \times 475 \times 25$ e) $2 \times 36 \times 2 \times 250$ f) $25 \times 2 \times 50 \times 4$

g) $2 \times 2 \times 15 \times 250$ h) $2 \times 853 \times 500$ i) $4 \times 952 \times 25$

4.

Printer	Printing Rate
A	1 page every 2 seconds
B	90 pages per minute
C	2 pages every second
D	160 pages in 2 minutes

Which printer is the fastest? Explain how you know.

5.

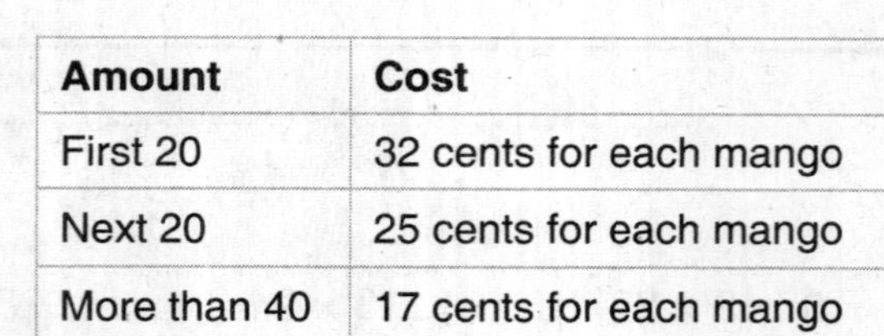

Amount	Cost
First 20	32 cents for each mango
Next 20	25 cents for each mango
More than 40	17 cents for each mango

The chart shows the price a grocery store pays for mangos.
How much would the following amounts cost?

a) 15 mangos

b) 30 mangos

c) 50 mangos

NS6-29: Concepts in Multiplication

1. You can multiply a 3-digit number by a 2-digit number using the method you learned previously.

Multiply.

a)

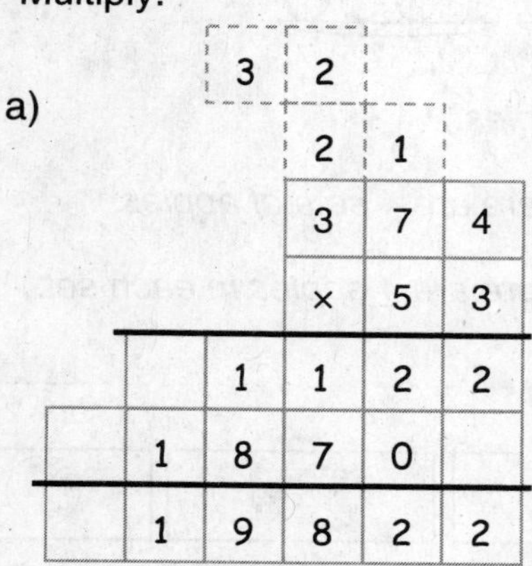

b)

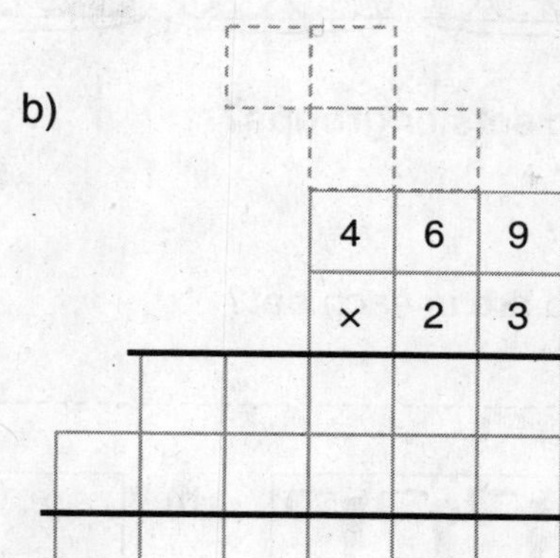

c)

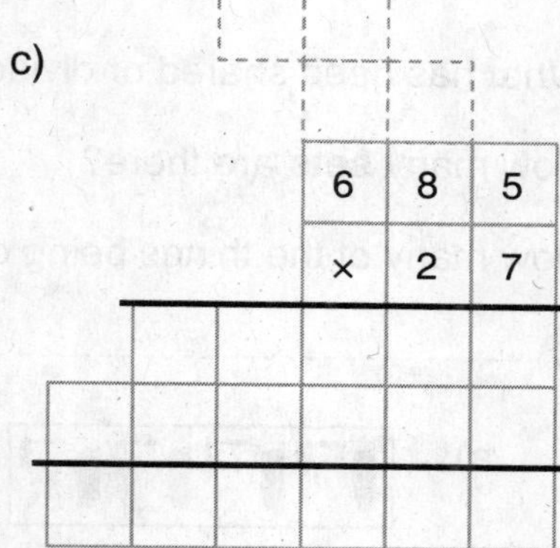

2. Cross out any number that is not a multiple of 4.

13   24   32   50   40   2   27

3. Write the odd multiples of 7 that are between 20 and 80.

4. What is the fifth prime number? Explain how you know.

5. Multiply.

a) 569 × 34   b) 792 × 87   c) 926 × 96   d) 5243 × 88

6. The Karakoran mountain range in Tibet pushes up 2 cm a year.
How much higher will the range be in 500 years?

7. Each basket holds 47 apples each. There are 326 baskets.
How many apples are there altogether?

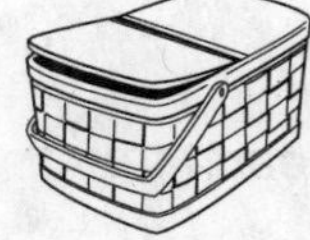

8. What is the largest factor of 24 that is less than 24?

9. Hassim plays basketball every week for 136 minutes.
He needs 1 350 minutes to get a job at the summer camp.
If he plays for 7 weeks, will he have enough hours?

10. Find the missing digits.

a) 3 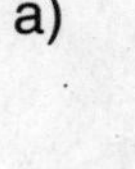 4 × 3 = 9 7 2

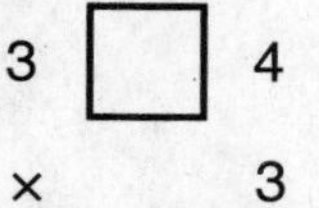

b) 7 ☐ 7 × 5 = 3 8 8 5

c) 2 5 2 × ☐ = 1 0 0 8

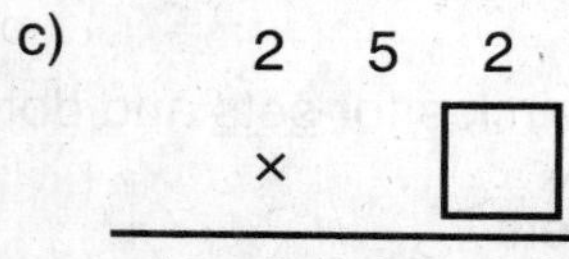

NS6-30: Sets

Abdul has 16 apples. A tray holds 4. There are 4 trays.

What has been shared or divided into **sets** or **groups**? *(Apples.)*

How many **sets** are there? *(There are 4 sets of apples.)*

How many of the things being divided are in each **set**? *(There are 4 apples in each set.)*

---

1. a)

What has been shared or divided into sets? ____________

How many sets? ______

How many in each set? ______

b)

What has been shared or divided into sets? ____________

How many sets? ______

How many in each set? ______

2.

	What has been shared or divided into sets?	How many sets?	How many in each set?
a) 8 books for each student 32 books 4 students			
b) 4 flowers in each vase 6 flower vases 24 flowers			
c) 5 apples on each tray 20 apples 4 trays			
d) 3 trees in each row 7 rows 21 trees			

3. Using circles for <u>sets</u> and dots for <u>things</u>, draw a picture to show…

a) 6 sets
3 things in each set

b) 4 groups
5 things in each group

c) 2 sets
9 things in each set

NS6-31: Two Ways of Sharing

Amanda has 16 cookies. There are two ways she can **share** (or divide) her cookies equally.

Method 1: She can decide how many sets (or groups) of cookies she wants to make.

Example:
Amanda wants to make 4 sets of cookies. She draws 4 circles. She then puts one cookie at a time into the circles until she has placed all 16 cookies.

Method 2: She can decide how many cookies she wants to put in each set.

Example:
Amanda wants to put 4 cookies in each set. She counts out 4 cookies. She keeps counting out sets of 4 cookies until she has placed all 16 cookies into sets.

---

1. Share **24** dots equally. How many dots are in each set?
HINT: Place one dot at a time.

a) 4 sets:

There are _____ dots in each set.

b) 6 sets:

There are _____ dots in each set.

2. Share the shapes equally among the sets.
HINT: Count the shapes first. Divide by the number of circles.

a)

b)

3. Share the squares equally among the sets.

4. Group the lines so that there are three lines in each set. Say how many sets there are.

a) There are _____ sets.

b) There are _____ sets

c) There are _____ sets.

5. Group **18** candies so that…

a) there are 9 candies in each set.

b) there are 6 candies in each set.

NS6-31: Two Ways of Sharing *(continued)*

6. In each question, fill in what you know. Write a question mark for what you don't know.

	What has been shared or divided into sets?	How many sets? or How many in each set?
a) Beth has 42 marbles. She puts 6 marbles in each jar.	marbles	There are 6 marbles in each set
b) 30 people in 6 cars.	people	There are 6 sets of people.
c) Jenny has 18 stickers. She gives them to her 2 sisters.		
d) Mike has 40 pictures. He puts 8 in each page of the album.		
e) 24 children are sitting at 3 tables.		
f) 35 flowers are in 5 vases.		

7. Divide the dots into sets.
HINT: If you know the number of sets, start by drawing circles for sets. If you know the number of things in each set, fill one circle at a time with the correct number of dots.

a) 21 dots; 3 sets

_____ dots in each set

b) 14 dots; 7 dots in each set

_____ sets

c) 36 dots; 9 dots in each set.

d) 20 dots; 4 sets.

NS6-32: Dividing by Skip Counting

You can solve the division problem **12 ÷ 4 = ?** by skip counting on the number line.

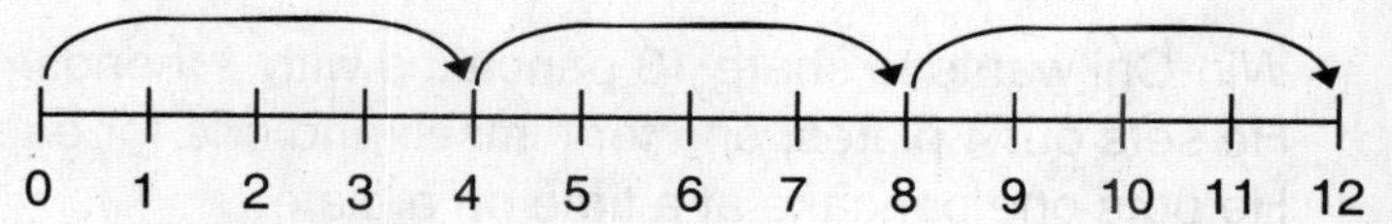

If you divide 12 into sets of size 4, how many sets do you get? The number line shows that it takes three skips of size 4 to get 12.

4 + 4 + 4 = 12 so... **12 ÷ 4 = 3**

---

1. Use the number line to find the answer to the division statement. Be sure to draw arrows to show your skip counting.

a) 0 1 2 3 4 5 6 7 8

8 ÷ 2 = ____

b)

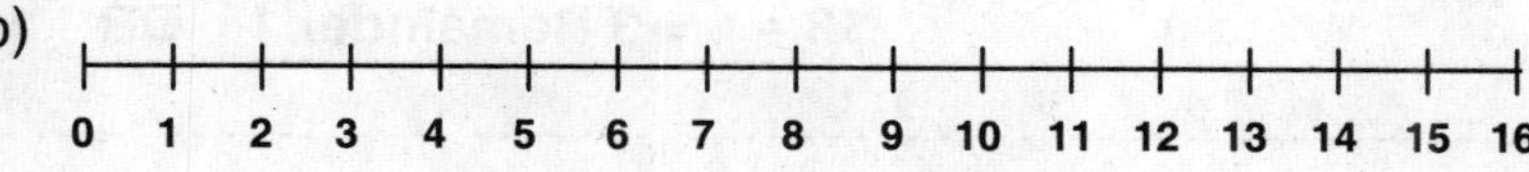

16 ÷ 8 = ____

2. What division statement does the picture represent?

a) 0 1 2 3 4 5 6 7 8 9 10 11 12 13 14 15

____

b)

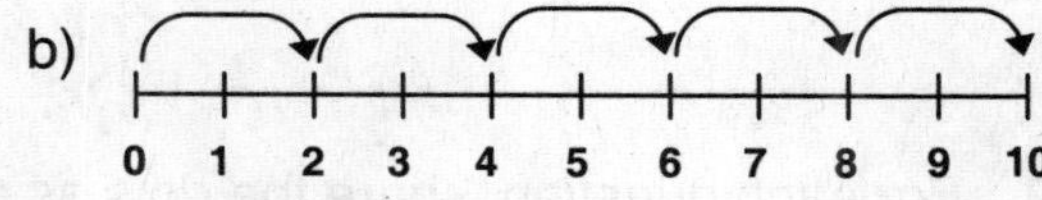

____

3. You can also find the answer to a division question by skip counting on your fingers.

For instance, to find **45 ÷ 9**, count by 9s until you reach 45… the number of fingers you have up when you say "45" is the answer.

9 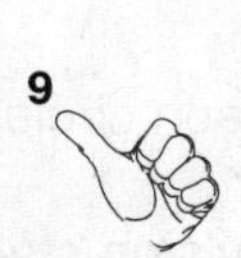

18 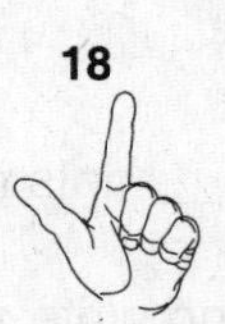

27 

36 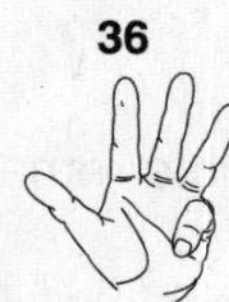

45 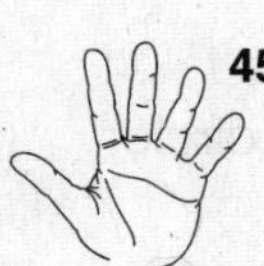

So 45 ÷ 9 = 5

Find the answers by skip counting on your fingers.

a) 35 ÷ 5 = ____ b) 12 ÷ 6 = ____ c) 32 ÷ 8 = ____ d) 21 ÷ 7 = ____ e) 45 ÷ 5 = ____

f) 36 ÷ 4 = ____ g) 25 ÷ 5 = ____ h) 42 ÷ 6 = ____ i) 27 ÷ 3 = ____ j) 16 ÷ 2 = ____

k) 36 ÷ 6 = ____ l) 35 ÷ 7 = ____ m) 18 ÷ 3 = ____ n) 21 ÷ 3 = ____ o) 40 ÷ 8 = ____

4. 24 flowers are in 6 bouquets. How many flowers in each bouquet? ________

5. 36 trees are in 9 rows. How many trees are in each row? ________

6. Amy uses 8 pencils in a month. How many months will she take to use 32 pencils? ________

NS6-33: Remainders

Win-Chi wants to share 13 pancakes with 3 friends.
He sets out 4 plates, one for himself and one for each of his friends.
He puts one pancake at a time on a plate.

There is one pancake left over.

Thirteen pancakes cannot be shared equally into 4 sets.
Each person gets 3 pancakes, but *one* is left over.
This is the remainder.

13 ÷ 4 = 3 Remainder 1 OR 13 ÷ 4 = 3 R1 **NOTE: R means "remainder"**

---

1. Can you share 9 pancakes equally onto 2 plates?
   Show your work using dots for pancakes and circles for plates.

2. For each question, share the dots as equally as possible among the circles.

   a) 10 dots in 3 circles

   ____ dots in each circle; ____ dots remaining

   b) 17 dots in 4 circles

   ____ dots in each circle; ____ dots remaining

3. Share the dots as equally as possible. Draw a picture and write a division statement.

   a) 13 dots in 3 circles

    13 ÷ 3 = 4 R1

   b) 19 dots in 3 circles

   c) 36 dots in 5 circles

   d) 33 dots in 4 circles

   e) 43 dots in 7 circles

4. Eight friends want to share 25 apples among them.
   How many apples will each friend get?
   How many will be left over?

5. Three siblings have more than 5 and less than 13 animal posters.
   They share the posters evenly with no remainder.
   How many posters do they have? (Show all the possible answers.)

6. Find four different ways to share 19 cookies into equal groups so that one is left over.

NS6-34: Long Division – 2-Digit by 1-Digit

Linda is preparing snacks for four classes.
She needs to divide 95 crackers into 4 groups.
She will use long division and a model to solve the problem.

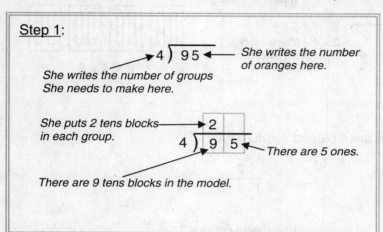

Step 1:

4) 95

She writes the number of groups She needs to make here. (4)

She writes the number of oranges here. (95)

She puts 2 tens blocks in each group. (2)

4) 9 5

There are 5 ones.

There are 9 tens blocks in the model.

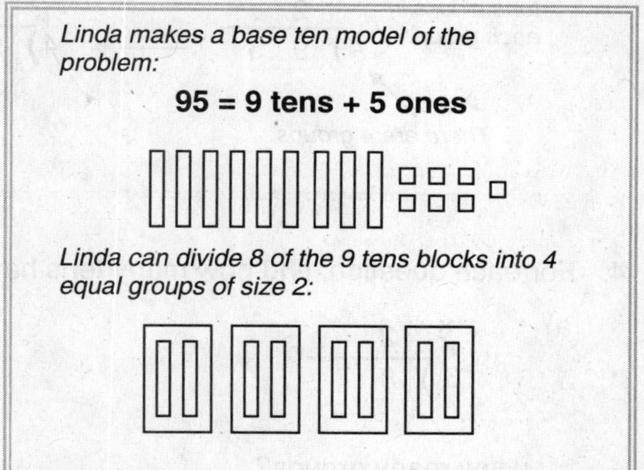

Linda makes a base ten model of the problem:
95 = 9 tens + 5 ones
Linda can divide 8 of the 9 tens blocks into 4 equal groups of size 2:

1. Linda has written a division statement to solve a problem.
How many groups does she want to make?
How many tens blocks and how many ones would she need to model the problem?

a) 2) 53

groups ______
tens blocks ______
ones ______

b) 5) 71

groups ______
tens blocks ______
ones ______

c) 4) 95

groups ______
tens blocks ______
ones ______

d) 5) 88

groups ______
tens blocks ______
ones ______

2. How many tens blocks can be put in each group?

a) 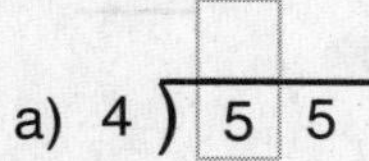 4) 5 5

b) 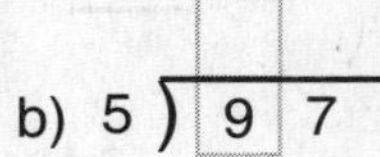 5) 9 7

c) 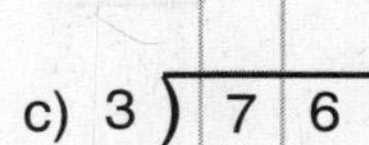 3) 7 6

d) 3) 8 9

e) 4) 9 2

f) 4) 4 8

g) 5) 9 7

h) 3) 8 1

i) 7) 8 5

j) 8) 9 6

3. For each division statement, write how many groups have been made and how many tens blocks are in each group.

a) 4) 8 7

groups ______
number of tens in each group ______

b) 3) 9 4

groups ______
number of tens in each group ______

c) 6) 7 4

groups ______
number of tens in each group ______

d) 2) 9 8

groups ______
number of tens in each group ______

Step 2:

There are 2 tens blocks in each group. → 2 over 4) 9 5 ← *There are 4 groups.*

→ 2 over 4) 9 5, with 8 below the 9

2 × 4 = 8 tens blocks have been placed.

In the model:

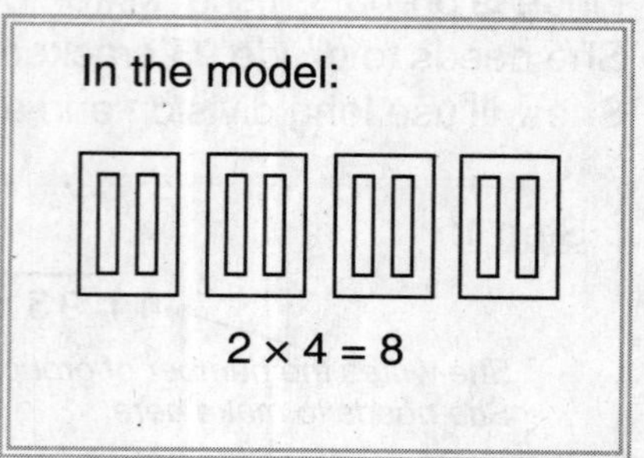

2 × 4 = 8

4. For each question, find how many tens have been placed by multiplying.

a)

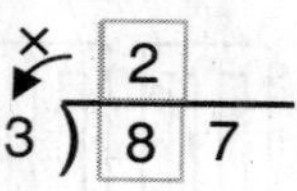

How many groups? ______

How many tens? ______

How many tens in each group? ______

How many tens placed altogether? ______

b) 2 over 4) 9 5

How many groups? ______

How many tens? ______

How many tens in each group? ______

How many tens placed altogether? ______

5. Use skip counting to find out how many tens can be placed in each group.
Then use multiplication to find out how many tens have been placed.

a) 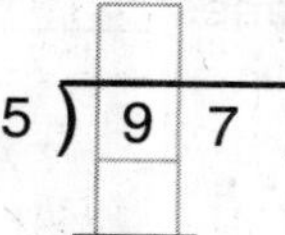
b) 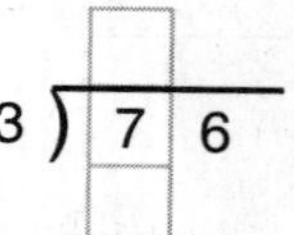
c) 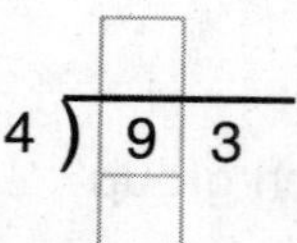
d) 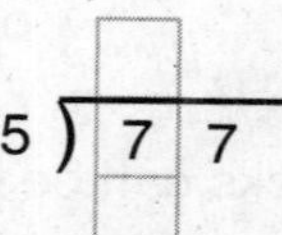
e) 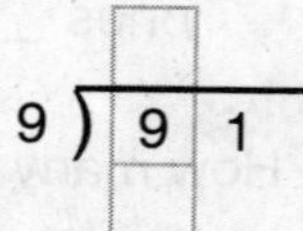

f) 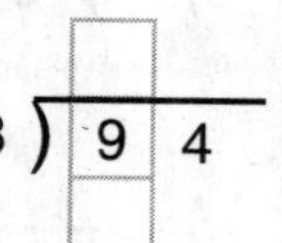
g) 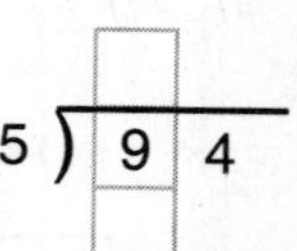
h) 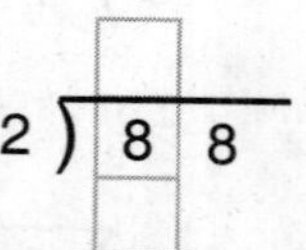
i) 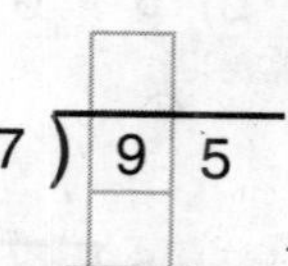
j) 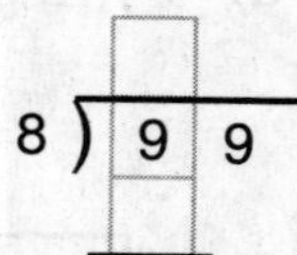

k) 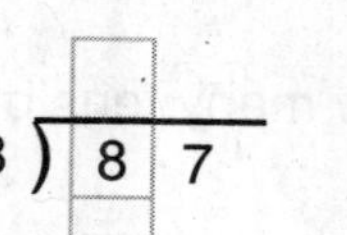
l) 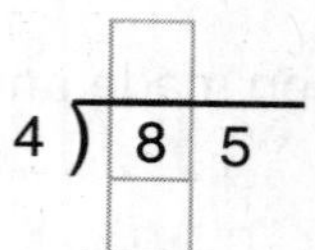
m) 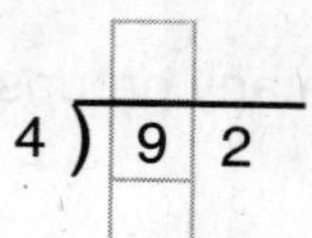
n) 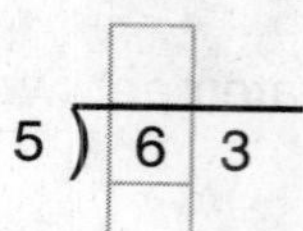
o) 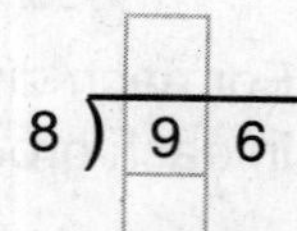

p) 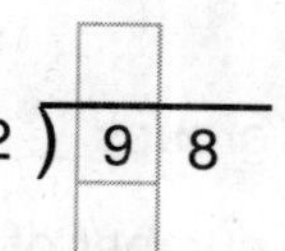
q) 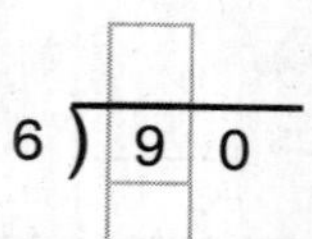
r) 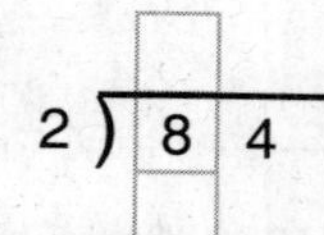
s) 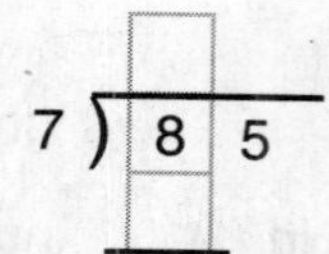
t) 3) 8 1

Step 3:

There are 9 tens blocks. Linda has placed 8.

She subtracts to find out how many are left over (9 – 8 = 1).

$$\begin{array}{r} 2 \\ 4\overline{)\,9\;5} \\ -8 \\ \hline 1 \end{array}$$

In the model:

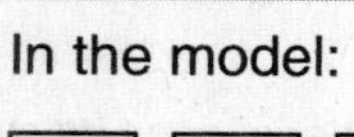

So there is 9 – 8 = 1 left over.

6. For each question below, carry out the first three steps of long division.

a) 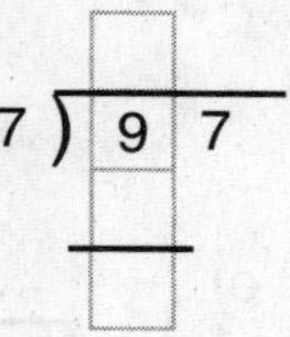
b) 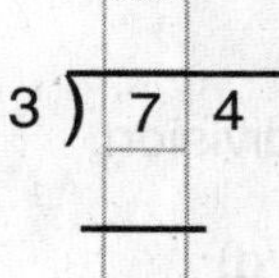
c) 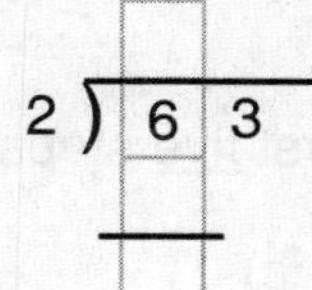
d) 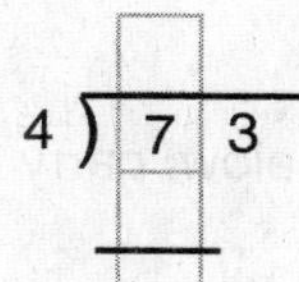
e) 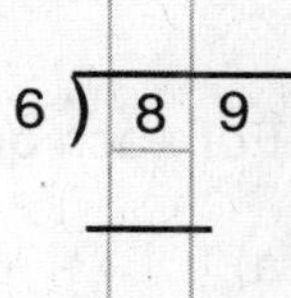

f) 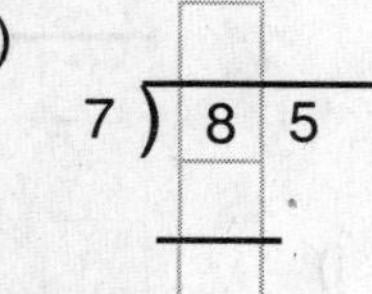
g) 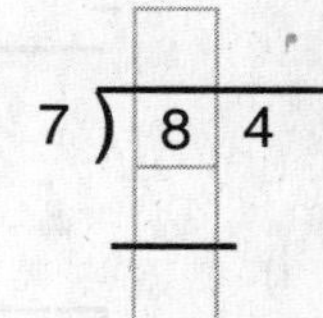
h) 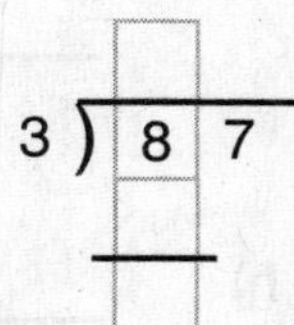
i) 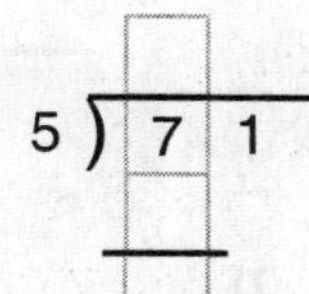
j) 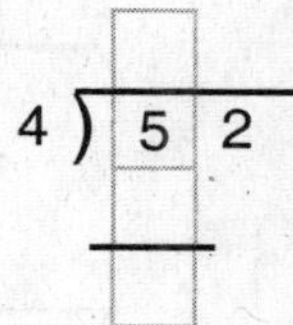

Step 4:

There is one tens block left over and 5 ones. So there are 15 ones left over. Linda writes the 5 beside the 1 to show this.

$$\begin{array}{r} 2 \\ 4\overline{)\,9\;5} \\ -8 \\ \hline 1 \end{array} \longrightarrow \begin{array}{r} 2 \\ 4\overline{)\,9\;5} \\ -8\;\downarrow \\ \hline 1\;5 \end{array}$$

There are this many ones still to place.

In the model:

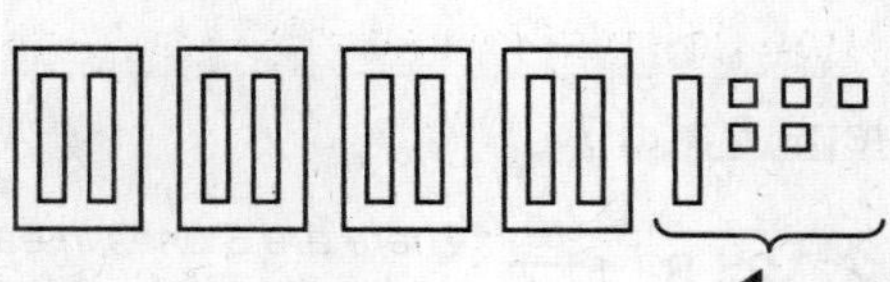

There are still 15 ones to place in 4 groups.

7. For each question below, carry out the first four steps of long division.

a) 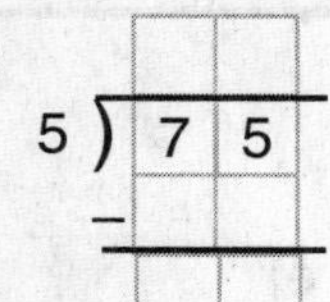
b) 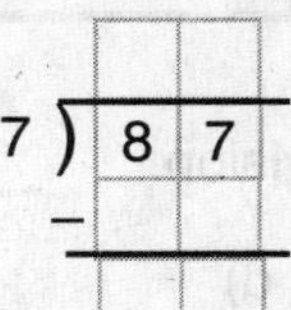
c) 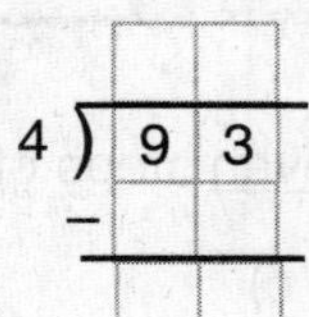
d) 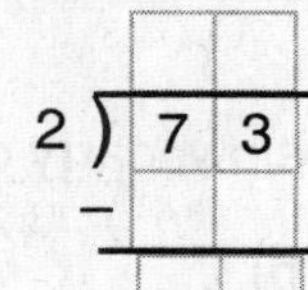
e) 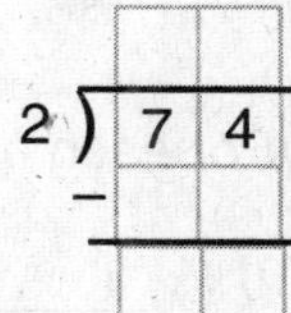

f) 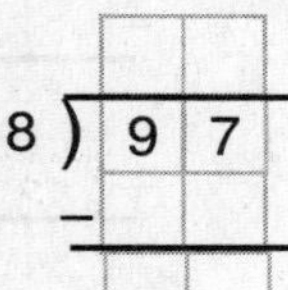
g) 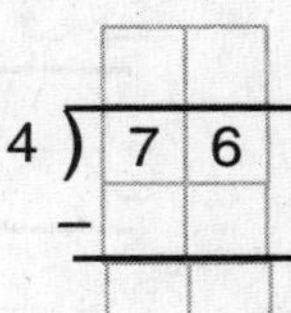
h) 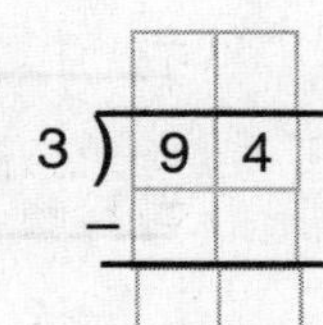
i) 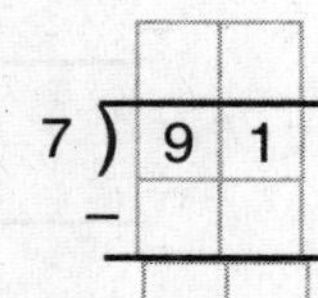
j) 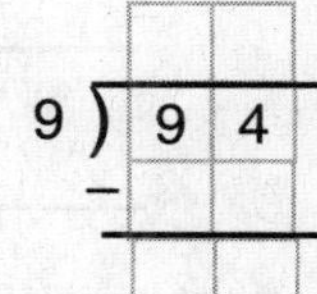

Step 5:

Linda finds the number of ones he can put in each group by dividing 15 by 4.

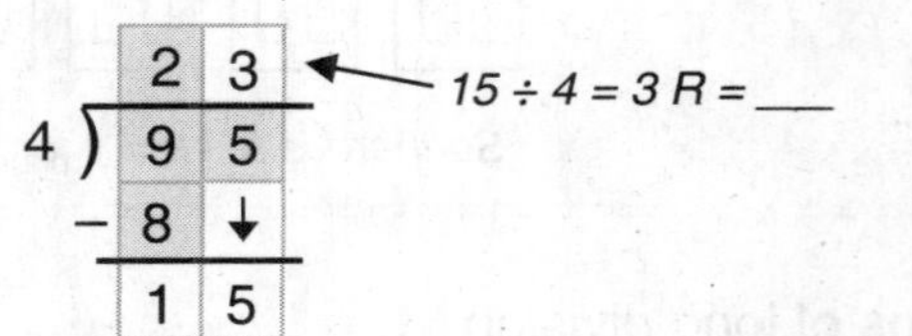

In the model:

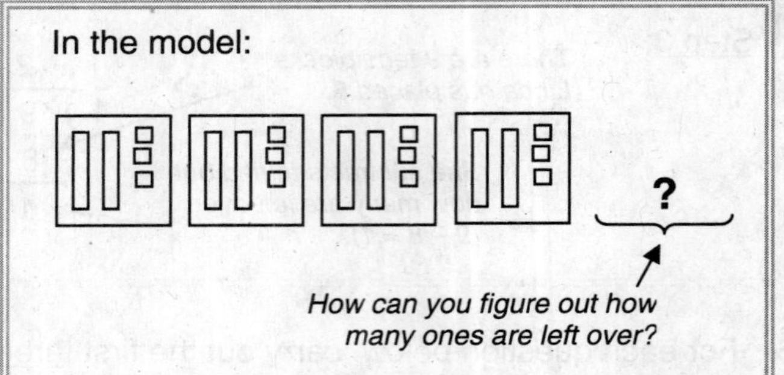

?
How can you figure out how many ones are left over?

8. For each question below, carry out the first five steps of long division.

a) 5) 9 4

b) 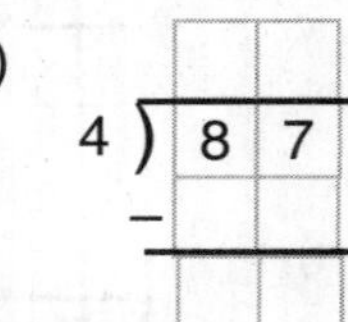

c) 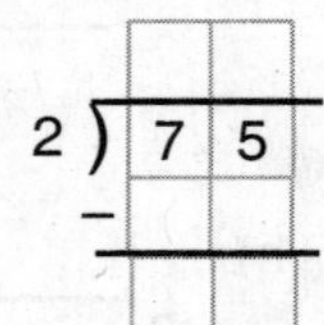

d) 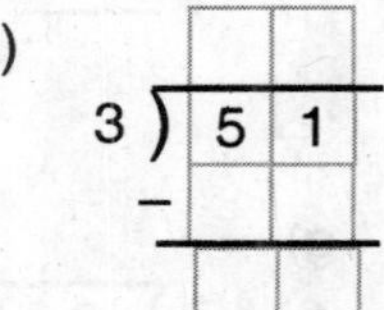

e) 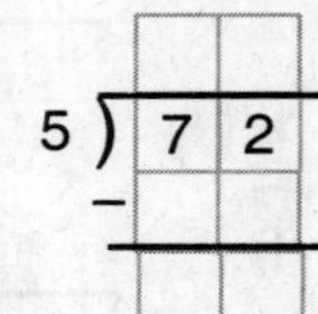

f) 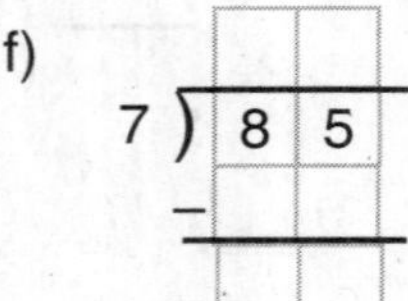

g) 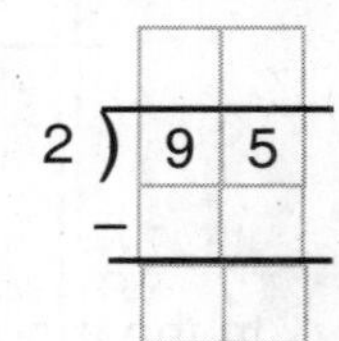

h) 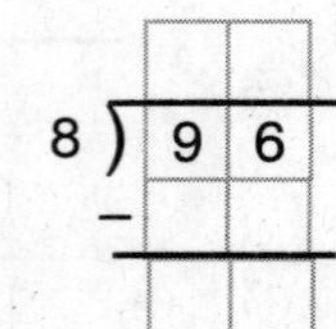

i) 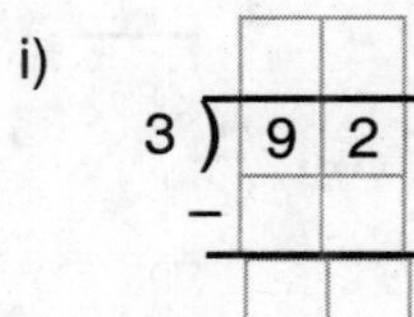

j) 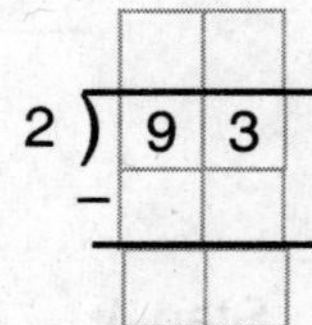

Steps 6 and 7:

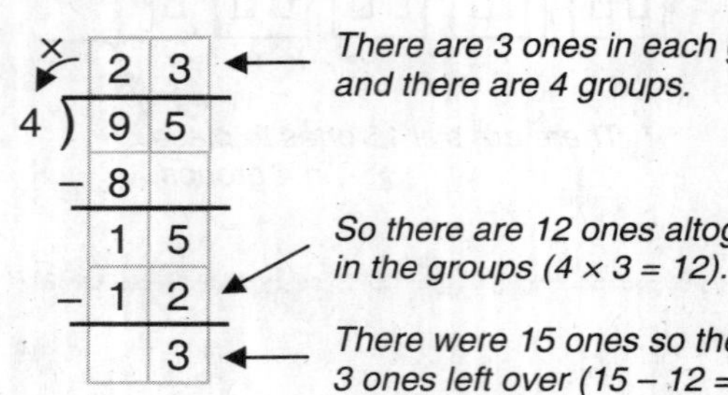

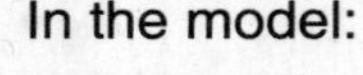

In the model:

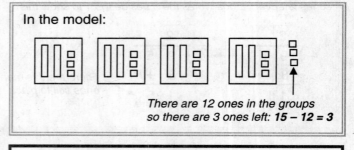

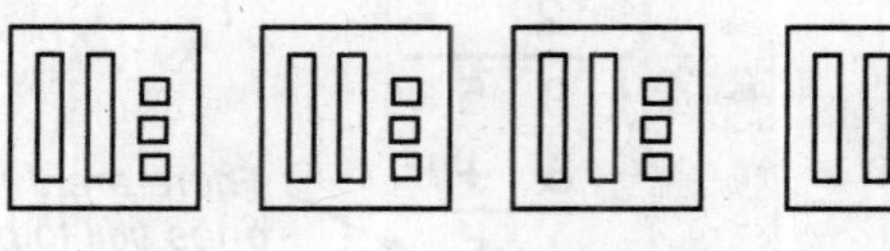

There are 12 ones in the groups so there are 3 ones left: ***15 – 12 = 3***

The division statement and the model both show that she can give each class 23 crackers with three left over.

9. For each question below, carry out all seven steps of long division.

a) 4) 6 5

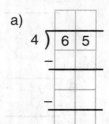

b) 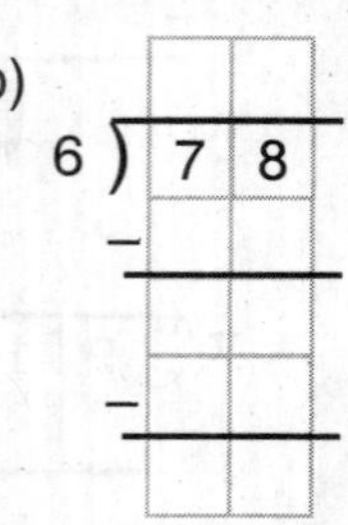

c) 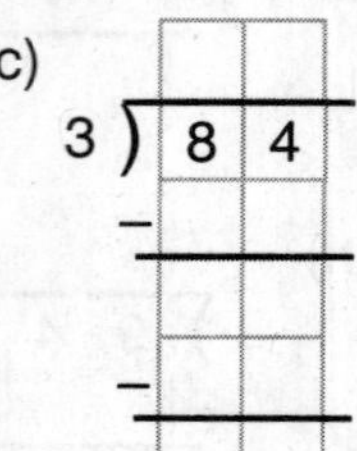

d) 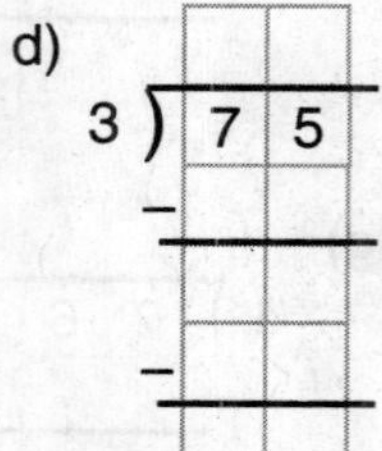

e) 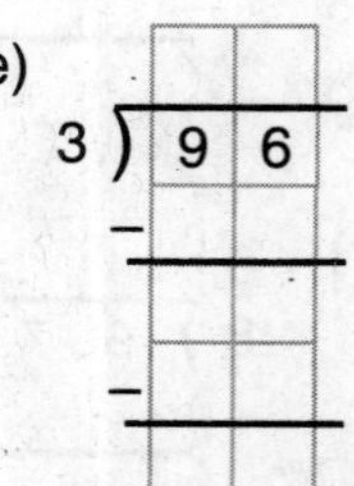

f) 4) 7 1
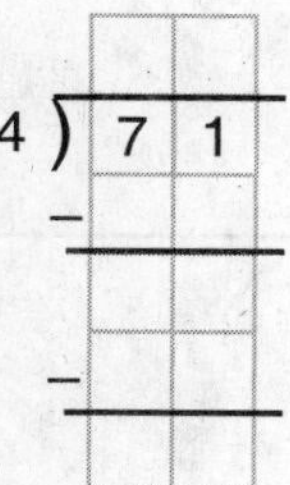

g) 5) 8 4

h) 8) 9 6
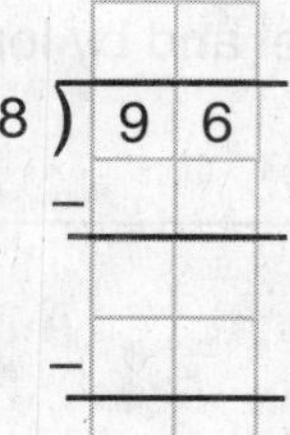

i) 7) 8 5
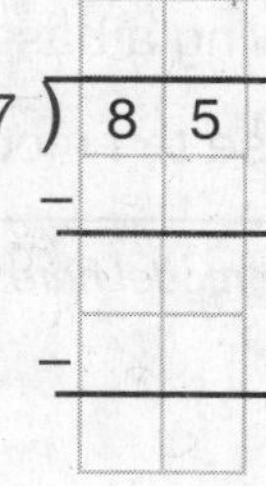

j) 9) 9 5
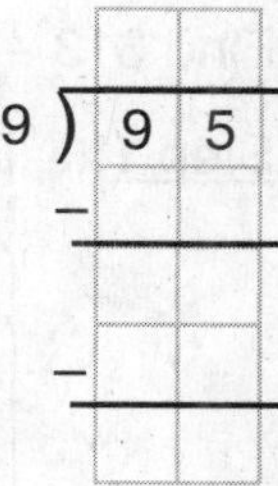

k) 6) 6 9
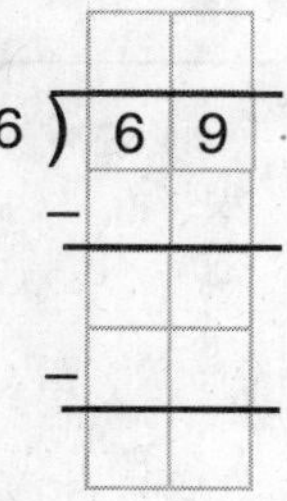

l) 4) 7 7
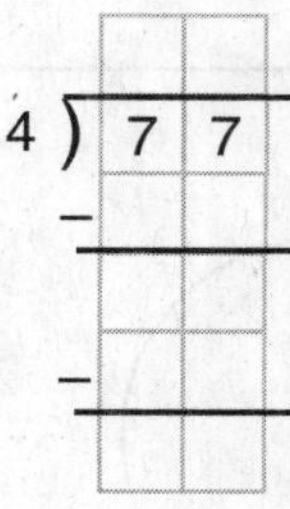

m) 9) 9 4
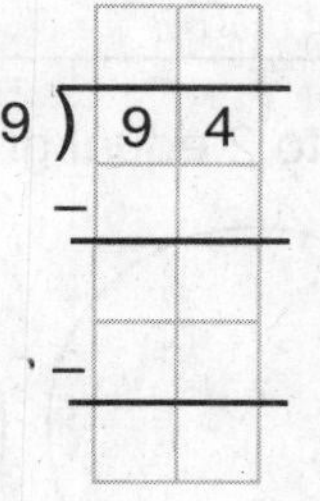

n) 5) 6 8
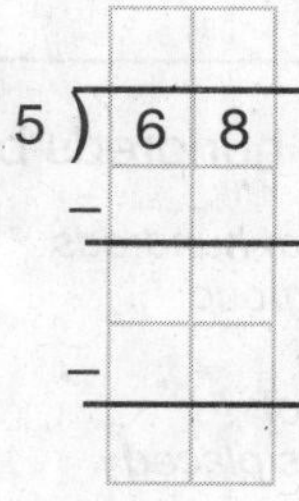

o) 6) 9 9
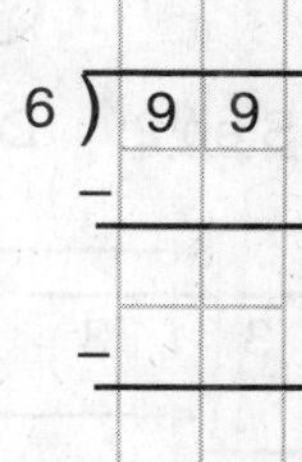

10. Alan put 99 sandwiches on platters of 8. How many sandwiches are left over?

11. How many weeks are in 84 days?

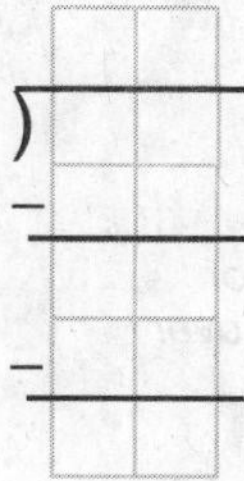

12. Elson arranges 97 books into 7 rows.

    How many rows can he make and how many books are left over?

13. Mita spent $91 to rent a canoe for a week.

    How much did the canoe cost each day?

14. 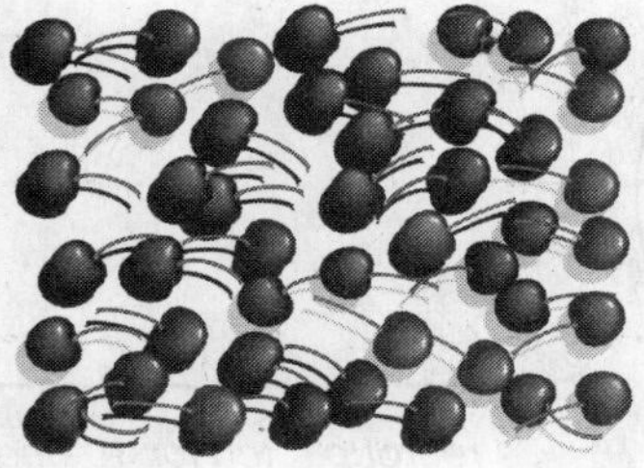

Saran divides 59 cherries equally among 4 friends

Wendy divides 74 cherries equally among 5 friends.

Who will have more cherries left over?

NS6-35: Long Division – 3- and 4-Digit by 1-Digit

1. Find 313 ÷ 2 by drawing a base ten model and by long division.

Step 1: Draw a base ten model of 313.

Step 2: Divide the hundreds blocks into 2 equal groups.

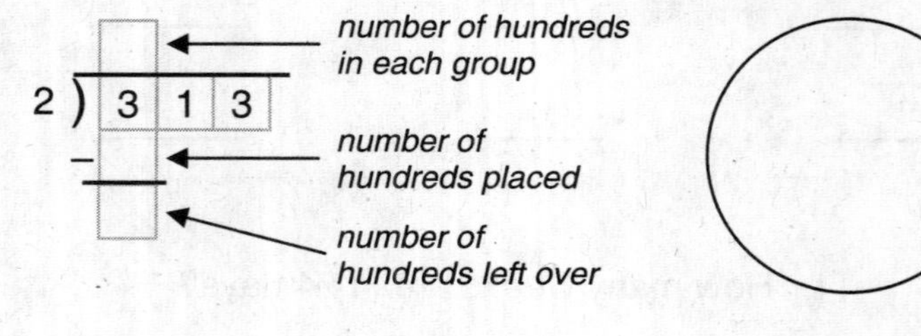

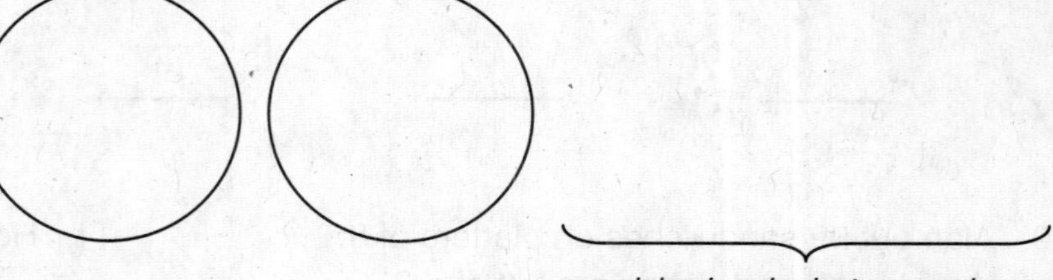

Step 3: Exchange the leftover hundreds block for 10 tens.

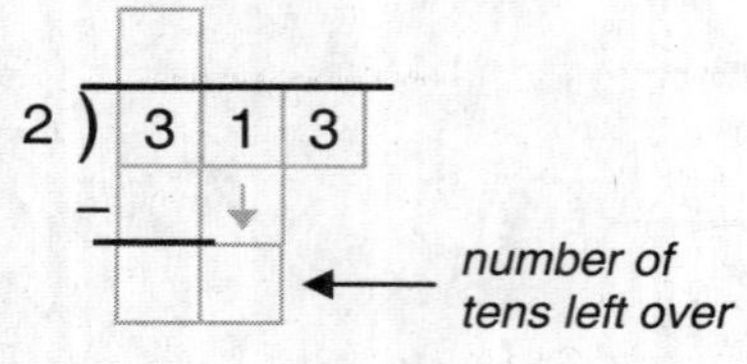

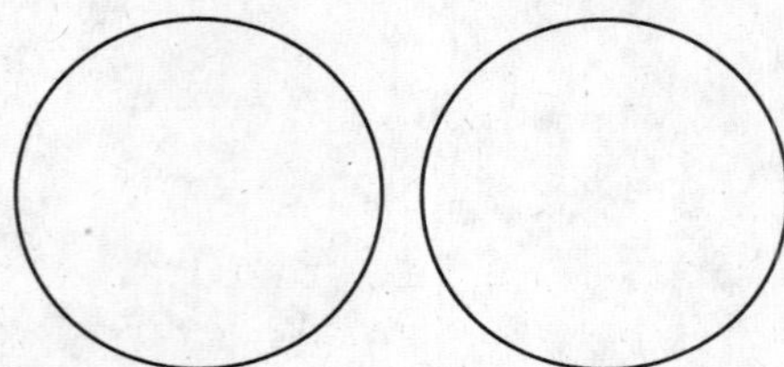

regroup a hundred as 10 tens

Step 4: Divide the tens blocks into two equal groups.

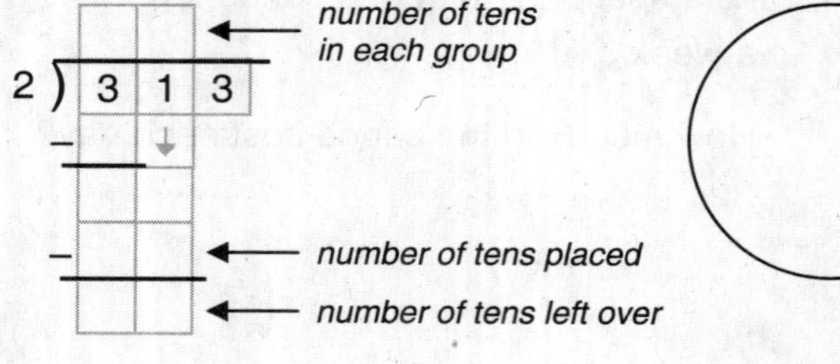

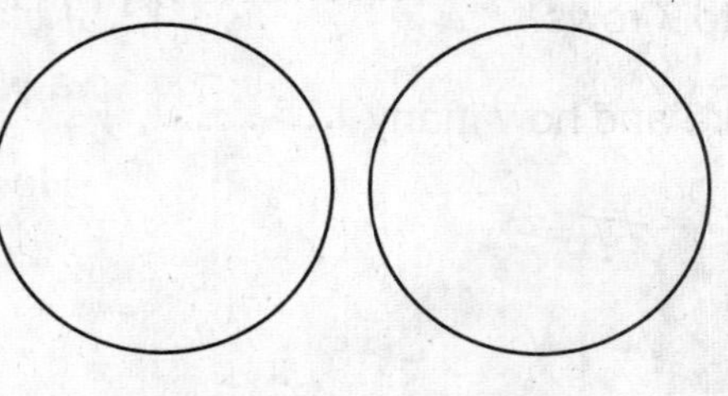

remaining tens and ones

Step 5: Exchange the leftover tens block for 10 ones.

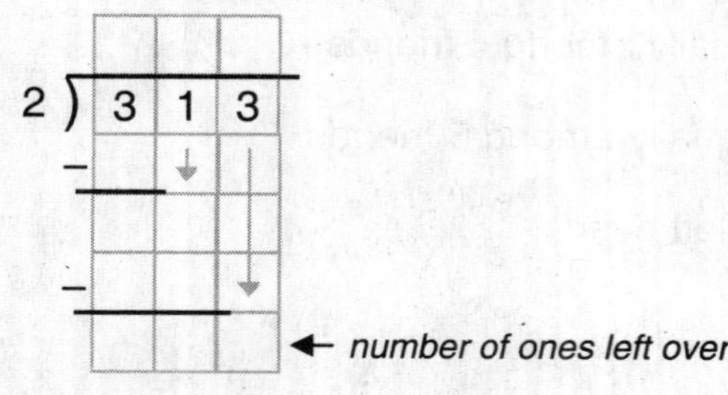

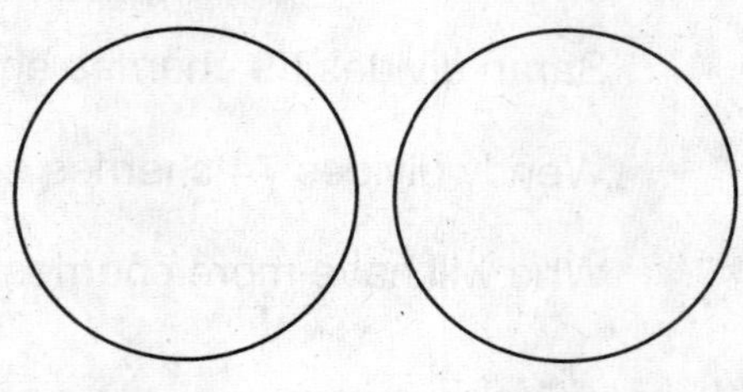

regroup a ten for 10 ones

<u>Steps 6 and 7</u>: Divide the ones into 2 equal groups.

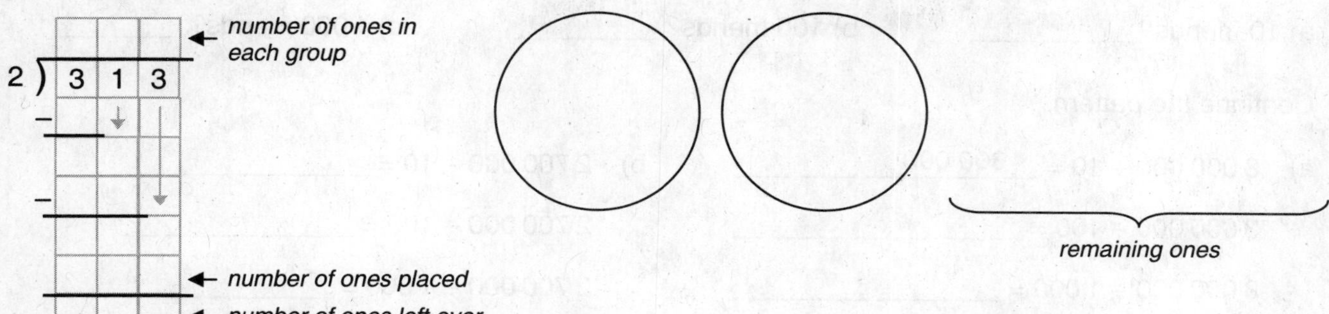

2. Divide.

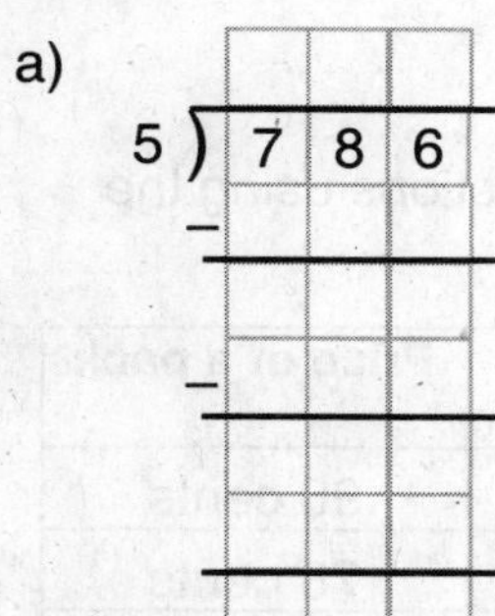

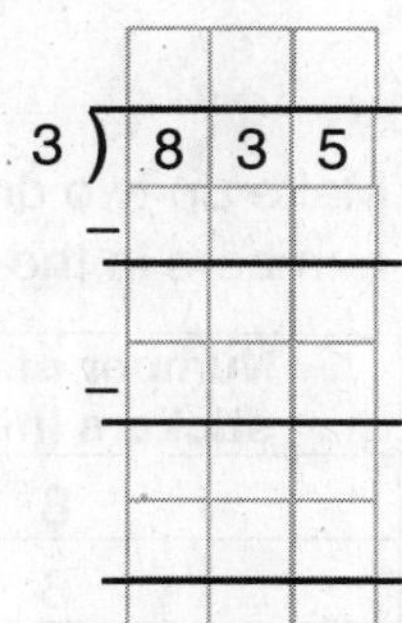

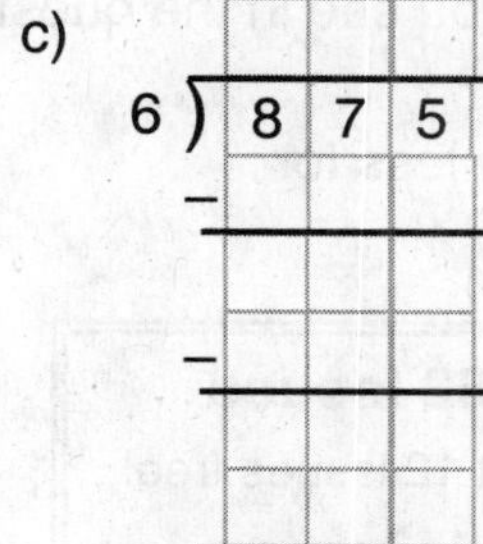

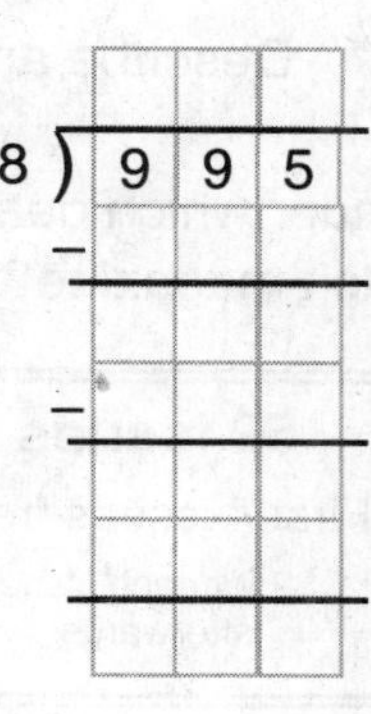

3. In each question below, there are fewer hundreds than the number of groups. Write a "0" in the hundreds position to show that no hundreds can be placed in equal groups. Then perform the division as if the hundreds had automatically been exchanged for tens.

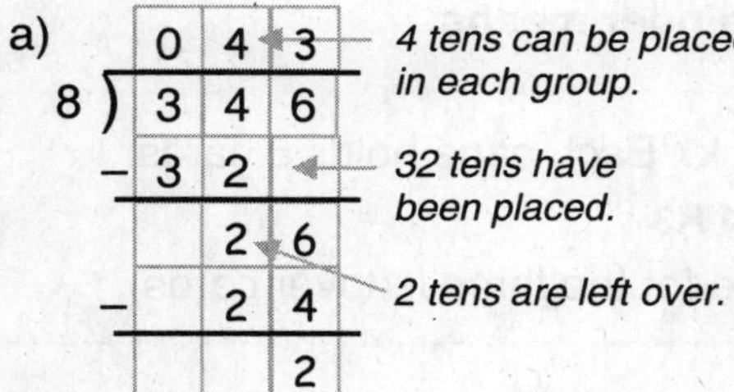

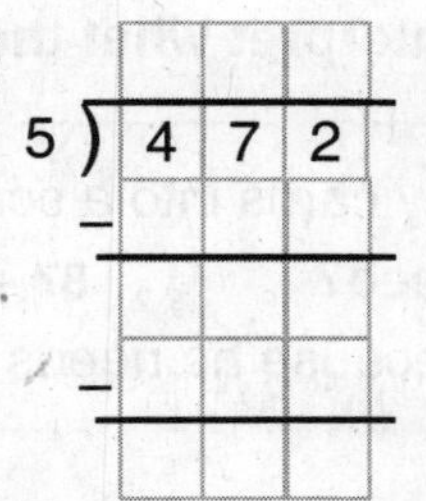

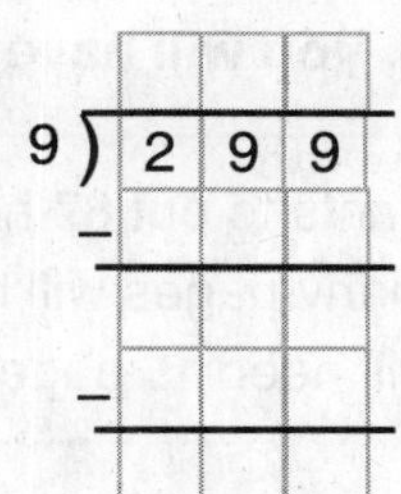

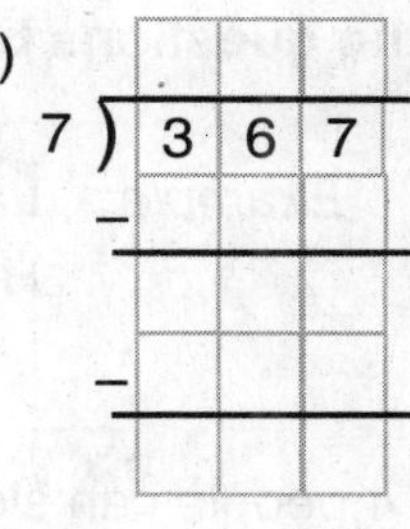

4. Divide.

a) $3 \overline{)115}$ b) $4 \overline{)341}$ c) $8 \overline{)425}$ d) $6 \overline{)379}$ e) $9 \overline{)658}$

f) $5 \overline{)1525}$ g) $5 \overline{)7523}$ h) $3 \overline{)5213}$ i) $4 \overline{)1785}$ j) $7 \overline{)2213}$

5. Karen swims 4 laps of a pool.
Altogether she swims 144 metres. How long is the pool?

6. The perimeter of a six-sided park is 732 km.
How long is each side of the park?

NS6-36: Topics in Division

1. How many pennies would each friend receive if you divided 3 000 pennies among …

a) 10 friends? ______ b) 100 friends? ______ c) 1 000 friends? ______

2. Continue the pattern.

a) 3 000 000 ÷ 10 = 300 000

3 000 000 ÷ 100 = ______

3 000 000 ÷ 1 000 = ______

3 000 000 ÷ 10 000 = ______

b) 2 700 000 ÷ 10 = ______

2 700 000 ÷ 100 = ______

2 700 000 ÷ 1 000 = ______

2 700 000 ÷ 10 000 = ______

3. Describe any patterns you see in the question 2.

4. Under which deal do you pay less for each magazine?

52 Issues First 4 issues free! $3 for each issue afterwards	**52 Issues** First 12 issues free! $4 for each issue after that

5. Make up two division questions using the numbers in the chart.

Number of animal stickers in a pack	Price of a pack
8	96 cents
6	78 cents
7	91 cents

In the questions below, you will have to interpret what the remainder means.

Example: Lars wants to put 87 hockey cards into a scrapbook. Each page holds 6 cards. How many pages will he need? **87 ÷ 6 = 14 R3**
Lars will need **15** pages (because he needs a page for the three leftover cards).

6. 4 people can sleep in a tent.
How many tents are needed for 58 people?

7. 6 friends share 83 stickers.
How many stickers does each friend receive?

8. A school cafeteria uses 7 loaves of bread each week.
In how many weeks and days will the cafeteria use 98 loaves of bread?

9. Esther is moving to a new apartment.
On each trip her car can carry 6 loads of boxes.
How many trips will she need to make to move 75 boxes?

Answer the following questions in your notebook.

1.  A bus carries 48 students. How many students can 65 buses carry?

2. If three oranges cost 69¢, how much do nine oranges cost?

3. a) Alice is between 20 and 40 years old. Last year, her age was a multiple of 4. This year, her age is a multiple of 5. How old is Alice?

   b) George is between 30 and 50 years old. Last year, his age was a multiple of 6. This year it is a multiple of 7. How old is George?

4. A family travelled in a car for 112 days. Gas costs $126 each week.

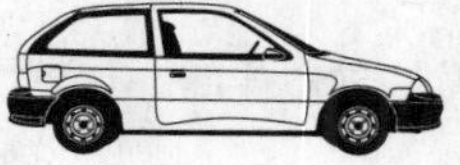

How much money did they spend on gas?

5. Can a prime number be divisible by 3? Explain.

6. What is the smallest whole number greater than 100 that is divisible by 99?

7. ☐ 5 6 9 ÷ 6 is about 400.

   What number could be in the box? Explain.

8. Kim buys cherries at a price of 3 for 10¢ and sells the cherries at a price of 5 for 20¢.
   How many cherries does she need to sell to make $1.00?
   HINT: What is the lowest common multiple of 3 and 5?

9. 3 360 trees are planted in 6 rows. How many trees are in each row?

10. There are two adults and two children in the Gordon family.
    The ticket price for a play was $12.50 for adults and $8.50 for children.
    How much money did the family have to pay for the tickets?
    If they received $8 in change, what amount did they pay with?

11. ➢ Choose a number less than 10 and greater than 0.
    ➢ If the number is even, halve it and add one. If the number is odd, double it.
    ➢ Again, if the new number is even, halve it and add one. If the new number is odd, double it.

    a) Continue the number snake for the example. What happens?
    b) Investigate which one-digit number makes the longest snake.
    c) Try starting a number snake with a two-digit number. What happens?

Example:
9
9 → 18
9 → 18 → 10

NS6-38: Rounding on a Number Line

1. Draw an arrow to the 0 or 10 to show whether the circled number is closer to **0 or 10**.

a) 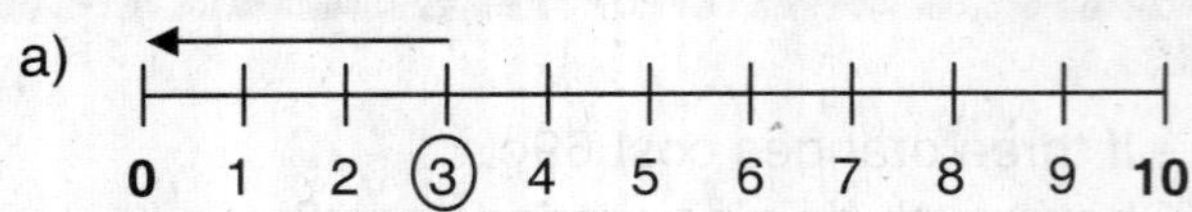

b) 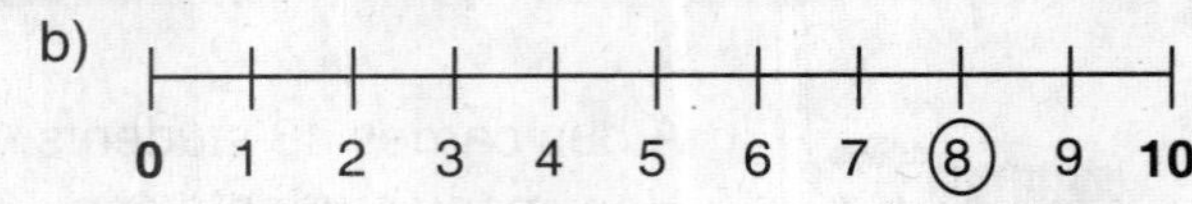

c) 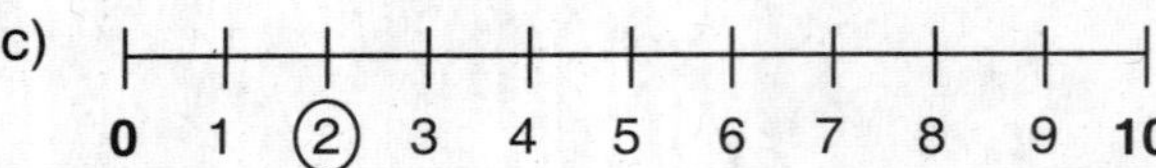

d) 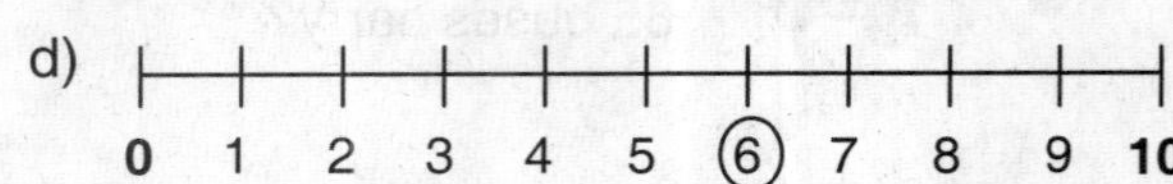

2. a) Which one-digit numbers are closer to i) 0? ______ ii) 10? ______

b) Why is 5 a special case? ______

3. Draw an arrow to show which multiple of ten you would round to. Then round each number to the nearest tens.

a) 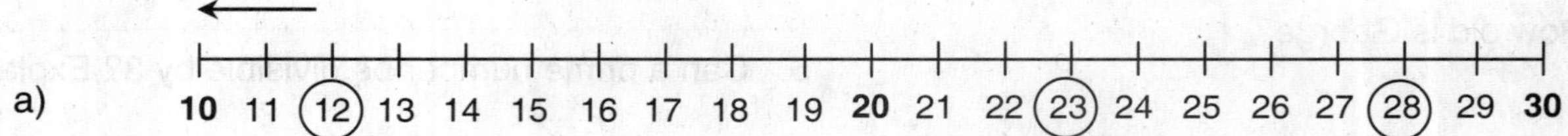

Round to 10 ______ ______

b) 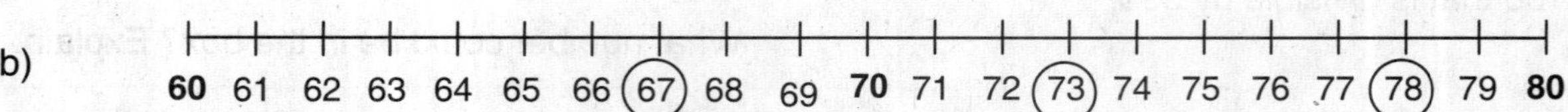

Round to ______ ______ ______

c) 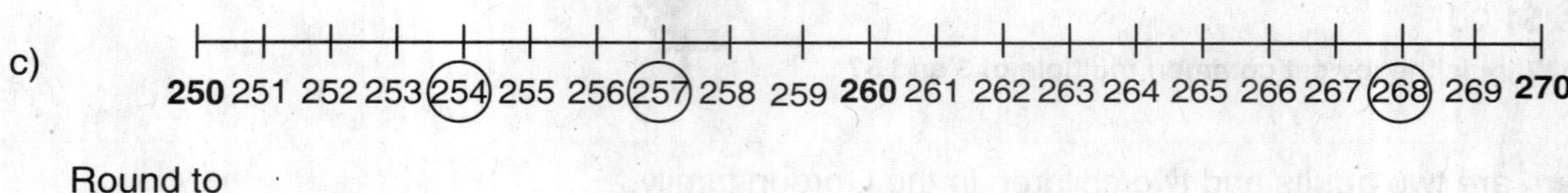

Round to ______ ______ ______

4. Circle the correct answer.

a) 21 is closer to 20 or 30

b) 12 is closer to 10 or 20

c) 38 is closer to 30 or 40

d) 75 is closer to 70 or 80

e) 252 is closer to 250 or 260

f) 586 is closer to 580 or 590

5. Draw an arrow to show whether the circled number is closer to 0 or 100.

a) 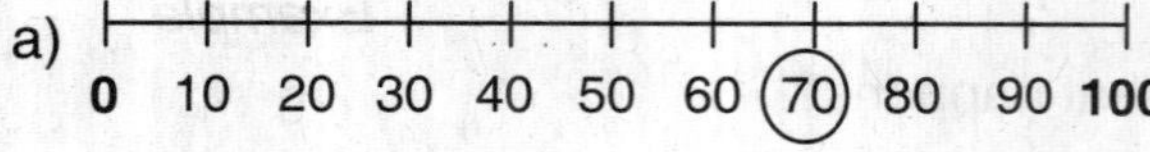

b) 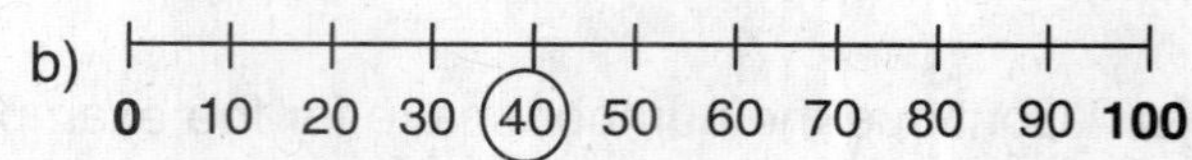

6. Is 50 closer to 0 or to 100? Why is 50 a special case?

______

NS6-38: Rounding on a Number Line *(continued)*

7. Circle the correct answer.

a) 70 is closer to: 0 or 100
b) 30 is closer to: 0 or 100
c) 60 is closer to: 0 or 100
d) 10 is closer to: 0 or 100

8. Show the approximate position of each number on the line. What multiple of 100 would you round to?

a) 642 b) 684 c) 793 d) 701

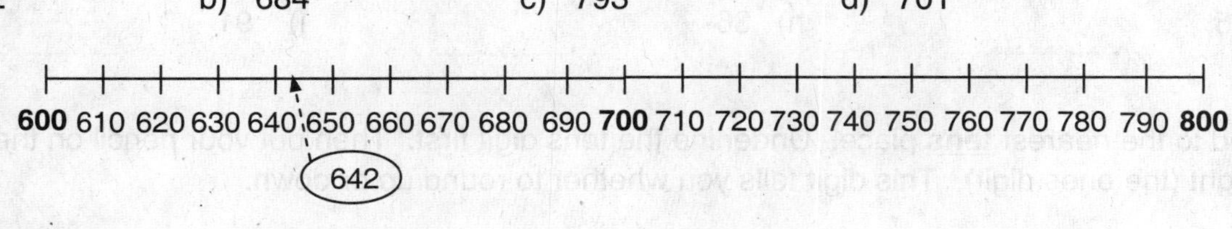

Round to ______

9. Circle the correct answer.

a) 164 is closer to: 100 or 200
b) 723 is closer to: 700 or 800
c) 678 is closer to: 600 or 700
d) 957 is closer to: 900 or 1 000

10. Draw an arrow to show whether the circled number is closer to 0 or 1 000.

a) 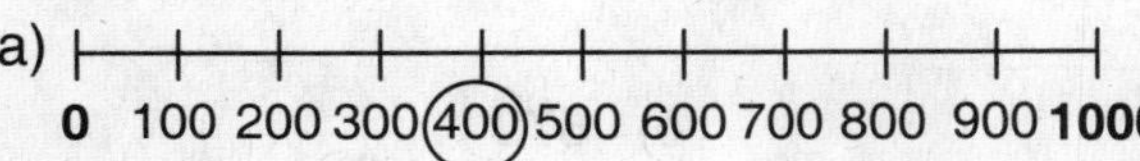

b) 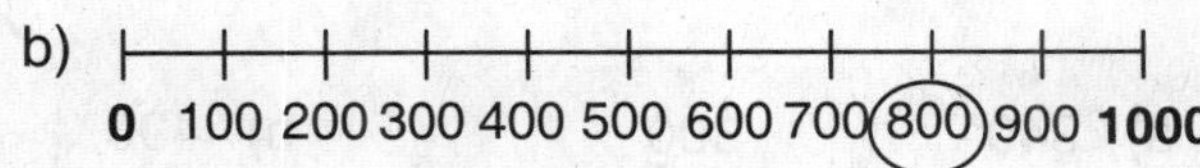

11. Circle the correct answer.

a) 100 is closer to 0 or 1 000
b) 900 is closer to 0 or 1 000
c) 600 is closer to 0 or 1 000

12. Draw an arrow to show which multiple of 1000 you would round to.

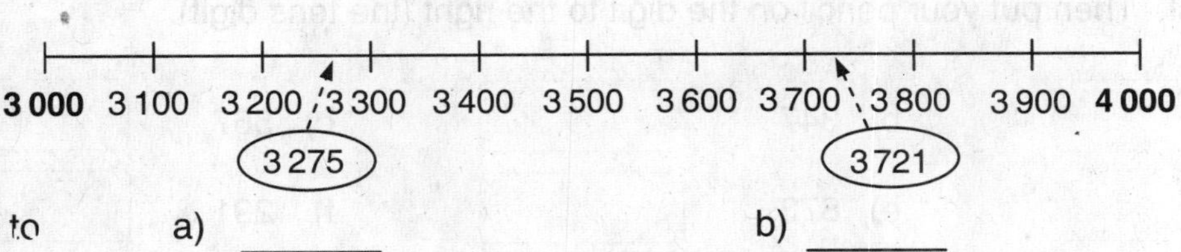

Round to a) ______ b) ______

13. Circle the correct answer.

a) 3 975 is closer to: 3 000 or 4 000
b) 8 123 is closer to: 8 000 or 9 000
c) 4 201 is closer to: 4 000 or 5 000
d) 2 457 is closer to: 2 000 or 3 000

14. Write a rule for rounding a four-digit number to the nearest thousands.

NS6-39: Rounding

1. Round to the nearest **tens** place.

> **REMEMBER:**
> If the number in the ones digit is:
> 0, 1, 2, 3 or 4 – you round down
> 5, 6, 7, 8 or 9 – you round up

a) 38 ☐ b) 46 ☐
c) 21 ☐ d) 62 ☐
e) 79 ☐ f) 81 ☐
g) 25 ☐ h) 36 ☐ i) 91 ☐

2. Round to the nearest **tens** place. Underline the tens digit first. Then put your pencil on the digit to the right (the ones digit). This digit tells you whether to round up or down.

a) 6<u>5</u>6 ↓ 660 b) 273 ☐ c) 152 ☐
d) 355 ☐ e) 418 ☐ f) 566 ☐
g) 128 ☐ h) 467 ☐ i) 338 ☐

3. Round the following numbers to the nearest **hundreds** place. Underline the hundreds digit first. Then put your pencil on the digit to the right (the tens digit).

a) <u>3</u>40 ↓ 300 b) 490 ☐ c) 570 ☐
d) 270 ☐ e) 160 ☐ f) 360 ☐
g) 460 ☐ h) 840 ☐ i) 980 ☐

4. Round the following numbers to the nearest **hundreds** place. As in the last question, underline the hundreds digit first. Then put your pencil on the digit to the right (the tens digit).

a) 167 ☐ b) 347 ☐ c) 567 ☐
d) 349 ☐ e) 873 ☐ f) 291 ☐

5. Round the following numbers to the nearest **thousands** place. Underline the thousands digit first. Then put your pencil on the digit to the right (the hundreds digit).

a) <u>4</u> 787 ↓ 5 000 b) 3 092 ☐ c) 7 697 ☐
d) 5 021 ☐ e) 2 723 ☐ f) 8 538 ☐

NS6-39: Rounding *(continued)*

6. Underline the digit you wish to round to. Then say whether you would round up or down.

a) *hundreds*

7	<u>3</u>	2	5

round up / (round down) — circled

b) *hundreds*

4	1	2	7

round up / round down

c) *tens*

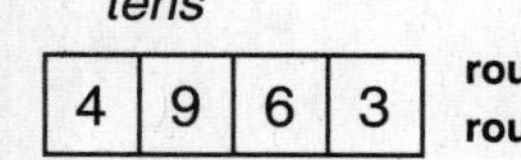

4	9	6	3

round up / round down

d) *thousands*

8	3	8	6	4

round up / round down

e) *ten thousands*

4	6	5	2	3

round up / round down

f) *ten thousands*

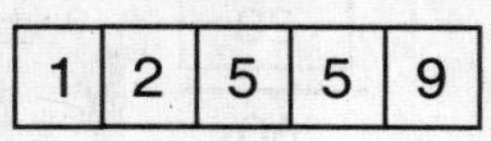

1	2	5	5	9

round up / round down

7. Complete the two steps from Question 6. Then follow the two steps below.

Round the digit underlined up or down.

- To round up add 1 to the digit.
- To round down keep the digit the same.

7	<u>3</u>	4	5
	3		

ru / (rd) — circled

The digits to the right of the rounded digit become zeroes.

The digits to the left remain the same.

7	<u>3</u>	4	5
7	3	0	0

ru / (rd) — circled

a) *thousands*

7	2	1	0	3

ru rd

b) *ten thousands*

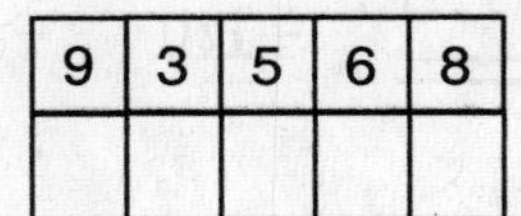

9	3	5	6	8

ru rd

c) *hundreds*

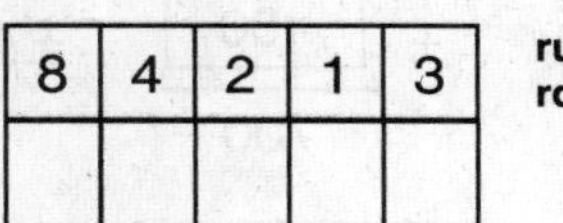

8	4	2	1	3

ru rd

d) *hundreds*

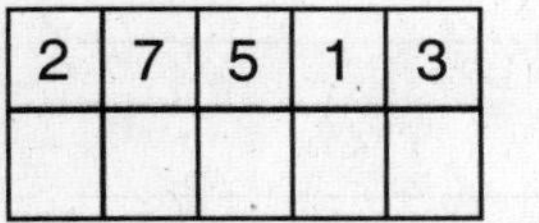

2	7	5	1	3

ru rd

e) *tens*

4	6	1	2	7	3

ru rd

f) *tens thousands*

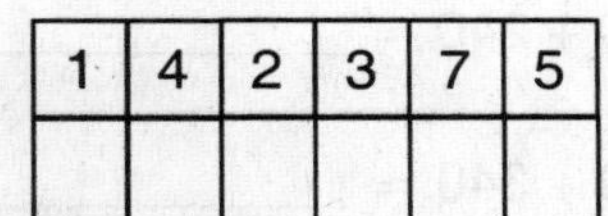

1	4	2	3	7	5

ru rd

8. Sometimes in rounding, you have to regroup.

Example: Round 3995 to the nearest hundred.

3	9	<u>8</u>	5
	10		

900 rounds to 1000.

3	<u>9</u>	8	5
4	0		

Regroup the 10 hundreds as 1 (thousand) and add it to the 3 (thousand).

3	<u>9</u>	8	5
4	0	0	0

Complete the rounding.

Round each number to the digit given (regroup if necessary).

a) 3 293 *tens* b) 5 921 *hundreds* c) 9 723 *thousands* d) 13 975 *tens*

e) 23 159 *hundreds* f) 999 857 *ten thousands* g) 395 321 *hundred thousands*

NS6-40: Estimating Sums and Differences

1. Estimate the sums and differences.

≈ ← Mathematicians use this symbol to mean ***"approximately equal to."***

a) 42 → 40
+ 23 → + 20
= 60

b) 28 → ___
+ 54 → + ___

c) 62 → ___
− 19 → − ___

d) 87 → ___
− 57 → − ___

e) 73 + 17 ≈ 70 + 20 = 90

f) 89 − 46 ≈ ______

g) 16 + 34 ≈ ______

h) 63 + 26 ≈ ______

i) 82 + 47 ≈ ______

j) 46 − 17 ≈ ______

k) 48 + 27 ≈ ______

l) 76 + 14 ≈ ______

m) 92 − 38 ≈ ______

2. Estimate by rounding to the nearest hundreds.

a) 290 → 300
+ 360 → + 400
= 700

b) 390 → ___
+ 460 → + ___

c) 630 → ___
− 170 → − ___

d) 840 → ___
− 550 → − ___

e) 680 + 160 ≈ ______

f) 470 − 220 ≈ ______

g 610 + 240 ≈ ______

h) 840 + 180 ≈ ______

i) 670 + 340 ≈ ______

j) 941 − 463 ≈ ______

k) 126 + 567 ≈ ______

l) 523 + 285 ≈ ______

BONUS

3. To estimate, round to the nearest thousands or ten thousands.

a) 1 275 → 1 000
+ 3 940 → + 4 000
= 5 000

b) 4 729 → ___
− 3 132 → − ___

c) 2 570 → ___
+ 6 234 → + ___

d) 29 753 → ___
− 23 123 → − ___

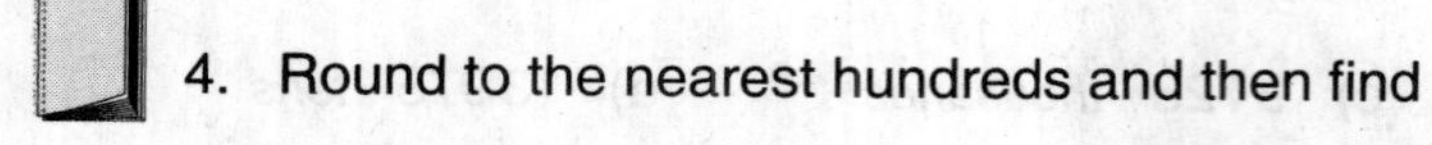

4. Round to the nearest hundreds and then find the sum or difference.

a) 3 272 + 1 976

b) 3 581 − 1 926

c) 64 857 − 42 345

NS6-41: Estimating

Answer the following questions in your notebook.

1. The population of Saskatchewan is 995 000 and the population of New Brunswick is 750 500. Estimate the difference in the two populations.

Saskatchewan

New Brunswick

2. The population of Newfoundland is 520 200 and the population of Prince Edward Island is 137 900.

   Estimate the total population of the two provinces.

Newfoundland

Prince Edward Island

3. Round 628 315 to the nearest:
   a) tens
   b) hundreds
   c) thousands
   d) ten thousands

4. Estimate the products by rounding to the leading digits.
   a) 32×75
   b) 492×81
   c) 307×12
   d) $2\,759 \times 812$

5. Estimate the following total amounts.
   a) 6 tapes at $4.99 a tape
   b) 5 pies at $3.12 a pie
   c) 8 books at $7.87 a book

6. Jacques multiplied a 1-digit number by a 3-digit number. The product was about 1 000.

   Describe three different pairs of numbers he might have multiplied.

7. The populations of New Brunswick and Nova Scotia are listed in an almanac as 750 000 and 936 900.

   What digit do you think these numbers have been rounded to? Explain.

Nova Scotia

8. There are 1 483 beads in a jar.

   It takes 58 beads to make a bracelet.

   Sandra estimates that she can make 30 bracelets.

   Is her estimate reasonable? Explain.

9. A supermarket sold 472 apples, 783 oranges, 341 pears, and 693 bananas.
   a) How many pieces of fruit did they sell in all?
   b) Use estimation to check your solution. Explain your estimation strategy.

10. To estimate the difference 1 875 – 1 432, should you round the numbers to the nearest thousands or the nearest hundreds? Explain.

NS6-42: Methods of Estimation

Answer the following questions in your notebook.

1. Predict which range each product or quotient will lie in before you perform the calculation.

A. 1 to 10	**B.** 11 to 100	**C.** 101 to 500	**D.** 501 to 1 000	**E.** above 1 000

a) 37×25 b) $4\,279 \div 70$ c) $13\,200 \div 600$ d) 45×87

2. Which method of estimation will work best for each calculation below? Justify your answers.

- Rounding
- Front-end estimation (round both numbers down to the leading digit)
- Rounding one number up and one number down

a) $657 + 452$ b) $891 + 701$ c) $425 + 375$ d) $395 - 352$

For which question does neither method work well?

3. Use any method of estimation you choose to judge whether the answer is reasonable. Then perform the calculation to check if the answer is correct.

a) $3\,875 + 2\,100 = 8\,257$ b) $37 \times 435 = 1\,285$ c) $9\,352 - 276 = 9\,076$

4. Some calculations are easy because …

You can group numbers that add to 10 or 100.

10 100
4⑦ + 3③ + 5(40) + 3(60)

You can do the calculation in steps.

$100 - 23$
$= 100 - 20 - 3$

You don't have to regroup.

$3 \times 213 = 639$

Which calculations below could you do mentally? Describe your method. For the harder calculations, say how you would estimate.

a) $3\,875 - 1\,325$ b) $800 - 53$ c) 876×9 d) $7\,521 + 9\,859$

e) 532×3 f) $321 + 587 + 413 + 379$ g) $42\,000 \div 70$

5. Write a number that could be rounded to:

a) 1 000 or 1 400.

b) 6 000 or 5 900 or 5 870.

6. How would you estimate …

a) the length of a row of 10 000 loonies?

b) the number of seconds in a year?

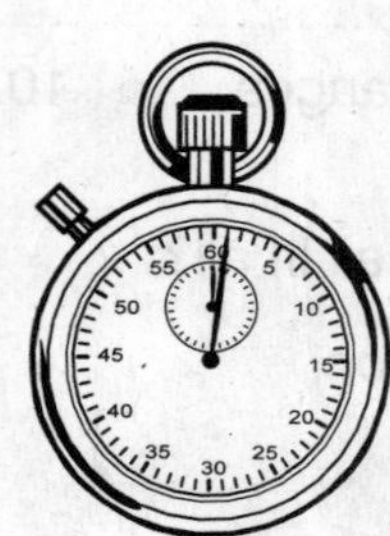

NS6-43: Integers

Temperature is recorded on a scale that includes **negative** and **positive** whole numbers.

These numbers are called **integers**.

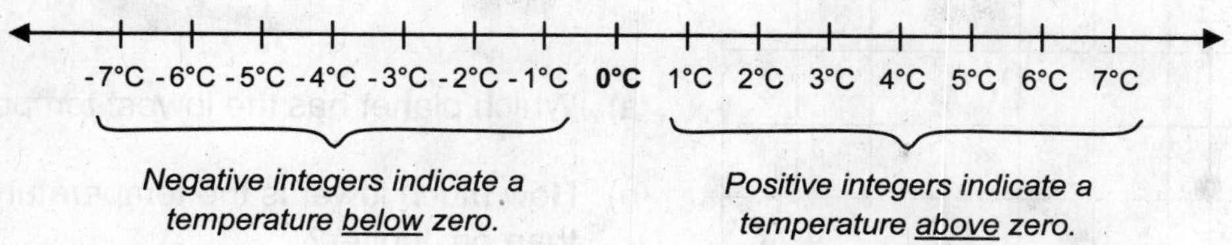

---

1. Write an integer for each days temperature.
   How much did the temperature change from day to day?
   (If the temperature fell, write a negative sign in front of your answer)

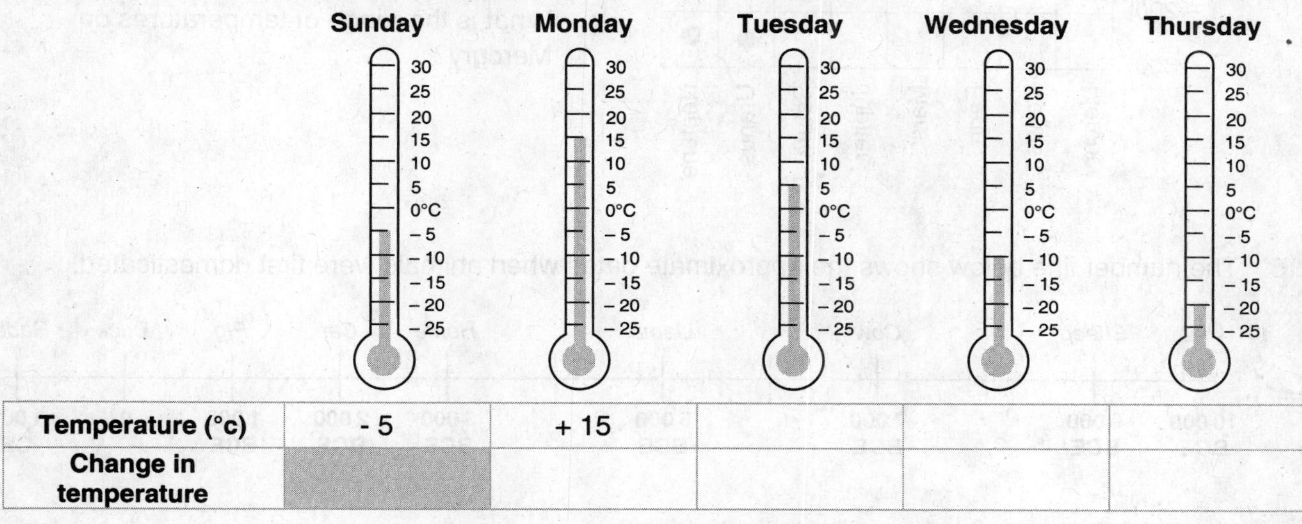

	Sunday	Monday	Tuesday	Wednesday	Thursday
Temperature (°c)	- 5	+ 15			
Change in temperature					

2.

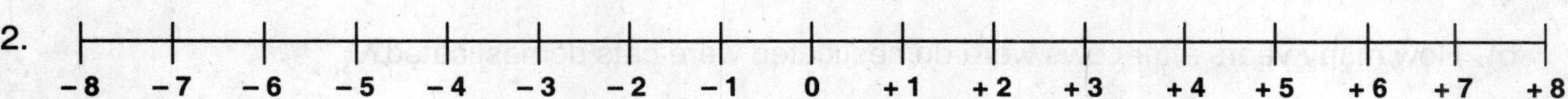

a) Mark the numbers on the number line.
   A: – 5 **B:** + 2 **C:** – 7 **D:** + 5 **E:** – 3

b) How many spaces apart are the numbers?
   i) – 5 and – 4: ________ ii) – 2 and + 3: ________ iii) + 6 and + 8: ________

c) How many negative numbers are greater than (ie. to the right of) – 4?

3. Leela recorded the winter temperatures shown in the chart.
   How much did the temperature change …

a) from Monday to Tuesday? ______

b) from Tuesday to Wednesday? ______

c) from Wednesday to Thursday? ______

Monday	Tuesday	Wednesday	Thursday
+ 5°C	– 2°C	– 7°C	+ 1°C

4. The chart shows the average temperature on the planets.

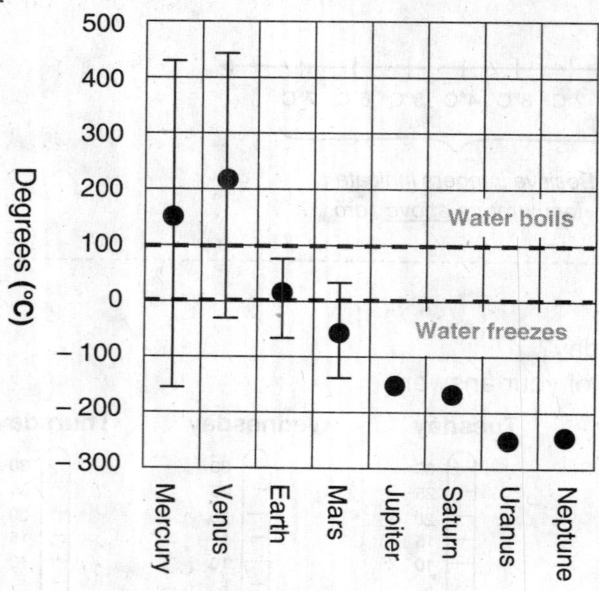

a) Which planet has the lowest temperature?

b) How much lower is the temperature on Uranus than on Jupiter?

c) The **range** of a set of numbers is the difference between the highest and lowest numbers.

What is the range of temperatures on Mercury?

5. The number line below shows the approximate dates when animals were first domesticated.

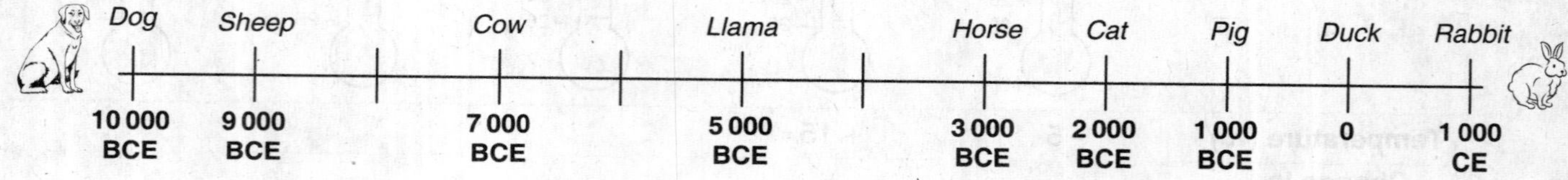

a) Which type of animal was domesticated first?

b) How many years after cows were domesticated were cats domesticated?

c) How many years after horses were domesticated were rabbits domesticated?

d) Pick two animals. How many years after the first animal was the second animal domesticated?

6. Mackerel live about 200 m below sea level.
Gulper eels live at 1 000 m below sea level.
Write integers for the depths where the animals live.
How far below the mackerel does the gulper eel live?

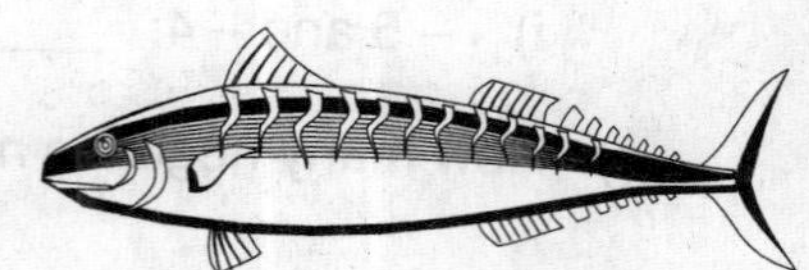

7. How many negative integers are greater than −6?

8. Why are −3 and +3 closer to each other than −4 and +4?

LSS6-1: Organized Lists

Many problems in mathematics and science have more than one solution.

If a problem involves two quantities, you can be sure you haven't missed any possible solutions if you list the values of one of the quantities in increasing order.

Example:

Find all the ways you can make 35¢ with dimes and nickels. Start with no dimes, then 1 dime, and so on up to 3 dimes (4 would be too many).

Then, count on by 5s to 35 to find out how many nickels you need to make 35¢.

Step 1:

dimes	nickels
0	
1	
2	
3	

Step 2:

dimes	nickels
0	7
1	5
2	3
3	1

---

1. Fill in the amount of pennies, nickels, dimes or quarters you need to…

a) Make 17¢

nickels	pennies
0	
1	
2	
3	

b) Make 45¢

dimes	nickels
0	
1	
2	
3	
4	

c) Make 23¢

nickels	pennies
0	
1	
2	
3	
4	

d) Make 32¢

dimes	pennies
0	
1	
2	
3	

e) Make 65¢

quarters	nickels
0	
1	
2	

f) Make 85¢

quarters	nickels

2.

quarters	nickels
0	
1	
2	

Ben wants to find all the ways he can make 60¢ using quarters and nickels. He lists the number of quarters in increasing order. Why did he stop at 2 quarters?

____

____

3. Make a chart to show all the ways you can make the given amount.

a) 90¢ using dimes and nickels

b) 125¢ using quarters and dimes

LSS6-1: Organized Lists *(continued)*

Example:

Alana wants to find all pairs of numbers that multiply to give 15.
There are no numbers that will multiply by 2 or 4 to give 15, so Alana leaves those rows in her chart blank.
The numbers in the last row of the chart are the same as those in the third row so Alana knows she has found all pairs.

1 × 15 = 15 **3 × 5 = 15**

1st Number	2nd Number
1	15
2	---
3	5
4	---
5	3

---

4. Find all pairs of numbers that multiply to give the number in bold.

a) **6**

First Number	Second Number

b) **8**

First Number	Second Number

5. Alicia wants to find all the ways she can make 70¢ using quarters and dimes.
One of the entries on her chart won't work. Which one is it?

quarters	dimes
0	
1	
2	

6. Find all the ways to make the amounts using quarters and dimes.
NOTE: Some entries on your chart may not work.

a) 80¢

quarters	dimes
0	
1	
2	

b) 105¢

quarters	dimes

7. Find all the widths and lengths of a rectangle with perimeter 12 units.

Width	Length
1	

8. Make a chart to find all the pairs of numbers that multiply to give.

a) 12 b) 14 c) 20 d) 24

PA6-19: Patterns with Increasing & Decreasing Steps

1. In the sequences below, the step or gap between the numbers increases or decreases. Can you see a pattern in the way the gap changes?

   Use the pattern to extend the sequence.

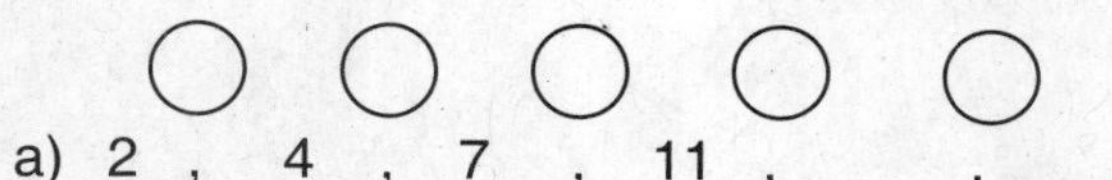

a) 2 , 4 , 7 , 11 , ____ , ____

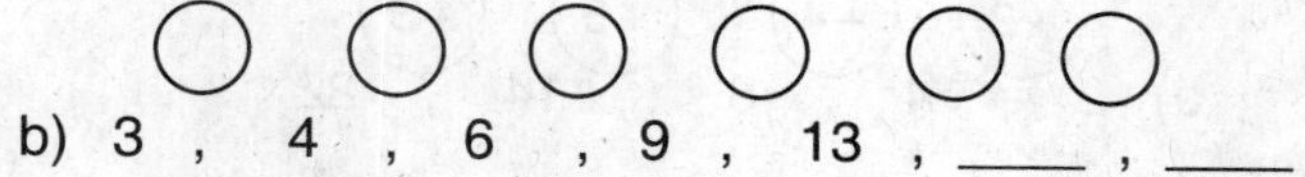

b) 3 , 4 , 6 , 9 , 13 , ____ , ____

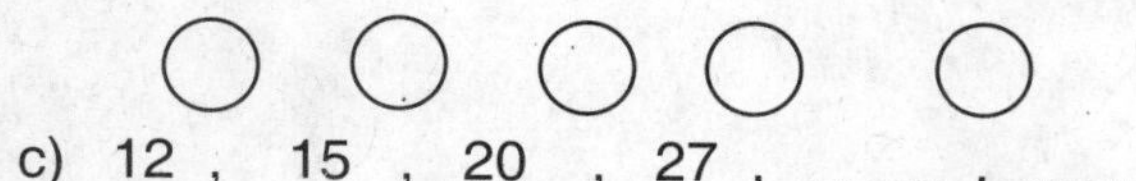

c) 12 , 15 , 20 , 27 , ____ , ____

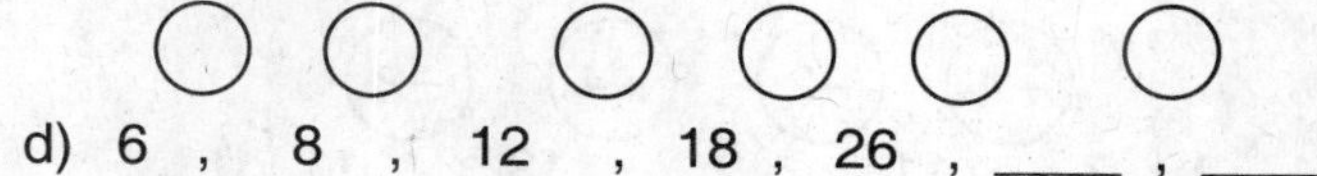

d) 6 , 8 , 12 , 18 , 26 , ____ , ____

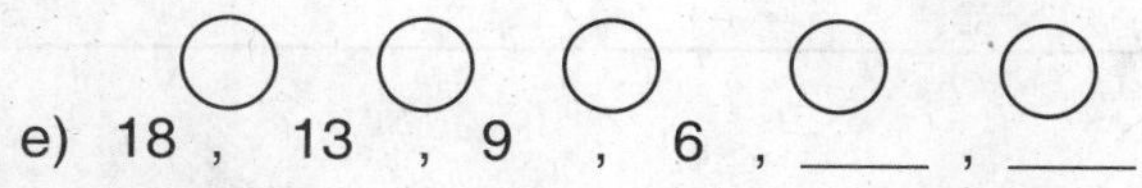

e) 18 , 13 , 9 , 6 , ____ , ____

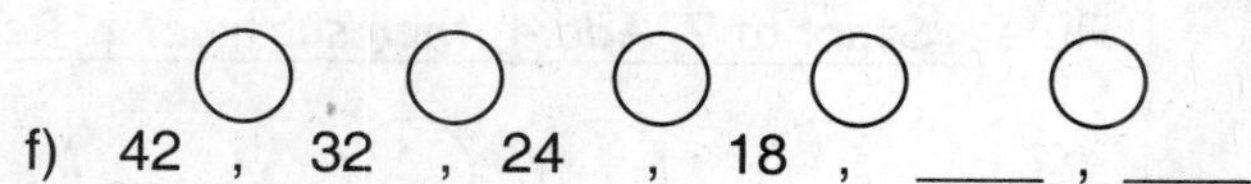

f) 42 , 32 , 24 , 18 , ____ , ____

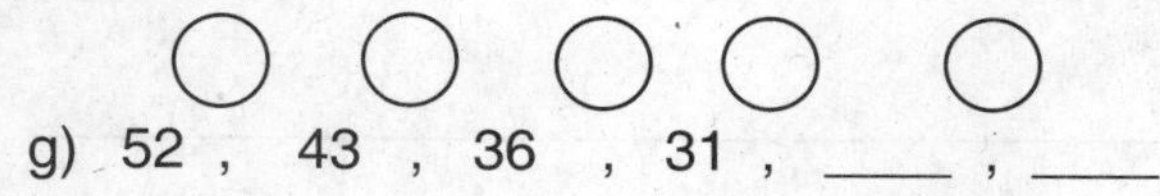

g) 52 , 43 , 36 , 31 , ____ , ____

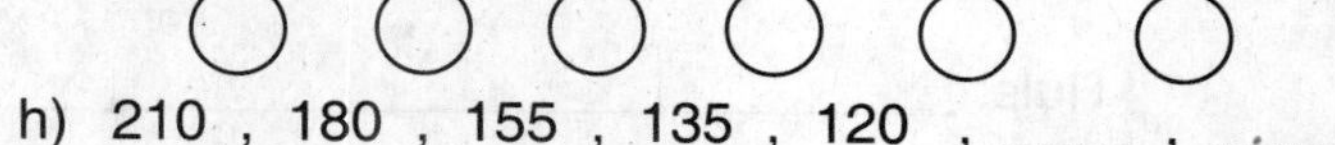

h) 210 , 180 , 155 , 135 , 120 , ____ , ____

2. Complete the T-table for Figure 3 and Figure 4. Then use the pattern in the gap to predict the number of triangles needed for Figures 5 and 6.

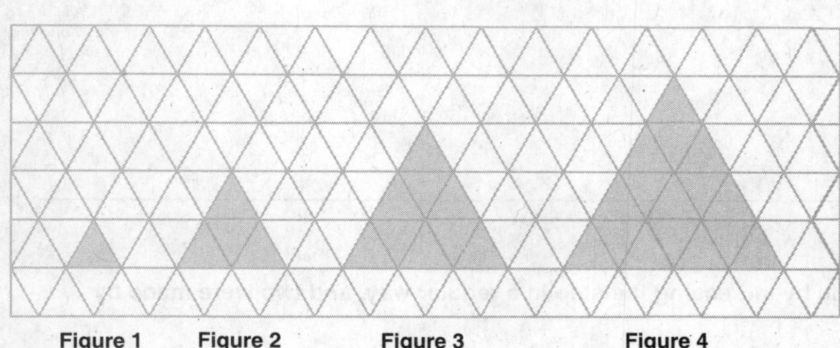

Figure 1 Figure 2 Figure 3 Figure 4

Figure	Number of Triangles
1	1
2	4
3	
4	
5	
6	

Write the number of triangles added each time here.

3. Make a T-table to predict how many blocks will be needed for Figure 6.

   HINT: Don't forget to count the hidden blocks.

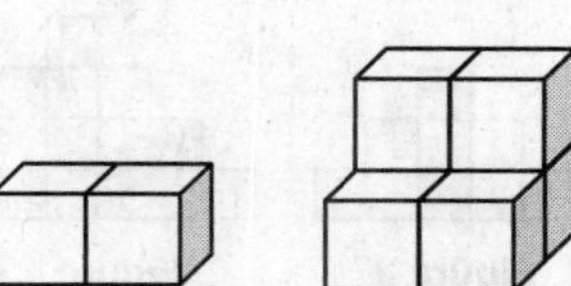

Figure 1 Figure 2

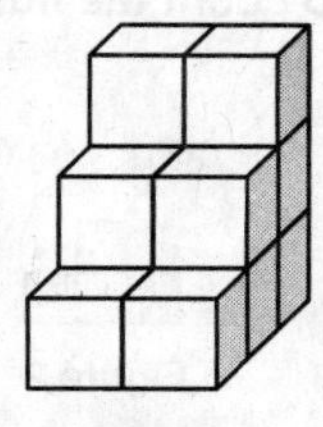

Figure 3

PA6-19: Patterns with Increasing & Decreasing Steps
(continued)

4. In each sequence below, the **step** changes in a regular way (it increases, decreases, or increases and decreases). Write a rule for each pattern.

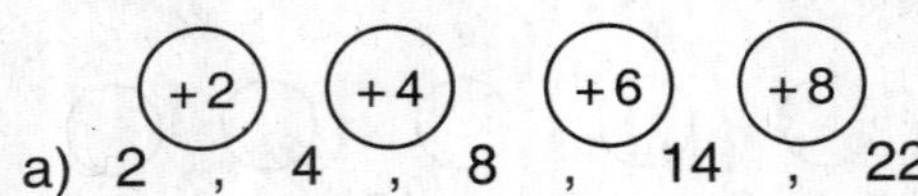

a) 2 , 4 , 8 , 14 , 22

Rule: Start at 2. Add 2, 4, 6 ... (the step increases by 2).

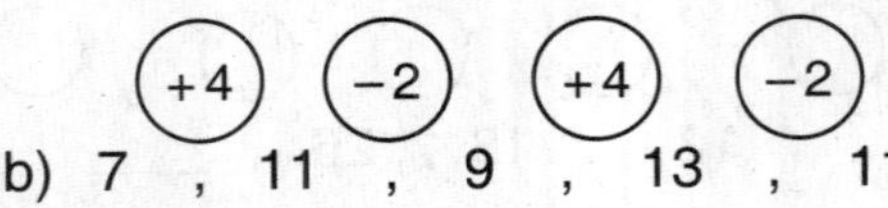

b) 7 , 11 , 9 , 13 , 11

Rule : Start at 7. Add 4, then subtract 2. Repeat.

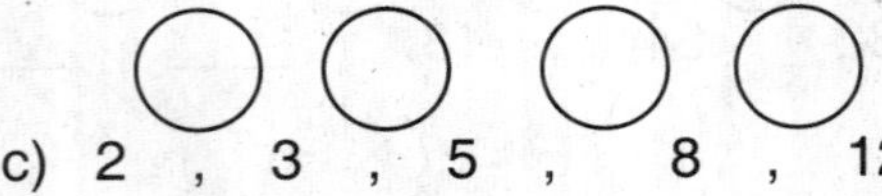

c) 2 , 3 , 5 , 8 , 12

Rule: __________

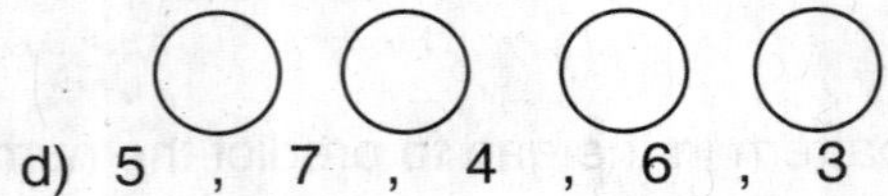

d) 5 , 7 , 4 , 6 , 3

Rule: __________

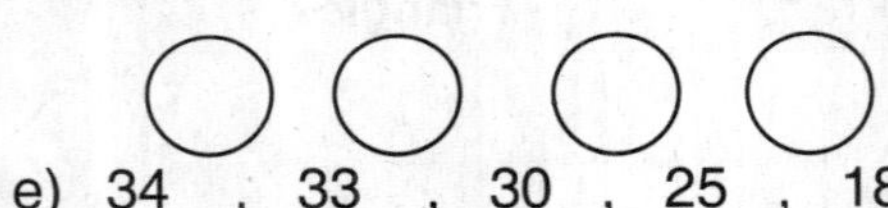

e) 34 , 33 , 30 , 25 , 18

Rule: __________

5. Write a rule for each pattern.
HINT: Two of these patterns were made by increasing the step in a regular way, and two were made by multiplication.

a) 2 , 5 , 10 , 17 b) 2 , 4 , 8 , 16 c) 1 , 3 , 9 , 27 d) 4 , 6 , 10 , 16

6. Write the number of shaded squares or triangles in each figure. Write a rule for the pattern. Use your rule to predict the number of shaded parts in the 5th figure.
HINT: To count the number of triangles in the last figure in b), try skip counting by 3s.

a)

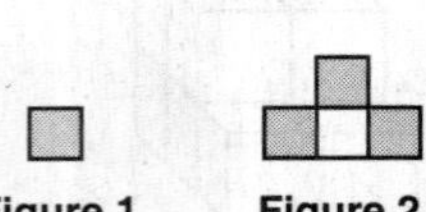

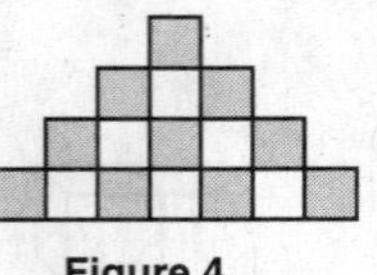

Figure 1 Figure 2 Figure 3 Figure 4

b)

Figure 1 Figure 2 Figure 3 Figure 4

7. Create a pattern with a step that increases and decreases.

PA6-20: Advanced Patterns

Answer the following questions in your notebook.

1. The dots show how many people can sit along each side of a table.

Number of Tables	Number of People

   a) Draw a picture to show how many people could sit at 4 and 5 tables. Then, fill in the T-table.

   b) Describe the pattern in the number of people. How does the step change?

   c) Extend the pattern to find out how many people could sit at 8 tables.

2. a) The Ancient Greeks investigated numbers that could be arranged in geometric shapes.

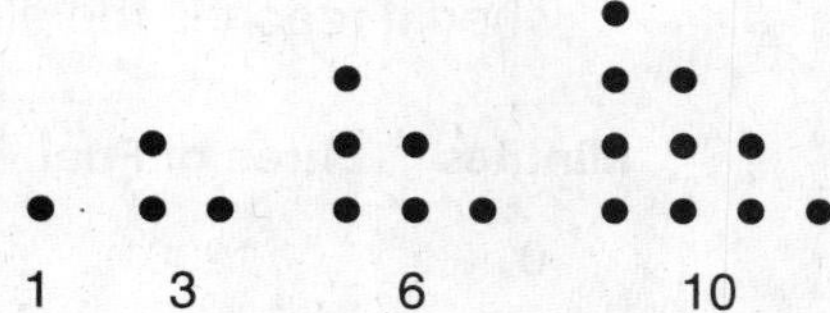

The first four **triangular** numbers are shown here to the left.

   i) Find the 5th and 6th triangular numbers by drawing a picture.

   ii) Describe the pattern in the triangular numbers. How does the step change?

   iii) Find the 8th triangular number by extending the pattern you found in ii).

   b) Repeat steps i) to iii) with the **square** numbers.

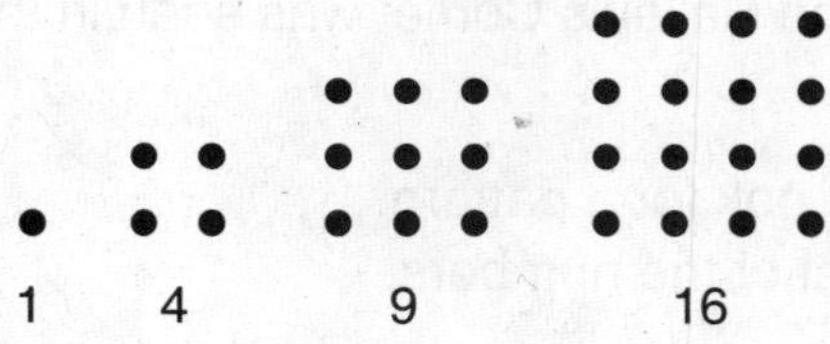

3. One of the most famous sequences in mathematics is the **Fibonacci sequence**, shown below.

   a) Find the gap between terms, then use the pattern in the gap to continue the sequence.

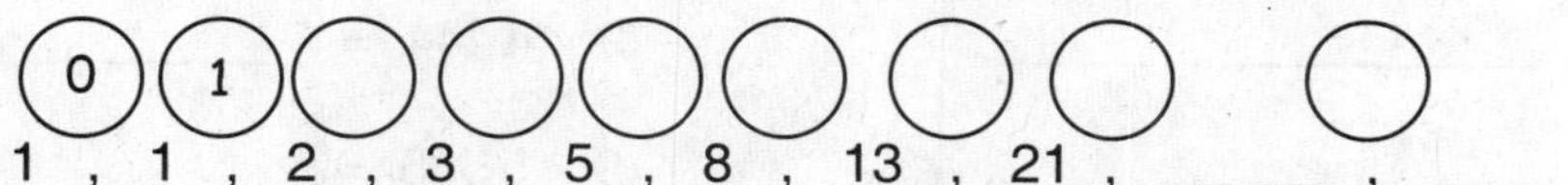

   b) What pattern do you see in the number of odd and even numbers in the Fibonacci sequence?

   c) Sum the first 4 odd Fibonacci numbers. Then sum the first 2 even numbers. What do you notice?

   d) Sum the first six odd Fibonacci numbers and the first three even numbers. What to you notice?

PA6-21: Patterns with Larger Numbers

1. Use addition or multiplication to complete the following charts.

a)

Years	Weeks
1	52
2	
3	
4	

b)

Years	Days
1	365
2	
3	

c)

Hours	Seconds
1	3600
2	
3	
4	

2. Water drains from two tanks at the rate shown in the chart below. Describe the pattern in the numbers in each column.

Which tank do you think will empty first?

Minutes	Tank 1	Tank 2
1	500 L	500 L
2	460 L	490 L
3	420 L	470 L
4	380 L	440 L

3. a) How much fuel will be left in the airplane after 25 minutes?

b) How far from the airport will the plane be after 30 minutes?

c) How much fuel will be left in the airplane when it reaches the airport?

Minutes	Litres of Fuel	km from Airport
0	1200	525
5	1150	450
10	1100	375

4. 

Halley's Comet returns to Earth every 76 years. It was last seen in 1986.

a) How many times will the comet be seen in the 2000s?

b) When was the first time Halley's Comet was seen in the 1900s?

5. Use multiplication to find the first few products. Look for a pattern. Use the pattern you've described to fill in the rest of the numbers.

a)

$37 \times 3 =$ ____________

$37 \times 6 =$ ____________

$37 \times 9 =$ ____________

$37 \times 12 =$ ____________

__________ = ____________

b)

$9 \times 2222 =$ ____________

$9 \times 3333 =$ ____________

$9 \times 4444 =$ ____________

$9 \times 5555 =$ ____________

__________ = ____________

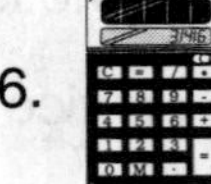

6. Using a calculator, can you discover any patterns like the ones in Question 5?

PA6-22: Equations

1. In a word problem an empty box can stand for an unknown quantity.
   Find the missing number in each problem and write it in the box.

a)
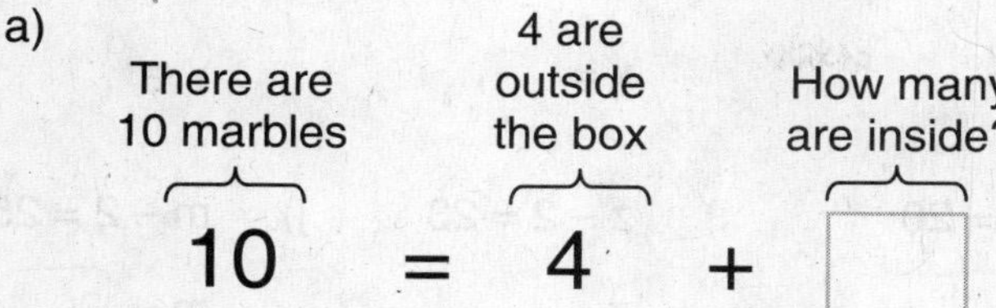
There are 10 marbles
4 are outside the box
How many are inside?
10 = 4 + □

b)
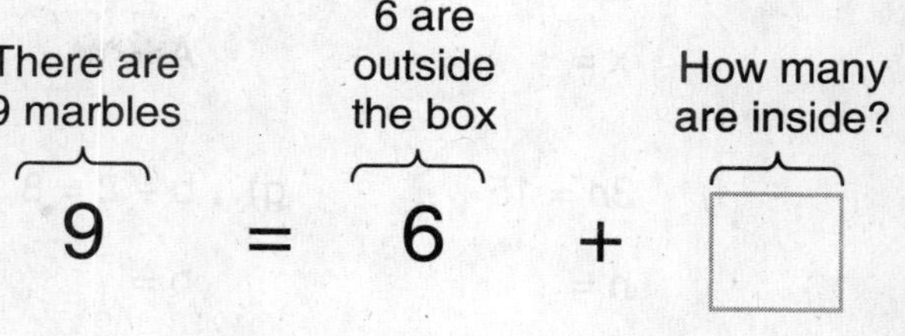
There are 9 marbles
6 are outside the box
How many are inside?
9 = 6 + □

c)
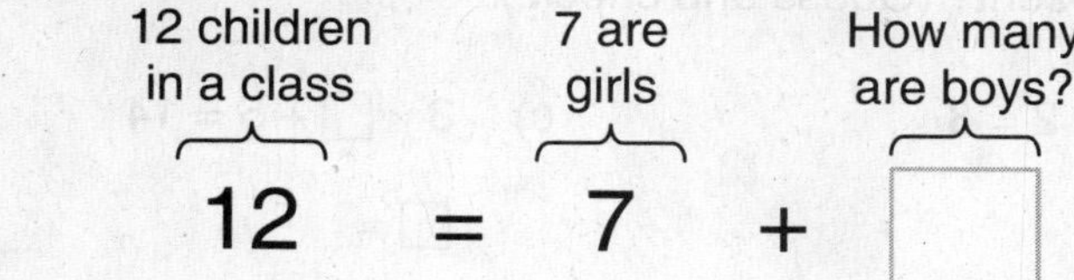
There are 12 children in a class
7 are girls
How many are boys?
12 = 7 + □

d) A cat had 7 kittens; 4 kittens are boys; How many are girls?

$7 = 4 + \square$

e)
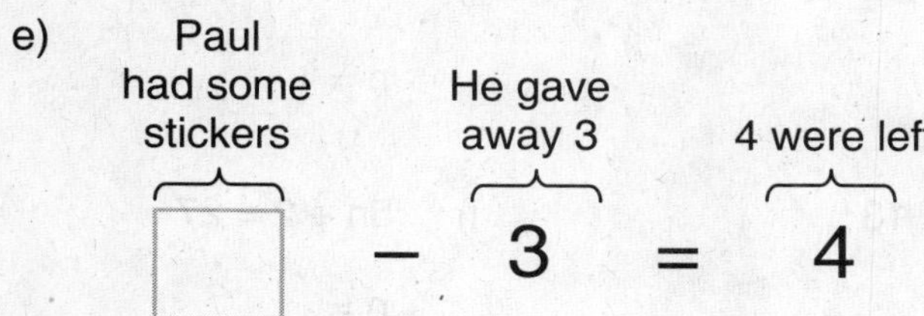
Paul had some stickers
He gave away 3
4 were left
□ − 3 = 4

f)
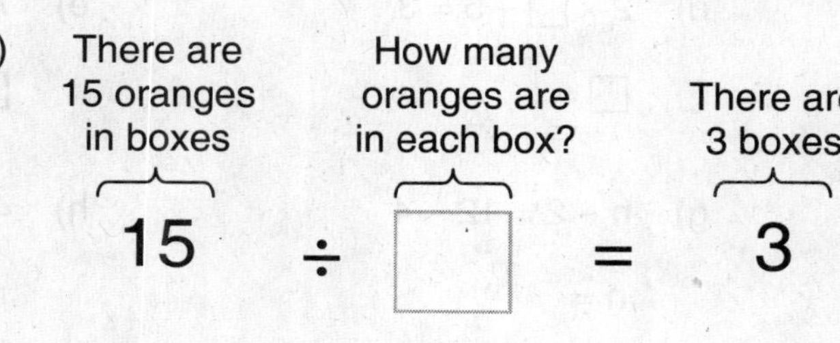
There are 15 oranges in boxes
How many oranges are in each box?
There are 3 boxes
15 ÷ □ = 3

2. Find the number that makes each equation true (by guessing and checking) and write it in the box.

a) $\square + 4 = 7$ b) $\square + 3 = 6$ c) $\square + 5 = 9$

d) $9 - \square = 6$ e) $17 - \square = 13$ f) $11 - \square = 9$

g) $2 \times \square = 6$ h) $5 \times \square = 15$ i) $3 \times \square = 9$

j) $\square \div 2 = 4$ k) $\square \div 5 = 3$ l) $\square \div 3 = 4$

m) $5 + 4 = 6 + \square$ n) $10 - 4 = \square + 5$ o) $\square + \square + 2 = 8$

3. Find two different answers for the following equation:

$\square + \square + \bigcirc = 5$ $\square + \square + \bigcirc = 5$

4. How many answers can you find for the equation: $\square + \square + \bigcirc = 9$?

PA6-23: Equations (Advanced)

1. What number does the letter represent?

a) $x + 3 = 9$ $x =$ ☐

b) $A - 3 = 5$ $A =$ ☐

c) $n + 5 = 11$ $n =$ ☐

d) $6x = 18$ $x =$ ☐

e) $y + 5 = 17$ $y =$ ☐

f) $3n = 15$ $n =$ ☐

g) $b \div 2 = 8$ $b =$ ☐

h) $4x = 20$ $x =$ ☐

i) $z - 2 = 23$ $z =$ ☐

j) $m - 2 = 25$ $m =$ ☐

2. What number does the box or the letter "n" represent? (Guess and check.)

a) $2 \times \square + 3 = 9$ $\square =$ ☐

b) $5 \times \square - 2 = 8$ $\square =$ ☐

c) $3 \times \square + 5 = 14$ $\square =$ ☐

d) $2 \times \square - 5 = 3$ $\square =$ ☐

e) $7 \times \square + 2 = 16$ $\square =$ ☐

f) $n + 5 = 4 + 10$ $n =$ ☐

g) $n - 2 = 12 - 4$ $n =$ ☐

h) $4n + 1 = 13$ $n =$ ☐

i) $5n + 2 = 27$ $n =$ ☐

3. Find x.

a) $x + x = 8$ $x =$ ______

b) $x + x + x = 12$ $x =$ ______

c) $x + x + x = 24$ $x =$ ______

4. Find all values of a and b (that are whole numbers) that make the equation true.

a) $a + b = 6$

b) $a \times b = 6$

c) $6 - a = b$

5. If $2a + 6 = 12$ and $2b + 6 = 14$, explain why b must be greater than a.

6. Write 3 different equations with solution 5.

7.

A	A	A	12
A	B	B	14
A	B	C	10

The shaded column shows the total of each row.

For instance $A + A + A = 12$

Find A, B, and C.

PA6-24: Variables

A **variable** is a letter or symbol (such as **x**, **n**, or **h**) that represents a number.

In the product of a number and a variable, the multiplication sign is usually dropped.

$3 \times T$ is written $3T$, and $5 \times z$ is written $5z$.

1. Write a numerical expression for the cost of renting a kayak …

Rent a kayak
$5 for each hour

a) 2 hours: 5 x 2 = 10 b) 4 hours: ________ c) 7 hours: ________

2. Write an expression for the distance a car would travel at …

a) Speed: 70 km per hour
Time: 3 hours
Distance: ________ km

b) Speed: 40 km per hour
Time: 2 hours
Distance: ________ km

c) Speed: 100 km per hour
Time: h hours
Distance: ________ km

3. Write an algebraic expression for the cost of renting a sailboat for …

Rent a sailboat
$7 per hour

a) h hours: ______ or ______ b) t hours: ______ or ______

c) x hours: ______ or ______ d) n hours: ______ or ______

4. Write an equation that tells you the relationship between the numbers in column A and column B.

a)

A	B
1	5
2	6
3	7

A + 3 = B

b)

A	B
1	3
2	6
3	9

2 × A = B

c)

A	B
1	8
2	9
3	10

____

d)

A	B
1	5
2	10
3	15

____

e)

A	B
1	8
2	16
3	24

____

5. Replace the letter in x in x + 5 = 9 with any other letter. Does the equation still give the same solution? Explain.

6. Write an equation for each problem. (Use a variable for the unknown)

a) In a class of 28 students, 15 are girls. How many students are boys?

b) Ramona had 48 stamps but gave some away. She kept 24. How many did she give away?

PA6-25: Graphs

1. For each set of points, write a list of ordered pairs, and then complete the T-table.

a)

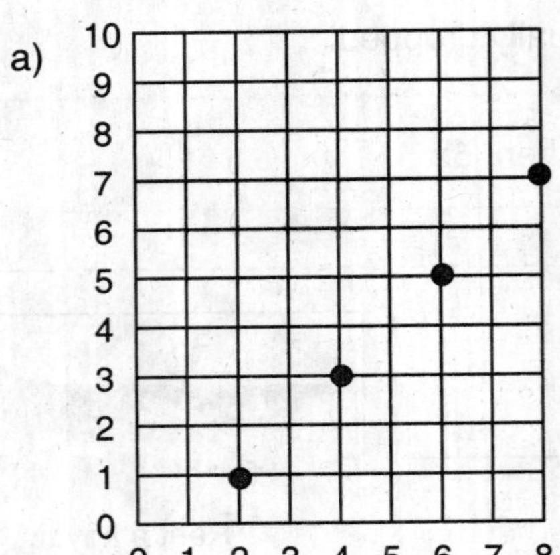

b)

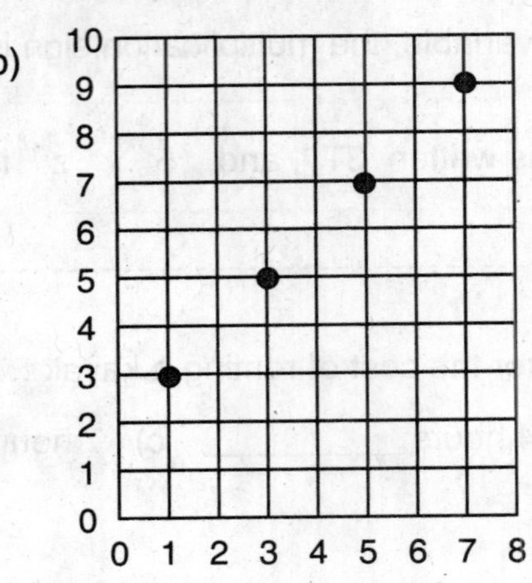

c)

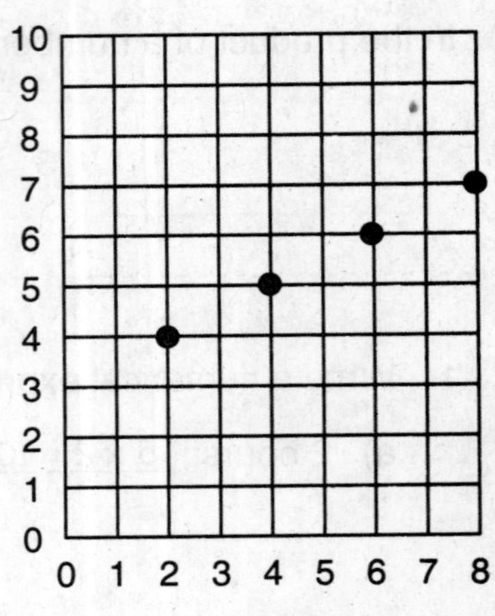

a)

Ordered Pairs	First Number	Second Number
(2 , 1)	2	1
(,)		
(,)		
(,)		

b)

Ordered Pairs	First Number	Second Number
(,)		
(,)		
(,)		
(,)		

c)

Ordered Pairs	First Number	Second Number
(,)		
(,)		
(,)		
(,)		

2. Mark four points on the line segments. Then write a list of ordered pairs, and complete the T-table.

a)

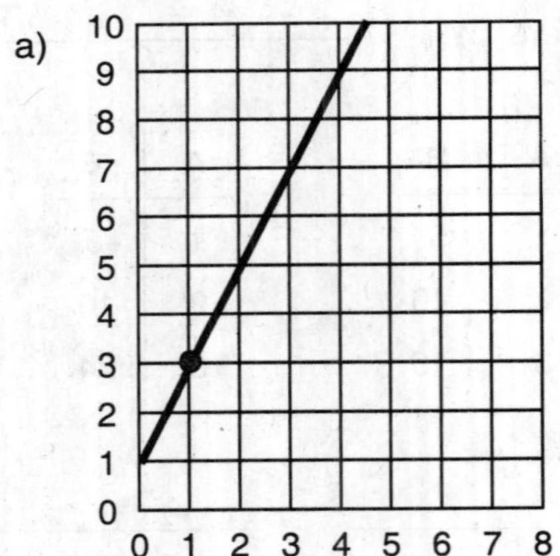

b)

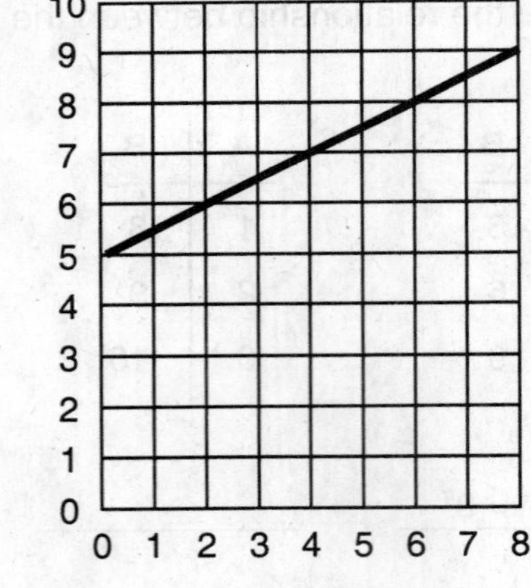

c)

a)

Ordered Pairs	First Number	Second Number
(1 , 3)	1	3
(,)		
(,)		
(,)		

b)

Ordered Pairs	First Number	Second Number
(,)		
(,)		
(,)		
(,)		

c)

Ordered Pairs	First Number	Second Number
(,)		
(,)		
(,)		
(,)		

3. Write a list of ordered pairs based on the T-table provided. Mark the ordered pairs on the graph and connect the points to form a line.

First Number	Second Number	
3	1	(,)
4	3	(,)
5	5	(,)
6	7	(,)

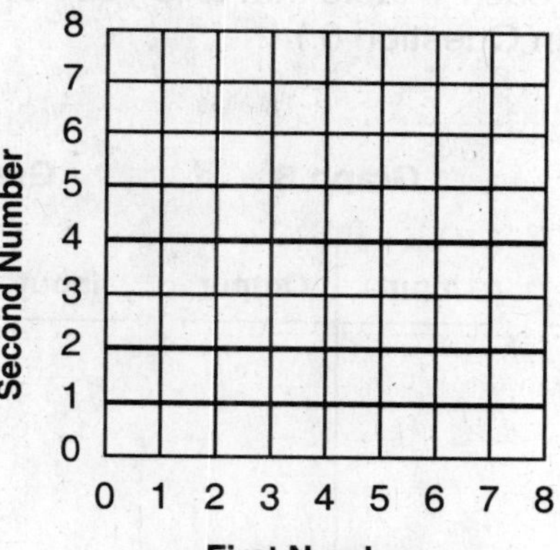

4. Draw a graph for each T-table (as in Question 3).
NOTE: Make sure you look carefully at the scale in part d).

a)

Input	Output
2	5
4	6
6	7
8	8

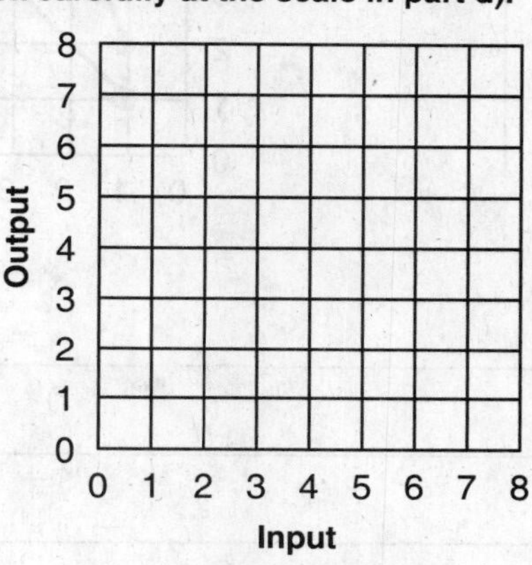

b)

Input	Output
1	7
2	6
3	5
4	4

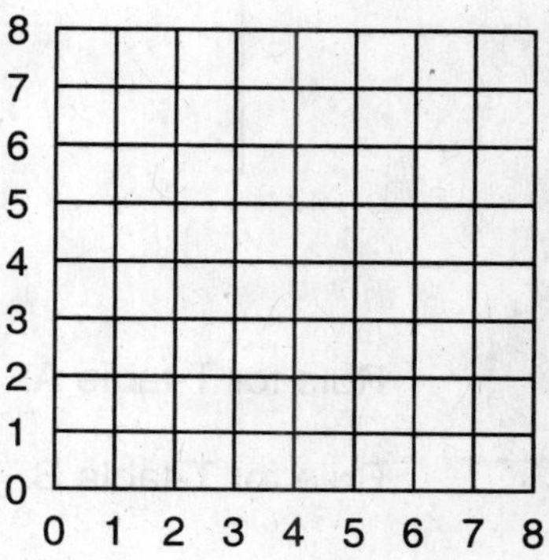

BONUS

c)

Input	Output
2	4
4	8
6	12
8	16

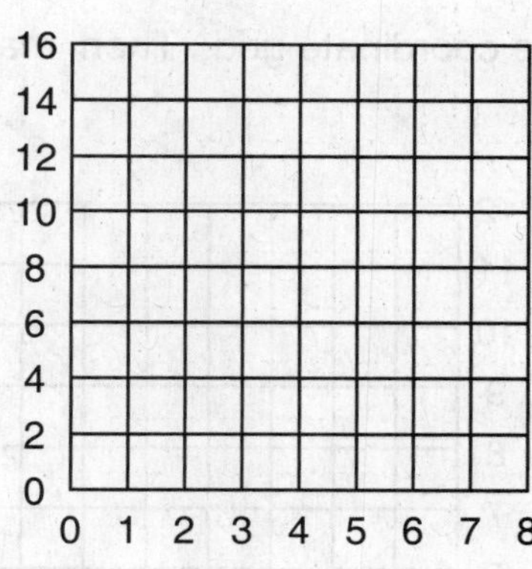

d)

Input	Output
1	6
3	8
5	10
7	12

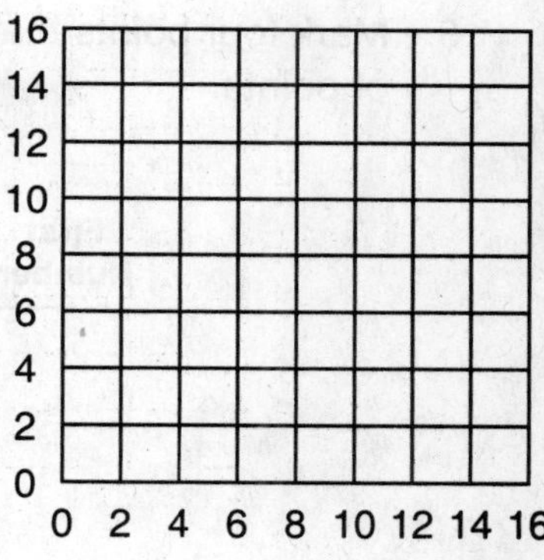

5. Draw a coordinate grid (like those above) on grid paper and plot the following ordered pairs: (1 , 2), (3 , 5), (5 , 8), and (7 , 11).

6. On grid paper, make a T-table and graph for the following rules.
   a) Multiply by 2 and subtract 1
   b) Multiply by 4 and subtract 3
   c) Divide by 2 and add 3

PA6-25: Graphs *(continued)*

7. Make a T-table for each set of points on the coordinate grid.
Write a rule for each T-table that tells you how to calculate the output from the input.
(See the rules in Question 6.)

Graph A

Input	Output

Graph B

Input	Output

Graph C

Input	Output

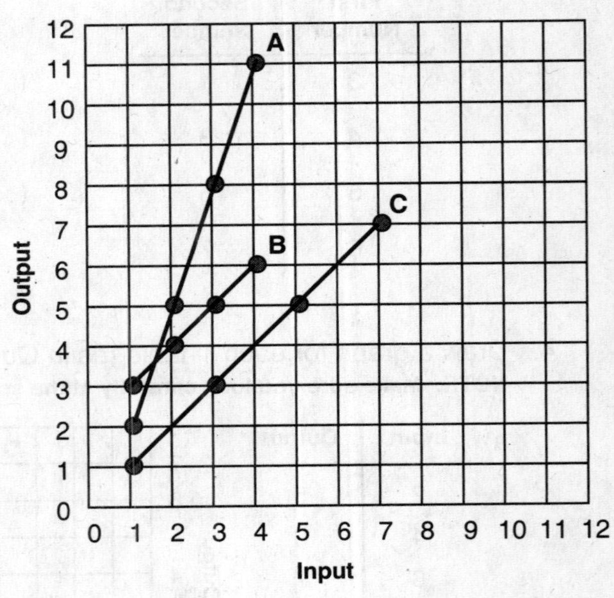

Rule for T-table A: ______________________________

Rule for T-table B: ______________________________

Rule for T-table C: ______________________________

8. Mark four points that lie on a straight line in the coordinate grid. Then, make a T-table for your set of points.

First Number	Second Number

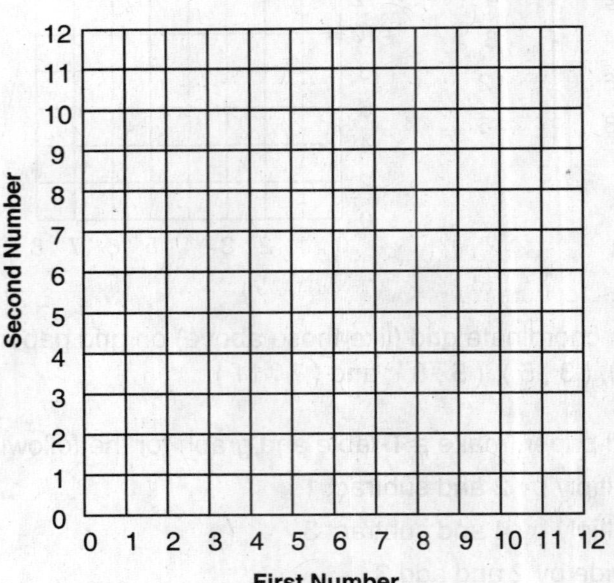

PA6-26: Interpreting Graphs (Advanced)

Answer these questions in your notebook.

1.

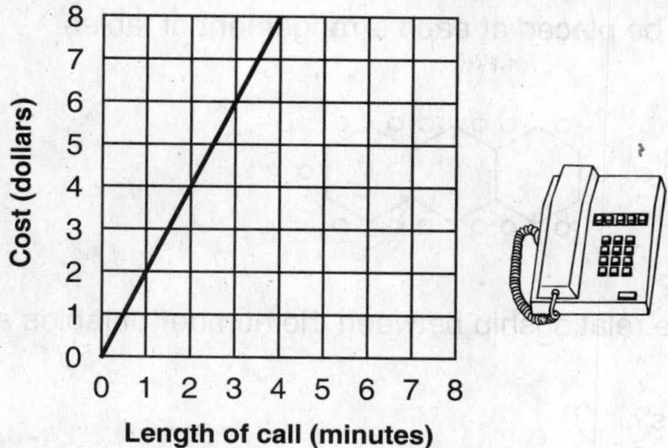

The graph shows the cost of making a long distance telephone call.

a) If you talked for 2 minutes, how much would you pay?

b) What is the cost for a minute call?

c) How much would you pay to talk for 10 minutes?

d) If you paid 6 dollars, how long would you be able to talk for?

e) How much would you pay to talk for 30 seconds?

2.

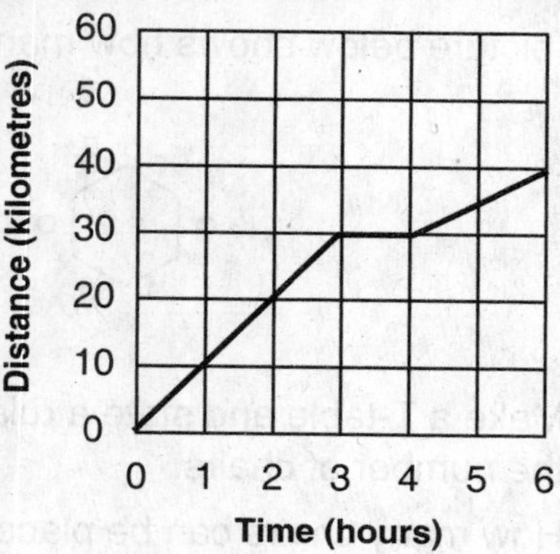

The graph shows the distance Kathy travelled on a cycling trip.

a) How far had Kathy cycled after 2 hours?

b) How far had Kathy travelled after 6 hours?

c) Did Kathy rest at all on her trip? How do you know?

d) When she was cycling, did Kathy always travel at the same speed?

3.

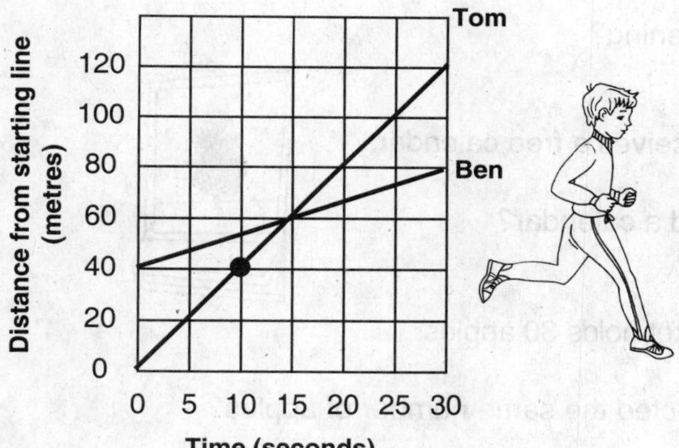

Ben and Tom run a 120 m race.

a) How far from the start was Tom after 10 seconds?

b) How far from the start was Ben after 15 seconds?

c) Who won the race? By how much?

d) How much of a head start did Ben have?

e) How many seconds from the start did Tom overtake Ben?

4.

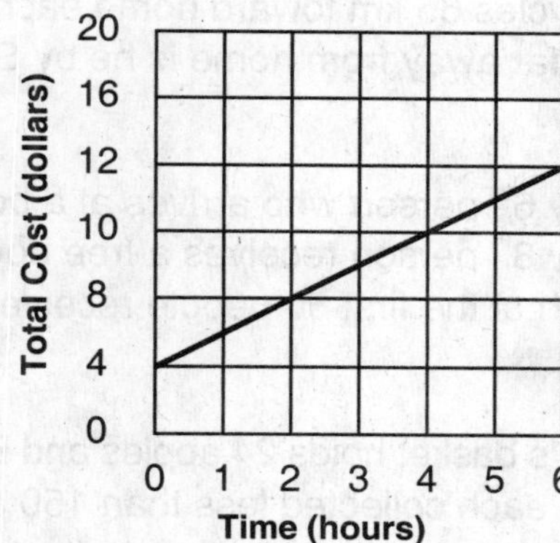

The graph shows the cost of renting a bike from Mike's store.

a) How much would you pay to rent the bike for:
i) 2 hours? ii) 4 hours? iii) 3 hours?

b) How much do you pay for the bike before you have even ridden it?

c) Dave's store charges $3.50 an hour for a bike. Whose store would you rent from if you wanted the bike for 3 hours? Explain.

PA6-27: Problems and Puzzles

Answer the following questions in your notebook.

1. The picture below shows how many chairs can be placed at each arrangement of tables.

   a) Make a T-table and state a rule that tells the relationship between the number of tables and the number of chairs.

   b) How many chairs can be placed at 12 tables?

2. Andy has $10 in his bank account.
   He saves 25 dollars each month.
   How much does he have in his account after 10 months?

3. A recipe calls for 5 cups of flour for every 6 cups of water.
   How many cups of water will be needed for 25 cups of flour?

4. Raymond is 400 km from home on Wednesday morning.
   He cycles 65 km toward home each day.
   How far away from home is he by Saturday evening?

5. Every 6th person who arrives at a book sale receives a free calendar.
   Every 8th person receives a free book.
   Which of the first 50 people receive a book and a calendar?

6. Anna's basket holds 24 apples and Emily's basket holds 30 apples.
   They each collected less than 150 apples.
   How many baskets did they collect if they collected the same number of apples?

7. a) How many shaded squares will be on the perimeter of the 10th figure? How do you know?

   b) How many white squares will be in a figure that has a shaded perimeter of 32 squares?

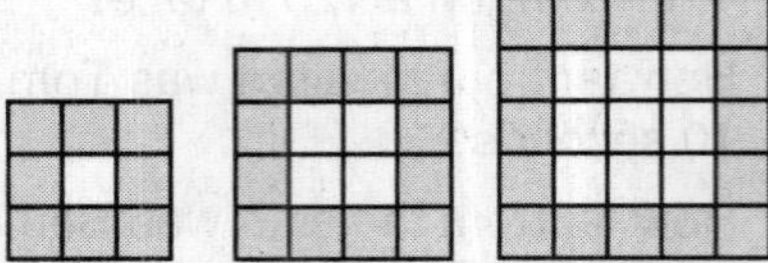

8. Gerome wants to rent a hockey rink for 6 hours. Which is the cheapest way to rent the rink:
   (i) pay a fee of $60 for the first hour and $35 for each hour after that? or (ii) pay $45 each hour?

PA6-27: Problems and Puzzles *(continued)*

9. What strategy would you use to find the 72nd shape in this pattern? What is the shape?

10. Paul shovelled sidewalks for 4 days.
Each day, he shovelled 3 more sidewalks than the day before.
He shovelled 30 sidewalks altogether.
How many sidewalks did he shovel on each of the days? **Guess and check!**

11. Make a chart with three columns to show:
   - the number of edges along a side of the figure,
   - the number of small triangles in the figure,
   - the perimeter of the figure.

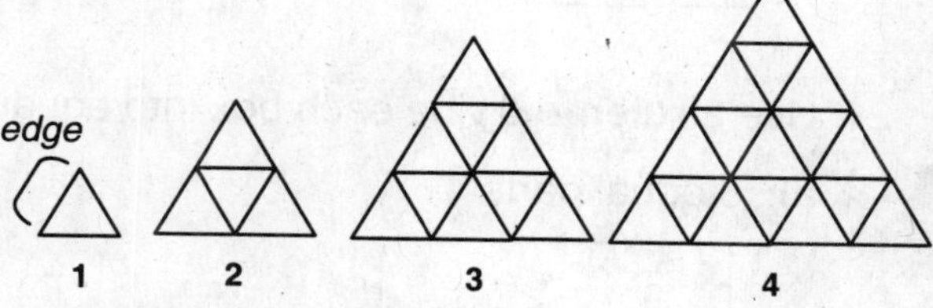

Describe the pattern in each column and any relationships between the columns of the chart.

12. The picture shows how the temperature changes at different heights over a mountain.

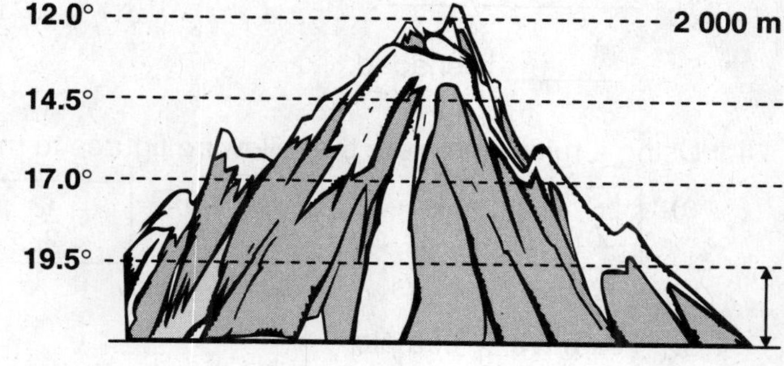

a) Does the temperature increase or decrease at greater heights?

b) What distance does the arrow represent in real life?

c) Measure the length of the arrow. What is the scale of the picture?

d) Do the numbers in the sequence of temperatures decrease by the same amount each time?

e) If the pattern in the temperature continued, what would the temperature be at:
(i) 3000 m? (ii) 4000 m?

13. Marlene says she will need 27 blocks to make Figure 7.
Is she right?
Explain.

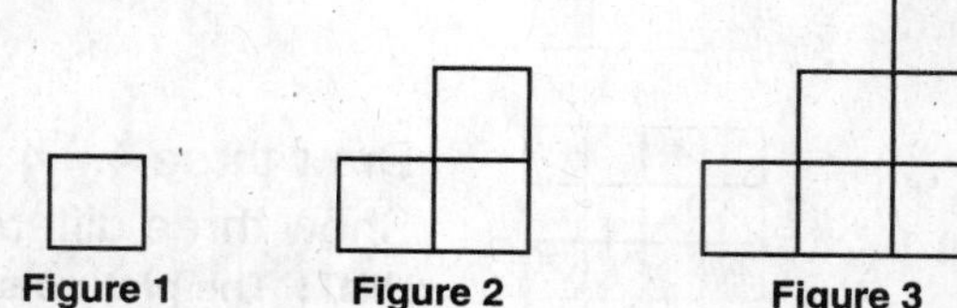

NS6-44: Equal Parts and Models of Fractions

Fractions name equal parts of a whole.

The pie is cut into 4 equal parts. 3 parts out of 4 are shaded.

$\frac{3}{4}$ of a pie is shaded.

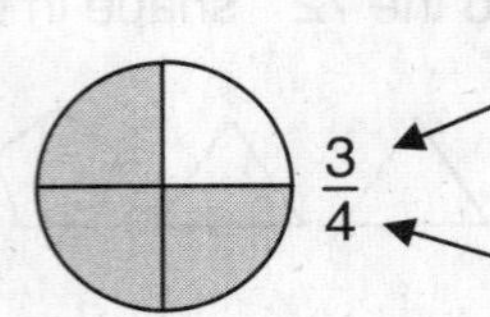

The **numerator** (3) tells you how many parts are counted.

The **denominator** (4) tells you how many parts are in a whole.

---

1. Name the following fractions.

a) 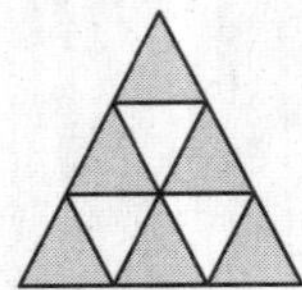
b) 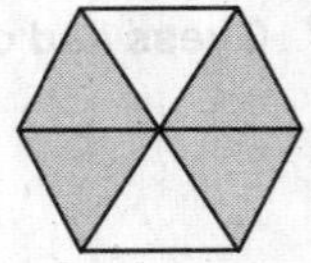
c) 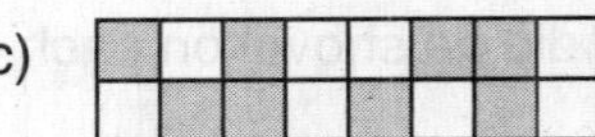
d) 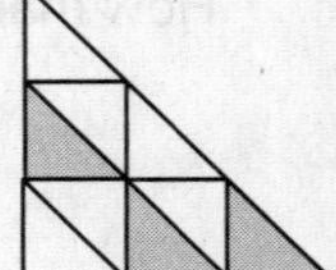

2. Use a **ruler** to divide each box into equal parts.

a) 3 equal parts

b) 10 equal parts

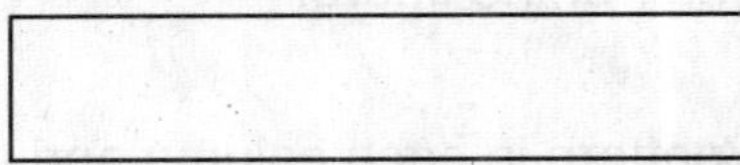

3. Using a **ruler**, find what fraction of each of the following boxes is shaded.

a) 

_________ is shaded.

b) 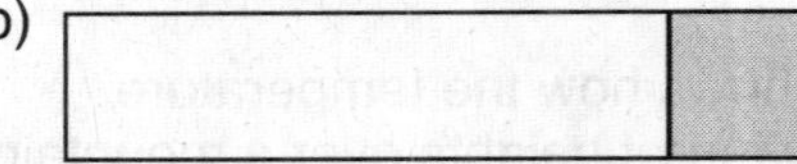

_________ is shaded.

4. Using a ruler, complete the following figures to make a whole.

a) $\frac{1}{4}$

b) 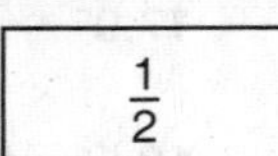

$\frac{1}{2}$

c) 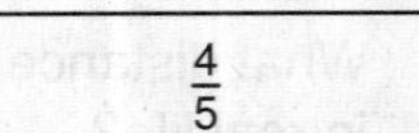

$\frac{4}{5}$

5. You have $\frac{5}{8}$ of a pie.

a) What does the bottom (denominator) of the fraction tell you?

b) What does the top (numerator) of the fraction tell you?

6. In your notebook explain why each picture does or does not show $\frac{1}{4}$.

a) 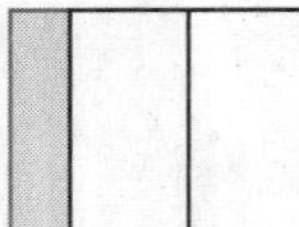
b) 
c) 
d) 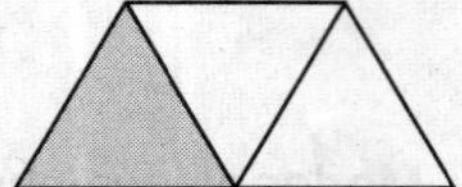

7. 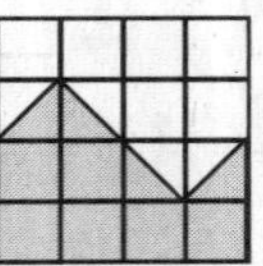

Draw three 4 × 4 grids on grid paper.
Show three different ways to shade half of the grid.
HINT: The picture shows one way.

NS6-45: Equal Parts of a Set

Fractions can name parts of a set: $\frac{3}{5}$ of the figures are pentagons, $\frac{1}{5}$ are squares and $\frac{1}{5}$ are circles.

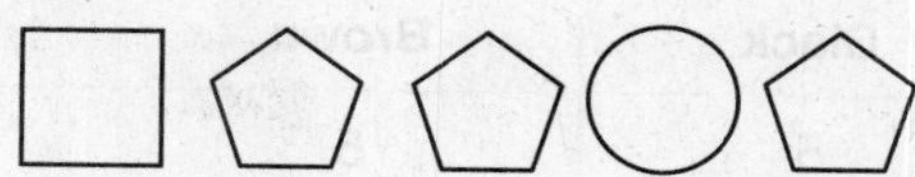

1. Fill in the blanks.

a) 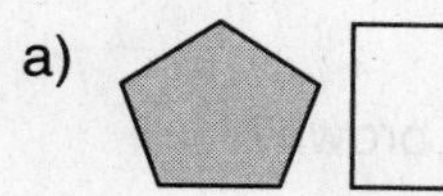 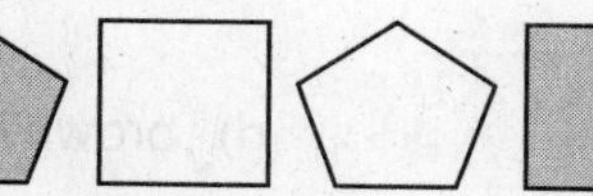 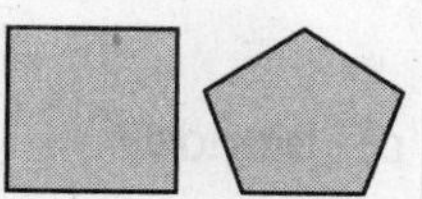

b)  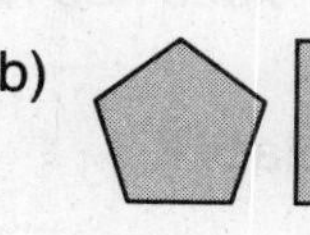 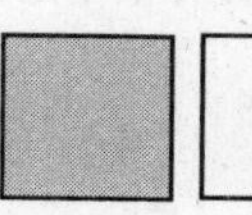 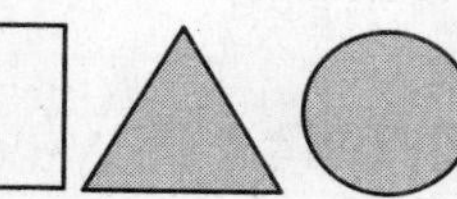

a) ______ of the figures are pentagons.

______ of the figures are shaded.

b) ______ of the figures are squares.

______ of the figures are shaded.

2. Fill in the blanks. 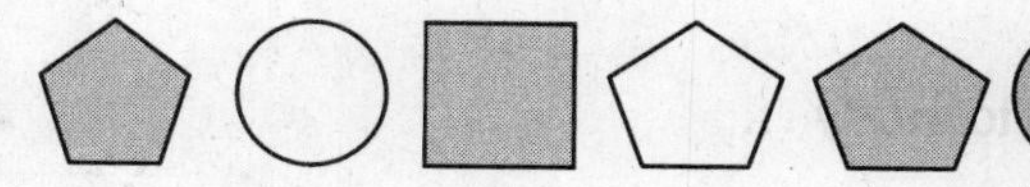

a) $\frac{4}{7}$ of the figures are ______________

b) $\frac{2}{7}$ of the figures are ______________

c) $\frac{1}{7}$ of the figures are ______________

d) $\frac{5}{7}$ of the figures are ______________

3. 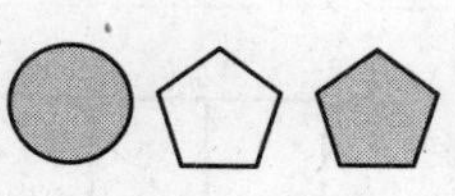 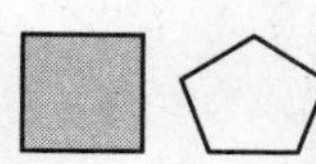 Describe this picture in two different ways using the fraction $\frac{3}{5}$.

4. A hockey team wins 6 games, loses 4 games, and ties one game.
What fraction of the games did the team ...

a) win? ______ b) lose? ______ c) tie? ______

5. A box contains 2 blue marbles, 3 red marbles, and 4 yellow marbles.

What fraction of the marbles are **not** blue? ______________

6. The chart shows the number of children with each given hair colour in a class.

Hair Colour	Black	Brown	Red	Blonde
Number of Children	5	5	1	3

What fraction of children in the class has hair that is ...

a) red? b) black? c) blonde? d) brown? 

7. There are 23 children in a class.
Each child chose to do a science project on animals or on plants.
The chart shows the number who chose each topic.

a) Fill in the missing numbers in the chart.

b) What fraction of the children chose to study ...

animals? plants? 

c) What fraction of the girls chose to study ...

animals? plants? 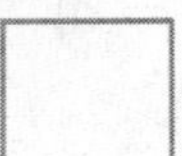

	Animals	Plants
Boys	7	4
Girls		
Children	12	

8. What fraction of the **squares** are on the **outside** of the figure? ______________

9. Write a **fraction** for each statement below.

 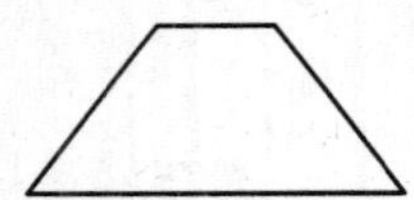 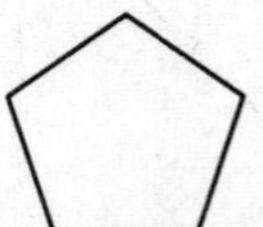 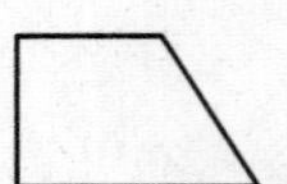 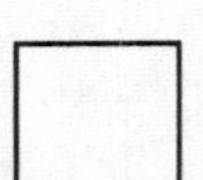 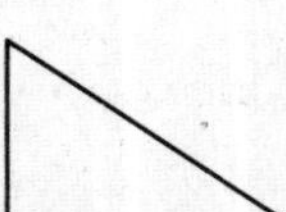 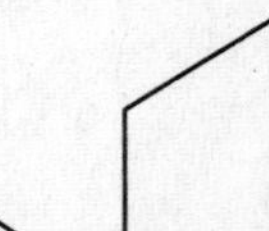

a) ☐ of the figures are pentagons.

b) ☐ of the figures have 4 vertices.

c) ☐ of the figures have exactly 2 right angles.

d) ☐ of the figures have exactly 1 pair of parallel sides.

10. Write two fractions statements for the figures in Question 9 above. Justify your answer.

NS6-46: Parts and Wholes

1. 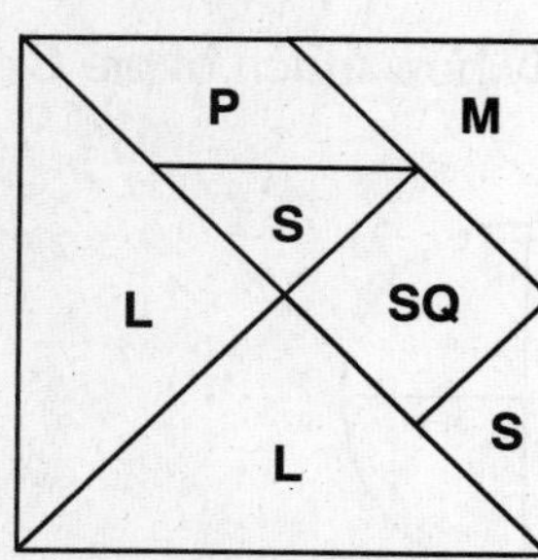

In a tangram ...

- 2 small triangles (**S**) cover a medium triangle (**M**)
- 2 small triangles (**S**) cover a square (**SQ**)
- 2 small triangles (**S**) cover a parallelogram (**P**)
- 4 small triangles (**S**) cover a large triangle (**L**)

What fraction of each shape is covered by a single small triangle?

a) 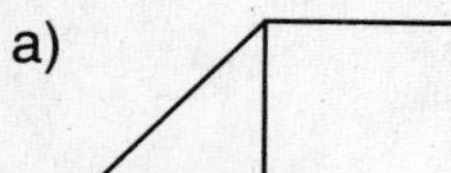

b) 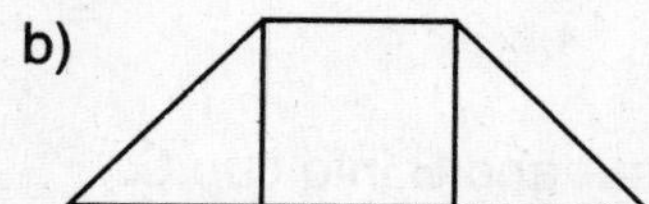

c) 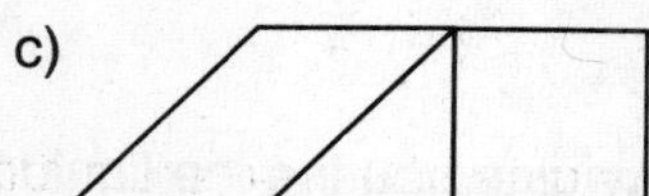

d) 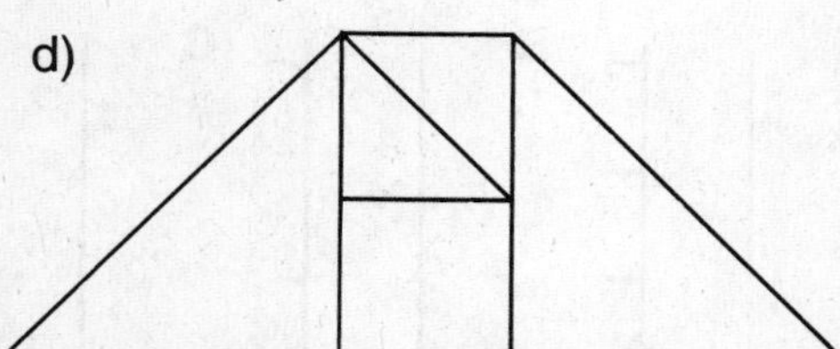

e) 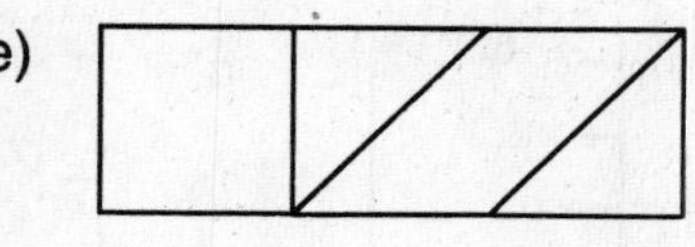

f) 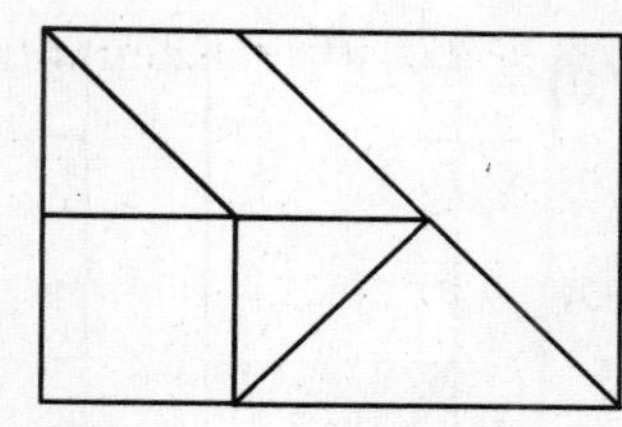

2. What fraction of each shape is shaded? Explain how you know.

a) 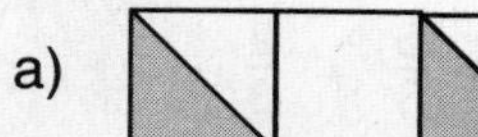

b) 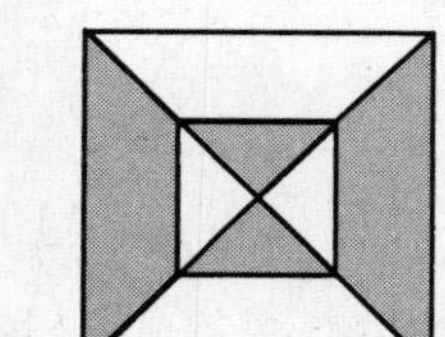

c) 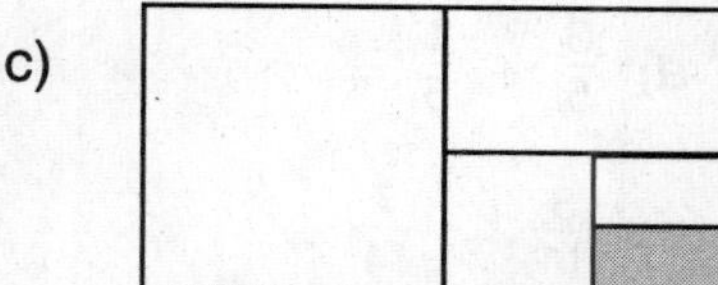

3. What fraction of the trapezoid is covered by a single small triangle?

Show your work.

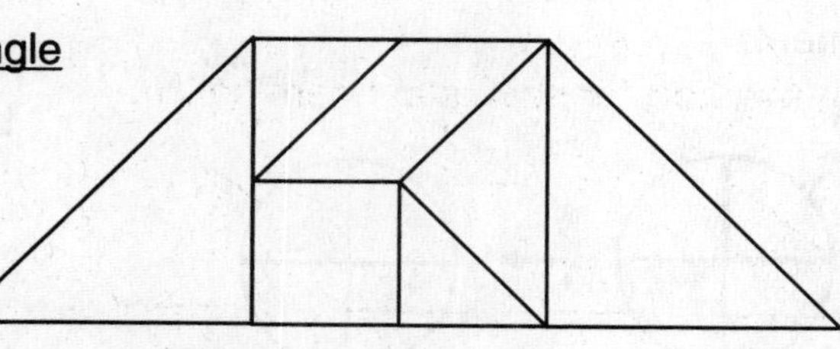

4. If  = red and ▒ = blue, approximately what fraction of each flag is shaded red? Explain.

a) 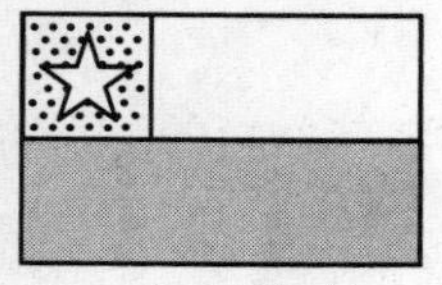

CHILE

b) 

CANADA

c) 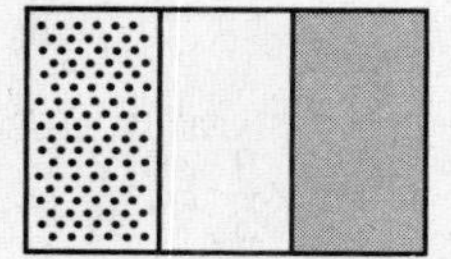

FRANCE

d) 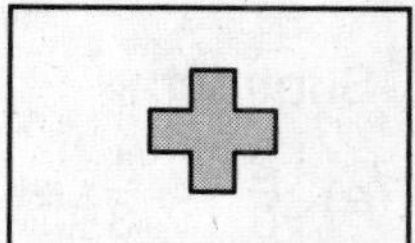

SWITZERLAND

NS6-47: Adding and Subtracting Fractions

1. Imagine moving the shaded pieces from pies A and B into pie plate C. Show how much of pie C would be filled and then write a fraction for pie C.

A B C

$\frac{1}{4}$ + $\frac{2}{4}$ = ___

2. Imagine pouring the liquid from cups A and B into cup C. Shade the amount of liquid that would be in C. Then complete the addition statements.

a)

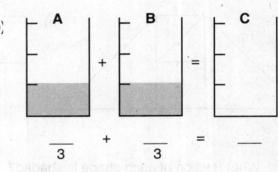

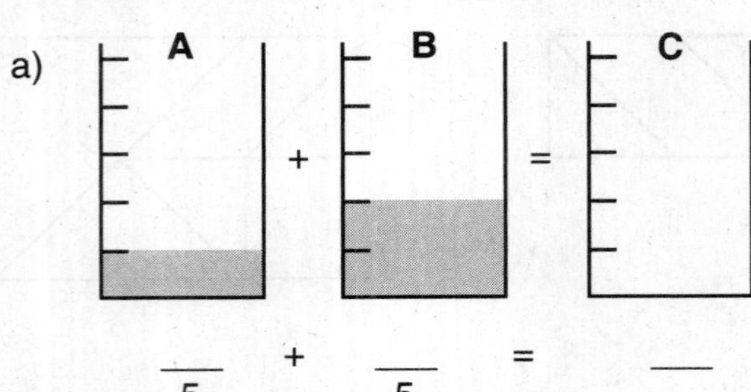

$\frac{\quad}{5}$ + $\frac{\quad}{5}$ = ___

b) A + B = C

$\frac{\quad}{3}$ + $\frac{\quad}{3}$ = ___

3. Add.

a) $\frac{3}{5} + \frac{1}{5} =$ b) $\frac{2}{4} + \frac{1}{4} =$ c) $\frac{3}{7} + \frac{2}{7} =$ d) $\frac{5}{8} + \frac{2}{8} =$

e) $\frac{3}{11} + \frac{7}{11} =$ f) $\frac{5}{17} + \frac{9}{17} =$ g) $\frac{11}{24} + \frac{10}{24} =$ h) $\frac{18}{57} + \frac{13}{57} =$

4. Show how much pie would be left if you took away the amount shown. Then complete the fraction statement.

a)

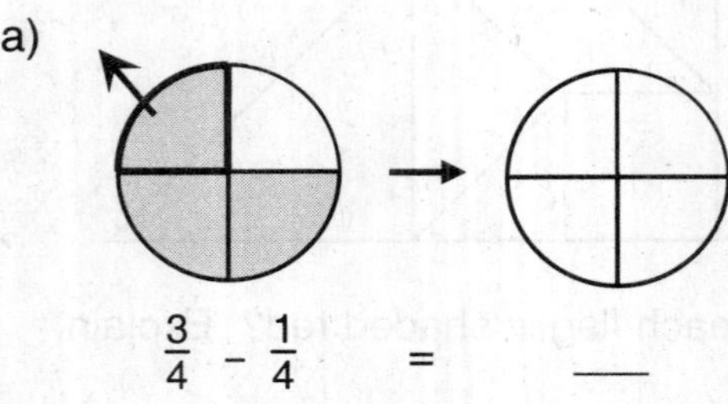

$\frac{3}{4} - \frac{1}{4}$ = ___

b)

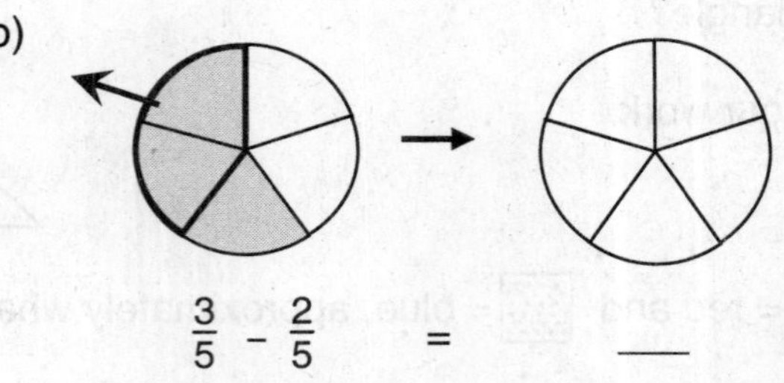

$\frac{3}{5} - \frac{2}{5}$ = ___

5. Subtract.

a) $\frac{2}{3} - \frac{1}{3} =$ b) $\frac{3}{5} - \frac{2}{5} =$ c) $\frac{6}{7} - \frac{3}{7} =$ d) $\frac{5}{8} - \frac{2}{8} =$

e) $\frac{9}{12} - \frac{2}{12} =$ f) $\frac{6}{19} - \frac{4}{19} =$ g) $\frac{9}{28} - \frac{3}{28} =$ h) $\frac{17}{57} - \frac{12}{57} =$

NS6-48: Ordering and Comparing Fractions

1. 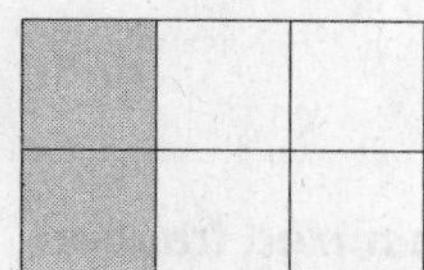 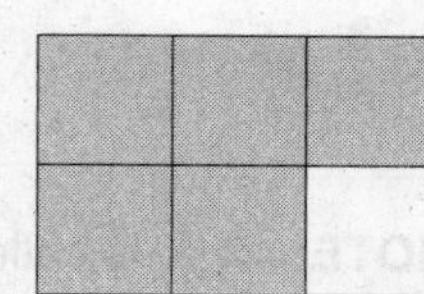

What fraction has a greater numerator, $\frac{2}{6}$ or $\frac{5}{6}$? ________

Which fraction is greater? ________

Explain your thinking: ____

____

2. Circle the greater fraction in each pair.

a) $\frac{5}{17}$ or $\frac{11}{17}$ b) $\frac{3}{17}$ or $\frac{4}{17}$ c) $\frac{11}{25}$ or $\frac{6}{25}$ d) $\frac{57}{115}$ or $\frac{43}{115}$

3. Two fractions have the same <u>denominators</u> (bottoms) but different <u>numerators</u> (tops). How can you tell which fraction is greater?

____

4. Write the fractions in order from least to greatest.

a) $\frac{4}{5}$, $\frac{1}{5}$, $\frac{3}{5}$ b) $\frac{9}{10}$, $\frac{2}{10}$, $\frac{1}{10}$, $\frac{5}{10}$

5. Circle the greater fraction in each pair.

a) $\frac{1}{7}$ or $\frac{1}{6}$ b) $\frac{8}{8}$ or $\frac{8}{9}$ c) $\frac{7}{300}$ or $\frac{7}{200}$

6. Fraction A and Fraction B have the same <u>numerators</u> (tops) but different <u>denominators</u> (bottoms). How can you tell which fraction is greater?

____

7. Write the fractions in order from least to greatest.

a) $\frac{1}{9}$, $\frac{1}{4}$, $\frac{1}{17}$ b) $\frac{2}{11}$, $\frac{2}{5}$, $\frac{2}{7}$, $\frac{2}{16}$ 

8. Circle the greater fraction in each pair.

a) $\frac{2}{3}$ or $\frac{2}{9}$ b) $\frac{7}{17}$ or $\frac{11}{17}$ c) $\frac{6}{288}$ or $\frac{6}{18}$

9. Which fraction is greater, $\frac{1}{2}$ or $\frac{1}{100}$? Explain your thinking.

10. Is it possible for $\frac{2}{3}$ of a pie to be bigger than $\frac{3}{4}$ of another pie? Show your thinking with a picture.

NS6-49: Mixed Fractions

William and Jessie ate three and three quarter pies altogether (or $3\frac{3}{4}$ pies).

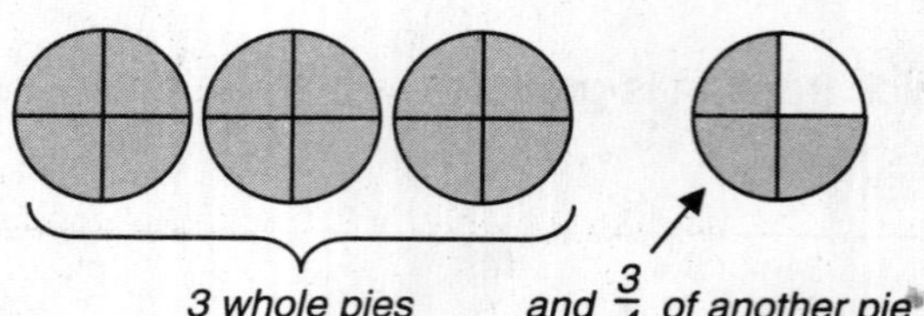

NOTE: $3\frac{3}{4}$ is called a **mixed fraction** because it is a mixture of a whole number and a fraction.

1. Write how many whole pies are shaded.

a) 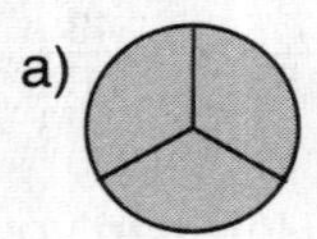 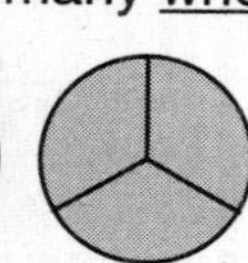 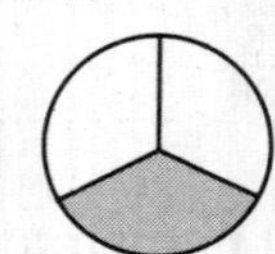

2 whole pies

b) 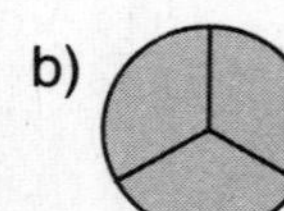 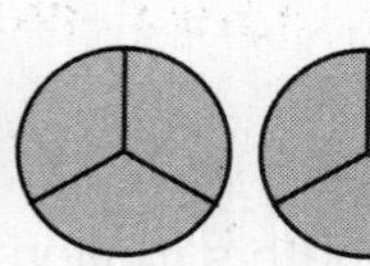 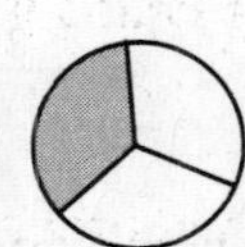

____ whole pies

c)  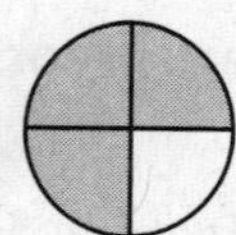

____ whole pie

2. Write each fraction as a mixed fraction.

a) 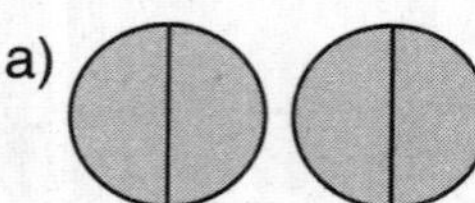 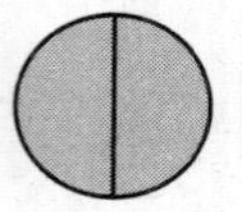 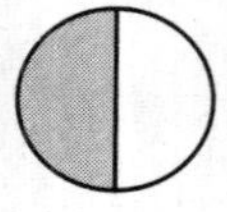 ____

b) 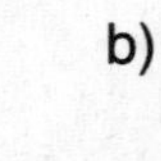 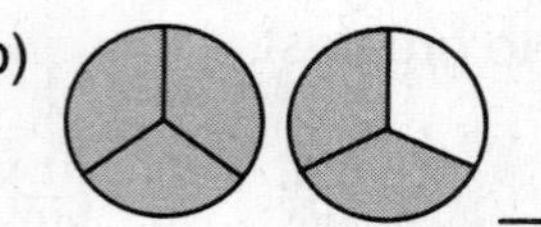 ____

c) 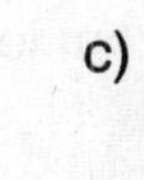 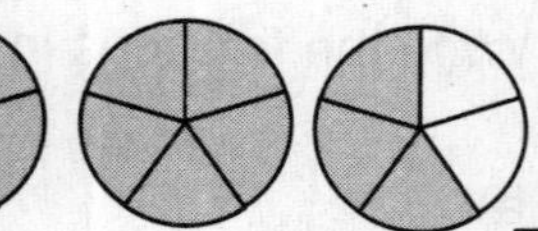 ____

d) 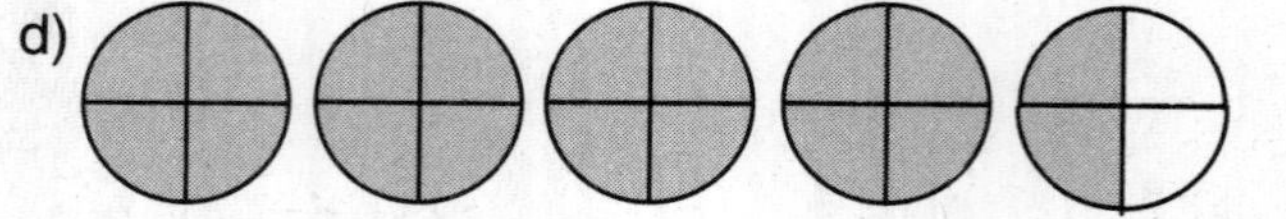 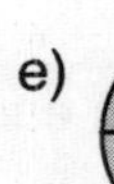 ____

e) 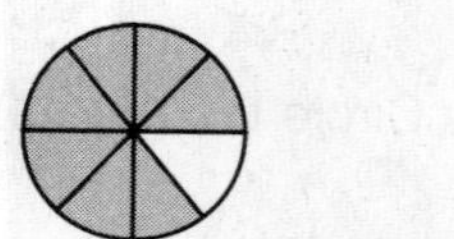 ____

f) 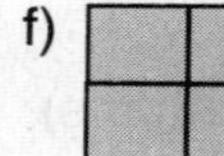 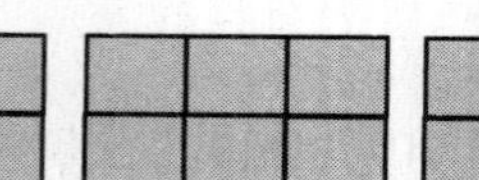 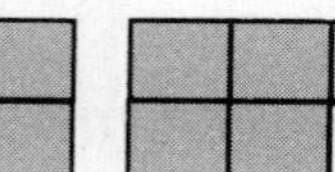 ____

g) 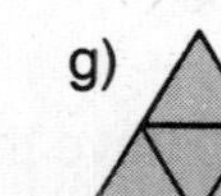  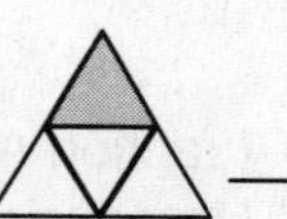 ____

3. Shade the amount of pie given in bold.
NOTE: There may be more pies than you need.

a) $\mathbf{2\frac{2}{3}}$ 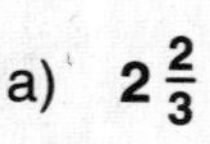 

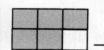

b) $\mathbf{3\frac{1}{4}}$ 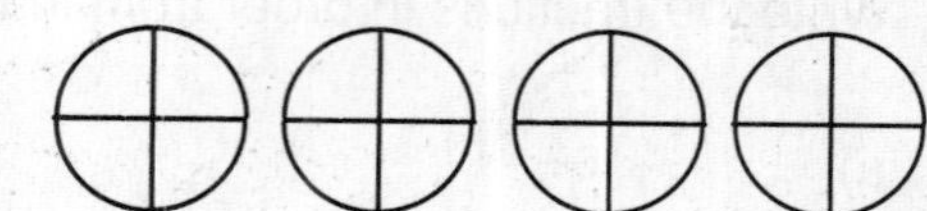

c) $\mathbf{1\frac{3}{4}}$ 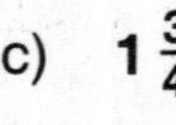 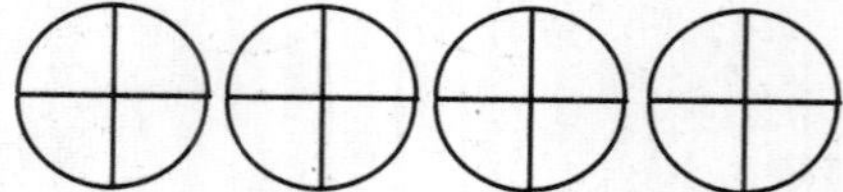

d) $\mathbf{2\frac{4}{5}}$ 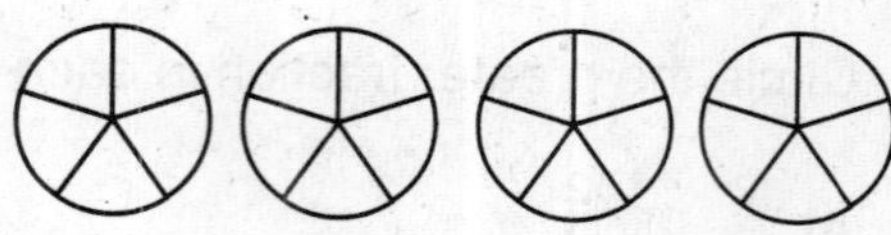

4. Sketch. a) $2\frac{1}{4}$ pies b) $3\frac{2}{3}$ pies c) $1\frac{1}{5}$ pies d) $3\frac{1}{6}$ pies

5. Which fraction represents more pie, $3\frac{2}{3}$ or $4\frac{1}{4}$?

6. Is $5\frac{3}{4}$ closer to 5 or 6?

NS6-50: Improper Fractions

Huan-Yue and her friends ate **9** quarter-sized pieces of pizza.

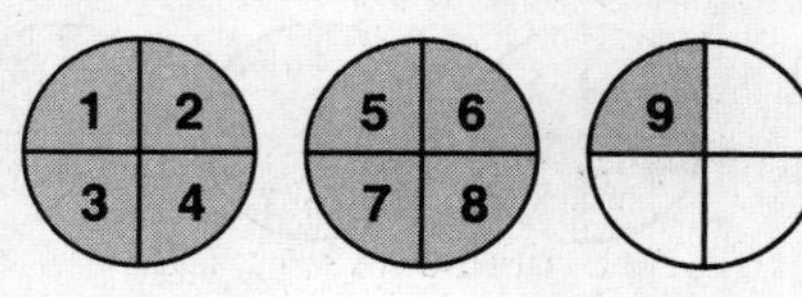

$\frac{9}{4} = 2\frac{1}{4}$

improper fraction *mixed fraction*

Altogether they ate $\frac{9}{4}$ pizzas.

When the numerator of a fraction is larger than the denominator, the fraction represents *more than a whole*. Such fractions are called **improper fractions**.

---

1. Write these fractions as improper fractions.

a) 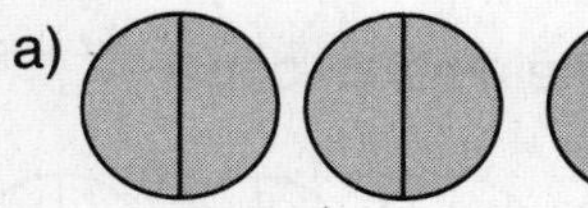 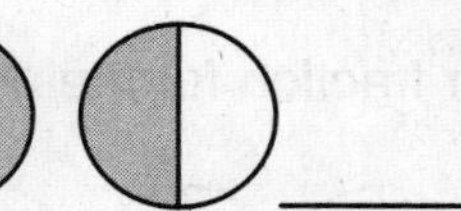 ______ b) 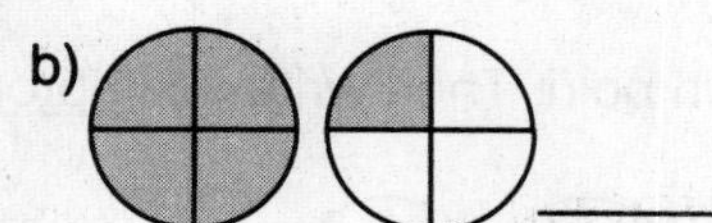 ______ c)  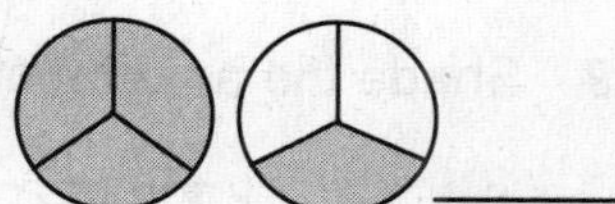 ______

d) 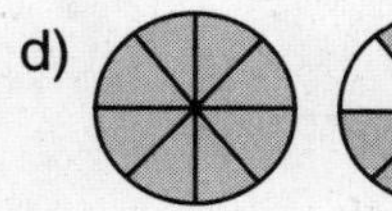 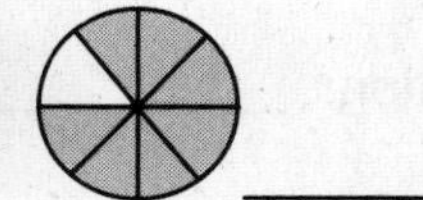 ______ e) 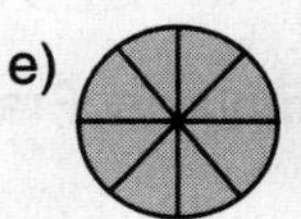 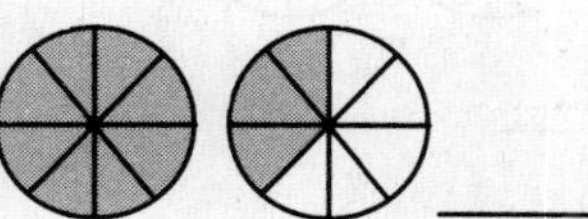 ______ f) 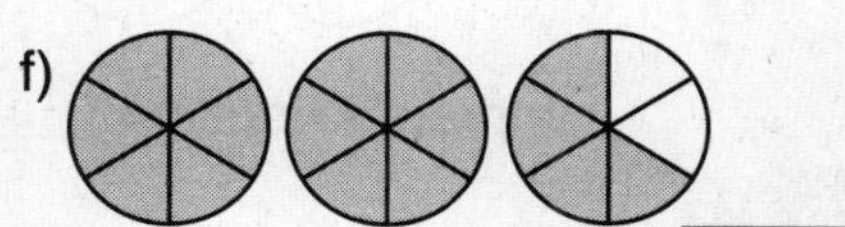 ______

g) 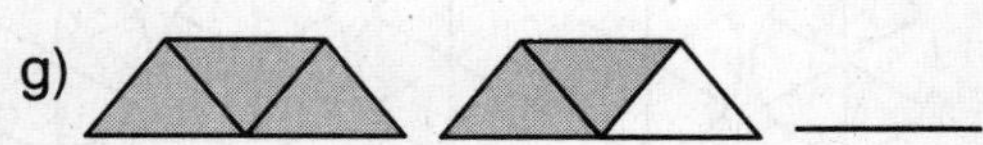 ______ h) 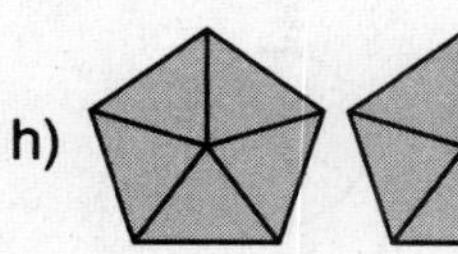 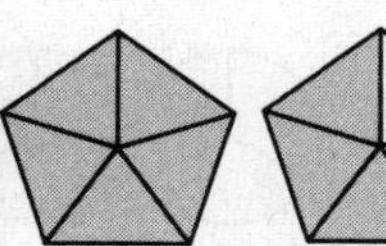 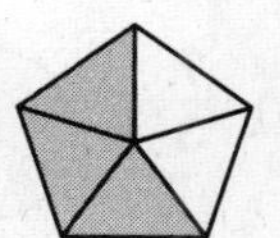 ______

2. Shade one piece at a time until you have shaded the amount of pie given in bold.

a) $\mathbf{\frac{5}{2}}$ 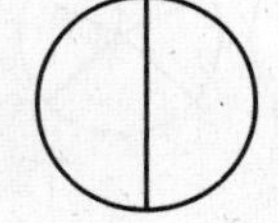 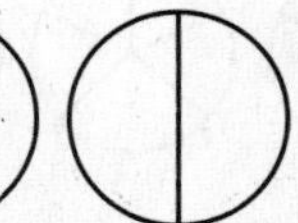  b) $\mathbf{\frac{9}{4}}$ 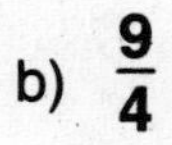 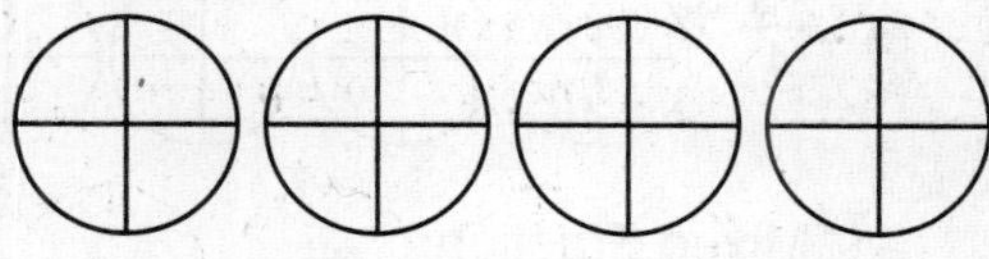

c) $\mathbf{\frac{10}{3}}$  d) $\mathbf{\frac{8}{4}}$ 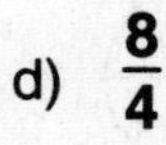 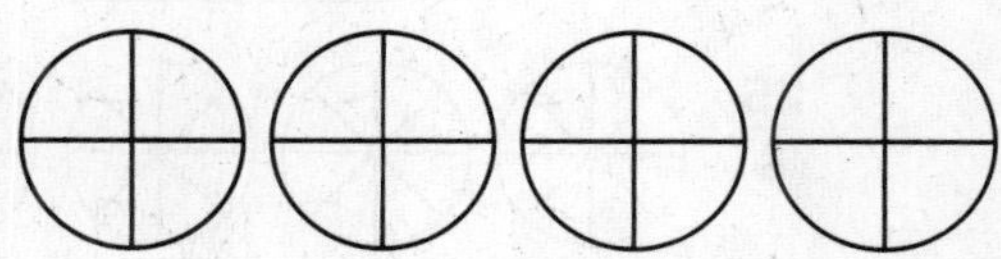

3. Sketch. a) $\frac{9}{4}$ pies b) $\frac{7}{3}$ pies c) $\frac{9}{2}$ pies d) $\frac{7}{6}$ pies

4. Which fraction represents more pie? $\frac{7}{4}$ or $\frac{9}{4}$? How do you know?

5. Which fractions are more than a whole? How do you know? a) $\frac{5}{7}$ b) $\frac{9}{8}$ c) $\frac{13}{11}$

NS6-51: Mixed and Improper Fractions

1. Write these fractions both as <u>mixed</u> fractions and as <u>improper</u> fractions.

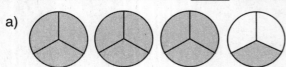

a) b)

c) 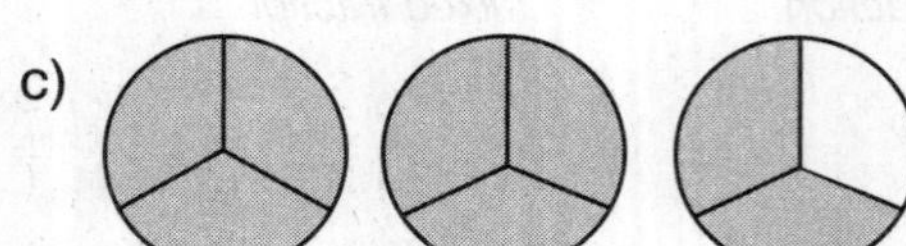 d) 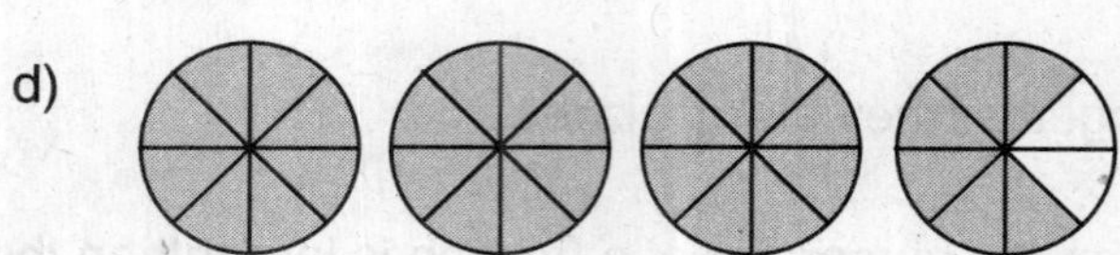

e) 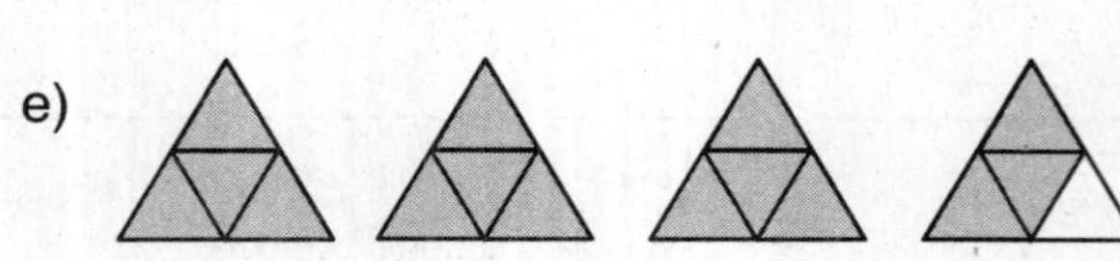 f) 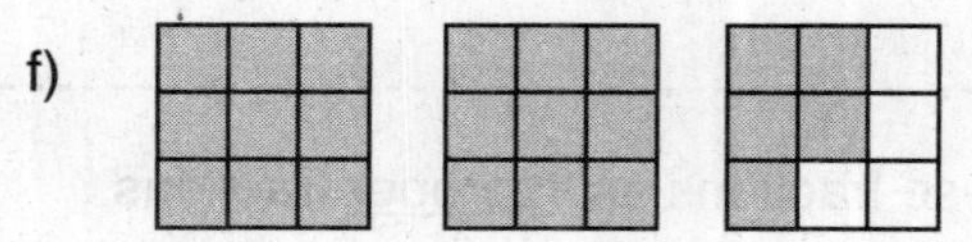

2. Shade the amount of pie given in bold. Then write an <u>improper</u> fraction for the amount of pie.

a) $\mathbf{3\frac{1}{2}}$ 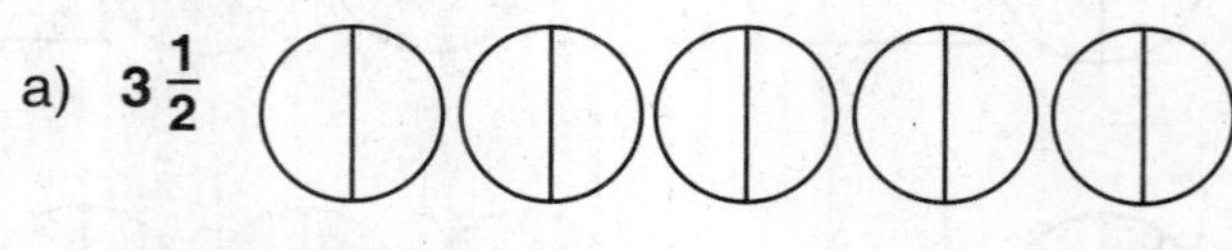

Improper Fraction: ________

b) $\mathbf{3\frac{3}{4}}$

Improper Fraction: ________

3. Shade the amount of pie given in bold. Then write a <u>mixed</u> fraction for the amount of pie.

a) $\mathbf{\frac{7}{3}}$ 

Mixed Fraction: ________

b) $\mathbf{\frac{19}{6}}$ 

Mixed Fraction: ________

c) $\mathbf{\frac{13}{4}}$ 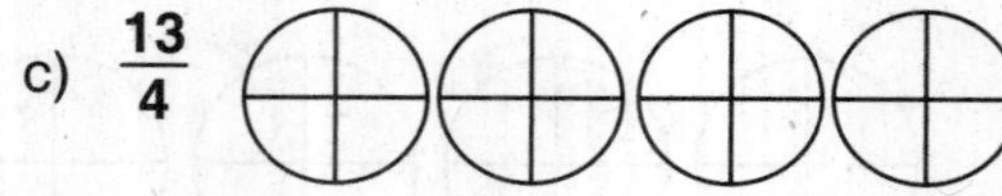

Mixed Fraction: ________

d) $\mathbf{\frac{13}{5}}$ 

Mixed Fraction: ________

e) $\mathbf{\frac{25}{8}}$ 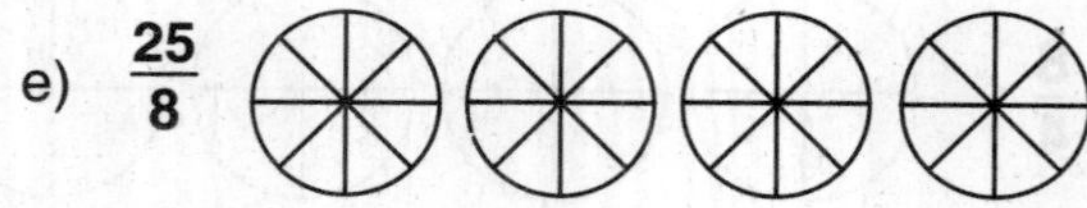

Mixed Fraction: ________

f) $\mathbf{\frac{19}{4}}$ 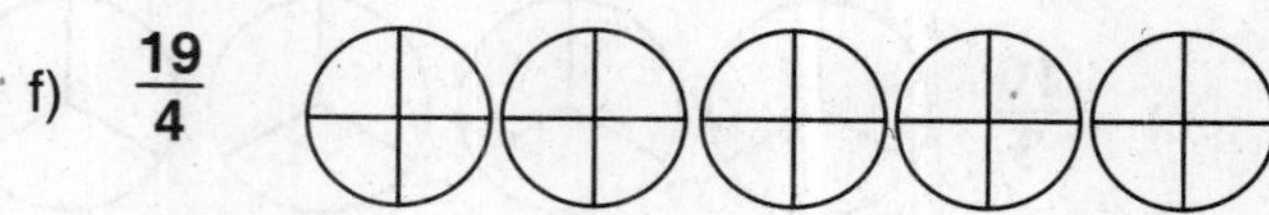

Mixed Fraction: ________

4. Draw a picture to find out which fraction is greater.

a) $2\frac{1}{2}$ or $\frac{3}{2}$ b) $2\frac{4}{5}$ or $\frac{12}{5}$ c) $\frac{15}{8}$ or $\frac{7}{3}$

5. How could you use division to find out how many <u>whole</u> pies are in $\frac{11}{3}$ of a pie? Explain.

NS6-52: Mixed Fractions (Advanced)

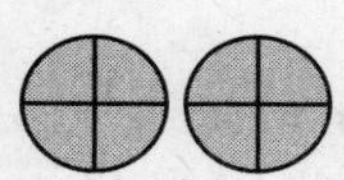

There are 4 quarter pieces in 1 pie.

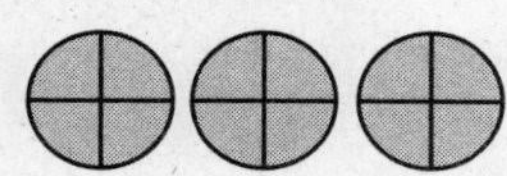

There are 8 (2 × 4) quarters in 2 pies.

There are 12 (3 × 4) quarters in 3 pies.

How many quarter pieces are in $3\frac{3}{4}$ pies?

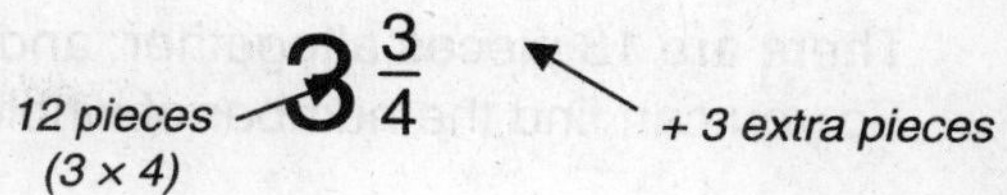

So there are 15 quarter pieces altogether.

---

1. Find the number of **halves** in each amount.

   a) 1 pie = ______ halves b) 2 pies = ______ halves c) 4 pies = ______ halves

   d) $3\frac{1}{2}$ pies = ______ halves e) $4\frac{1}{2}$ pies = ______ halves f) $5\frac{1}{2}$ pies = ______

2. Find the number of **thirds** in each amount.

   a) 1 pie = ______ thirds b) 2 pies = ______ thirds c) 4 pies = ______ thirds

   d) $1\frac{1}{3}$ pies = ______ thirds e) $2\frac{2}{3}$ pies = ______ f) $5\frac{2}{3}$ pies = ______

3. A box holds 4 cans.

   a) 2 boxes hold ______ cans b) $2\frac{1}{4}$ boxes hold ______ cans c) $3\frac{3}{4}$ boxes hold ______ cans

4. A box holds 6 cans.

   a) $2\frac{1}{6}$ boxes hold ______ cans b) $2\frac{5}{6}$ boxes hold ______ cans c) $3\frac{1}{6}$ boxes hold ______ cans

5. Write the following mixed fractions as improper fractions.

   a) $2\frac{1}{3} = \frac{\quad}{3}$ b) $5\frac{1}{2} = \frac{\quad}{2}$ c) $4\frac{2}{3} = \frac{\quad}{3}$ d) $6\frac{1}{4} = \frac{\quad}{4}$

6. Envelopes come in packs of 6.
   Alice used $2\frac{5}{6}$ packs.
   How many envelopes did she use? ______

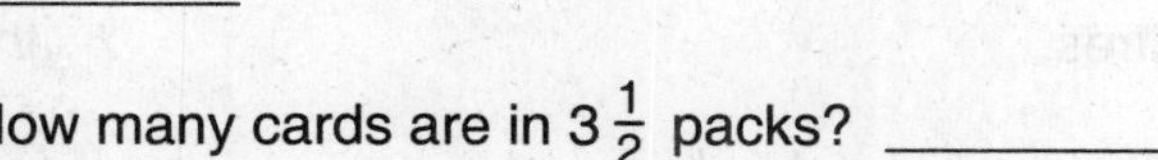

7. Baseball cards come in packs of 8. How many cards are in $3\frac{1}{2}$ packs? ______

8. Maia and her friends ate $2\frac{3}{4}$ pizzas. How many quarter-sized pieces did they eat? ______

9.

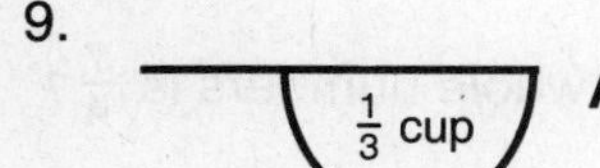

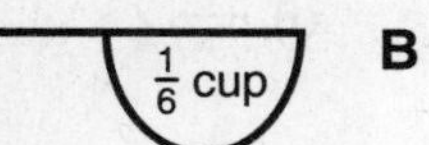

Cindy needs $2\frac{2}{3}$ cups of flour.

   a) How many scoops of cup A would she need? ______

   b) How many scoops of cup B would she need? ______

NS6-53: Mixed & Improper Fractions (Advanced)

How many whole pies are there in $\frac{13}{4}$ pies?

There are 13 pieces altogether, and each pie has 4 pieces.
So you can find the number of whole pies by dividing 13 by 4: **13 ÷ 4 = 3 remainder 1**

There are 3 whole pies and 1 quarter left over, so: $\frac{13}{4} = 3\frac{1}{4}$

---

1. Find the number of whole pies in each amount by dividing.

a) $\frac{4}{2}$ pies = ______ whole pies b) $\frac{6}{2}$ pies = ______ whole pies c) $\frac{12}{2}$ pies = ______ whole pies

d) $\frac{6}{3}$ pies = ______ whole pies e) $\frac{15}{3}$ pies = ______ whole pies f) $\frac{8}{4}$ pies = ______ whole pies

2. Find the number of whole and the number of pieces remaining by dividing.

a) $\frac{5}{2}$ pies = ___2___ whole pies and ___1___ half pies = ___$2\frac{1}{2}$___ pies

b) $\frac{11}{3}$ pies = ______ whole pies and ______ thirds = ______ pies

c) $\frac{10}{3}$ pies = ______ whole pies and ______ thirds = ______ pies

d) $\frac{9}{2}$ pies = ______ whole pies and ______ half pies = ______ pies

3. Write the following improper fractions as mixed fractions.

a) $\frac{3}{2}$ = b) $\frac{9}{2}$ = c) $\frac{8}{3}$ = d) $\frac{15}{4}$ = e) $\frac{22}{5}$ =

4. Write a mixed and improper fraction for the number of litres.

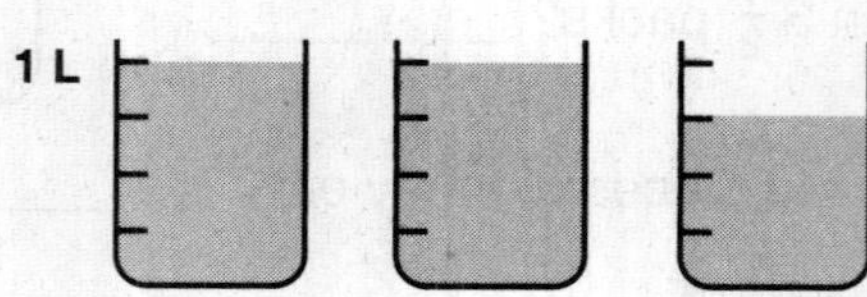

5. Write a mixed and improper fraction for the length of the rope.

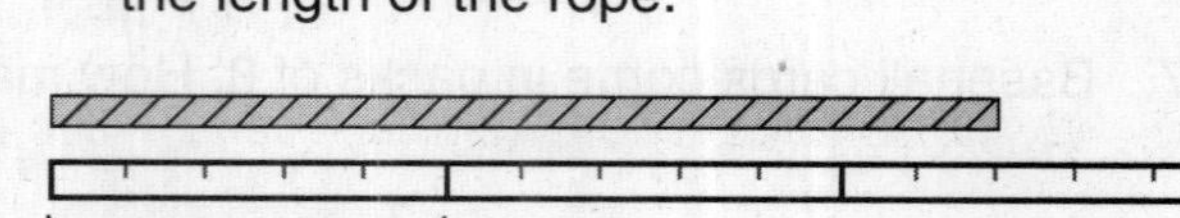

6. Which is greater: $\frac{7}{3}$ or $\frac{5}{2}$? How do you know?

7. Between which two whole numbers is $\frac{7}{4}$?

8. How much greater than a whole is … a) $\frac{10}{7}$? b) $\frac{6}{5}$? c) $\frac{4}{3}$? d) $\frac{11}{10}$?

NS6-54: Equivalent Fractions

Aidan shades $\frac{2}{6}$ of the squares in an array: 

He then draws heavy lines around the squares to group them into 3 equal groups: 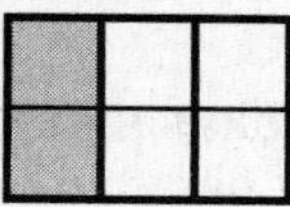

He sees that $\frac{1}{3}$ of the squares are shaded.

The pictures show that two sixths are equal to one third: $\frac{2}{6} = \frac{1}{3}$

Two sixths and one third are **equivalent fractions**.

---

1. Group the squares to make an equivalent fraction.

a) 

$\frac{6}{10} = \frac{}{5}$

b) 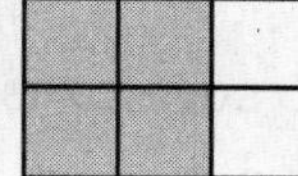

$\frac{4}{6} = \frac{}{3}$

c) 

$\frac{10}{12} = \frac{}{6}$

2. 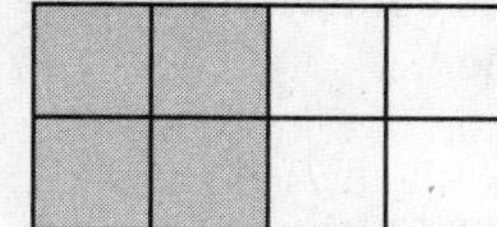 Write three equivalent fractions for the amount shaded here.

________ ________ ________

3. Group the buttons to make an equivalent fraction.

a)  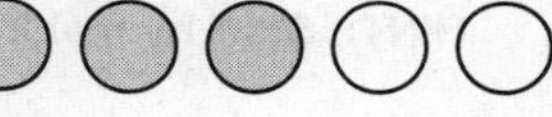

$\frac{4}{6} = \frac{}{}$

b)  

$\frac{3}{6} = \frac{}{}$

c)   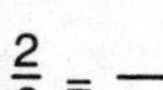

$\frac{2}{6} = \frac{}{}$

d)  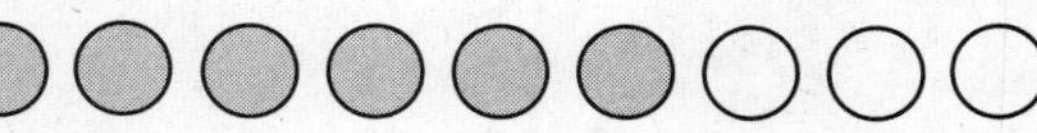

$\frac{6}{9} = \frac{}{}$

e)  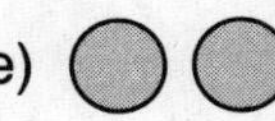

$\frac{6}{10} = \frac{}{}$

4. Cut each pie into smaller pieces to make an equivalent fraction.

a) 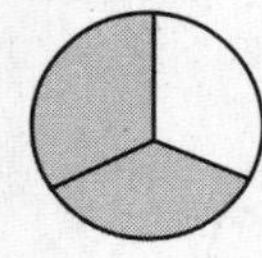

$\frac{2}{3} = \frac{}{6}$

b) 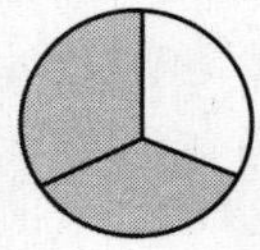

$\frac{2}{3} = \frac{}{9}$

c) 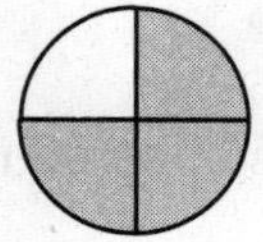

$\frac{3}{4} = \frac{}{12}$

5. a) Draw lines to cut the pies into …

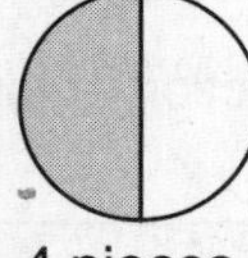

4 pieces

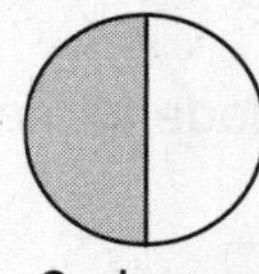

6 pieces

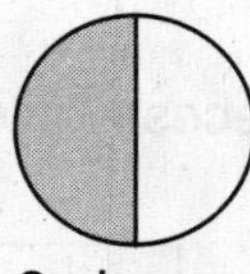

8 pieces

b) Then fill in the numerators of the equivalent fractions.

$\frac{1}{2} = \frac{}{4} = \frac{}{6} = \frac{}{8}$

6. Draw shaded and unshaded circles (as in Question 3). Group the circles to show …

a) six eighths is equivalent to three quarters

b) four fifths is equivalent to eight tenths

NS6-55: Models of Equivalent Fractions

Anne makes a model of $\frac{2}{5}$ using 15 squares as follows:

First she makes a model of $\frac{2}{5}$ using shaded and unshaded squares (leaving space between the squares).

Step 1: ■ ■ □ □ □

$\frac{2}{5}$ of the squares are shaded. She then adds squares one at a time until she has placed 15 squares.

Step 2: ■■ ■■ □□ □□ □□

Step 3: ■■■ ■■■ □□□ □□□ □□□

From the picture, Anne can see that $\frac{2}{5}$ of a set of 15 squares is equivalent to $\frac{6}{15}$ of the set.

---

1. Draw a model of $\frac{2}{3}$ using 12 squares. The question is started for you.

   HINT: Place the extra squares beside the ones already drawn, one square at a time.

   ■ ■ □

2. Draw a model of $\frac{3}{5}$ using 10 squares.

   HINT: Start by making a model of $\frac{3}{5}$.

3. Draw a model of $\frac{3}{4}$ using 8 squares.

4. $\frac{5}{6}$ of a pizza is covered in olives.
   $\frac{1}{3}$ of the pizza is covered in mushrooms.
   Each piece has a topping. Complete the picture.
   How many pieces are covered in olives **and** mushrooms? ____

5. If box C was cut into 12 pieces, how many pieces would you shade to make a fraction equivalent to A and B?

   A B C

NS6-56: Fractions of Whole Numbers

Dan has 6 cookies. He wants to give $\frac{2}{3}$ of his cookies to his friends. To do so, he shares the cookies equally onto 3 plates:

There are 3 equal groups, so each group is $\frac{1}{3}$ of 6.

There are 2 cookies in each group, so $\frac{1}{3}$ of 6 is 2.

There are 4 cookies in two groups, so $\frac{2}{3}$ of 6 is 4.

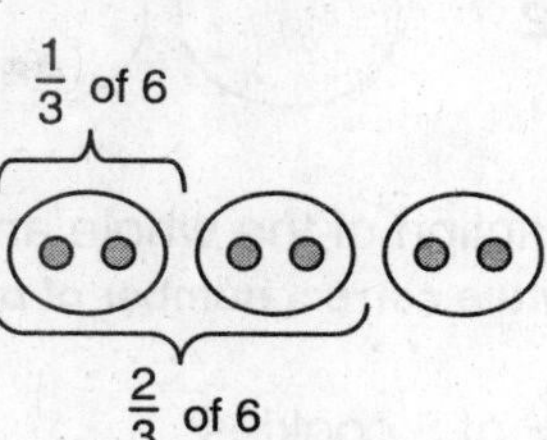

---

1. Write a fraction for the amount of dots shown. The first one has been done for you.

a) 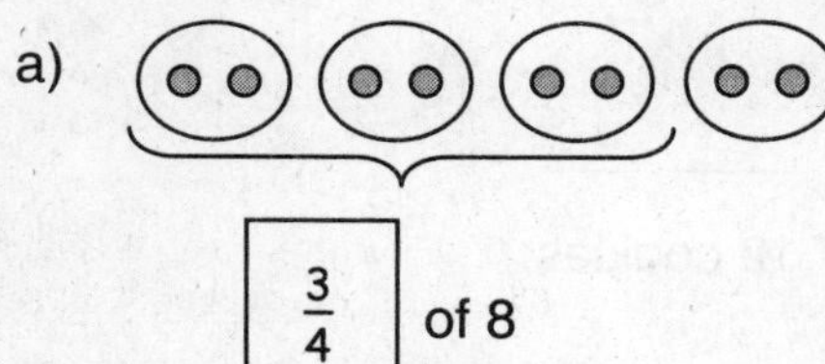

$\frac{3}{4}$ of 8

b) 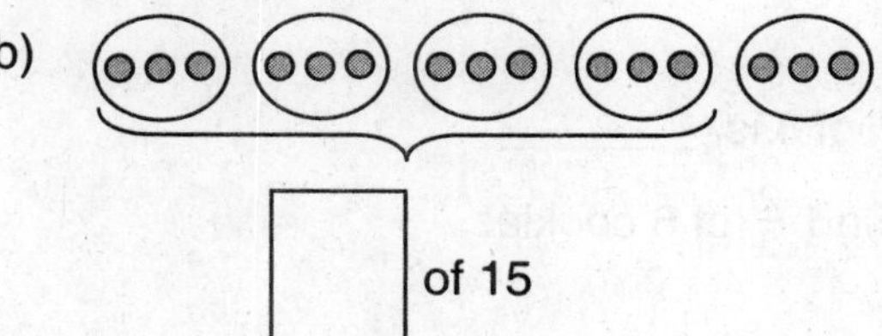

☐ of 15

2. Fill in the missing numbers.

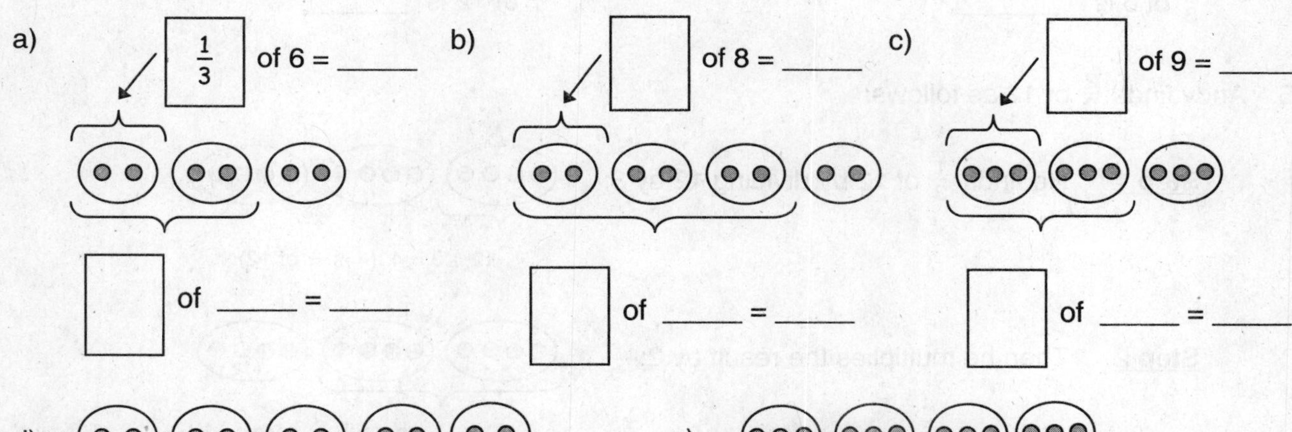

d) 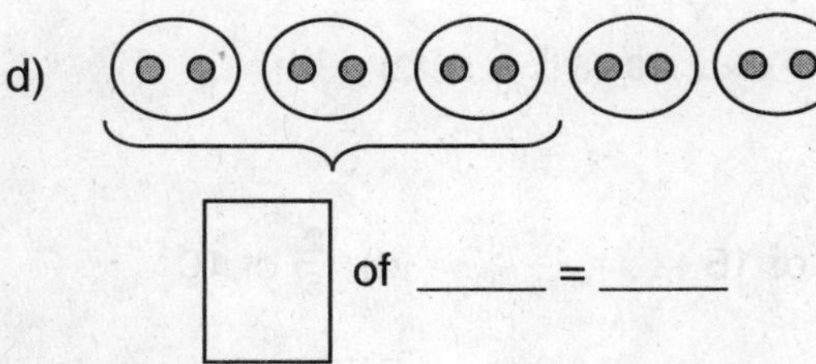

☐ of ______ = ______

e) 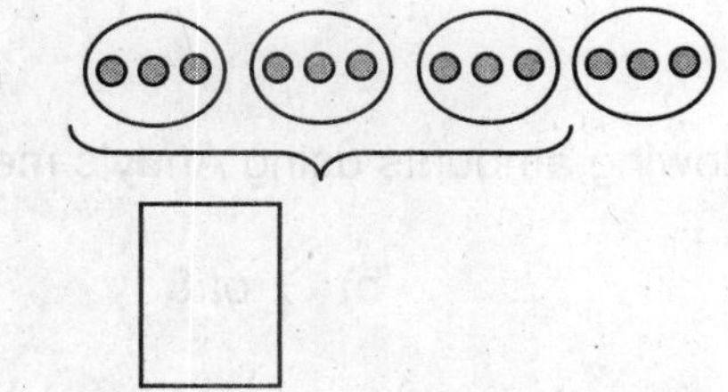

3. Draw a circle to show the given amount. The first one has been done for you.

a) $\frac{2}{3}$ of 6

b) $\frac{3}{4}$ of 8

c) $\frac{3}{5}$ of 10

d) $\frac{3}{4}$ of 12

4. Fill in the correct number of dots in each circle, then draw a larger circle to show the given amount.

a) $\frac{2}{3}$ of 12   b) $\frac{2}{3}$ of 9

5. Find the fraction of the whole amount by sharing the cookies equally.
HINT: Draw the correct number of plates then place the cookies one at a time. Then circle the correct amount.

a) Find $\frac{1}{4}$ of 8 cookies.

$\frac{1}{4}$ of 8 is ________

b) Find $\frac{1}{2}$ of 10 cookies.

$\frac{1}{2}$ of 10 is ________

c) Find $\frac{2}{3}$ of 6 cookies.

$\frac{2}{3}$ of 6 is ________

d) Find $\frac{3}{4}$ of 12 cookies.

$\frac{3}{4}$ of 12 is ________

6. Andy finds $\frac{2}{3}$ of 12 as follows:

Step 1 He finds $\frac{1}{3}$ of 12 by dividing 12 by 3:

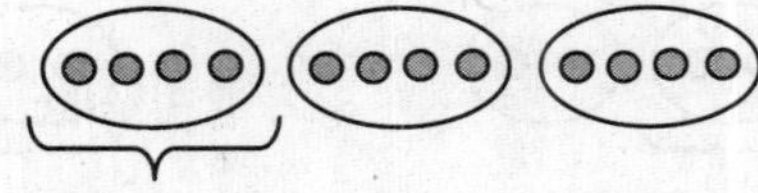

12 ÷ 3 = 4 (4 is $\frac{1}{3}$ of 12)

Step 2 Then he multiplies the result by 2:

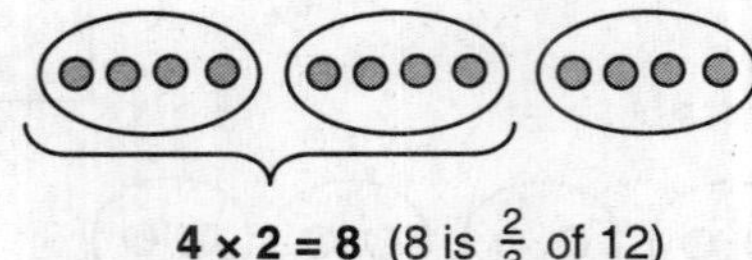

4 × 2 = 8 (8 is $\frac{2}{3}$ of 12)

Find the following amounts using Andy's method.

a) $\frac{2}{3}$ of 9 ________
b) $\frac{3}{4}$ of 8 ________
c) $\frac{2}{3}$ of 15 ________
d) $\frac{2}{5}$ of 10 ________

e) $\frac{3}{5}$ of 25 ________
f) $\frac{2}{7}$ of 14 ________
g) $\frac{1}{6}$ of 18 ________
h) $\frac{1}{2}$ of 12 ________

i) $\frac{3}{4}$ of 12 ________
j) $\frac{2}{3}$ of 21 ________
k) $\frac{3}{8}$ of 16 ________
l) $\frac{3}{7}$ of 21 ________

7. a) Shade $\frac{2}{5}$ of the boxes. b) Shade $\frac{2}{3}$ of the boxes. c) Shade $\frac{3}{4}$ of the boxes.

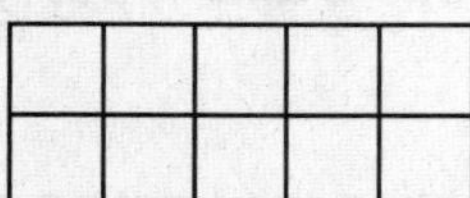
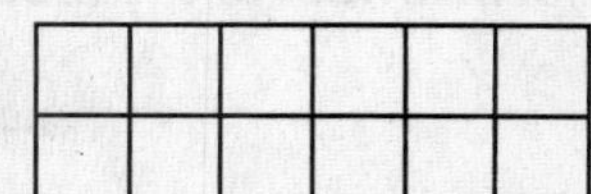
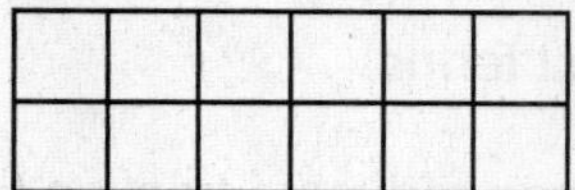

8. a) Shade $\frac{1}{4}$ of the boxes. Draw stripes in $\frac{1}{6}$ of the boxes.

b) Shade $\frac{1}{3}$ of the boxes. Draw stripes in $\frac{1}{6}$ of the boxes. Put dots in $\frac{1}{8}$ of the boxes.

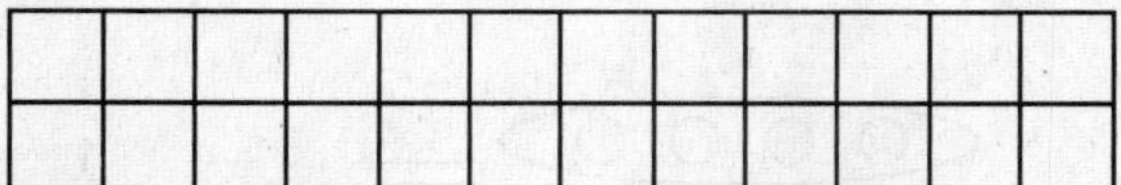
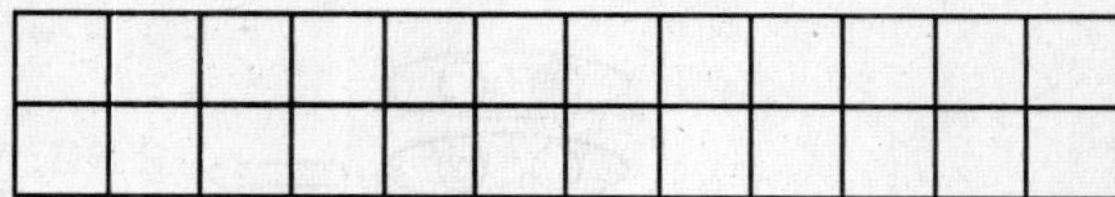

9. 15 children are on a bus. $\frac{3}{5}$ are girls. How many girls are on the bus? ____________

10. A kilogram of lichees costs \$8. How much would $\frac{3}{4}$ of a kilogram cost? ____________

11. Gerald has 12 apples. He gives away $\frac{3}{4}$ of the apples.

a) How many apples did he give away? __________ b) How many did he keep? __________

12. Shade $\frac{1}{3}$ of the squares.

Draw stripes in $\frac{1}{6}$ of the squares.

How many squares are blank?

13. Evelyn has 20 marbles.
$\frac{2}{5}$ are blue. $\frac{1}{4}$ are yellow. The rest are green.
How many are green?

14. Ed started studying at 9:10. He studied for $\frac{2}{3}$ of an hour.
At what time did he stop studying?

15. Marion had 36 stickers.
She kept $\frac{1}{6}$ for herself and divided the rest evenly among 5 friends.
How many stickers did each friend get?

16. Which is longer: 17 months or $1\frac{3}{4}$ years?

17. Linda had 12 apples.
She gave $\frac{1}{4}$ of them to Nandita. She gave 2 to Amy.

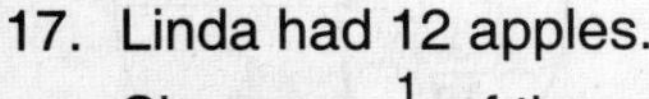

She says that she has half left. Is she correct?

NS6-57: Reducing Fractions

A fraction is reduced to **lowest terms** when the only whole number that will divide into its numerator and denominator is the number 1. $\frac{2}{4}$ is *not* in lowest terms (because 2 divides into 2 and 4) but $\frac{1}{2}$ is in lowest terms.

You can reduce a fraction to lowest terms by dividing a set of counters representing the fraction into equal groups. (You may have to group counters several times before the fraction is in lowest terms.)

Step 1: Count the number of counters in each group.

Step 2: Divide the numerator and denominator of the fraction by the number of counters in each group.

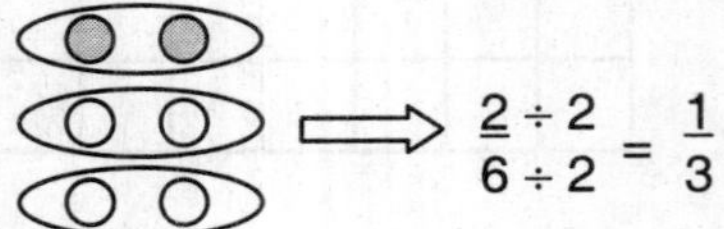

$\frac{2 \div 2}{6 \div 2} = \frac{1}{3}$

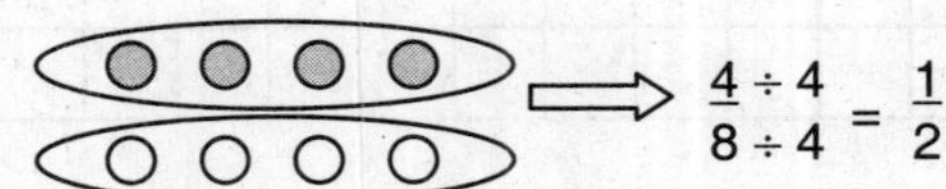

$\frac{4 \div 4}{8 \div 4} = \frac{1}{2}$

1. Reduce these fractions by grouping.

a) 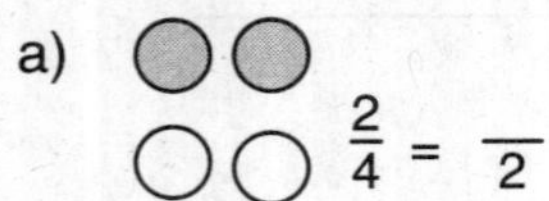 $\frac{2}{4} = \frac{}{2}$

b) 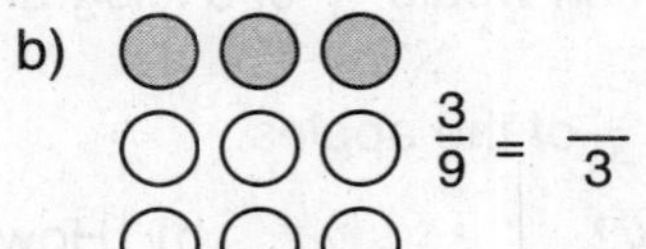 $\frac{3}{9} = \frac{}{3}$

c) 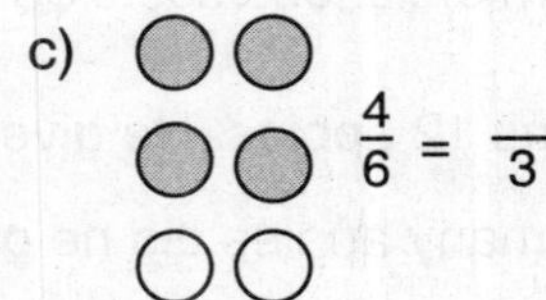 $\frac{4}{6} = \frac{}{3}$

2. Show how you would reduce the fractions by dividing.

a) $\frac{2 \div}{4 \div} = $ ____ b) $\frac{3 \div}{9 \div} = $ ____ c) $\frac{4 \div}{6 \div} = $ ____

3. Reduce the fractions below by dividing.

a) $\frac{2}{10} = $ — b) $\frac{2}{6} = $ — c) $\frac{2}{8} = $ — d) $\frac{2}{12} = $ —

e) $\frac{3}{9} = $ — f) $\frac{3}{15} = $ — g) $\frac{4}{12} = $ — h) $\frac{6}{9} = $ —

i) $\frac{4}{6} = $ — j) $\frac{10}{15} = $ — k) $\frac{20}{25} = $ — l) $\frac{8}{12} = $

4. The pie chart show how the children in a Grade 6 class get to school. What fraction of the children …

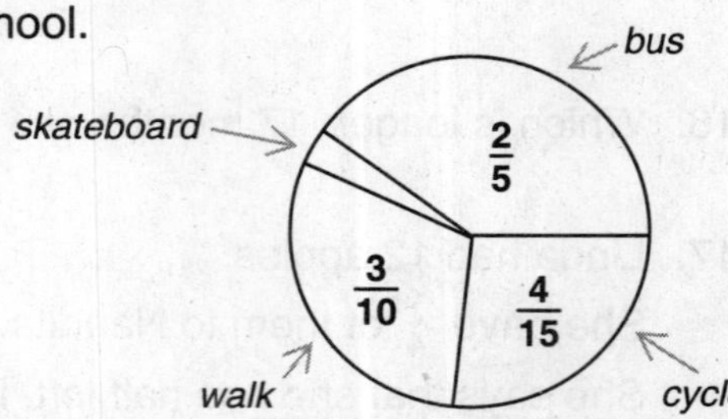

a) walk to school? 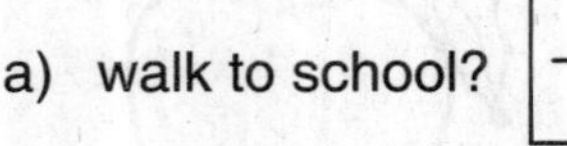

b) take the bus? 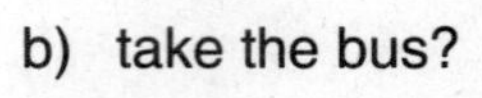 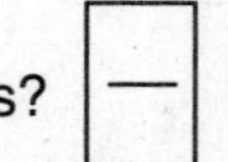

c) skateboard? 

d) cycle?

1.

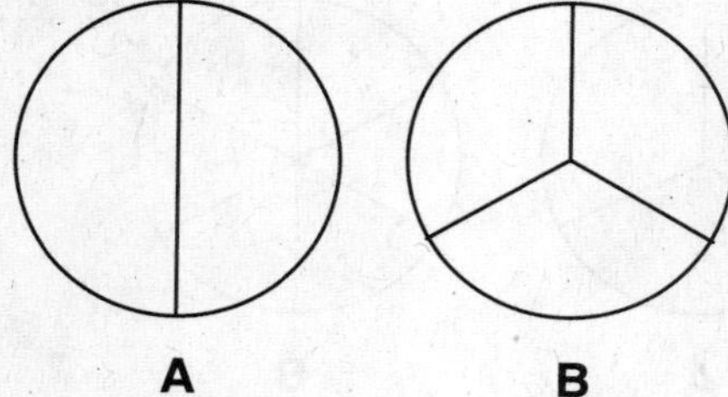

How many pieces are in pie A? ______

How many pieces are in pie B? ______

Find the LCM of the number of pieces in pies A and B: **LCM =** ______

Cut pie A and pie B into this many pieces.

How many pieces did you cut each piece of pie A into? ______

How many pieces did you cut each piece of pie B into? ______

2.

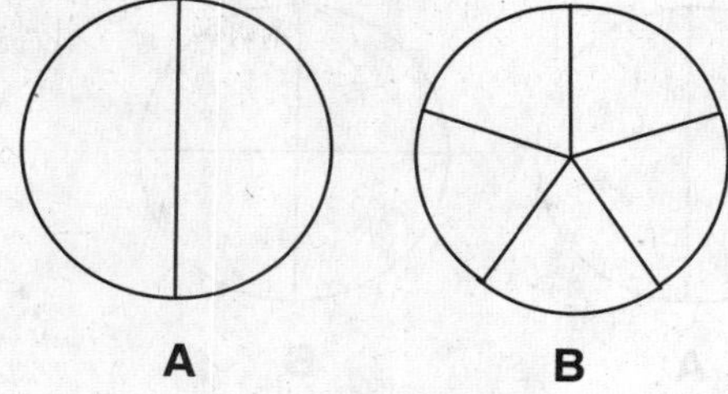

How many pieces are in pie A? ______

How many pieces are in pie B? ______

Find the LCM of the number of pieces in pies A and B: **LCM =** ______

Cut pie A and pie B into this many pieces.

How many pieces did you cut each piece of pie A into? ______

How many pieces did you cut each piece of pie B into? ______

3.

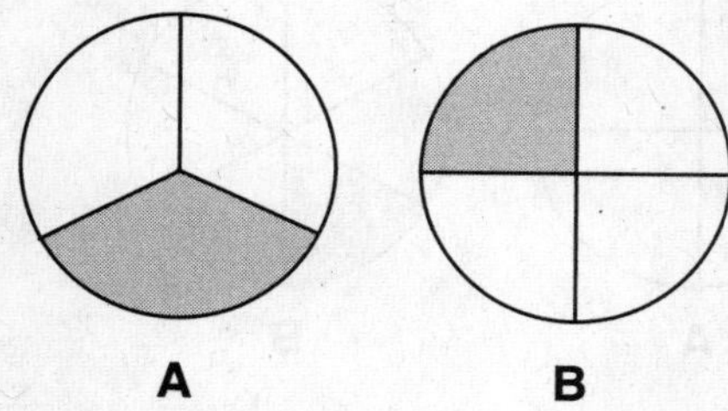

Write the name of each fraction.

A - ______________ B - ______________

Find the LCM of the number of pieces in pies A and B: **LCM =** ______

Cut each pie into the same number of pieces, given by the LCM.

Now write a new name for each fraction.

A - ______________ B - ______________

4.

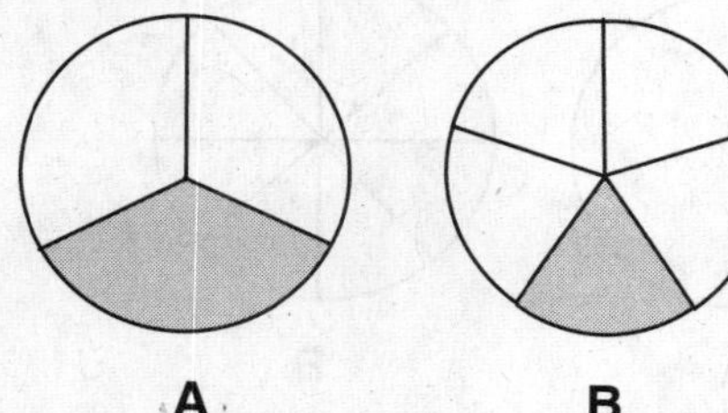

Write the name of each fraction.

A - ______________ B - ______________

Find the LCM of the number of pieces in pies A and B: **LCM =** ______

Cut each pie into the same number of pieces, given by the LCM.

Now write a new name for each fraction.

A - ______________ B - ______________

NS6-58: Lowest Common Multiples in Fractions *(continued)*

5.

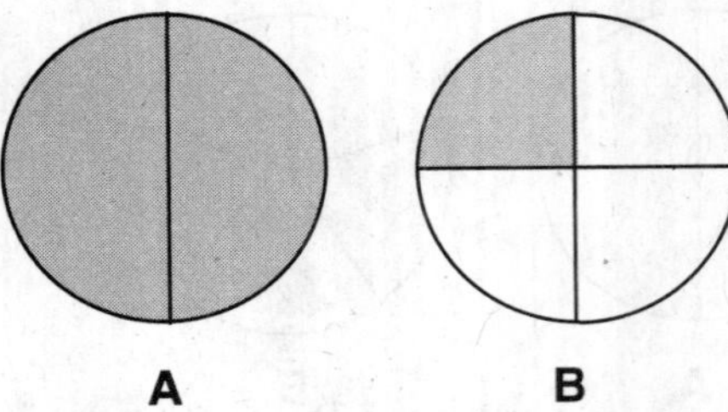

Write the name of each fraction.

A - ______________ B - ______________

Find the LCM of the number of pieces in pies A and B: **LCM =** ______

Cut each pie into the same number of pieces, given by the **LCM**.

Now write a new name for each fraction.

A - ______________ B - ______________

6.

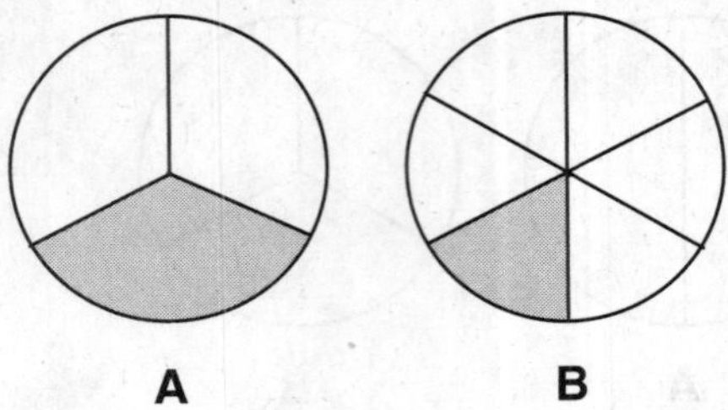

Write the name of each fraction.

A - ______________ B - ______________

Find the LCM of the number of pieces in pies A and B: **LCM =** ______

Cut each pie into the same number of pieces, given by the **LCM**.

Now write a name for each fraction.

A - ______________ B - ______________

7.

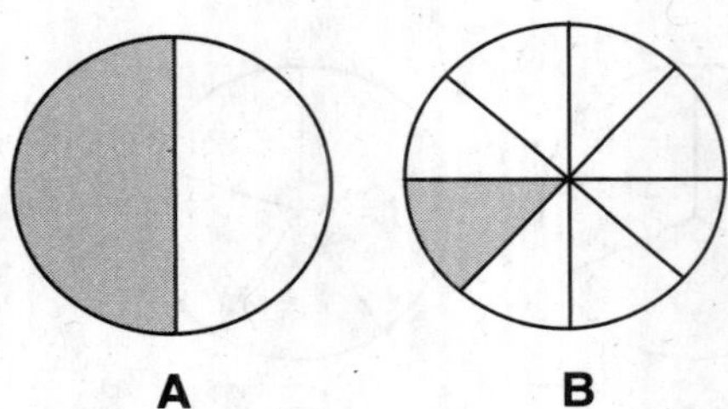

Write the name of each fraction.

A - ______________ B - ______________

Find the LCM of the number of pieces in pies A and B: **LCM =** ______

Cut each pie into the same number of pieces, given by the LCM.

Now write a new name for each fraction.

A - ______________ B - ______________

8.

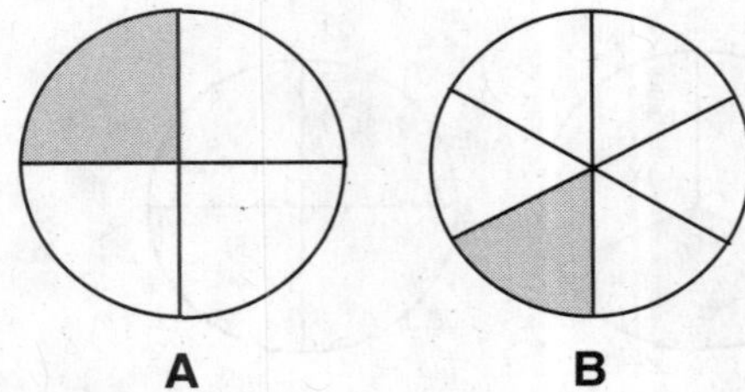

Write the name of each fraction.

A - ______________ B - ______________

Find the LCM of the number of pieces in pies A and B: **LCM =** ______

Cut each pie into the same number of pieces, given by the LCM.

Now write a new name for each fraction.

A - ______________ B - ______________

NS6-59: Comparing and Ordering Fractions

Use the fraction strips below to answer Questions 1 to 3.

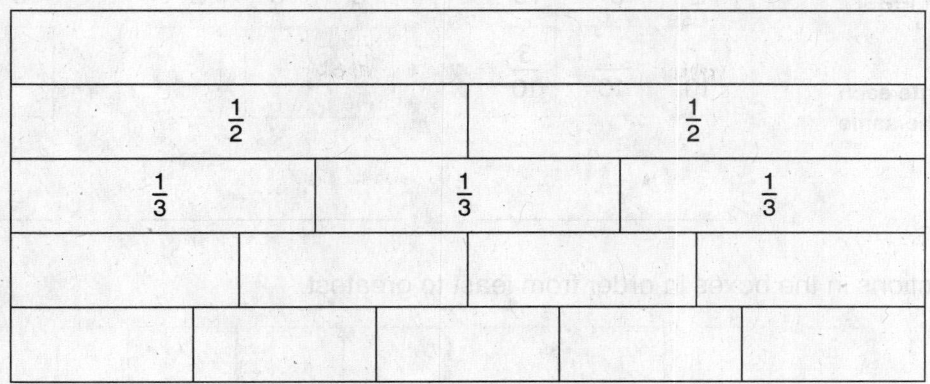

1. Fill in the missing numbers on the fraction strips above. Then write > (greater than) or < (less than) between each pair of numbers below.

   a) $\frac{2}{3} \square \frac{3}{5}$ b) $\frac{3}{4} \square \frac{1}{2}$ c) $\frac{2}{5} \square \frac{3}{4}$ d) $\frac{3}{4} \square \frac{4}{5}$

2. Circle the fractions that are greater than $\frac{1}{3}$.

   $\frac{3}{5}$ $\frac{2}{5}$ $\frac{1}{2}$

3. Circle the fractions that are greater than $\frac{1}{2}$.

   $\frac{2}{3}$ $\frac{2}{5}$ $\frac{3}{4}$

4. Turn each fraction into an equivalent fraction so that both fractions have the same denominator (by finding the LCM of both denominators). Then write =, <, or > between the two fractions.

   a) $\frac{5 \times 1}{5 \times 2} \square \frac{7}{10}$

   $\frac{5}{10} < \frac{7}{10}$

   b) $\frac{1}{2} \square \frac{3}{10}$ c) $\frac{3}{4} \square \frac{7}{8}$ d) $\frac{11}{20} \square \frac{2}{5}$

   e) $\frac{2}{3} \square \frac{4}{5}$ f) $\frac{1}{2} \square \frac{2}{3}$ g) $\frac{3}{4} \square \frac{2}{3}$ h) $\frac{2}{3} \square \frac{6}{9}$

   i) $\frac{3}{4} \square \frac{4}{5}$ j) $\frac{1}{7} \square \frac{5}{21}$ k) $\frac{17}{35} \square \frac{3}{5}$ l) $\frac{4}{5} \square \frac{5}{6}$

NS6-60: Comparing and Ordering Fractions (Advanced)

1. Write the fractions in order from least to greatest.

HINT: First write each fraction with the same denominator.

a) $\frac{1}{2}$ $\frac{2}{5}$ $\frac{3}{10}$ b) $\frac{1}{3}$ $\frac{5}{6}$ $\frac{1}{2}$ c) $\frac{5}{8}$ $\frac{1}{2}$ $\frac{3}{4}$

$\frac{\square}{10}$ $\frac{\square}{10}$ $\frac{3}{10}$

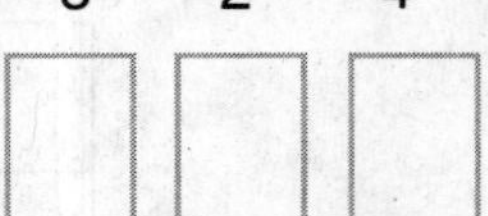

______ ______ ______

2. Write the fractions in the boxes in order from least to greatest.

0 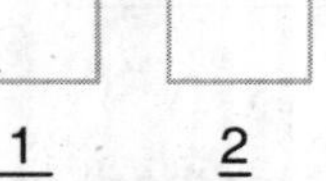 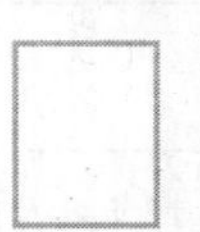 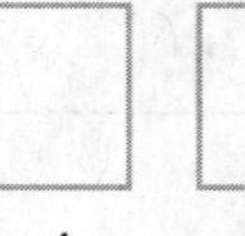   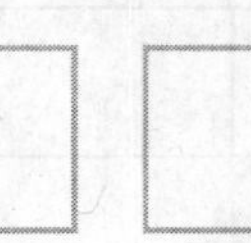  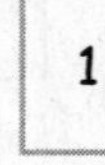 1

$\frac{1}{10}$ $\frac{2}{5}$ $\frac{9}{10}$ $\frac{4}{5}$ $\frac{3}{5}$ $\frac{3}{10}$ $\frac{1}{5}$ $\frac{1}{2}$ $\frac{7}{10}$

3. Equivalent fractions are said to be in the same **family**. Write two fractions in the same family as the fraction in each triangle.

a) $\frac{1}{2}$ b) $\frac{1}{3}$ 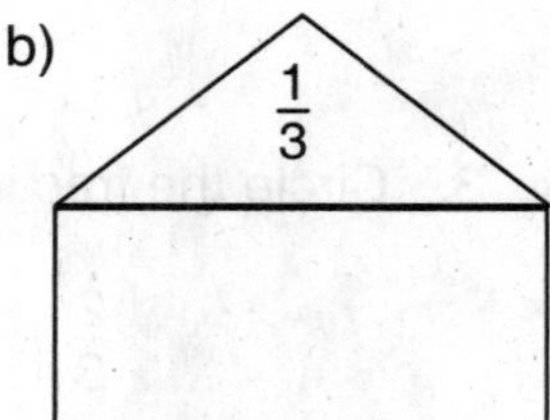 c) $\frac{3}{4}$ 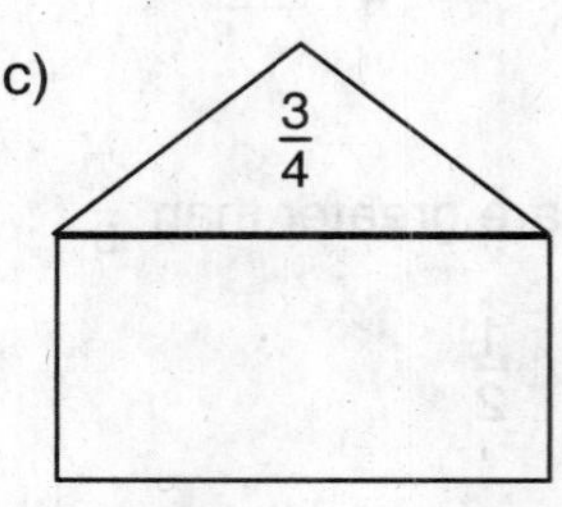 d) $\frac{2}{5}$ 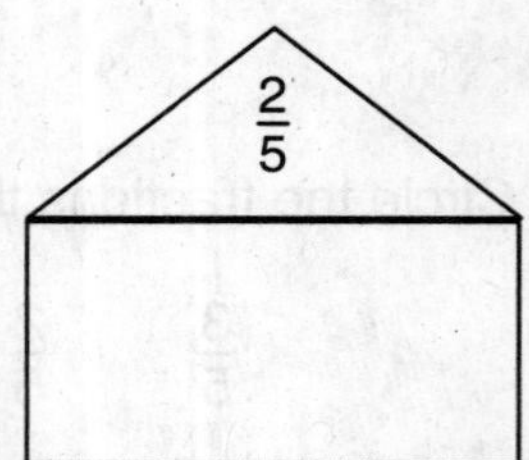

4. In each question, circle the pair of fractions that are in the same family.

a) $\frac{1}{2}$ $\frac{4}{6}$ $\frac{5}{10}$ b) $\frac{2}{3}$ $\frac{4}{6}$ $\frac{1}{4}$ c) $\frac{3}{15}$ $\frac{16}{20}$ $\frac{4}{5}$

5. Fill in the missing fractions in the sequence.
HINT: Give all the fractions the same denominator.

$\frac{1}{6}$ $\frac{1}{3}$ $\frac{1}{2}$ ☐ $\frac{5}{6}$ ☐

6. Explain how you know $\frac{1}{3}$ is greater than $\frac{1}{8}$.

7. Find 2 fractions from the fraction family of $\frac{4}{12}$ with numerators smaller than 4.

8. Find 5 fractions from the fraction family of $\frac{12}{24}$ with numerators smaller than 12.

9. A recipe for soup calls for $\frac{2}{3}$ of a can of tomatoes.
A recipe for spaghetti sauce calls for $\frac{5}{6}$ of a can.
Which recipe uses more tomatoes?

NS6-61: Word Problems

Answer the following questions in your notebook.

1. Anne had 1 hour for lunch.
   She played for $\frac{3}{5}$ of an hour and read for $\frac{1}{10}$ of an hour.
   a) How many minutes did she have left to eat lunch?
   b) What fraction of an hour was this?

Colour	Number of Walls Painted
White	10
Yellow	5
Blue	4
Green	1

2. a) What fraction of the walls were painted green?
   b) What colour was used to paint one fifth of the walls?
   c) What colour was used to paint one half of the walls?

3. Charles left for school at 7:10 am. He walked for $\frac{2}{5}$ of an hour to his friend's house, and then another $\frac{3}{5}$ of an hour to school. At what time did he arrive at school?

4. The pie chart shows the times of day when a lizard is active.

Awake but Inactive

Asleep

Awake and Active

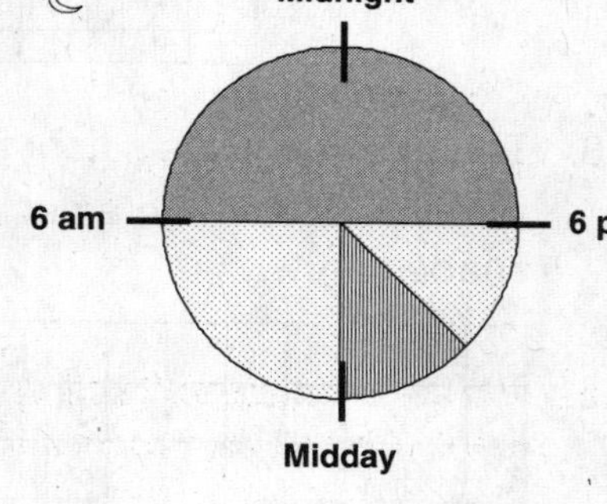

   a) What fraction of the day is the lizard…
      i) awake but inactive ii) asleep iii) awake and active
   b) How many hours a day is the lizard…
      i) awake but inactive ii) asleep iii) awake and active

5. John, Brian, Eldad, and Ahmed bought some pizzas.
   They ate the following fractions of a pizza (in no particular order): $\frac{2}{10}$, $\frac{2}{5}$, $\frac{7}{10}$, $\frac{6}{5}$
   There were 5 slices left over.
   a) How many pizzas did they buy?

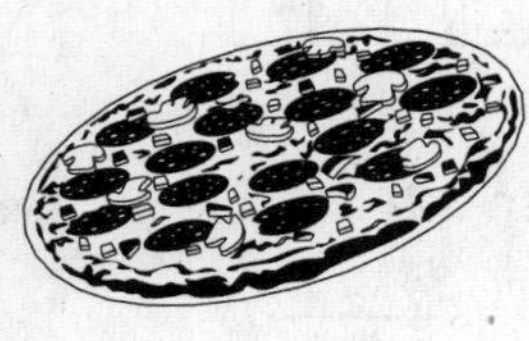

   b) • Eldad ate $\frac{1}{5}$ of a pizza.
      • Ahmed ate $\frac{7}{10}$, which was 3 more slices than Brian.
      • John ate more than one pizza.
   How much pizza did each boy eat?

6. A box holds 9 cans. The box is $\frac{2}{3}$ full.
   How many cans are in the box?

NS6-62: Decimal Hundredths

Fractions with denominators that are multiples of ten (tenths, hundredths) commonly appear in units of measurement.

- A millimetre is a tenth of a centimetre (10 mm = 1 cm)
- A centimetre is a tenth of a decimetre (10 cm = 1 dm)
- A decimetre is a tenth of a metre (10 dm = 1 m)
- A centimetre is a hundredth of a metre (100 cm = 1 m)

REMEMBER:

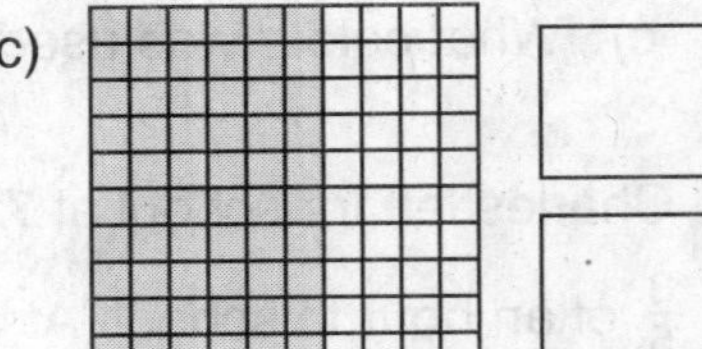

Decimals are short forms for fractions: .73 has 7 tenths (= 700 hundredths) plus 3 more hundredths.

---

1. Write a fraction and a decimal for each picture.

a)  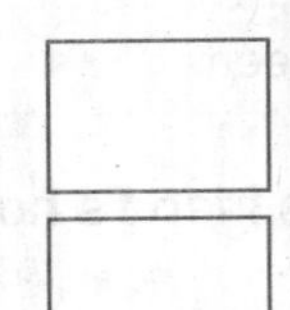

b) 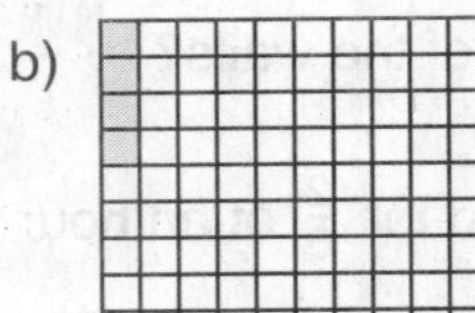 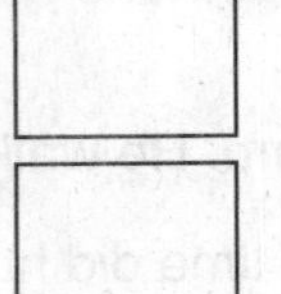

c)

2. Convert the fraction to a decimal. Then shade.

a) $\frac{39}{100}$ = 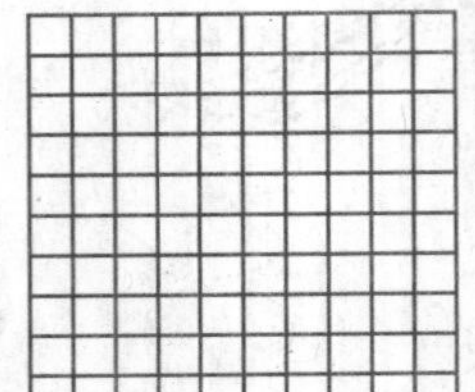

b) $\frac{65}{100}$ =

c) $\frac{7}{100}$ = 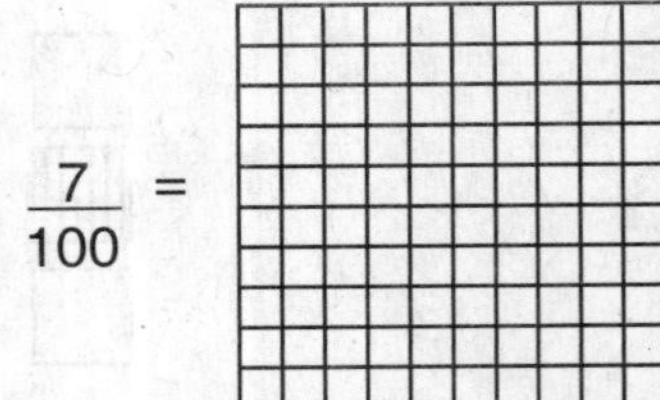

3. The picture shows a floor plan of a zoo. Write a fraction and a decimal for each shaded part:

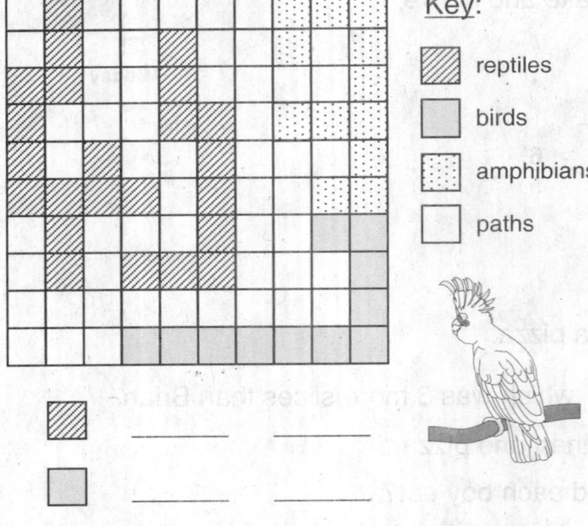

4. Make your own floor plan for a zoo. Write a fraction and a decimal for each shaded part:

NS6-63: Tenths and Hundredths

1. Draw lines around the columns to show tenths as in a). Then, write a fraction and a decimal to represent the number of shaded squares.

a) 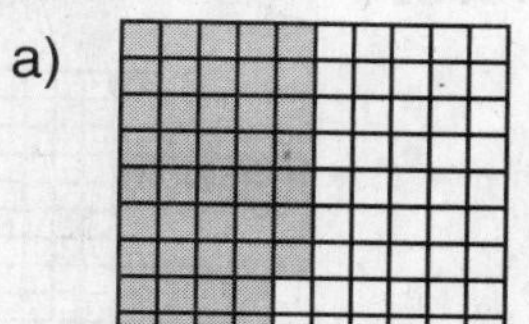 = 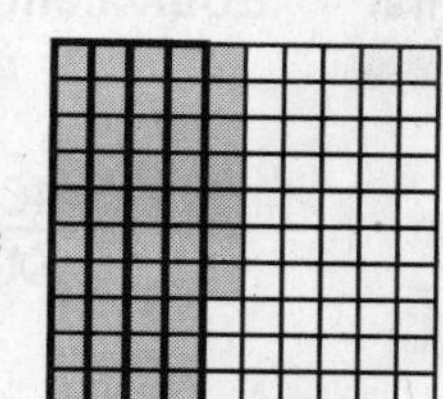

47 hundredths = 4 tenths ___ hundredths

$\frac{47}{100}$ = . 4 7

b) 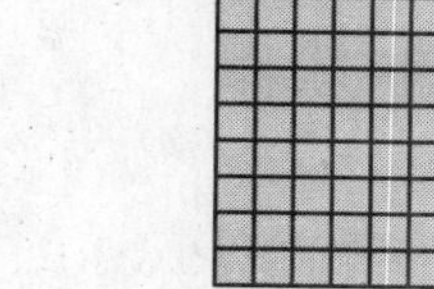 = 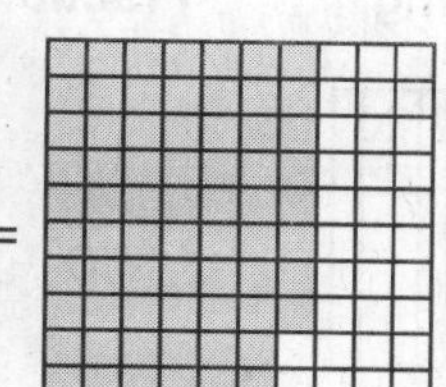

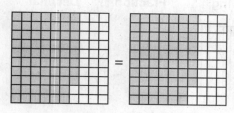

___ hundredths = ___ tenths ___ hundredths

$\frac{\quad}{100}$ = . ___ ___

c) 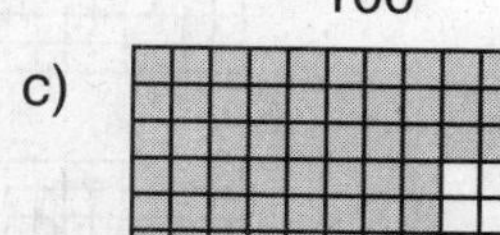 = 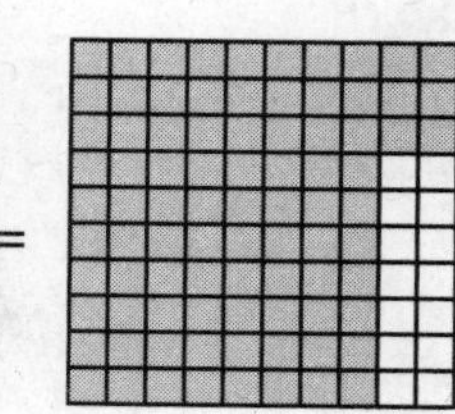

___ hundredths = ___ tenths ___ hundredths

$\frac{\quad}{100}$ = . ___ ___

d) 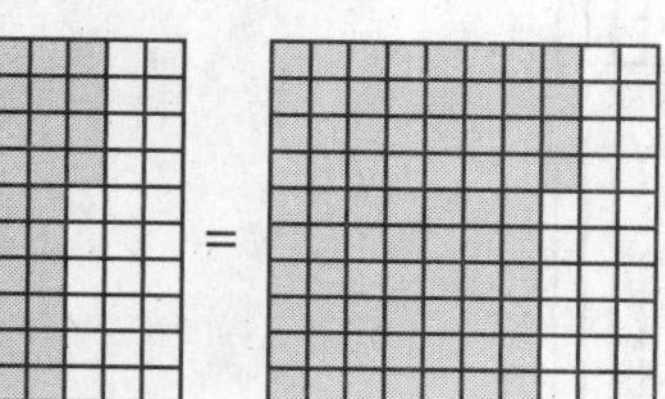

___ hundredths = ___ tenths ___ hundredths

$\frac{\quad}{100}$ = . ___ ___

2. Fill in the blanks.

a) 43 hundredths = ___ tenths ___ hundredths

$\frac{43}{100}$ = . 4 3

b) 28 hundredths = ___ tenths ___ hundredths

$\frac{\quad}{100}$ = . ___ ___

c) 66 hundredths = ___ tenths ___ hundredths

$\frac{\quad}{100}$ = . ___ ___

d) 84 hundredths = ___ tenths ___ hundredths

$\frac{\quad}{100}$ = . ___ ___

e) 9 hundredths = ___ tenths ___ hundredths

$\frac{\quad}{100}$ = . ___ ___

f) 30 hundredths = ___ tenths ___ hundredths

$\frac{\quad}{100}$ = . ___ ___

3. Describe each decimal in two ways.

a) .52 = 5 tenths 2 hundredths

= 52 hundredths

b) .55 = ___ tenths ___ hundredths

= ______________________

c) .40 = ___ tenths ___ hundredths

= ______________________

d) .23 = ___ tenths ___ hundredths

= ______________________

e) .02 = ___ tenths ___ hundredths

= ______________________

f) .18 = ___ tenths ___ hundredths

= ______________________

NS6-64: Changing Tenths to Hundredths

1. Fill in the chart below. The first one has been done for you.

Drawing	Fraction	Decimal	Equivalent Decimal	Equivalent Fraction	Drawing
	$\frac{4}{10}$	0.4	0.40	$\frac{40}{100}$	

2. Write a fraction for the number of hundredths. Then count the shaded columns and write a fraction for the number of tenths.

a) 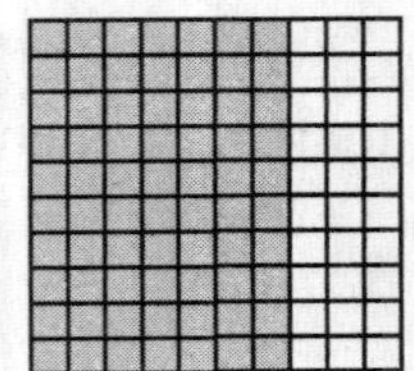

$\frac{\quad}{100} = \frac{\quad}{10}$

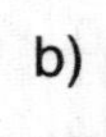

b) 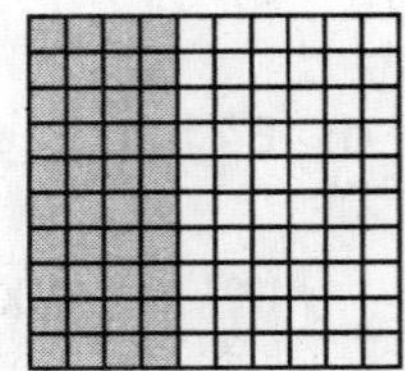

$\frac{\quad}{100} = \frac{\quad}{10}$

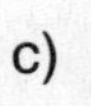

c) 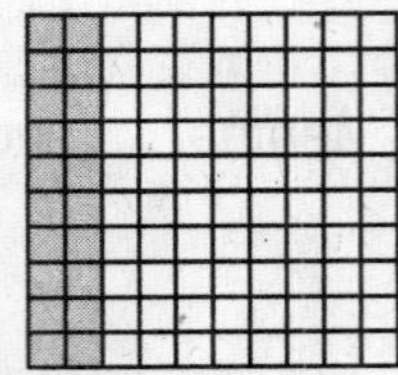

$\frac{\quad}{100} = \frac{\quad}{10}$

d) 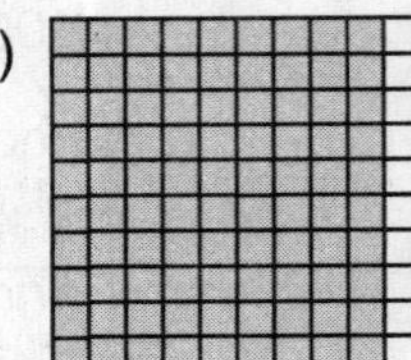

$\frac{\quad}{100} = \frac{\quad}{10}$

3. Fill in the missing numbers. **REMEMBER:** $\frac{10}{100} = \frac{1}{10}$

a) $.5 = \frac{5}{10} = \frac{\quad}{100} = .\_\_\ \_\_$

b) $.\_\_ = \frac{3}{10} = \frac{\quad}{100} = .30$

c) $.\_\_ = \frac{9}{10} = \frac{\quad}{100} = .90$

d) $.\_\_ = \frac{8}{10} = \frac{\quad}{100} = .\_\_\ \_\_$

e) $.\_\_ = \frac{\quad}{10} = \frac{40}{100} = .\_\_\ \_\_$

f) $.\_\_ = \frac{\quad}{10} = \frac{70}{100} = .\_\_\ \_\_$

g) $.\_\_ = \frac{4}{10} = \frac{\quad}{100} = .\_\_\ \_\_$

h) $.\_\_ = \frac{6}{10} = \frac{\quad}{100} = .\_\_\ \_\_$

i) $.3 = \frac{\quad}{10} = \frac{\quad}{100} = .\_\_\ \_\_$

NS6-65: Decimals, Money and Measurements

A **dime** is **one tenth** of a dollar. A **penny** is one **hundredth** of a dollar.

10¢ 1¢

1. Express the value of each decimal in four different ways.

a) .64

6 dimes 4 pennies

6 tenths 4 hundredths

64 pennies

64 hundredths

b) .72

c) . 43

d) .04

2. A **decimetre** is **one tenth** of a metre. A **centimetre** is a **hundredth** of a metre.
Express the value of each measurement in four different ways.

a) .28 m

2 decimetres 8 centimetres

b) .13 m

3. Express the value of each decimal in 4 different ways.
HINT: First add a zero in the hundredths place.

a) .6 ____ dimes ____ pennies

____ tenths ____ hundredths

____ pennies

____ hundredths

b) .8 ____ dimes ____ pennies

____ tenths ____ hundredths

____ pennies

____ hundredths

4. Express the value of each decimal in four different ways. Then circle the greater number.

a) .27 ____ dimes ____ pennies

____ tenths ____ hundredths

____ pennies

____ hundredths

b) .3 ____ dimes ____ pennies

____ tenths ____ hundredths

____ pennies

____ hundredth

5. George says .63 is greater than .8 because 63 is greater than 8. Can you explain his mistake?

NS6-66: Changing Notation: Fractions and Decimals

1. Fill in the missing numbers.

a) 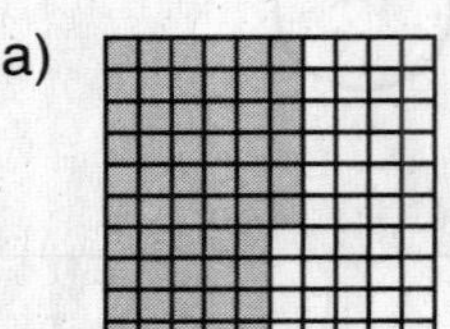
b) 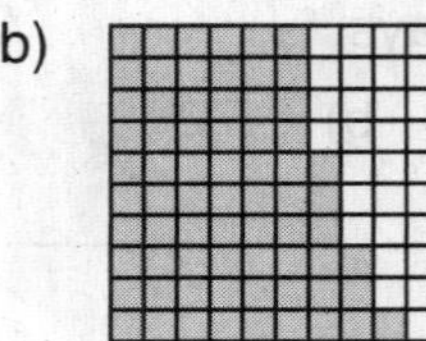
c) 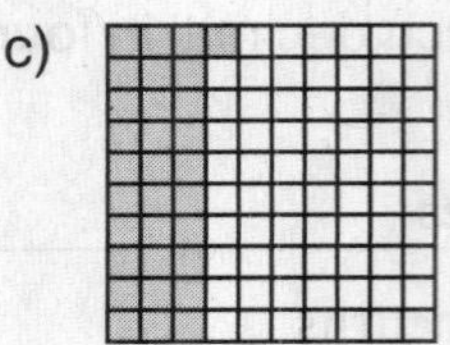
d) 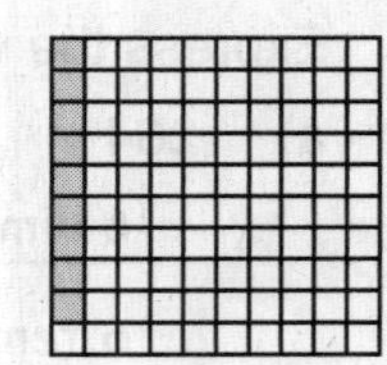

tenths	hundredths

tenths	hundredths

tenths	hundredths

tenths	hundredths

$\frac{}{100}$ = . ____ ____ (tenths, hundredths) $\frac{}{100}$ = . ____ ____ $\frac{}{100}$ = . ____ ____ $\frac{}{100}$ = . ____ ____

2. Write the following decimals as fractions.

a) .3 = $\frac{}{10}$ b) .5 = $\frac{}{10}$ c) .8 = $\frac{}{10}$ d) .2 = $\frac{}{10}$ e) .1 = $\frac{}{10}$

f) .34 = $\frac{}{100}$ g) .39 = $\frac{}{100}$ h) .77 = $\frac{}{100}$ i) .86 = $\frac{}{100}$ j) .61 = $\frac{}{100}$

k) .7 = l) .34 = m) .06 = n) .4 = o) .04 =

p) .6 = q) .46 = r) . 25 = s) .93 = t) .06 =

3. Change the following fractions to decimals.

a) $\frac{2}{10}$ = . ____ b) $\frac{4}{10}$ = . ____ c) $\frac{3}{10}$ = . ____ d) $\frac{9}{10}$ = . ____

e) $\frac{93}{100}$ = . f) $\frac{78}{100}$ = . ___ ___ g) $\frac{66}{100}$ = . h) $\frac{5}{100}$ = . ___ ___

4. Circle the equalities that are incorrect.

a) $.36 = \frac{36}{100}$ b) $.9 = \frac{9}{100}$ c) $.6 = \frac{6}{10}$ d) $\frac{27}{100} = .27$ e) $\frac{3}{100} = .03$

f) $.75 = \frac{74}{100}$ g) $.40 = \frac{40}{10}$ h) $.75 = \frac{75}{100}$ i) $.08 = \frac{8}{100}$ j) $.03 = \frac{3}{10}$

5. Write as a decimal.

a) 8 tenths 2 hundredths = b) 0 tenths 9 hundredths =

6. Write .46 as a fraction in lowest terms. Explain how you found your answer.

NS6-67: Decimals and Fractions Greater Than One

A hundreds block may be used to represent a whole. 10 is one tenth of 100, so a tens block represents one tenth of the whole. 1 is one hundredth of 100, so a ones block represents one hundredth of the whole.

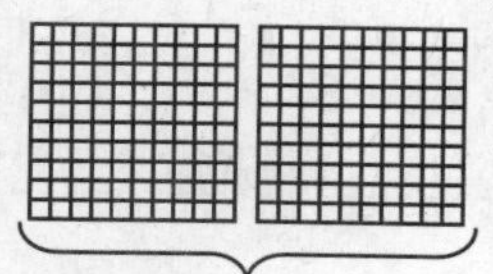
2 wholes

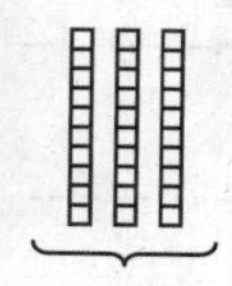
3 tenths

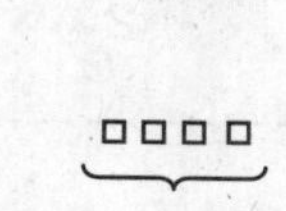
4 hundredths

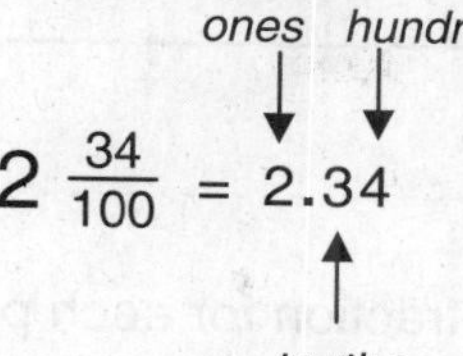

$2\frac{34}{100} = 2.34$

NOTE: A mixed fraction can be written as a decimal.

1. Write a mixed fraction and a decimal for the base ten models below.

a) 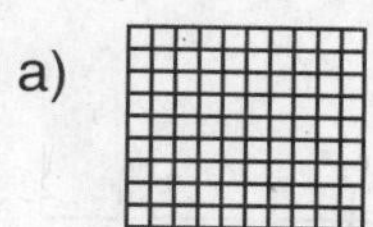  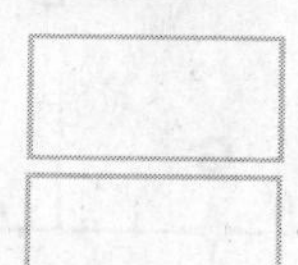

b) 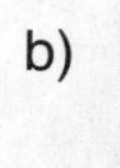 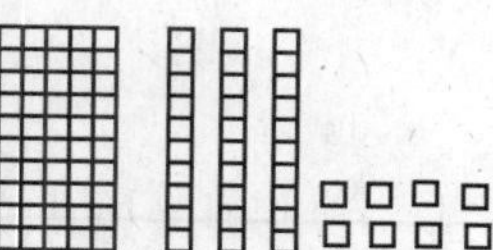 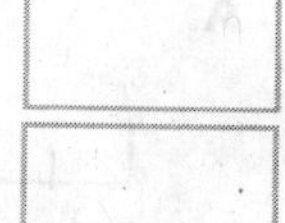

c)  

d) 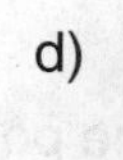 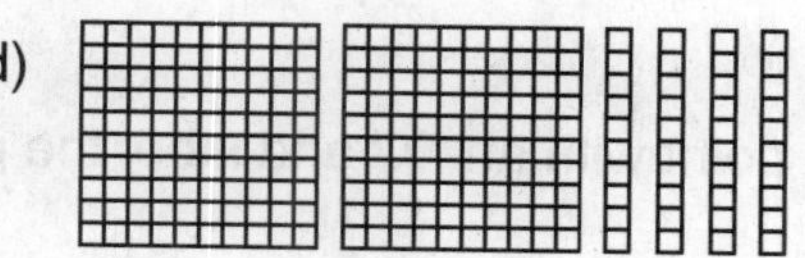 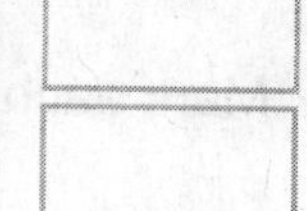

e) 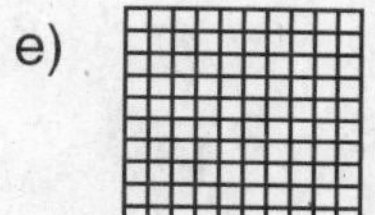 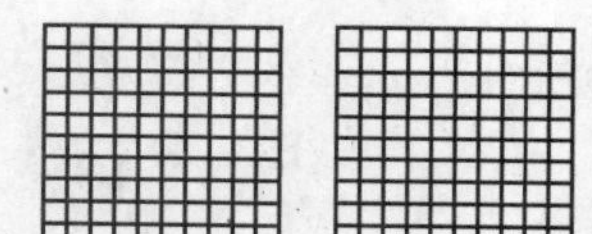 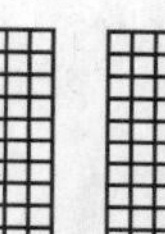 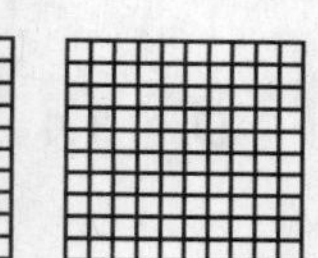 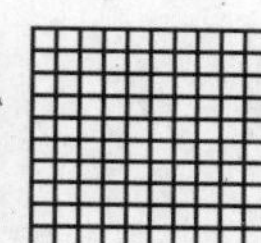 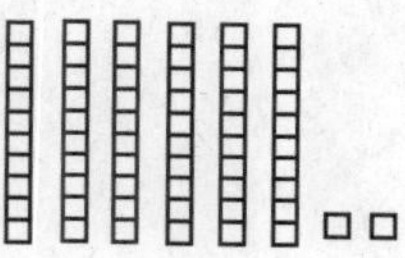 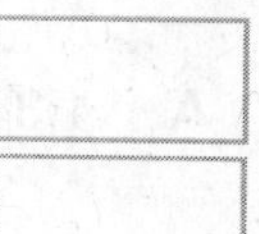

2. Draw a base ten model for the following decimals.

a) 3.21 b) 1.62

3. Write a decimal and a mixed fraction for each of the pictures below.

a) 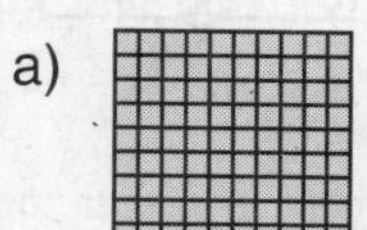 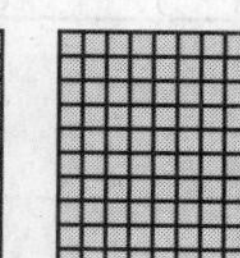 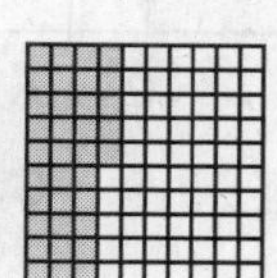 

b) 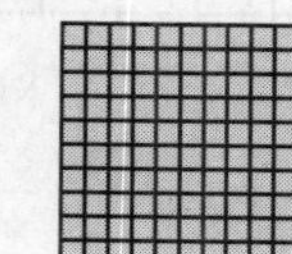 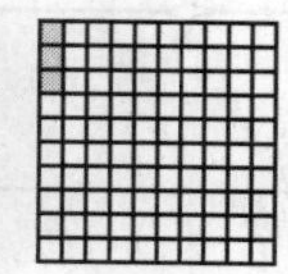 

4. Write a decimal for each of the mixed fractions below.

a) $1\frac{32}{100}$ = b) $2\frac{71}{100}$ = c) $8\frac{7}{10}$ = d) $4\frac{27}{100}$ =

e) $3\frac{7}{100}$ = f) $17\frac{8}{10}$ = g) $27\frac{1}{10}$ = h) $38\frac{5}{100}$ =

5. Which decimal represents a greater number?
Explain your answer with a picture.

a) 6 tenths or 6 hundredths? b) .8 or .08? c) 1.02 or 1.20?

NS6-68: Decimals and Fractions On Number Lines

This number line is divided into tenths. The number represented by Point A is $2\frac{3}{10}$ or 2.3.

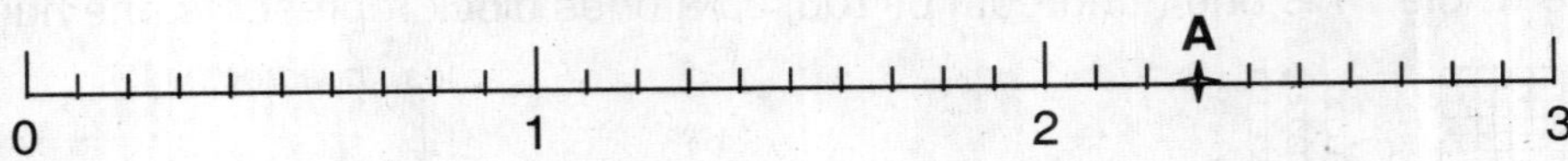

---

1. Write a fraction or a mixed fraction for each point.

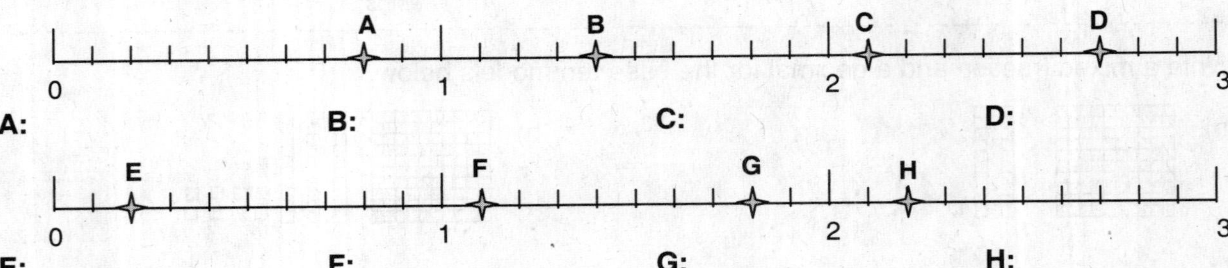

A: B: C: D:

E: F: G: H:

2. Mark each point with an "X" and label the point with the correct letter.

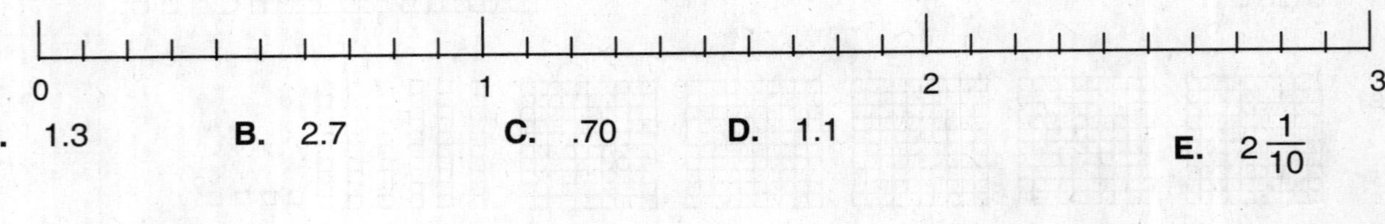

A. 1.3 **B.** 2.7 **C.** .70 **D.** 1.1 **E.** $2\frac{1}{10}$

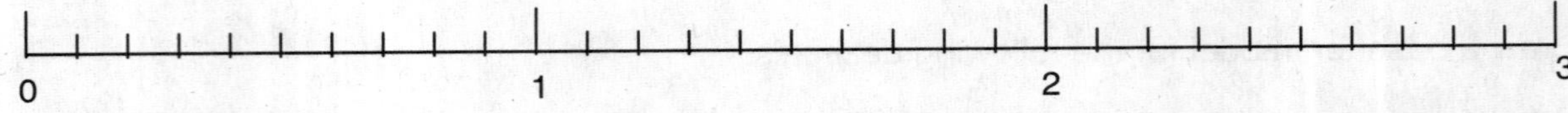

F. one and three tenths **G.** nine tenths **H.** one and one tenth **I.** two decimal nine

3. Write the name of each point as a decimal in words.

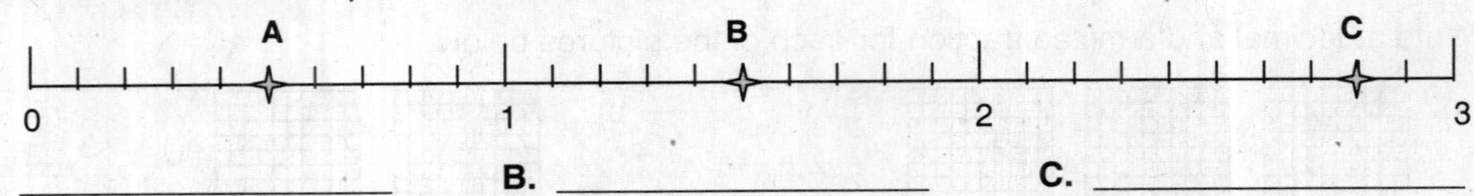

A. ____________ **B.** ____________ **C.** ____________

4. Mark the decimals on the number lines.

a) **0.6** b) **1.2**

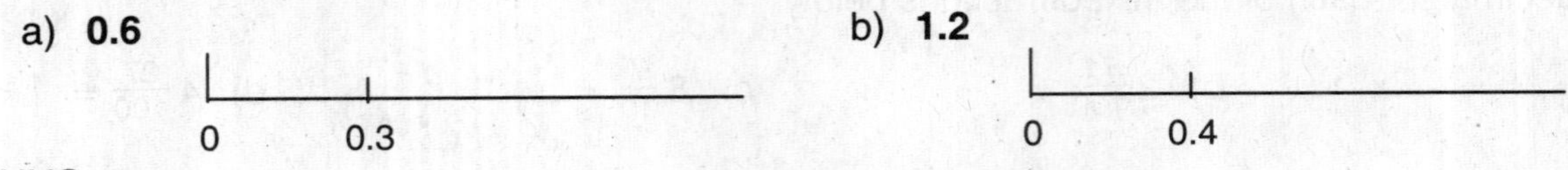

BONUS

5. Mark the following fractions and decimals on the number line.

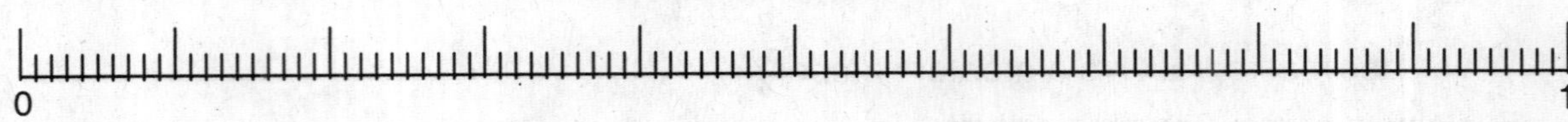

A. .72 **B.** $\frac{34}{100}$ **C.** .05 **D.** $\frac{51}{100}$

NS6-69: Comparing and Ordering Fractions and Decimals

1.

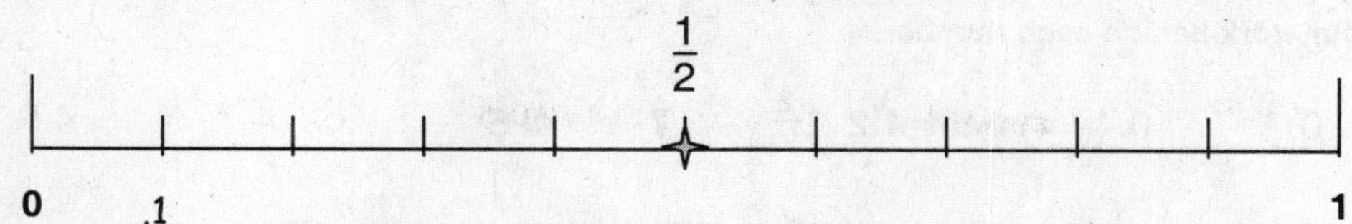

a) Write a decimal for each point marked on the number line. (The first decimal is written for you.)

b) Which decimal is equal to one half? $\frac{1}{2}$ =

2. Use the number line in Question 1 to say whether each decimal is closer to "zero," "a half," or "one."

a) .3 is closer to ________ b) .7 is closer to ________ c) .8 is closer to ________

d) .9 is closer to ________ e) .1 is closer to ________ f) .2 is closer to ________

3.

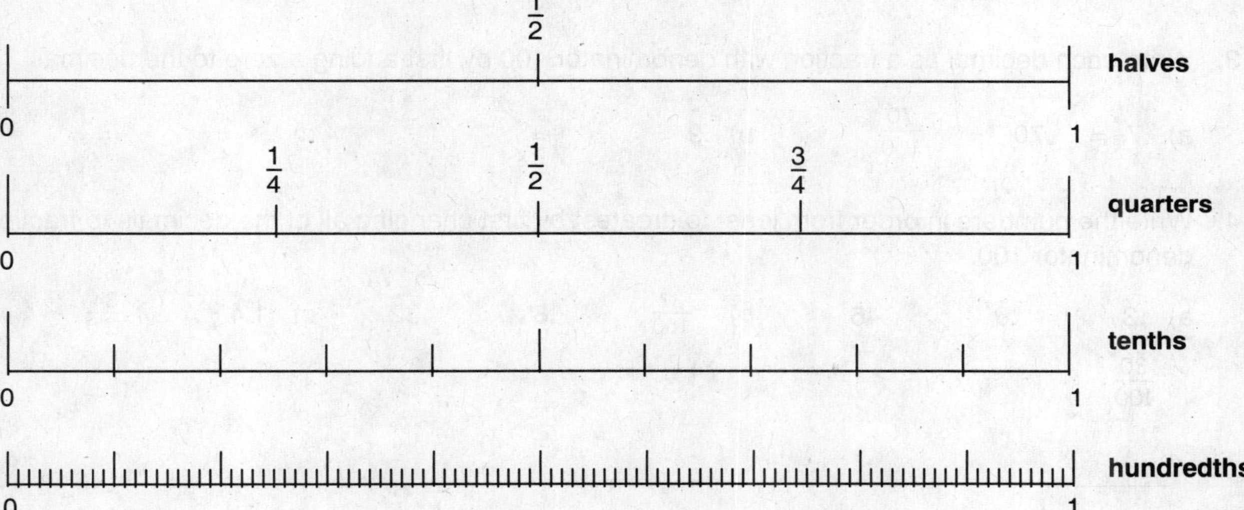

Use the number lines above to compare the numbers given. Write < (less than) or > (greater than) between each pair of numbers.

a) 0.7 ☐ $\frac{3}{4}$ b) 0.4 ☐ $\frac{7}{10}$ c) 0.8 ☐ $\frac{1}{2}$ d) 0.2 ☐ $\frac{1}{4}$

e) 0.4 ☐ $\frac{1}{2}$ f) 0.35 ☐ $\frac{1}{4}$ g) 0.07 ☐ $\frac{1}{2}$ h) $\frac{3}{4}$ ☐ .65

4. Which whole number is each decimal or mixed fraction closest to: "zero," "one," "two," or "three"?

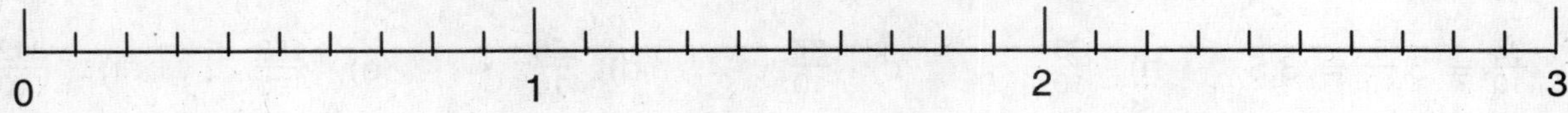

a) 2.4 is closest to ________ b) 2.8 is closest to ________ c) $1\frac{3}{10}$ is closest to ________

NS6-70: Ordering Fractions and Decimals

1. Write the numbers in order by first changing each decimal to a fraction with a denominator of 10.
NOTE: Show your work beside each number.

a) 0.6 $\frac{6}{10}$ 0.7 0.4 b) 1.2 $1\frac{2}{10}$ 3.7 3.5 c) 4.7 4.5 $4\frac{3}{10}$

____________ ____________ ____________

2. Ali says: "To compare .6 and .42, I add a zero to .6:

$.6 = 6 \textit{ tenths} = 60 \textit{ hundredths} = .60$

60 (hundredths) is greater than 42 (hundredths).

So .6 is greater than .42."

Add a zero to the decimal expressed in tenths. Then circle the greater number in each pair.

a) .4 .32 b) .72 .8 c) .32 .2

3. Write each decimal as a fraction with denominator 100 by first adding a zero to the decimal.

a) .7 = .70 = $\frac{70}{100}$ b) .9 = __ = __ c) .1 = 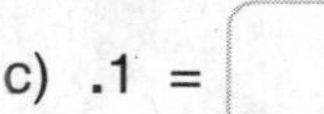 __ = __

4. Write the numbers in order from least to greatest by first changing all of the decimals to fractions with denominator 100.

a) .3 .9 .45 b) $\frac{37}{100}$ .8 .32 c) 1.4 $1\frac{34}{100}$ 1.35

$\frac{30}{100}$  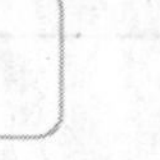

____________ ____________ ____________

5. Change $\frac{27}{10}$ to a mixed fraction by shading the correct number of pieces.

   Mixed Fraction: ______

6. Change the following improper fractions to mixed fractions.

a) $\frac{25}{10}$ b) $\frac{37}{10}$ c) $\frac{86}{10}$ d) $\frac{60}{10}$ e) $\frac{186}{100}$ f) $\frac{175}{100}$

7. Change the following improper fractions to decimals by first writing them as mixed fractions.

a) $\frac{35}{10} = 3\frac{5}{10} = 3.5$ b) $\frac{38}{10}$ c) $\frac{87}{10}$ d) $\frac{53}{10}$ e) $\frac{153}{100}$ f) $\frac{342}{100}$

8. Which is greater, $\frac{23}{10}$ or 2.4? Explain.

9. Write 5 decimals greater than 1.32 and less than 1.4.

10. 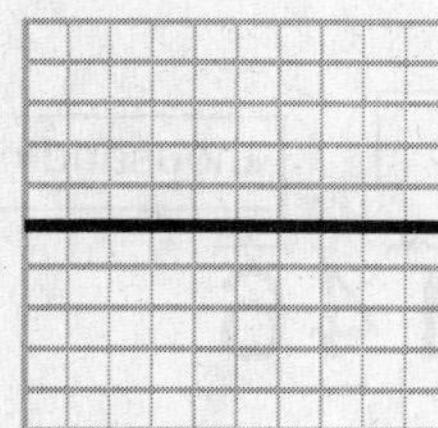

Shade $\frac{1}{2}$ of the squares. Write 2 fractions and 2 decimals for $\frac{1}{2}$.

Fractions: $\frac{1}{2} = \frac{\quad}{10} = \frac{\quad}{100}$

Decimals: $\frac{1}{2}$ = .____ = .____

11. 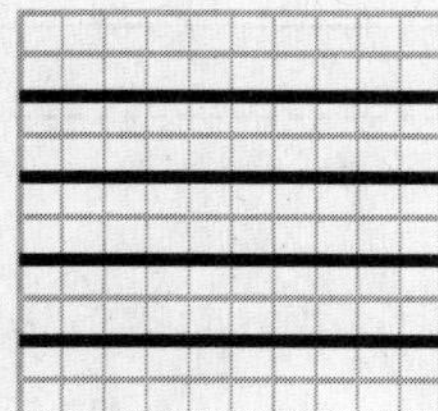

Shade $\frac{1}{5}$ of the boxes. Write 2 fractions and 2 decimals for $\frac{1}{5}$.

Fractions: $\frac{1}{5} = \frac{\quad}{10} = \frac{\quad}{100}$

Decimals: $\frac{1}{5}$ = .____ = .____

12. Write equivalent fractions.

a) $\frac{2}{5} = \frac{\quad}{10} = \frac{\quad}{100}$ b) $\frac{3}{5} = \frac{\quad}{10} = \frac{\quad}{100}$ c) $\frac{4}{5} = \frac{\quad}{10} = \frac{\quad}{100}$.

13. 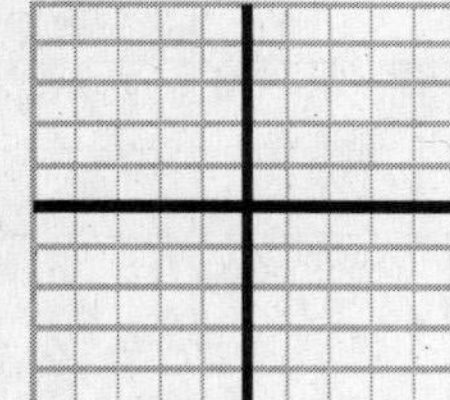

Shade $\frac{1}{4}$ of the squares. Write a fraction and a decimal for $\frac{1}{4}$ and $\frac{3}{4}$.

Fraction: $\frac{1}{4} = \frac{\quad}{100}$ *Decimal:* $\frac{1}{4}$ = .____

Fraction: $\frac{3}{4} = \frac{\quad}{100}$ *Decimal:* $\frac{3}{4}$ = .____

14. Circle the greater number.

HINT: First change all fractions and decimals to fractions with denominator 100.

a) $\frac{3}{4}$ .72 b) $\frac{1}{2}$ .53 c) $\frac{3}{5}$ .87

$\frac{75}{100}$

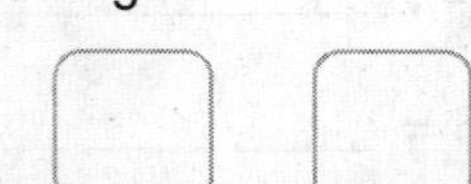

15. Write the numbers in order from least to greatest. Explain how you found your answer.

a) .8 .42 $\frac{3}{4}$ b) $\frac{1}{2}$ $\frac{4}{5}$ .35 c) $\frac{3}{5}$ .45 $\frac{1}{2}$

16. How does knowing that $\frac{1}{4} = 0.25$ help you find the decimal form of $\frac{3}{4}$?

17. Explain how you know 0.65 is greater that $\frac{1}{2}$.

NS6-71: Thousandths

If a thousands cube is used to represent a whole number, then a hundreds block represents a tenth, a tens block represents a hundredth, and a ones block represents a thousandth of a whole.

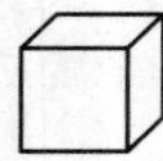
1 whole

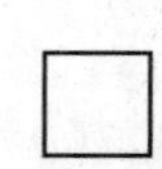
1 tenth

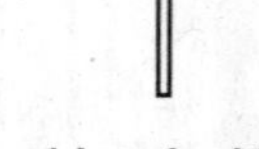
1 hundredth

1 thousandth

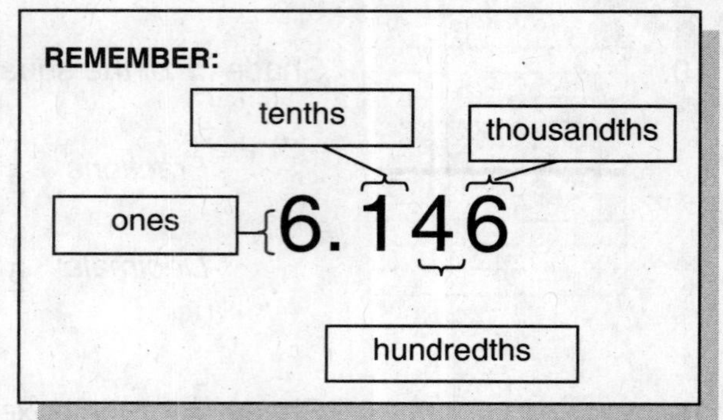

1. Beside each number, write the place value of the underlined digit.

a) 3.2<u>7</u>4 b) 9.27<u>3</u> c) 2.<u>5</u>37

d) 7.12<u>9</u> e) <u>5</u>.214 f) 8.<u>9</u>78

2. Write the following numbers into the place value chart. The first one has been done for you.

	ones	tenths	hundredths	thousandths
a) 6.512	6	5	1	2
c) 7.03				
e) 1.763				
g) 6.38				
i) 5.813				

	ones	tenths	hundredths	thousandths
b) 6.354				
d) 1.305				
f) 0.536				
h) 8				
j) 0.13				

3. Write the following decimals as fractions.

a) .652 = b) .372 = c) .20 = d) .002 =

4. Write each decimal in expanded form.

a) .237 = 2 tenths + 3 hundredths + 7 thousandths

b) .325 = ____________________

c) 6.336 = ____________________

5. Write the following fractions as decimals.

a) $\frac{49}{100}$ = b) $\frac{50}{100}$ = c) $\frac{758}{1000}$ = d) $\frac{25}{1000}$ =

6. Compare each pair of decimals by writing < or > in the box.
HINT: Add zeroes wherever necessary to give each number the same number of digits after the decimal point.

a) .375 ☐ .378 b) .233 ☐ .47 c) .956 ☐ .1

d) .27 ☐ .207 e) .7 ☐ .32 f) .8 ☐ .516

NS6-72: Adding Hundredths

1. Write a fraction for each shaded part. Then add the fractions, and shade your answer. The first one has been done for you.

a) 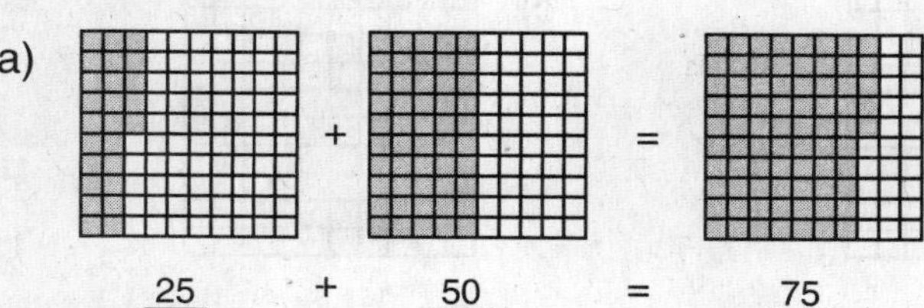

$\frac{25}{100} + \frac{50}{100} = \frac{75}{100}$

b) 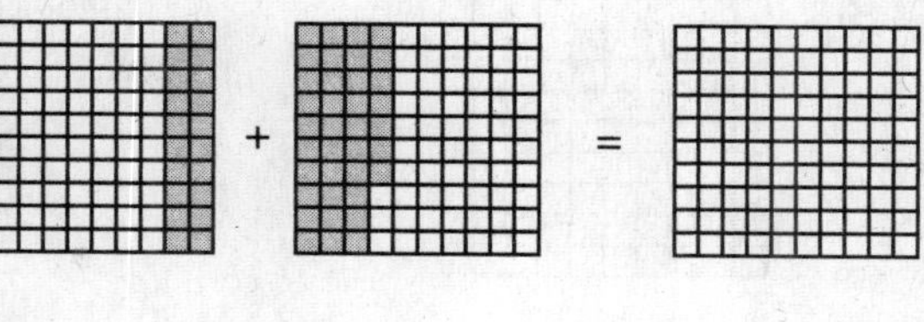

c) d) 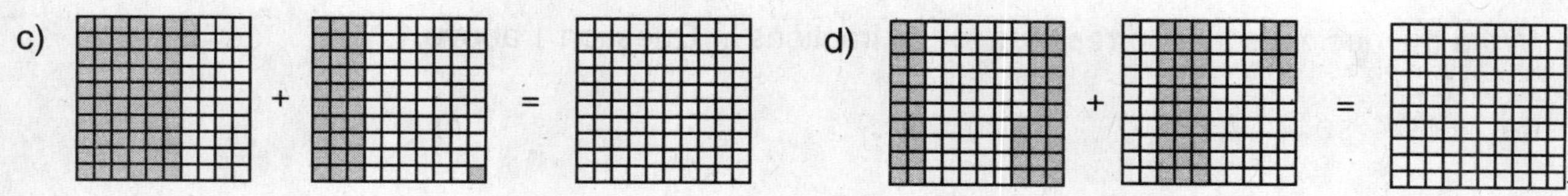

2. Write the decimals that correspond to the fractions in Question 1 above.

a) .25 + .50 = .75	b)
c)	d)

3. Add the decimals by lining up the digits. Be sure that your final answer is expressed as a decimal.

a) 0.32 + 0.57 =

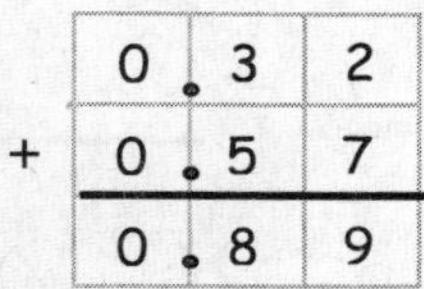

b) 0.91 + 0.04 =

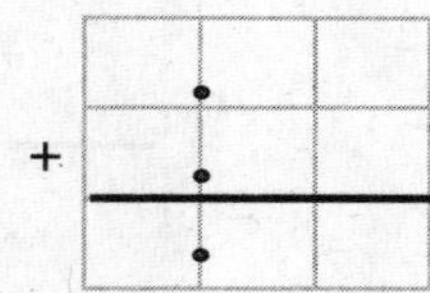

c) 0.42 + 0.72 =

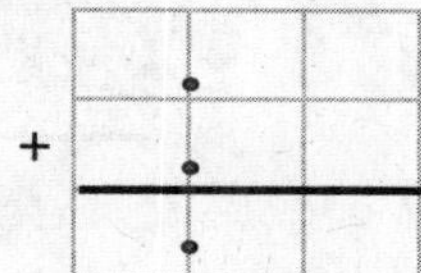

d) 0.22 + 0.57 =

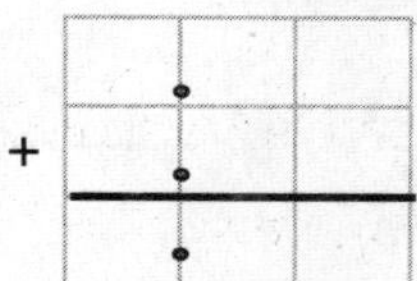

e) 0.3 + 0 .36 =

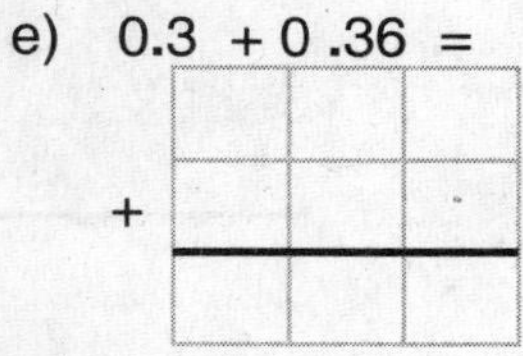

f) 0.5 + 0.48 =

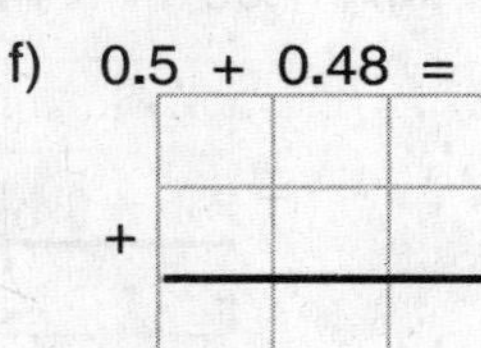

g) 0.81 + 0.58 =

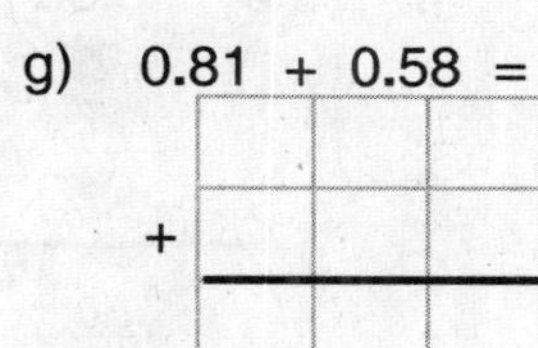

h) 0.46 + 0.22 =

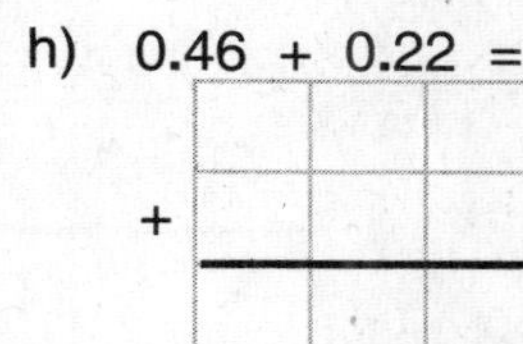

4. Line up the decimals and add the following numbers.

a) 4.32 + 2.17 b) 3.64 + 5.23 c) 9.46 + 3.12 d) 0.87 + 0.02 e) 4.8 + 0.31

5. Each wing of a butterfly is 3.72 cm wide. It's body is .46 cm wide. How wide is the butterfly?

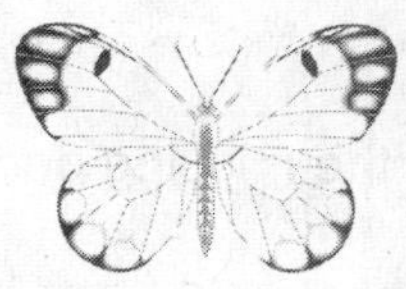

6. Anne made punch by mixing .63 litres of juice with .36 litres of ginger ale. How many litres of punch did she make?

NS6-73: Subtracting Hundredths

1. Subtract by crossing out the correct number of boxes.

a) 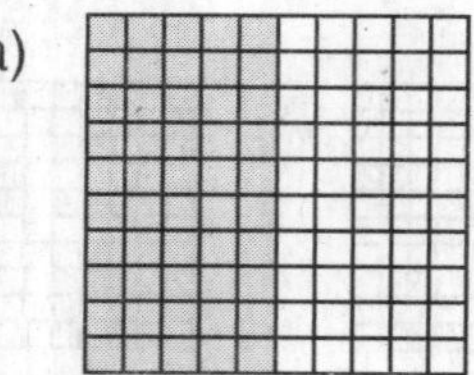

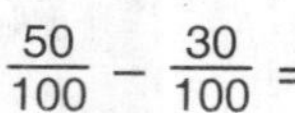

$\frac{50}{100} - \frac{30}{100} =$

b) 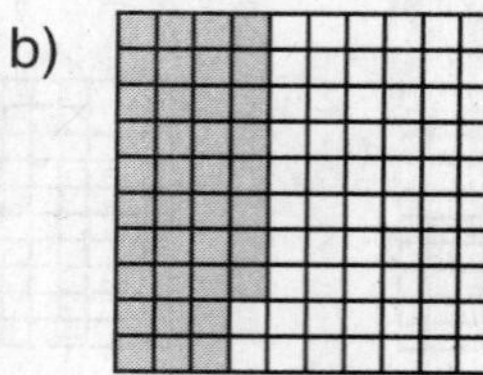

$\frac{38}{100} - \frac{12}{100} =$

c) 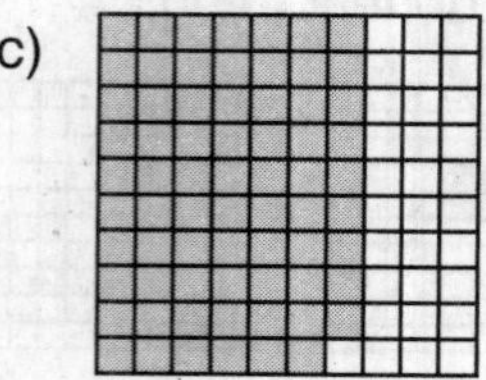

$\frac{69}{100} - \frac{34}{100} =$

2. Write the decimals that correspond to the fractions in Question 1 above.

a) .50 - .30 = .20	b)	c)

3. Subtract the decimals by lining up the digits.

a) 0.53 − 0.21 =

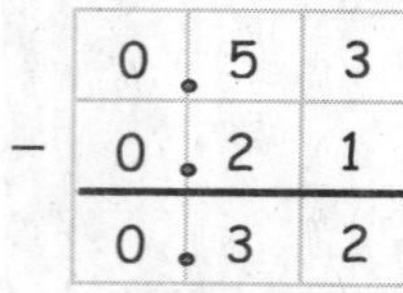

b) 0.88 − 0.34 =

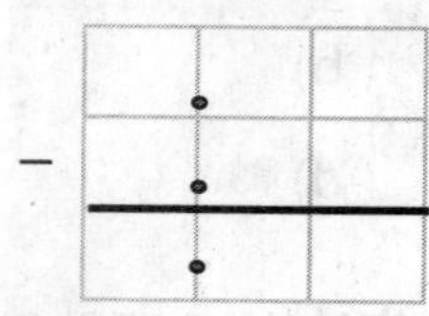

c) 0.46 − 0.23 =

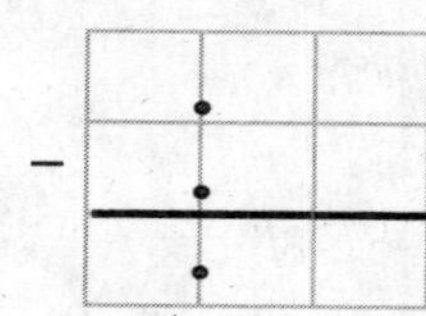

d) 0.75 − 0.21 =

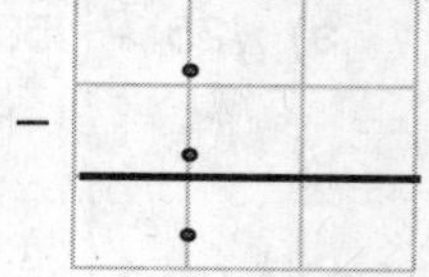

e) 0.33 − .17 =

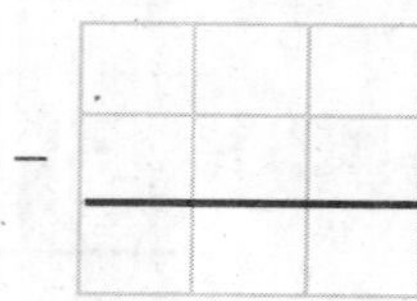

f) 0.64 − 0.38 =

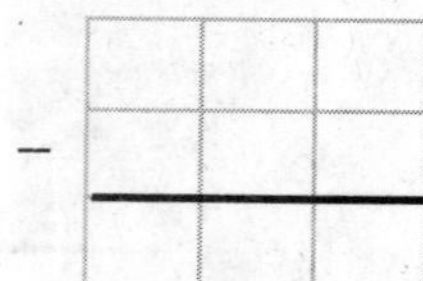

g) 0.92 − 0.59 =

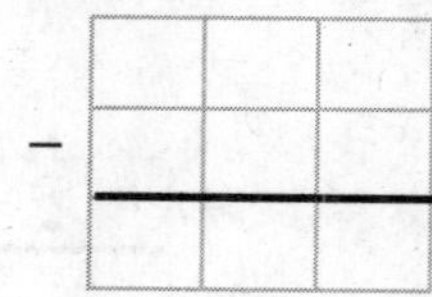

h) 0.53 − 0.26 =

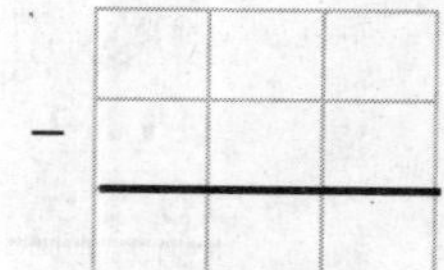

i) 1.00 − .82 =

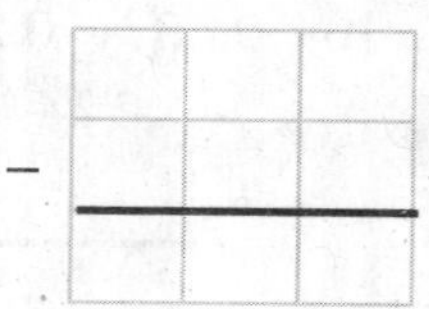

j) 1.00 − 0.36 =

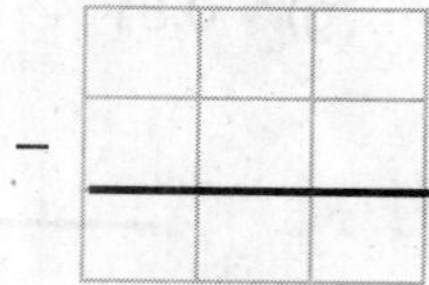

k) 1.00 − 0.44 =

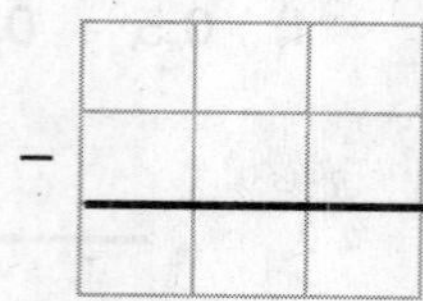

l) 1.00 − 0.29 =

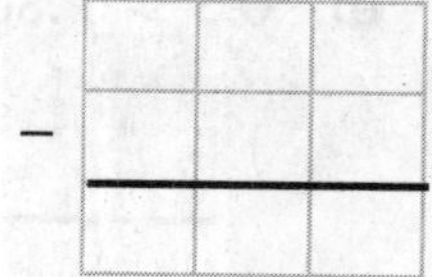

4. Subtract the following decimals.

a) .82 − .45 b) .97 − .38 c) .72 − .64 d) .31 − .17

e) .58 − .3 f) .62 − .6 g) .98 − .03 h) .53 − .09

5. Find the missing decimal in each of the following.

a) 1 = .35 + ☐ b) 1 = .72 + ☐ c) 1 = .41 + ☐

NS6-74: Adding and Subtracting Decimals

1. Add by drawing a base ten model. Then, using the chart provided, line up the decimal points and add.
NOTE: Use a hundreds block for a whole and a tens block for one tenth.

a) 1.23 + 1.12

b) 1.46 + 1.33

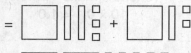

=

=

	ones	tenths	hundredths
+			

	ones	tenths	hundredths
+			

2. Draw a model of the greater number. Then subtract by crossing out blocks as shown in part a).

a) 2.35 – 1.12 = 1.23

b) 3.24 – 2.11

3. Add or subtract.

a)

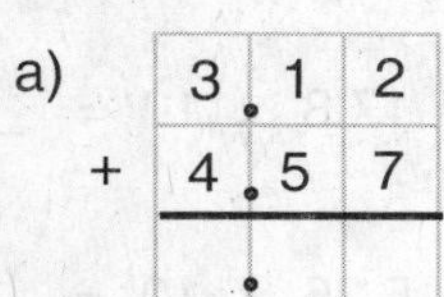

b)

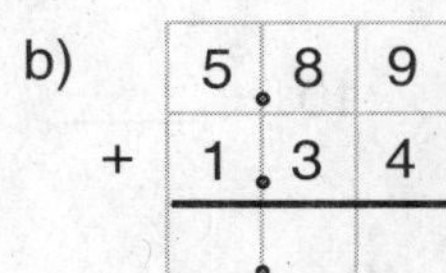

c)

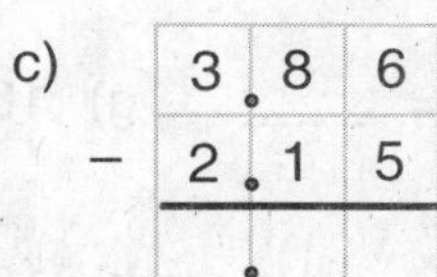

d)

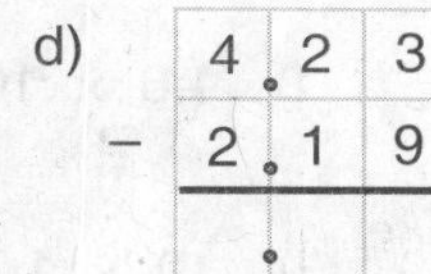

e)

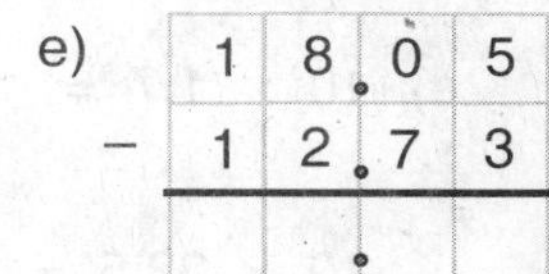

4. Subtract each pair of numbers by lining up the decimal points.

a) 7.87 – 4.03 b) 9.74 – 6.35 c) 2.75 – .28 d) 28.71 – 1.4 e) 17.9 – 4.29

5. The average temperature in Jakarta is 30.33°C and, in Toronto, it is 11.9°C.
How much warmer is Jakarta than Toronto?

6. Mercury is 57.6 million kilometres from the Sun.
Earth is 148.64 million kilometres from the Sun.

How much farther from the Sun is the Earth?

7. Continue the patterns. a) .2, .4, .6, ____, ____, ____ b) .3, .6, .9, ____, ____, ____

NS6-75: Multiplying Decimals by 10

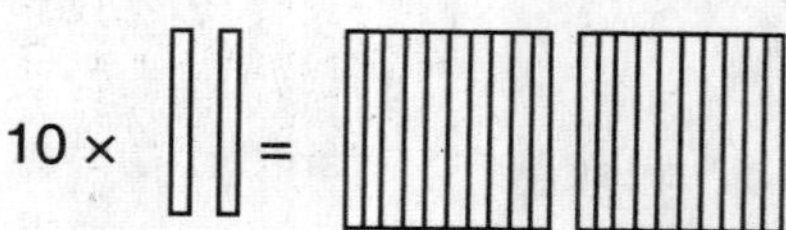

If a hundreds block represents 1 whole, then a tens block represents 1 tenth (or 0.1).

10 tenths make 1 whole: $10 \times 0.1 = 1.0$

---

1. Multiply the number of tens blocks by 10. Then show how many hundreds blocks you would have. The first one is done for you.

a) 10 × [2 tens blocks] = [2 hundreds blocks]

$10 \times 0.2 =$ 2

b) 10 × [3 tens blocks] =

$10 \times 0.3 =$ ______

c) 10 × [6 tens blocks] =

$10 \times 0.6 =$ ______

2. Multiply.

a) $10 \times .5 =$ ____ b) $10 \times .7 =$ ____ c) $10 \times 1.4 =$ ____ d) $10 \times .9 =$ ____

e) $10 \times 1.7 =$ ____ f) $1.6 \times 10 =$ ____ g) $18.2 \times 10 =$ ____ h) $17.3 \times 10 =$ ____

i) $10 \times 23.5 =$ ____ j) $10 \times 1.72 =$ ____ k) $10 \times 42.6 =$ ____ l) $5.36 \times 10 =$ ____

3. To change from dm to cm, you multiply by 10 (there are 10 cm in 1 dm).

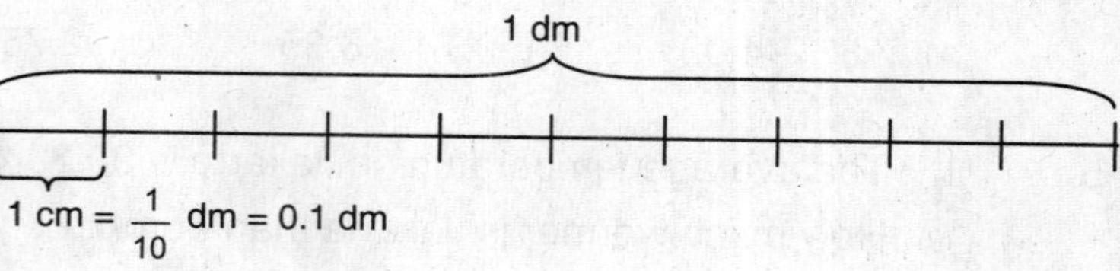

Find the answers.

a) .6 dm = ______ cm b) .8 dm = ______ cm c) 1.6 dm = ______ cm

4. 10×3 can be written as a sum: 3 + 3 + 3 + 3 + 3 + 3 + 3 + 3 + 3 + 3.
Write $10 \times .3$ as a sum and skip count by .3 to find the answer.

5. A dime is a tenth of a dollar (10¢ = $0.10).
Draw a picture or use play money to show that 10 × $0.20 = $2.00.

NS6-76: Multiplying Decimals by 100 and 1000

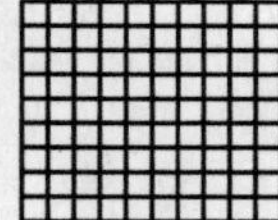 = 1.0 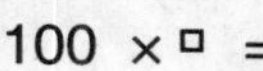 = 0.01  100 × □ = 

If a hundreds block represents 1 whole then a ones block represents 1 hundredth (or .01).

100 hundredths makes 1 whole:
100 × .01 = 1.00

---

1. Write a multiplication statement for each picture.

a) 100 ×  = 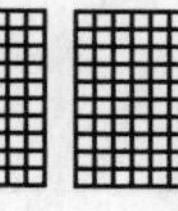

100 × .02 = ______

b) 100 ×  = 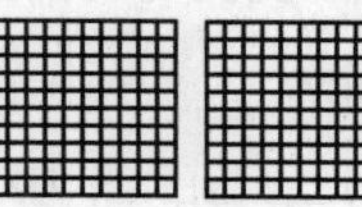

______ = ______

2. The picture shows why the decimal shifts two places to the right when multiplying by 100.

100 × 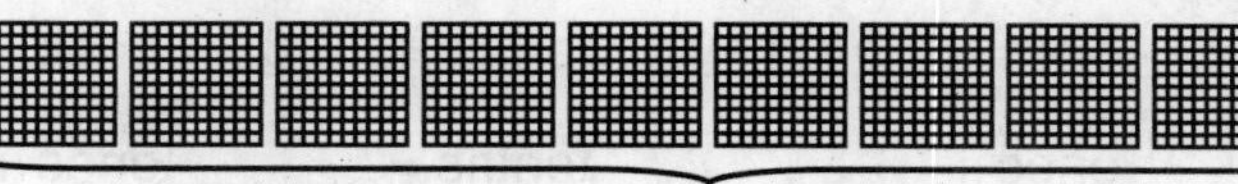 

= 100 × 0.12 = 12 100 × 0.1 = 10 100 × 0.02 = 2

In each case shift the decimal 2 places to the right.

a) 100 × .7 = 70 b) 100 × 1.8 = ______ c) 100 × 4.6 = ______

d) 100 × 5.9 = ______ e) 100 × 2.3 = ______ f) 100 × 4.0 = ______

g) 100 × 0.16 = ______ h) 100 × 0.69 = ______ i) 100 × 0.07 = ______

3. Multiply.

a) 100 × .07 = 7 b) 100 × .06 = ______ c) 100 × .67 = ______ d) .95 × 100 = ______

e) 100 × 1.82 = ______ f) 100 × 4.07 = ______ g) 100 × .50 = ______ h) 100 × .7 = ______

i) 100 × 1.8 = ______ j) 100 × .35 = ______ k) 100 × .64 = ______ l) .95 × 100 = ______

4. a) What do 1000 thousandths add up to? ______ b) What is 1000 × .001? ______

5. Look at your answer to Question 4 b).
How many places right does the decimal shift when you multiply by 1000? ______

6. Multiply the numbers by shifting the decimal.

a) 1000 × .86 = ______ b) 1000 × .325 = ______ c) 1000 × 1.329 = ______

d) 1000 × .76 = ______ e) 1000 × 8.25 = ______ f) 1000 × 7.5 = ______

NS6-77: Multiplying Decimals by Whole Numbers

The picture shows how to multiply a decimal by a whole number.

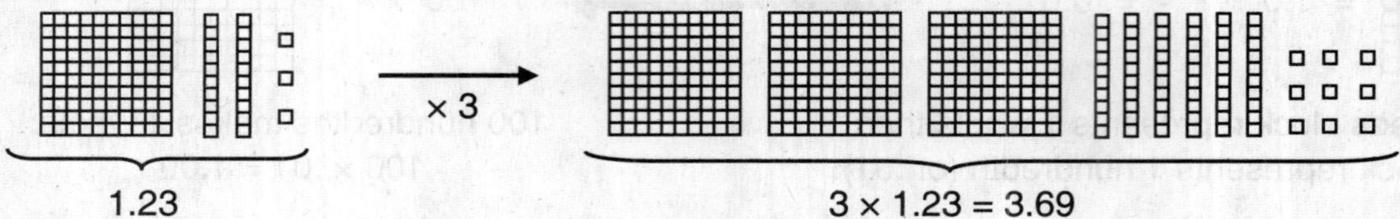

HINT: Simply multiply each digit separately.

---

1. Multiply mentally.

   a) 2 × 1.43 = ______ b) 3 × 1.2 = ______ c) 5 × 1.01 = ______ d) 4 × 2.1 = ______

   e) 2 × 5.34 = ______ f) 4 × 2.1 = ______ g) 3 × 3.12 = ______ h) 3 × 4.32 = ______

2. Multiply by exchanging tenths for ones (the first one is done for you).

   a) 6 × 1.4 = 6 × 1 = 6 ones + 6 × 4 = 24 tenths = 8 ones + 4 tenths = 8.4

   b) 3 × 2.5 = ________ ones + ________ tenths = ______ ones + ______ tenths = ______

   c) 3 × 2.7 = ________ ones + ________ tenths = ______ ones + ______ tenths = ______

   d) 4 × 2.6 = ____

3. Multiply by exchanging tenths for ones or hundredths for tenths.

   a) 3 × 2.51 = ______ ones + ______ tenths + ______ hundredths

   = ______ ones + ______ tenths + ______ hundredths = ______

   b) 4 × 2.14 = ______ ones + ______ tenths + ______ hundredths

   = ______ ones + ______ tenths + ______ hundredths = ______

   c) 5 × 1.41 = ______ ones + ______ tenths + ______ hundredths

   = ______ ones + ______ tenths + ______ hundredths = ______

4. Multiply. In some questions you will have to regroup twice.

a) 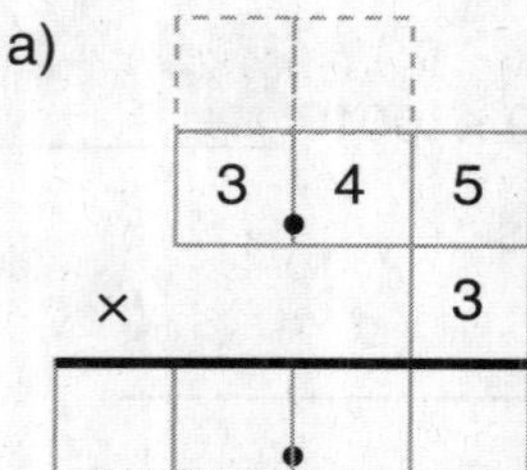

b) 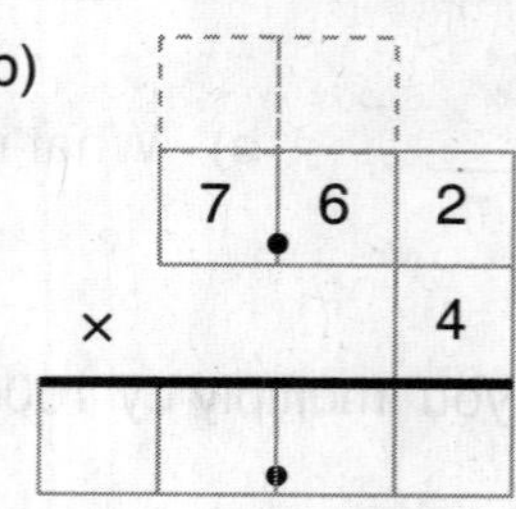

c) 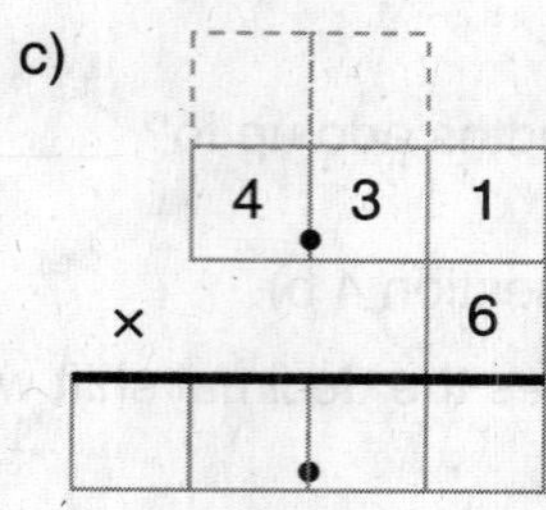

d) 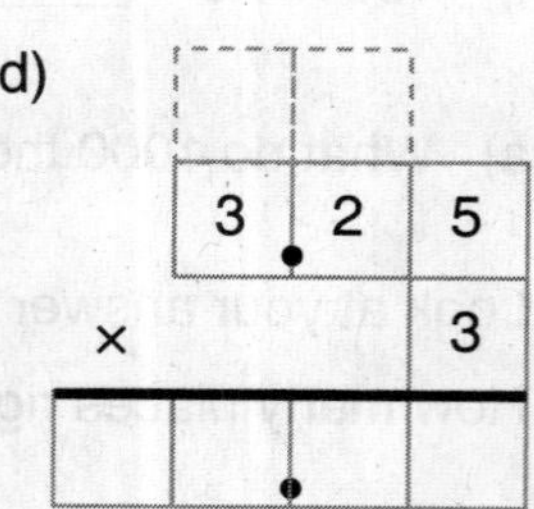

5. In your notebook, find the products.

   a) 5 × 2.1 b) 3 × 8.3 c) 5 × 7.5 d) 9 × 2.81 e) 7 × 3.6 f) 6 × 3.4

   g) 4 × 3.2 h) 5 × 6.35 i) 6 × 3.95 j) 8 × 2.63 k) 3 × 31.21 l) 4 × 12.32

NS6-78: Dividing Decimals by 10 and 100

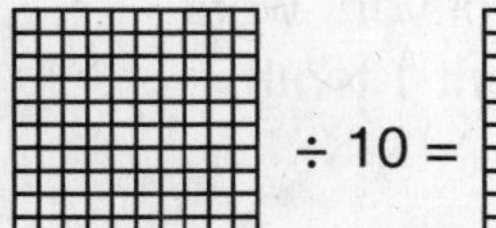 ÷ 10 = 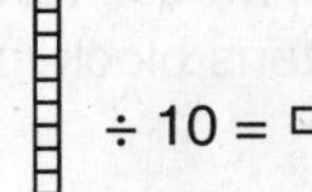 ÷ 10 = □ 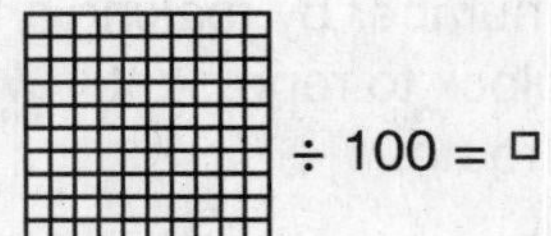 ÷ 100 = □

Divide 1 whole into 10 equal parts – each part is 1 tenth:
1.0 ÷ 10 = 0.1

Divide 1 tenth into 10 equal parts – each part is 1 hundredth:
0.1 ÷ 10 = 0.01

Divide 1 whole into 100 equal parts – each part is 1 hundredth:
1.0 ÷ 100 = 0.01

When you divide a decimal by 10 the decimal shifts one place to the left:

0 . 7 ÷ 10 = .07 7 . 0 ÷ 10 = .7

When you divide a decimal by 100 the decimal shifts two places to the left.

7 . 0 ÷ 100 = .07

---

1. Complete the picture and write a division statement for each picture.

a)  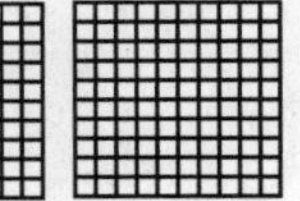 ÷ 10 = 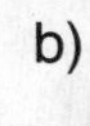

2.0 ÷ 10 = .2

b) 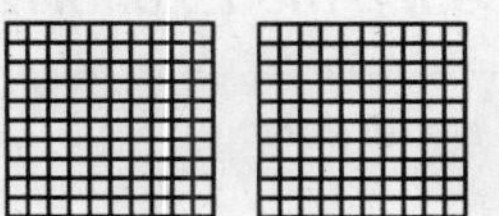 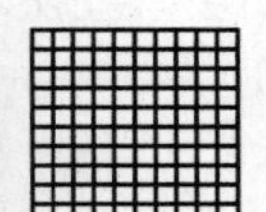 ÷ 10 =

________ = ________

c)  ÷ 10 = □□□

.3 ÷ 10 = ________

d)  ÷ 10 =

________ = ________

e)  ÷ 10 =

________ = ________

2. Complete the picture and write a division statement (the first one is done for you).

a) 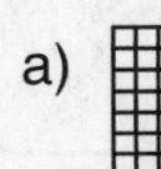 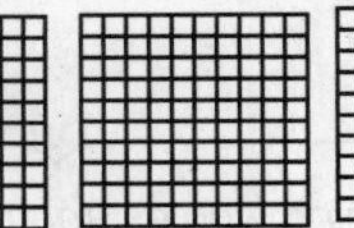 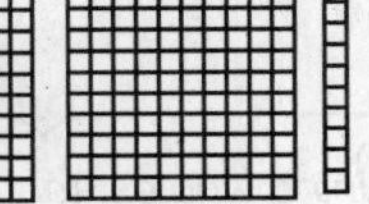 ÷ 10 = 

2.3 ÷ 10 = .23

b) 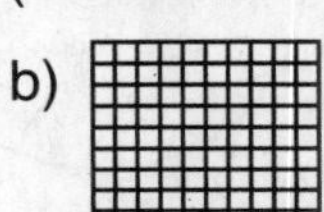 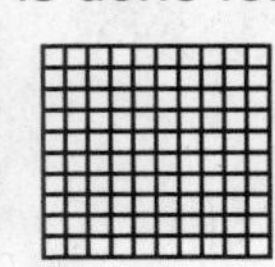 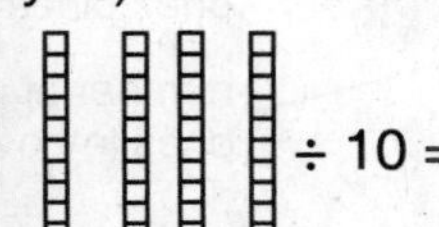 ÷ 10 =

________ = ________

3. Shift the decimal one or two places to the left by drawing an arrow as shown in 3 a).
HINT: If there is no decimal, add one to the right of the number first.

a) 0.3 ÷ 10 = .03 b) 0.5 ÷ 10 = ______ c) 0.7 ÷ 10 = ______ d) 1.3 ÷ 10 = ______

e) 7.6 ÷ 10 = ______ f) 12.0 ÷ 10 = ______ g) 9 ÷ 10 = ______ h) 6 ÷ 10 = ______

i) 42 ÷ 10 = ______ j) 17 ÷ 10 = ______ k) .9 ÷ 10 = ______ l) 27.3 ÷ 10 = ______

m) 3.0 ÷ 100 = ______ n) 6.2 ÷ 100 = ______ o) .7 ÷ 100 = ______ p) 17.2 ÷ 100 = ______

4. Explain why 1.00 ÷ 100 = .01 using dollar coins as a whole.

5. A wall 3.5 m wide is painted with 100 stripes of equal width.
How wide is each stripe?

6. 5 × 3 = 15 and 15 ÷ 5 = 3 are in the same fact family.
Write a division statement in the same fact family as 10 × 0.1 = 1.0.

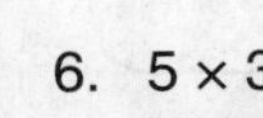

NS6-79: Dividing Decimals by Whole Numbers

You can divide a decimal by a whole number by making a base ten model. Keep track of your work using long division. Use a hundreds block to represent 1 whole, a tens block to represent 1 tenth, and a ones block to represent 1 hundredth.

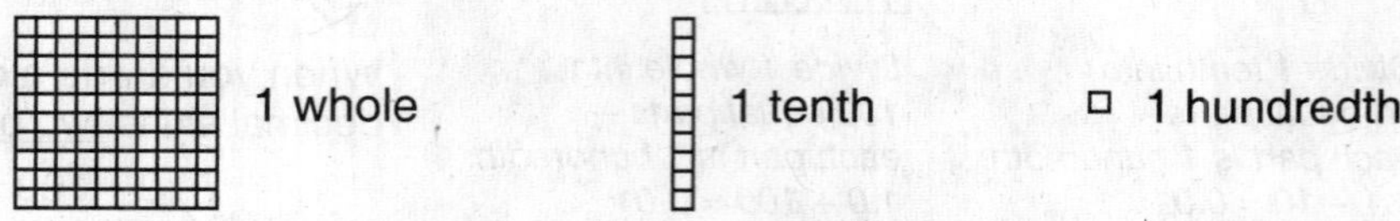

1. Find **5.12 ÷ 2** by drawing a base ten model and by long division.

Step 1: *Draw a base ten model of 5.12.*

Step 2: *Divide the whole blocks into 2 equal groups.*

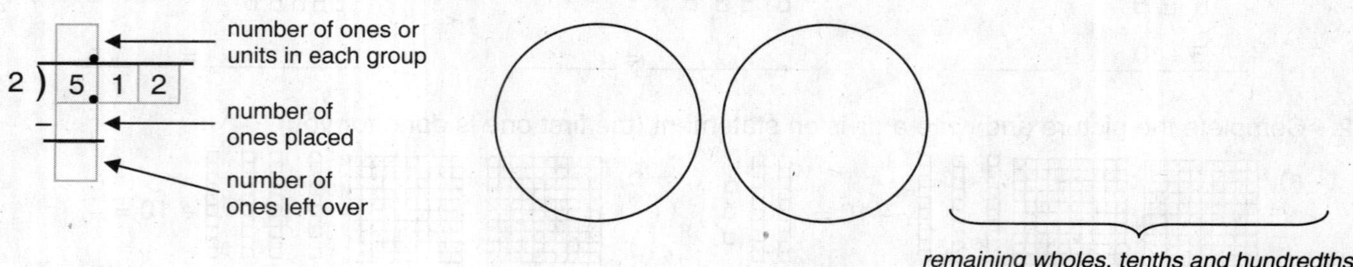

Step 3: *Exchange the left over whole blocks for 10 tenths.*

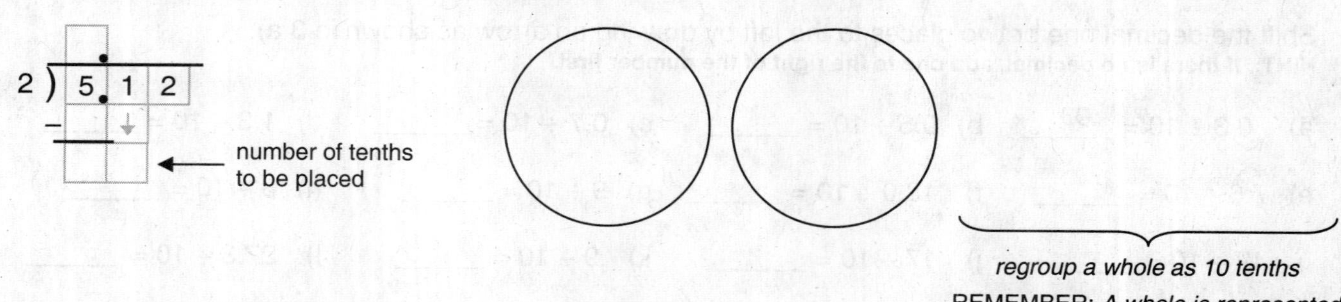

Step 4: *Divide the tenths blocks into 2 equal groups.*

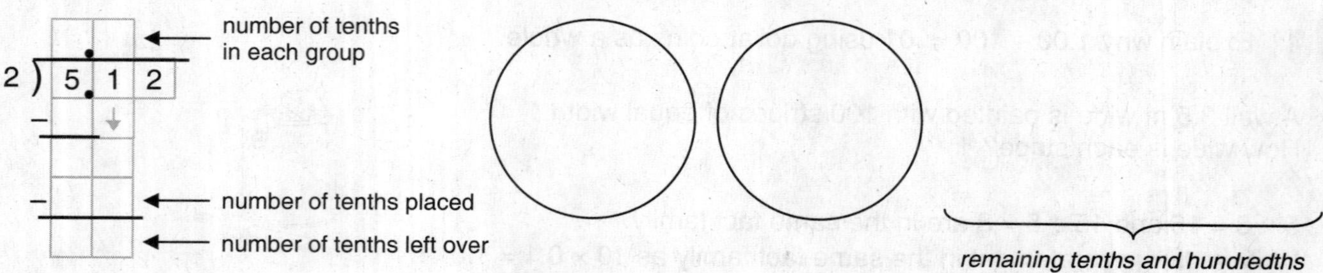

Step 5: *Regroup the left over tenth block as 10 hundredths.*

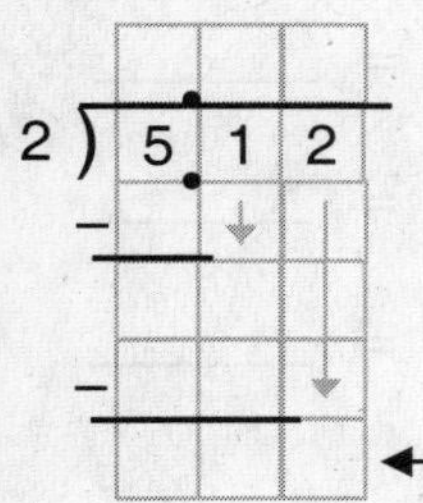

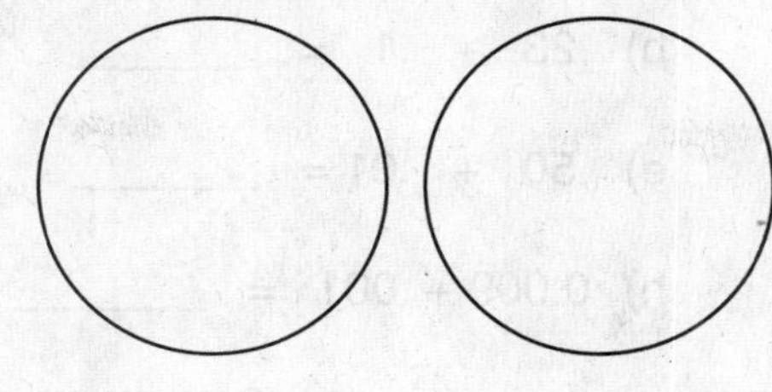

exchange a tenth for 10 hundredths

Steps 6 and 7: *Divide the hundredths into 2 equal groups.*

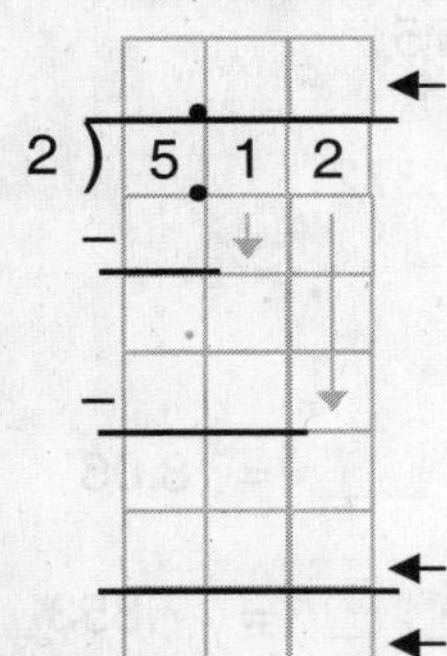

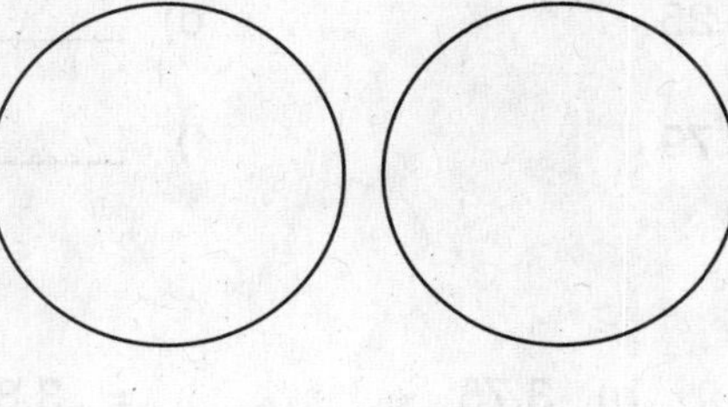

remaining hundredths

2. Divide.

a) 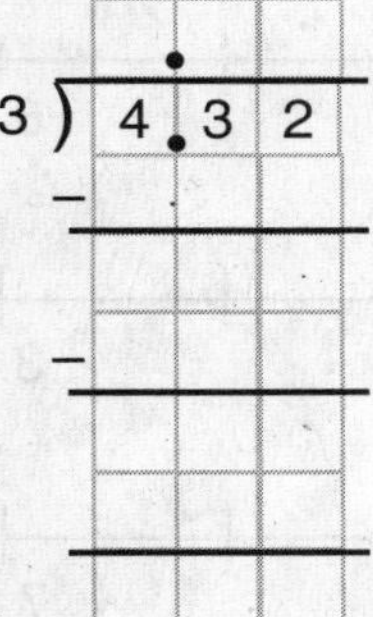

b) 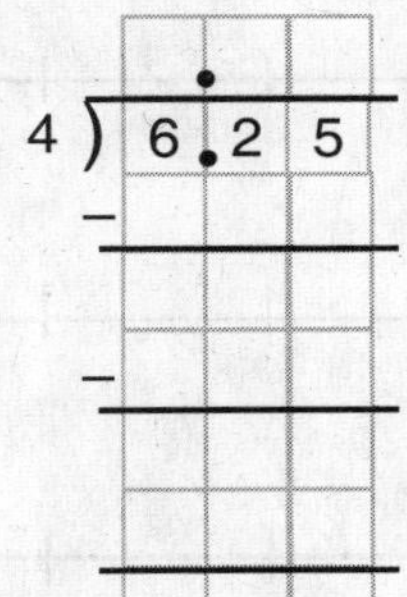

c) 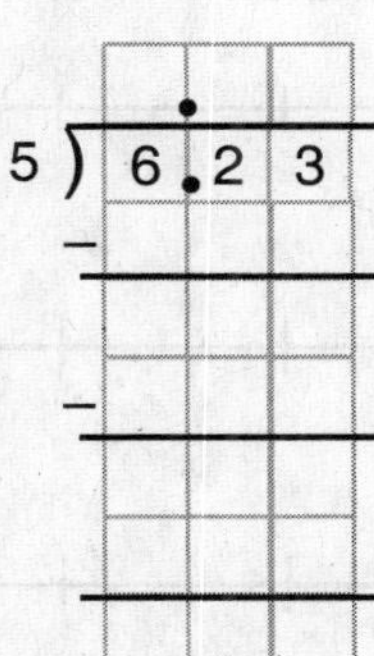

d) 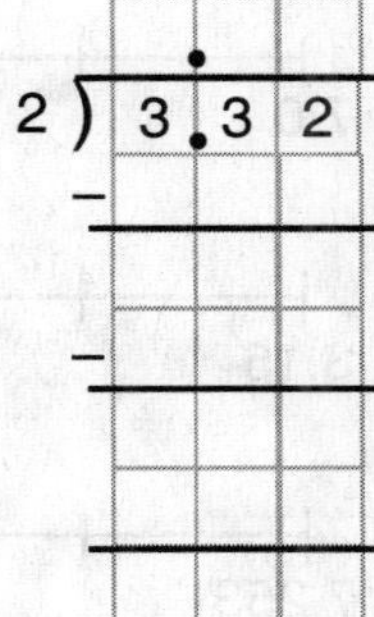

3. Divide. a) 8) 1.44 b) 7) 9.4 c) 8) 2.72 d) 9) 6.13 e) 5) 20.5

4. Five apples cost $2.75. How much does each apple cost?

5. Karen cycled 62.4 km in 4 hours. How many kilometres did she cycle in an hour?

6. Four friends earn a total of $29.16 shovelling snow. How much does each friend earn?

7. Which is a better deal: 6 pens for $4.98 or 8 pens for $6.96?

8. James divides 3.4 m of rope into 6 equal parts. Each part is a whole number of decimetres long.
   a) How long is each part? b) How many decimetres of rope are left over?

NS6-80: Differences of 0.1, 0.01, and 0.001

1. Fill in the blanks.

a) .74 + .1 = _______ b) .23 + .1 = _______ c) .09 + .1 = _______

d) .79 + .1 = _______ e) .50 + .01 = _______ f) 2.79 + .01 = _______

g) 3.056 + .001= _______ h) 0.009 + .001 = _______ i) 2.372 + .01 = _______

2. Fill in the blanks.

a) _______ is .1 more than .4 b) _______ is .1 more than 0.9

c) _______ is .1 more than 3.25 d) _______ is .01 more than .75

e) _______ is .01 more than .79 f) _______ is .001 more than .372

3. Fill in the blanks.

a) 2.34 + _______ = 2.35 b) 3.75 + _______ = 3.85 c) 8.07 − _______ = 8.06

d) 6.92 − _______ = 6.82 e) 3.957 + _______ = 3.967 f) 7.852 + _______ = 7.853

4. Fill in the missing numbers on the number lines.

a) 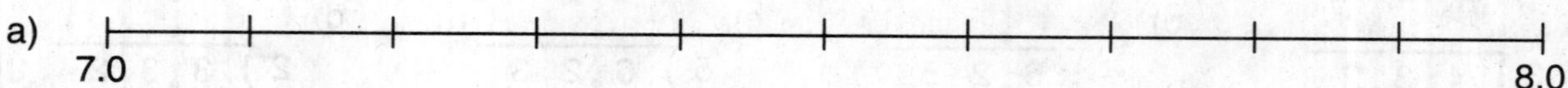
7.0 8.0

b) 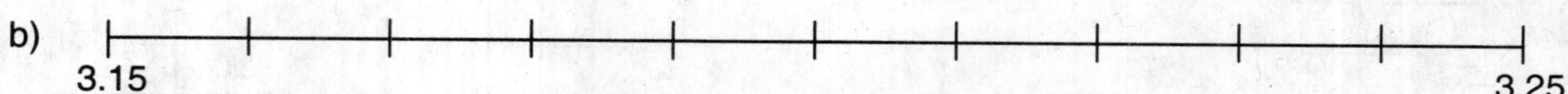
3.15 3.25

c) 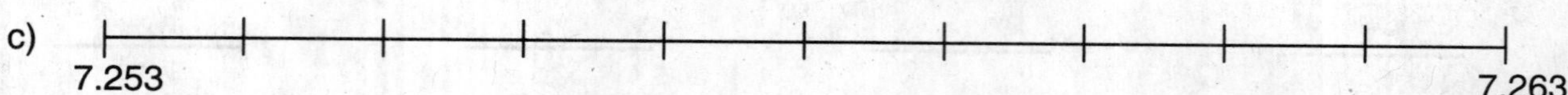
7.253 7.263

5. Continue the patterns.

a) .3, .4, .5, _______, _______, _______ b) 9.6, 9.7, 9.8 , _______, _______, _______

c) 2.5, 2.6, 2.7, _______, _______, _______ d) 4.34, 4.35, 4.36 _______, _______, _______

e) 2.96, 2.97, 2.98, _______, _______, _______ f) 1.234, 1.235 , _______, _______

6. Fill in the blanks.

a) 7.9 + .1 = _______ b) 2.9 + .1 = _______ c) 6.95 + .1 = _______

d) 2.69 + .01 = _______ e) 3.99 + .01 = _______ f) 7.299 + .001 = _______

NS6-81: Place Value and Rounding

1. Round to the nearest whole number.

a) 26.408 b) 38.97 c) 59.962 d) 71.001

2. Round to the nearest tenth.

a) 26.54 b) 47.946 c) 49.874 d) 38.96

3. Estimate by rounding to the nearest whole number.

a) 94.7 ÷ 5.2
Estimate.
☐ ÷ ☐ = ☐

b) 2.96 × 8.147
Estimate.
☐ × ☐ = ☐

c) 4.51 × 0.86
Estimate.
☐ × ☐ = ☐

4. Estimate by rounding each number to the nearest whole number. Use your estimate to say which answers are reasonable.

a) 32.7 + 4.16 = 73.8 b) 0.7 × 8.3 = 5.81 c) 9.2 × 10.3 = 947.6

d) 97.2 ÷ 0.9 = .8 e) 88.2 ÷ 9.8 = 9 f) 54.3 − 18.6 = 35.7

5. Calculate each answer from Question 4. Were your predictions correct?

6. 5.3 is said to be precise to the tenths. Any number from 5.25 to 5.34 could round it. What numbers could round to 7.2?

7. Which measurement would need to be taken to the nearest tenth?

a) Height of a building (metres).
b) Distance shot put is thrown in Olympic Games (metres).
c) Length of the Canada/U.S. border (kilometres).

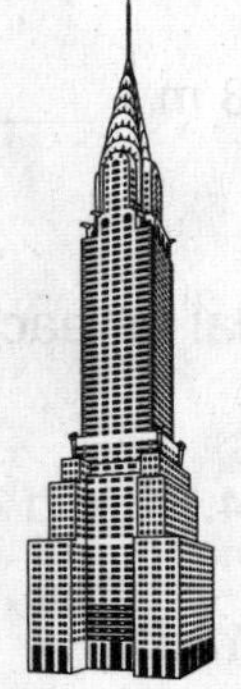

8. What amount is represented by the tenths digit?

a) 3.54 m b) 6.207 km c) 4.69 dm

d) 4.6 million e) $17.46 f) 83.4 cm

NS6-82: Decimals Review

The size of a unit of measurement depends on which unit has been selected as the whole.

A millimetre is a **tenth** of a centimetre,
but it is only a **hundredth** of a decimetre.
REMEMBER: A decimetre is 10 centimetres.

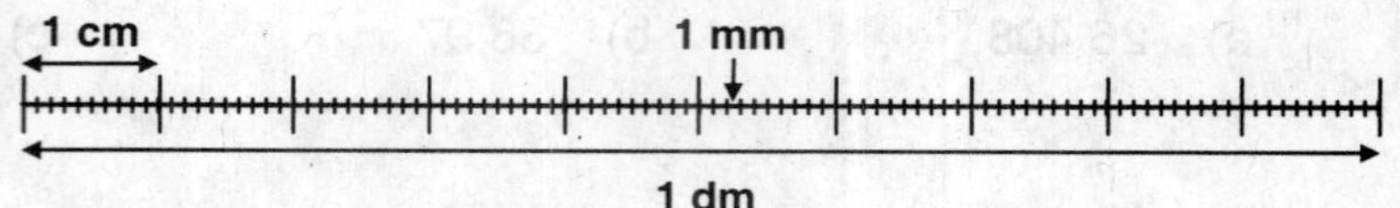

1. Draw a picture in the space provided to show 1 tenth of each whole.

a) 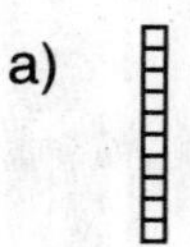

1 whole 1 tenth

b) 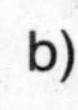 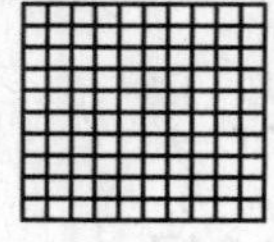

1 whole 1 tenth

c) 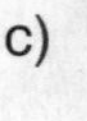 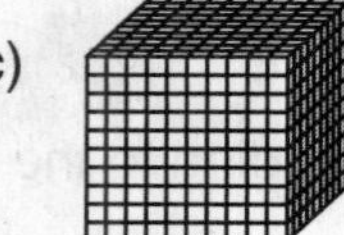

1 whole 1 tenth

2. Write each measurement as a fraction and then as a decimal.

a) 1 cm = $\frac{1}{10}$ dm = .1 dm

b) 100 mm = ☐ m = ____ m

c) 1 mm = ☐ cm = ____ cm

d) 16 mm = ☐ cm = ____ cm

e) 77 mm = ☐ dm = ____ dm

f) 83 cm = ☐ m = ____ m

3. Add the measurements by first changing the smaller unit into a decimal in the larger unit.

a) 5 cm + 7.3 dm = 0.5 dm + 7.3 dm = 7.8 dm

b) 5 cm + 3.2 dm = ____

c) 8 mm + 5.7 cm = ____

d) 33 cm + 1.64 m = ____

e) 685 cm + 12.3 m = ____

f) 982 cm + 1.5 m = ____

4. Write a decimal for each description. Some questions have more than one answer.

a) Between 4.31 and 4.34 

b) Between 2.60 and 2.70 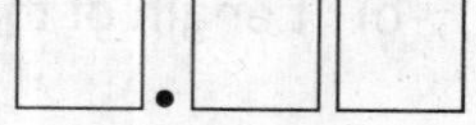

c) Between 13.75 and 13.8 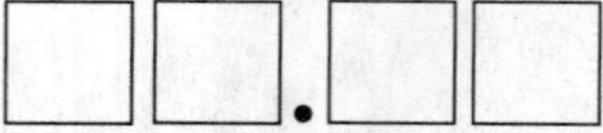

d) Between 9.7 and 9.8 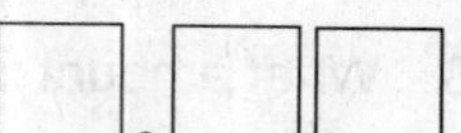

e) One tenth greater than 5.23 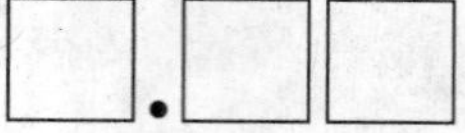

f) One hundredth less than 4.00 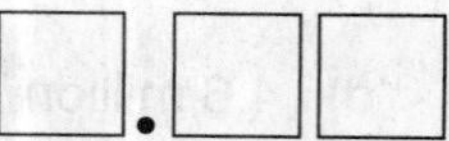

5. Add.

a) 4 000 + 300 + 7 + 0.01 = ____________

b) 20 000 + 300 + 30 + 0.2 + .04 = ____________

c) 300 000 + 20 000 + 5000 + 70 + 0.1 + 0.09 + 0.006 = ____________

6. Write < or > to show which decimal is greater.

a) 4.9 ☐ 4.6 b) 3.45 ☐ 3.35 c) 1.9 ☐ 1.26 d) 0.7 ☐ 0.524

7. Put a decimal in each number so that the digit **7** has the value $\frac{7}{10}$.

a) 5 7 2 b) 1 0 7 c) 2 8 7 5 9 d) 7

8. Use the digits 5, 6, 7, and 0 to write a number between the given numbers.

a) .567 < ____________ < .576 b) 5.607 < ____________ < 5.760

9. Write three decimals between .3 and .5: ________ ________ ________

10. Write –, +, ×, or ÷ in the circle.

a) 62.57 ◯ 10 = 72.57 b) 19.2 ◯ 10 = 192 c) 9 ◯ 10 = .9

11. Write the decimals in order from least to greatest. Explain your answer for c).

a) .37 .275 .371 b) .007 .07 .7 c) 1.29 1.3 2.001

12. Use the number line to estimate which fraction lies in each range.

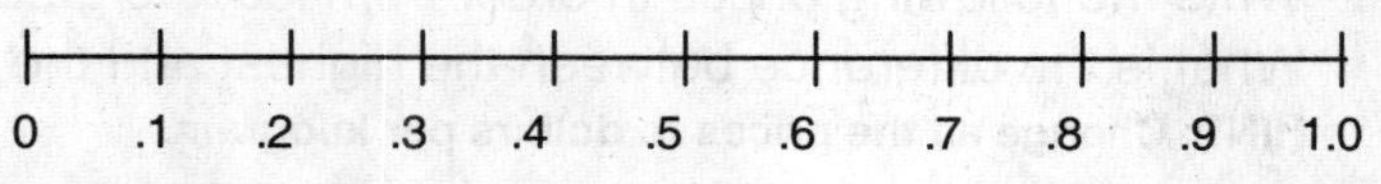

Fractions: 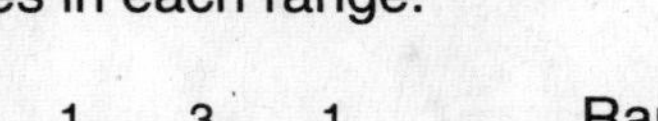 $\frac{1}{2}$, $\frac{1}{3}$, $\frac{3}{4}$, $\frac{1}{10}$

Ranges:

A	B	C	D	E
0 to .2	.2 to .4	.4 to .6	.6 to .8	.8 to 1.0

13. Is 6 a reasonable estimate for 8 × .72? Explain.

14. How do you know that 10 × 87.3 is 873 and not 8 730?

15. Charge 1.25 hours to a mixed fraction in lowest terms, then to a time in minutes.

NS6-83: Word Problems with Decimals

Answer the following questions in your notebook.

1. Explain how you would change 5.47 m into cm.
HINT: How many centimetres are in $\frac{47}{100}$ of a metre?

2. $0.68 means 6 dimes and 8 pennies.
Why do we use the decimal notation for money?
What is a dime a tenth of?
What is a penny a hundredth of?

3. The wind speed in Vancouver was 26.7 km/h on Monday, 16.0 km/h on Tuesday and 2.4 km/h on Wednesday.
What was the average wind speed over the 3 days?

4. 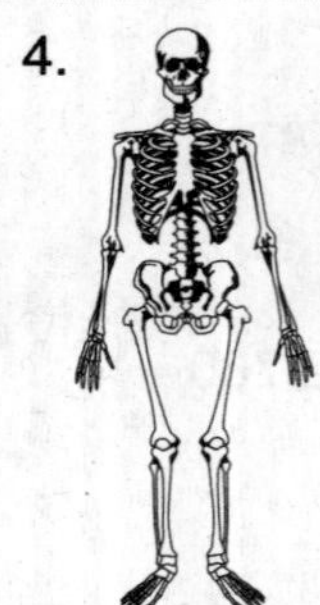
The tallest human skeleton is 2.7 m high and the shortest is 60 cm high. What is the difference in the heights of the skeletons?

5.

Star	Distance from the Sun in light years
Alpha Centauri	4.3
Barnard's Star	6.0
L726-8	8.8
Sirius	9.5
61 Cigni	11.0

A light year is 9.5 trillion kilometres.
NOTE: This is the distance light travels in one year.

a) If you travelled from the Sun to Barnard's Star, how many trillion km would you have travelled?

b) Which star is just over twice as far from the Sun as Alpha Centauri?

6. Food moves through the esophagus at a rate of .72 km per hour.
How many metres per hour is this?

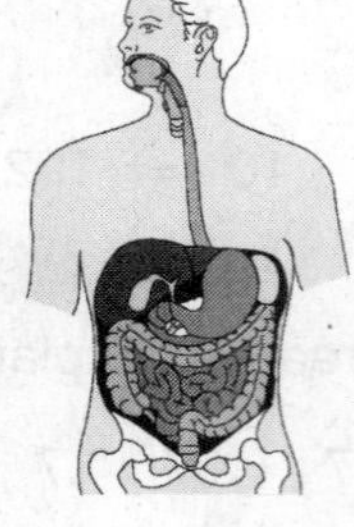

7. Write the following prices in order from least to greatest.
What is the difference between the highest and the lowest prices?
HINT: Change all the prices to dollars per kilogram.

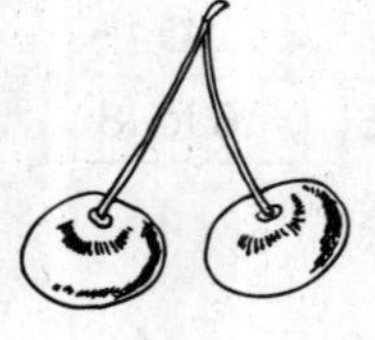

A: Cherries – 59¢ for each 100 g

B: Watermelon – $3.90 for each kg

C: Strawberries – $0.32 for each 100 g

D: Blueberries – $3.99 for each 500 g

NS6-84: Unit Rates

A rate is a comparison of two quantities in different units.

In a **unit rate**, one of the quantities is equal to one.

For instance, "1 apple costs 30¢" is a unit rate.

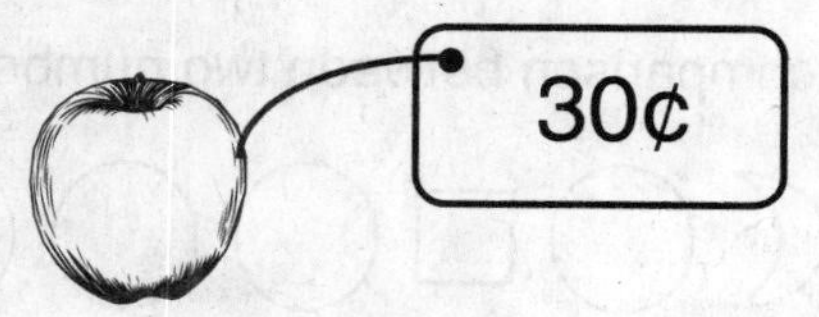

---

1. Fill in the missing information.

a) 17 km in 1 hour

_______ km in 3 hours

b) 1 book costs $4.95

4 book costs _______

c) 2 teachers for 75 students

6 teachers for _______

d) 5 mangoes cost $4.95

1 mango costs _______

e) 4 mangoes cost $12

1 mango costs _______

f) 6 pears cost $4.92

1 pear costs _______

2. Find the unit rate.

a) 4 kg of rice for 60 cups of water.

1 kg of rice for _______ cups of water.

b) 236 km in 4 hours.

_______ km in 1 hr.

c) 6 cans of juice cost $1.98

1 can costs _______

3. Use a ruler to find out the height of each animal. (One centimetre represents 50 cm in real life.)

a) Kangaroo

Height of picture in cm: _______

Height of animal in m: _______

b) Height of picture in cm: _______

Height of animal in m: _______

Horse

c) Height of picture in cm: _______

Height of animal in m: _______

Giraffe

4. Ron earns $66 babysitting for six hours. How much does he earn in an hour?

____

5. Tina earns $75 cutting lawns for 5 hours. How much does she earn in an hour?

____

NS6-85: Introduction to Ratios

A **ratio** is a comparison between two numbers.

1. 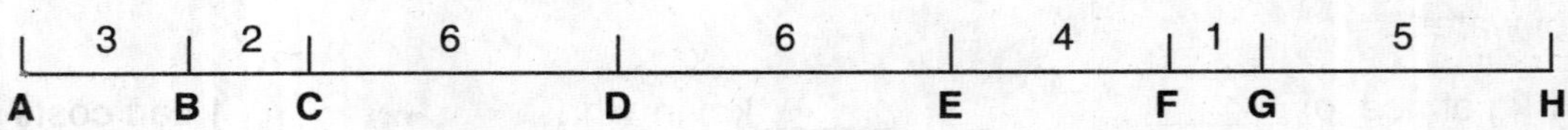

a) The ratio of moons to circles is _____ : _____

b) The ratio of triangles to moons is _____ : _____

c) The ratio of cylinders to squares is _____ : _____

d) The ratio of squares to circles is _____ : _____

e) The ratio of squares to moon is _____ : _____

f) The ratio of squares to figures is _____ : _____

2. Write the number of vowels compared to the number of consonants in the following words.

a) apple 2 : 3

b) banana ____ : ____

c) orange ____ : ____

d) pear ____ : ____

3. Write the ratio of the lengths.

A	3	B	2	C	6	D	6	E	4	F	1	G	5	H

a) AB to DE _____ : _____

b) BC to CD _____ : _____

c) EF to FG _____ : _____

d) EF to BC _____ : _____

e) AB to GH _____ : _____

f) CD to FG _____ : _____

4. To make punch, you need …

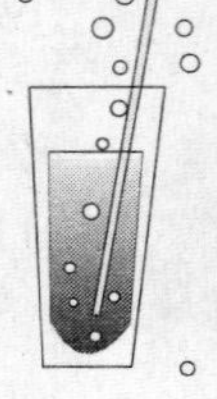

- 4 L of ginger ale
- 2 L of orange juice
- 3 L of mango juice

What is the ratio of ginger ale to punch?

____

5. 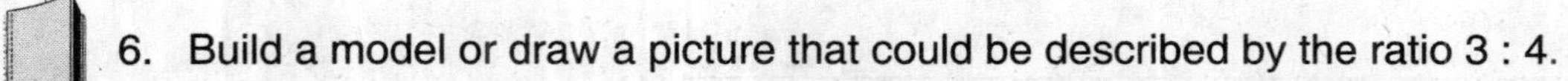

a) In the above pattern, what does the ratio 2 : 3 describe?

____

b) What does the ratio 5 : 10 describe?

____

6. Build a model or draw a picture that could be described by the ratio 3 : 4.

NS6-86: Equivalent Ratios

1. The picture shows that the ratio of apples to bananas on a grocery shelf is:

8 apples to every 6 bananas

OR

4 apples to every 3 bananas.

Group the fruit to show two equivalent ratios.

a)

_______ to every _______

or _______ to every _______

b)

_______ to every _______

or _______ to every _______

2. Starting with the ratio 2 triangles to every 3 squares, Talia created a sequence of equivalent ratios. Fill in the missing figures and ratios.

Triangles	△△	△△ △△	△△ △△ △△	
Squares	□□□	□□□ □□□		□□□ □□□ □□□ □□□
Ratio	2 : 3			

3. Starting with the ratio given, write a sequence of five ratios that are all equivalent.

a) 3 : 4 = 6 : 8 =   :   =   :   =   :

b) 2 : 5 =

4. Find the missing terms. a) 3 : 4 = ____ : 8 b) 5 : 7 = 10 : ____ c) 2 : 5 = ____ : 25

A recipe for granola calls for 2 cups of raisins for every 3 cups of oats.

How many cups of raisins will Eschi need for 12 cups of oats?

She writes a sequence of equivalent ratios to find out.

NOTE: She multiplies both terms in the ratio 2 : 3 by 2, then by 3, then by 4.

2 : 3 = 4 : 6 = 6 : 9 = 8 : 12

Eschi needs 8 cups of raisins.

5. Solve each problem by writing a sequence of equivalent ratios (as in the example above).

a) A recipe calls for 5 cups of oats for every 3 cups of raisins.
How many cups of oats are needed for 12 cups of raisins?

b) 2 cm on a map represent 11 km.
How many km do 8 cm on the map represent?

c) Six bus tickets cost $5.
How much will 18 tickets cost?

NS6-87: Finding Equivalent Ratios

There are 3 boys for every 2 girls in a class of 20 children.

To find out how many boys are in the class, write a sequence of ratios.

3 boys : 2 girls = 6 boys : 4 girls = 9 boys : 6 girls = 12 boys : 8 girls

Stop when the terms of the ratio add to 20.

12 boys + 8 girls = 20 students. So there are 12 boys in the class.

1. Write a sequence of ratios to solve each problem. The first one is started for you.

   a) There are 5 boys for every 4 girls in a class of 27 children.
   How many girls are in the class?

   5 : 4 = 10 : 8 =

   b) There are 3 red fish for every 5 blue fish in an aquarium.
   With 24 fish, how many fish are blue?

   c) A recipe for punch calls for 3 L of orange juice for every 2 litres of mango juice.
   How many litres of orange juice are needed to make 15 litres of punch?

Five subway tickets cost $4. Kyle wants to know how much 20 tickets will cost. He writes the ratio of tickets to dollars as a fraction. Then, he finds an equivalent fraction by multiplying:

Step 1:	Step 2:	Step 3:	Step 4:
$\frac{4}{5} = \frac{?}{20}$	$\frac{4}{5} = \frac{}{20}$	$\frac{4}{5} \xrightarrow{\times 4} \frac{}{20}$ (× 4)	$\frac{4}{5} \xrightarrow{\times 4} \frac{16}{20}$ (× 4)

2. Solve the following ratios. Draw arrows to show what you multiply by.

a) $\frac{3}{4} \xrightarrow{\times 5} \frac{}{20}$ (× 5) b) $\frac{1}{5} = \frac{}{25}$ c) $\frac{2}{5} = \frac{}{20}$ d) $\frac{6}{7} = \frac{}{35}$

e) $\frac{3}{4} = \frac{}{16}$ f) $\frac{2}{3} = \frac{}{12}$ g) $\frac{15}{25} = \frac{}{100}$ h) $\frac{5}{9} = \frac{}{45}$

BONUS

NOTE: Sometimes, in the questions below, the arrow may point from right to left.

3. a) $\frac{15}{} \xleftarrow{\times 5} \frac{3}{4}$ (× 5) b) $\frac{10}{} = \frac{2}{5}$ c) $\frac{9}{} = \frac{3}{7}$ d) $\frac{10}{15} = \frac{}{3}$

e) $\frac{4}{5} = \frac{}{15}$ f) $\frac{2}{3} = \frac{}{9}$ g) $\frac{}{45} = \frac{2}{5}$ h) $\frac{}{20} = \frac{7}{10}$

NS6-88: Word Problems (Advanced)

In a pet shop, there are 3 cats for every 2 dogs. If there are 12 cats in the shop, how many dogs are there?

Solution:

Step 1:
Write, as a fraction, the ratio of the two things being compared.

$$\frac{3}{2}$$

Step 2:
Write, in words, what each number stands for.

$$\begin{matrix}\text{cats} \\ \text{dogs}\end{matrix}\ \frac{3}{2}$$

Step 3:
On the other side of an equals sign, write the *same* words, on the *same* levels.

$$\begin{matrix}\text{cats} \\ \text{dogs}\end{matrix}\ \frac{3}{2} = \frac{\quad}{\quad}\ \begin{matrix}\text{cats} \\ \text{dogs}\end{matrix}$$

Step 4:
Re-read the question to determine which quantity (i.e. number of cats or dogs) has been given (in this case, cats) – then place that quantity on the proper level.

$$\begin{matrix}\text{cats} \\ \text{dogs}\end{matrix}\ \frac{3}{2} = \frac{12}{\quad}\ \begin{matrix}\text{cats} \\ \text{dogs}\end{matrix}$$

Step 5:
Solve the ratio.

Solve the following questions in your notebook.

1. There are 2 apples in a bowl for every 3 oranges.
   If there are 9 oranges, how many apples are there?

2. Five bus tickets costs $3.
   How many bus tickets can you buy with $9?

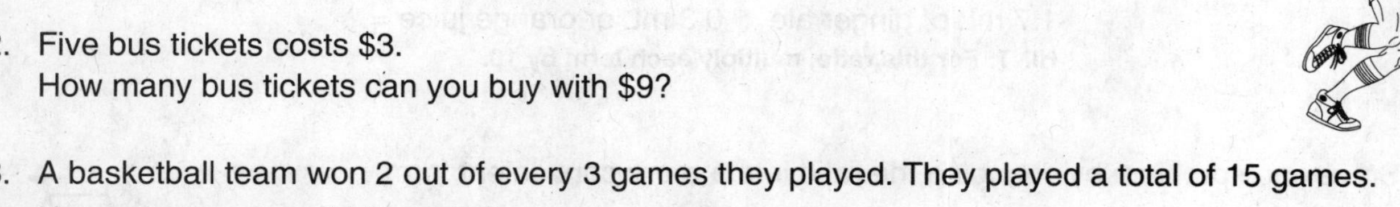

3. A basketball team won 2 out of every 3 games they played. They played a total of 15 games.
   How many games did they win?
   NOTE: The quantities are "games won" and "games played."

4. To make fruit punch, you mix 1 litre of orange juice with 2 litres of pineapple juice.
   If you have 3 litres of orange juice, how many litres of pineapple juice do you need?

5. Nora can run 3 laps in 4 minutes.
   At that rate, how many laps could she run in 12 minutes?

6. The ratio of boys to girls in a class is 4:5.
   If there are 20 boys, how many girls are there?

7. 2 cm on a map represents 5 km in real life.
   If a lake is 6 cm long on the map, what is its actual size?

NS6-89: Advanced Ratios

Tony can paint 3 walls in $\frac{1}{2}$ an hour. He wants to know how many walls he can paint in 5 hours.

He first changes the ratio $\frac{1}{2}$: 3 to a more convenient form by doubling both terms of the ratio.

$\frac{1}{2}$ hour : 3 walls = 1 hour : 6 walls

Then he multiplies each term by 5.

1 hour : 6 walls = 5 hours : 30 walls

Tony can paint 30 walls in 5 hours.

---

1. Change each ratio so the number on the left is a whole number.

a)  $\frac{1}{2}$ hour : 2 km walked =

b)  $\frac{1}{4}$ cup of flour : 2 cups of potatoes =

c) $\frac{1}{3}$ hour : 3 km rowed =

d)  $\frac{1}{3}$ cup of raisins : 2 cups of oats =

e) 0.3 km : 1 litre of gas used =

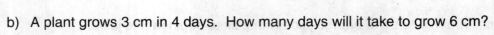

f)  1.7 mL of ginger ale : 0.3 mL or orange juice =

HINT: For this ratio, multiply each term by 10.

2. Solve each problem by changing the ratio into a more convenient form.

a) Rhonda can ride her bike 3 km in $\frac{1}{4}$ of an hour. How far can she ride in 2 hours?

b) A plant grows 3 cm in 4 days. How many days will it take to grow 6 cm?

3. 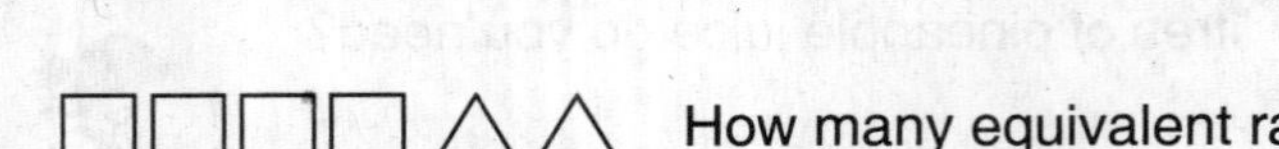 How many equivalent ratios can you write for this array?

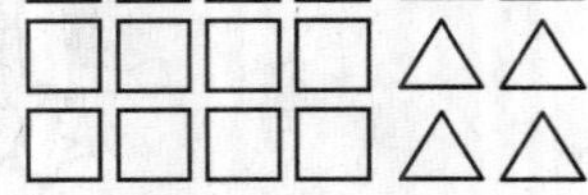

4. For each ratio below write an equivalent ratio with one term equal to 20.

a) 4 : 6 b) 3 : 5 c) 4 : 5 d) 10 : 30

5. In a class of 30 students there are 10 girls. Explain why the ratio of girls to boys is 1 to 2.

NS6-90: Percents

A **percent** is a ratio that compares a number to 100.

The term percent means "out of 100" or "for every 100." For instance, 84% on a test means 84 out of 100.

You can think of percent as a short form for a fraction with 100 in the denominator, e.g. $45\% = \frac{45}{100}$

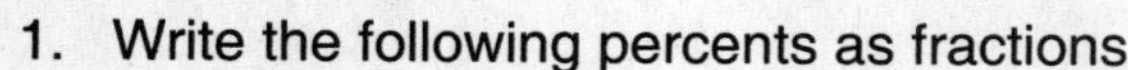

1. Write the following percents as fractions.

a) 7% b) 92% c) 5% d) 15%

e) 50% f) 100% g) 2% h) 7%

2. Write the following fractions as percents.

a) $\frac{2}{100}$ b) $\frac{31}{100}$ c) $\frac{52}{100}$ d) $\frac{100}{100}$

e) $\frac{17}{100}$ f) $\frac{88}{100}$ g) $\frac{2}{100}$ h) $\frac{1}{100}$

3. Write the following decimals as percents, by first turning them into fractions. The first one has been done for you.

a) $.72 = \frac{72}{100} = 72\%$ b) .27 c) .04

4. Write the fraction as a percent by changing it to a fraction over 100. The first one has been done for you.

a) $\frac{3^{\times 20}}{5_{\times 20}} = \frac{60}{100} = 60\%$ b) $\frac{2}{5}$

c) $\frac{4}{5}$ d) $\frac{1}{4}$

e) $\frac{3}{4}$ f) $\frac{1}{2}$

g) $\frac{3}{10}$ h) $\frac{7}{10}$

i) $\frac{17}{25}$ j) $\frac{7}{20}$

k) $\frac{3}{25}$ l) $\frac{19}{20}$

m) $\frac{23}{50}$ n) $\frac{47}{50}$

NS6-90: Percents *(continued)*

5. Write the following decimals as a percents. The first one has been done for you.

a) $.2 = \frac{2}{10}\,\substack{\times 10 \\ \times 10} = \frac{20}{100} = 20\%$

b) .5

c) .7

d) .9

6. What percent of the figure is shaded?

a) 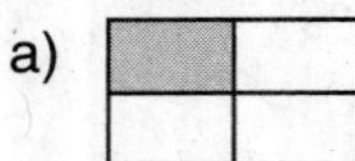

b) 

c) 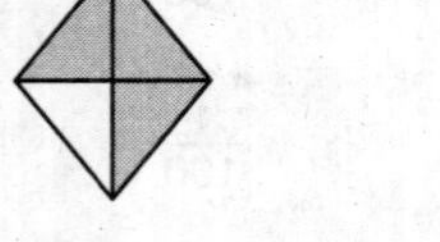

d)

7. Change the following fractions to percents by first reducing them to lowest terms.

a) $\frac{9}{15}\,\substack{\div 3 \\ \div 3} = \frac{3}{5} = \frac{3}{5}\,\substack{\times 20 \\ \times 20} = \frac{60}{100} = 60\%$

b) $\frac{12}{15}$

c) $\frac{3}{6}$

d) $\frac{7}{35}$

e) $\frac{21}{28}$

f) $\frac{18}{45}$

g) $\frac{12}{30}$

h) $\frac{10}{40}$

i) $\frac{20}{40}$

j) $\frac{16}{40}$

k) $\frac{60}{150}$

l) $\frac{45}{75}$

NS6-91: Visual Representations of Percents

1. Fill in the chart below. The first one has been done for you.

Drawing				
Fraction	$\frac{23}{100}$	$\frac{\_\_}{100}$	$\frac{45}{100}$	$\frac{\_\_}{100}$
Decimal	0. 2 3	0.__ __	0.__ __	0.81
Percent	23%	63%	____ %	____ %

Use a ruler for Questions 2 to 5.

2. Shade 50% of each box.

a) 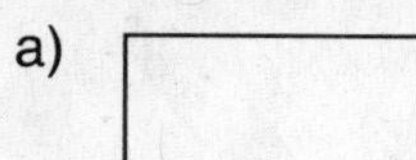

b) 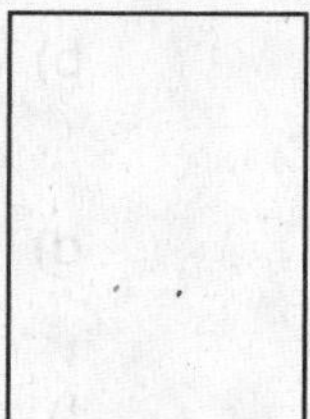

c) 

3. Shade 25% of each box.

a) 

b) 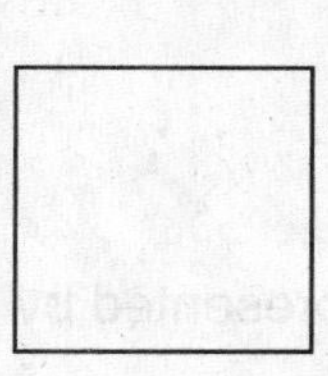

4. The triangle is 50% of a parallelogram. Show what 100% might look like.

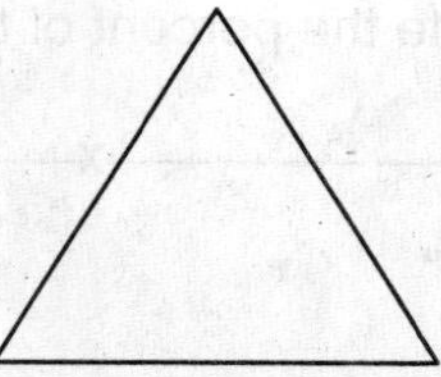

5. Colour 50% of the rectangle blue, 40% red, and 10% green.

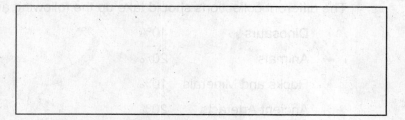

6. a) Write a fraction for the part shaded: _____

b) Write the fraction with a denominator of 100: _____

c) Write a decimal and percent for the part shaded: _____ _____

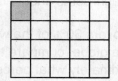

NS6-91: Visual Representations of Percents *(continued)*

7. Write a fraction and a percent for each division of the number line.

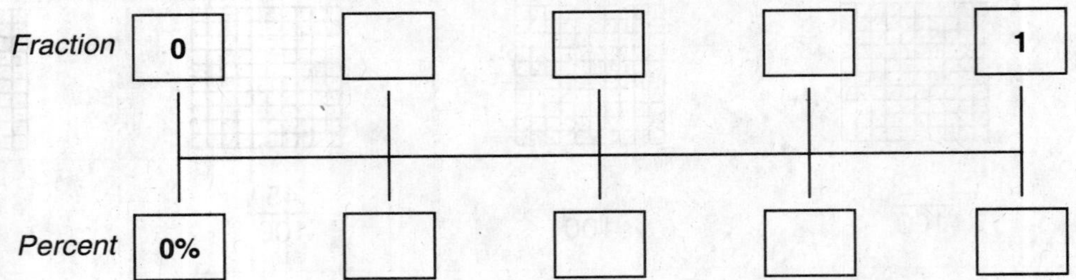

8. Draw marks to show 25%, 50%, and 75% of the line segment.

a) ______________________ b) ______________________

c) ______________________ d) ______________________

9. Extend each line segment to show 100%.

a) 50%

b) 25%

c) 20%

d) 75%

e) 0% 60%

f) 0% 80%

g) 0% 10%

h) 0% 50%

10. Estimate the percent of the line segment represented by each mark.

a)
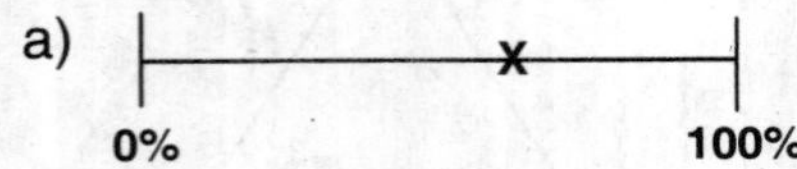

b)
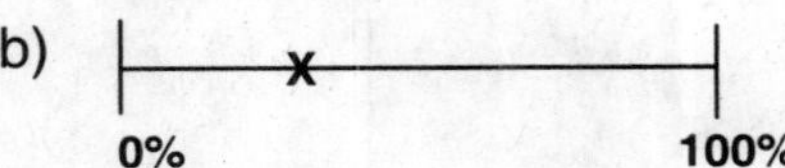

11. Draw a rough sketch of a floor plan for a museum.

The different collections should take up the following amounts of space:

- Dinosaurs 40%
- Animals 20%
- Rocks and Minerals 10%
- Ancient Artefacts 20%

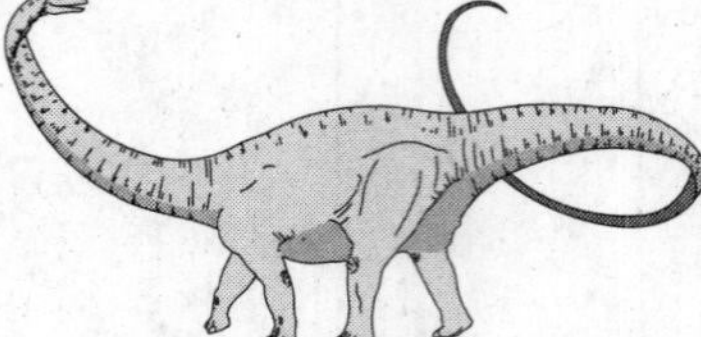

Washrooms should take up the final 10% of the floor space.

12. Asia covers 30% of the world's land mass.
Using a globe, compare the size of Asia to the size of Australia.
Approximately what percent of the world's land mass does Australia cover?

NS6-92: Comparing Decimals, Fractions, & Percents

1. From the list below, choose the percent to which each fraction is closest.

10%	25%	50%	75%	100%

a) $\frac{3}{5}$ ______ b) $\frac{4}{5}$ ______ c) $\frac{2}{5}$ ______ d) $\frac{2}{10}$ ______

e) $\frac{1}{10}$ ______ f) $\frac{4}{10}$ ______ g) $\frac{9}{10}$ ______ h) $\frac{4}{25}$ ______

i) $\frac{11}{20}$ ______ j) $\frac{16}{20}$ ______ k) $\frac{37}{40}$ ______ l) $\frac{1}{12}$ ______

2. Write <, > or = between the following pairs of numbers. The first one has been done for you.
HINT: Change each pair of numbers to a pair of fractions with the same denominator.

a) $\frac{1}{2}$ ☐ 47%

$\frac{50 \times 1}{50 \times 2}$ ☐ $\frac{47}{100}$

$\frac{50}{100}$ > $\frac{47}{100}$

b) $\frac{1}{2}$ ☐ 53%

c) $\frac{1}{4}$ ☐ 23%

d) $\frac{3}{4}$ ☐ 70%

e) $\frac{2}{5}$ ☐ 32%

f) .27 ☐ 62%

g) .02 ☐ 11%

h) $\frac{1}{10}$ ☐ 10%

i) $\frac{19}{25}$ ☐ 93%

j) $\frac{23}{50}$ ☐ 46%

k) .9 ☐ 10%

l) $\frac{11}{20}$ ☐ 19%

3. Write each set of numbers in order from least to greatest by first changing each number to a fraction.

a) $\frac{3}{5}$, 42% , .73

b) $\frac{1}{2}$, .73 , 80%

c) $\frac{1}{4}$, .09 , 15%

d) $\frac{2}{3}$, 57% , .62

NS6-93: Finding Percents

If you use a thousands cube to represent 1 whole, you can see that taking $\frac{1}{10}$ of a number is the same as dividing the number by 10 – the decimal shifts one place left.

$\frac{1}{10}$ of 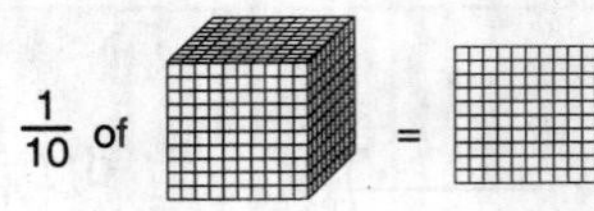

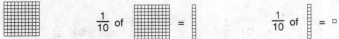

$\frac{1}{10}$ of 1 = .1

$\frac{1}{10}$ of 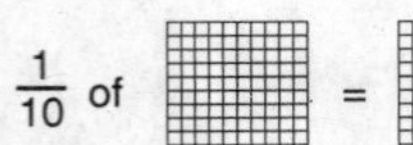

$\frac{1}{10}$ of .1 = .01

$\frac{1}{10}$ of =

$\frac{1}{10}$ of .01 = .001

---

1. Find $\frac{1}{10}$ of the following numbers by shifting the decimal. Write your answers in the boxes provided.

a) 4 b) 7 c) 32 d) 120 e) 3.8 f) 2.5

2. 10% is short for $\frac{1}{10}$. Find 10% of the following numbers.

a) 9 b) 5.7 c) 4.05 d) 6.35 e) .06 f) 21.1

3. You can find percents that are multiples of 10 as follows.

Example: Finding 30% of 21 is the same as finding 10% of 21 and multiplying the result by 3.

<u>Step 1</u>: 10% of 21 = 2.1

<u>Step 2</u>: 3 × 2.1 = 6.3 → so 30% of 21 = 6.3

Find the percents using the method above.

a) 40% of 15
i) 10% of 15 =
ii) 4 × = ______

b) 60% of 25
i) 10% of ____ =
ii) ____ × = ______

c) 90% of 2.3
i) 10% of ____ =
ii) ____ × = ______

d) 60% of 35
i) 10% of ____ =
ii) ____ × = ______

e) 40% of 24
i) 10% of ____ =
ii) ____ × = ______

f) 20% of 1.3
i) 10% of ____ =
ii) ____ × = ______

NS6-94: Finding Percents (Advanced)

35% is short for $\frac{35}{100}$. To find 35% of 27, Sadie finds $\frac{35}{100}$ of 27.

Step 1: She multiplies 27 by 35.

	2	3
	2	7
×	3	5
1	3	5
8	1	0
9	4	5

Step 2: She divides the result by 100.

945 ÷ 100 = 9.45

So 35% of 27 is 9.45.

---

1. Find the following percents using Sadie's method.

a) 45% of 32

Step 1:

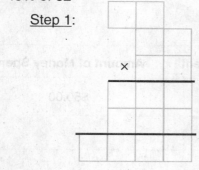

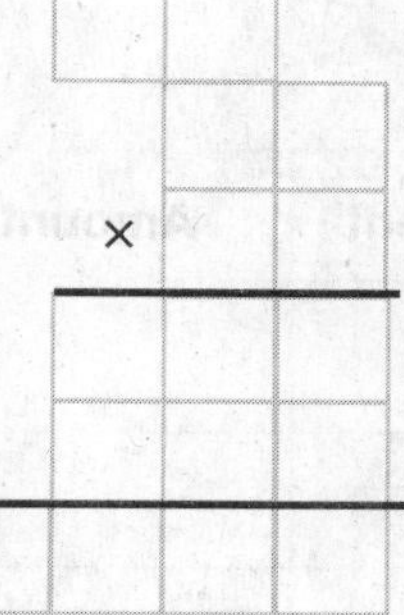

Step 2:

_______ ÷ 100 =

So _______ of _______ is _______.

b) 28% of 63

Step 1:

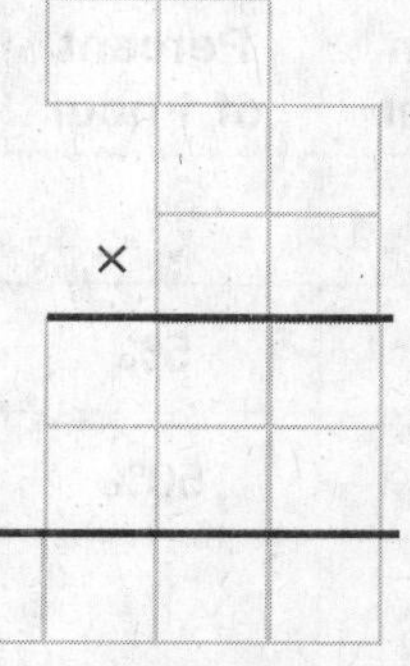

Step 2:

_______ ÷ 100 =

So _______ of _______ is _______.

2. Find the following percents using Sadie's method.

a) 13% of 9 b) 52% of 7 c) 65% of 8 d) 78% of 9

e) 23% of 42 f) 17% of 68 g) 37% of 80 h) 62% of 75

3. 25% is equal to $\frac{1}{4}$ and 75% is equal to $\frac{3}{4}$. Find …

a) 25% of 80 b) 25% of 280 c) 25% of 12 d) 75% of 20 e) 75% of 320

NS6-95: Percents: Word Problems

1. Find the missing percent of each child's stamp stamp collection that comes from other countries.
HINT: Change all fractions to percents.

a) Anne's collection:

Canada	USA	Other
40% = 40%	$\frac{1}{2}$ = 50%	= 10%

b) Brian's collection:

Canada	England	Other
80%	$\frac{1}{10}$	

c) Juan's collection:

Mexico	USA	Other
$\frac{1}{2}$	40%	

d) Lanre's collection:

Canada	Nigeria	Other
22%	$\frac{3}{5}$	

e) Faith's collection:

Jamaica	Canada	Other
$\frac{3}{4}$	15%	

f) Carlo's collection:

France	Italy	Other
$\frac{3}{4}$	10%	

2. A painter spends $500.00 on art supplies. Complete the chart.

	Fraction of Money Spent	Percentage of Money Spent	Amount of Money Spent
Brushes			$50.00
Paint	$\frac{4}{10}$		
Canvas		50%	

3. Indra spent 1 hour doing homework. The chart shows the time she spent on each subject.
   a) Complete the chart.
   b) How did you find the amount of time spent on math?

Subject	Fraction of 1 hour	Percent of 1 hour	Decimal	Number of minutes
English	$\frac{1}{4}$		.25	15
Science	$\frac{1}{20}$	5%		
Math		50%		
French			.20	

4. Roger wants to buy a deck of cards that costs $8.00. The taxes are 15%. How much did he pay in taxes?

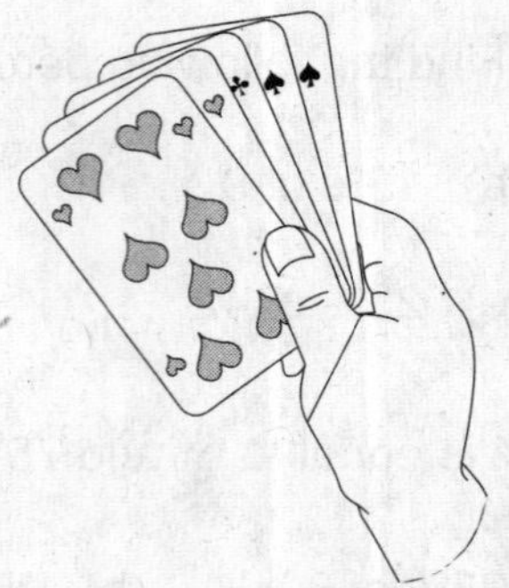

5. There are 15 boys and 12 girls in a class. $\frac{3}{4}$ of the girls have black hair, and 60% of the boys have black hair. How many children have black hair?

NS6-96: Fractions, Ratios, and Percents

1. Write the number of girls (**g**), boys (**b**), and children (**c**) in each class.

   a) There are 8 boys and 5 girls in a class. **b**: ______ **g**: ______ **c**: ______

   b) There are 4 boys and 7 girls in a class. **b**: ______ **g**: ______ **c**: ______

   c) There are 12 boys and 15 girls in a class. **b**: ______ **g**: ______ **c**: ______

   d) There are 9 girls in a class of 20 children. **b**: ______ **g**: ______ **c**: ______

   e) There are 7 boys in a class of 10 children. **b**: ______ **g**: ______ **c**: ______

2. Write the number of boys, girls and children in each class.
   Then write the fraction of children who are boys and the fraction who are girls in the boxes provided.

   a) There are 5 boys and 6 girls in a class. **b**: ______ [____] **g**: ______ [____] **c**: ______

   b) There are 15 children in the class. 8 are boys. **b**: ______ [____] **g**: ______ [____] **c**: ______

3. Write the fraction of children in the class who are boys and the fraction who are girls.

   a) There are 5 boys and 12 children in the class. **b**: [____] **g**: [____]

   b) There are 3 boys and 2 girls in the class. **b**: [____] **g**: [____]

   c) There are 9 girls and 20 children in the class. **b**: [____] **g**: [____]

   d) The ratio of boys to girls is 5:9 in the class. **b**: [____] **g**: [____]

   e) The ratio of girls to boys is 7:8 in the class. **b**: [____] **g**: [____]

   f) The ratio of boys to girls is 10:11 in the class. **b**: [____] **g**: [____]

4. From the information given, determine the number of girls and boys in each class.

   a) There are 20 children in a class. $\frac{2}{5}$ are boys.

   b) There are 42 children. $\frac{3}{7}$ are girls.

   c) There are 15 children.
   The ratio of girls to boys is 3:2.

   d) There are 24 children.
   The ratio of girls to boys is 3:5.

NS6-96: Fractions, Ratios, and Percents *(continued)*

Answer the following questions in your notebook.

5. Find the number of boys and girls in each classroom.
   a) In classroom A, there are 25 children: 60% are girls.
   b) In classroom B, there are 28 children. The ratio of boys to girls is 3 : 4.
   c) In classroom C, there are 30 children. The ratio of boys to girls is 1 : 2.

6. For each question below, say which classroom has more girls.
   a) In classroom A, there are 40 children. 60% are girls.
      In classroom B, there are 36 children. The ratio of boys to girls is 5 : 4.
   b) In classroom A, there are 28 children. The ratio of boys to girls is 5 : 2.
      In classroom B, there are 30 children. $\frac{3}{5}$ of the children are boys.

7. In the word "Whitehorse"…
   a) … what is the ratio of vowels to consonants?
   b) … what fraction of the letters are vowels?
   c) … what percent of the letters are consonants?

8. Look at the circle graph. Estimate the fraction of pets of each typed owned according and complete the chart.

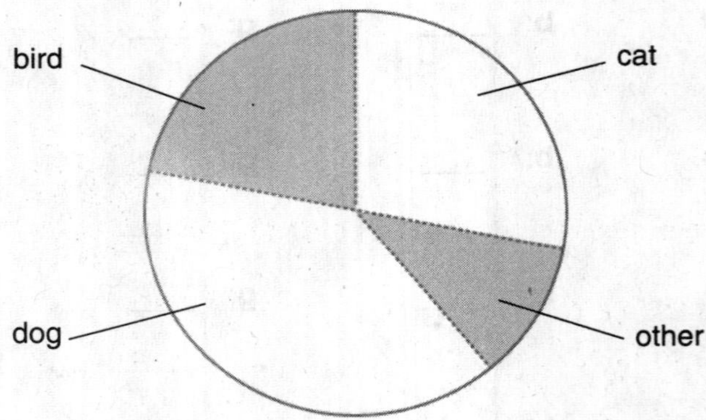

Pets		
Type	**Fraction out of 100**	**Percent**
dog		
cat		
bird		
other		

9. Write the amounts in order from least to greatest: $\frac{1}{20}$, 20% , 0.2. Show your work.

10. Kevin has 360 hockey cards.
    30% are Toronto Maple Leaf cards, and $\frac{1}{2}$ are Montreal Canadien cards. The rest are Vancouver Canuck cards.
    How many of each type of card does he have?

11. What percent of a metre stick is 37 cm? Explain.

NS6-97: Concepts in Careers and the Media

Answer the following questions in your notebook.

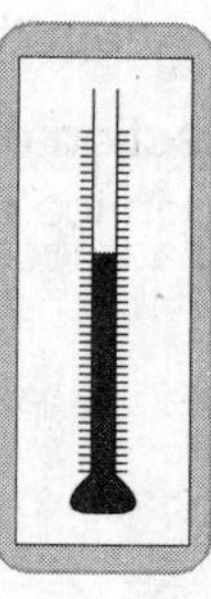

1. *Meteorologists* study the weather.
   The world's highest temperature in the shade was recorded in Libya in 1932.
   The temperature reached 58°C.

   a) How long ago was this temperature recorded?

   b) On an average summer day in Toronto, the temperature is 30°C.
   How much higher was the temperature recorded in Libya?

   c) The lowest temperature recorded (in Antarctica) was – 89°C.
   What is the difference between the lowest and the highest temperatures recorded?

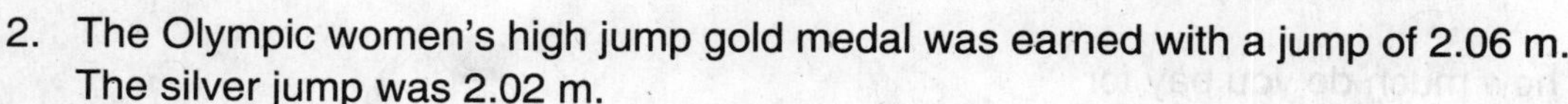

2. The Olympic women's high jump gold medal was earned with a jump of 2.06 m.
   The silver jump was 2.02 m.

   a) Round both jumps to the nearest tenth.

   b) Make up two jumps which would round to the same number (when rounded to the tenths).

   c) Why are Olympic high jumps measured so precisely?

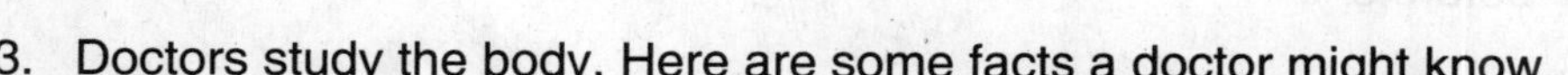

3. Doctors study the body. Here are some facts a doctor might know.

   a) FACT: "The heart pumps about 0.06 L of blood with each beat."
   About how many times would the heart need to beat to pump a litre of blood?

   b) FACT: "All of the blood passes through the heart in a minute."
   How many times would the blood pass through the heart in a day?

   c) FACT: "Bones make up about 15% of the weight of the body."
   How much would the bones of a 62 kg person weigh?

   d) FACT: "The brain is 85% water."
   What fraction of the brain is not water?

   e) FACT: "The most common type of blood is Type O blood.
   45% of people have Type O blood."
   About how many children in a class of 24 kids would have Type O blood?

NS6-98: Word Problems (Advanced)

Answer the following questions in your notebook.

1. 98% of Antarctica is covered in ice.

   What fraction of Antarctica is not covered in ice?

2. A ball is dropped from a height of 100 m. Each time it hits the ground, it bounces $\frac{3}{5}$ of the height it fell from. How high did it bounce…

   a) on the first bounce?

   b) on the second bounce?

3. The peel of a banana weighs $\frac{1}{8}$ of the total weight of a banana.

   If you buy 4 kg of bananas at $0.60 per kg …

   a) how much do you pay for the peel?

   b) how much do you pay for the part you eat?

4. The price of a soccer ball is $8.00. If the price rises by $0.25 each year,

   How much will the ball cost in 10 years?

5. Janice earned $28.35 on Monday.

   On Thursday, she spent $17.52 for a shirt.

   She now has $32.23.

   How much money did she have before she started work Monday?

6. Anthony's taxi service charges $2.50 for the first kilometre and $1.50 for each additional km.

   If Bob paid $17.50 in total, how many km did he travel in the taxi?

7. There are three apartment buildings in a block.

   - Apartment A has 50 suites.
   - Apartment B has 50% more suites than Apartment A.
   - Apartment C has twice as many suites as Apartment B.

   a) How many suites do Apartment B and Apartment C have?

   b) How many suites do the three apartments have altogether?

NS6-98: Word Problems (Advanced) *(continued)*

Answer the following questions in your notebook.

8. Six classes at Queen Victoria P.S. are going skating.

There are 24 students in each class. The teachers ordered 4 buses, which each hold 30 students. Will there be enough room? Explain.

9. It took Cindy 20 minutes to finish her homework: she spent $\frac{2}{5}$ of the time on math and $\frac{2}{5}$ of the time on history.
   a) How many minutes did she spend on math and history?
   b) How many minutes did she spend on other subjects?
   c) What percent of the time did she spend on other subjects?

10. How many months old is a $1\frac{1}{2}$-year-old child?

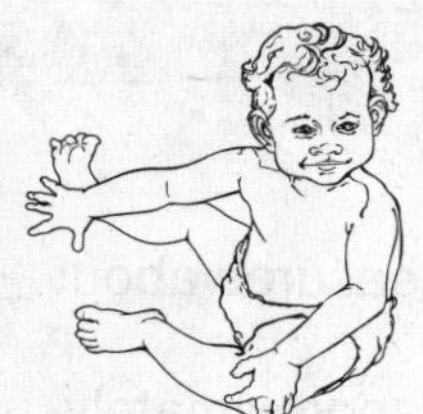

11. Philip gave away 75% of his hockey cards.
    a) What fraction of his cards did he keep?
    b) Philip put his remaining cards in a scrapbook. Each page held 14 cards and he filled 23 pages.
    How many cards did he put in the book?
    c) How many cards did he have before he gave part of his collection away?

12. Find the mystery numbers.
    a) I am a number between 15 and 25.
    I am a multiple of 3 and 4.
    b) I am a number between 20 and 30.
    My tens digit is 1 less than my ones digit.
    c) Rounded to the nearest tens I am 60.
    I am an odd number.
    The difference in my digits is 2.

13. A pentagonal box has a perimeter of 3.85 m. How long is each side?

14. Tony bought a binder for $17.25 and a pen for $2.35. He paid 15% in taxes.
How much change did he receive from $25.00?

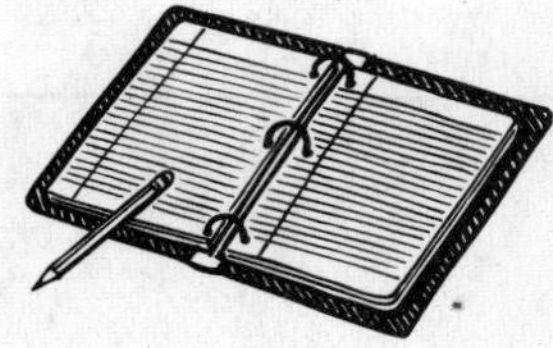

15. Tom spent $500 on furniture: he spent $\frac{3}{10}$ of the money on a chair, $50.00 on a table and the rest on a sofa.
What fraction and what percent of the $500.00 did he spend on each item?

ME6-1: Millimetres and Centimetres

If you look at a ruler with millimetre measurements, you can see that 1 cm is equal to 10 mm.

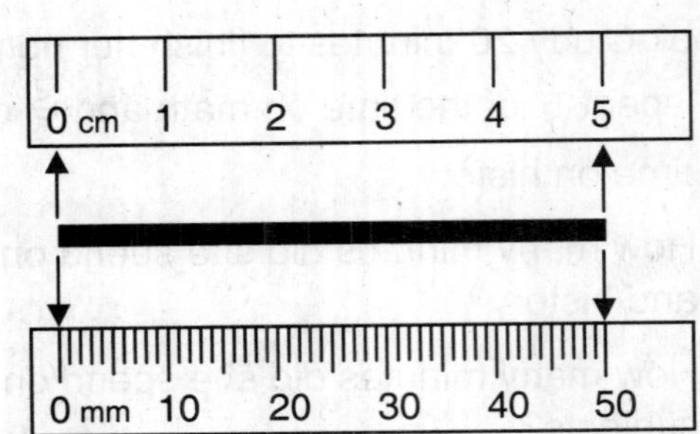

Measure the line in mm and cm.

The line is _____ cm long, or _____ mm long.

To convert a measurement from cm to mm,

we have to multiply the measurement by _____.

---

1. Your little finger is about 1 cm or 10 mm wide. Measure the objects below using your little finger. Then convert your measurement to mm.

a) 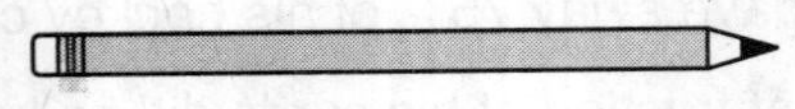

This pencil measures about _____ little fingers.

So, the pencil is approximately _____ mm long.

b) 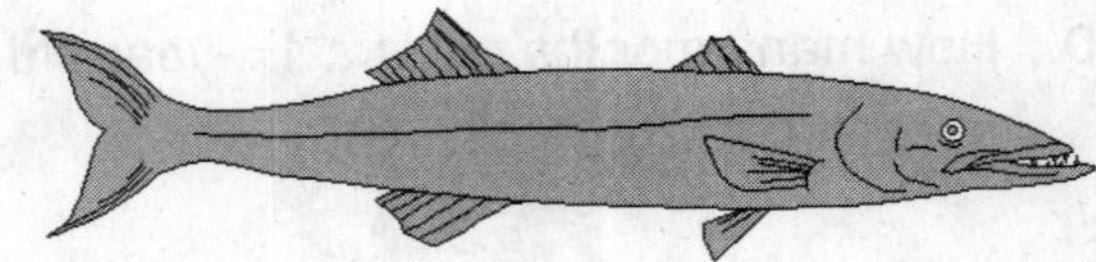

This barracuda measures about _____ little fingers.

So, the picture is approximately _____ mm long.

2. Find the distance between the two arrows on each ruler.

a) 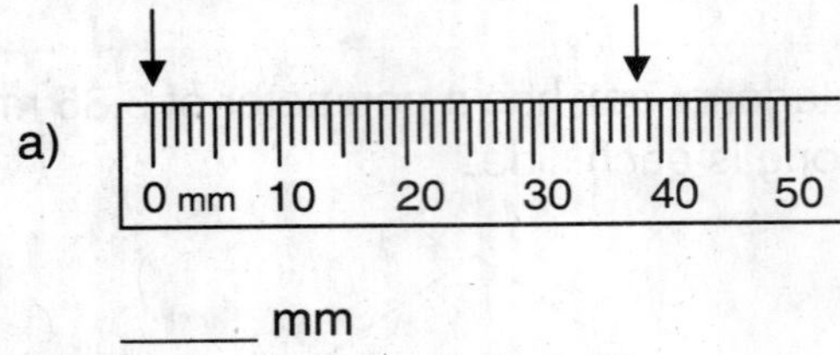

_____ mm

b)

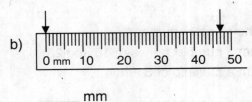

_____ mm

3. Use a ruler to draw the following lines to the exact millimetre.

a) Draw a line 27 mm long.

b) Draw a line 52 mm long.

4. a) Which is longer…

i) Line A 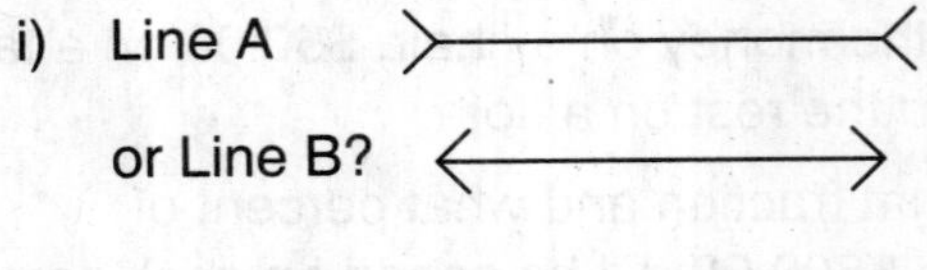 or Line B?

____

ii) The height of the hat or the brim of the hat? 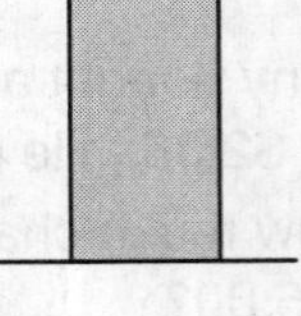

____

b) Measure the lengths in mm to check.

5. Estimate whether each line is <u>less</u> than 40 mm or <u>more</u> than 40 mm.
Place a checkmark in the appropriate column.
Then measure the actual length.

	Less than 40 mm	More than 40 mm
a)		
b)		
c)		

Actual Lengths: a) _____ mm b) _____ mm c) _____ mm

6. 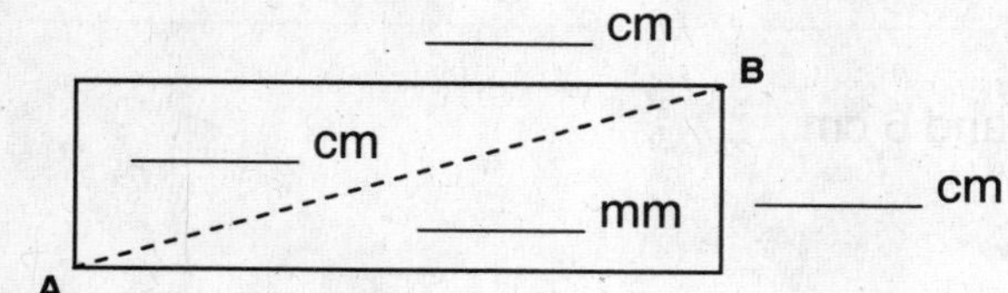

Measure the sides of the rectangle (in cm).

Then measure the distance between the two diagonal corners in cm and mm.

NOTE: Your answer in cm will be a decimal.

7. How many millimetres (mm) are there in one centimetre (cm)? _____________

8. To change a measurement from centimetres (cm) into millimetres (mm), what should you <u>multiply</u> by?

____

9. Fill in the missing numbers.

mm	cm
	13
	32

mm	cm
	8
	18

mm	cm
	213
	170

mm	cm
	9
	567

10. To change a measurement from mm to cm what should you <u>divide</u> by? _____________

a) 50 ÷ 10 = _____ b) 80 ÷ 10 = _____ c) 3200 ÷ 10 = _____ d) 430 ÷ 10 = _____

e) 460 mm = _______ cm f) 60 mm = _______ cm g) 580 mm = _______ cm

11. Convert. a) 4 cm = _______ mm b) 18 cm = _______ mm c) _______ cm = 130 mm

12. Circle the greater measurement in each pair of measurements below.
First, convert one of the measurements so that both units are the same.

a) 5 cm 70 mm b) 83 cm 910 mm c) 45 cm 53 mm

d) 2 cm 12 mm e) 60 cm 6200 mm f) 72 cm 420 mm

ME6-1: Millimetres and Centimetres *(continued)*

13. Using your ruler, draw a second line so that the pair of lines are the given distance apart.

	Distance apart in cm	Distance apart in mm
a) | |	4	40
b) |	3	____
c) |	____	80
d) |	7	____

14. In the space provided, draw a line that is between 5 and 6 cm.

How long is your line in mm? ________

15. Write a measurement in mm that is between …

a) 7 and 8 cm: _____ mm b) 12 and 13 cm: ________ c) 27 and 28 cm: ________

16. Write a measurement in a whole number of cm that is between …

a) 67 mm and 75 mm: ___ cm b) 27 mm and 39 mm: ______ c) 52 mm and 7 cm: ______

17. Draw a line that is a whole number of centimetres long and is between …

a) 35 and 45 mm b) 55 and 65 mm c) 27 and 33 mm

18. Rebecca says 7 mm is longer than 3 cm because 7 is greater than 3. Is she right?

19. Carl has a set of sticks: some are 7 cm long and some are 4 cm long.

Example: This picture (not drawn to scale) shows how he could line up the sticks to measure 19 cm: 7 cm | 4 cm | 4 cm | 4 cm

Draw a sketch to show how Carl could measure each length by lining the sticks up end to end.

a) 8 cm b) 11 cm c) 22 cm d) 26 cm e) 25 cm

20. Show how Carl could make these measurements using his sticks.
HINT: you may need to subtract.

a) 3 cm b) 1 cm c) 20 mm d) 50 mm e) 17 cm

BONUS:
f) Can you find two different solutions for each measurement?

ME6-2: Decimetres

A **decimetre** is a unit of length equal to 10 cm.

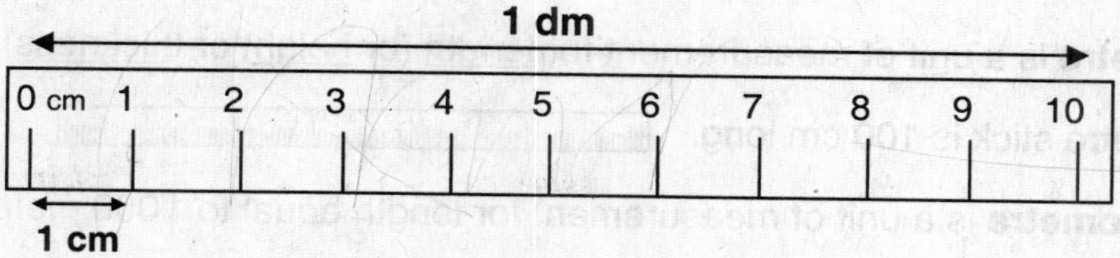

1. Place a checkmark in the correct column.
HINT: You can use the picture at the top of the page to help you estimate.

	Less than 1 dm	More than 1 dm
My leg		✓
The length of an eraser	✓	
My pencil		✓
The height of the classroom door		✓

2. 1 decimetre = 10 centimetres.

3. What fraction of a decimetre (dm) is a centimetre? 1/10

4. To change a measurement from dm to cm, what should you multiply by? ________

5. To change a measurement from cm to dm what should you divide by? ________

6. Find the numbers missing from the following charts.

cm	dm
120	12
	31
	42

cm	dm
80	
	620
300	

cm	dm
530	
	1
950	

7. In the space provided, draw a line that is between 1 and 2 decimetres long.

a) How long is your line in cm? ________ b) How long is your line in mm? ________

8. Write a measurement in cm that is between …

a) 3 and 4 dm ________ b) 6 and 7 dm ________ c) 9 and 10 dm ________

9. Write a measurement in dm that is between …

a) 62 and 72 cm ________ b) 37 and 45 cm ________ c) 48 and 73 cm ________

10. How many dm are in 100 cm? ________

11. There are 10 mm in 1 cm. There are 10 cm in 1 dm. How many mm are in 1 dm? ________

ME6-3: Metres and Kilometres

A **metre** is a unit of measurement for length (or height or thickness) equal to 100 cm.

A metre stick is 100 cm long.

A **kilometre** is a unit of measurement for length equal to 1 000 metres.

Here are some measurements you can use for estimating in metres.

*about **2** metres:* the height of a (tall) adult

*about **10** metres:* the length of a school bus

*about **100** metres:* the length of a football field

1. Find (or think of) an object in your classroom or outside that is approximately …

   a) 2 metres long ____________ b) 3 metres long ____________

2. Fourteen basketball players can lie head to foot along a basketball court.

   What is the court's length in metres? ____________

3. a) How many adults do you think could lie head to foot across your classroom? ____________

   b) Approximately how wide is your classroom (in metres)? ____________

4. a) About how many school buses high is your school? ____________

   b) About how high is your school (in metres)? ____________

5. A small city block is about 100 m long.

   Name a place you can walk to from your school: ____________

   Approximately how many metres away from the school is the place you named? ____________

6. The number line represents 1 km. Mark the following distances on the line:

   A 200 m **B** 50 m **C** 550 m **D** 825 m **E** 110 m

   0 km ———————————————— 1 km

7. About how many football fields long is a kilometre?

8. You can travel 1 km if you walk for 15 minutes at a regular speed.

   Name a place that is about 1 km from your school.

ME6-4: Comparing Units

1. Finish the table by following the pattern.

m	1	2	3	4	5	6
dm	10	20				
cm	100	200				
mm	1000	2000				

2. To convert a measurement from metres to centimetres, you multiply by ____________.

3. To convert a measurement from metres to millimetres, you multiply by ____________.

4. Convert the following measurements.

m	cm
8	
70	

m	mm
5	
17	

cm	mm
4	
121	

dm	cm
32	
5	

5. Convert the measurement given in cm to a measurement using multiple units.

a) 423 cm = ___ m _____ cm b) 514 cm = ___ m _____ cm c) 627 cm = ___ m _____ cm

d) 673 cm = ___ m _____ cm e) 381 cm = ___ m _____ cm f) 203 cm = ___ m _____ cm

6. Convert the following multiple units of measurements to a single unit.

a) 2 m 83 cm = _______ cm b) 3 m 65 cm = _______ cm c) 4 m 85 cm = _______ cm

d) 9 m 47 cm = _______ cm e) 7 m 4 cm = _______ cm f) 6 m 40 cm = _______ cm

7. Change the following measurements to multiple units then to decimal notation.

a) 546 cm = __5__ m __46__ cm = __5.46__ m b) 217 cm = ____ m ______ cm = _______ m

c) 783 cm = ____ m ______ cm = _______ m d) 608 cm = ____ m ______ cm = _______ m

e) 72 cm = ____ m ______ cm = _______ m f) 7 cm = ____ m ______ cm = _______ m

8. Why do we use the same decimal notation for dollars and cents and for metres and centimetres?

9. Michelle says that to change 6 m 80 cm to centimetres, you multiply the 6 by 100 and then add 80. Is Michelle correct? Why does Michelle multiply by 100?

ME6-5: Changing Units

1. Measure the line below in mm, cm, and dm:

_______ mm   _______ cm   _______ dm

a) Which of the units (mm, cm, or dm) is: largest? __________ smallest? __________

b) Which unit did you need more of to measure the line, the larger unit or the smaller unit?

____

c) To change a measurement from a **larger** to a **smaller** unit, do you need …

(i) more of the smaller units, or   (ii) **fewer** of the smaller units?

____

2. Fill in the missing numbers.

a) 1 cm = ______ mm   b) 1 dm = ______ cm

d) 1 dm = ______ mm   d) 1 m = ______ dm

e) 1 m = ______ cm   f) 1 m = ______ mm

Units **decrease** in size going **down** the stairway:

m
dm
cm
mm

- 1 step down = 10 × smaller
- 2 steps down = 100 × smaller
- 3 steps down = 1 000 × smaller

3. Change the measurements below by following the steps.

a) Change 3.5 cm to mm

i) The new units are 10 times smaller

ii) So I need 10 times more units

iii) So I multiply by 10

3.5 cm = 35 mm

b) Change 7.2 cm to mm

i) The new units are ____ times __________

ii) So I need ____ times __________ units

iii) So I __________ by ____

7.2 cm = ____ mm

c) Change 2.6 dm to cm

i) The new units are ____ times __________

ii) So I need ____ times __________ units

iii) So I __________ by ____

2.6 dm = ____ cm

d) Change 7.53 cm to mm

i) The new units are ____ times __________

ii) So I need ____ times __________ units

iii) So I __________ by ____

7.53 cm = ____ mm

REMEMBER: There are 1 000 g in a kg and 1 000 mg in a g.

e) Change 3.4 mm to cm

i) The new units are _____ times_________

ii) So I need _____ times ____________ units

iii) So I ________________________ by _____

3.4 mm = _____ cm

f) Change 8.53 kg to g

i) The new units are _____ times __________

ii) So I need _____ times ____________ units

iii) So I ________________________ by _____

8.53 kg = _____ g

g) Change 5.2 g to mg

i) The new units are _____ times __________

ii) So I need _____ times ____________ units

iii) So I ________________________ by _____

5.2 g = _____ mg

h) Change 2.14 g to kg

i) The new units are _____ times __________

ii) So I need _____ times ____________ units

iii) So I ________________________ by _____

2.14 g = _____ kg

4. Change the units by following the steps in Question 3 mentally.

a) 4 m = __________ dm b) 1.3 dm = __________ mm c) 20 cm = __________ mm

5. A decimetre of ribbon costs 5¢.
How much will 90 cm cost?

6. Emily's books weigh 2.1 kg, 350 g, and 1253 g.
Her backpack can hold 4 kg.
Can she carry all three books?

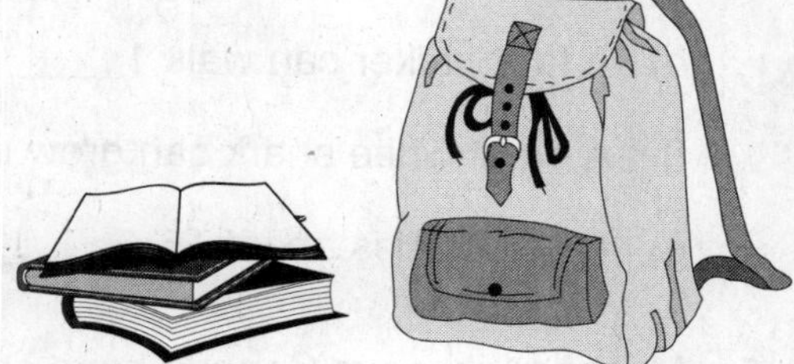

7. The width of a rectangle is 57 cm and its length is 65 cm.
Is the perimeter of the rectangle greater or less than 2.4 m?

8. How is the relation between kilograms and grams similar to the relation between kilometres and metres?

9. How is the relation between milligrams and grams similar to the relation between millimetres and metres?

ME6-6: Appropriate Units of Length

1. Match the word with the symbol.
   Then match the object with the appropriate unit of measurement.

a)

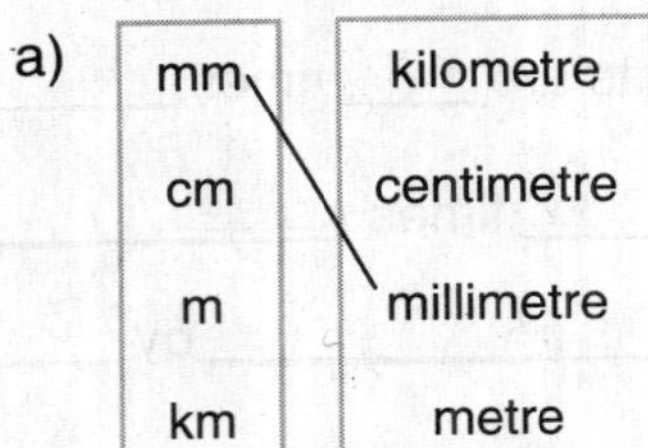

Symbol	Word	Object
mm	kilometre	length of a bee's antenna
cm	centimetre	width of a swimming pool
m	millimetre	distance of a marathon
km	metre	diameter of a drum

b)

Symbol	Word	Object
km	metre	length of a ruler
cm	millimetre	thickness of a nail
m	kilometre	diameter of the moon
mm	centimetre	length of a soccer field

2. Circle the unit of measurement that makes the statement correct.
   a) A very tall adult is about 2 **dm** / **m** high.
   b) The width of your hand is close to 1 **dm** / **cm**
   c) The Calgary Tower is 191 **cm** / **m** high.

3. Nicholas measured some objects, but forgot to include the units. Add the appropriate unit.
   a) bed: 180 ____ b) car: 2 ____ c) hat: 25 ____ d) toothbrush: 16 ____ e) driveway: 11 ____

4. Choose which unit (km, m, or cm) belongs to complete each sentence.
   a) Canada's entire coastline is 202 080 _______ long.
   b) Mount Logan, in the Yukon Territory, is 5 959 _______ high.
   c) Water going over the Della Falls in British Columbia drops 440 _______.
   d) A teacher's desk is about 200 _______ long.
   e) A fast walker can walk 1 _______ in 10 minutes.
   f) A great white shark can grow up to 4 _______.
   g) A postcard is about 15 _______ long.

5. Most provinces in Canada have an official tree and an official bird.
   Change each measurement below to the smallest unit used.
   Then order the trees from tallest to shortest.

Tree	Height	In the Smallest Units
White Birch (*Saskatchewan*)	2 m	
Lodgepole Pine (*Alberta*)	3 050 cm	
Western Red Cedar (*British Columbia*)	59 m	
Red Oak (*Prince Edward Island*)	24 m	

1. ____________
2. ____________
3. ____________
4. ____________

6. Order the official birds from longest to shortest.

Bird	Length	In the Smallest Units
Atlantic Puffin (*Newfoundland & Labrador*)	34.5 cm	
Great Horned Owl (*Alberta*)	63.5 cm	
Snowy Owl (*Quebec*)	66 cm	
Great Gray Owl (*Manitoba*)	0.55 m	

1. ________
2. ________
3. ________
4. ________

7. Mark each measurement on the number line with an "X." The first one is done for you.

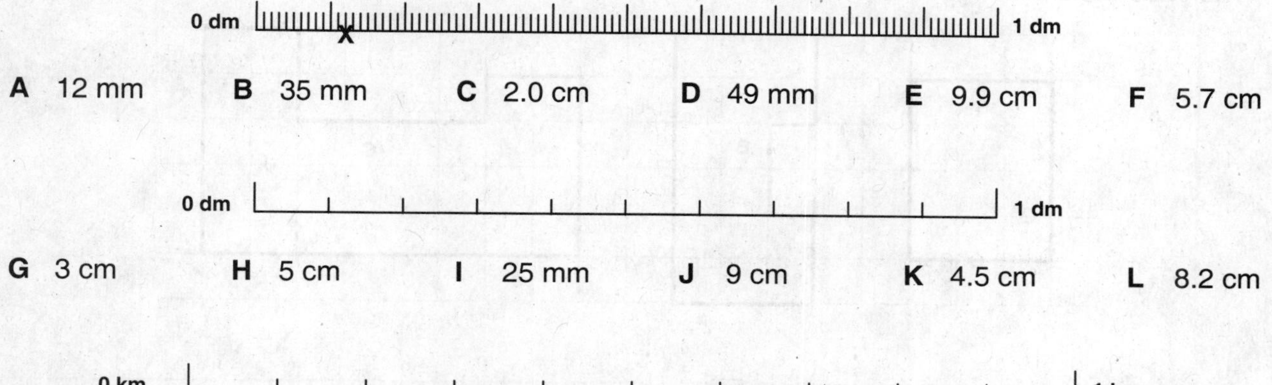

A 12 mm **B** 35 mm **C** 2.0 cm **D** 49 mm **E** 9.9 cm **F** 5.7 cm

0 dm — 1 dm

G 3 cm **H** 5 cm **I** 25 mm **J** 9 cm **K** 4.5 cm **L** 8.2 cm

0 km — 1 km

M 200 m **N** 500 m **O** 700 m **P** 350 m **Q** 850 m **R** 630 m **S** 90 m

8. Fill in the numbers in the correct places below (select from the box).

a) The 1988 Winter Olympics skiing competitions took place at Nakiska, which is ________ **km** from Calgary.
The highest point at Nakiska is ________ **m** above sea level.
The longest run down the mountain is ________ **km.**

3.3	83	2 260

b) The Red River is ________ **km** long.
In 1997 it flooded and rose ________ **m.**
Winnipeg was protected by a ________ **km** floodway that was built around the city.

7.5	47	877

9. Name an object in your classroom that has …

a) a thickness of about 20 mm: ________ b) a height of about 2 m: ________

ME6-7: Exploring Perimeter

1. Each edge is 1 cm long. Write the total length of each side in cm as shown in the first figure. Then write an addition statement and find the perimeter.

a)

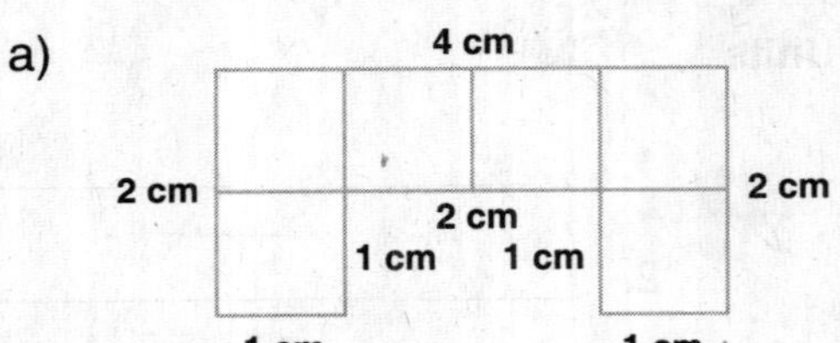

b)

Perimeter: ____________________

Perimeter: ____________________

2. Each edge is 1 unit long. Write the length of each side beside the figure (don't miss any edges!). Then use the side lengths to find the perimeter.

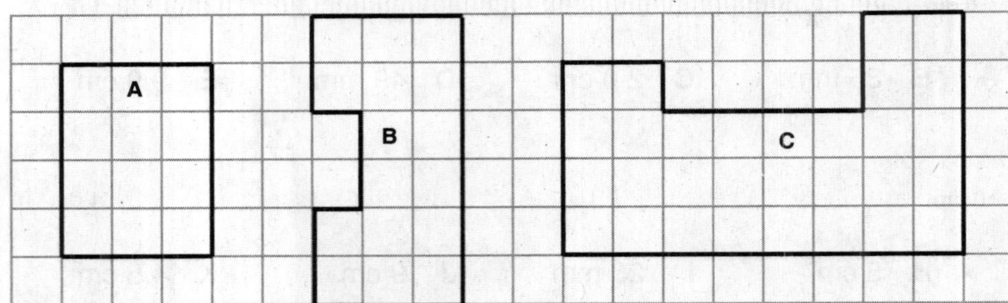

3. Draw your own figure and find the perimeter.

4. Draw two different shapes with a perimeter of 12 units.

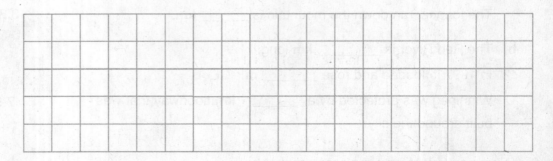

5. On grid paper, draw your own figures and find their perimeters. Try making letters or other shapes!

ME6-8: Measuring Perimeter

1. Measure the perimeter of each figure in cm using a ruler.

a)

b) 

c) 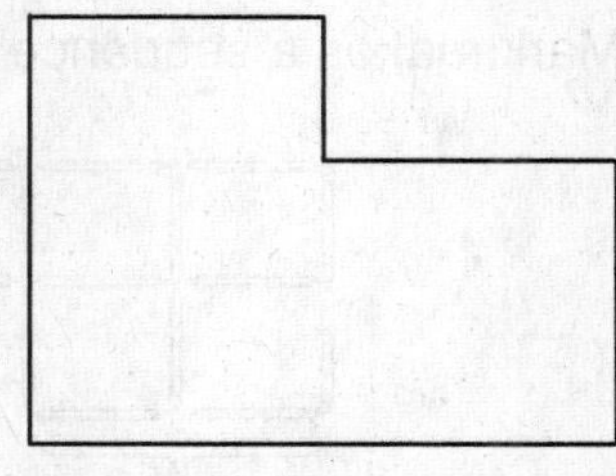

Perimeter: ________ Perimeter: ________ Perimeter: ________

2. Find the perimeter of each shape. Be sure to include the units in your answer.

a)

b) 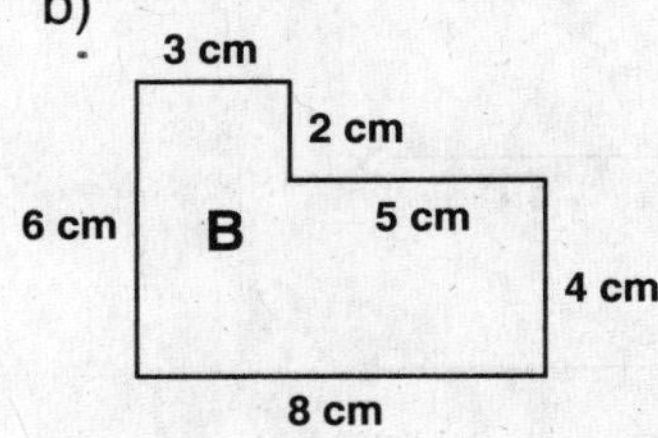

c) 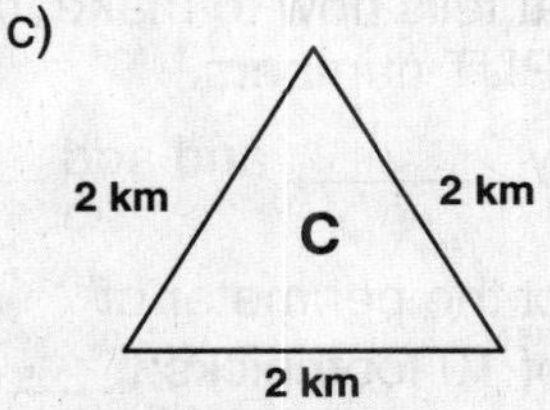

d) 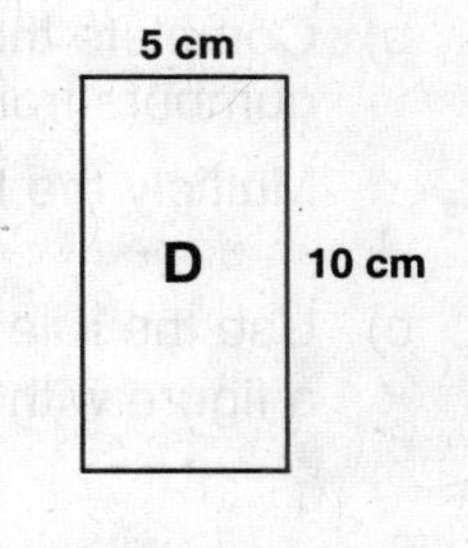

Perimeter: ______ Perimeter: ______ Perimeter: ______ Perimeter: ______

e) Write the letters of the shapes in order from greatest perimeter to least perimeter.
HINT: Make sure you look at the units!

____

3. Your little finger is about 1 cm wide. Estimate, then measure, the perimeter of each shape in cm.

a)

b) 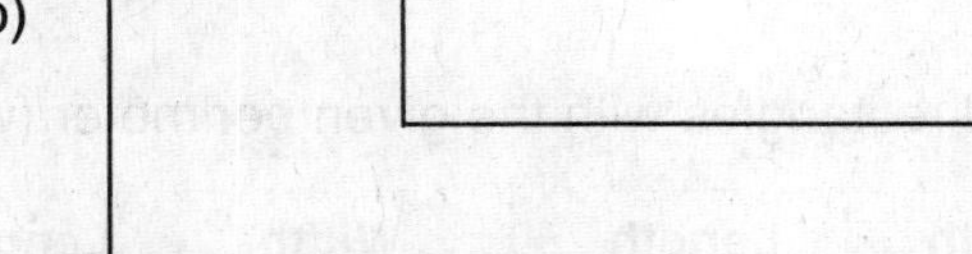

Estimated Perimeter: ____________ Estimated Perimeter: ____________

Actual Perimeter: ____________ Actual Perimeter: ____________

4. Show all the ways you can make a rectangle using …
   a) 10 squares
   b) 12 squares
   c) Can you make a rectangle with 7 squares?
   d) Which of the rectangles in b) has the greatest perimeter? What is the perimeter?

5. Draw three different figures with perimeter 10.
NOTE: The figures don't have to be rectangles.

6. A rectangle has perimeter 1 m. Each longer side is 36 cm. How long is each shorter side?

7. A rectangle is twice as wide as it is long.
What is the ratio of the width to the perimeter of the rectangle?

ME6-9: Investigating Perimeter

1. Mark makes a sequence of figures with toothpicks.

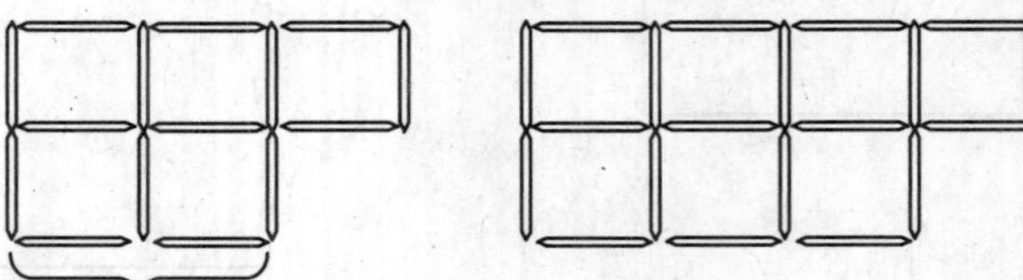

a) Complete the chart.

b) Complete the rule that tells how to make the OUTPUT numbers from the INPUT numbers.
Multiply the INPUT by ________ and add ________.

c) Use the rule to predict the perimeter of a figure with a base of 10 toothpicks: ____________

INPUT *Number of toothpicks in base*	**OUTPUT** *Perimeter*
2	10

2. Add one square to the figure so that the perimeter of the new figure is 12 units.
NOTE: Assume all edges are 1 unit.

a) 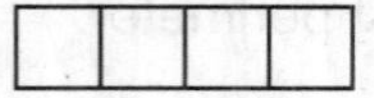

Original Perimeter = ____ units
New Perimeter = 12 units

b) 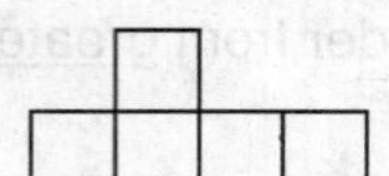

Original Perimeter = ____ units
New Perimeter = 12 units

c) 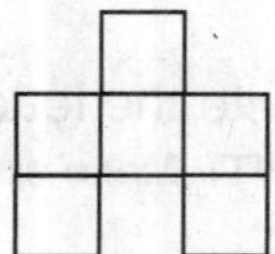

Original Perimeter = ____ units
New Perimeter = 12 units

3. Find all rectangles with the given perimeter (with lengths and widths that are whole numbers).

Width	**Length**

Perimeter = 6 units

Width	**Length**

Perimeter = 12 units

Width	**Length**

Perimeter = 16 units

Width	**Length**

Perimeter = 18 units

4. Repeat steps a) to c) of Question 1 for the following patterns.

a) 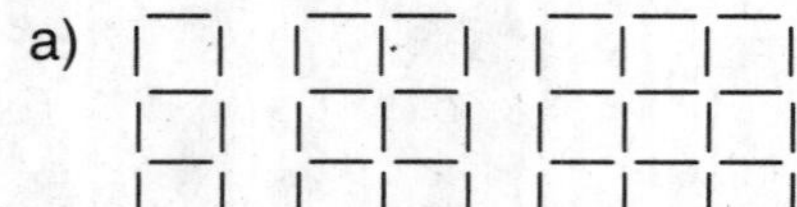

b)

5. Emma says the formula 2 × (length + width) gives the perimeter of a rectangle. Is she correct?

ME6-10: Area in Square Centimetres

Shapes that are flat are called **two-dimensional** (2-D) shapes.

The **area** of a 2-dimensional shape is the amount of space it takes up.

A **square centimetre** is a unit for measuring area. A square with sides of 1 cm has an area of one square centimetre. The short form for a square centimetre is cm^2.

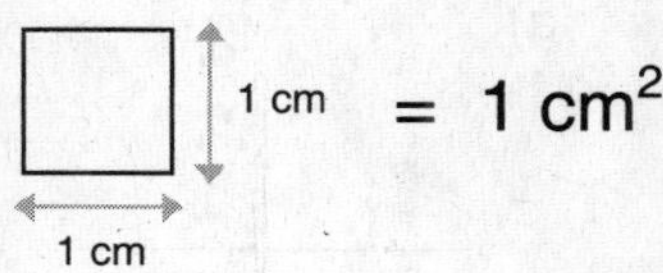

1. Find the area of these figures in square centimetres.

a) 

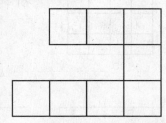

b) 

c) 

Area = ________ cm^2 Area = ________ cm^2 Area = ________ cm^2

2. Using a ruler, draw lines to divide each rectangle into square centimetres.

a) 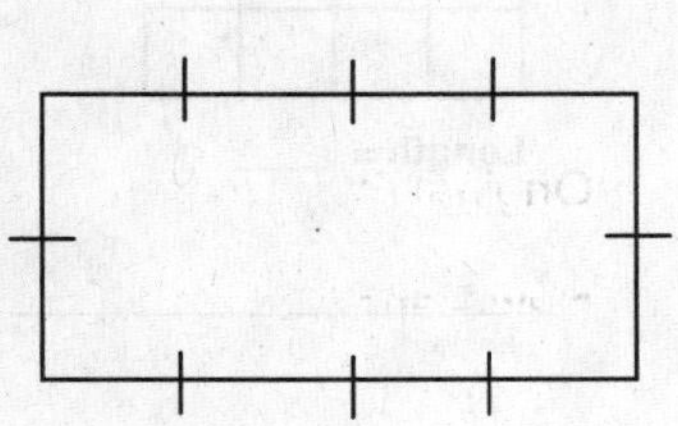

b) 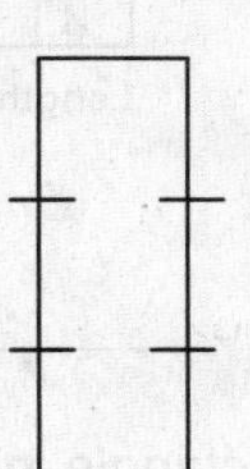

c) 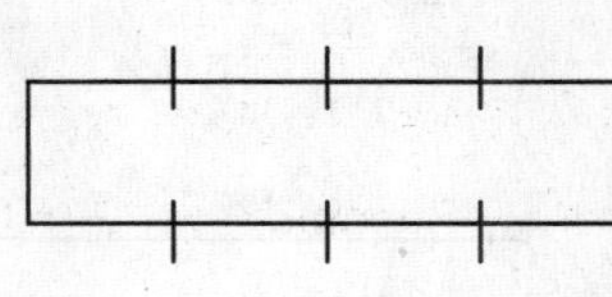

Area = ________ cm^2 Area = ________ cm^2 Area = ________ cm^2

3. How can you find the area (in square units) of each of the given shapes?

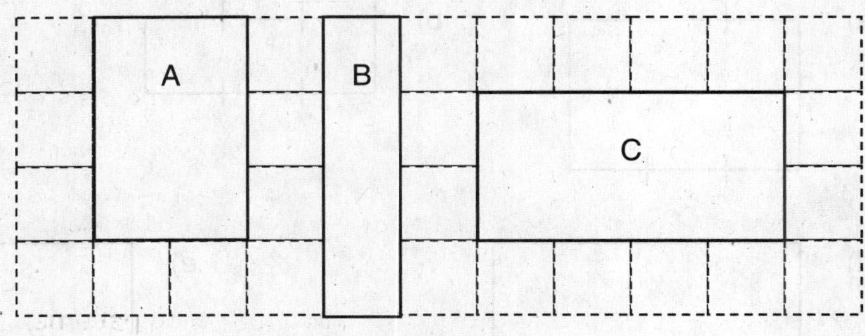

Area of **A** = ________   Area of **B** = ________   Area of **C** = ________

4. Draw three different shapes that have an area of 10 cm^2 (the shapes don't have to be rectangles).

5. Draw several shapes and find their area and perimeter.

6. Draw a rectangle with an area of 12 cm^2 and perimeter of 14 cm.

ME6-11: Area of Rectangles

1. Write a multiplication statement for each array.

a) 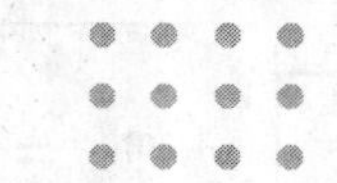 ______

b)  ______

c)  ______

d)  ______

2. Draw a dot in each box. Then write a multiplication statement that tells you the number of boxes in the rectangle.

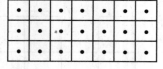

a) 3 × 7 = 21

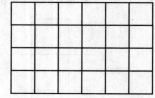

b) 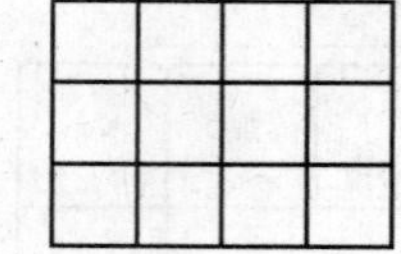 ______

c) 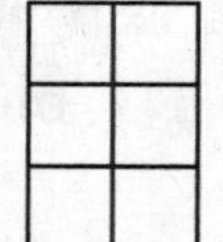 ______

d)  ______

3. Write the number of boxes along the width and length of each rectangle.
Then write a multiplication statement for the area of the rectangle (in square units).

a) 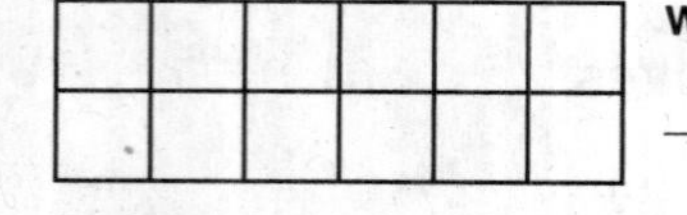
Width = ____
Length = ____

______

b) 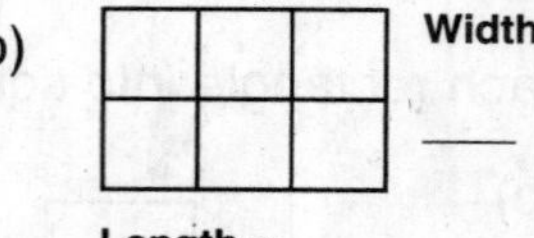
Width = ____
Length = ____

______

c) 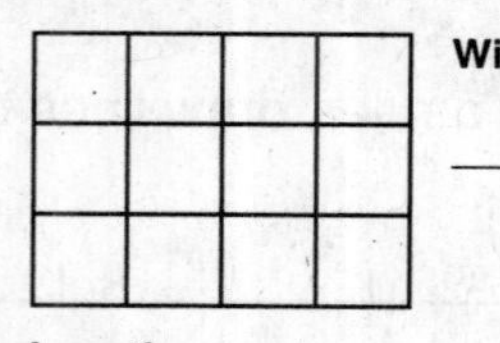
Width = ____
Length = ____

______

4. Using a ruler, draw lines to divide each rectangle into squares.
Write a multiplication statement for the area of the boxes in cm^2.
NOTE: You will have to mark the last row of boxes yourself using a ruler.

a) 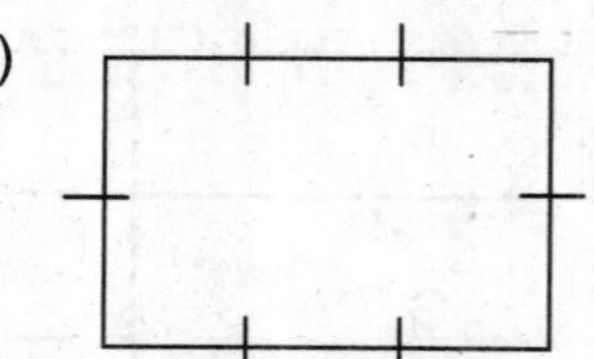

b) 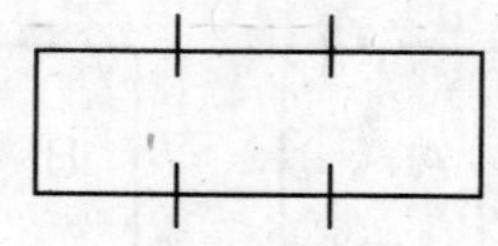

c) 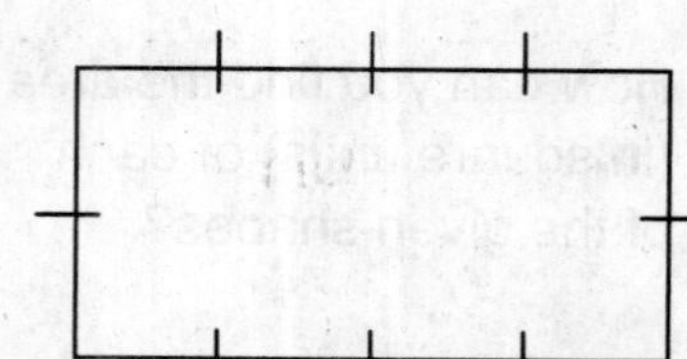

d) 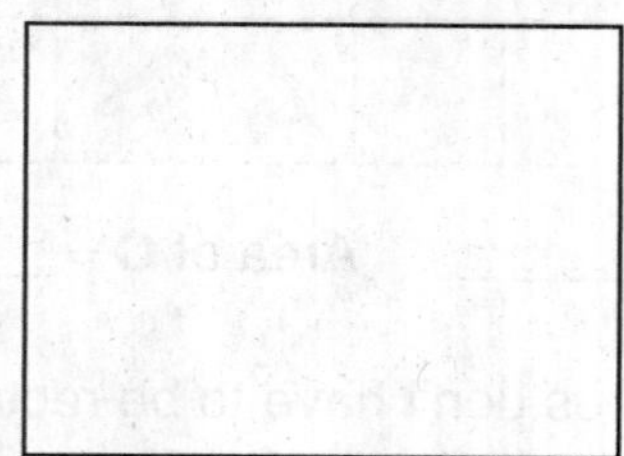

e) 

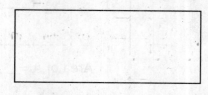

5. If you know the length and width of a rectangle, how can you find its area?

______

ME6-12: Exploring Area

1. Measure the length and width of the figures then find the area.

a) ____________ b) ____________ c) ____________

2. Find the area of a rectangle with the following dimensions:

a) width: 6 m length: 7 m ____________

b) width: 3 m length: 7 m ____________

c) width: 4 cm length: 8 cm ____________

3. a) Calculate the area of each rectangle. Be sure to include the units.

A: 3 m, 7 m — Area: ________

B: 4 cm, 5 cm — Area: ________

C: 11 m, 6 m — Area: ________

D: 15 km, 10 km — Area: ________

b) By letter, create an ordered list of the rectangles from greatest to least area: ____________

4. A rectangle has an area of 18 cm^2 and a length of 6 cm. How can you find its width?

____

5. A rectangle has an area of 24 cm^2 and a width 8 cm. What is its length? ____________

6. A square has an area of 25 cm^2. What is its width? ____________

7. a) Write the lengths of each side on the figure.

b) Divide the figure into two boxes.

c) Calculate the area by finding the area of the two boxes.

Area Box 1: ________ Area of Box 2: ________

TOTAL Area: ________

8. Using grid paper, create two different rectangles with an area of 12 square units.

ME6-13: Comparing Area and Perimeter

1. For each shape below, calculate the perimeter and area of each shape, and write your answers in the chart below. The first one has been done for you.
NOTE: The edge of each grid square represents 1 cm.

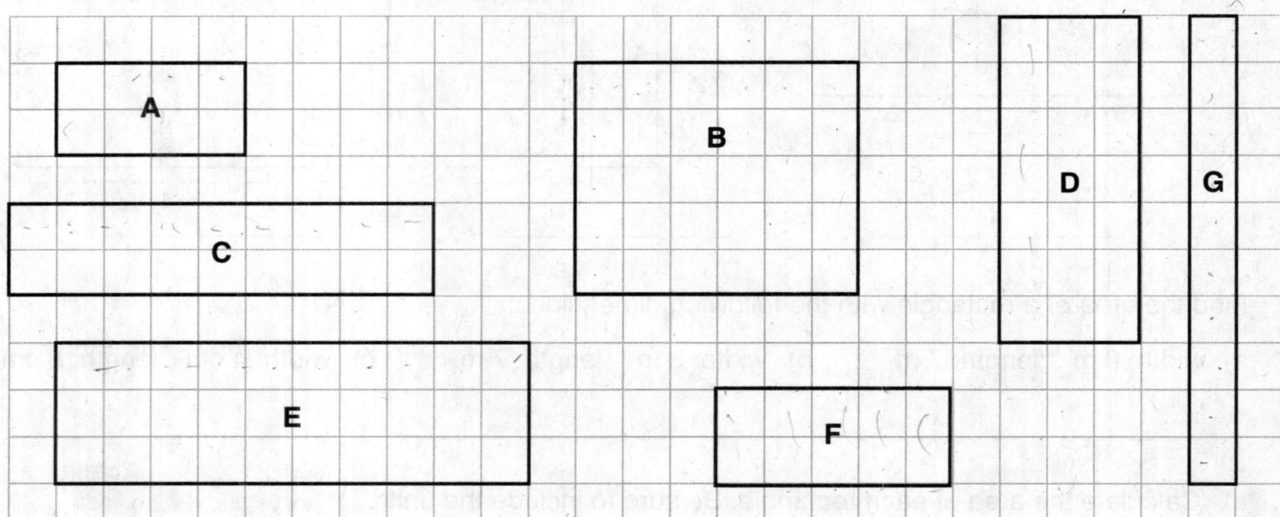

Shape	Perimeter	Area
A	2 + 4 + 4 + 2 = 12 cm	2 × 4 = 8 cm²
B	5+6+5+6=22cm	5×6=30cm²
C	2+9+9+2=22cm	2×9=18cm²
D	3+7+7+3=20 cm	3×7=21cm²
E	3+10+10+3=26cm	3×10=30cm²
F	2+5+5+2=14cm	2×5=10cm²
G	1+10+10+1=22cm	10×1=10cm²

2. Shape C has a greater perimeter than shape D. Does it also have greater area? no

3. Name two other shapes where one has a greater perimeter and the other, a greater area:
A and G

4. Write the shapes in order from greatest to least perimeter: E, B, C, G, D, F, A

5. Write the shapes in order from greatest to least area: B, E, D, C, F, G,

6. Are the orders in Questions 4 and 5 the same? no they are not

7. What is the difference between perimeter and area? for the perimeter you add up all the sides, for the Area you times tow sides

12
10
22

ME6-14: Area and Perimeter

1. Measure the length and width of each rectangle, and then record your answers in the chart below.

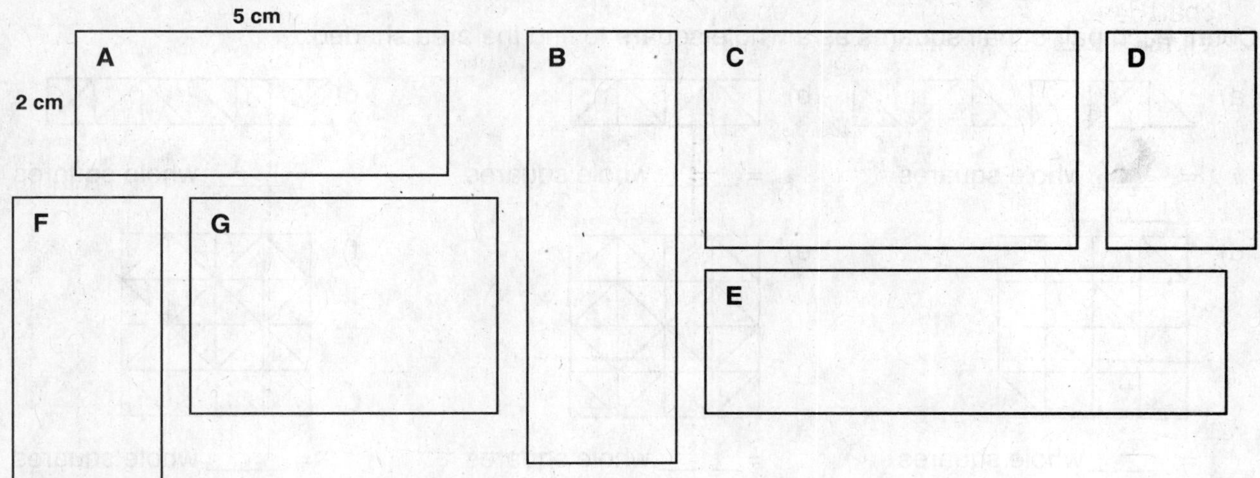

Rectangle	Estimated Perimeter	Estimated Area	Length	Width	Actual Perimeter	Actual Area
A	cm	cm^2	cm	cm	cm	cm^2
B						
C						
D						
E						
F						
G						

2. Measure the perimeter and find the area for each rectangle below with a ruler.

a)

Perimeter = ______ cm

Area = ______ cm^2

b)

Perimeter = ______ cm

Area = ______ cm^2

c)

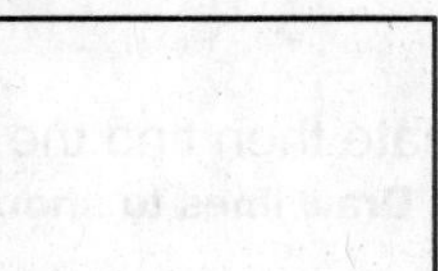

Perimeter = ______ cm

Area = ______ cm^2

3. Find the area of the rectangle using the clues.
   a) Width = 2 cm; Perimeter = 10 cm; Area = ?
   b) Width = 4 cm; Perimeter = 18 cm; Area = ?

4. Draw a square on grid paper with the given perimeter. Then find the area of the square.
   a) Perimeter = 12 cm; Area = ?
   b) Perimeter = 20 cm; Area = ?

5. On grid paper, draw a rectangle with …
   a) an area of 10 square units and a perimeter of 14 units.
   b) an area of 8 square units and a perimeter of 12 units.

ME6-15: Area of Polygons and Irregular Shapes

1. Two half squares cover the same area as a whole square .

Count each pair of half squares as a whole square to find the area shaded.

a) = 3 whole squares

b) = 2 whole squares

c) = 3 whole squares

d)

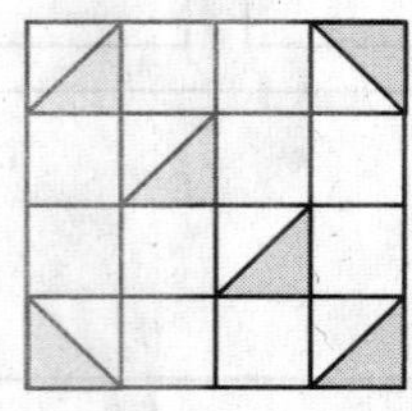

= 4 whole squares

e) = 5 whole squares

f) = 11 whole squares

g)

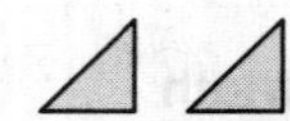

= 13 whole squares

h) = 10 whole squares

i)

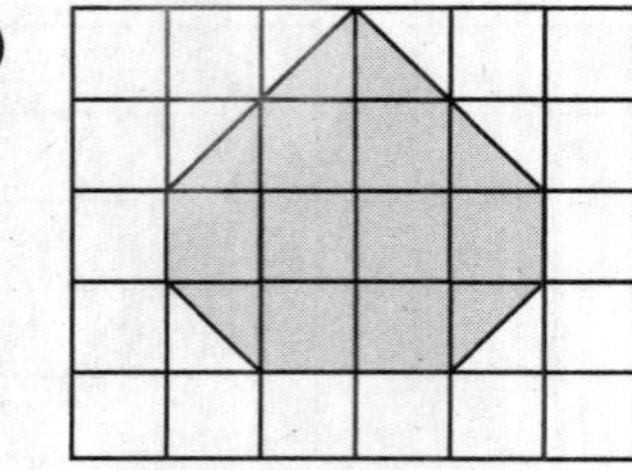

= 7.5 whole squares

j)

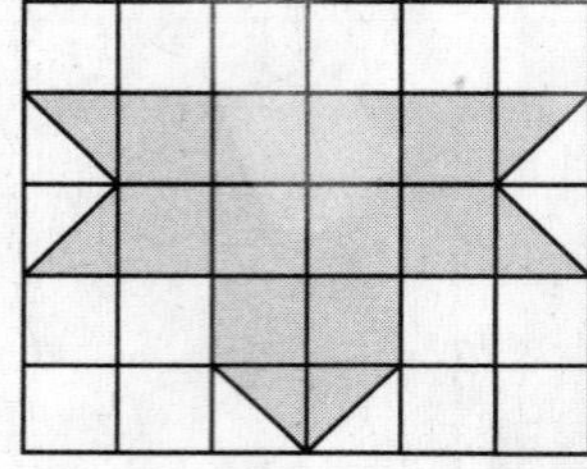

= 6 whole squares

k)

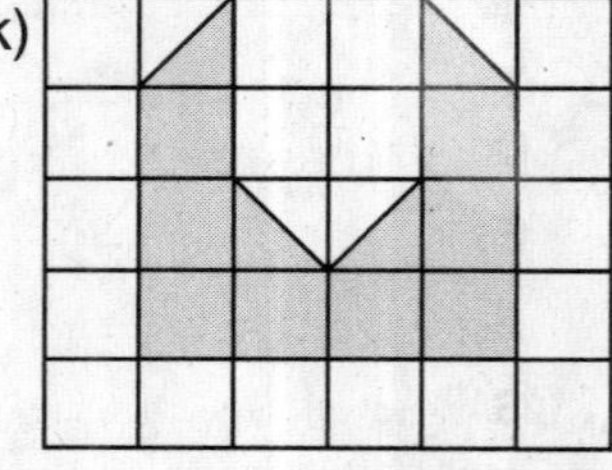

= 7.5 whole squares

2. Estimate then find the area of each figure in square units.
HINT: Draw lines to show all the half squares.

a)

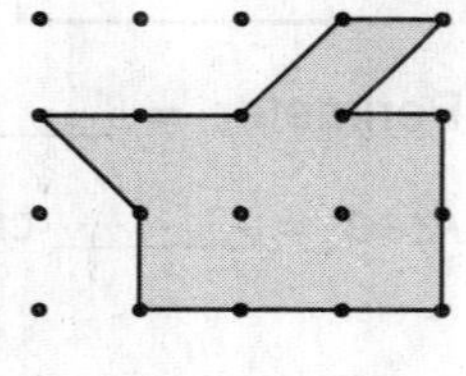

b)

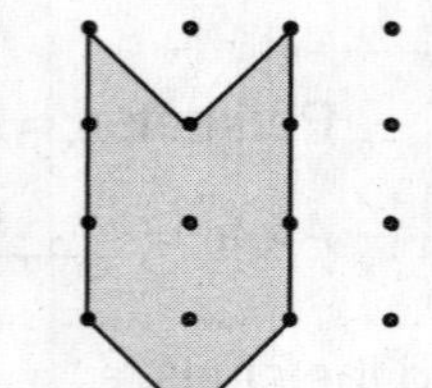

c)

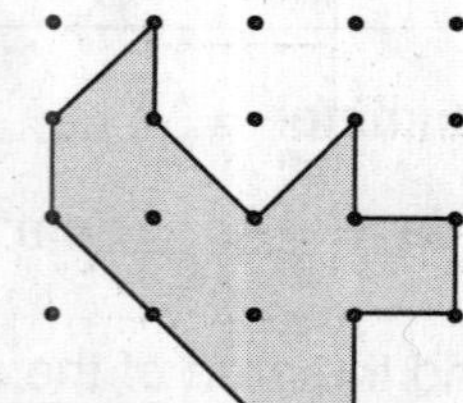

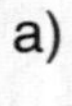

3. For each picture say whether the shaded area is <u>more</u> than, <u>less</u> than, or <u>equal</u> to the unshaded area. Explain how you know.

a)

b) equal

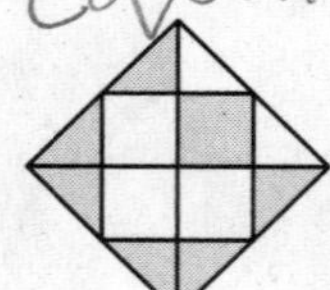

c) less

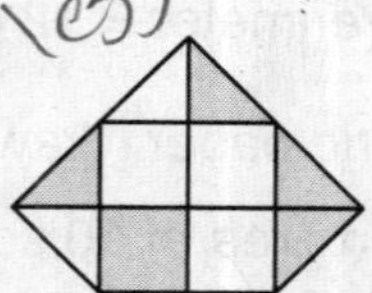

4. 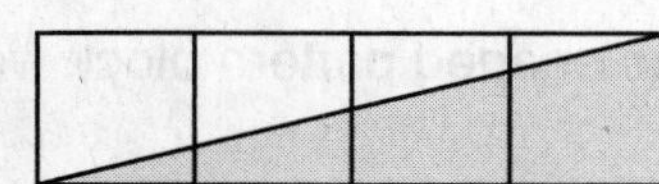

a) What fraction of the rectangle is the shaded part? ______

b) What is the area of the rectangle in square units? ______

c) What is the area of the shaded part? ______

5. Find the shaded area in square units.

a)  b)  c)  d) 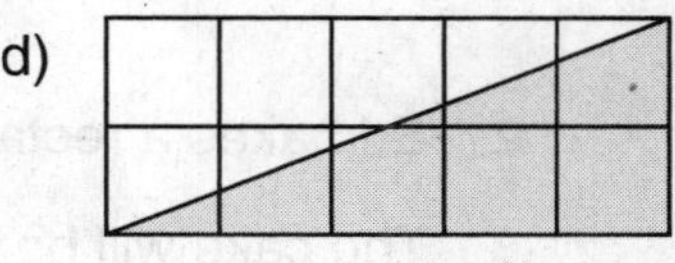

______ ______ ______ ______

6. Draw a line to divide each shape into two triangles or a triangle and a rectangle. Then calculate the area of each shape.

 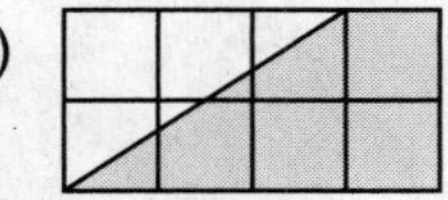 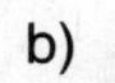 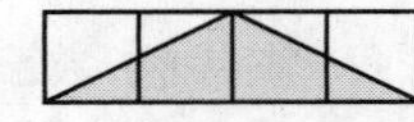  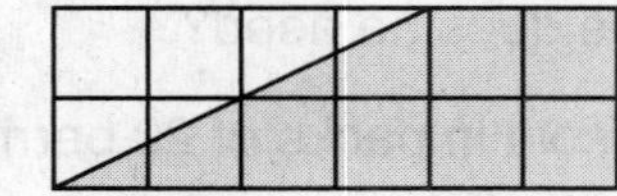 d) 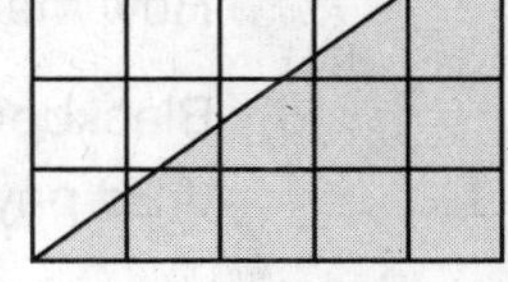

7. Calculate the area of each shape.

 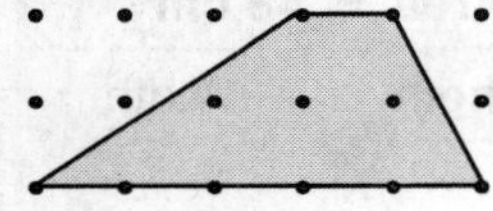 b) 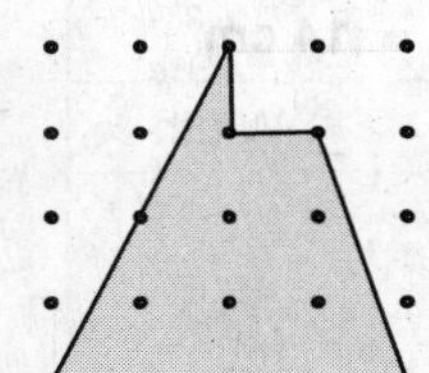 c) 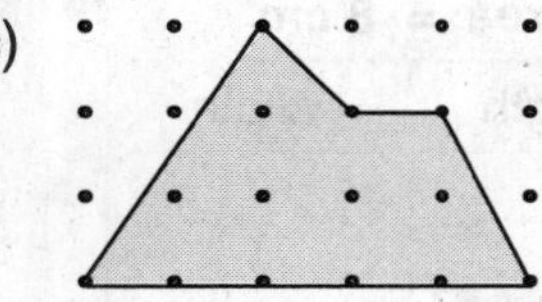

8. Each of the shaded shapes below represents ½ a square. How many total squares do they add up to?
REMEMBER: Two ½ squares = 1 full square.

a) 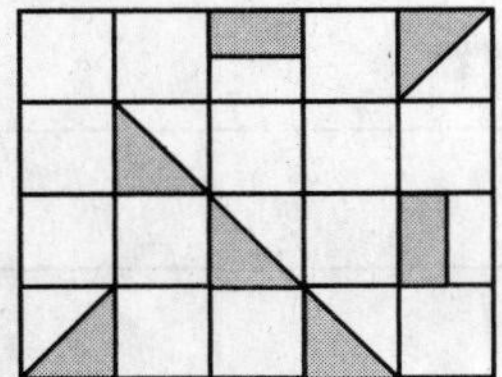

______ half squares

______ total squares

b) 

______ half squares

______ total squares

c) 

______ half squares

______ total squares

9. Fill in the blanks to find the total area. The first one has been done for you.

a) 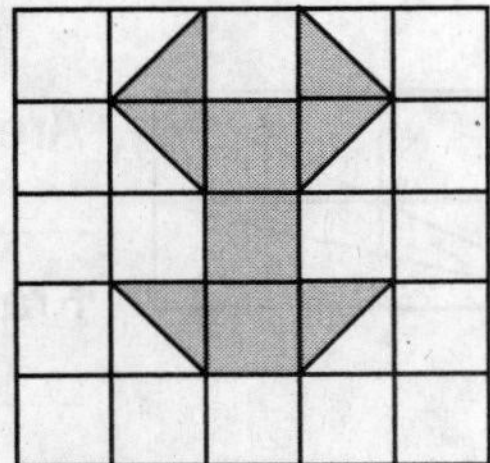

3 full squares

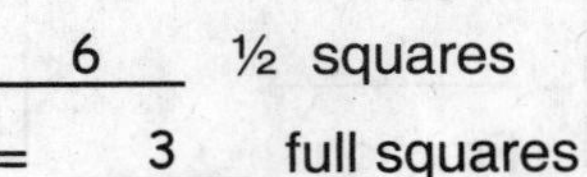

6 ½ squares

= 3 full squares

Area = 3 + 3 = 6

b) 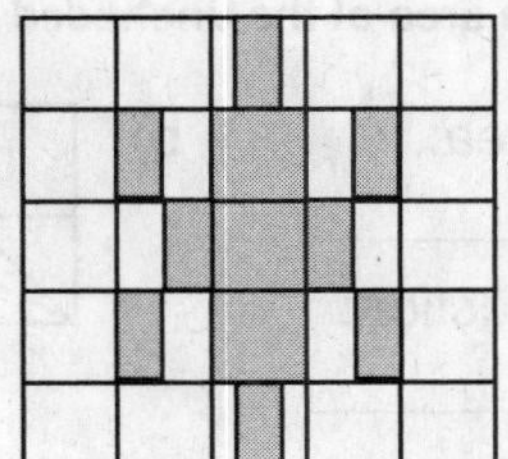

______ full squares

______ ½ squares

= ______ full squares

Area =

ME6-16: Problems and Puzzles

1. 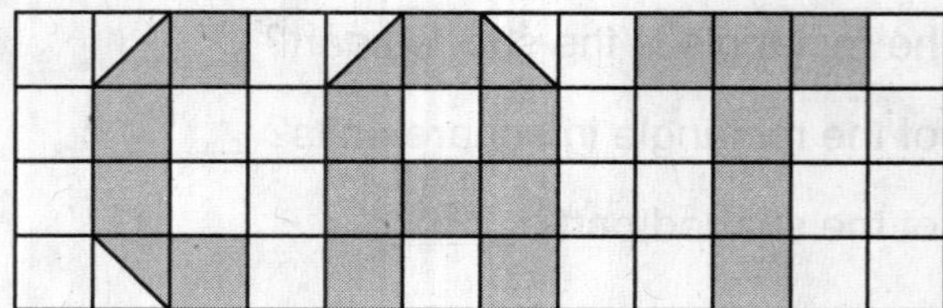

a) Find the area of the shaded pattern block word.

b) There are 48 squares in the grid. How can you use your answer above to find the number of unshaded squares (without counting them)?

2. Ed bakes a rectangular birthday cake for his Dad.

The cake will be cut into twenty-four 5 × 5 cm pieces.

a) What is the area of the cake?

b) The width of the cake is 20 cm. What is its length?

c) Ed puts blackberries on the perimeter of the cake, 2 blackberries on each 5 cm. How many berries does he need?

d) Blackberries are sold in packs of 20 berries. Each pack costs $2.99. If Ed pays for the blackberries with a 10-dollar bill, how much change does he get?

3. A rectangle's length and width are both whole numbers, where the length is greater than the width. Find possible sizes for the rectangle, given the areas below.

Area = 8 cm^2	
Length	Width

Area = 14 cm^2	
Length	Width

Area = 18 cm^2	
Length	Width

4. Name something you would measure in …

a) square metres ________________

b) square kilometres ________________

BONUS

5. Find the area of the shaded part. Then, say what fraction of the grid is shaded.

HINT: How can you use the area of the unshaded part and the area of the grid?

a) 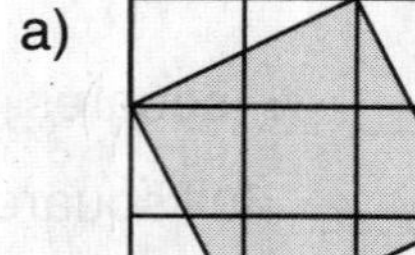 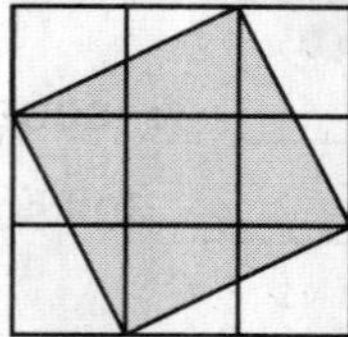 Area: ________ Fraction: ________

b) 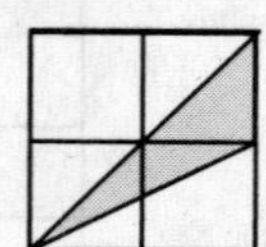 Area: ________ Fraction: ________

c) 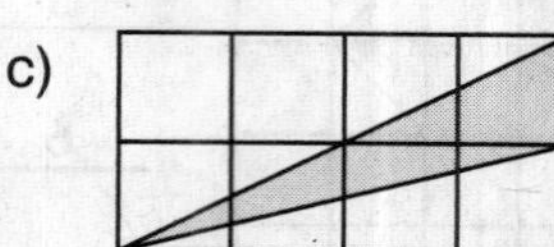 Area: ________ Fraction: ________

ME6-17: Area of Parallelograms

1. The rectangle was made by moving the shaded triangle from one end of the parallelogram to the other:

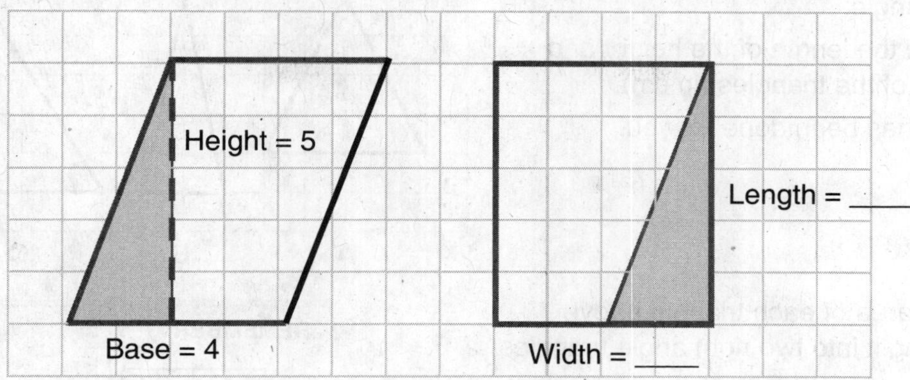

a) Is the area of the rectangle the same as the area of the parallelogram? ____________

How do you know? ____________

____

b) Fill in the width of the rectangle.

What do you notice about the base of the parallelogram and the width of the rectangle?

____

c) Fill in the length of the rectangle.

What do you notice about the height of the parallelogram and the length of the rectangle?

____

d) Recall that, for a rectangle: Area = length × width.

Can you write a formula for the area of a parallelogram using the base and height?

1. Measure the height of the parallelograms using a protractor and a ruler.

Measure the base using a ruler.

Find the area of the parallelogram using your formula from Question 1 d) above.

a)

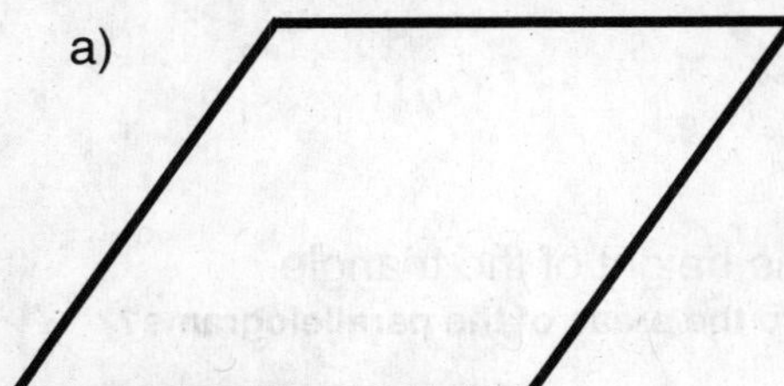

b)

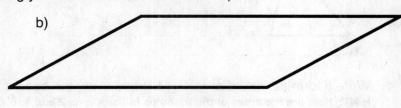

3. Find the area of the following parallelograms.

a) Base = 5 cm
Height = 7 cm

b) Base = 4 cm
Height = 3 cm

c) Base = 8 cm
Height = 6 cm

d) Base = 3.7 cm
Height = 6 cm

ME6-18: Area of Triangles

1. a) Draw a dotted line to show the height of the triangle.
Then find the length of the height and the base of the triangles (in cm).
The first has been done for you.

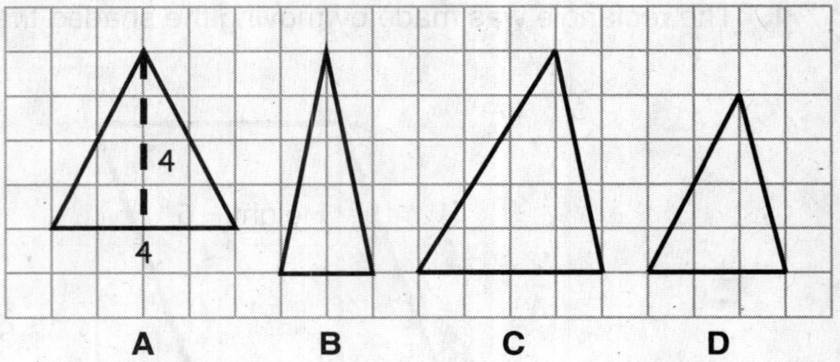

b) Find the area of each triangle above by dividing it into two right angle triangles.

Area of A: __________ Area of B: __________

Area of C: __________ Area of D: __________

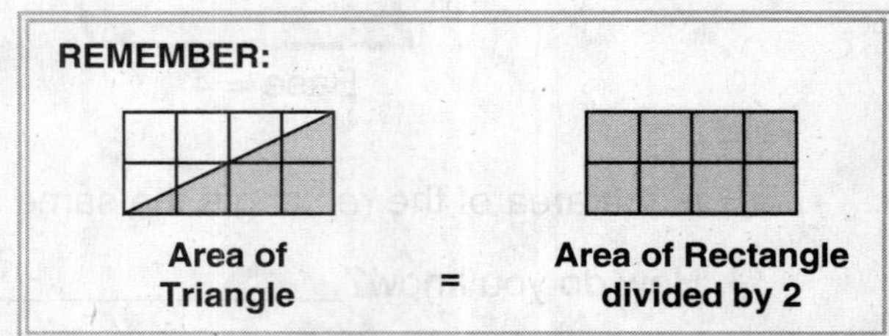

REMEMBER:
Area of Triangle
=
Area of Rectangle divided by 2

2. Parallelogram B was made by joining two copies of Triangle A together.
How can you find the area of Triangle A?
HINT: Use what you know about the area of parallelograms.

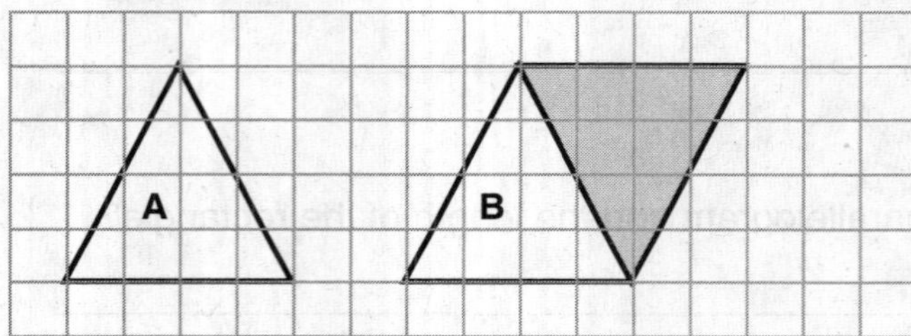

____

____

____

3. Find the area of the triangle by joining two copies of the triangle together to form a parallelogram as in Question 2.

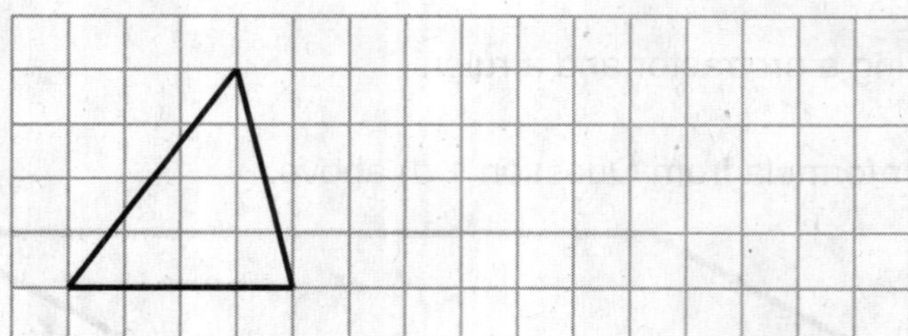

4. Write a formula for the area of a triangle using the base and the height of the triangle.
HINT: How are the areas of the triangles in Questions 2 and 3 related to the areas of the parallelograms?

____

5. Show how you would calculate the area of Triangle A in Question 1 using your formula.

____

ME6-19: Investigations

1. On the previous page, you discovered the formula:

Area of Triangle = (base × height) ÷ 2

Find the area of a triangle with the dimensions.

a) Base = 6 cm
Height = 2 cm
Area =

b) Base = 4 cm
Height = 3 cm
Area =

c) Base = 6 cm
Height = 4 cm
Area =

d) Base = 3.2 cm
Height = 8 cm
Area =

2. Previously, you discovered the formula:

Area of a Parallelogram = base × height

Find the area of a parallelogram with the dimensions.

a) Base = 5 cm
Height = 7 cm
Area =

b) Base = 10 cm
Height = 17 cm
Area =

c) Base = 3.5 cm
Height = 9 cm
Area =

d) Base = 2.75 cm
Height = 8 cm
Area =

3. Measure the base and height of the triangle using a ruler. Then find the area of the triangle.

a)

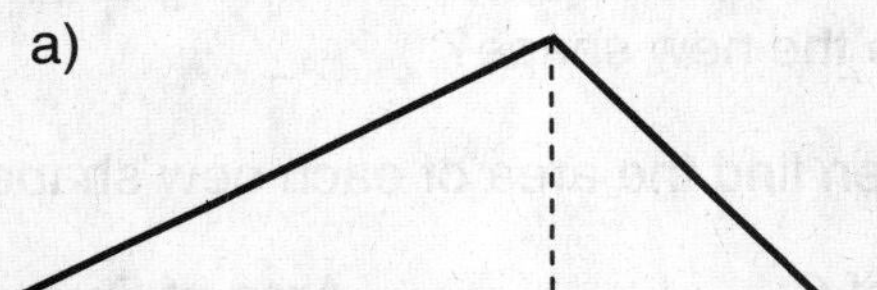

b)

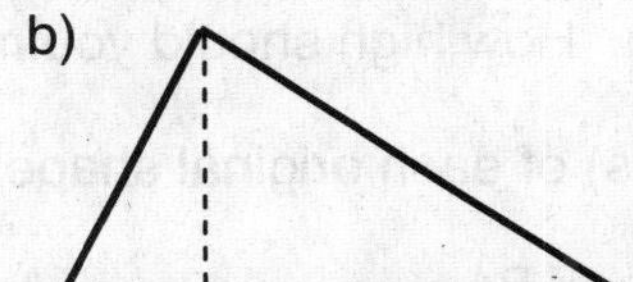

c)

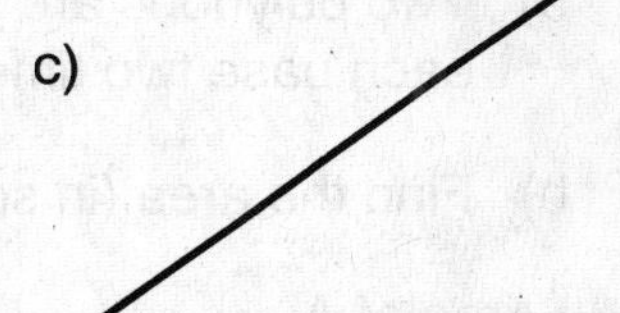

4. Find the area of each shape by subdividing it into triangles and rectangles.

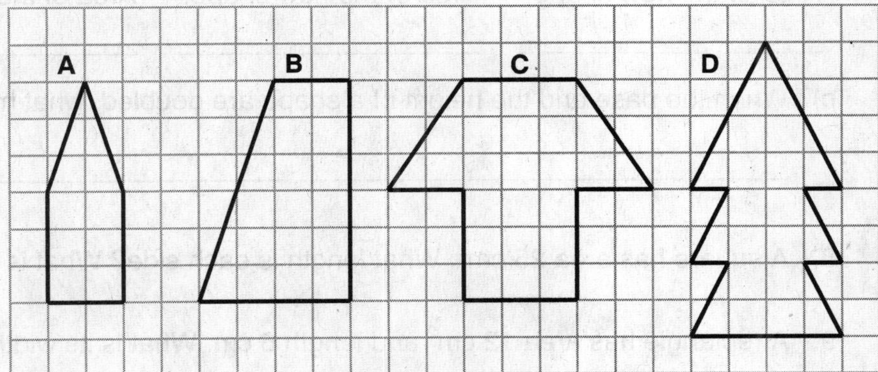

5. Draw a line to cut the figure into two rectangles.
Calculate the area of the two rectangles and add the areas to get the area of the figure.

4
3
4
7
4
8

ME6-19: Investigations *(continued)*

6. Find the measurements of the sides that are not labelled.
Then calculate the perimeter and area of each figure.
CAREFUL: Not all sides have been provided with measurements.

a) 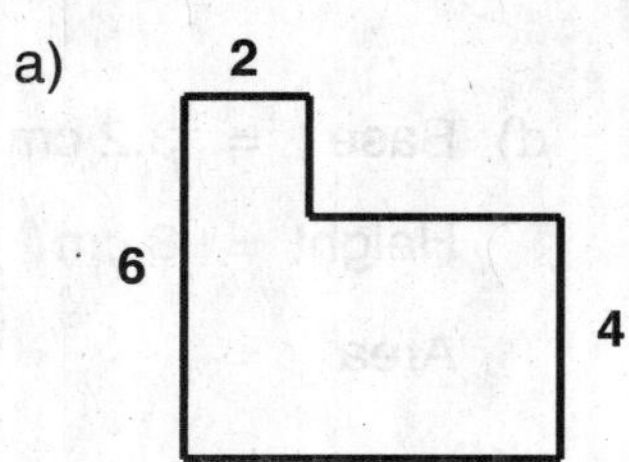

Perimeter: ______

Area: ______

b) 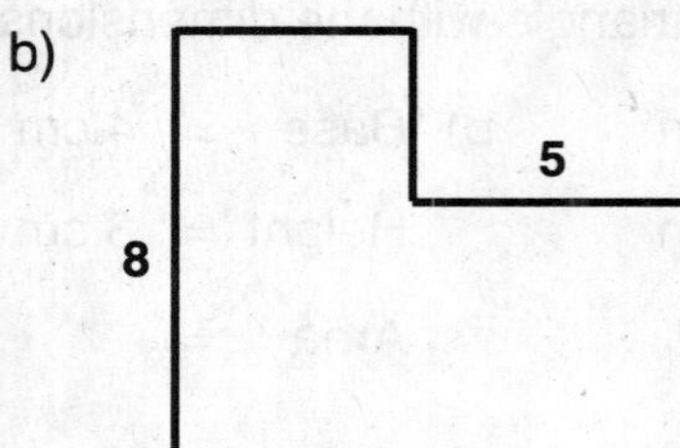

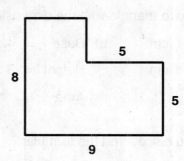

Perimeter: ______

Area: ______

7. 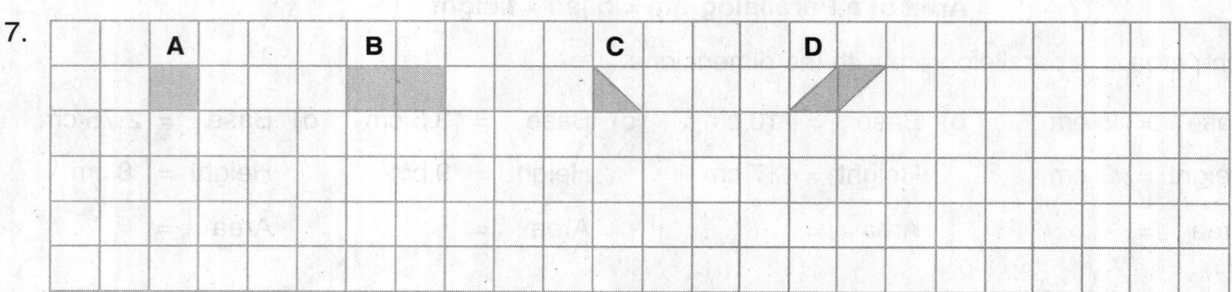

a) Two polygons are similar if they are the same shape. Draw a shape similar to the original, making each base two times as long. How high should you make the new shape?

b) Find the area (in square units) of each original shape. Then find the area of each new shapes.

Area of A: ________ Area of B: ________ Area of C: ________ Area of D: ________

Area of the new shape: ________ Area of the new shape: ________ Area of the new shape: ________ Area of the new shape: ________

c) When the base and the height of a shape are doubled, what happens to the area of the shape?

____

8. A square has area 25 cm^2. What length is each side? What is its perimeter?

9. A rectangle has area 12 cm^2 and length 6 cm. What is its width? What is its perimeter?

10. A parallelogram has base 10 cm and area 60 cm^2. How high is the parallelogram?

11. Draw a rectangle on grid paper. Draw a second rectangle with sides that are twice as long. Is the perimeter of the larger rectangle 2 times or 4 times the perimeter of the smaller rectangle?

12. On grid paper, draw two different rectangles. Make the one with the smaller area have the greater perimeter.

ME6-19: Investigations *(continued)*

Answer the following questions in your notebook.

13. Each square on the grid represents an area of 25 cm^2.
What is the area of each figure?
How do you know?

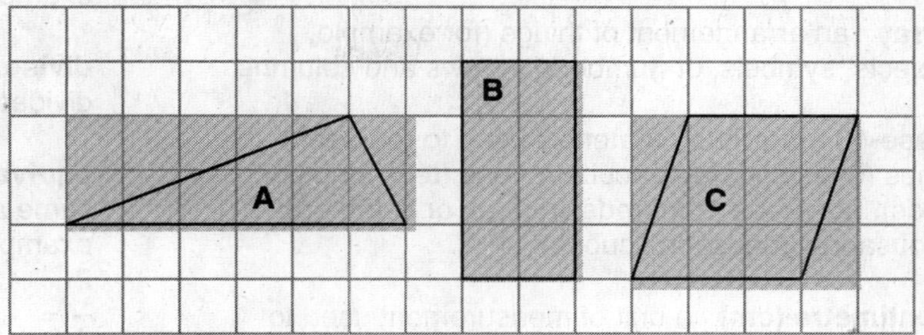

14. Each edge on the grid represents 0.5 cm.
Is the perimeter of the rectangle greater than or less than 14.5 cm?
How do you know?

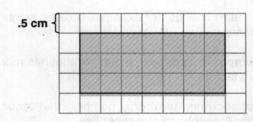

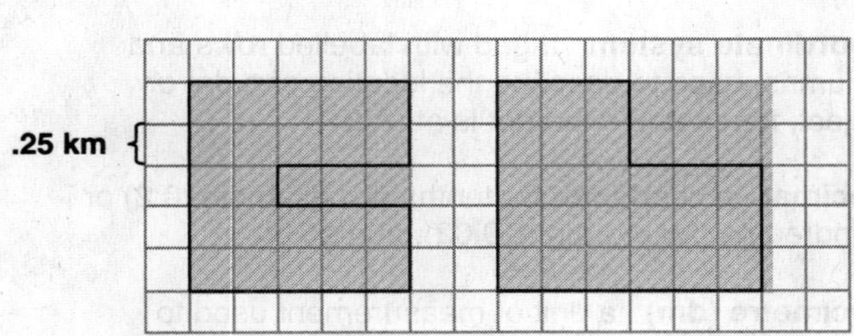

15. The picture shows plans for two parks.
What is the perimeter of each park?

.25 km

16. What fraction of the area of the rectangle is the triangle?
How do you know?

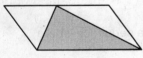

17. What fraction of the area of the parallelogram is the area of the triangle?
How do you know?

18. The area of the shaded triangle is 8 m^2. What is the perimeter of the square?
How do you know?

19. The area of a triangle is 20 cm^2, and its base is 10 cm.
What is the height of the triangle? How can you check your answer?

20. Alex is doing a science project on swimming pools. What could he measure using …

a) metres (m)?　　b) metres squared (m^2)?　　c) metres cubed (m^3)?

area the amount of space occupied by the face or surface of an object

array an arrangement of things (for example, objects, symbols, or numbers) in rows and columns

base-10 materials materials used to represent ones (ones squares or cubes), tens (tens strips or rods), hundreds (hundreds squares or flats), and thousands (thousands cubes)

centimetre (cm) a unit of measurement used to describe length, height, or thickness

column things (for example, objects, symbols, numbers) that run up and down

composite number a number that has more than two factors

consecutive numbers numbers that occur one after the other on a number line

coordinate system a grid with labelled rows and columns, used to describe the location of a dot or object, for example the dot is at (A,3)

decimal a short form for tenths (for example, 0.2) or hundredths (for example, 0.02), and so on

decimetre (dm) a unit of measurement used to describe length, height, or thickness; equal to 10 cm

decreasing sequence a sequence where each number is less than the one before it

denominator the number on the bottom portion of a fraction; tells you how many parts are in a whole

diagonal things (for example, objects, symbols, or numbers) that are in a line from one corner to another corner

difference the "gap" between two numbers; the remainder left after subtraction

divide to find how many times one number contains another number

dividend in a division problem, the number that is being divided or shared

divisible by containing a number a specific number of times without having a remainder (for example, 15 is divisible by 5 and 3)

divisor in a division problem, the number that is divided into another number

equivalent fractions fractions that represent the same amount, but have different denominators (for example, $\frac{2}{3} = \frac{4}{6}$)

estimate a guess or calculation of an approximate number

expanded form a way to write a number that shows the place value of each digit (for example, 27 in expanded form can be written as 2 tens + 7 ones, or 20 + 7)

factor tree a diagram that uses branches (lines) to show prime factorization

factors whole numbers that are multiplied to give a product

fraction a number used to name a part of a set or a region

growing pattern a pattern in which each term is greater than the previous term

improper fraction a fraction that has a numerator that is larger than the denominator; this represents more than a whole

increasing sequence a sequence where each number is greater than the one before it

integer a whole number that is either positive, negative, or zero

kilometre (km) a unit of measurement for length; equal to 1000 cm

leading digit the first (non-zero) digit in a number

line graph a way to display data; often used to represent the relationship between two variables; has a vertical and a horizontal axis, labels, and data points connected by a line

litre (L) a unit of measurement to describe capacity; equal to 1000 mL

lowest common multiple (LCM) the least nonzero number that two numbers can divide into evenly (for example, 6 is the LCM of 2 and 3)

metre (m) a unit of measurement used to describe length, height, or thickness; equal to 100 cm

mililitre (mL) a unit of measurement used to describe capacity

millimetre (mm) a unit of measurement used to describe length, height, or thickness; equal to 0.1 cm

mixed fraction a mixture of a whole number and a fraction

model a physical representation (for example, using base-10 materials to represent a number)

multiple of a number that is the result of multiplying one number by another specific number (for example, the multiples of 5 are 0, 5, 10, 15, and so on)

multiply to find the total of a number times another number

number line a line with numbers marked at intervals, used to help with skip counting

numerator the number on the top portion of a fraction; tells you how many parts are counted

pattern (repeating pattern) the same repeating group of objects, numbers, or attributes

perfect square the result of a number multiplied by itself

perimeter the distance around the outside of a shape

prime factorization a number written as a product of prime numbers

prime number a number that has only two factors: itself and 1

product the result from multiplying two or more numbers together

quotient the result from dividing one number by another number

regroup to exchange one place value for another place value (for example, 10 ones squares for 1 tens strip)

remainder the number left over after dividing or subtracting (for example, 10 ÷ 3 = 3 R1)

row things (for example, objects, symbols, or numbers) that run left to right

set a group of like objects

skip counting counting by a number (for example, 2s, 3s, 4s) by "skipping" over the numbers in between

square centimetre (cm2) a unit of measurement used to describe area

sum the result from adding two or more numbers together

term a number in a sequence

term number the position of a term in a sequence

T-table a chart used to compare two sequences of numbers

unit rate a comparison of two quantities where one quantity is equal to 1

variable a letter or symbol that represents a number

Venn diagram a diagram containing circles, used to organize items according to attributes; the parts of the circles that overlap represent items that share attributes

Patterns & Algebra 1

Worksheet PA6-1

1. a) Gap = 3; 11, 14, 17
   b) Gap = 6; 19, 25, 31
   c) Gap = 5; 17, 22, 27
2. a) 23 cm
   b) 5 days

Worksheet PA6-2

1. a) Gap = – 3; 9, 6, 3
   b) Gap = – 6; 14, 8, 2
   c) Gap = – 5; 37, 32, 27
2. $9
3. 46 stamps

Worksheet PA6-3

1. a) 49, 53, 57
   b) 76, 84, 92
   c) 80, 83, 86
2. a) 19, 16, 13
   b) 30, 28, 26
   c) 73, 67, 61
4. c)
5. Sanjukta is right.

Worksheet PA6-4

1. a) 5
   b) 3
   c) 6
2. a) 2
   b) 5
   c) 1
3. a) Subtract 7
   b) Add 8
   c) Add 4
4. a) 67, 72, 77; Add 5
   b) 69, 66, 63; Subtract 3
   c) 860, 872, 884; Add 12
5. a) Hannah
   b) Tim – subtracts instead of adds; Jack – adds 5 instead of 6.

Worksheet PA6-5

1. a) Start at 2 and add 6 each time.
   b) Start at 3 and add 6 each time.
   c) Start at 1 and add 5 each time.
2. a) 42
   b) 29
   c) 27
3. a) Yes (31)
   b) No (39)
   c) Yes (33)
4. a) 19 shapes needed
   b) 11 shapes needed

Worksheet PA6-6

1. a) 8
   b) 13
   c) 9
2.

Figure	Line Segments
1	9
2	17
3	25

   a) 33
   b) 41
3.

Figure	Tri.	Seg.
1	3	7
2	6	13
3	9	19
4	12	25

   a) 31
   b) 37
4. 33 cm
5. $69
6. a) 3 L
   b) 9 L
   c) 7 hours
7. $32
8. a) 14 triangles
   b) No (she needs 16)
9. Merle (who saved $85; Alex saved $77)

Worksheet PA6-7

1. a) 23
   b) 66
2. No
3. a) 16
   b) 16, 21
   c) 18, 21, 27
4. Table 1: Rule - Add 2. 3 – 17
   Table 2: Rule – Add 4. 3 – 33
5. a) 42 pentagons
   b) 72 triangles and 36 pentagons
   c) 72 triangles
6. a) i) a baby
   ii) tiger
   b) 4 weeks = 28 days

Worksheet PA6-8

1. 3 km
2. 100 km
3. 15 L
4. 25 km
5. 25 km
6. 3 m
7. 3 hours
8. 30 cm
9. 12 m

Worksheet PA6-9

1. a) 12
   b) 12
2. b) 20
   c) 9
3. 24th day

Worksheet PA6-10

2. a) Across rows: add 2
   Down columns: add 4
   Diagonal (l to r): add 6
   Diagonal (r to l): add 2
   b) Across rows: add 6
   Down columns: add 6
   Diagonal (l to r): add 12
   Diagonal (r to l): stay the same
   c) Across rows: add 4
   Down columns: subtract 4
   Diagonal (l to r): stay the same
   Diagonal (r to l): subtract 8
5. a) 3rd row
   b) 5th column
   c) Start at 0 and add 5; Start at 4 and add 2

Worksheet PA6-11

1. 15
2. a)

2	**7**	6
9	5	**1**
4	3	**8**

   b)

6	**13**	**8**
11	9	**7**
10	5	12

   c)

6	**20**	10
16	12	**8**
14	**4**	18

3. The number at the top of the pyramid is the sum of the two numbers beneath it.
4. a) 6
   b) 8
   c) 11

Worksheet PA6-12

2. a) 4 × s = t
   b) 5 × s = t
   c) 2 × s = t
3. a)

squares	rectangles
1	4
2	8
3	12

4 × s = r

   b)

rectangles	triangles
1	6
2	12
3	18

6 × r = t

   c)

squares	rectangles
1	8

2	16
3	24

8 × s = r

4. No, Wendy would need 42 triangles (skip count by 6's seven times).

7.

	Row	Chairs
a)	1	7
	2	8
	3	9
b)	1	10
	2	11
	3	12

8. b) Add 7; r + 7 = c
   c) Add 8; r + 8 = c

9.

	Row	Chairs
a)	1	5
	2	6
	3	7

r + 4 = c

b)	1	2
	2	3
	3	4

r + 1 = c

10.

	Input	Output
a)	1	5
	2	6
	3	7
b)	5	1
	6	2
	7	3
c)	3	18
	5	30
	6	36

11. a) Add 4 to each input.
   b) Add 5 to each input.
   c) Multiply the input by 7.

Worksheet PA6-13

1.

Vertical Lines	Horizontal Lines
1	3
2	6
3	9

Multiply the input by 3.

2.

Crosses	Triangles
1	2
2	4
3	6

Multiply the input by 2.

3.

Suns	Moons
1	2
2	3
3	4

Add 1 to the input.

4.

Light Hexagons	Dark Hexagons
1	2
2	4
3	6

Multiply the input by 2.

5.

Diamonds	Stars
1	2
2	3
3	4

Add 1 to the input.

6.

Hexagons	Triangles
1	2
2	4
3	6

Multiply the input by 2.

7. 18 hexagons are needed (skip count by 2's nine times).

Worksheet PA6-14

1. a) 3 × Figure Number
   b) 2 × Figure Number
   c) Ignore question or point out it's not a direct variation.
2. Circle a) and c).

Worksheet PA6-15

1. a) i) 2 × FN
      ii) 2 × FN + 1
   b) i) 4 × FN
      ii) 4 × FN + 2
   c) i) 2 × FN
      ii) 2 × FN + 1

Worksheet PA6-16

1.

	Input	Output
a)	1	7
	2	11
	3	15
b)	1	5
	2	7
	3	9
c)	1	9
	2	14
	3	19

Worksheet PA6-17

1. a) Multiply by 4 and add 5
   b) Multiply by 2 and add 1
   c) Multiply by 3 and add 4
2. a) Multiply by 5 and add 4
   b) Multiply by 6 and add 6
   c) Multiply by 4 and add 2
3. a) Multiply by 5 and subtract 1
   b) Multiply by 3 and subtract 2
   c) Multiply by 4 and subtract 2
4. a) Multiply by 5 and subtract 3
   b) Multiply by 6 and subtract 3
   c) Add 4
5. a) Multiply by 5 and add 2
   b) Multiply by 2 and subtract 1
   c) Add 6

Worksheet PA6-18

1. a) 2 × FN + 2
   Figure 9: 20 triangles
   b) 2 × FN + 1
   Figure 11: 23 line segments
   c) 2 × FN + 1
   Figure 10: 21 squares

Number Sense 1

Worksheet NS6-1

1. a) Tens
   b) Millions
   c) Hundred thousands
   d) Hundreds
2. a) Thousands
   b) Millions
   c) Ones
   d) Ones
3.

a)	2	3	1	6	9	5	3
b)			6	2	5	0	7
c)	5	6	0	4	8	9	1
d)				1	3	9	9

Worksheet NS6-2

1. a) 2; 70; 800; 4 000; 50 000; 600 000
   b) 7; 30; 500; 8 000; 20 000; 100 000
2. a) 70
   b) 700
   c) 700
   d) 700 000
3. a) 500
   b) 30 000
   c) 80
   d) 70 000

Worksheet NS6-3

1. a) 2 435
   b) 3 316
   c) 2 328
2. a) 3 thousands, 4 hundreds, 6 tens, 8 ones
   b) 1 thousand, 5 hundreds, 4 tens, 2 ones
   c) 2 thousands, 6 hundreds, 5 tens, 9 ones
3. a) 4 438
   b) 2 494

Worksheet NS6-4

1. a) 2 millions + 5 hundred

thousands +
3 ten thousands +
6 thousands +
7 hundreds +
8 tens + 4 ones

b) 6 millions +
2 hundred thousands +
3 ten thousands +
5 thousands +
4 hundreds +
1 ones

c) 3 millions +
5 ten thousands +
6 thousands +
2 hundreds +
6 ones

2. a) 70 000 + 2 000 + 600 + 10 + 3
   b) 30 + 6
   c) 500 + 20 + 6
   d) 10 000 + 2 000 + 300 + 50 + 2
3. a) 6 747
   b) 868
   c) 3 032
   d) 56 493
4. a) 40
   b) 80
   c) 700
   d) 200
5. a) 4 000 + 300 + 50 + 4
   4 thousands +
   3 hundreds + 5 tens + 4 ones
   b) 2000 + 600 + 4
   2 thousands +
   6 hundreds +
   4 ones
7. 11
8. 7
10. 1 000

Worksheet NS6-5

1. a) 735 > 725
   b) 527 > 427
2. a) 83 **76**2
   b) 27**3** 605
   c) 614 85**8**
   d) **4**83 250
3. a) 641 5**9**7
   b) 38**9** 583
   c) **6**03 470
   d) 621 4**9**2
4. a) >
   b) <
   c) >
   d) <

Worksheet NS6-6

1. a) 10 more
   b) 100 less
   c) 10 more
   d) 10 more
2. a) 1 000 less
   b) 1 000 less
   c) 1 000 less
   d) 1 000 more
3. a) 1 000 more
   b) 1 000 less
   c) 10 000 less
   d) 10 000 more
4. a) 100 000 more
   b) 10 000 less
   c) 10 000 more
   d) 100 000 less
5. a) 10 000 less
   b) 100 less
   c) 10 000 more
   d) 10 000 less
6. a) 3 792
   b) 39 827
   c) 3 882
   d) 14 023
7. a) 236
   b) 28 583
   c) 39 045
   d) 42 227
8. a) 10
   b) 100
   c) 10
   d) 100
9. a) 6437, 6447
   b) 49 640, 50 640
   c) 624 843
   d) 28 383
10. a) 827 325 is 10 less than 827 335
    b) 482 305 is 100 000 greater than 382 305
    c) 915 778 is 10 000 less than 925 778

Worksheet NS6-7

1. a) 254, **416**
   b) **3 128**, 2 209
2. a) Forty-eight
   b) 3 508
   c) Ninety-four
   d) 662
3. a) 67, 68, 76, 78, 86, **87**
   b) 24, 29, 42, 49, 92, **94**
   c) 20, 25, 50, **52**
4. a) 6 432
   b) 9 874
   c) 4 210
5. a) 84 321
   b) 98 521
   c) 65 431
6.

	Greatest	Least
a)	87 521	12 578
b)	95 321	12 359
c)	53 310	10 335

The in-between numbers will vary.

7. a) 683 759, 693 231, 693 238
   b) 42 380, 47 832, 473 259
   c) 385 290, 532 135, 928 381
   d) 195, 2 575, 38 258
8. 9 999
9. a) >
   b) <
   c) >
   d) <
10. a) Ottawa
    b) 414 284, 662 401, 774 072
11. a) 999
    b) 9 999
    c) 99 999
12. There are **2** correct answers, example: 42 310 and 42 130
13. Answers will vary – number will begin with 6 digit and end with either the 5 or 7 digit; the second digit can be 4, 5 or 7.
14. a) 4
    b) 2

Worksheet NS6-8

1. a) 4 tens + 12 ones = 5 tens + 2 ones
   b) 2 tens + 18 ones = 3 tens + 8 ones
2. a) 5 tens + 3 ones
   b) 8 tens + 5 ones
   c) 1 tens + 4 ones
   d) 2 tens + 7 ones
3.

	Hundreds	Tens
b)	6 + 2 = 8	4
c)	3 + 1 = 4	5
d)	6 + 3 = 9	6

4. a) 6 hundreds + 8 tens + 9 ones
   b) 2 hundreds + 7 tens + 5 ones
   c) 10 hundreds + 8 tens + 9 ones
5.

	Thou-sands	Hun-dreds
b)	3 + 1 = 4	2
c)	8 + 2 = 10	0

6. a) 7 thousands +
   3 hundreds +
   2 tens + 5 ones
   b) 6 thousands +
   4 hundreds +
   2 tens + 6 ones
   c) 9 thousands +
   5 hundreds +
   3 tens
7. a) 3 thousands +
   3 hundreds +
   2 tens + 5 ones
   b) 5 thousands +
   2 hundreds +
   8 tens + 6 ones
   c) 5 ten thousands +
   7 thousands +
   5 hundreds +

7 tens + 8 ones

8. Yes. Teresa needs 6 590 blocks to build her model. She has 6 700 blocks, so she can build it.

Worksheet NS6-9

1. a)

tens	ones
2	6
3	6
5	12
6	2

b)

tens	ones
5	7
2	7
7	14
8	4

2. a) 1, 3
Final answer: 33
b) 1, 0
Final answer: 60
c) 1, 6
Final answer: 76
d) 1, 2
Final answer: 92

3. a) 71
b) 81
c) 91
d) 102

Worksheet NS6-10

1. 4 hundreds + 8 tens + 3 ones;
2 hundreds + 4 tens + 5 ones;
6 hundreds + 12 tens + 8 ones;
7 hundreds + 2 tens + 8 ones

2. a) 617
b) 826
c) 746
d) 846

3. a) 491
b) 617
c) 418
d) 624

4. a) 795
b) 729
c) 941
d) 419

Worksheet NS6-11

1. 5 thousands + 4 hundreds + 8 tens + 6 ones;
3 thousands + 7 hundreds + 1 tens + 3 ones;
8 thousands + 11 hundreds + 9 tens + 9 ones;
9 thousands + 1 hundreds + 9 tens + 9 ones

2. a) 7 395
b) 7 158
c) 9 378
d) 8 097

3. a) 9 914
b) 6 838
c) 6 815
d) 2 749

4. a) 6 981
b) 6 377
c) 9 828
d) 10 017

5. a) 9 895
b) 9 831
c) 8 848
d) 9 630

6. a) 6 728
b) 91 628
c) 474 917
d) 748 188

7. a) 828
b) 1 111
c) 6666
d) 58 285

Worksheet NS6-12

1.

	Tens	Ones
a)	4	13
b)	5	15
c)	3	15
d)	4	13

2. a) 45
b) 28
c) 37
d) 18

3. a) Help;
8 is less than 9.
b) No;
4 is greater than 3.
c) Help;
5 is less than 7.
d) No;
8 is greater than 2.

4. a) 185
b) 482
c) 373
d) 241

5. a) 536
b) 124
c) 308
d) 355

6. a) 478
b) 478
c) 473
d) 337

7. a) 2 832
b) 2 721
c) 2 850
d) 7 221

8. a) 1 714
b) 3 062
c) 5 081
d) 28 211

9. a) 7 779
b) 3 759
c) 2 768
d) 2 678

10. a) 532
b) 68
c) 3 514
d) 4 889

Worksheet NS6-13

1. 70 are girls
2. 453 stamps
3. 8110 km
4. 1 007 509 people
5. 168 cans
6. 85 years
7. Answers will vary: The difference between a three-digit number and its reverse number is always 198 because regardless of the numbers, there will always be 198 numbers in-between.
8. 256 km
9. 250 km

Worksheet NS6-14

1. a) Newfoundland, Ellesmere Island, Vancouver Island, Baffin Island
b) 398 590 km^2
c) 87 376 km^2
d) No.

2. a) 87 645
b) 56 748; 56 784
c) There are 16 correct answers. Example: 86 754
d) 68 754

3. 844 400

5. a) Depends upon the year (currently 462 years).
b) Copernicus' book to Galileo's discovery of Jupiter's moons: 67 years;
Galileo's discovery of the moons to Isaac Newton's law of gravity: 57 years.

Worksheet NS6-15

1. b) 4 rows;
4 dots in each row;
4 × 4 = 16
c) 4 rows;
5 dots in each row;
4 × 5 = 20

2. a) 4 × 3 = 12
b) 2 × 5 = 10
c) 5 × 3 = 15
d) 7 × 2 = 14

3. a)
• • • • •
• • • • •
b)
• • • • • •
• • • • • •
• • • • • •
c)
• • • • •
• • • • •
• • • • •
• • • • •
d)
• • • • • • • •

4. a) 1 × 6;
2 × 3;
3 × 2;
6 × 1

b) 1 × 8;
2 × 4;
4 × 2;
8 × 1

c) 1 × 9;
3 × 3;
9 × 1

d) 1 × 10;
2 × 5;
5 × 2;
10 × 1

5. **6**: 1, 2, 3, 6
8: 1, 2, 4, 8
9: 1, 3, 9
10: 1, 2, 5, 10
12: 1, 2, 3, 4, 6, 12

Worksheet NS6-16

1. a) 1
b) No
2. 2, 3, 5, 7
3. 12, 14, 15, 16, 18
4. 29
5. 11, 13, 17, 27, 29
6. Primes:
2, 3, 5, 7, 11, 13, 17, 19, 23, 29, 31, 37, 41, 43, 47, 53, 59, 61, 67, 71, 73, 79, 83, 89, 97
7. 11, 13;
17, 19;
5, 7

Worksheet NS6-17

1. a) 1, 5, 25
b) 1, 2, 4, 8
c) 1, 2, 3, 4, 6, 12
d) 1, 2, 4, 8, 16
2. Composite numbers:
30, 32, 33, 34, 35, 36
3. a) Any primes less than 20
b) 6, 8, 10, 14
c) 16
4. Cross out: 19, 34, 50
5. 10, 20, 30
7. 15, 21, 27, 33, 39
8. 3
9. 37
10. 5

Worksheet NS6-18

1. a) Bottom row:
2, 3, 2
b) Bottom row:
2, 2, 2, 2
c) Bottom row:
3, 2, 2, 2
2. a) 5 × 2 × 2
b) 3 × 3 × 2
c) 2 × 2 × 2
d) 7 × 2
3. a) 5 × 3 × 2
b) 3 × 3 × 2 × 2
c) 3 × 3 × 3
d) 2 × 2 × 2

Worksheet NS6-19

1. a) 5 × 3 tens
= 15 tens
= 150
b) 3 × 4 tens
= 12 tens
= 120
2. a) 3 × 6 tens
= 18 tens
= 180
b) 6 × 5 tens
= 30 tens
= 300
c) 4 × 5 tens
= 20 tens
= 200
d) 5 × 4 tens
= 20 tens
= 200
3. a) 15; 150; 1 500
b) 6; 60; 600
c) 12; 120; 1 200
d) 20; 200; 2 000
4. a) 210
b) 150
c) 120
d) 240
6. 18 000

Worksheet NS6-20

1. a) 2 × 20 + 2 × 5
b) 3 × 10 + 3 × 5
2. a) 5 × 10 + 5 × 3
= 50 + 15
= 65
b) 4 × 20 + 4 × 1
= 80 + 4
= 84
c) 3 × 40 + 3 × 3
= 120 + 9
= 129
d) 2 × 400 + 2 × 30 + 2 × 2
= 80 + 60 + 4
= 864
3. a) 36
b) 156
c) 78
d) 147
4. a) 3 284
b) 2 169

Worksheet NS6-21

1. a) 153
b) 246
c) 124
d) 204
2. a) 189
b) 300
c) 305
d) 188

Worksheet NS6-22

1. a) 1, 2
b) 1, 5
c) 2, 0
d) 3, 6
2. a) 12
b) 15
c) 20
d) 36
3. a) 70
b) 90
c) 90
d) 75

Worksheet NS6-23

1. a) 468
b) 399
2. a) 164
b) 868
c) 936
d) 248
3. a) 454
b) 864
c) 672
d) 872
4. a) 728
b) 906
c) 968
d) 855
5. a) 670
b) 2 947
c) 792
d) 1 206
6. a) 228
b) 888
c) 969

Worksheet NS6-24

1. a) 150
b) 150
c) 1 500
d) 1 500
2. a) 1
b) 2
c) 3
3. a) 60;
600;
6 000;
60 000
b) 360;
3600;
36 000;
360 000
c) 850;
8 500;
85 000;
850 000
4. a) 190
b) 560
c) 830
d) 4 200
5. a) 10 × 30 = 300
b) 10 × 20 = 200
c) 10 × 60 = 600
d) 10 ×70 = 700
6. $456
7. a) 1 000
b) 10 000
8. 25 723 dimes

Worksheet NS6-25

1. a) 3 × 10
b) 4 × 10
c) 7 × 10
d) 5 × 10
2. a) 2 × 10 × 33

b) 2 × 10 × 21
c) 3 × 10 ×17

3. a) 2 × 240 = 480
b) 3 × 320 = 960
c) 4 × 120 = 480
d) 5 × 410 = 2 050

4. a) 990
b) 1 200
c) 1 600
d) 1 360

5. a) 40 × 60 = 2 400
b) 30 × 70 = 2 100
c) 30 × 80 = 2 400
d) 60 × 50 = 3 000

Worksheet NS6-26

1. a) 60 (carry 1)
b) 20 (carry 4)
c) 60 (carry 1)
d) 90

2. a) 810
b) 1 200
c) 1 380
d) 1 840

3. b) 30 × 20 + 30 × 3 = 600 + 90 = 690
c) 40 × 30 + 40 × 2 = 1 200 + 80 = 1 280

Worksheet NS6-27

1. a) 72
b) 108
c) 258
d) 248

2. a) 1 360
b) 900
c) 4 140
d) 1 680

3. a) 210; 700
b) 91; 390
c) 128; 1 600
d) 225; 1 350

4. a) 728
b) 3 672
c) 3 268
d) 1 701

5. a) 1 530
b) 1 216
c) 3 848
d) 1 836

6. a) 805
b) 5 184
c) 1 075
d) 3 654

Worksheet NS6-28

1. 50, 90, 32, 56, 36, 34, 70, 110, 78

2. b) Yes

3. a) 350
b) 15 120
c) 29 000
d) 47 500

4. C is the fastest.
Converting to the same units (pages/second):
A – 0.5
B – 1.5
C – 2
D – 1.33

5. a) 15 × $0.32 = $4.80
b) 20 × $0.32 + 10 × $0.25 = $8.90
c) 20 × $0.32 + 20 × $0.25 + 10 × $0.17 = $13.10

Worksheet NS6-29

1. a) 16 328
b) 10 787
c) 18 495

2. Cross out: 13, 50, 2, 27

3. 15, 21, 27, 33, 39

4. 11

5. a) 19 346
b) 68 904
c) 88 896
d) 461 384

6. 1 000 cm

7. 15 322

8. 12

9. No (952 minutes)

10. a) 2
b) 1
c) 4

Worksheet NS6-30

1. a) Cups; 2; 4
b) Candy; 3; 2

2. a) Candy; 4; 8
b) Flowers; 6; 4
c) Cake; 4; 5
d) Trees; 7; 3

Worksheet NS6-31

1. a) 6
b) 4

2. a) 4 dots per set
b) 3 dots per set

3. 3 dots per set

4. a) 3 sets
b) 7 sets
c) 4 sets

5. a) 2 sets of 9
b) 3 sets of 6

6. c) Stickers; 2 sets
d) Pictures; 8 per set

7. a) 7
b) 2
c) 4
d) 5

Worksheet NS6-32

1. a) 4
b) 2

2. a) 18 ÷ 3 = 6
b) 8 ÷ 2 = 4

3. a) 7
b) 2
c) 4
d) 3

4. 4

5. 4

6. 4

Worksheet NS6-33

1. No (1 remainder)

2. a) 3; 1
b) 4; 1

3. a) 13 ÷ 3 = 4 R1
b) 19 ÷ 3 = 6 R1
c) 36 ÷ 5 = 7 R1
d) 33 ÷ 4 = 8 R1

4. 25 ÷ 8 = 3 R1

5. 3 groups of 3;
3 groups of 4;
3 groups of 2;

6. 2 groups of 9;
3 groups of 6;
6 groups of 3;
9 groups of 2

Worksheet NS6-34

1. a) 2; 5; 3
b) 5; 7; 1
c) 4; 9; 5
d) 5; 8; 8

2. a) 1
b) 1
c) 2
d) 2

3. a) 2 groups; 4 tens in each group
b) 3 groups; 3 tens in each group
c) 1 group; 6 tens in each group
d) 2 groups; 4 tens in each group

4. a) 3 groups; 8 tens; 2 tens in each group; 6 tens altogether
b) 4 groups; 9 tens; 2 tens in each group; 8 tens altogether

5. a) 1; 4
b) 2; 6
c) 2; 8
d) 1; 5

6. a) 1; 7; 2
b) 2; 6; 1
c) 3; 6; 0
d) 1; 4; 3

7. a) 1; 5; 25
b) 1; 7; 17
c) 2; 8; 13
d) 3; 6; 13

8. a) 18; 5; 44
b) 21; 8; 07
c) 37; 6; 15

d) 17; 3; 21
9. a) 16 R1
b) 13
c) 28
d) 25
10. 6 are left over
11. 12 weeks
12. 13 rows; 6 books left over
13. $13
14. 14 cherries each; 4 left over, Wendy

Worksheet NS6-35

2. a) 156 R1
b) 278 R1
c) 145 R5
d) 124 R3
3. b) 94 R2
c) 33 R2
d) 52 R3
4. a) 38 R1
b) 85 R1
c) 53 R1
d) 63 R1
5. 36 m
6. 122 km

Worksheet NS6-36

1. a) 300
b) 30
c) 3
2. a) 30 000, 3 000, 300
b) 270 000, 27 000, 2 700, 270
4. First deal. ($144 vs $160)
6. 58 ÷ 4 = 14 R2 so 15 tents will be needed for 58 people
7. 13 stickers each; 5 remaining
8. 14 weeks
9. 75 ÷ 6 = 12 R3 so 13 trips are needed to move all the boxes

Worksheet NS6-37

1. 3 120
2. 207¢
3. a) 25
b) 49
4. $2 016
5. Yes. (Prime number 3); otherwise, no.
6. 198
7. 2
8. 150
9. 560
10. Ticket cost: $42; Amount paid with: $53

Worksheet NS6-38

1. a) 0, ←
b) 10, →
c) 10, →
d) 0, ←
2. a) i) 1, 2, 3, 4
ii) 6, 7, 8, 9
b) Equal distance between 0 and 10
3. a) 10, ←
20, ←
30, →
b) 70 →
70 ←
80 →
c) 250 ←
260 →
270 →
4. a) 20
b) 10
c) 40
d) 70
5. a) 100
b) 0
6. Equal distance to both 0 and 100.
7. a) 100
b) 0
c) 100
d) 0
8. a) 700
b) 700
c) 800
d) 700
9. a) 200
b) 700
c) 700
d) 1 000
10. a) 0
b) 1 000
11 a) 0
b) 1 000
c) 1 000
12. a) 3 000
b) 4 000
13. a) 4 000
b) 9 000
c) 4 000
d) 2 000
14. If the last three digits are a number between 0 and 499, keep the first digit the same and change the other digits to 0.
If the last three digits are a number between 500 and 999, increase the first digit by 1 and change the other digits to 0.

Worksheet NS6-39

1. a) 40
b) 50
c) 20
d) 60
2. a) 660
b) 270
c) 150
d) 360
3. a) 300
b) 500
c) 600
d) 300
4. a) 200
b) 300
c) 600
d) 300
5. a) 5 000
b) 3 000
c) 8 000
d) 5 000
6. a) r.d.
b) r.d.
c) r.d.
d) r.u.
7. a) r.d. 72 000
b) r.d. 90 000
c) r.d. 84 200
d) r.d. 27 500
8. a) 3 290
b) 5 900
c) 10 000
d) 13 980

Worksheet NS6-40

1. a) 40 + 20 = 60
b) 30 + 50 = 80
c) 60 – 20 = 40
d) 90 – 60 = 30
2. b) 400 + 500 = 900
c) 600 – 200 = 400
d) 800 – 600 = 200
3. b) 5 000 – 3 000 = 2 000
c) 3 000 + 6 000 = 9 000
d) 30 000 – 20 000 = 10 000
4. a) 3 300 + 2 000 = 5 300
b) 3 600 – 2 000 = 1 600
c) 64 900 – 42 300 = 22 600

Worksheet NS6-41

1. 250 000
2. 660 000
3. a) 628 320
b) 628 300
c) 628 000
d) 630 000
4. a) 30 × 80 = 2 400
b) 500 × 80 = 40 000
c) 300 × 10 = 3 000
d) 3 000 × 800 = 2 400 000
5. a) 6 × $5 = $30
b) 5 × $3 = $15
c) 8 × $8 = $64
6. Answers will vary: 1 × 999; 2 × 498; 3 × 333
7. Hundreds (the last non-zero digit of either number)
8. 60 × 30 = 1800; so her estimate is a little high

9. a) 2 289
10. Rounding to the nearest hundreds gives a better estimate

Worksheet NS6-42

1. a) E
   b) D
   c) B
   d) E
3. a) Too high
   b) Too low
   c) Correct
4. a) 2 550
   b) 747
   c) 7 884
   d) 17 380

Worksheet NS6-43

1.

M	T	W	R	F
-5	15	5	-10	-20
	20	5	-15	10

2. b) i) 1
   ii) 5
   iii) 2
   c) 3
3. a) 7 degrees
   b) 5 degrees
   c) 8 degrees
4. a) Uranus
   b) About 10 to 20 degrees
   c) About 280 degrees
5. a) Dog
   b) 5 000 years
   c) 2 000 years
6. Mackerel: – 200 m
   Gulper Eel: – 1 000 m
   8oo m lower
7. Infinity
8. Because there are closer to zero.

Logic and Systematic Search

Worksheet LSS6-1

1. a)

nickels	pennies
0	17
1	12
2	7
3	2

b)

dimes	nickels
0	9
1	7
2	5
3	3
4	1

c)

nickels	pennies
0	23
1	18
2	13
3	8
4	3

d)

dimes	pennies
0	32
1	22
2	12
3	2

2.

quarters	nickels
0	12
1	7
2	2

He stops at 2 quarters because 3 quarters is 75¢ (and larger than 60¢).

3. a)

Dimes	Nickels
0	18
1	16
2	14
3	12
4	10
5	8
6	6
7	4
8	2
9	0

b)

quarters	dimes
0	25
1	20
2	15
3	10
4	5
5	0

4. a)

1st number	2nd number
1	6
2	3
3	2
4	-

b)

1st number	2nd number
1	8
2	4
3	-
4	2

5.

quarters	dimes
0	7
1	-
2	2

6. a)

quarters	dimes
0	8
1	-
2	3

b)

quarters	dimes
0	-
1	8
2	-
3	3

7.

S 1	S 2	S 3
1	1	10
2	2	8
3	3	6
5	5	2

8. a)

1st number	2nd number
1	12
2	6
3	4
4	3
6	2
12	1

b)

1st number	2nd number
1	14
2	7
7	2
14	1

c)

1st number	2nd number
1	20
2	10
4	5
5	4
10	2
20	1

d)

1st number	2nd number
1	24
2	12
3	8
4	6
6	4
8	3
12	2
24	1

Patterns & Algebra 2

Worksheet PA6-19

1. a) Gap: 2, 3, 4, 5, 6
   Pattern: 16, 22
   b) Gap: 1, 2, 3, 4, 5, 6
   Pattern: 18, 24
   c) Gap: 3, 5, 7, 9, 11
   Pattern: 36, 47
   d) Gap: 2, 4, 6, 8, 10, 12
   Pattern: 36, 48
2.

Fig	# Tri	# Added
1	1	
2	4	3
3	9	5
4	16	7
5	25	9
6	36	11

3. 42
4. c) + 1, + 2, + 3, + 4

Rule: Start at 2. Add 1, 2, 3 … (the step increases by 1)

d) + 2, – 3, + 2, – 3
Rule: Start at 5. Add 2 and then subtract 3. Repeat.

5. a) Start at 2. Add 3, 5, 7 … (the step increases by 2)
b) Start at 2. Multiply by 2.
c) Start at 1. Multiply by 3.
d) Start at 4. Add 2, 4, 6 … (the step increases by 2)

6. a) Figure 1: 1
Figure 2: 3
Figure 3: 6
Figure 4: 10
Rule: Start at 1. Add 2, 3, 4 … (the step increases by 1)
So Figure 5: 15
b) Figure 1: 1
Figure 2: 3
Figure 3: 9
Figure 4: 27
Rule: Start at 1. Multiply by 3.
So Figure 5: 81

Worksheet PA6-20

1. a) 5 people at 1 table, 6 at 2 tables, 9 at 3 tables, 10 at 4 tables, 13 at 5 tables
b) The gap is 1, 3, 1, 3.
c) 13 + 1 + 3 + 1 = 18

2. a) i) 15, 21
ii) The gap between numbers increases by 1 every term.
iii) 21 + 7 + 8 = 36
b) i) 25, 36
ii) The gap between numbers increases by 2 every term.

3. a) The gap starts 0, 1, 1, 2, 3, 5, 8, which is the same as the sequence. So the gap continues 13, 21, and the sequence continues 34, 55.
b) The pattern is odd-odd-even.
c) They are the same.
d) They are the same.

Worksheet PA6-21

1. a)

Years	Weeks
1	52
2	104
3	156
4	208

b)

Years	Days
1	365
2	730
3	1 095

c)

Hours	Seconds
1	3 600
2	7 200
3	10 800
4	14 400

2. Tank 1 empties at a constant rate of 40 units per minute. Tank 2 empties at a rate of 10, 20, 30, …, etc. units per minute. So Tank 2 will empty first.

3. a) After 25 minutes, the airplane will have 950 litres of fuel.
b) After 30 minutes, the plan will be 75 km from the airport.
c) When the plane reaches the airport, it will be carrying 850 litres of fuel.

4. a) 13 Times
b) 1910

5. a) 37 × 3 = 111
37 × 6 = 222
37 × 9 = 333
37 × 12 = 444
37 × 15 = 555
b) 9 × 2222 = 19 998
9 × 3333 = 29 997
9 × 4444 = 39 996
9 × 5555 = 49 995
9 × 6666 = 59 994

Worksheet PA6-22

1. a) 6
b) 3
c) 5
d) 3

2. a) 3
b) 3
c) 4
d) 3

3. 1 + 1 + 3 = 5
2 + 2 + 1 = 5
0 + 0 + 5 = 5

4. 1 + 1 + 7 = 9
2 + 2 + 5 = 9
4 + 4 + 1 = 9
0 + 0 + 9 = 9

Worksheet PA6-23

1. a) x = 6
b) A = 8
c) n = 6
d) x = 3

2. a) □ = 3
b) □ = 2
c) □ = 3
d) □ = 4

3. a) X = 4
b) X = 4
c) X = 8

4. a) Assuming that a and b are positive:
1 + 5 = 6
2 + 4 = 6
3 + 3 = 6
4 + 2 = 6
5 + 1 = 6
b) 1 × 6 = 6
2 × 3 = 6
3 × 2 = 6
6 × 1 = 6
c) 6 – 1 = 5
6 – 2 = 4
6 – 3 = 3
6 – 4 = 2
6 – 5 = 1

7. A = 4
B = 5
C = 1

Worksheet PA6-24

1. a) 5 × 2 = 10
b) 5 × 4 = 20
c) 7 × 4 = 28

2. a) 70 × 3 = 210
b) 40 × 2 = 80
c) h × 100 = 100h

3. a) 7 × h = 7h
b) 7 × t = 7t
c) 7 × x = 7x
d) 7 × n = 7n

4. a) A + 3 = B
b) 2 × A = B
c) A + 7 = B
d) B = A + A×4

5. Yes it does.

Worksheet PA6-25

1. a)

O.P	1st	2nd
(2,1)	2	1
(4,3)	4	3
(6,5)	6	5
(8,7)	8	7

b)

(1,3)	1	3
(3,5)	3	5
(5,7)	5	7
(7,9)	7	9

c)

(2,4)	2	4
(4,5)	4	5
(6,6)	6	6
(8,7)	8	7

2. a)

O.P	1st	2nd
(1,3)	1	3
(2,5)	2	5
(3,7)	3	7
(4,9)	4	9
(0,1)	0	1

b)

(0,5)	0	5
(2,6)	2	6
(4,7)	4	7
(6,8)	6	8

(8,9)	-8	-9

c)

(0,0)	0	0
(1,3)	1	3
(2,6)	2	6
(3,9)	3	9

3. *Ordered pairs:*
(3, 1), (4, 3), (5, 5), (6, 7)

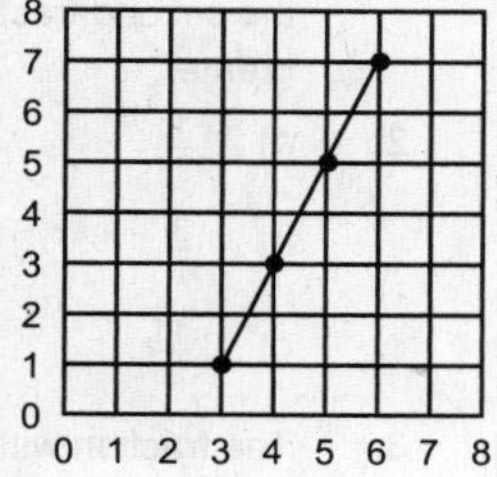

4. a)

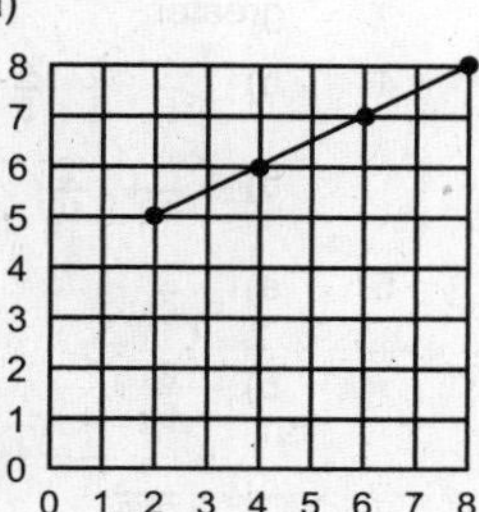

b)

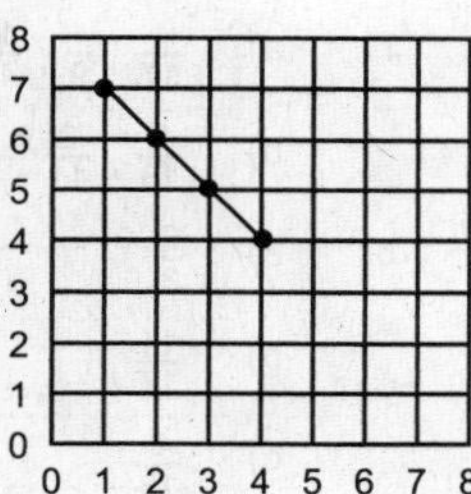

c)

d)

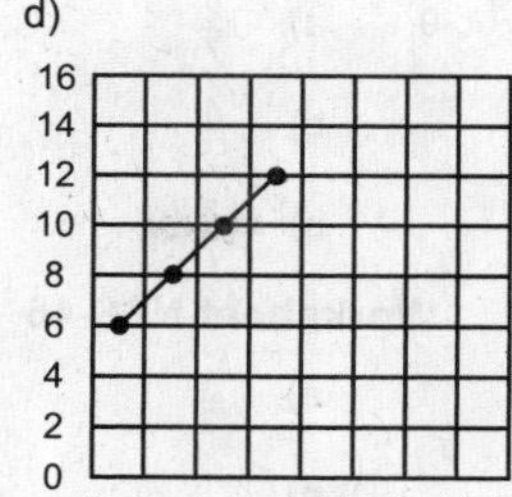

5. Graphs will vary depending on scales chosen.

Sample answer:

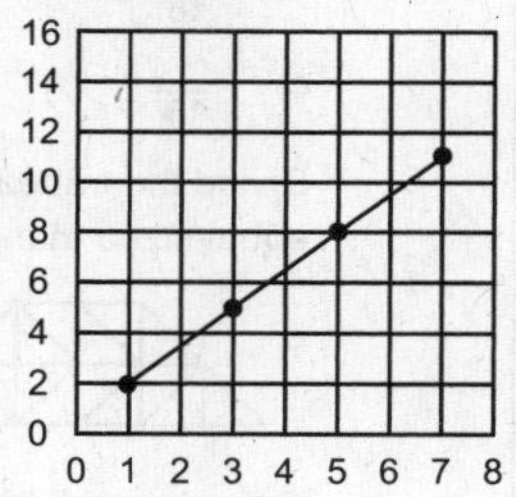

6. Answers will vary depending on input numbers selected.

a)

Input	Output
1	1
2	3
3	5
4	7

b)

Input	Output
1	1
2	5
3	9
4	13

c)

Input	Output
2	4
4	5
6	6
8	7

7. A:

Input	Output
1	2
2	5
3	8
4	11

RULE for T-table A: Start at 1, multiply by 3 and subtract 1.

Repeat.

B:

Input	Output
1	3
2	4
3	5
4	6

RULE for T-table B: Start at 1, add 2

C:

Input	Output
1	1
3	3
5	5
7	7

RULE for T-table C: Output = Input (or multiply by 1)

Worksheet PA6-26

1. a) $4.00
   b) $2.00
   c) $20.00
   d) 3 minutes
2. a) 20 km
   b) 40 km
   c) Yes, Kathy rested for an hour (between hours 3 and 4). Here, the distance didn't change.
   d) No – Kathy traveled faster between hours 0 and 3 than she did between hours 4 and 6.
3. a) 40 metres
   b) 60 metres
   c) Tom won the race by 40 metres.
   d) Ben had a 40 metre head start.
4. a) i) $8.00
   ii) $10.00
   iii) $9.00
   b) $4.00
   c) To rent a bike for 3 hours from Dave's store would cost $10.50. At Mike's store it would be $9.00, so Mike's store is the better choice for a 3-hour rental.

Worksheet PA6-27

1. a)

Tables	Chairs
1	6
2	10
3	14
4	18

Rule:
Start at 6 and add 4.

   b) 50
2. $260.00
3. 140 km
4. 30 cups of water
5. The 24th and the 48th receive both a book and a calendar.
6. Counting by 24's and 30's, you see that 120 is divisible by both numbers (and it's less than 150). So they each collected 120 apples: Anna collected 5 baskets of 24 and Emily collected 4 baskets of 30.
7. a) There will be 44 shaded squares on the perimeter, and we know this since # shaded pieces = 4 × figure # + 4 (or, in this specific case, 4 × 10 + 4).
   b) There will be 49 white squares:
   32 – 4 = 28
   28 ÷ 4 = 7
   (this gives us the figure # we need)
   And, in Figure 7, there are 7 × 7 = 49 white squares.
8. As such, Method A will cost Gerome $215 for 6 hours (5 × $35 + $40) and Method B will cost him $270 (6 × $45). So Method A is cheaper.
9. The core pattern is 5 shapes in length and the closest multiple of

5 to 72 – without going over – is 70 (14 × 5), with remainder 2.

So, to find the 72nd shape, look at the 2nd shape of the core pattern: it is a pentagon.

10. Paul shovelled the following # of sidewalks each day:

Day 1: 3

Day 2: 6

Day 3: 9

Day 4: 12

11.

	# E	# T	P
1	1	1	3
2	2	4	6
3	3	9	9
4	4	16	12

Patterns in columns –

- # of edges increases by 1 each time;
- # of triangles increases by 3, then by 5, then by 7, etc… (step increases by 2 each time);
- Perimeter increases by 3 each time.

12. a) Decreases
b) 500 metres
c) 1 cm = 500 m
d) Yes (decreases by 2.5° each time)

13. No, Marlene isn't right. She will need 28 blocks to make Figure 7 (since 1 + 2 + 3 + 4 + 5 + 6 + 7 = 28).

Number Sense 2

Worksheet NS6-44

1. a) $\frac{6}{9}$
b) $\frac{4}{6}$
c) $\frac{8}{16}$

2. a) 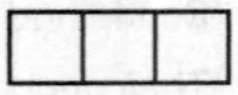

b) 

3. a) $\frac{2}{3}$
b) $\frac{1}{5}$

4. a) 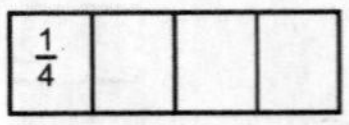

b) 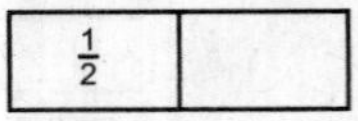

c) 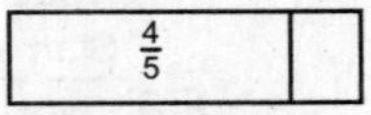

5. a) The total number of pieces
b) The number of pieces that are shaded

6. a) Doesn't show $\frac{1}{4}$: the pieces aren't all the same size.
b) Doesn't show $\frac{1}{4}$: the circle is cut into three pieces.
c) $\frac{1}{4}$

Worksheet NS6-45

1. a) $\frac{3}{5}$, $\frac{3}{5}$
b) $\frac{2}{5}$, $\frac{4}{5}$

2. a) Pentagons, or unshaded
b) circles
c) squares

3. $\frac{3}{5}$ are shaded;
$\frac{3}{5}$ are pentagons

4. a) $\frac{6}{11}$
b) $\frac{4}{11}$
c) $\frac{1}{11}$

5. $\frac{7}{9}$

6. a) $\frac{1}{14}$
b) $\frac{5}{14}$
c) $\frac{3}{14}$

7. a) 5, 7, 11
b) $\frac{12}{23}$, $\frac{11}{23}$
c) $\frac{5}{12}$, $\frac{7}{12}$

8. $\frac{8}{9}$

9. a) $\frac{2}{7}$
b) $\frac{4}{7}$
c) $\frac{3}{7}$

Worksheet NS6-46

1. a) $\frac{1}{3}$
b) $\frac{1}{4}$
c) $\frac{1}{5}$

2. a) $\frac{2}{6}$
b) $\frac{8}{16}$
c) $\frac{1}{16}$

3. Divide the trapezoid into equal-sized triangles:

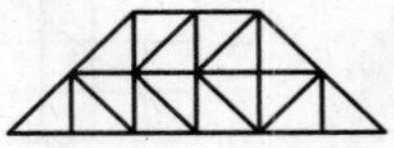

A single small triangle = $\frac{1}{16}$ of the figure.

4. a) $\frac{1}{2}$
b) $\frac{2}{3}$
c) $\frac{1}{3}$

Worksheet NS6-47

1. $\frac{3}{4}$

2. a) $\frac{3}{5}$
b) $\frac{2}{3}$

3. a) $\frac{4}{5}$
b) $\frac{3}{4}$
c) $\frac{5}{7}$

4. a) $\frac{2}{4}$
b) $\frac{1}{5}$

5. a) $\frac{1}{3}$
b) $\frac{1}{5}$
c) $\frac{3}{7}$

Worksheet NS6-48

1. Greater numerator: $\frac{5}{6}$

Greater fraction: $\frac{5}{6}$

Thinking will vary –

Example:
Each rectangle is divided into the same number of pieces, and each piece is the same size. Since only two pieces are shaded in the first rectangle, and five are shaded in the second, we know that the second fraction is greater.

2. a) $\frac{11}{17}$
b) $\frac{3}{7}$
c) $\frac{11}{25}$

3. The fraction with the *larger* numerator is greater.

4. a) $\frac{1}{5}$, $\frac{3}{5}$, $\frac{4}{5}$
b) $\frac{1}{10}$, $\frac{2}{10}$, $\frac{5}{10}$, $\frac{9}{10}$

5. a) $\frac{1}{6}$
b) $\frac{8}{8}$
c) $\frac{7}{200}$

6. The fraction with the *smaller* denominator is greater.

7. a) $\frac{1}{17}$, $\frac{1}{9}$, $\frac{1}{4}$
b) $\frac{2}{16}$, $\frac{2}{11}$, $\frac{2}{7}$, $\frac{2}{5}$

8. a) $\frac{2}{3}$
b) $\frac{11}{17}$
c) $\frac{6}{18}$

9. $\frac{1}{2} = \frac{50}{100} > \frac{1}{100}$

10. Yes, since the pies can be very different sizes:

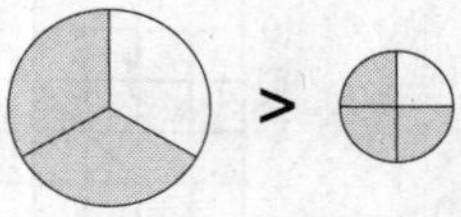

Worksheet NS6-49

1. b) 3
c) 1

2. a) $2\frac{1}{2}$
b) $1\frac{2}{3}$

c) $2\frac{3}{5}$

5. $4\frac{1}{4}$ represents more pie – you can tell by looking at the "whole" part of the fraction: 4 > 3

6. It is closer to 6.

Worksheet NS6-50

1. a) $\frac{5}{2}$
   b) $\frac{5}{4}$
   c) $\frac{4}{3}$

4. $\frac{9}{4}$ represents more pie – since the denominators are the same, you can simply compare the numerators: 9 > 7

5. Fractions b) and c) are more than a whole – you can tell this since their numerators are greater than their denominators.

Worksheet NS6-51

1. a) $3\frac{1}{3}$, $\frac{10}{3}$
   b) $2\frac{3}{4}$, $\frac{11}{4}$
   c) $2\frac{2}{3}$, $\frac{8}{3}$

2. a) $\frac{7}{2}$
   b) $\frac{15}{4}$

3. a) $2\frac{1}{3}$
   b) $3\frac{1}{6}$
   c) $3\frac{1}{4}$

4. a) $2\frac{1}{2}$
   b) $2\frac{4}{5}$
   c) $4\frac{15}{8}$

5. 11 ÷ 3 = 3 R2 – so there are 3 whole pies in the fraction

Worksheet NS6-52

1. a) 2 halves
   b) 4 halves
   c) 8 halves

2. a) 3 thirds
   b) 6 thirds
   c) 12 thirds

3. a) 8 cans
   b) 9 cans
   c) 15 cans

4. a) 13 cans
   b) 17 cans
   c) 19 cans

5. a) $\frac{7}{3}$
   b) $\frac{11}{2}$
   c) $\frac{14}{3}$

6. 17

7. 28

8. 11

9. a) 8
   b) 16

Worksheet NS6-53

1. a) 2
   b) 3
   c) 6

2. b) 3; 2; $3\frac{2}{3}$
   c) 3; 1; $3\frac{1}{3}$

3. a) $1\frac{1}{2}$
   b) $4\frac{1}{2}$
   c) $2\frac{2}{3}$

4. $2\frac{3}{4}$, $\frac{11}{4}$

5. $2\frac{2}{5}$, $\frac{12}{5}$

6. $\frac{5}{2}$;
   convert to mixed fraction;
   $\frac{5}{2} = 2\frac{1}{2}$;
   $\frac{7}{3} = 2\frac{1}{3}$;
   $2\frac{1}{2} > 2\frac{1}{3}$

7. Between 1 and 2

8. a) $\frac{3}{7}$
   b) $\frac{1}{5}$
   c) $\frac{1}{3}$

Worksheet NS6-54

1. a) $\frac{3}{5}$
   b) $\frac{2}{3}$
   c) $\frac{5}{6}$

2. $\frac{4}{8}$, $\frac{2}{4}$, $\frac{1}{2}$

3. a) $\frac{2}{3}$
   b) $\frac{1}{2}$
   c) $\frac{1}{3}$

4. a) $\frac{4}{6}$
   b) $\frac{6}{9}$
   c) $\frac{9}{12}$

5. b) $\frac{1}{2} = \frac{2}{4} = \frac{3}{6} = \frac{4}{8}$

Worksheet NS6-55

4. 1 piece

5. 4 pieces

Worksheet NS6-56

1. b) $\frac{4}{5}$

2. a) 2, $\frac{2}{3}$, 6, 4
   b) $\frac{1}{4}$, 2, $\frac{3}{4}$, 8, 6
   c) $\frac{1}{3}$, 3, $\frac{2}{3}$, 9, 6
   e) $\frac{3}{4}$ of 12 = 9

5. a) 2
   b) 5
   c) 4

6. a) 9 ÷ 3 = 3
   3 × 2 = 6
   b) 8 ÷ 4 = 2 × 3 = 6
   c) 15 ÷ 3 = 5 × 2 = 10

9. 9

10. $6.00

11. a) 9
    b) 3

12. 6

13. $20 \times \frac{2}{5}$ = 8 blue;
    $20 \times \frac{1}{4}$ = 5 yellow;
    8 + 5 = 13;
    20 – 13 = 7 green

14. $60 \times \frac{2}{3}$ = 40;
    9:10 + :40 = 9:50

15. $36 \times \frac{1}{6}$ = 6; 36 – 6 = 30;
    30 ÷ 5 = 6

16. $1\frac{3}{4}$ yrs. = 12 + $\frac{3}{4}$ × 12 = 12 + 9 = 21 mos.; 21 mos. > 17 mos.

17. $12 \times \frac{1}{4}$ = 3 + 2 = 5; 12 – 5 = 7; 7 > 6 which is $\frac{1}{2}$ × 12; no

Worksheet NS6-57

1. a) $\frac{1}{2}$
   b) $\frac{1}{3}$
   c) $\frac{2}{3}$

2. a) $\div\frac{2}{2} = \frac{1}{2}$
   b) $\div\frac{3}{3} = \frac{1}{3}$
   c) $\div\frac{2}{2} = \frac{2}{3}$

3. a) $\frac{1}{5}$
   b) $\frac{1}{3}$
   c) $\frac{1}{4}$

4. a) $\frac{1}{4}$
   b) $\frac{2}{5}$
   c) $\frac{3}{20}$

Worksheet NS6-58

1. 2, 3, 6, 3, 2

2. 2, 5, 10, 5, 2

3. $\frac{1}{3}$, $\frac{1}{4}$, 12, $\frac{4}{12}$, $\frac{3}{12}$

4. $\frac{1}{3}$, $\frac{1}{5}$, 15, $\frac{5}{15}$, $\frac{3}{15}$

5. $\frac{1}{2}$, $\frac{1}{4}$, 4, $\frac{2}{4}$, $\frac{1}{4}$

6. $\frac{1}{3}$, $\frac{1}{6}$, 6, $\frac{2}{6}$, $\frac{1}{6}$

7. $\frac{1}{2}$, $\frac{1}{8}$, 8, $\frac{4}{8}$, $\frac{1}{8}$

8. $\frac{1}{4}$, $\frac{1}{6}$, 12, $\frac{3}{12}$, $\frac{2}{12}$

Worksheet NS6-59

1. a) >
   b) >
   c) <

2. $\frac{3}{5}$, $\frac{2}{5}$, $\frac{1}{2}$

3. $\frac{2}{3}$, $\frac{3}{4}$

4. b) $\frac{5}{5} \frac{x}{x} \frac{1}{2}$; $\frac{5}{10} > \frac{3}{10}$
   c) $\frac{2}{2} \frac{x}{x} \frac{3}{4}$; $\frac{6}{8} < \frac{7}{8}$

Worksheet NS6-60

1. a) $\frac{5}{10}$, $\frac{4}{10}$, $\frac{3}{10}$; $\frac{3}{10}$, $\frac{4}{10}$, $\frac{5}{10}$
   b) $\frac{2}{6}$, $\frac{5}{6}$, $\frac{3}{6}$; $\frac{2}{6}$, $\frac{3}{6}$, $\frac{5}{6}$
   c) $\frac{5}{8}$, $\frac{4}{8}$, $\frac{6}{8}$; $\frac{4}{8}$, $\frac{5}{8}$, $\frac{6}{8}$
2. $\frac{1}{10}$, $\frac{1}{5}$, $\frac{3}{10}$, $\frac{2}{5}$, $\frac{1}{2}$, $\frac{3}{5}$, $\frac{7}{10}$, $\frac{4}{5}$, $\frac{9}{10}$
3. a) $\frac{3}{6}$, $\frac{4}{8}$
   b) $\frac{3}{9}$, $\frac{4}{12}$
   c) $\frac{6}{8}$, $\frac{9}{12}$
4. a) $\frac{1}{2}$, $\frac{5}{10}$
   b) $\frac{2}{3}$, $\frac{4}{6}$
   c) $\frac{16}{20}$, $\frac{4}{5}$
5. $\frac{4}{6}$, $\frac{6}{6}$ or $\frac{2}{3}$, 1
6. $\frac{1}{3} = \frac{8}{24}$; $\frac{1}{8} = \frac{3}{24}$; $\frac{8}{24} > \frac{3}{24}$
7. $\frac{3}{9}$, $\frac{2}{6}$, $\frac{1}{3}$
8. $\frac{10}{20}$, $\frac{9}{18}$, $\frac{8}{16}$, $\frac{7}{14}$, $\frac{6}{12}$, $\frac{5}{10}$, $\frac{4}{8}$, $\frac{3}{6}$, $\frac{2}{4}$, $\frac{1}{2}$
9. spaghetti sauce

Worksheet NS6-61

1. a) 18
   b) $\frac{3}{10}$
2. a) $\frac{1}{20}$
   b) blue
   c) white
3. 8:10 am
4. a) i) $\frac{1}{2}$
      ii) $\frac{1}{8}$
      iii) $\frac{3}{8}$
   b) i) 12
      ii) 3
      iii) 9
5. a) 3
   b) Eldad ate 2; Ahmed ate 7; Brian ate 4; John ate 12 slices.
6. 6

Worksheet NS6-62

1. a) 66/100, 0.66
   b) 4/100, 0.04
   c) 60/100, 0.6
2. a) 0.39
   b) 0.65
   c) 0.07
3. 0.23
   0.11
   0.12
   0.54

Worksheet NS6-63

1. a) 47 hundredths = 4 tenths 7 hundredths
   $\frac{47}{100} = 0.47$
   b) 68 hundredths = 6 tenths 8 hundredths
   68/1000 = 0.68
   c) 86 hundredths = 8 tenths 6 hundredths
   86/100 = 0.86
2. a) 43 hundredths = 4 tenths 3 hundredths
   $\frac{43}{100} = 0.43$
   b) 28 hundredths = 2 tenths 8 hundredths
   28/100 = 0.28
   c) 66 hundredths = 6 tenths 6 hundredths
   66/100 = 0.66
3. a) 0.52 = 5 tenths 2 hundredths = 52 hundredths
   b) .55 = 5 tenths 5 hundredths = 55 hundredths
   c) .40 = 4 tenths 0 hundredths = 40 hundredths

Worksheet NS6-64

1. 5/10, 0.5, 0.50, 50/100
   8/10, 0.8, 0.80, 80/100
   10/10, 1.0, 1.00, 100/100
2. a) 70/100 = 7/10
   b) $\frac{40}{100} = \frac{4}{10}$
   c) $\frac{20}{100} = \frac{2}{10}$
3. a) .5, $\frac{50}{100}$, .50
   b) .3, $\frac{30}{100}$, .30
   c) .9, $\frac{90}{100}$, .90

Worksheet NS6-65

1. b) 7 dimes 2 pennies, 7 tenths 2 hundredths, 72 pennies, 72 hundredths
   c) 4 dimes 3 pennies, 4 tenths 3 hundredths, 43 pennies, 43 hundredths
2. a) 2 decimetres 8 centimetres, 2 tenths 8 hundredths of a metre, 28 centimetres, 28 hundredths of a metre
   b) 1 decimetre 3 centimetres, 1 tenth 3 hundredths of a metre, 13 centimetres, 13 hundredths of a metre
3. a) 6 dimes 0 pennies, 6 tenths 0 hundredths, 60 pennies, 60 hundredths
   b) 8 dimes 0 pennies, 8 tenths 0 hundredths, 80 pennies, 80 hundredths
4. a) 2 dimes 7 pennies, 2 tenths 7 hundredths, 27 pennies, 27 hundredths
   b) 3 dimes 0 pennies, 3 tenths 0 hundredths, 30 pennies, 30 hundredths
   .3 is greater than .27
5. .63 = 63/100, which is less than 80/100 = .8

Worksheet NS6-66

1.

	Tenths	Hund.
a)	5	6
b)	6	10
c)	3	1
d)	0	9

$\frac{56}{100} = 0.56$
$\frac{70}{100} = 0.70$
$\frac{31}{100} = 0.31$
$\frac{9}{100} = 0.09$

2. a) 3/10
   b) 5/10
   c) 8/10
3. a) 0.20
   b) 0.40
   c) 0.30
4. Circle: (a) (c) (d) (e) (h)
5. a) 0.82
   b) 0.09
6. .46 = 23/50

Worksheet NS6-67

1. a) $1\frac{21}{100}$, 1.21
   b) $1\frac{38}{100}$, 1.38
   c) $\frac{59}{100}$, .59
3. a) $2\frac{35}{100}$, 2.35
   b) $1\frac{3}{100}$, 1.03
4. a) 1.32
   b) 2.71
   c) 8.7
5. a) 6 tenths because it is equal to 60 hundredths which

is greater than 6 hundredths

b) .8 because it is equal to 80 hundredths which is greater than 8 hundredths

c) 1.20 because it is equal to 1 and 20 hundredths which is greater than 1 and two hundredths

Worksheet NS6-68

1. A: $\frac{8}{10}$
   B: $1\frac{4}{10}$
   C: $2\frac{1}{10}$
   D: $2\frac{7}{10}$
   E: $\frac{2}{10}$
   F: $1\frac{1}{10}$
   G: $1\frac{8}{10}$
   H: $2\frac{2}{10}$

3. A: five tenths
   B: one and five tenths
   C: two and eight tenths

Worksheet NS6-69

1. a) .1, .2 , .3, .4, .5, .6, .7, .8, .9
   b) .5

2 a) a half
   b) a half
   c) one

3. a) <
   b) <
   c) >

4. a) 2
   b) 3
   c) 1

Worksheet NS6-70

1. a) 0.4, 0.6, 0.7
   b) 1.2, 3.5, 3.7
   c) $4\frac{3}{10}$, 4.5, 4.7

2. a) 0.40
   b) 0.80
   c) 0.32

3. a) $0.7 = 0.70 = \frac{70}{100}$
   b) $0.9 = 0.90 = \frac{90}{100}$
   c) $0.1 = 0.10 = \frac{10}{100}$

4. a) 0.3 0.45 0.9
   b) 0.32 $\frac{37}{100}$ .80
   c) $1\frac{34}{100}$ $1\frac{35}{100}$ 1.4

5. $2\frac{7}{10}$

6. a) $2\frac{5}{10}$
   b) $3\frac{7}{10}$
   c) $8\frac{6}{10}$

7. b) $3\frac{8}{10}$, 3.8
   c) $8\frac{7}{10}$, 8.7

8. $\frac{23}{10} = 2.3$; $2.4 > 2.3$

9. possible answers: 1.33, 1.34, 1.35, 1.36, 1.37, 1.38. 1.39

10. $\frac{1}{2} = \frac{5}{10} = \frac{50}{100}$
    $\frac{1}{2} = .5 = .50$

11. $\frac{1}{5} = \frac{2}{10} = \frac{20}{100}$
    $\frac{1}{5} = .2 = .20$

12. a) $\frac{2}{5} = \frac{4}{10} = \frac{40}{100}$
    b) $\frac{3}{5} = \frac{6}{10} = \frac{60}{100}$
    c) $\frac{4}{5} = \frac{8}{10} = \frac{80}{100}$

13. $\frac{1}{4} = \frac{25}{100} = 0.25$
    $\frac{3}{4} = 75/100 = .75$

14. a) $\frac{3}{4}$
    b) .53
    c) .87

15. a) .42 $\frac{3}{4}$ .8
    b) .35 $\frac{1}{2}$ $\frac{4}{5}$
    c) .45 $\frac{1}{2}$ $\frac{3}{5}$

16. 3/4 is 1/4 + 1/4 + 1/4. So 3/4 is .25 + .25 + .25, which is .75.

17. 0.65 = 65/100, which is greater than 1/2 = 50/100.

Worksheet NS6-71

1. a) hundredths
   b) thousandths
   c) tenths

2. a) 6, 5, 1, 2
   b) 6, 3, 5, 4
   c) 7, 0, 3, 0

3. a) $\frac{652}{1000}$
   b) $\frac{372}{1000}$
   c) $\frac{20}{100}$

4. a) 2 tenths + 3 hundredths + 7 thousandths
   b) 3 tenths + 5 hundredths + 2 thousandths
   c) 6 ones + 3 tenths + 3 hundredths + 6 thousandths

5. a) .49
   b) .50
   c) .758

6. a) <
   b) <
   c) >

Worksheet NS6-72

1. b) .30 + .37 = .67
   c) .62 + .31 = .93

2. a) $\frac{25}{100} + \frac{50}{100} = \frac{75}{100}$
   b) $\frac{30}{100} + \frac{37}{100} = \frac{67}{100}$
   c) $\frac{62}{100} + \frac{31}{100} = \frac{93}{100}$

3. b) .95
   c) 1.14

4. a) 6.49
   b) 8.87
   c) 12.58

5. 7.9 cm

6. .99 L

Worksheet NS6-73

1. a) $\frac{20}{100}$
   b) $\frac{26}{100}$
   c) $\frac{35}{100}$

2. b) .38 – .12 = .26
   c) .69 – .34 = .35

3. b) .54
   c) .23

4. a) .37
   b) .59
   c) .08

5. a) .65
   b) .28
   c) .59

Worksheet NS6-74

1. a) 2.35
   b) 2.79

2. b) 1.13

3. a) 7.69
   b) 7.23
   c) 1.71

4. a) 3.84
   b) 3.39
   c) 2.47

5. 18.43 degrees warmer

6. 91.04 million kilometres

7. a) .8, 1.0, 1.2
   b) 1.2, 1.5, 1.8

Worksheet NS6-75

1. b) 3
   c) 6

2. a) 5
   b) 7
   c) 14

3. a) 6
   b) 8
   c) 16

4. .3 + .3 + .3 + .3 + .3 + .3 + .3 + .3 + .3 + .3 = 3

6. Multiplying by 10 exchanges tenths for ones.

Worksheet NS6-76

1. a) 2
   b) 100 × .03 = 3

2. b) 180
   c) 460

3. a) 7
   b) 6
   c) 67

4. a) 1
   b) 1

5. three

6. a) 860
   b) 325
   c) 1 329

Worksheet NS6-77

1. a) 2.86
   b) 3.6
   c) 5.05
2. b) 6, 15, 7, 5, 7.5
   c) 6, 21, 8, 1, 8.1
3. a) 6, 15, 3, 7, 5, 3, 7.53
   b) 8, 4, 16, 8, 5, 6, 8.56
   c) 5, 20, 5, 7, 0, 5, 7.05
4. a) 1, 1, 10.35
   b) 2, 30.48
   c) 1, 25.86
5. a) 10.5
   b) 24.9
   c) 37.5

Worksheet NS6-78

1. b) 3.0 ÷ 10 = .3
   c) .3 ÷ 10 = .03
2. b) 2.4 ÷ 10 = .24
3. b) .05
   c) .07
4. Dividing by 100 shifts the decimal two places to the left. A dollar divided 100 ways yields a penny.
5. .035 m
6. 1.0 ÷ 10 = .1

Worksheet NS6-79

1. b) 2, 4, 1
   c) 2, 4, 11
2. a) 1.44, 3, 13, 12, 12, 12, 0
   b) 1.56, 4, 22, 20, 25, 24, 1
   c) 1.24, 5, 12, 10, 23, 20, 3
3. a) .18
   b) 1.3, R .3
   c) .34
4. 55¢
5. 15.6 km
6. $7.29
7. 6 pens for $4.99
8. a) 5 dm
   b) 4 dm

Worksheet NS6-80

1. a) .84
   b) .33
   c) .19
2. a) .5
   b) 1.0
   c) 3.35
3. a) 0.01
   b) 0.1
   c) 0.01
4. a) 7.1, 7.2, 7.3, 7.4, 7.5, 7.6, 7.7, 7.8, 7.9
   b) 3.16, 3.17, 3.18, 3.19, 3.20, 3.21, 3.22, 3.23, 3.24
   c) 7.254, 7.255, 7.256, 7.257, 7.258, 7.259, 7.260, 7.261, 7.262
5. a) .6, .7, .8
   b) 9.9, 10.0, 10.1
   c) 2.8, 2.9, 3.0
6. a) 8.0
   b) 3.0
   c) 7.05

Worksheet NS6-81

1. a) 26
   b) 39
   c) 60
2. a) 26.5
   b) 47.9
   c) 49.9
3. a) 95, 5, 19
   b) 3, 8, 24
   c) 5, 1, 5
4. a) 37, not reasonable
   b) 8, reasonable
   c) 90, not reasonable
5. yes
6. Any number from 7.15 to 7.24
7. a) no
   b) yes
   c) no
8. a) 0.5 m
   b) 0.2 km
   c) 0.6 dm

Worksheet NS6-82

2. a) $\frac{1}{10}$, .1
   b) $\frac{1}{10}$, .1
   c) $\frac{1}{10}$, .1
3. b) 0.5 dm + 3.2 dm = 3.7 dm
   c) 0.8 cm + 5.7 cm = 6.5 cm
5. a) 4 307.01
   b) 20 330.24
   c) 325 070.196
6. a) >
   b) >
   c) >
7. a) 5.72
   b) 10.7
   c) 28.759
8. a) .5706
   b) 5.670 or 5.706
9. any number from .31 to .49 for numbers in the hundredths
10. a) +
    b) ×
    c) ÷
11. a) .275, .37, .371
    b) .007, .07, .7
    c) 1.29, 1.3, 2.001
12. C, B, D, D
13. Yes; it is the product rounded to the nearest unit.
14. Multiplying by 10 moves the decimal one place to the right.
15. 1.25 hours = 75 minutes

Worksheet NS6-83

1. Multiply by 100.
2. Because Canadian currency has a base 10 system; one dollar; one dollar
3. 15.03 km/h
4. 2.1 m
5. a) 57 trillion km
   b) L726-8
   c) Barnard's star
6. 720 metres per hour
7. $3.20/kg, $3.90/kg, $5.90/kg, $7.98/kg, $4.78

Worksheet NS6-84

1. a) 51
   b) $19.80
   c) 225
2. a) 15
   b) 59
   c) $0.33
4. $11
5. $15

Worksheet NS6-85

1. a) 2:6
   b) 1:2
   c) 3:3
2. a) 2:3
   b) 3:3
   c) 3:3
3. a) 3:6
   b) 2:6
   c) 4:1
4. 4:9
5. a) ratio of triangles to circles
   b) ratio of squares to all figures

Worksheet NS6-86

1. a) 6 to 4 or 3 to 2
   b) 10 to 8 or 5 to 4
2. 2:3, 4:6, 6:9, 8:12
3. a) 3:4 = 6:8 = 12:16 = 24:32 = 48: 64
   b) 2:5 = 4:10 = 8:20 = 16:40 = 32: 80
4. a) 6
   b) 14
   c) 10
5. a) 20 cups
   b) 44 km
   c) $15

Worksheet NS6-87

1. a) 5:4 = 15:12; 15 + 12 = 27; 12 girls
   b) 3:5 = 6:10 = 9:15; 9 + 15 = 24; 15 blue fish
   c) 3:2 = 6:4 = 9:6; 9 + 6 = 15; 9 L orange juice
2. a) $\frac{15}{20}$
   b) × 5 →; $\frac{5}{25}$
   c) × 4 →; $\frac{8}{20}$
3. a) $\frac{15}{20}$
   b) $\frac{10}{25}$
   c) $\frac{9}{21}$

Worksheet NS6-88

1. 6 apples
2. 15 bus tickets
3. 10 games
4. 6 litres
5. 9 laps
6. 25 girls
7. 15 km

Worksheet NS6-89

1. a) 1:4
   b) 1:8
   c) 1:9
2. a) 22 km
   b) 8 days
3. 12:6, 8:4, 6:3, 4:2, 2:1
4. a) 20:30
   b) 12:20
   c) 20:25 or 16:20
5. If there are 30 students and 10 of them are girls, 30 – 10 = 20 are boys. The ratio of girls to boys is 10:20 = 1:2.

Worksheet NS6-90

1. a) $\frac{7}{100}$
   b) $\frac{92}{100}$
   c) $\frac{5}{100}$
2. a) 2%
   b) 31%
   c) 52%
3. b) $\frac{27}{100}$ = 27%
   c) $\frac{4}{100}$ = 4%
4. b) $\frac{40}{100}$ = 40%
   c) $\frac{80}{100}$ = 80%
5. b) = $\frac{5}{10}$ = $\frac{50}{100}$ = 50%
   c) = $\frac{7}{10}$ = $\frac{70}{100}$ = 70%
6. a) 25%
   b) 20%
   c) 75%
7. b) = $\frac{4}{5}$ = $\frac{80}{100}$ = 80%
   c) = $\frac{1}{2}$ = $\frac{50}{100}$ = 50%

Worksheet NS6-91

1. b) $\frac{63}{100}$, .63
   c) .45, 45%
6. a) $\frac{1}{20}$
   b) $\frac{5}{100}$
   c) .05, 5%
7. $\frac{1}{4}$, 25%;
   $\frac{1}{2}$, 50% ;
   $\frac{3}{4}$, 75% ;
   1, 100%
10. a) 60%
    b) 30%
12. About 5%

Worksheet NS6-92

1. a) 50%
   b) 75%
   c) 50%
2. b) $\frac{50}{50}\frac{\times 1}{\times 2}$; $\frac{50}{100}$ < $\frac{53}{100}$
   c) $\frac{25}{25}\frac{\times 1}{\times 4}$; $\frac{25}{100}$ > $\frac{23}{100}$
3. a) $\frac{60}{100}$, $\frac{42}{100}$, $\frac{73}{100}$
   $\frac{42}{100}$, $\frac{60}{100}$, $\frac{73}{100}$
   b) $\frac{50}{100}$, $\frac{73}{100}$, $\frac{80}{100}$
   c) $\frac{25}{100}$, $\frac{9}{100}$, $\frac{15}{100}$;
   $\frac{9}{100}$, $\frac{15}{100}$, $\frac{25}{100}$

Worksheet NS6-93

1. a) .4
   b) .7
   c) 3.2
2. a) .9
   b) .57
   c) .405
3. a) i) 1.5
   ii) 1.5, 6
   b) i) 25, 2.5
   ii) 6, 2.5, 15
   c) i) 2.3, .23
   ii) 9, .23, 2.07

Worksheet NS6-94

1. a) i) 1, 32, 34, 160, 1280, 1 440
   ii) 1 440, 14.4, 45%, 32, 14.4
   b) i) 2, 63, 28, 504, 1260 1764
   ii) 1 764, 17.64, 28%, 63, 17.64
2. a) 1.17
   b) 3.64
   c) 5.2
3. a) 20
   b) 70
   c) 3

Worksheet NS6-95

1. b) 80%, 10%, 10%
   c) 50%, 40%, 10%
2. Brushes: $\frac{1}{10}$, 10%;
   Paint: 40%, $200.00;
   Canvas: $\frac{5}{10}$, $250.00
3. a) English: 25%;
   Science: .05, 3;
   Math: $\frac{1}{2}$, .50, 30;
   French: $\frac{1}{5}$, 20%, 12
   b) a half hr = 30 min
4. $1.20
5. 18

Worksheet NS6-96

1. a) 8, 5, 13
   b) 4, 7, 11
   c) 12, 15, 27
2. a) 5, $\frac{5}{11}$; 6, $\frac{6}{11}$, 11
   b) 8, $\frac{8}{15}$, 7, $\frac{7}{15}$, 15
3. a) $\frac{5}{12}$ boys, $\frac{7}{12}$ girls
   b) $\frac{3}{5}$ boys, $\frac{2}{5}$ girls
   c) $\frac{11}{20}$ boys, $\frac{9}{20}$ girls
4. a) 8 boys, 12 girls
   b) 24 boys, 18 girls
   c) 6 boys, 9 girls
5. a) 10 boys, 15 girls
   b) 12 boys, 16 girls
6. a) A
   b) B
7. a) 4:6
   b) 4/10
   c) 60%
9. 1/20 = 5/100
   20% = 20/100
   0.2 = 2/10 = 20/100
10. 108 Maple Leafs cards
    180 Canadiens cards
    72 Canucks cards
11. 37%, since 1 cm is 1/100 = 1% of a metre

Worksheet NS6-97

1. a) 76 years ago (from 2008)
   b) 28 degrees higher
   c) 147 degrees
2. a) gold: 2.1 m
   b) silver: 2.0 m
   c) Because the difference between the best jumps is so small
3. a) About 17 times
   b) 1 440 times
   c) About 9.3 kg

Worksheet NS6-98

1. 2%
2. a) 60 m
   b) 36 m

3. a) $.30
   b) $2.10
4. $10.50
5. $21.40
6. 11 km
7. a) 225
   b) 275
8. No; there are only 120 bus seats for 144 students.
9. a) 8 + 8 = 16
   b) 4
   c) 20%
10. 18 months
11. a) $\frac{1}{4}$
    b) 322
    c) 1 288
12. a) 24
    b) 23
    c) 57
13. .77 m
14. $2.46
15. chair: $\frac{3}{10}$, 30%;
    table: $\frac{1}{10}$; 10%;
    sofa: $\frac{3}{5}$, 60%

Measurement

Worksheet ME6-1

1. a) 5 fingers: 50 mm
   b) 7 fingers: 70mm
2. a) 38 mm
   b) 47 mm
4. a) i) Same length (30 mm)
   ii) Same length (20 mm)
5. a) 38 mm
   b) 15 mm
   c) 60 mm
6. Diagonal:
   5.2 cm, 52 mm
   Sides:
   5 cm, 1.5 cm
7. 10
8. 10
9. 130; 320; 80; 180; 2 130;
   1 700; 90; 5 670
10. a) 5
    b) 8
    c) 320
11. a) 40
    b) 180
    c) 13
12. a) 70 mm
    b) 910 mm
    c) 45 cm
13. b) 30 mm
    c) 8 cm
16. a) 7 cm
    b) 3 cm
    c) 6 cm
17. a) 4 cm (40 mm)
    b) 6 cm (60 mm)
    c) 3 cm (30 mm)
18. No: 3 cm = 30 mm which is longer than 7 mm
19. a) 5 cm + 3 cm
    b) 5 cm + 3 cm + 3 cm
    c) 5 cm + 5 cm + 3 cm + 3 cm + 3 cm + 3 cm

Worksheet ME6-2

2. 10 cm
3. $\frac{1}{10}$
4. 10
5. 10
6. 310; 420; 8; 6 200; 30; 53; 10; 95
9. a) 7 dm
   b) 4 dm
   c) Answers may vary: 5 dm, 6 dm or 7 dm
10. 10
11. 100

Worksheet ME6-3

2. 30 m
7. 10

Worksheet ME6-4

1. 30, 300, 3 000;
   40, 400, 4 000;
   50, 500, 5 000;
   60, 600, 6 000
2. 100
3. 1 000
4. 800, 7 000;
   5 000, 17 000;
   40, 1 210;
   320, 50
5. a) 4 m 23 cm
   b) 5 m 14 cm
   c) 6 m 27 cm
6. a) 283 cm
   b) 365 cm
   c) 485 cm
7. a) 546 cm = 5 m 46 cm = 5.46 m
   b) 2 m 17 cm = 2.17 m
   c) 7 m 83 cm = 7.83 m
8. Because 100 cents = 1 dollar and 100 cm = 1 m
9. Yes, Michelle is correct. She multiplies 6 m by 100 in order to convert the measure to cm (since there are 100 cm in a metre).

Worksheet ME6-5

1. a) Largest = dm; Smallest = mm
   b) smaller
   c) more
2. a) 10 mm
   b) 10 cm
   c) 100 mm
3. b) 10, smaller, 10, more, multiply, 10, 72
   c) 10, smaller, 10, more, multiply, 10, 26
4. a) 40 dm
   b) 130 mm
   c) 200 mm
5. 45¢
6. Yes (Total weight = 3.703 kg)
7. Greater (2.44 m)
8. 1 000 g = 1 kg
   1 000 m = 1 km
9. 1 000 mg = 1 g
   1 000 mm = 1 m

Worksheet ME6-6

1. a) mm = millimetre = length of bee's antenna;
   cm = centimetre = diameter of a drum;
   m = metre = width of a swimming pool;
   km = kilometre = distance of a marathon
   b) km = kilometre = diameter of the moon;
   cm = centimetre = length of a ruler;
   m = metre = length of a soccer field;
   mm = millimetre = thickness of a nail
2. a) m
   b) dm
   c) m
3. a) cm
   b) m
   c) cm
4. a) km
   b) m
   c) m
5. 1. Western Red Cedar
   2. Lodgepole Pine
   3. Red Oak
   4. White Birch
6. 1. Snowy Owl
   2. Great Horned Owl
   3. Great Gray Owl
   4. Atlantic Puffin
8. a) 83 km, 2 260 m, 3.3 km
   b) 877 km, 47 m, 7.5 km

Worksheet ME6-7

1. a) 2 + 4 + 2 + 1 + 1 + 2 + 1 + 1 = 14 cm
   b) 3 + 6 + 3 + 2 + 1 + 2 + 1 + 2 = 20 cm
2. A: 14 units

B: 20 units
C: 28 units

Worksheet ME6-8

1. 10 cm; 8 cm; 14 cm
2. a) 24 m
   b) 28 cm
   c) 6 km
   d) 30 cm
   e) C – A – D – B
3. a) P = 18 cm
   b) P = 16 cm
4. a) 10 × 1; 2 × 5
   b) 12 × 1; 2 × 6; 3 × 4
   c) Yes; 1 × 7
6. 14 cm
7. 2:6 or 1:3

Worksheet ME6-9

1. a) 2, 10
   3, 12
   4, 14
   5, 16
   6, 18
   b) 2, 6
   c) 26
3. P = 6:
   W = 1, L = 2
   P = 12:
   W = 1, L = 5;
   W = 2, L = 4
   P = 16:
   W = 1, L = 7;
   W = 2, L = 6;
   W = 3, L = 5
   P = 18:
   W = 1, L = 8;
   W = 2, L = 7;
   W = 3, L = 6;
   W = 4, L = 5
4. a) i) 1, 8
   2, 10
   3, 12
   4, 14
   5, 16
   ii) 2, 6
   iii) 26
   b) i) 1, 8
   2, 12
   3, 16
   4, 20
   5, 24
   ii) 4, 4
   iii) 44
5. Yes, she is correct.

Worksheet ME6-10

1. a) 8 cm^2
   b) 8 cm^2
   c) 9 cm^2
2. a) 8 cm^2
   b) 3 cm^2
   c) 4 cm^2
3. A = 6 cm^2
   B = 4 cm^2
   C = 8 cm^2

Worksheet ME6-11

1. a) 4 × 3 = 12
   b) 2 × 3 = 6
   c) 3 × 2 = 6
2. b) 3 × 4 = 12
   c) 3 × 2 = 6
3. a) W = 2, L = 6; Area = 12 sq units
   b) W = 2, L = 3; Area = 6 sq units
   c) W = 3, L = 4; Area = 12 sq units
4. a) 2 cm × 3 cm = 6 cm^2
   b) 1 cm × 3 cm = 3 cm^2
   c) 2 cm × 4 cm = 8 cm^2
5. Area = L × W

Worksheet ME6-12

1. a) 2 cm × 5 cm = 10 cm^2
   b) 1 cm × 3 cm = 3 cm^2
   c) 3 cm × 5 cm = 15 cm^2
2. a) 42 m^2
   b) 21 m^2
   c) 32 cm^2
3. a) A: 21 m^2
   B: 20 cm^2
   C: 66 m^2
   D: 150 km^2
   b) D – C – A – B
4. Divide 18 by 6: 3 cm
5. 3 cm
6. 5 cm
7. There are two options.

OPTION #1

Box 1: 
Area
= 2 × 2
= 4 square units

Box 2: 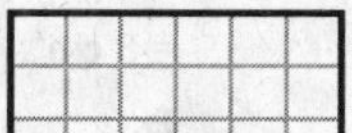
Area
= 3 × 6
= 18 square units

Total Area (Option #1)
= 4 + 18
= 22 square units

OPTION #2

Box 1: 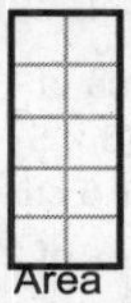
Area
= 5 × 2
= 10 square units

Box 2: 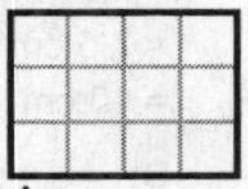
Area
= 3 × 4
= 12 square units

Total Area (Option #2)
= 10 + 12
= 22 square units

Worksheet ME6-13

1.

Shape	P	A
B	22 cm	30 cm^2
C	22 cm	18 cm^2
D	20 cm	21 cm^2
E	26 cm	30 cm^2
F	14 cm	10 cm^2
G	22 cm	10 cm^2

2. No
3. D & G
4. E; B, C & G; D; F; A
5. E & B; D; C; F; G; A
6. No

Worksheet ME6-14

1.

	L	W	P	A
A	5	2	14	10
B	2	6	16	12
C	5	3	16	15
D	2	3	10	6
E	7	2	18	14
F	2	4	12	8
G	4	3	14	12

2. a) 14 cm, 10 cm^2
   b) 8 cm, 3 cm^2
   c) 10 cm, 6 cm^2
3. a) 6 cm^2
   b) 20 cm^2
4. a) 9 cm^2
   b) 25 cm^2
5. a) 2 × 5 rectangle
   b) 2 × 4 rectangle

Worksheet ME6-15

1. a) 3 whole squares
   b) 2 whole squares
   c) 3 whole squares
   g) 4 whole squares
   h) 5 whole squares
   i) 11 whole squares
   j) 13 whole squares
   k) 10 whole squares
2. a) 7.5 square units
   b) 6 square units
   c) 7.5 square units
3. a) More
   b) Equal
   c) Less
4. a) $\frac{1}{2}$
   b) 4 square units
   c) 2 square units
5. a) 1 square units
   b) 3 square units
   c) 3 square units
6. a) 5 square units
   b) 2 square units
   c) 8 square units
7. a) 6 square units
   b) 8.5 square units
   c) 8.5 square units

8. a) 7 half squares = 3.5 total squares
   b) 9 half squares = 4.5 total squares
   c) 14 half squares = 7 total squares
9. b) 3 full squares; 8 half squares = 4 full squares
   Area = 3 + 4 = 7

Worksheet ME6-16

1. a) 20 square units
   b) 48 – 20 S = 28 U
2. a) 24 × 25 = 600 cm^2
   b) 600 ÷ 20 = 30 cm
   c) Perimeter = 20 + 30 + 20 + 30 = 100 cm, so he needs 100 ÷ 5 × 2 = 40 blackberries.
3.

	Length	Width
8 cm^2	4	2
	8	1
14 cm^2	7	2
	14	1

	Length	Width
18 cm^2	6	3
	9	2
	18	1

5. a) 5; $\frac{5}{9}$
   b) 1; $\frac{1}{4}$
   c) 2; $\frac{1}{4}$

Worksheet ME6-17

1. a) Yes
   b) 4
   c) 5
   d) Area = B × H
2. a) 12 cm^2
   b) 14 cm^2
3. a) 35 cm^2
   b) 12 cm^2
   c) 48 cm^2

Worksheet ME6-18

1. a) Measurements should be:

	Base	Height
B	2	5
C	4	5
D	3	4

   b) **A:**
   Area of 1st triangle
   = (2 × 4) ÷ 2
   = 4 cm^2
   Area of 2nd triangle
   = (2 × 4) ÷ 2
   = 4 cm^2
   Total Area of A
   = 4 cm^2 + 4 cm^2
   = 8 cm^2
   B:
   Area of 1st triangle
   = (1 × 5) ÷ 2
   = 2.5 cm^2
   Area of 2nd triangle
   = (1 × 5) ÷ 2
   = 2.5 cm^2
   Total Area of B
   = 2.5 cm^2 + 2.5 cm^2
   = 5 cm^2
   b) **C:**
   Area of 1st triangle
   = (3 × 5) ÷ 2
   = 7.5 cm^2
   Area of 2nd triangle
   = (1 × 5) ÷ 2
   = 2.5 cm^2
   Total Area of C
   = 7.5 cm^2 + 2.5 cm^2
   = 10 cm^2
   D:
   Area of 1st triangle
   = (2 × 4) ÷ 2
   = 4 cm^2
   Area of 2nd triangle
   = (1 × 4) ÷ 2
   = 2 cm^2
   Total Area of D
   = 4 cm^2 + 2 cm^2
   = 6 cm^2
2. Area of Triangle A = Area of Parallelogram B ÷ 2
3. Area of Parallelogram = 4 × 4 = 16
   So, the area of the triangle is half of 16 – or 8 square units.
4. A = (Base × Height) ÷ 2
5. Area of Triangle A
   = (4 × 4) ÷ 2
   = 16 ÷ 2
   = 8 square units

Worksheet ME6-19

1. a) 6 cm^2
   b) 6 cm^2
   c) 12 cm^2
2. a) 35 cm^2
   b) 170 cm^2
   c) 31.5 cm^2
3. a) 6 cm^2
   b) 4 cm^2
   c) 6 cm^2
4. A. 9 square units
   B. 18 sq. units
   C. 24 sq. units
   D. 20 sq. units
5. Area = 44 sq. units
6. a) P = 24 units
   A = 28 sq. units
   b) P = 34 units
   A = 57 sq. units
7. b)

Shape	Area	New Shape Area
A	1	4
B	2	8
C	.5	2
D	1	4

   c) The shape's area is quadrupled (multiplied by 4).
8. 5 cm; 20 cm
9. 2 cm; 16 cm
10. 6 cm
11. 2 times
13. A: 150 cm^2
    B: 200 cm^2
    C: 225 cm^2
14. Less (P = 10 cm)
15. 6.5 km; 5.5 km
16. $\frac{1}{2}$
17. $\frac{1}{2}$
18. 16 m
19. 4 cm